A Narrative of a Visit to the Australian Colonies ... Illustrated by three maps, fifteen etchings, and several wood-cuts.

James Backhouse

In spite of the pity and anger Backhouse and Walker felt at the sufferings of indigenous peoples, it is unlikely they could have seen how their own activities were part of the British colonising imperative. Backhouse eventually returned home to grow trees and travel further in ministry. As a nurseryman, he began to supply the increasing domestic demand for imported Australian plants, without any awareness of the respect due to the indissoluble spiritual kinship of these life-forms for Aboriginal peoples.

<u>encounters</u>

Earth is their religion or spirituality — the substance ⊕ focus of their entire physical expression

Robert Cock = payed rent for privilege of living on Aboriginal land

It seems that being a Quaker did not preclude a certain mental block when it came to the issue of white land ownership versus black land rights.

(John Woolman).

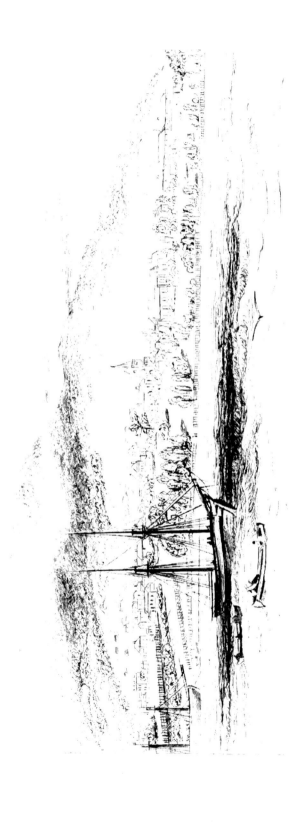

A NARRATIVE

OF

A VISIT

TO THE

AUSTRALIAN COLONIES,

BY

JAMES BACKHOUSE.

ILLUSTRATED BY THREE MAPS, FIFTEEN ETCHINGS,

AND SEVERAL WOOD-CUTS.

LONDON:

HAMILTON, ADAMS, AND CO. PATERNOSTER ROW.

YORK: JOHN L. LINNEY, LOW OUSEGATE.

MDCCCXLIII.

YORK: PRINTED BY JOHN L. LINNEY.

43.

8. 9

12.

CONTENTS.

CHAPTER X.

CHAPTER XI.

CHAPTER XII.

CHAPTER XIII.

CHAPTER XIV.

CHAPTER XV.

CHAPTER XVI.

CHAPTER XVII.

CHAPTER XVIII.

CHAPTER XIX.

CHAPTER XX.

CHAPTER XXVI.

CHAPTER XXVII.

CHAPTER XXVIII.

CHAPTER XXIX.

CHAPTER XXX.

CHAPTER XXXI.

CHAPTER XXXII.

CHAPTER XXXIII.

CHAPTER XXXIV.

CHAPTER XXXV.

CHAPTER XXXVI.

APPENDIX.

LIST OF PLATES, &c.

* *In this map, the names of Counties are in open, Roman Capitals; those of Hundreds and Principal Places, in plain, Roman Capitals; and those of Parishes in Italic Capitals.*

ERRATA.

Page. Line.

60—3rd from foot, for "their feeling," read *this feeling.*

98—13th from top, for "linestone," read *limestone.*

112—7th from top, for "thes mall," read *the small.*

113—4th from foot, for "Oxtalis," read *Oxalis*

150—13th from foot, for "prisoners," read *pensioners.*

158—foot of plate, for "Sidney, N. S. Wales," read *Hobart Town, V. D. Land.*

267—8th from foot, for "diforme," read *difforme.*

286—10th from foot, for "19th of 8th mo. 1837," read *page* 486.

410—19th from top, for "calamifolium," read *calamiforme.*

427—6th from top, for   do.   do.

553—2nd from foot, for "1341," read 1841.

lvii—6th from foot, for "as in the case," read *as is the case.*

INTRODUCTION.

The Visit to the Australian Colonies, a Narrative of which is contained in the following pages, occupied a period of six years, terminating with 1838. It was undertaken, solely, for the purpose of discharging a religious duty. During its course, the writer kept a Journal, in which, having been trained to habits of observation, records were made, not only on religious subjects, but also, on such as regarded the productions of the Countries visited, the state of the Aborigines, and of the Emigrant and Prisoner Population, &c.

From this Journal, the Narrative has been prepared, regard being generally had, to the point of time at which the record was made; but this has sometimes been deviated from, in order to give a more concise and clear view of a subject, and to avoid repetition. A copious Appendix is added to the work, containing a variety of documents, connected with subjects introduced into the Narrative.

The writer was accompanied in this visit, by his friend George Washington Walker, of Newcastle-upon-Tyne; who united in the service, under the belief, that he also, was called to this work. Under impressions of religious duty, the subject was brought before the meetings for discipline, of the Society of Friends, to which the writer and his Companion respectively belonged; and they received Certificates of the unity of these meetings with them, in regard to their proposed visit. As these certificates are introduced in Appendix. A. further notice on this point is unnecessary here.

A feeling of Christian interest, on behalf of a company of Pensioners, emigrating to Van Diemens Land, induced the writer and his friend, to make the voyage to that Colony, on board a vessel, in which a number of these people were passengers. In the Australian Colonies, J. Backhouse and G. W. Walker visited a large proportion of the country Settlers, in their own houses, holding religious meetings with such of them as they could collect, almost every evening, in the course of their journeys. These journeys were generally performed on foot; this mode of travelling being the most independent, and giving the easiest access to that part of the prisoner population, assigned to the Settlers, as servants. In towns, meetings were held for the promotion of religion and good morals, to which the Inhabitants were invited; and many visits of a religious character were paid to Penal Establishments. To avoid repetition, the particular notice of many of these visits and interviews, is omitted in the Narrative, generally when nothing occurred to inform or instruct, of a character different from what had been previously noticed.

For the purpose of conveying more distinct ideas on various subjects, than could be conveyed by words, three maps, with fifteen etchings, on steel, and several woodcuts have been introduced into this volume. The one, at page 158, was inadvertently entitled, by the engraver, "A Chain Gang going to work, near Sidney, New South Wales," instead of, "at Hobart Town, Van Diemens

Land." In many respects, this plate would correctly represent the Ironed Gangs of Sydney, or any other part of New South Wales, as well as the Chain Gangs in Van Diemens Land, or the Penal Settlements of these Colonies; but it was originally drawn from the Hulk Chain Gang, at Hobart Town. For this error, and a few others, that will be found in the volume, some of which are noticed in the list of *Errata*, it is hoped that the reader will make due allowance.

As dates are of considerable importance to be observed, in works on newly-occupied and rapidly advancing countries, those of the month and year have been placed at the heads of the pages. Should any extracts be made from this volume, the writer hopes that they may be accompanied by the dates, where these have a bearing upon the subject treated of.

The Settlements on the south coast of Australia have made rapid advances since the visits here recorded, but as the writer was, in great measure, cut off from communication with the Australian regions, by a subsequent sojourn in Southern Africa, he apprehends that he shall not render his readers a service, by going out of the line of his own observations, and commenting upon these changes, respecting which, he supposes, that the public are in possession of better information, from other sources, than he has it in his power to communicate. For a similar reason, he has refrained from observations on some modifications of the Penal Discipline, of New South Wales and Van Diemens Land, which are of recent date.

In the course of the Narrative, the term Savages is sometimes used in reference to the Aborigines of the countries visited; but it is only intended, by this term, to designate human beings, living on the wild produce of the earth, and destitute of any traces of civilization; and by no means, to convey the idea, that these people are more cruel than the rest of the human race, or of inferior intellect.

A hope is entertained by the writer, that this volume may convey a measure of useful information, and excite some interest on behalf of the Aborigines, and the Emigrant and Prisoner Population of Australia, as well as suggest important considerations, in connexion with the relation of man to his Creator and Redeemer. Under this hope, and with the desire, that the perusal of the work may be attended by the divine blessing, without which, nothing can be of any real benefit, the volume is submitted to the attention of the reader.

York, 15th of 12th mo. 1842.

NARRATIVE.

CHAPTER I.

Voyage to Van Diemens Land.—Embarkation —Emigrant Pensioners.—Dis-
orderly conduct.—Intemperance.—The Ocean.—Bottled Water.—Petrels.—
Coast of Spain.—Birds.—Storm.—Danger.—Equator.—Sunset.—Trinidad
and Martin Vaz.—Funeral.—Whales.—Fishes.—Albatross.—African Coast.—
Cape Town.—Schools.—Slavery.—Public Institutions.—Religious Meeting.—
Departure.—L'Agullas Bank.—Southern Ocean.—Birds.—Religious Labours.
—Coast of V. D. Land.—Colour of the Sea.—Piratical Vessel.—Sharks.—Bad
Bay.—Arrival at Hobart Town.

ALL necessary arrangements for a long voyage having previously been made, we embarked in St. Katharine's Dock,
London, on the 3rd of the 9th month, 1831, on board the
Science—a fine barque, of 236 tons, William Saunders, master. A few of our friends accompanied us to Gravesend,
where we anchored that afternoon, and others joined us there
on the following day, with whom we went to meeting, at
Rochester.   In this, the last assembly for public worship
which we attended in our native land, we were favoured to
feel much of the comfort of the Holy Spirit, and of confirmation respecting our projected voyage being undertaken in the
divine counsel.

In the cabin of the Science, there were two other passengers; and in the steerage, forty-six Chelsea pensioners, who
had commuted their pensions for an advance of four years'

B

payment; nine women, chiefly pensioners' wives; six children, and a young man, whom one of the pensioners had
befriended. These, with the crew, amounted to above eighty
persons.

On the 5th, some of the pensioners received a part of their
advance from the Government, to enable them to purchase
necessaries for the voyage, for which purpose some of them
went on shore; but they wasted their money in strong drink,
and returned on board so much intoxicated, that the necessity
of preventing others doing the same, was obvious. The men
became very unruly, but were appeased by the women being
allowed to go on shore to make purchases, and by a boat
with supplies of clothing, bedding, &c. being sent off to the
ship.—In the evening we proceeded further down the river,
and, on the 6th, dropped anchor off Deal. Here the men
were determined to go on shore, and were taken from the
vessel by Deal boatmen, in spite of remonstrance and threats
from the captain: many of them came back intoxicated, but
one returned no more.

We sailed from the Downs on the 9th, and from that time
till we reached the Cape of Good Hope, few days passed
without some of the pensioners being intoxicated and quarrelling: sometimes but few were sober; and, occasionally,
the women were as bad as the men. Three times the captain
was seized by different men, who threatened to throw him
overboard. One man was nearly murdered by one of his fellows, and all kinds of sin prevailed among them. A fruitful
source of this disorder was a daily allowance to each person
of about five liquid ounces of spirits. Some saved it for a few
days, and then got drunk with it: some purchased it from
others, and so long as their money lasted, or they could sell
their clothes, were constantly intoxicated. The general excitement produced by this quantity of spirits, made them
irritable in temper, and seemed to rouse every corrupt passion
of the human mind. To all expostulation, the constant reply
was: "We are free men, and it is our own: we have paid
for it, and have a right to do as we please with it."

From having been long accustomed to act in obedience
to military discipline, instead of upon principle, these men

were generally as incapable of taking care of themselves,
when temptation was in the way, as children; and the
state of confusion they were in was often appalling. From
first going on board we read to them twice a day from the
Bible or religious tracts. This was nearly the only time they
were quiet. At first some of them tried to stop us by making
a noise, but finding we proceeded without noticing them, they
ceased: and at the conclusion of the voyage, some of them
acknowledged, that the time of our reading had been the only
time in which they had had any comfort.

On arriving at the Cape of Good Hope, the captain delivered three of the most disorderly men to the civil authorities: two of them were detained, and three others and a
woman of bad character, left the vessel of their own accord.
Those who remained on board conducted themselves better
after we got to sea again, notwithstanding several of them
had become of evil notoriety during our short stay in Cape
Town.

But to return to our voyage. On the 16th of 9th month,
in the evening, we now and then caught a glimpse of the
light on the Lizard Point, Cornwall; which was the last
trace we saw of our native shores. Several of the pensioners
had begun to repent of having embarked, before reaching
this point! On the 17th, we were out of soundings, and the
ocean presented the dark blue colour that prevails where it
is unfathomably deep. The circle of view, not being broken
by other objects, appeared very limited. From the ordinary
elevation of a ship's deck, this circle is only estimated at
about eight miles in diameter. The night of the 18th was
stormy, and we were in some danger from want of skill in the
second mate, in whose watch the vessel was "taken aback"
in a squall. On the 19th, our water began to be very
disagreeable; and we found bottled spring-water, of which
we brought out a good stock, a great luxury. Many Stormy
Petrels followed the vessel on the 20th, and at various subsequent periods. These little birds, which are about the size of
a swallow, have a propensity to keep about the wake or track
of a ship in windy weather, and before, as well as during a
storm; therefore when they follow a vessel in calm weather,

they are considered as the harbingers of a breeze: but notwithstanding this, they are frequently to be seen in the same situation in continued fine weather, especially about meal times, when various crumbs of refuse food are cast overboard, which, floating into the wake of the vessel, are picked up with avidity by these lively little birds, that skim over the surface, sometimes alighting upon the unbroken waves, and running upon them with their webbed feet, balancing themselves by means of their wings, which they hold erect, and ready for flight.

We were off Cape Finisterre, on the N. W. coast of Spain, on the 21st; some of the land seemed of considerable elevation. On the 8th of 10th month, we entered the Torrid Zone; and saw a few Flying-fish; the first living creatures, except the Petrels, that we had seen for many days. A Swallow also cheered us by a visit: it flew many times around the vessel. A great number of Black and White Gulls, and some Porpoises, were seen in the evening. On the 17th, we lost the trade winds, that had urged us on rapidly for many days, and reached a latitude where squalls, often attended by thunder and heavy rain, and dead calms and variable breezes, frequently follow each other in quick succession, the thermometer varying from 78o to 82° in the shade. During a severe squall on the 25th, large patches of phosphorescent light were seen on the surface of the ocean for a short time: they presented a scene of great beauty, the interest of which was not diminished by the raging of the sea. The Swallow noticed on the 8th, and another which joined it, perished in the storm. On the 25th, we were in considerable danger, in consequence of the second mate getting intoxicated, and falling asleep in his watch, when the wind was strong, and only an inexperienced youth, at the wheel by which the vessel is steered. The mate was in consequence degraded from his office.

26th of 10th month, we crossed the Equator in 27° west longitude. None of those disagreeable scenes took place, that are often exhibited on such occasions, and that are as heathenish in their origin as in their practice; in which Neptune is represented by some person, and ceremonies are

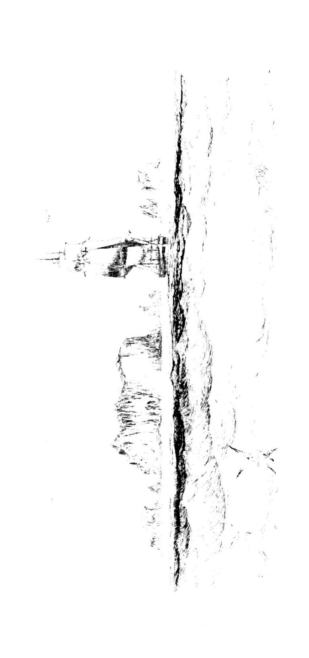

performed, outrageous to Christianity and to civilization. We passed under the vertical sun on the 2nd of 11th mo. having had a fine breeze since crossing the equator. Within the tropics, the sky at sunset frequently presents a scene of great beauty, in the softest tints. Blue is the prevailing colour in the zenith; nearer the horizon, verdigris green is shaded into rose colour, and sometimes into glowing red; with which also some of the patches of rich brown cloud of various shade are tinged. A purple shade is cast over the ocean, which is seldom rough; and the atmosphere being of a pleasant warmth, the effect of the whole is remarkably soothing and luxurious.

On the 4th of 11th mo. we passed between the rocks of Martin Vaz and the little island of Trinidad, off the coast of South America. As we approached them, the swell became bolder, and some Terns and Black Gulls, and a few Boobies were seen. The sight of land was cheering, notwithstanding, it was only that of an uninhabited island, and of the grotesque rocks occupied by sea fowl, depicted in the annexed etching.

On the 12th, the remains of an old man of some piety, named John Salmon, were committed to the deep. He had been in declining health from the time he came on board. His situation among a number who were swift to do evil, was painful, but he bore it patiently. On being inquired of, a short time before he died, if he felt peaceful, he replied, that he was very comfortable; and on being asked, if all his hope was in Christ, he said, "O yes! it had need." Last night, the corpse, wrapped in a blanket and sewed up in a hammock, with three eighteen pound shots to make it sink, was brought on deck, placed upon a hatch turned upside down, and covered with a union jack. This morning it was removed to the quarter-deck, around which the passengers and crew were seated. A flag was hoisted half-mast high, and the vessel was laid to, or made still upon the waters. The Captain read the funeral service of the Episcopal Church for such occasions; and when he came to the words, "Commit the remains, &c. to the deep," the men who were stationed for the purpose, removed the union jack, raised the head of the hatch, and launched the corpse over the ship's side into the ocean, in which it instantly sunk. At this moment a cry of

distress burst from the widow of the deceased, but she soon
became collected again, and the Captain proceeded with the
service.   He afterwards addressed the company on the folly
of wasting their lives in riot and excess, and I added an
exhortation to "watch and be sober:" but nevertheless,
some of the pensioners were again intoxicated before night!

The seaman who was lately raised to the office of second
mate, betrayed his trust on the 17th, and persuaded one of
the boys to steal liquor, with which they both got drunk, and
he consequently forfeited his place.—On the 27th, a sail was
in sight, which proved to be the Borneo, of London, on a
whaling voyage.   Whales had frequently been seen for some
time past, and at one time, a shoal of Porpoises of vast
extent passed us, swimming in a westerly direction, at a very
rapid rate.   The Borneo captured two whales while within
sight.   One of them spouted blood to a great height when
struck, and dragged the boat at a fearful rate, almost round
the circle of our horizon.   After the whale was towed alongside the vessel, we went on board, and inspected the huge
animal, which was of the same species as those taken in the
northern latitudes: it is called in this hemisphere the Right
Whale.   A shark was already at its side watching for prey.
The Humpbacked and the Fin Whales have also been occasionally seen of late, and the Right Whale in considerable numbers.
They make a noise resembling that occasioned by the escape
of steam from the boiler of a steam engine, but this is not
heard at a great distance: their heads are often beset with
barnacles.   The near view of these enormous animals, rising
majestically to the surface of the ocean, and spouting clouds
of spray, whilst the water is pouring off their ample sides, is
very interesting.   Within the warmer southern latitudes,
a number of Pilot-fish frequently accompanied us, swimming
rapidly, either close before the bow, or after the stern of the
vessel.   They are about the size of mackerel, and are marked
with alternate dark and silvery bands.   A sharp nosed fish
supposed to be a Sword-fish, about nine feet long, followed us for several days.   Several thick, dark-coloured fish
about a foot and a half long, were frequently swimming close
by the rudder.   Sometimes small Dolphins were playing

about the vessel; and numerous Flying-fish, of two species, darted from the bosom of the deep, and made aerial excursions of various length, sometimes of more than a hundred yards, endeavouring to escape the voracity of Bonitas and Albacores, which frequently sprung out of the water after them. The Flying-fish, which are about the size of small herrings, and of a silvery hue, often meet an enemy in the air, in the long-winged Wandering Albatross; which, in small numbers, and of plumage so varied as to admit of the individual birds being identified, accompanied us in this part of our voyage, sailing almost motionless on the wing.

On the 2nd of 12th mo. we sighted the coast of Africa, off Saldanha Bay; from whence we beat up past Dassen and Robben Islands, into Table Bay, which we entered on the 5th. The sea broke heavily on Dassen Island, which is low and sandy, and against the main land; the coast of which appeared hilly, with mountains remote from the shore. Some of the slopes near the sea were very sandy, and the hills looked arid and brown, except where there were patches of cultivation. About Table Bay, the scenery is very beautiful. Hills of moderate elevation, with a few scattered farms, bound the northern side: on the east is an extensive sandy flat; beyond which, at a distance of about 30 miles, rise the peaked and rugged mountains of Hottentot's Holland. And on the south, at the foot of Table Mountain, which is 3,582 feet high, with the Devil's Hill to the left, and the Lion's Hill to the right, Cape Town, with its clean-looking, white houses, interspersed with trees, is situated. The ships and boats in the bay, the houses scattered along the shore, and the numerous sea fowl—Gulls, Albatrosses, Terns, Divers, and Penguins—flying and swimming around, contribute to cheer the eye which has for many weeks looked upon little, but the unvarying circle of the dark blue ocean.—The Penguins are unable to fly on account of the shortness of their wings, but these serve as fins to impel them through the water, in which they swim with their bodies submerged.

On the 6th, we went on shore, and became the guests of Dr. and Jane Philip; from whom, as well as from some other

Christian friends, before strangers to us, we received much kind attention. Dr. Philip introduced us to the Governor, Sir Galbraith Lowry Cole, who received us politely, and permitted us to land some cases of religious books and tracts for gratuitous distribution, free of duty, and without subjecting the vessel to port charges, more than are usual on putting into the bay merely for refreshments. We also received a kind welcome from John Bell, the Colonial Secretary, and from several other persons of influence.

In company with Dr. Philip, we visited several schools and other public institutions for the amelioration of the human race. One of the infant schools contained a set of interesting children of the upper class, who were all of white complexion: the separation between these and the other ranks was effected by a higher rate of payment. In the lower school there was a lively group, of varied shade of skin, including the children of the fair European, the brown Hottentot, and the Black of various nations, torn from his native land, by the ruthless hand of slavery. The animated countenances of all colours, and the prompt and pertinent answers the children gave, shewed intellectual powers, that under such cultivation, promised well for future days.

Slavery, with its train of abominations, was still in existence at this period in Cape Town. I one day saw a young man attempting to sell a coloured child, which I had ground to believe was his own; and the reason he then retained it was, that he could not get his price!—Several times we rode in a carriage driven by a young man of white skin, good person and agreeable countenance, whom benevolence had placed in a situation to earn the price of the cost of his own freedom. This circumstance forcibly reminded me of the question: "Who maketh thee to differ from another, and what hast thou that thou didst not receive?" It was not the young man's fault that he was born a slave: it was not my merit that I was born free. I felt thankful under the conviction that God was increasing the friends of the oppressed, and opening the eyes of men to see the incompatibility of slavery with the Gospel.

At a committee meeting of the Philanthropic Institution,

for redeeming female children from slavery, it was deeply interesting to see sprightly children, the age of my own, brought forward to be sold for manumission. As I watched a slave mother who held a little girl by each hand, and observed her animated countenance, lighted up by the hope of obtaining the boon of liberty for her offspring, the question recurred to me, Why were these children born in bondage and mine born free? Was it only because the oppressor laid his unhallowed hand upon their parents, and because mine, by divine mercy, were saved from such oppression? A reckless persecutor was indeed permitted to cast one of my predecessors into prison, because he dared not to violate his conscience; and to keep him there till his days were ended by the severity, long before he had attained to my own age; but this entailed no curse on me or on my children. The persecutor bore the curse! But were men to act on the great Christian principle, "Whatsoever ye would that men should do unto you, do ye even so unto them;" there would be neither persecution nor slavery.

We visited the noble Library, the reading room of which is open to all classes, also the College, Hospital, and Prisons. We attended a meeting for the formation of a Temperance Society, and were present at a meeting for religious purposes in the chapel of the London Missionary Society. In this meeting my companion spoke for the first time in the line of gospel ministry. I was also favoured with an opportunity to express my Christian interest on behalf of those assembled, in whose company we felt the force of the declaration "God is no respecter of persons: but in every nation he that feareth him, and worketh righteousness is accepted of him."

On the 15th, having parted from our kind friends in Cape Town, with earnest desires that many more might be added to those already labouring to spread the knowledge of Christ, and to ameliorate the condition of their fellow-men, we returned on board the Science, being accompanied by Dr. Philip, who before he left us, prayed vocally for our preservation.

On the 18th, we were again out of sight of land; which,

while it was in view, was so attractive as to keep us too unsettled to attend much to other things. In the evening a breeze, which we had had during the day, increased into a gale, and as we were in the act of crossing L'Agullas Bank, which lies off Cape L'Agullas—the southermost point of Africa—the waves were magnificently bold. Sometimes we were in a deep hollow, and the next minute mounted on the top of a lofty billow, which, as it approached, seemed ready to swallow us up; but the buoyancy of the vessel occasioned it to rise over the surge; in mounting which, the masts would form an angle of, perhaps, 45 degrees with the horizon, in an opposite direction to that in which the billow advanced: on reaching its top the inclination was suddenly reversed, the wind at the same time pressing the vessel against the receding mass of water, which boiled from under the leeward side, or sometimes flowed over a portion of the deck. Sometimes the top of a broken billow struck against the ship's side, and covered half the vessel with spray. Now and then a shower fell, but often the sun shone brightly on the agitated scene, illuminating the spray from the tops of the broken, dark blue waves, with the colours of the rainbow, and sometimes shewing light of emerald green through the unbroken water. Vast numbers of Stormy Petrels were sailing on the wing, within a few yards of the stern of our bark, and numerous Wandering Albatrosses were flying around, or occasionally settling on the surface of the boisterous ocean, and riding with careless dignity over the highest billows, scarcely regarding their surfy tops.

When custom has taken away the nervous excitement occasioned by the rolling of the ship, it is surprising how little the mind recognizes danger under such circumstances; and " how thoughtless still the thoughtless seem." For my own part, I enjoyed the spectacle; but the remembrance, that He who rules over all is our Father, merciful and kind, regarding us for good, was necessary for the enjoyment: and the knowledge, that such scenes were often the preludes of a summons to the bar of eternal judgment, rendered it to me, a time of deep searching of heart; and one in which self was deeply abased under a sense of unworthiness; notwithstanding a capacity was granted to trust in Jesus for mercy.

Our voyage was made between the 39th and 45th degrees of south latitude. Most of the way we had a strong breeze, and the weather so cold that we found it needful to use warmer clothing than we had been accustomed to wear in England.—Persons making voyages of this kind ought not only to be provided with warm clothing, but with such as is adapted for wet weather at sea.—Fin, Spermaceti, and Right Whales were often seen in this part of the voyage, also the Wandering and the Black Albatross. The latter is the bolder bird, though the smaller species. One taken, measured 3ft. from the tip of the bill to that of the tail, and 7ft. from the extremity of one wing to that of the other. Sometimes a few Sooty and other Petrels were also seen, and on the 10th of 1st month, 1832, when upwards of 100 miles south of the island of Amsterdam, a Penguin passed us. To the south of New Holland we saw a Fishing Eagle chasing the Albatrosses, and observed long pieces of sea weed.

On the first day of the week, during the voyage, we regularly assembled the pensioners along with such of the ship's company as could be present, and imparted religious instruction to them, according to the fresh ability, from time to time afforded us. On these occasions we read to them from the Holy Scriptures; directed them to the convictions of the Divine Spirit on their own minds, condemning them for sin; counselled them to seek mercy with God through a crucified Redeemer; and often prayed with them for the continuance of the long-suffering of the Most High. When approaching the land of our destination, under a fresh sense of duty, we had religious interviews with them singly or in families, in which several of them were much contrited.

On the 4th of 2nd month, we were cheered by the sight of Van Diemens Land, which we made opposite Port Davey, in consequence of the south-easterly direction of the wind. We had not seen land for fifty days, but had become so much accustomed to the solitude of the ocean, as to feel reconciled to it, and at home upon its bosom.—The water this morning presented the olive colour, common where the

depth is fathomable, or to use a sea term " within soundings."
It has this colour generally, from the Cape of Good Hope to
about opposite the island of Amsterdam.—A small sail was
seen to the northward.   The number of vessels sighted since
we left England, has only been about six.   One of these, in
the Atlantic, was of piratical appearance and suspicious
movements.   We had no defence but in the Lord; our trust
was in him; we lifted up our hearts to him in prayer for
protection; and were separated by a thunder storm from
the object of our fears, when it seemed to be bearing down
upon us: thus, if these fears were not groundless, were we
" delivered from unreasonable and wicked men."

The south-west coast of V. D. Land is mountainous.
Some of its features reminded us of the north front of the
Cleveland-hills of Yorkshire, but it is more lofty and rugged,
and the scattered herbage and bushes upon it looked as
brown as an English heath.—Large bubbles ascended in slow
succession to the surface of the ocean, while we were becalmed opposite Port Davey; numerous animalcules were sporting
on the surface, and fringed Jelly-fishes tinged with purple or
crimson, were swimming at various depths.   Several sharks
were cruising around the vessel.—In the course of our
voyage, a few Grey Sharks, 6 to 8ft. long, were captured by
means of hooked lines, baited with pork.   When a vessel is
making four knots, or miles, an hour, a shark cannot take
the bait; because the voracious animal is under the necessity
of turning on one side to sieze its prey, and before this can
be effected, the bait has passed beyond reach.   To remedy
this the bait was hawled close under the stern, and line given
out, so as to render the bait still upon the water; it was
then immediately seized.   One of these sharks had several
Sucking-fish adhering to it, some of them within its gills.
These fish when suffered to fasten on the hand, produced a
strange and unpleasant sensation.   The heart of the Shark
being taken out of the body, and put into a bucket of salt
water, continued to beat for several minutes.

During the night of the 6th, we passed to the south of
V. D. Land.   The sea again assumed its dark blue colour.
Three large Grampuses came close to the vessel: they made

a snorting noise, but did not eject water like the larger species of the whale tribe. A breeze on the morning of the 7th carried us to the south of the Mew Stone—a large conical rock a few miles from the shore. The mountains on the south coast are rugged, and some of them peaked. Patches of snow were lying on a lofty one near South Cape. Wood covered their sides and reached in some places to the water's edge. We were in danger of being driven into Bad Bay, after passing too close to the Acteon Reef,—possibly through an opening in it,—but were enabled to escape from this perilous position by a sudden change of wind accompanying a thunder storm. After being thus mercifully delivered from this peril, and having rounded the rocky islets fronting Tasman's Head, the wind, before daylight was quite gone, resumed its former position, and we proceeded up Storm Bay, along the east side of Bruny Island, as far as Fluted Cape—a fine mass of columnar basalt.—Having the advantage of a bright moon we continued our course until so dazzled by numerous fires of large extent, consuming the adjacent woods, as to be unable to see our way. The vessel was therefore kept "standing off and on" till day light.

Early in the morning of the 8th of 2nd mo. we entered the Derwent; and at a short distance from Hobart Town, took in a pilot, who brought us to anchor in Sulivans Cove. Our feelings were those of reverent thankfulness to the Great Preserver of men, for having brought us safely over the great deep; and our prayers earnest for the continuance of his care over us, and for ability to go in and out acceptably before him.

CHAPTER II.

HOBART Town, the capital of Tasmania or Van Diemens Land, is beautifully situated on undulating ground by the side of an estuary called the Derwent, from its resemblance to the lake of that name in Cumberland—In 1831, the number of its inhabitants was 8,360. In 1837 it had become augmented to 14,461, and was still rapidly increasing. The streets are spacious, and most of them cross at right angles. The houses are chiefly brick, and covered with shingles that have the appearance of slates: they stand separately in little gardens, except in a few of the streets best situated for business, and extend over several low hills at the foot of Mount Wellington, which is 4,000 feet high, and covered with wood, except where bassaltic cliffs protrude near the top.—The view from the town toward the sea is exceedingly beautiful, extending over many miles of water, enlivened by shipping and bounded by woody hills, on which the greenness of numerous patches of cultivated ground, ornamented by white-washed cottages, has taken the place of the sombre forest. The sketch of this picturesque spot forming the frontispiece of this volume, was taken by my friend Charles Wheeler, in 1833. Since that period it has undergone several alterations, and a tall cupola has been substituted for the spire of the Episcopal place of worship.

Soon after we came to anchor in Sulivans Cove, on which the town stands, several persons came on board to enquire for intelligence from England, and among them a merchant, on whom we had letters of credit. With him we went on shore, and he introduced us to the Lieutenant Governor, Col. George Arthur; to whom we delivered a letter of introduction from Lord Goderich, the Secretary of State for the Colonies, commending us to the protection of the Lieut. Governor, and requesting him to forward, what Lord Goderich was pleased to call, our benevolent object, so far as he could consistently with the public good. Our first interview with Col. Arthur, gave us a favourable impression of his character, as a Governor and as a Christian, which further acquaintance with him strongly confirmed: he took great interest in the temporal and spiritual prosperity of the Colonists, and in the reformation of the prisoner population, as well as in the welfare of the surviving remnant of the native Black Inhabitants; and he assured us that every facility should be granted us, in attempts to further any of these objects.

In the evening we returned on board the Science, and the chief mate requested us to wake him at 10 o'clock, that he might see the lights of the steerage passengers put out; some of them having been on shore and having returned intoxicated: he had been kept up during the past two nights, in consequence of the position of the vessel in regard to the land; and now, when 10 o'clock arrived and he had been a short time asleep, we found it impracticable to awake him. After vainly trying a variety of expedients, some of which made him speak, but without consciousness, we extinguished the lights ourselves, the captain being on shore. The mate slept soundly till five in the morning, when he awoke in terror, under a vague idea of neglect of duty.

2nd mo. 9th. We went on shore with John Leach, a young man from Bradford, Yorkshire, professing with the Wesleyans, who came to V. D. Land under an apprehension of religious duty: at this time he worked as a journeyman cabinet maker three days in the week for his support, and devoted the remainder of his time to religious purposes.—We made calls on several persons to whom we had letters of introduction, and engaged a lodging in Liverpool Street, near the entrance into the Government Domain.—When walking in the town, my companion met one of his nephews, whose residence was in a distant part of the island, and who was greatly surprised to see his relative, having had no notice of his intention to visit this part of the world. This unexpected interview was mutually agreeable; for thus far from home, (and every one in this country calls his native land Home) the mind clings with increased attachment to every tie and every recollection.

12th. We sat down together to wait upon the Lord, in our own sitting room, and were joined by the captain of a vessel who had lately taken some of the Aborigines to Flinders Island, where they are provided for by the Government.—We continued the practice of holding our meetings for worship, on first days and once in the course of the week, for a considerable period by ourselves, unless, as on this occasion, any one casually stepped in. In the evening we accepted an invitation from the Lieut. Governor, to take tea with him and his family—a numerous and interesting group. After tea, at the request of the Lieut. Governor, I read to them the 6th chapter of John, the servants being likewise assembled at the evening devotion of the family; and after a subsequent pause, I also expressed a few words, on the importance of an individual participation in the bread which came down from heaven, which Christ declared to be his flesh, that he would give for the life of the world. We were favoured on this occasion, to feel comfort from the Lord, especially in a short interval of silence, which terminated in vocal prayer.

15th. The little vessel which we saw on the 4th instant, proved to be the Liberty, she arrived at Hobart Town yesterday: we went on board of her to day, and learned from the captain that she was built out of the wreck of the Betsy and Sophia, which sailed from London on the 4th of the 6th month, 1831, on a whaling expedition, and which had gone to the Island of Desolation or Kerguelens Land, to take a kind of seal called the Sea Elephant: she had nearly completed her cargo from the blubber of this animal and that of the Black Whale, and was coming out of one of the bays, when she unshipped her rudder, and in spite of all exertions, went to leeward upon the rocks, and became a wreck: the papers and stores were saved, and the latter were sufficient to serve four months; but calculating upon the uncertainty of escaping for a long time from these inhospitable shores, the men immediately took to the scanty allowance of 2lbs of biscuit each, with about 4lbs. of pork per week, for the whole nineteen men; two of whom had been brought from Prince Edward's Island, where they had been left by the captain of another ship. They used the flesh of Sea Elephants and of birds, to supply the deficiency in other food. They were wrecked on the 16th of 3rd mo. 1831. After being on the island about a month, they began to build their little vessel, which they named "The Liberty;" and in which fourteen of them sailed on the 12th of the 12th mo. Their sufferings made many of them thoughtful, and they kept up religious service on board. They made this voyage in the latitude of 44° S. and had plenty of wind. Three times they had heavy gales, but their little bark, which had one mast and was about twenty tons burden, rode so well over the billows, that they shipped no seas; but they had almost constantly to work the pumps. They reached Macquarie Harbour, on the west coast of this Island, when they had only 6lbs. of biscuit left. It was late when they arrived at the Penal Settlement, and the Commandant was in bed; the captain therefore remained till morning before seeing him, but was furnished with comfortable accommodation. When he awoke, and found himself in a house, he said it was long before he could realize his situation, or be sure that he was not dreaming. The Commandant treated this crew with great kindness, and a pious minister addressed them so movingly in the chapel, that the hardy sailor said, "There was hardly any body there that did not cry." They were furnished with a plentiful supply of provisions, and sailed from Macquarie Harbour on the 4th inst. and were favoured to arrive here in good health, after a voyage of about 3,500 miles. Five men whom they left on the island, were afraid to come in the Liberty; the provision and ammunition were therefore

divided with them.   A vessel was afterwards sent from
V. D. Land, to bring these men away, but they had been
previously taken off by an American Whaler.

16th. We went on board the Elizabeth, in company with
Captain Forster, the chief police magistrate, to whom we had
been introduced by the Governor, and witnessed the examination of part of the convicts, just arrived from England in
this ship. A variety of questions were put to them relating
to the crimes for which they had been sentenced to transportation, the number of times they had previously been apprehended, the causes of their apprehension, the punishments
they had received, the state of their families, what their
parents were, whether they could read or write, their occupation, &c. of all which a record is kept. The Government
was already in possession of information on many of these
subjects, but further particulars are often elicited after
the arrival of the prisoners. The convicts are assigned as
servants to the colonists, and the vacancies occasioned by
any others having obtained tickets-of-leave are first supplied; the rest are then assigned to the service of such
as apply for them, except in cases of second transportation, when they are mostly sent to a penal settlement.—
In the present instance, a man was brought out a second
time; but on account of his having behaved well on the
voyage, and some other circumstances in his favour, he was
ordered by the Governor into a chain-gang; where, if he
continue to improve, he will after a certain time be assigned
to private service.

Dr. Martin, the Surgeon-superintendent, who came out
with the ship, went over it with us : it had been kept
so clean and well ventilated, that it was perfectly free
from unpleasant smell, notwithstanding the prisoners, 220
in number, had slept in it last night.—The boys were
separated from the men, and a system of discipline and
instruction was pursued amongst them, that was attended
with very pleasing results. Some of the convicts were
employed by the Doctor as assistants and monitors. Out
of 120 of the prisoners, 76 could not read; and many of
them seemed never to have had any care bestowed upon them

before. Several of them learned to read and write, and improved in their conduct upon the passage.

Dr. Martin's system of discipline does not exclude corporal punishment in extreme cases; but it unites firmness with kindness, and such an appeal to the convictions, as brings a sense of its justice with the exercise of coercion. The prisoners of good behaviour, particularly the boys, were encouraged by a reward, of a little more time on deck than the others. I was much gratified with the inspection of this ship: it in no degree diminished the interest I have felt for this degraded part of the human family: and I thought it very evident, that persons coming out under religious impressions, might be very useful in assisting the surgeons, in the discharge of the important duties that devolve upon them in convict vessels. On mentioning my views to Dr. Martin, he said he should have been very glad of such help; and I apprehend such would be the general feeling of the surgeons employed in this service. It is impracticable for them personally to superintend the adults and the boys at the same time, when they are confined in separate places.

20th. We went to the Penitentiary to see the convicts from on board the Elizabeth, examined by the Lieut. Governor, who spoke to several of them individually: he alluded to the degraded state into which they had brought themselves by their crimes; this he justly compared to a state of slavery; he gave them counsel regarding their future conduct, warning them particularly against the influence of bad company, and of drunkenness; and told them they might regard the door of a public house, through which many of them had come into their present situation, as the entrance to a jail; that their conduct would be narrowly watched, and if it should be bad, they would be severely punished, put to work in a chain-gang, or sent to a penal settlement, where they would be under very severe discipline; or their career might be terminated on the scaffold. That, on the contrary, if they behaved well, they would in the course of a proper time, be indulged with a ticket-of-leave, which would permit them to reap the profit of their own labour: that if they should still persevere in doing well, they would then become eligible for a conditional pardon, which would give them the liberty of the colony: and that a further continuance in good conduct, would open the way for a free pardon, which would liberate those who received it, to return to their native land.   That the masters to whom they were assigned, would in the meantime, provide them a sufficiency of food, clothing, and bedding; and that the Government expected them to labour for their masters without wages, and to do it cheerfully.

After the Lieut. Governor had concluded, I begged leave to say a few words, and my request was readily granted. I endeavoured to enforce what the Governor had said, pointing out its bearing upon their immortal interests; also directing their attention to their own experience, in regard to the cause of the sins for which they stood convicted before a human tribunal, and of many others, of which they were guilty in the sight of God, at whose judgment-seat they must all stand.   This cause, I suggested to them, was their neglecting to confer with their own consciences, and I recommended them to the daily exercise of this duty, in order that they might understand their need of the help of the Holy Spirit, to resist sin, and of the atonement of a Saviour for pardon, and thus be prepared to pray for help and pardon in the name of Jesus, who came to save men *from* their sins, and not *in* them; and in order that they might keep these things in remembrance, I recommended them daily to read their Bibles.

Several of the convicts who arrived by the Elizabeth, had belonged to a society of thieves in London, who limited their number to forty members, admitted by their captain, at any age, but preferring the young.   They were distinguished by marks, which had occasionally been changed because others had imitated them.   They met at certain times to be trained to expertness in pocket-picking, and to divide their booty, which was expended in dissipation and profligacy, unless any of their number were in prison; in which case a portion was devoted to paying counsel for them on their trial.   Several other such societies are said to exist in the metropolis of England.   Some of the juvenile prisoners had been confined on board a hulk before being sent to V. D. Land. In this situation they appeared to have corrupted each other greatly. There is much ground to apprehend that the juvenile hulks are nurseries of vice and crime.

22nd. I had some conversation with a person who was brought to the Colony in 1804, at the time that Lieut. Governor Collins first formed a settlement in V. D. Land. At that period she was but a child; and on landing was lodged with some others under a blanket supported by sticks, near the place where the Commissariat-office now stands in Hobart Town, which at that time was covered with wood. After spending a night there, they were removed to the spot where the village of New Town now stands, and lodged in a hollow tree. Here they were first visited by the Aborigines, with whom the children were often left, and who treated them kindly. Provisions becoming scarce, the people often cooked maritime plants collected on the sea shore, which bear to this day, the name of Botany Bay Greens. Sometimes they collected for food the crap or refuse of the blubber of whales, out of which the oil had been taken by whaling vessels, and which was washed up on the shores. At length the pressure of hunger was so great, as to oblige the Governor to give leave to some of the convicts, to go into the country and shift for themselves. Many of these committed outrages upon the natives, whose animosity toward the white people thus became excited at an early period, notwithstanding many years elapsed before they were in open hostilty.

23rd. We visited the House of Correction for females, termed the Factory, a considerable building of several wards, with apartments for the Superintendent, and a chapel. It contains about 230 prisoners, who are employed in picking and spinning wool, and in washing for the Hospital, Orphan-school, &c. Most of the inmates sleep in hammocks, and every thing about the place is very clean. On being sent hither for misconduct, the women are dressed in a prison garb and have their hair cut off, which they esteem a great punishment; and in some cases they are subjected to solitary confinement.

25th. We occupied a little leisure by a walk to one of the

woody hills near the town, which was clothed with the Gum trees—species of *Eucalyptus*—of large size, having foliage somewhat like willows, and growing among grass and small shrubs. Many trees were lying on the ground, and in various stages of decay. Smaller trees, called here Honey Suckle, She Oak, Cherry Tree, and Wattle, were interspersed among the others, and the ground was decorated with *Leptospermam scoparium, Correa virens, Indigofera australis,* and *Epacris impressa;* the last of which resembles heath with white, pink, or crimson flowers. The trees in this country often bear the name of others belonging to the Northern Hemisphere. Thus the Honey-suckle of the Australian regions is generally some species of *Banksia,* often resembling a fir in growth, but having foliage more like a holly; and the Cherry-tree is an *Exocarpos*—a leafless, green, cypress-like bush, with small red or white fruit, bearing the stone outside!—The vallies here are termed gullies. In one of these we set up from among some dead wood, two Opossums and some animals called Bandicoots, both about the size of rabbits. Some pretty birds were sporting among the branches, gay butterflies fluttering among the flowers, and a Mole-cricket, enlivened by a recent shower, was merrily chirping in the ground. Grasshoppers with wings of black and yellow were very numerous, so as to be injurious to vegetation; and among the rocks, and on the trunks of trees, little dark lizards were plentiful, basking in the clear sunshine.

26th. We visited a chain-gang of upwards of 100 prisoners, at Bridgewater, 11 miles from Hobart Town; they were employed under the superintendence of a military officer, in making a raised causeway across a muddy flat in the Derwent, and were generally in good health, notwithstanding the water here is not of the best quality; but like much in the colony, contains a large quantity of alumine. A guard of soldiers under arms stood over the prisoners while we addressed them in the barrack yard. They were quiet and attentive, and we were well satisfied in having gone to see them.

27th. We walked to the Government-garden, which is situated on the beautiful banks of the Derwent, about a mile from the town, and comprises several acres, enclosed with a wall, except on the side next the river. The climate is almost too cold for grapes and cucumbers, but apples, pears, quinces, mulberries, and walnuts, succeed better than in England. Oaks, ashes, and sycamores, raised from English seed, attain to three or four feet the first year. Bees have been lately introduced: the first hive swarmed sixteen times this summer! Many of the little shrubs which ornament English greenhouses are natives of this country, so that the gardens here have the advantage of having them in the open ground; and to these are added several from Africa and New-South-Wales: here also are some fine, young Norfolk Island Pines.

28th. We looked into the King's School, conducted on the National School plan; in which there are upwards of forty boys, who pay from 4d. to 1s. a week, but attend irregularly.—The inefficiency of this school occasioned it to be subsequently remodelled under a more efficient teacher.—In a walk in the evening, on a partially cleared hill, in the environs of the town, we had conversation with several assigned prisoners, who were breaking up plots of ground for their respective masters. On remarking to one of them, that he had perhaps found his way to this country "through the door of a public-house:" he replied with some feeling, "You say right; and if I had known sooner what I know now, perhaps I should not have come here at all." Another said, with an expression of pleasure, that on his way out, he had learned to read the Testament, and that he thought he could read the tracts we had given him. Another, that he had lately become aware of his danger from sin, and was now seeking peace. On the remark being made, that peace was offered to man on the condition of repentance toward God, and faith toward our Lord Jesus Christ; and that when it was obtained, the help of the Holy Spirit must be sought, for ability to walk in the right way, he added, "Yes, and we must not grieve the Holy Spirit." One of these men became pious, and after some years made a profession with the Society of Friends: he subsequently became free, and continued to conduct himself creditably to his religious profession.

29th. We walked to Elizabeth Town, usually called New Norfolk, in consequence of a number of persons, formerly residing on Norfolk Island, being settled in the neighbourhood. The distance from Hobart Town is about 22 miles, by the road, which is a pretty good one for carriages ; and, which passing through the little villages of New Town, O'Briens Bridge, and Glenorchy, winds under the mountains by the side of the Derwent, which retains the appearance of a chain of picturesque lakes most of the way. It is navigable for small vessels to New Norfolk, where it is about as wide as the Thames at Battersea. The mountains are clothed with wood ; but in many places the timber is not so thick as to exclude the growth of grass. Some narrow flats of good land, partially cultivated, occur near the river. The rocks exposed by cutting the road are basalt and sandstone, or more dense silicious formations, and limestone imbedding marine fossils. A considerable piece of road has been recently cut near New Norfolk, by a chain-gang, stationed in three poor looking huts, into one of which we stepped, to give the men a few tracts. They were without Bibles, which one of them remarked, they might often spend half an hour advantageously in reading. This we represented to one of the Episcopal Chaplains of the Colony, who caused the deficiency to be supplied, and placed some copies of the Scriptures at our disposal, to apply in other cases of need. Evening closed in, very dark, before we reached our destination, and the noise of strange birds, lizards and frogs, became great, and very striking to an English ear. We passed several neat farm houses, and some decent inns on the way, and at the end of our journey found accommodation at the Bush Inn, little inferior to that of decent inns, a step below first-rate, in England.

3rd mo. 1st. The site of New Norfolk is so laid out, that the streets will cross at right angles. The houses were at this time about thirty in number, exclusive of an Episcopal place of worship and an unfinished hospital. We visited the latter, which contained about forty patients, under the superintendence of one of the Colonial Surgeons. We also visited a respectable boarding-school, of about twenty fine looking

boys, kept by a young man with whose family I was acquainted in England.

2nd. We returned to Hobart Town, calling at a few small
cottages on the Sorell-rivulet; where we reasoned with the
occupants on "temperance, righteousness, and judgment to
come." Learning that there was "a marked tree road," or a
way through "the bush," as the forest is termed in this
country, marked by pieces of bark being chopped off the
sides of trees, we ventured to take it; and though the distance was five miles, and it was extremely hilly and rough,
the variety was pleasant. Some of the species of Gum-tree
have deciduous bark, and consequently white trunks; these
are generally blackened at the base by fire, that has been
kindled to clear off the underwood and long-grass, at various
intervals; long strips of bark hang from the branches, and
great numbers of dying and dead trees, the wreck of ages, lie
on the ground in these forests. The only quadruped we saw
was an Opossum. A flock of Black Cockatoos were screaming and tearing off the bark from dead trees, to obtain the
grubs on which they feed. Near the main road, a prisoner
was at work splitting the wood of the Peppermint-tree, a
species of *Eucalyptus*, into posts and rails: he was one who,
as well as his master and family, had been recently awakened
to the inportance of eternal things, by the labours of John
Leach, and belonged to a little congregation of Wesleyans, at
O'Briens Bridge. The warmth of feeling of the master was
like that described by the apostle Paul, in some of the early
converts to Christianity; who, he says, "If it had been
possible, would have plucked out their own eyes, and given
them to him."

5th. Apprehending it would be right for us to take the
first opportunity of visiting the penal settlement, at Macquarie Harbour, we conferred with the Lieut. Governor, on
the subject, and received his sanction.—6th. We accompanied the Lieut. Governor to the Old Orphan School, and
to an unfinished building, designed for the better accommodation of this institution. The latter is prettily situated near
New-town, and is intended for about six hundred children.

On the 7th, we went to New Norfolk by a coach, which

changed horses at the Black Snake Inn, on the road; and on the 8th, accompanied by Robert Officer, the surgeon in charge of the Hospital, made calls on several of the inhabitants, and visited a Government School at the Back River. On the 9th, we accompanied George Dixon, an old school-fellow of mine, and three of his nieces, to his house at Green Valley, on the Lower Clyde, travelling twenty seven miles on foot, by the side of a little cart, drawn by four oxen and driven by a prisoner, and proceeding at the rate of about two miles and a half per hour, along a road, a large part of which was a mere cart track. Much of the country was settled: it consisted of hills, generally covered with open grassy forest, and interspersed with little patches of cultivated ground. In locations of land of two or three thousand acres, it is seldom that as many hundreds have been tilled. Large portions are of woody and rocky hills that cannot be ploughed, but on which sheep feed. In this country, these animals keep in good health in the woods, the climate being exceedingly dry. Where the ground is free from timber, the grass is in tufts, often not covering more than one-third of the surface.

On the way we looked into a school near Macquarie Plains, and called at the huts of a chain-gang, employed at a place called the Deep Gulley, in cutting a point of land, so as to admit the road to pass by the side of the Derwent. At this place coal is visible, in narrow strata alternating with sandstone and shale. On Macquarie Plains we called on John Terry, an emigrant from Yorkshire, who has a corn mill at New Norfolk, and who was here shearing his sheep. He is a scrupulously honest man, who left England at a time when farmers were suffering adversity, and notwithstanding many difficulties that he has had to contend with, he thinks his circumstances have been greatly improved by the change. A few miles beyond his cottage is the Woolpack Inn; the sitting-room of which would not disgrace a market town in England. We called also at the hut of a Scotchman, to get a drink of water, no more being to be had for nine miles. Here we met a person of our acquaintance, who, like many other young men, on first arriving in the colony, was too much excited with the notion of shooting Kangaroos and

Parrots, to settle down at once to some useful occupation. In the course of this excursion for amusement, he sustained an injury by falling from a horse, that long disabled him from earning a livelihood.　Pursuing our route over low hills, some clear of wood and others covered with Black Wattle, *Acacia affinis*, yielding a gum like Gum Arabic, we at length reached Green Valley, where we received a hearty greeting from Agnes Dixon, a native of Lewis, one of the Western Islands of Scotland, who soon prepared a refreshing cup of tea; after which, we gladly resigned our weary limbs and blistered feet to rest.

George Dixon emigrated to this colony eleven years ago, he was trained to agricultural pursuits, and has brought a portion of his location of land into cultivation, both in the growth of wheat and other grain; he has also formed a good garden, which is well stocked with fruit trees and has a Hawthorn hedge.　The common fences of the country are formed of logs, branches, or posts and rails.　His house is built of split wattles, plastered and whitewashed, the roof projecting in front and resting on wooden pillars so as to form a verandah, a common style of building in this country.　The house consists of two front rooms with boarded floors, and two behind,—a kitchen and store room,—floored with stone.　His land consists of basaltic hills with grassy forest, and he has about a mile of frontage on the Clyde, which at this season of the year is little more than a chain of pools—called here lagoons —of various length and depth, and about 30 ft. in width. In winter this becomes a considerable river.　Some parts of its banks are open, others bushy, and some rocky.　In one place a rock like a steeple stands between a cliff and the margin of the river; this is depicted in the annexed etching, which presents also a fair representation of the woody hills of Tasmania, and their white barked Gum-trees. G. Dixon's shepherd is a prisoner, but a man of religious sensibility: he became a thief from the influence of intoxicating drink, but does not shew any dishonesty when he abstains: he had a ticket-of-leave, but lost it, in consequence of being persuaded to drink a glass of porter, which immediately revived his thieving propensity.

We remained in the district of the Clyde, which is a branch of the Derwent, till the 19th, and in the course of this time visited the recently laid-out towns of Bothwell, on the upper, and Hamilton, on the lower part of the river, as well as many of the settlers in the surrounding country, and on another branch of the Derwent, called the Ouse.

Bothwell has already a small Episcopal place of worship, built of stone, an inn of two stories, of brick, about thirty houses, of wood, and a small jail, of the same material. Several of the settlers in the vicinity are persons of respectability from various parts of the United Kingdom; a few of them are remarkable for their piety: two have water-mills a little above the town. Hamilton, at this time consisted of a water-mill and about ten houses, occupied chiefly by artizans of various kinds, who are a great accommodation to the settlers of the surrounding district; and such of them as are sober and industrious make a respectable livelihood.

The country about Bothwell is hilly. Basalt is the prevailing rock, but some of the hills are sandstone; and near the river in a place below the town, the sandstone forms projections; under which, prisoners who had escaped into the woods, and who in this country are termed Bush-rangers, formerly found concealment. These people plundered the settlers and committed other outrages; but most of these outlaws have been captured or shot. Many of the hills about Hamilton are also basaltic, some of them are remarkably red, and bare of wood at the top, which is often of a vivid green, from being covered with Chick-weed of the same species that is troublesome in the gardens of England. She-oak—*Casuarina quadrivalvis,* is the prevailing tree on these hills: it seldom grows in contact: its trunk is about 10 ft. high, and 5 ft. round; its head spherical, 10 or 15 ft. in diameter, and consisting of pendulous, leafless, green, jointed twigs, resembling horse-tail weed. From the neighbourhood of Hamilton a range of rocky mountains is visible to the west, beyond which the country is high and little known, and toward the centre of the island, a high craggy mountain, called the Peak of Teneriffe, is very conspicuous. Among the hills, and on the tops of some of them are level tracts, which bear the name of marshes or plains, but the latter term is often used in Tasmania to signify lands clear of trees, even where the surface is far from level.

When a place is first occupied by a settler, a hut of the simplest kind is formed, often like a mere roof resting on the ground; and when other needful things have been effected, one of upright logs is built, and covered with shingles. This is usually divided into two rooms; one of which is fitted up with broad rough shelves, for sleeping berths; and the other, which has a square recess for a fireplace, built of stones, at the outer end, and continued into a rude chimney a little higher than the roof, is used for a cooking and sitting room. The crevices between the logs either remain open, or are filled with wool or some other material. A square opening, closing with a shutter, admits light into each room, and short logs of wood or rude benches, serve for seats. Many families that have been brought up in England in respectable circumstances, live for several years in a hut of this description, until they can find time and means to build themselves a better habitation; and a hut of this kind is generally to be seen contiguous to a better house, and is occupied by the male servants, who are mostly prisoners.

Perhaps a chief reason why some persons make a better livelihood here than in England, is, because they submit to live at a much smaller expense. The original settlers having had free grants of land, subject only to a quit-rent, had also no rent to pay; but no free grants of land are now made. The lowest sum for which land is sold by the Government is £5 per acre. Although convict servants are sentenced to work without wages, they cost a settler in one way or another, from £20 to £25 a year, including maintenance, clothing, &c.

Agricultural operations are carried on in this country by means of oxen, horses being scarce. Cattle are bred in the bush, where they become very wild. Many of the settlers are expert in hunting them into enclosures, and subduing them to the yoke. Brush Kangaroos are numerous here on the more woody hills; and the Vulpine Opossum—the Common Opossum of this land—abounds. Both are injurious to the corn. The Opossums live in holes in the Gum-trees, and

feed chiefly on their leaves : they are shot in considerable
numbers on moonlight nights to diminish them, and for
the sake of their fur, which is very thick and warm.
When shot they sometimes hang by their prehensile tails,
by which they can lay firm hold of a branch. While
warm, their fur readily comes off, but it becomes fast when
they are cold. The skins sell for about four pence
each, and are black, brown, or grey. Birds of various
kinds also abound in this country ; among them may be
enumerated Green Parrots, that are great pests in gardens,
Nonpareil Parrots, that are very troublesome in corn fields,
and pick about on the roads, Green Paroquets, that frequent
farm yards, Lemon-crested Cockatoos, which are likewise a
great annoyance to the farmer, several species of Crow
and Magpie, also the Wattle-bird, the Miner, the Wedge-
tailed Eagle, &c. The Emu is now extinct in this part of
the island.

In the course of one of our walks, we passed the remains
of a hut that was burnt about two years ago, by the
Aborigines of the Ouse or Big River district. An old man
named Clark lost his life in it, but a young woman escaped ;
she rushed from the fire and fell on her knees before the
natives, one of whom extinguished the flames which had
caught her clothes, and beckoned to her to go away.
They killed a woman on the hill behind the hut. A few
weeks after, they surrounded the house of G. Dixon, who
received a spear through his thigh, in running from a barn
to his house. Previously to this period, the natives had visited this neighbourhood peaceably and excited no alarm.
They have now been removed to Flinders Island ; but a
detachment of soldiers, such as was placed in various situations to defend the settlers against the Aborigines, still
remains at Elengowen, near the house of a fine old Scotch
woman, named Jacobina Burns ; who emigrated from her
own country many years ago, and has induced several of her
relatives to follow her. She has improved her circumstances,
and is noted for hospitality, which is indeed a very general
virtue among the settlers in this land.

While at Green Valley, walking alone, and meditating on

the clear evidence I had had of its being my religious duty to visit this part of the world, for many years before the right time seemed to be come for me to set out, and querying within myself as to how we should proceed, so as to be found acting in accordance with the divine will, the words "Go through the breadth of the land," were impressed on my mind with such authority as left no doubt but this was the counsel of the Lord, mercifully granted for our direction. For the Lord still condescends to lead about and instruct those who put their trust in him; notwithstanding it may seldom be by impressions exactly of this kind; but more frequently by a constraining sense of his will independent of any distinct form of words, or by the overruling of his providence.

3rd mo. 19th, we visited a little agricultural settlement called the Hollow Tree, and a place named Cockatoo Valley, celebrated for the fineness of its timber, which is chiefly of the kinds called Stringy-bark and Peppermint. Some saw-yers were at work here. Their hut was entirely built of large slabs of bark, which are obtained from several species of *Eucalyptus*, and serve many useful purposes. At the Wool-pack Inn, in returning toward Hobart Town, we obtained beds made up on wooden sofas, for the use of each of which two shillings a night was charged, this also was the price of each of our meals.

20th. The mornings are cold at this autumnal season, but mid-day is as warm as an English summer. Numbers of Piping Crows called also White Magpies, were hopping about near the inn, and raising their whistling notes to each other at an early hour, and the chattering of Miners, Wattle birds, Black Magpies, and Paroquets was very enlivening to us on our journey. On the way to New Norfolk, which we reached in time for the coach to Hobart Town, we had interviews with the Deep-gulley-road-gang, in three detachments; whose attention we called to the end of their being, the incapacity of persons whose affections are estranged from God, and set on carnal things, to enjoy heaven, and the consequent necessity of being born again of the Spirit, by yielding to its convictions, which produce repentance. toward God and faith toward Jesus Christ.

CHAPTER III.

WE remained in Hobart Town till the 7th of 5th month; and were much occupied in putting religious tracts and books into circulation, visiting the prisons, conversing with various persons, on the eternal interests of man, and holding or attending meetings for the promotion of religion and morality. During this period we became acquainted with several pious persons; one of whom, Captain William Jacob, from India, was temporarily residing in this island, on account of his health; Van Diemens Land being much resorted to by invalids from India, and often with great benefit, from its fine, dry, salubrious climate. Another, was a drummer, who went into the army at fourteen years of age, and had remained in it fourteen years. He said he had spent much of his time in sin, but had now learned the value of his Bible, and was glad when opportunity offered, to retire into the bush to read it alone : he had found peace of mind through faith in Christ, but was in a situation requiring great watchfulness, to retain the sense of the Divine presence being with him. Another, was a young man, who, when in London, sometimes stepped into Friends' Meeting House, in White Hart Court; where a solemn feeling pervaded his mind, without his knowing from whence it arose; but as he supposed the congregation while sitting in silence, were exercised in examining the state of their own hearts before the Lord, he endeavoured to be similarly occupied.

We several times visited the prisoners in the Penitentiary, who assembled for religious purposes in a mess-room accommodating about 450 at a time: their quietness and attention were very striking; notwithstanding many of them wore chains, the least clink was rarely to be heard; many of them appeared truly grateful for a little religious counsel extended in Christian sympathy.

The Penitentiary contains upwards of 600 prisoners: it is the great receptacle of convicts on their arrival in the Colony: those returned from assigned service for misconduct, or other causes, are also sent here; and those retained for some of the public-works are likewise lodged in this place. Considering the class of its inmates, they are under good discipline. They are sent out in the morning under overseers and guards, to work on the roads, and in the various departments, as sawyers, carpenters, builders, &c. and they are all mustered and locked up at night. This precaution renders property remarkably secure in Hobart Town; where formerly robbery was very common. The Penitentiary has a large day-room, and numerous sleeping wards. The men are lodged on two tiers of barrack-bedsteads. These are large platforms without any separation, which is a great evil. In every room there is a man in charge, who is answerable for the conduct of the rest; but it is rare for one to dare to complain of the misconduct of his fellow. Each individual has a bed, blanket, and coverlet; and the place is well ventilated and clean. A tread-mill is attached to this building, which serves the purpose of special punishment, and grinds corn for the institution.—At a subsequent period, a large addition was made to this prison, including a number of solitary cells, and an Episcopal chapel, part of which is open also to the public.

In the latter part of the 4th month, a Temperance Society was first established in Hobart Town, but not without considerable opposition. The Lieut. Governor became its Patron; and the senior Colonial Chaplain, stated, in support of the object, that he had attended between three

D

and four hundred criminals to execution, nineteen out of twenty of whom, had been drawn into the commission of the crimes for which they forfeited their lives, either directly or indirectly by intemperance.

On the 15th of 4th month, we held a meeting with some sawyers, in their huts, at a place called the Kings Pits, on the ascent of Mount Wellington, at an elevation of about 2,000 feet, and about four miles from the town. These people seemed a little interested in the counsel given them, and received a few tracts gratefully. The forest among which they are residing is very lofty: many of the trees are clear of branches for upwards of 100 feet. It caught fire a few months ago, and some of the men narrowly escaped. The trees are blackened to the top, but are beginning to shoot again from their charred stems. The brushwood is very thick in some of these forests. A shower of snow fell while we were at the place. *Acacia Oxycedrus*, 10 feet high, was in flower on the ascent of the mountain. This, along with numerous shrubs of other kinds, formed impervious thickets in some places; while, in others, *Epacris impressa*, displayed its brilliant blossoms of crimson and of rose colour.

The brook that supplies Hobart Town with water, flows from Mount Wellington through a valley at the foot of the mountain. Here the bed of the brook is rocky, and so nearly flat as scarcely to deserve the name of The Cascades, by which this place is called. Many dead trees and branches lie across the brook, by the sides of which grows *Drymophila cyanocarpa*—a plant, allied to Solomon's Seal, producing sky-blue berries on an elegantly three-branched, nodding top. *Dianella cærulea*—a sedgy plant—flourishes on the drier slopes: this, as well as *Billardiera longiflora*—a climbing shrub, that entwines itself among the bushes—was now exhibiting its violet-coloured fruit. In damp places, by the side of the brook, a princely tree-fern, *Cybotium Billardieri*, emerged through the surrounding foliage. A multitude of other ferns, of large and small size, enriched the rocky margins of the stream, which I crossed upon the trunk of one of the prostrate giants of

B BL

the forest, a Gum-tree of large dimensions, which had been uprooted by some blast from the mountain; and in its fall, had subdued many of the neighbouring bushes, and made a way where otherwise the forest would have been inaccessible. On descending from this natural bridge, to examine a tree-fern, I found myself at the foot of one of their trunks, which was about 5 feet in circumference and 10 in height. The lower part was a mass of protruding roots, and the upper part clothed with short remains of leaf-stalks, looking rough and blackened: this was surmounted by dead leaves hanging down, and nearly obscuring the trunk from distant view: above was the noble crest of fronds, or leaves, resembling those of *Asplenium Filix-fœmina* in form, but exceeding 11 feet in length, in various degrees of inclination between erect and horizontal, and of the tenderest green, rendered more delicate by the contrast with the dark verdure of the sur-rounding foliage. At my feet were several other ferns of large size, covering the ground, and which, through age and their favourable situation, had attained root-stocks a foot in height, crowned by circles of leaves three times that length. Other plants of tree-fern, at short distances, concealed from my view, by their spreading fronds, the foliage of the lofty evergreens that towered a hundred feet above them. The trunk of one of the tree-ferns was clothed with a *Trichomanes* and several species of *Hy-menophyllum*—small membranaceous ferns of great delicacy and beauty. On a rocky bank adjoining, there were other ferns, with creeping roots, that threw up their bright green fronds at short distances from each other, decorating the ledges on which they grew. In the deepest recesses of this shade I could enjoy the novel scene—ferns above, below, around—without fear of molestation; no dangerous beasts of prey inhabiting this interesting island. The annexed etching will give the reader some idea of a tree-fern, many species of which exceed in beauty the stately palms of warmer climates.

5th mo. 7th, 1832. Having obtained a letter of introduc-tion from the Lieut. Governor to Major Baylee, the com-mandant of the Penal Settlement, at Macquarie Harbour;

and other necessary arrangements having been made for our passage on board the Government brig Tamar, we embarked, after dining with the senior colonial chaplain, William Bedford, and his family, from whom we received much kind attention during our sojourn in V. D. Land. The vessel not sailing till the 10th, we spent the evening at the house of Nathaniel Turner, the Wesleyan Minister stationed at Hobart Town, in company with John Allen Manton, a Wesleyan Missionary, also proceeding to Macquarie Harbour. At N. Turner's we also met the teachers of four sabbath schools, containing together about 200 children. Two of these schools are in Hobart Town, and the others at Sandy Bay and O'Briens Bridge. After the teachers had transacted the business of their monthly meeting, we had a solemn and highly favoured religious opportunity; in which, in the fresh feeling of heavenly love, I endeavoured to encourage them to live under a sense of the divine presence, and to seek to the Lord for counsel and direction, in order that their well-intended labours might be blessed.

There were in the cabin of the Tamar, John Burn, the captain for the voyage, Henry Herberg, the mate, David Hoy, a ship's carpenter, Jno. A. Manton, George W. Walker, and myself. Ten private soldiers and a sergeant, as guard, occupied a portion of the hold, in which there were also provisions for the Penal Settlement, and a flock of sheep. Two soldiers' wives and five children were in the midships. Twelve seamen, several of whom were convicts, formed the crew; and 18 prisoners under sentence to the Penal Settlement completed the ship's company. The last occupied a jail, separated from the hold by wooden bars, filled with nails, and accessible only from the deck by a small hatchway. One of the soldiers on guard stood constantly by this hatchway, which was secured by three bolts across the opening, two walked the deck, the one on one side returning with his face toward the prison, at the time the other was going in the opposite direction, and two were in the hold, seated in view of the jail. The prisoners wore chains, and only two of them were allowed to come on deck at a time

for air; these were kept before the windlas and not
allowed to converse with the seamen. This was rigidly
observed, in consequence of two of these men having, at a
former period, been parties in the seizure of a vessel named
the Cypress, making the same voyage; which was carried
off to the coast of China or Japan. They put the persons,
now our captain and mate, on shore, along with several
others, in Recherche Bay, at the mouth of D'Entrecasteaux
Channel; from whence they reached Hobart Town with
great difficulty. The jail occupied by these men was not
high enough for them to stand erect in, but they could
stretch themselves on the floor, on which they slept, being
each furnished with a blanket.

On the 8th, I paid my first visit to the prisoners, just after
they had been searched, lest they should have concealed any
implements for effecting their escape. After enquiring respecting their health, I told them that if they had no objection, I
would read them a chapter in the Bible, and desired to
know if there was any one in particular they would prefer.
One of them replied, there was some very good reading in
Isaiah. I opened the book, and read the 42nd chapter, and
at the conclusion commented upon it, pointing out the effect
of sin, the object of the coming of the Saviour, and his
power, not only to deliver out of darkness and the prison-
house, in a spiritual sense, but also in an outward one;
expressing my conviction, that if they would attend to that
grace which reproved them for evil, they would be led to
repentance, and into that faith in Christ, through which they
would obtain forgiveness of sin, and a capacity to love and
serve God; that this would produce such an effect upon
their conduct, as to restrain them from evil, and enable them
to work righteousness, procure them a remission of their
sentence, and introduce them to peace and joy, beyond any
thing of which they could form an idea while in the service of
Satan, whom, I did not doubt, they had found in their own
experience to be a liar, as they had been tempted by him to
expect pleasure from sin, but had found in its stead
trouble and loss. Several of them were attentive and
appeared thoughtful, and on taking leave, one of them placed

his hand to my foot and helped me to ascend from the prison.

The day the Tamar sailed was very fine. The Science, by which we came to V. D. Land, was passing down the Derwent at the same time, on her voyage for England; we parted from her on entering D'Entrecasteaux Channel, little anticipating the disaster by which she was lost off Cape Horn; where she was struck by a heavy sea, that swept away four of her men, and left the remainder, who were ultimately rescued by another ship, in a forlorn and perilous situation.—The various bays and islands of D'Entrecasteaux Channel, with their wood-covered hills looked beautiful. We came to anchor in the evening off Mount Royal. Numbers of fish called Flat-head and Rock Cod were taken. The former is firm, and resembles in figure the Bull-head of English rivers, but weighs about 1½lb. The other is softer than the English cod, and weighs from 3 to 7lbs. When stewed with but little water it nearly dissolves, and makes very palatable soup;—at least so we sometimes found it when at sea, and having little but salt meat.

11th. Anchor was weighed early, and passing between the Acteon Islands and Recherche Bay—a navigation requiring great care—we rounded the Whales-head, and came into the open sea. The evening was beautifully fine. We passed close by the Mew Stone by moonlight. Jelly-fish, such as are said to be food of the whale, and resembling glass-beads, were in myriads in the day time, and at night the sea was illuminated by phosphorescent species. Sometimes we heard the cry of a small Penguin common in this vicinity, known by the name of the Jackass Penguin.

12th. About two o'clock in the morning, the wind changed to N.W. At four it blew a violent gale, attended by lightning, thunder, and rain. We had just advanced far enough to be able to enter the middle harbour of Port Davey, by its northern opening, which is to the south of the northermost conical rock in the annexed sketch. The rocky island between that, and the southermost of the three conical rocks to the south, shuts this harbour in from

the open sea. We came to anchor in the middle of a bason a
mile and a half across, surrounded by hills, with little wood.
One on the north, which may be 800 feet high, called Spring
Hill, exhibits little but white quartz rock; which is abundant
every where around. There were trees, many of which
appeared to be dead, on the distant mountains. This was the
first time we had taken refuge in a harbour in an uninhabited
country; but solitary as it was, we were thankful for the
refuge from the storm.

We remained in Port Davey seventeen days. During this
time the wind was contrary, and often blew with great
violence; sometimes threatening to drive the vessel on shore,
notwithstanding it was moored with two heavy chain cables.

During our stay the sheep were placed on a small island,
on which were a few bushes and some coarse rushy herbage,
such as was also the covering of much of the adjacent
shores.

There were low Gum-trees on some of the hills, and the
brushwood in some of the gullies was very thick, as it was also
toward the sea beach; on which, here and there, logs of the
Huon Pine, a fine species of timber, were washed up.
Several low shrubs of the *Epacris* tribe were growing in the
clefts of Spring Hill: among them a species of *Richea* with a
single head, resembling a pine-apple plant, mounted on a
stick 6 feet high; two species of *Decaspora*—thyme-like
bushes, with flattened purple berries, and *Prinotes cerinthoides*—a straggling little shrub, with cylindrical, inflated,
pendulous blossoms, an inch long, of a deep rose colour.

I once ascended Spring Hill alone, taking the rocky part of it,
which is composed of projections of white quartz, sometimes
tinged with pink or blue, amongst which I could climb as on
a rude stair-case. Being sheltered from observation by the
rocky spires, I came among a flock of White Cockatoos,
which are too shy knowingly to admit the presence of a
stranger: they chattered to each other, and shook their
beautiful lemon-coloured crests with an amusing degree
of consequence, until at length I threw a stick among them,
which dispersed the assembly. Much of the ground running

back from the top of this hill, was perforated by a land-lobster, the size of a prawn; its holes were carried up with conical towers of earth about a foot high. This animal seems common in this wet part of Van Diemens Land.

One of my objects in this excursion was to endeavour to ascertain, if there existed beyond Bathurst Harbour—the sheet of water east of where the Tamar was lying—a lake doubtfully laid down on some maps; but this object was frustrated, by the coming on of a fog and heavy rain, just as I had reached a remote peak, from which I had hoped to see the desired spot. Previously, however, I had noticed the sea breaking on the south coast, at a much shorter distance, than I had expected from the map.—The top of the peak was composed of large blocks of white quartz, with thick scrub between them. From one to another of these I skipped to the opposite side of the peak; and from thence descending, passed through a thick scrub as high as my shoulders, hoping to reach the vessel by a nearer cut; but I had not proceeded far, before a deep woody ravine obstructed my course: and now was put to proof, the advantage of having my mind stayed on the Lord; the feeling of whose good presence had been with me in my solitary wandering, and in my musing upon the novel scenes presented by his creation in this part of the world; for had I become agitated I should probably have been lost. Evening was drawing on, I was alone and several miles from my companions; the scrub through which I had come had closed as I had left it, and it was necessary to retrace my steps. Fixing my heart more steadfastly on the Lord, in prayer, and taking the bearing of a prominent rock by a compass, which in all my wanderings I carried in a pocket opposite to that occupied by my watch, I patiently parted the opposing scrub with my hands, now somewhat weakened by fatigue; and after some time, again reached the rocky peak, which I mounted under such a sense of my Heavenly Father's love, as I hope not soon to forget, and which comforted and invigorated me, and constrained me, on bended knees, to give him thanks.

The fog parted a few times, and opened a fine view of the northern harbour of Port Davey, the Davey River, Mount de

Wit, and other mountains in that direction. Losing little time in observations, and being favoured to find my way across the rocks in safety, I took to my heels upon the more open ground, and came in sight of the Tamar before the sun had set. I was much surprised not to see the boat off, as I had requested the men who came on shore for water in the morning, to come for me in the evening, saying, they might then expect to see me somewhere on the face of Spring Hill. Like men of their class, they had so little regarded the instructions, that when inquired of, a few hours after, they could give no account of me. My companion had become uneasy at my absence; and, at length, I saw him with some seamen leave the vessel in a boat and come toward the shore, and heard the V. D. Land cry of Cooey, borrowed from the Aborigines, to which I answered; but to my dismay, saw the boat again pushed from the land. Not having taken into account that sound does not readily descend, they had concluded, as they did not hear me, that I was not there. No time was to be lost. I left the rocky part of the mountain for a slope on which I hoped to run; but on reaching it, my feet slipped among a fungus resembling moistened glue—a species of *Tremella?*—with which the ground had become covered during the rain. I arose and fell until my legs shook under me; and giving up the hope of standing, I launched off in a sitting posture; and besmeared with this slimy vegetable, passed rapidly to the bottom of the hill. Here again I ran and shouted: my voice reached far over the still water, and the boat, to my great comfort, returned. I met it in the sea, for the purpose of washing my clothes, that previously, for several hours, had been soaked with rain, which fell at times so heavily that I had had no occasion to stoop to drink during the whole day.

While detained in Port Davey, we made an excursion, in the ship's boat, with the carpenter, to examine the northern entrance into the bason in which the Tamar lay. It proved sufficiently deep for ships of moderate size; but there is a sunken rock half a mile N. and by West of the largest pyramidal rock, which is called by the seamen Big Caroline. We also went into the southern opening, called Kelleys River,

which is an estuary 5 or 6 miles long, 1 broad, and from 2 to
3 fathoms deep, and consequently only fit for boats.   There
were several Black Swans upon it.   These birds are abundant
in this neighbourhood in the breeding season.   Among the
scrub on the shore there was a flock of Black Cockatoos.
The Wombat—a burrowing, herbivorous animal, in figure
somewhat like a small bear,—abounds in this neighbourhood:
its flesh, when young, resembles that of the hare.

We likewise visited the Davey River, or northern harbour;
in which, under a point from the west, in the turn toward
Cockburn Cove, vessels sometimes take shelter from a
southerly gale.   Oysters are obtained at low tides in this
cove, on the smooth waters of which, Pelicans, Red-bills,
and Gulls were swimming.   On the north of it there is mica
rock containing Garnets.   Here we spent a night by a large
fire, sheltered by a few bushes, near to heaps of oyster shells,
accumulated from time immemorial by the Aborigines, who
occasionally resort hither.   The middle of the night was
stormy and wet.   The distant mountains were covered with
snow in the morning.

Fishing formed a frequent occupation on board the Tamar.
Rock-cod and occasionally eels about 5 feet long and 14 inches
round, were caught.   Sometimes a small shark would take
the bait; and we had to expostulate with the soldiers against
a cruel practice they adopted, of running a stick through the
breathing apparatus of these animals, and in this state throwing them overboard to perish.   This was done in the spirit of
revenge, because of the annoyance, as they not only spoiled
the baits, but drove away the fish.   We succeeded in convincing the men that they were wrong in giving way to this
spirit, and that it was their duty either to kill the sharks by
the most speedy means or to liberate them, as they had as
much right to take the baits, as the soldiers had to take
the fish; seeing that in so doing, they only followed an
instinct given by their Creator.   One of the species is spotted,
and is called in this country, the Nurse.

Reading in the cabin, and the religious instruction of the
respective groups of the prisoners, sailors, soldiers, and soldiers'

wives and children, also occupied portions of the time we were delayed here, which without employment, would have been tedious. In pleading with some of these people on the importance of a practical application of the doctrines of the Gospel, by those who profess to be christians, we desired them to judge of the corrupt state of their own hearts, at least, by that token which was obvious to others; viz., the practice of cursing and swearing. They took our counsel in good part; and whether changed from principle or not, became more circumspect.

There was something peculiarly interesting and affecting to my mind, in bringing the sound of the Gospel into this desolate part of the earth; where perhaps, since the days in which the world itself was called into existence, it was never before heard; and in proclaiming it as the message of mercy, to the people we brought with us—the only human beings in the place—whose hearts appeared to be as desolate as the hills by which we were surrounded.

5th mo. 29th. The wind having become more favourable, the sheep were brought on board, and while preparation was making for sailing, G. W. Walker and the carpenter landed me on one of the islets at the mouth of the harbour, to cut Native Parsley and a variety of shrubs for provender. This islet is composed of a substance resembling Asbestos, and is fronted on the inside by vertical veins of quartz. In the middle is a deep cove with a hole through to the outside, the surf beating against which forms a jet of spray within many feet high, resembling the blowing of a whale. We boarded the Tamar on her passage out, and were soon again at sea, where the fair wind failed, and we stood off the land for the night.

On the morning of the 30th, we had a view of Point Hibbs, and of a high, domed rock named the Pyramid. A series of heavy gales in the course of the four succeeding days, drove us far northward of our port. When we were laid to, the wind blew the topsail out of the bolt-rope, and while it was undergoing repair, we beat down the rocky coast with sails only just sufficient to enable us to keep off the shore. Scarcely anything was cooked during this period, and few

persons on board were disposed to eat.   Most of the time we
kept in our berths, which were warm and dry.   The motion
of the vessel was too great to allow a person to walk, or even
to stand without hold, and we were unable from this cause
combined with sickness, to wash or shave.

Some Black and Wandering Albatrosses were continually
soaring around us; and a flock of the beautiful Petrels, called
Cape Pigeons, kept close to our stern, generally on the wing,
but often swimming, or running on the water after anything
cast from the ship.   The wind howls, and the sea rages in
vain to these birds.   They keep on the wing in the fiercest
tempests, and swim with ease on the most boisterous waves.
It was a trying time for all on board, especially for the poor
women and children; into whose quarters the water several
times found its way in torrents.   The perplexities that sometimes arose, occasioned some of the soldiers to quarrel and
swear, even when the vessel seemed ready to be overwhelmed;
so inveterate was this evil habit!   It was a season of trial
both of our faith and patience; but the belief that we were
in our right places was sustaining.

On the morning of the 4th of 6th month, land was descried
through the hazy atmosphere, and all sail was made with a
varying but generally favourable wind, till we came distinctly
in view of Cape Sorell, at the entrance of Macquarie Harbour.
On approaching nearer, we were thrown into much perplexity,
no signal being made from the pilot's station for an hour and
a half, either to approach nearer or to stand off.   During this
time we stood backward and forward outside the dangerous
bar, which is of wide extent, while the sea was again getting
up.   At length, when about to run back for shelter to Port
Davey, we were descried, and a signal to enter was hoisted.
We immediately stood in, and in a few minutes the opportunity to return was past.   The pilot put off, knowing better
than ourselves, our danger: his boat could only be seen now
and then above the billows; but he was soon alongside, and
ordered all the sails to be squared, that we might go right
before the wind.   On coming on board, he commanded the
women and children below, and then came to me, and advised
me to go below also.   I replied, that if we were lost I should

like to see the last of it, for the sight was awfully grand.
Laying hold of a rope at the stern, he said, "Then put your
arm round this rope and don't speak a word." To my companion he gave similar instructions, placing him at the opposite
quarter. A man was sent into the chains on each side, with
the sounding lead. The pilot went to the bows, and nothing
was now to be heard through the roar of the wind and waves,
but his voice calling to the helmsman, the helmsman's answer,
and the voices of the men in the chains, counting off the
fathoms as the water became shallower.. The vessel was cast
alternately from one side to the other, to prevent her sticking
on the sand, in which case the billows would have run over
her, and have driven her upon a sand-bank a mile from the
shore, on which they were breaking with fury. The fathoms
decreased, and the men counted off the feet, of which we drew
7½, and there were but seven in the hollow of the sea, until
they called out eleven feet. At this moment a huge billow
carried us forward on its raging head into deep water. The
pilot's countenance relaxed: he looked like a man reprieved
from under the gallows, and coming aft, shook hands with
each individual, congratulating them on a safe arrival in
Macquarie Harbour.

We now soon entered into the inlet, which is about twenty-
five miles long, and from three to seven miles broad, by a
narrow passage between two rocks, called "The Gates," or
from the nature of the settlement, "Hells Gates;" many of
the prisoners recklessly asserting that all who entered in
hither, were doomed to eternal perdition. We had a fine sail
up the Harbour; and on arriving off Sarahs Island, about
twenty miles from the entrance, were boarded by the commissariat officer, surgeon, &c.—all anxious to hear what was
going on in the world, they having had no tidings for more
than three months. They gave us a hearty welcome, and
conveyed us to the Settlement, where I became the guest of
Major Baylee, and G. W. Walker took up his quarters with
our fellow-voyager, J. A. Manton; for whom, as missionary,
a house was in readiness.

After a short time spent in conversation, each of us retired
to rest, thankful to the Lord, who had answered the prayers

put up to him on the raging seas, for deliverance from the stormy tempest; when the billows, spiritually as well as outwardly, at times went over our heads. We cried unto God, who commands the winds and the seas and they obey him. We called to mind the situation of the disciples of his Son, when he was asleep in a tempest and they were afraid, and remembered, that when he arose and rebuked the wind, there was a great calm. We put our trust in his name, and renewed our confidence in the Father of mercies through him. Our minds became comforted by his Holy Spirit: we laid us down and slept, being sensible that he sustained us. And now that he had permitted us again to land in safety, we could adopt the language of the Psalmist. " Bless the Lord, O my soul, and all that is within me, bless his holy name. Bless the Lord, O my soul, and forget not all his benefits: who forgiveth all thine iniquities; who healeth all thy diseases; who redeemeth thy life from destruction; who crowneth thee with loving kindness and tender mercies."

We remained 17 days at the settlement on Sarahs Island, making occasional excursions to the out-posts; and, notwithstanding, the place has since been abandoned, on account of its distance from Hobart Town, and the difficulty of access to it, and the prisoners have been transferred to Port Arthur, on Tasmans Peninsula, I propose in the ensuing chapter to introduce some notice of it, and of the discipline of the prisoners, as being an interesting portion of the nearly uninhabited, western side of V. D. Land, and exhibiting a specimen of the discipline of one of the older Penal Settlements.

CHAPTER IV.

Macquarie Harbour did not present the desolate appearance
which we had been given to expect. The mountains along the
east side are not nearly so bare as those of Port Davey, the
rock only projecting above the soil on the tops of the highest.
The most striking mountains are Mount Discovery, to the
south, Mount Sorell, to the east, and Mount Zeehaan and
Heemskerk, to the north. The herbage on their sides is
coarse and deep; it looks grassy from a distance, but probably may not be so in reality. The scrub of the gullies runs
into deep wood on the lower grounds. Deep wood also
clothes many of the hills. The prevalence of Myrtle—*Fagus
Cunninghamii*—and other trees of dark foliage, gives a very
sombre appearance to the forests. These extend also over
the low hills at the foot of the mountains, and up the west
side of the harbour, about ten miles, toward Cape Sorell.
Behind the mountains on the east of Macquarie Harbour, rises
a magnificent, snow covered range; the most striking point
of which is the Frenchmans Cap, having the form of a
quarter of a sphere, perpendicular on the south, and towering
to 5,000 feet above the level of the sea. This is probably
the highest point of V. D. Land. The south end of the
harbour is more level and less woody. A wide inlet called
Birches River opens into it, and a little to the east, the
Gordon River, which is navigable for 30 or 40 miles, but

closely hemmed in by scrub and mountains to a great distance. Lime, which is rare in Tasmania, is obtained from the upper part of this river. On the east side is an inlet called Kelleys Bason, and near the northern extremity, is Kings River. The scrub in the gullies and many parts of the forest is extremely thick, and very deep: it comes so close to the water's edge, as generally to render the shores of the harbour and tributary rivers inaccessible.

Sarahs Island has a strikingly verdant appearance. The little paddocks, interspersed among the buildings and lofty paled fences, that give the whole island the look of a fortified place, vie in verdure with English meadows.—The capacity of the country about Macquarie Harbour, for cultivation, does not however appear to be great. Such lands as are sufficiently clear to admit of being ploughed, are peaty and wet; but probably they might be made to produce grass and vegetables. No attempts have been made to raise any kind of grain; and the humidity of the climate of the western part of V. D. Land, does not promise success to this branch of agriculture. Sheep do not thrive here; and at one time nearly half of the goats kept at the settlement died.

The timber about Macquarie Harbour is very fine. Huon Pine, supposed to be a species of *Dacrydium*, which is much valued for ship-building and general purposes, abounds on the eastern side: the wood is closer grained and more durable than White American Pine, and has an aromatic smell. This tree attains to about 100 feet in height, and 25 in circumference, and is of a pyramidal form: the branches from the trunk are a little below horizontal, and are clothed with numerous, slender, pendant, scaly branchlets, of lively green, serving the purpose of leaves, as in the Cypress and Arbor-vitæ. Celery-topped Pine—*Thalamia asplenifolia*—so called from the resemblance of a branch clothed with its dilated leaves, to the leaf of Celery, is well calculated for masts. Myrtle, allied to Beech, but with leaves more like Dwarf Birch, is suited for keels. Light-wood—*Acacia Melanoxylon*—clothed with leaf-like spurious foliage, resembling the leaves of a Willow, is also fine timber, and its roots make beautiful veneering. It derives this name from swimming in water, while the other woods of V. D. Land, except the pines, generally sink; in some parts of the Colony it is called Black-wood, on account of its dark colour. Other timber trees are known here by the names of Pink-wood, *Carpodontos lucida*, Hard-wood, a species of *Olea*, Sasafras, *Athosperma moschata*, Stink-wood, *Zieria arborescens*, &c. Forest Tea Tree, a species of *Leptospermum*, is valued for fuel; some crooked portions of its trunk are finely veined, and well adapted for fancy-work. The black substance forming part of the stems of tree ferns, is used for reeding, in inlaying, for which purpose it is superior to Ebony. Respectable hats have been manufactured from the shavings of some species of Acacia, as well as from broad leaved sedges, *Lepidosperma gladiata;* the leaves being first boiled and bleached.

Notwithstanding the fine scenery of Macquarie Harbour, it was a gloomy place in the eyes of a prisoner, from the privations he suffered there, in being shut out from the rest of the world, and restricted to a limited quantity of food, which did not include fresh meat; from being kept under a military guard; from the hardship he endured, in toiling almost constantly in the wet, at felling timber and rolling it to the water, and from other severe labour, without wages, as well as from the liability to be flogged or subjected to solitary confinement, for small offences.

Out of 85 deaths that occurred here in eleven years, commencing with 1822, only 35 were from natural causes; of the remainder, 27 were drowned, 8 killed accidentally, chiefly by the falling of trees, 3 were shot by the military, and 12 murdered by their comrades. There is reason to believe that some of these murders were committed for the purpose of obtaining for the murderers, and those who might be called upon as witnesses on their trials, a removal from this place, though at the ultimate cost of the life of the murderers, and without a prospect of liberation on the part of the others! Some of the prisoners who returned hither with us in the Tamar, had been witnesses in such a case; but they had had the privilege of the change, for a time, to the penitentiary at Hobart Town! These circumstances, with the fact, that within the eleven years, 112 prisoners had eloped from

E

this settlement, proved also that its privations were felt to be very great.

Escape from Macquarie Harbour was well known to be a difficult and very hazardous undertaking, and very few who attempted it, reached the settled parts of the Colony. Out of the 112 who eloped, 62 were supposed to have perished in the bush, and 9 were murdered by their comrades on the journey, for a supply of food. For this purpose, the party proposing to attempt traversing the formidable forest, selected a weak minded man, and persuaded him to accompany them; and when the slender stock of provisions which they had contrived to save from their scanty rations, was exhausted, they laid violent hands on their victim. One party when lately apprehended near the settled districts, had in their possession, along with the flesh of a Kangaroo, a portion of that of one of their comrades! An appalling evidence of how easily man, in a depraved state, may descend even to cannibalism.

Of the small number who reached the settled part of the country, some were immediately apprehended; a few became formidable marauders, and were ultimately shot or executed; others escaped to New South Wales, but continuing their evil practices, were transported to Norfolk Island; and of the remainder, who were an inconsiderable number, the circumstances remain doubtful.

In the earlier days of this settlement flagellation was the chief punishment, and the reformation of the prisoners seemed hopeless. There is ground to believe the example of some of those under whose charge they were placed was at that period also of a deteriorating character. The first missionary sent here found a chief officer living in open profligacy, and saw so little prospect, under such circumstances, of being able to do any good among the prisoners, that he returned by the same vessel to Hobart Town.

Of latter time the administration of corporal punishment was much diminished, and that of solitary confinement increased, with evident advantage. Major Baylee also expostulated with the parties, and convinced them that he would not administer punishment without cause: this greatly

increased his influence, and obtained for him such respect
and esteem, that he could go about the settlement, unattended,
with perfect confidence.

The following abstract exhibits the average of the returns
of punishment for 1826, 7 and 8, and for 1829, 30, and 31.

Years.	No. of Prisoners in the Settlement	No. of Prisoners sentenced.	No. of Lashes inflicted.	No. of days of solitary confinement.
1826,27,28	312.	188.	6280.	5.
1829,30,31	255.	56.	973.	209.

The removal of a few prisoners from Macquarie Harbour,
on account of good conduct, before the expiration of their
sentence, had a decidedly good effect upon the others; and
the labours of William Schofield, the first missionary who
became resident there, were, through the divine blessing,
crowned with encouraging success. He found a difficulty in
prevailing upon the men to cherish hope; but when this was
once effected, they began to lay hold of the offers of mercy
through a crucified Redeemer, and some remarkable instances
of change of character ensued. On conversing with some
of the reformed prisoners, they said, that the change of
heart they had undergone had altered the face of the settlement in their eyes: it had ceased to wear the gloom by
which it was formerly overcast. Two, to whom it had been
so irksome as to tempt them to run away, said, they were
now well satisfied, and thankful they had been sent there.
Others who had been placed in the less laborious part of
the establishment, because of good conduct, were, at their
own request, allowed to return to their old employments,
which they preferred on account of being less exposed to
temptation; saying, they were less afraid of labour than
of sin.

A man who lost his arm some time ago, was awakened
to a sense of his sinful condition, whilst in imminent danger
from this accident. He said the the Lord found him when he
sought Him not, yet so strongly did he feel his own desperate
wickedness, that he could entertain no hope, until he was

reminded of the mercy extended to Manasseh, Mary Mag-
dalene, and others of similar character. He told me he
had been guilty of housebreaking, and many other crimes,
for which he said he had been three times sentenced to this
settlement; he said also that the gallows was no terror to him,
and that he was so hardened, that he did whatsoever he
wished, in defiance of the laws of God and man, till the Lord
visited him, and brought him low. He afterwards ranked
amongst those, who having been forgiven much, love much.
The alteration in his conduct was noticed by all around him:
the Commandant said his very voice was changed; formerly it
was ferocious, now it was mild; formerly he was contentious
and addicted to fighting, now he was gentle and peaceable;
formerly he was so given to swearing, and the habit of it had
such power over him, that, after he had turned to the Lord,
if any thing irritated him, he had to lay his hand upon his
mouth that he might not swear; now he was to be found
warning others against this sin.

The men who had turned from their evil ways, were allowed
to sit in a room used for an adult-school, in order that they
might not be disturbed in reading and meditation, by those
who still remained in folly, and would be disposed to deride
them; and this man, on account of his infirmity, was allowed likewise to retire alone to one of the caves in
the base of the island, to meditate and pray. Though he
had lost an arm, he was not idle, but employed himself in
carrying wood for fuel, after it was landed from the boat. I
invited him to show me his cave; he readily consented,
and led me down a steep and slippery path at the back
of the island. The cave was damp on one side, and
had a honeycomb-like incrustation upon it: its sloping roof
was dry, a few old palings formed its loose floor, and a cold
wind blew through it from a small opening at its farther
extremity. I could not stand upright in it, but entered by
stooping; he followed, and we sat down upon its floor, and
conversed for a while on the mercy of God to sinners, in
sending his Son into the world to save them, and in calling
them by his Spirit to come unto Him.

This cold and forlorn place was much prized by its

occupant, in it, (to use his own words,) he contrasted his privilege, in being allowed to meditate in quiet, and to wait for the Spirit's influence, with the privations of those who in former ages wandered in sheepskins and goatskins, in deserts and mountains, and in dens and caves of the earth, being destitute, afflicted, tormented. Before quitting the place we kneeled before the Lord, and I prayed for this "brand plucked out of the burning," as well as for myself. When I ceased, he prolonged the voice of supplication, ascribing glory, honour, and praise to Him that liveth for ever and ever, who in the riches of his mercy had called him out of darkness into his marvellous light, and translated him from the kingdom of Satan, into the kingdom of his own dear Son. In the course of conversation, this monument of divine goodness, desired that I would tell audacious sinners of the mercy that God had shown to him; and assure them that he found such comfort and pleasure in righteousness, as he never could have thought of whilst he remained in sin. When he became awakened he found himself in ignorance also, and since that time he had learned to read.

But though a few were to be found at this settlement who had turned to the Lord, and were bringing forth fruits meet for repentance, and most conducted themselves pretty well under the discipline exercised over them, there was still great depravity existing: many were so far under the dominion of the devil, as to be led captive by him at his will. The effect of the corruption of human nature, increased by indulgence in sin, produced a description of character liable to fall into temptation whenever it came in the way, and far from being always restrained by the fear of punishment.

The number of prisoners at the settlement at the time of our visit, including the out-gangs, was 177; formerly it was about 300. Many of them were employed on Sarahs Island, in ship-building, and others at out-stations, chiefly as a wood-cutting gang at Philips Creek, where they were superintended by a constable, and lodged in huts of the humblest construction; but these, being furnished with good fires, were not very uncomfortable, particularly when the inmates whitewashed them, and kept them clean. On conversing with the men of this gang respecting the hope of remission of sentence on good conduct, one man, with tears in his eyes, said, he had been there 10 years: he seemed cast down almost below hope. We assured them of the pleasure it gave the Lieutenant Governor, to remit their sentence, when they gained a character to warrant his doing so, and encouraged them to seek for a change of heart, by repentance toward God, and faith toward our Lord Jesus Christ, as a foundation for such a character. On being asked, one man said, that their ration of provision was not sufficient for them at such hard work; and though their general appearance was healthy, yet when they were engaged in heaving timber, and rolling it down to the water, and other fatiguing labour, it might often fail in appeasing the cravings of exhausted nature.

The timber they cut was chiefly Huon Pine. No beasts of burden were allowed at Macquarie Harbour. In order to get the felled timber to the water, a way had to be cleared, and to be formed with logs and branches; over this, straight trunks of trees were laid in the manner of the slips or skids, used in launching ships. Upon these the timber was rolled by the prisoners, sometimes to a great distance. These roads were termed Pine-roads.—If any of the men proved unruly at the out-stations, the constable lit a fire, the smoke of which was observed by the sentinel at the settlement, from whence assistance was promptly sent. Except sometimes as a punishment, the men were not in irons, for if they had been, they could not have performed their work. The boat which put us ashore at Philips Creek, was ordered to push off as soon as it had landed us, and to remain off until we were ready to return, lest any of the prisoners should seize it, and attempt their escape; circumstances of this sort having occurred. At a short distance from Philips Creek, is Philips Island, the soil of which is peaty loam: it had for some years been cultivated with potatoes. Here seven men were employed under a constable. The constable being a prisoner, who had conducted himself so as to gain confidence. A steep path led from the shore, and passing the huts, extended

across the island: it was planted on each side with native
shrubs, and rendered firm by pieces of the trunks of tree-
ferns, cut in lengths, and laid at short distances one from
another; of these, some of the steps were also formed on the
steepest part of the ascent.   The huts were almost overgrown
with the Macquarie Harbour Vine, a luxuriant climber, bearing small acid fruit.   We walked over the island, and
down one of its sides, which was woody, and which exhibited the finest tree-ferns we had seen, and in great
profusion.   They were of two kinds, one of which we
did not meet with elsewhere   Some of their larger fronds
or leaves were thirteen feet long, making the diameter
of the crest twenty-six feet.   The stems were of all degrees
of elevation, up to twenty-five or thirty feet; some of them,
at the lower part, were as stout as a man's body: those of
Cybotium Billardieri were covered with roots to the outside:
the whole length of those of the other species—*Alsophila australis*—was clothed with the bases of old leaves, which were
rough, like the stems of raspberries, closely tiled over each
other, and pointing upwards.   There was also a number of
other ferns of humble growth: two species of the beautiful
genus *Glichenia* had tough, wiry stems, which were used in
the settlement, for making bird-cages.

The general health of the prisoners at Macquarie Harbour
was good.   Seldom more than three of them were in the
hospital at a time.   The average of deaths did not amount
to more than one in 35 per annum, including those by
violence and accident.   These circumstances, the more remarkable in men whose habits had been dissipated, might
reasonably be attributed to spare diet and hard labour, in a
mild though humid climate, and seclusion from strong drink.
But whether from the limited supply of food, or from
being restricted to the use of salt meat, or from some other
cause, the surgeon remarked, that when the men became
ill, the tone of their constitution was so low that they were
difficult to recover.   Some of them were affected with
scurvy for long after leaving the settlement.

The common temperature of the winter at Macquarie
Harbour, was 43° in clear weather, when the wind was from

the south, and 52° when cloudy with the wind from the
north. Frost and great heat were of rare occurrence. Rain
was said to have fallen on five days out of seven, during ten
months in the year, from the formation of the settlement
in 1822.

The prisoners had no allowance of spirits at this station;
but rewards for little extra services were sometimes given
them by the officers, in this pernicious article; the
allowance of which to the latter and to the military
generally, was a great evil, and the source of much
misconduct.

Several of the prisoners who returned to Hobart Town in
the Tamar, had been first transported to Bermuda; but in
consequence of a mutiny in which they were implicated, they
were subsequently sent to V. D. Land. They preferred
Bermuda, because they had there an allowance of fresh
meat and rum, and some money for present use, as well as a
sum reserved till the expiration of their sentence.

During our stay at Macquarie Harbour, we received great
kindness and attention from the Commandant, who afforded
us all the information we desired respecting the discipline of
the Settlement, and gave us free access to the prisoners, both
for ascertaining their feelings, and for the purpose of imparting religious instruction. The other officers also were kindly
attentive. On the 21st of the 6th month, we left them
with feelings of gratitude, not soon to be effaced, and sailed to
Wellington Head, near the entrance of the harbour; having
in the jail several prisoners returning from the settlement;
they were not under strict guard, as the vessel was proceeding in the direction in which they desired to go, and
had no stock of provisions on board to tempt them to try to
carry her off.

The wind proving unfavourable, we were detained eighteen
days at Wellington Head; in the course of which we visited
the Pilot Station, and adjacent parts of the coast; and
daily had religious opportunities in the jail, with the crew of
the vessel, the military, and the prisoners. The jail was now
so much occupied with timber as to render it difficult to
crowd into it, and it was also dirty and dark; and the only

lamp we had, gave barely sufficient light to read by; but the comforting sense of our Heavenly Father's love, which often attended our minds, made up for all privations. One of the prisoners, who, for some time past had exhibited much religious thoughtfulness, a few times joined his exhortations to ours, and pleaded with his fellows, on the necessity of preparing for the awful day of the Lord. He began by telling them, that they had known him when he indulged in sin as much as any of them; but that they must have marked the change which had taken place in his conduct and character; and he could assure them, that he was much happier in walking in the fear of the Lord than ever he had been in sin; he therefore entreated them to turn to the Lord and seek mercy through that Saviour, in whom he had found mercy.

The person acting as steward on board the Tamar was transported when 14 years old. He attributed his early turpitude, to the influence of bad company, which led him to use strong drink and disobey his father, and to practice many other evils. When gambling with his associates on a First-day, at the suggestion of one of the party, they robbed a young man who happened to pass. For this offence several of them were transported. Though he had forsaken his evil ways and was now filling an honourable post, he still felt keenly the bitter consequences of his former vices, for which he was still in bondage.

6th mo. 22nd. We had the crew of the pilot-boat assembled, along with the persons on board the Tamar, and, after reading a portion of Scripture to them, spoke on the importance of avoiding to ridicule religion in their companions or others, who might be disposed to attend to its duties; we also exhorted them to consider what would be the feeling respecting having given way to such ridicule, when reflecting upon it, on a death bed.

The pilot put us on shore on the north beach, upon the sand of which we walked a few miles, in company with the mate, and picked up some small Helmet-shells, and specimens of a large digitated sponge. Several Black-fish—a small species of whale—were driven upon this beach in the late storm. A spaniel dog that accompanied us, rolled itself on the partially decomposed carcase of each of these as he came at it; I could not discover for what object.

Parties of Aborigines resort hither at certain seasons. They cross the mouth of the harbour on floats, in the form of a boat, made of bundles of the paper-like bark of the Swamp Tea-tree, lashed side by side, by means of tough grass. On these, three or four persons are placed, and one swims on each side, holding it with one hand. These Aborigines are said to be shy, but not to have committed any outrage. One of them exchanged a girl of about fourteen years of age, for a dog, with the people at the Pilot Station; but the girl not liking her situation was taken back, and the dog returned.

23rd. We went on shore close by the vessel, and on the way to the Pilot Station passed some large patches of a species of *Blandfordia*—a lily-like plant, with a crest of scarlet tubular flowers—which abounds also at Port Davey.

We afterwards traversed a portion of the beach, open to the sea on the south, near Cape Sorell. It consisted of numerous little bays; some sandy, others shingly, some rocky, and others covered thickly with decomposing kelp of enormous size, the smell of which was very disagreeable. Multitudes of maggots are produced in it, on which flocks of White Cockatoos feed, that roost among the large bushes on the shore. Ducks and other sea-fowl also find a plentiful supply of food in the maggots, which are floated off in abundance by the rising tide. The rotten kelp affords a manure to the peaty garden of the pilot, so congenial to the growth of potatoes, that those grown there exceed the best I ever saw in England.—There was a lichen on the neighbouring hills, of the same race as the Reindeer-moss, but of a texture resembling delicate net-work. In the abundant rain, it was distended into masses resembling cauliflowers. Like some of its congeners, it seemed as if it might be used for food: its taste was insipid, and I found no inconvenience from eating it.

We remained all night at the pilot's house, and in the morning had a meeting with the men, in which we were

made deeply sensible of the goodness and mercy of the
Lord; before whom we also spent some time in silent waiting, greatly to our comfort.

27th.   In a walk, I found the scrub so thick and entangled, that I was under the necessity of cutting my
way through it with the back of a saw; but when weary
of doing this, I waded past it in the salt-water.—In some
places, in this wet country, cyperaceous plants, which somewhat resemble rushes, entwine themselves among the larger
shrubs, and ascend to their tops, and lichens hang to a great
length from the boughs of some of the trees.   The sand-
banks at the mouth of Macquarie Harbour are covered with
Boobialla, a species of *Acacia*, the roots of which run far in
the sand.   Black Cockatoos and some other birds enlivened
the bush.   Sometimes large White Eagles were seen sitting
on boughs overhanging the water, watching for fish.

On the 9th of 7th mo. the Commandant and the Surgeon
paid us a visit; they had previously sent us a fresh stock
of provisions from the Settlement, those with which we
originally set out being nearly consumed; and now, after
waiting eighteen days for a fair wind, we crossed the bar
without touching; and soon passed the northernmost rocks
of Cape Sorell.   The following evening we were in sight
of South West Cape.   We laid-to till daylight on the
11th, and then entered D'Entrecasteaux Channel; where,
on passing some whalers, they informed us that we were
reported in Hobart Town to be lost.   In consequence of
adverse winds we were unable to relieve our friends from
anxiety on this point till the 13th, when we were favoured
again to land in safety and received many greetings.

Our old lodging being engaged, arrangements were made
for a temporary residence with Thomas J. and Sarah Crouch,
a pious young couple, who received us into their family in
Christian good-will, and to whose house we continued to
resort, as lodgers, for several years.

CHAPTER V.

WE remained in Hobart Town a month; in the course of which,
in compliance with a request from the Lieutenant Governor,
we presented him with a report on the state of the Penal
Settlement at Macquarie Harbour; the substance of which is
contained in the preceding remarks.

Our meetings for worship, during this period, were often
attended by pious persons in an inquiring state of mind,
to whom we were enabled to impart religious counsel.
We had also discussions with some of them on the principles
of the Society of Friends, which we endeavoured to show
were those of the Gospel practically carried out.

When taking a meal with pious persons, I was frequently
requested to give thanks. This being intended as a mark of
Christian courtesy to a stranger minister, I received it as
such; but we found it necessary to explain, that it was our
practice on such occasions, to endeavour to feel thankful, but
not to give expression to their feeling on behalf of ourselves
and others, unless under such a sense of divine influence as
warranted the belief that it was done in spirit and in truth.

Though, in the course of our travels, we were sometimes present when thanksgiving was uttered in a formal way, which left upon the mind, the impression, that God was drawn nigh unto with the lip, while the heart was far from him ; yet we were often sensible of a measure of the influence of the Holy Spirit, when thanksgiving was devoutly uttered by those who were in the constant practice of using expression on such occasions. Nevertheless, when we were present, where the attention of the company was individually turned to the Lord, in a short period of silence, in order to feel thankful, and to acknowledge this feeling in the secret of the heart, we were sensible of a greater measure of divine influence, which comforted our minds, under the belief that the Father of mercies condescended more decidedly, to mark this homage with approbation.

One of the pensioners who came to this land by the Science, died in the Hospital about this time. He came under powerful convictions for sin, on the passage hither, and appeared to find a measure of peace through faith in Christ, and to be seeking help from God, in a humble frame of mind. At that time he abstained from drunkenness, but he could not be persuaded to give up taking his ration of spirits, alleging that the water was bad, and required qualifying. He had formerly been affected with dropsy, and having kept alive an appetite for intoxicating drink, his old shipmates succeeded, after he landed, in prevailing upon him to drink largely. This soon produced a recurrence of the disease, and again brought darkness over his mind, and in his last days, nothing could be learned to afford any ground of hope in his death.

Meeting with a young man who had thoughts of entering the artillery, I endeavoured to dissuade him. Nothing seems to me more clear, than that if we 'do to others as we would that they should do to us,' we cannot fight ; and that if we love our neighbour as ourselves, we cannot make war upon him. That if the keeping of the commandments of Jesus be a proof of our love to him, it is impossible to make war, and love him ; for this evil is as much opposed to his commandment, ' If thine enemy hunger, feed him, and if he thirst, give him drink,' as darkness is to light. It seems a vain attempt to elude the force of this injunction, by saying it applies to persons, and not to nations. Is not this making the commandment of none effect by the tradition of men?

8th mo. 15th. We crossed the Derwent to Kangaroo Point—a distance of about three miles—in an open boat; and travelled along a cart track through the Bush, to the house of a Government Surveyor on Clarence Plains, whose wife was our fellow-passenger from England. Here we were received with that hospitality for which the settlers in this country are justly celebrated, and of which we largely partook during our journeying among them. There are several houses in this direction; but as is generally the case in this country, most of the land is unenclosed, grassy forest. The few fields which are near the houses are fenced with posts and rails.

16th. We visited one of the Government Schools, many of which are established in different parts of the Island. They are generally imperfectly organized on the plan of the English National Schools, which is far from working well with the small and irregular attendance general in this country. This originates in the lack of interest, induced by the schools being free, the want of a proper value for education on the part of parents, the unsettled and undisciplined habits which prevail extensively, and from the circumstances in which the settlers in a newly-occupied country are generally placed. Many of the people in this district were formerly resident on Norfolk Island; from whence they were removed by the Government: they have had too little education themselves to be able to estimate its value for their children.

17th. We visited a chain-gang stationed at Kangaroo Point, consisting of twenty-nine men, employed in making roads, &c. While speaking to the men as they sat on the ground at the dinner hour, a Scorpion came out of a log upon their fire, and attempted in vain to escape from the heat; it became affected with convulsive movements, by which its tail struck its back. Probably something of this kind may have given rise to the notion, that a scorpion commits suicide by stinging itself when surrounded by fire. Scorpions are common in this country among decayed timber; they are of small size, and their sting is not much worse than that of a wasp. A green, venomous Centipede, about three inches long, is found in similar situations, and among stones. Its bite is considered worse than the sting of the scorpion, producing gangrenous inflammation; but from the habits of these animals, which sting only in self-defence, and seek retirement, accidents rarely happen by them.

18th. Having received an invitation from a settler named Robert Mather, to pay him a visit at Lauderdale, on Muddy Plains, we made our way to his house, crossing a salt marsh, on the side of which were large bushes of Shrubby Samphire. R. Mather sent notice to his neighbours, of our wish to have a meeting with them, and walked with us to the house of an industrious, sober couple, who, while prospering in temporal things, did not forget the importance of those that are spiritual. A well-worn bible was lying on their table, and the woman told us, that as she became unable to do needlework by candle-light, she spent much of her evenings in reading this precious book to her family. Her husband was a marine, and is a pensioner. He was formerly addicted to the use of spirits, till, like many others in this country, he would bring rum home in a bucket, and drink it neat out of a pint tin. This, his wife would not allow, and he had the good sense to submit to her better government, by which he has become greatly raised in circumstances and in comfort. They have a neat, clean brick house, two tidy children, and a thriving garden, clear of weeds.—The hills on the peninsula of Muddy Plains abound with Blue Gum, Peppermint, and She-Oak: some of these trees as well as another kind called He-Oak, are also plentiful on the lower grounds.

19th. We had a meeting on R. Mather's premises, with about twenty-five persons, some of whom were prisoners, in which the people were warned against habitual sins. Drunkenness and swearing were particularly adverted to, as openly dishonouring God and serving the devil.

20th. Accompanied by R. Mather, we called on several of the settlers, many of whom are of the poorer class, to whom we spoke on the importance of attending to their spiritual concerns, and gave some tracts, for which they appeared grateful. We dined with a respectable family living

in a hut of the humblest structure, who increased their means
of support, by converting into lime, such shells as have accumulated in great abundance on the shore of Ralphs Bay. At
this place we met with William Gellibrand—a settler residing on a peninsula in the Derwent called South Arm,—and
accepting an invitation to visit his establishment, proceeded
thither in a lime boat. W. Gellibrand's house is situated
near the northern extremity of the peninsula : it commands
a view of Ralphs Bay and the Derwent, backed by the
woody hills on the shore, with Hobart Town at the distance
of 9 miles. This part of South Arm is a little elevated.
Basaltic and grit rocks project on its steep sides ; on which
Gulls and Shags roost in great numbers. Peach and almond
trees are coming into blossom in the well-stocked garden.
The native grass of the country is thin ; but the land in
tillage yields a fair return. The intelligent proprietor pays
more attention than most persons, to the comfort and
morals of his assigned servants. This attaches them to
him, and raises a tone of feeling in their minds congenial
to their reformation. On conversing with one of these men,
who has had an unusual measure of privilege during the time
he has been a prisoner, respecting the comparative difficulties
he might expect on becoming free, his sentence expiring in
a few days ; he remarked, " But, Sir, Liberty is sweet !"

21st. We returned to the main land, and dined with an
interesting family of Independents. Here we first partook
of Kangaroo, the taste of which is somewhat intermediate
between that of beef and mutton : it is usually served up
with bacon in a kind of hash called "a steamer."

22nd. Accompanied by a son of R. Mather, we visited
the settlers around the Pipeclay Lagoon, which opens into the
sea, and on the shores of which were lying the remains of
some Box and Cow-fishes. These are about four inches long,
and are encased in coats of mail ; having apertures for their
mouths, eyes, fins and tails. One of the people on whom
we called is said to be an illicit dealer in spirits, or what
is called in the Colony, the keeper of a " Sly-grog-shop."
These are a description of persons that are a great nuisance,
but it is difficult to obtain evidence against them, and

they are rather numerous in the Australian Colonies, especially in remote places.

23rd. Proceeding across a salt marsh to the shores of Frederick Henry Bay, we saw the Princess Royal—a vessel with female emigrants from England—driving from her anchors, in a violent storm of wind and snow. She was perceived also by some persons on the opposite side of the bay, who lighted a fire as a signal, on a point, behind which was a mud bed; on this, the ship went safely on shore in the night, the helmsman attending to an instruction received from the land, in a welcome English tongue, when those on board knew not on what coast they were driving. We took refuge from the snow storm in the house of a settler from Uxbridge, by whom we were hospitably entertained; and afterward proceeded to Glen Ayr, the residence of William de Gillern, which we made out when almost dark, by following the barking of a dog, and where we felt the value of a kind welcome, after a walk of 15 miles in snow, wet and mire.

24th. The snow was about three inches thick in the morning; but defending ourselves against the frequent showers, we went to Richmond, to arrange for holding a meeting. The court-house was readily granted for the purpose by William T. Parramore, the Police Magistrate; who also ordered a constable to invite the inhabitants. The court-house at this time was used as a place of worship by the Episcopalians and Wesleyans. The town of Richmond consisted of the court-house, a jail, a windmill, and about 30 dwelling-houses, three of which were inns. It is prettily situated, at the extremity of an inlet called the Sweet Water.

In the evening we returned to Glen Ayr. The snow among trees in full foliage, presented a novel appearance to an Englishman.—All the trees and shrubs of this country are evergreens; and with the exception of the little patches of land that have been cleared by settlers, may be said to cover the whole country. The thermometer at Richmond was at 27° several times this winter.

25th. We returned to Richmond, and called upon John H. Butcher, a magistrate, residing in an unfinished stone

F

house near the town; who, when he came to this country, brought a variety of fruit trees, packed and stowed at the bottom of the ship's hold. The Ribstone Pippin, French Crab, Golden Harvey, and a few other sorts of choice apples, survived the voyage, and have stocked the gardens of the Colony, in which fruits of this kind are produced in greater abundance and perfection than in England. People in this country often occupy houses as soon as they are built, and finish them as they have opportunity. In the earlier days of the colony J. H. Butcher, as well as many others, was robbed of much of what was available in his house, by Bush-rangers; but these marauders have been so reduced, that the inhabitants now live in such security, as often to be without fastenings to their doors and windows.

26th. We had a religious interview with the prisoners in the jail, and a meeting with the inhabitants in the court-house. In the latter, it did not seem to be my place to express much; nevertheless I was well satisfied in having appointed the meeting; believing that if people were directed to wait more singly upon the Lord, they would not omit assembling for worship because no minister was present, as some did to-day, when their minister was prevented from arriving by the stormy weather. It is a hurtful thing to lean upon man, in that which is a duty to God, and which ought to be performed in spirit and in truth.

27th. Accompanied by J. H. Butcher, we visited some of the settlers upon the Coal River. The district which bears this name is remarkably rich and fertile: it consists chiefly of extensive grassy levels, and gentle undulations, thinly timbered, and bounded by more thickly wooded hills, of various height and form. In this district there is a striking variety in the settlers. One of them is an intelligent man from one of the West India islands, who is improving a beautiful park-like estate, on which he has put up about 17 miles of post and rail fence, at the rate of £70 per mile, by free, and £60 by convict labour. Another was a prisoner, in the earlier days of the Colony: he became free and obtained a location of land, but retained such a love for strong drink as was incompatible with advancement in the scale of society. Few of this class have retained their possessions; and the greater strictness in the penal discipline of latter years, combined with the new regulations, which put a stop to the granting of land, and only allow it to become the property of settlers by purchase, now precludes such men from becoming proprietors. The day was bright and pleasant. Numbers of little green Parrots were extracting honey from the flowers of the Black-butted Gumtree; and *Anguillaria dioica,* a little, purple-spotted, whiteblossomed, bulbous plant, was decorating a sunny bank, as one of the first harbingers of spring.

28th. We have lodged a few nights at the Lenox Arms, a good inn, but with higher charges than in England. This evening we returned to Glen Ayr, after attending a meeting for the formation of a Temperance Society, and visiting some caves, in a range of hills near Richmond, called the Oven Hills. Formerly they were the resort of a horde of bushrangers, the name of the chief of whom was Michael Howe. These hills are of silicious sandstone, and are clothed chiefly with thin grass, and Gum and She Oak trees.

29th. We visited Orielton, a fine estate, on which a considerable quantity of land has been brought into cultivation. Our guide thither was a prisoner constable, from Birmingham. On remarking to him, that we met with many prisoners from that place, he replied, that many of them were persons who had formed bad habits, beginning with drinking; and that they were often drawn into this practice by having their wages paid at public-houses, or by the wages of several being paid to one man, which occasioned them to resort to public-houses for change, in order to divide the sum. From Orielton we went to Sorell Town, and became the guests of James Norman, one of the Colonial Chaplains, with whom we became acquainted in Hobart Town.

30th. Sorell Town, often called Pitt Water, from being situated on a little gulf of that name, has a neat Episcopal place of worship, a parsonage, a Government School-house, and a watch-house of stone, as well as about 50 houses and cottages, most of which are of wood. There is likewise

near the town, a bird-cage windmill,—a lively object, and
rare in this country.   The land in the vicinity is considered
the richest in the Colony; some of it is said to have produced sixteen crops of wheat in succession, many of them
self-sown : but this careless sort of agriculture, has in some
places allowed Perennial Cress, an imported plant that has
become a troublesome weed, to take almost exclusive possession of the land.—An estate of 400 acres is now on sale.
The price asked is £2,000—a large sum for this country.
A meeting was held for the formation of a Temperance
Society : it was the first for a philanthropic purpose ever
held in the place.

31st. We visited the lower settlement on Pitt Water, and
dined with James Gordon, a native of Middleton Tyas,
Yorkshire, who was acquainted with some of the older
branches of my family, and was one of the first persons
who welcomed me to this land, where a knowledge of
family connexions, is a source of great interest, often producing pleasant recollections. At his house we found
several of the females landed from the Princess Royal, and
formed an acquaintance with Charles Price, an Independent
Minister, who came out as superintendent of the female
emigrants, and had much trouble with some disorderly individuals, who were injudiciously put on board, to the
destruction of the comfort of all the others.   In the evening
we had a meeting with a small company in the Government
School-house at Sorell Town.

9th mo. 1st. Accompanied by J. H. Butcher, who again
joined us at Sorell Town, we visited a number of the
settlers to the north of that place, to invite them to a meeting. Some of these were born on Norfolk Island and others
in this Colony ; and, as is the case in numerous instances,
these are less intemperate than many originally from Europe.
—The view from behind Sorell Town is striking and beautiful. Undulating, cultivated ground, divided into fields
by post and rail fences, and ornamented by the scattered
dwellings of settlers, stretches in various directions among
the woody hills, except to the south, where the lively-
looking little town stands on the shore of Pitt Water, in

which are several small islands. On its further side is a long and narrow woody point of land, over which are seen the sea in Frederick Henry Bay, the hills of Tasmans Peninsula and Muddy Plains, and more remotely, those of Bruny Island. In the distance, surmounting the lower hills to the west, Mount Wellington, the top of which is still covered with snow, bounds the interesting picture. The weather has become as fine as that of 5th month, in England. Many little flowers begin to enamel the ground, one of which is too much like an English daisy not to excite the pleasing recollections associated with that little flower. Others, by their form and colour, bespeak the antipodes of England: and "strange bright birds" of the parrot tribe, as they exhibit in the sun their brilliant plumage of crimson, yellow, blue, and green, remind the British spectator, that he is in a foreign land; his ears are also assailed by the strange sound of their screaming voices, and by the unceasing noise of frogs and crickets, the former of which often rival that of a spinning mill.

By the day of the week, it is a year since we sailed from London. The time seems to have gone rapidly, though we have passed through a great variety of scenes. On the 5th, it will be a year since we saw the face of a member of our own Society, to which we do not feel the less attached on that account. The remembrance of the last meeting we were at, with our fellow professors, is still fresh in our recollection. The Comforter, who powerfully affected our minds at that time, is still, through the mercy of God in Christ Jesus, present with us, to bless and to keep us; so that from season to season we can acknowledge that the Lord hath dealt bountifully with us.

On the 2nd we had a meeting with about 70 persons, in the school-house at Sorell Town, and on the 3rd, after a rough passage over the Bluff Ferry, and a walk of nine miles through the bush, we re-crossed the Derwent, in a large boat, from Kangaroo Point, to Hobart Town, where we were cheered by letters from our friends in England.

CHAPTER VI.

WITH the exception of holding a meeting with a road party at a place called Robleys Barn, and another with the inhabitants of Clarence Plains, in a school-house, on the east side of the Derwent, we remained in Hobart Town till the 25th of 9th month. In the mean time, a few persons began to meet with us frequently for public worship; among these was a member of our Society, who came out to the Swan River, but not succeeding there, proceeded to V. D. Land, and took up his residence in Hobart Town, where he has not found it easy to obtain a livelihood. At the conclusion of one of our meetings, a young man informed me, that he felt burdened in mind from not having expressed something that had impressed him, believing that he ought to have communicated it. I therefore requested the company again to take their seats; and he proceeded in a humble but feeling manner, to comment on the declaration of Christ, "My yoke is easy and my burden is light;" saying, he had felt it so, when he had waited on the Lord for strength; but that when he had attempted in his own will and strength to perform religious acts, he had become burdened by them. At another time, after I had made some remarks on the advantage of allowing the mind to dwell under the

influence of the Holy Spirit, in silence, after vocal supplication, a good old Wesleyan observed, that the remarks
reminded him of the expressions in the parable of the Sower,
"Immediately Satan cometh and taketh away that which was
sown." This, he said, he had often noticed to be the case,
in passing immediately from religious exercises to conversation, without taking time to dwell under the impressions
produced.

25th. Having received the sanction of the Lieutenant
Governor, to visit the Establishment for the Aborigines
on Flinders Island (Great Island, of Maps) in Bass's Straits,
we embarked in the Charlotte Cutter, John Thornloe,
a young man from Doncaster, commanding her for the
voyage. The little cabin was in such confusion when
we went on board, that during much of the day, which
was wet, we could do little to advantage but stand still and
exercise patience, till others got their luggage out of the way.
In the evening the cutter drifted against the Challenger Man-
of-war, in the dark. Without discovering, so far as we
could make out, that the Cutter was a Government vessel,
the officers and men on board that ship, exerted themselves
with civility and kindness, and cleared us without cutting
a rope.

26th. Early in the morning we sailed, and in the evening, passed Cape Raoul or Basaltes, a magnificent mass of
perpendicular basaltic columns, forming the south west point
of Tasmans Peninsula.

27th. We put into Port Arthur, a penal settlement
lately formed to receive prisoners from one, recently given up
on Maria Island.—The Clarence bound for England put in
here to-day, to deliver up three prisoners, found on board
after sailing from Hobart Town; who had stowed themselves
away in the hope of escaping.—Port Arthur is much of the
same character as Macquarie Harbour, but being newly
formed, it is less organized.—Allowing such of the prisoners
as conducted themselves well at this place, a few square
yards of ground for gardens, and a small quantity of tea and
sugar, had a very beneficial influence upon their conduct,
but these indulgences being considered incompatible with

the rigid nature of the discipline intended to be maintained at such stations, were after a time withdrawn.

28th. We again proceeded on our voyage, but got to sea with great difficulty. At one time the cutter " missed stays." Though little of a sailor, I saw the only alternative was to get way upon the vessel, by running directly toward a rock near us, and on which there was a danger of being wrecked, and then to try again. The commander of the vessel, though an intrepid young man, had turned pale with fear, but on my promptly pointing out the possibility of escape by this means, he recovered his courage, and made the effort, which proved successful ; the vessel answered her helm, and we glided safely past the point of impending of danger. In the course of the day we rounded Cape Pillar and Tasmans Island, which is also of columnar basalt, and in the evening were off the Hippolyte Rocks. Near Cape Pillar we fell in with the barque Bolina, of London, on her passage from New Zealand. Along the coast many Gannets were diving for fish, which they dart upon from a considerable height in the air. Albatrosses, Cape Pigeons, and Blue and Stormy Petrels, were seen at intervals. Large flocks of Mutton-birds were flying about Tasmans Island at sunset.

29th. We beat up between Maria Island and the main land. The coast of the latter was steep and woody. Some parts of Maria Island are lofty : the northern end is 3,000 feet high, and steep : the island is divided into two portions by a low sandy neck. Black-fish, Gannets, and Mutton-birds were seen ; and in the evening, we were cheered by lights on the coast, at the house of a settler, and at a whaling station, in Spring Bay. The last proved of great service in directing the course of the cutter, which dropped anchor at midnight, the wind having failed.

30th. We had reading on deck. The company, among whom were a few other passengers, did not exhibit much appearance of religion, but some of them showed evidence of the want of it. One of the crew, a prisoner having a ticket of leave, who had been educated in a school on the system of the British and Foreign School Society, at Norwich, said he had not met with any of his school-fellows in this Colony, except one of his own brothers. These men, as well as some others, retain a sense of the kindness they met with from Joseph John Gurney, Peter Bedford, Elizabeth Fry, and some others of our friends in England, such as gives us a more ready access to their best feelings.

In the afternoon we again made sail, passed Green Island, which has been stocked with Rabbits, and made a course outside the White Rock, off Oyster Bay, on which the kind of Seal that affords rich fur, is occasionally taken. In Spring Bay one of the people fishing, brought up a species of Octopodia, an animal of the Cuttle-fish tribe, with eight arms, which in this specimen were 15 inches long. These it fixed to whatever came in its way, by means of circular, saucer-like suckers. It travelled with its mouth, which is in the centre of the arms and like the beak of a parrot, downward, and its red body of about 3 inches long, and like an oval fleshy bag, upward. Between these, its large eyes were very conspicuous. Its strange appearance and remarkable movements, excited no small degree of surprise among our company.

10th mo. 1st. Mutton Birds were in such vast flocks, that, at a distance, they seemed as thick as bees when swarming.—The wind became adverse, and fearing lest we should be driven out to sea, we ran into Schouten Passage, and brought up under Freycinets Peninsula, in Oyster Bay, where we went on shore. One of the soldiers, going as a guard to Flinder's Island, shot a Black Swan, on a lagoon running parallel with the beach. The hills on the peninsula are red, porphyritic granite, as are also some of those on Schouten Island; but, on the inside of the latter, which is about four miles across, the newer formations occur vertically. On the hills, are the Blue Gum, the Oyster Bay Pine, and the *Callitris pyramidalis,* which is a Cypress-like tree.—The bush here was gay with various shrubs, among which were several species of *Acacia, Boronia* and *Hibbertia,* some of the *Epacris* tribe, *Pomaderris elliptica,* with large clusters of small sulphur coloured blossoms, and *Comesperma volubilis,* a beautiful climber, the flowers of which, in spring, hang in blue festoons, among the bushes, in all parts of V. D. Land.

2nd. The wind continuing adverse, the cutter remained at anchor. Some of the men procured another Black Swan and some eggs. I took a solitary walk among the hills, in the course of which I was brought into close self-examination, and given to feel afresh the importance of watchfulness and prayer, and of the continued exercise of faith in Christ; thus the traversing of the uninhabited wilds, to observe the works of Him, whose all-seeing eye beholds us in the deepest solitudes, as well as in the most crowded haunts of men, was made conducive to my spiritual advantage.

3rd. This morning I took three fine Flat-heads, which, with a Swan's egg, contributed toward an abundant breakfast: the latter is rather inferior to the egg of a common fowl. In the forenoon the anchor was weighed, and sail made; but just when we got near the outside of the passage, the wind failed, and left us drifting from side to side for several hours, so that it was necessary from time to time, to tow the head of the vessel round by means of a boat, to keep her from drifting against the terrific, granite rocks, which are too perpendicular to allow of anchorage near them. The dangers of a calm do not appear to be much less in such a situation, than those of a storm. Though no one expressed fear, anxiety was marked on many countenances, during this time of suspense, from which we were at length favoured to be relieved by the turn of the tide, which carried us out to sea.

7th. During the last three days, we have been beating up the coast against a contrary wind. Yesterday the brig Helen, from the Isle of France to Sydney, with sugar, sent a boat to the Charlotte, and obtained a bag of biscuit, having run short of this necessary article. A Right Whale, a shark, and numerous flocks of birds, were seen. The flocks of Mutton-birds sometimes formed dense lines near the horizon, that might have been mistaken for rocks or land. Their flight is usually low; they move their wings smartly a few times, and then soar with them motionless for a considerable distance, except in turning or changing their altitude, which they effect by altering the position of their wings. A flock of them was swimming off Eddystone Point. In the course of the forenoon we dropped anchor in 13 fathoms water, under Swan Island, in Banks's Strait, to avoid drifting back with the strong tide. To the south we had the low sandy shore of Cape Portland, with low woody and grassy hills further distant; and to the north, Clarkes Island, and Cape Barren Island, with its lofty peaks.

The superstition of sailors often leads them to attribute a tedious voyage to having some unlucky person in the vessel. On hearing one of them remark, that we must have some Jonah on board, I took occasion to observe, that it would be well if we had not many worse than Jonah; for he was remarkable for disobedience to the Lord in one instance, but I feared, that in our company, there were those who were disobedient in many.—There is little ear for religious instruction, but no profession to despise it. I have been much restrained in mind in regard to expression on religious subjects, and have felt the force of the declaration "Where the Spirit of the Lord is there is liberty;" the reverse of which is also true. Here, there is a want of regard for this Spirit, and little ear to hear. Nevertheless there are two individuals on board, who say little, but spend much of their time in reading the Bible and hymns, whom we look upon with some comfort. The wreck of a brig that was lately lost, it is said, in consequence of drunkenness, was still lying on Swan Island.

As soon as the tide served, we again made sail; and passing the west end of Clarkes Island, came safely to anchor in Horse-shoe Bay, under the east shore of Preservation Island.

8th. Early in the morning, five Pelicans and some Cape Barren Geese, were upon the beach of Preservation, not far from two huts belonging to James Munro, an old sealer, who, with a native black woman named Jumbo, is the only permanent resident on the Island. We went on shore and paid them a visit, and had an interview also with three other sealers, and three female Aborigines, casually here, on their way to the coast of New Holland, where, on a number of small islands, they still obtain Fur Seals. These animals have become rare in the Australian seas compared to what they were a few years since, when they were destroyed in vast numbers, often in the breeding season.   On Guncarriage and Woody Islands, a few miles distant, several other sealers are residing, with female Aborigines, who assist in the management of their boats, take Mutton-birds, and do other kinds of work for these men. Some of the sealers exhibit the recklessness frequent in the character of sailors, in a superlative degree.   The women were dressed in frocks made of the skins of the Wallaby, a small species of Kangaroo.   One of them presented neck-laces of shells to my companion and myself; these she dropped into our hands as she passed, appearing to wish to avoid receiving any acknowledgment.

Preservation Island is low, and surrounded by round-topped, grey, granite rocks, except in a few places, where there are small sandy bays: it is covered with grass, barilla and nettles, and a large portion of it is so thickly bur-rowed by Mutton-birds, that it is difficult to walk without breaking into their holes.   J. Munro raises wheat, potatoes, and other vegetables near his house, which is sheltered by a few Tea-trees, the only ones on the island: he also rears goats, pigs and fowls ; and by means of these, added to the collecting of birds and their eggs, obtains a subsistence. Black Snakes sometimes take possession of the burrows of the Mutton-birds.   We saw one of these formidable animals, more than five feet long, and gave it a blow that made it rear its head with a threatening aspect.   As the only switch we could raise was a feeble one of Cape Barren Tea-bush, it was not thought expedient to repeat the blow, and the animal soon took refuge in a neighbouring hole.   A sister of Jumbo lost her life by the bite of a Black Snake, in her hand.   When taking Mutton-birds, the natives put a stick into the burrows and listen, to distinguish whether snakes or birds are the occupants.

9th.   Notwithstanding the wind was adverse, J. Thornloe

determined to attempt proceeding, having heard that the settlement on Flinders Island was suffering for want of provisions; he therefore sailed from Preservation, and by the assistance of J. Munro, as pilot, passed Long Island, Badger Island, Chapel Island, and a number of others, and succeeded in reaching the anchorage under Green Island, the nearest place of safety to the settlement, at which a vessel could lie.

On approaching Flinders Island, a smoke was observed on the shore, which we afterwards learned was a signal to the boats of the Settlement that were out, where they could not see the cutter. Two boats soon came off, in which were the Commandant, Ensign William J. Darling, and A. Mc'Lachlan, the surgeon of the Establishment for the Aborigines. The arrival of the Charlotte was hailed with joy, the white inhabitants of the settlement having been reduced in supplies, to potatoes and oatmeal, and the Aborigines, who do not like oatmeal, to potatoes and rice; so that had it not been for the supply of Mutton-birds which they were able to obtain, they would have been greatly straitened. Happily their tea and sugar also, were not exhausted; for of tea, as a beverage, the Aborigines are not less fond than the Europeans, from whom they have acquired this taste.

Before proceeding with my Journal, I will introduce a brief notice of Van Diemens Land and its Aboriginal Inhabitants, and of their history up to the time we first visited them on Flinders Island.

CHAPTER VII.

VAN DIEMENS LAND was discovered by Abel Jansen
Tasman, in 1642; he supposed it to be a part of the
Australian Continent, and named it in honour of Anthony
Van Diemen, at that time Governor General of the Dutch
possessions in the East Indies.   It was ascertained to be an
island in 1798, by Dr. Bass, and taken possession of by
the English in 1803, by Lieutenant Bowen.   The first
Lieutenant Governor arrived in 1804, and removed the seat
of Government from the original settlement at Risdon, or
Rest-down, on the east bank of the Derwent, to the present
site, which he named Hobart Town, after Lord Hobart.

The island lies between 41° 20' and 43° 40' south latitude,
and between 144° 40' and 148° 20' east longitude : its length
is about 210 miles, from north to south, and its breadth 150
from east to west; it is very mountainous and covered with
forest, which in many parts is extremely thick, but in others
open and grassy.   The original inhabitants, whose forefathers
had occupied it from time immemorial, were of the Negro
race.   They were of moderate stature, dark olive colour,
and had black, curly, woolly hair.   They were few in

number, probably never more than from 700 to 1,000, their habits of life being unfriendly to increase. Excepting on the west coast, they had no houses, but in inclement weather took shelter in the thicker parts of the forest, in the vallies or near the sea. They wore no clothes, but sometimes ornamented themselves by strips of skin with the fur on, which they wore around the body, arms, or legs. To enable them to resist the changes of the weather, they smeared themselves from head to foot with red ochre and grease. The men also clotted their hair with these articles, and had the ringlets drawn out like rat-tails. The women cropped their hair as close as they could with sharp stones or shells.

These people formed a few tribes, differing a little in dialect and habits; they were destitute of any traces of civilization; their food consisted of roots and some species of fungus, with shell-fish, grubs, birds, and other wild animals. The latter they took by means of the simplest missiles, or by climbing trees; they cooked them by roasting, and daily removed to a fresh place, to avoid the offal and filth that accumulated about the little fires which they kindled daily, and around which they slept. In this state, the first European visitants of their island, found them, and mistaking some peculiarities in their manners for stupidity, set them down as lower in intellect than other human beings.

In the early days of the Settlement of V. D. Land by the English, a party of the Aborigines made their appearance near Risden, carrying boughs of trees in token of peace, and were fired at by order of a timid officer, who became alarmed at their visit. Several of them were killed, and the rest fled in alarm. Though they did not forget this act of outrage, they were long before they became hostile.

The opinion seems general that the misconduct of Europeans gave rise to the aggressions of the Aborigines. These aggressions, however, produced retaliation on the part of the Whites, who shot many of the Aborigines, sometimes through fear, and there is reason to apprehend, sometimes through recklessness. At length, the Aborigines finding themselves in danger, and their hunting grounds occupied by the intruders into their country, determined to attempt to expel them. For this purpose they set fire to houses, and speared persons at unawares, until there were few families in the Island, who had not sustained some injury, or lost some member by them: the woody nature of the country afforded them ready concealment in thus carrying forward their attacks.

About 1828, a part of the Colony, was declared to be under martial law, as regarded the Aborigines, and about two years after, a military expedition was undertaken, with the intention of driving all those in the south-east part of the island, to Tasmans Peninsula. This project, which a better knowledge of the country and the people, proved a most absurd one, happily ended in no greater evil than the expenditure of a considerable sum of money, and the sojourn of a large proportion of the male, white inhabitants, for a few weeks, in " the bush," with little or no loss of life on either side. A "cordon" was formed across the country, but it was found impossible to keep the people in a line among the rocks, ravines and thickets, with which the island abounds, and the Aborigines stole through the ranks in the night, and escaped safely into the rear of their pursuers.

At length George Augustus Robinson, a benevolent individual, professing to be actuated by a sense of religious duty, offered to go into the woods, attended only by a few of the native Blacks, who had become domesticated, and had lived with him for a time on Bruny Island, and from whom he had acquired some knowledge of their language, and to endeavour to conciliate the Aborigines, and to persuade them to give themselves up to the protection of the Government, on condition of being well provided for, on an island in Bass's Straits. This project was considered by most, as one of madness, but it met the patronage of the Lieutenant Governor, and the Senior Colonial Chaplain, as well as of a few others, and Robinson set forth on his mission of mercy, and succeeded in his object. He was sometimes exposed to considerable danger, and had difficulty in obtaining interviews with the alarmed natives; but in order to inspire them with confidence, he put away every thing that they could mistake for weapons, and approached them with extended hands, even when the Blacks who accompanied him, shrunk back through fear.

The first of these people who became conciliated, were placed on Swan Island, which, being bare of wood and much exposed, was soon found unsuitable. They were therefore removed to Guncarriage Island, but this was also found too small, and it did not afford wild animals for their support, in case of need. They were at one time in danger of starvation from the failure of their provisions, which were irregularly supplied from the colony, but they were relieved by a small quantity of potatoes obtained from some sealers. Their next removal was to a place on Flinders Island, where their wants were better attended to, and where we found them in 1832. And here, their number received accessions from various parties successively conciliated, but it never became large, as few of them had children, and many of them, before being removed hither, had attained to the average period of the duration of their lives.

Flinders Island is of granite, and is about 130 miles in circumference; mountainous and rocky. The lofty parts are sterile, but the lower hills are covered with timber, chiefly Blue Gum. The lower grounds in various places are clothed with tall scrub, intermixed with She-oak and other trees. The open, grassy parts are not numerous, but some portions are capable of cultivation. The Wallaby, a small species of Kangaroo, abounds here, as do also various kinds of wildfowl.

A considerable number of the Aborigines were upon the beach when we landed, close by the Settlement, but they took no notice of us until requested to do so by W. J. Darling; they then shook hands with us very affably. It does not accord with their ideas of proper manners to appear to notice strangers, or to be surprised at any novelty. On learning that plenty of provisions had arrived by the cutter, they shouted for joy. After sunset they had a "corrobery" or dance around a fire, which they kept up till after midnight, in testimony of their pleasure.

G

In these dances the Aborigines represented certain events, or the manners of different animals: they had a horse dance, an emu dance, a thunder and lightning dance, and many others. In their horse dance, they formed a string, moving in a circle, in a half stooping posture, holding by each others loins, one man at the same time going along, as if reining in the others, and a woman as driver, striking them gently as they passed. Sometimes their motions were extremely rapid, but they carefully avoided treading one upon another. In the emu dance, they placed one hand behind them, and alternately put the other to the ground and raised it above their heads, as they passed slowly round the fire, imitating the motion of the head of the emu when feeding. In the thunder and lightning dance, they moved their feet rapidly, bringing them to the ground with great force, so as to produce a loud noise, and make such a dust as rendered it necessary for spectators to keep to windward of the group. Each dance ended with a loud shout, like a last effort of exhausted breath. The exertion used, made them very warm, and occasionally one or other plunged into the adjacent lagoon. One of their chiefs stood by to direct them, and now and then turned to the bystanders and said, " Narra, coopa corrobery "—very good dance—evidently courting applause.

10 mo. 10th. Several of the Aborigines came into the Commandant's hut, when we were at breakfast, and seated themselves quietly on stools, or on the floor; they did not offer to touch anything, but expressed pleasure on receiving a little tea or bread. They have a great dislike to butter or anything fat. At their own meals, they have learned to use tin cans and dishes, of which they take some care. On their first settlement, they threw away these articles as soon as their meals were over, and it was a matter of no small trouble, and exercise of patience to gather them together again. Fuel was at first collected by their white attendants, to boil the water for their tea, but when their taste for this article became strong, they were told, that they must either bring fuel for themselves or go without tea; and by means of this kind they were led to exertion in supplying

their own wants. They now collect fuel cheerfully, and assist in cooking, making bread, &c., and a soldier's wife teaches the women to wash.—In the course of the day a sealer from Guncarriage Island, came and took away a child that he had had by a native woman, now married to a man of her own nation, on the Settlement: he would not be persuaded to leave the little girl under the care of its mother, who was greatly distressed at parting with it.

Late in the evening we visited the Aborigines in the three huts or "breakwinds" that have been erected for them; these are built of spars, and thatched with rushes: they resemble roofs, and have an aperture along the ridge, for the escape of smoke. These, with a few cottages of similar materials, for the soldiers and prisoner boats-crew, and some weather-board huts, occupied by the Commandant, Surgeon, &c., and a tent used by a Surveyor, form the Settlement at this place, which is called The Lagoons. In each of the huts of the natives, there were fires along the centre, around which they were lying, in company with their dogs, which are good tempered like themselves. On our entering the people sat up, and began to sing their native songs—sometimes the men, at others the women—with much animation of countenance and gesture. This they kept up to a late hour: they are said often to continue their singing till midnight. To me, their songs were not unpleasing: persons skilled in music consider them harmonious.

11th. The men having been requested to cease from wearing "bal-de-winny," that is red ochre and grease, in their hair, they had signified a willingness to do so, if they might have some other covering for their heads; and to-day, according to a previous agreement, Scotch Caps were distributed among them, with which they were much delighted. In these they seemed to perceive a similarity to the head-dress of the military, and they immediately arranged themselves in a rank! They are very docile, and having noticed that the soldiers always went to inform the Commandant when going off the Settlement, they have adopted a similar practice, of their own accord. They neither exhibit the intellectual nor the physical degradation, that have been attributed to them. Naked human beings, when in a lean condition, are forlorn looking creatures; but many of these people have become plump, and are partially clothed, and these circumstances have removed much of what was forbidding to a civilized eye.

The Blacks make symmetrical cuttings on their bodies and limbs, for ornament. They keep the cuts open by filling them with grease, until the flesh becomes elevated. Rows of these marks, resembling necklaces around the neck, and similar ones on the shoulders, representing epaulets, are frequent. Rings representing eyes are occasionally seen on the body, producing a rude similitude of a face. They also wear necklaces formed of Kangaroo-sinews rolled in red ochre, and others of small spiral shells. They likewise wear the bones of deceased relatives around their necks, perhaps more as tokens of affection than for ornament; and these are also used as charms. They are commonly leg or jaw bones, wrapped with strings rolled in grease and ochre, the ends only protruding; but there is a couple here who lost their only child in infancy, and its skull is generally to be seen suspended on the breast either of its father or its mother. A man who had a head-ache to-day, had three leg bones fixed on his head, in the form of a triangle, for a charm. The shells for necklaces are of a brilliant, pearly blue: they are perforated by means of the eye-teeth, and are strung on a kangaroo-sinnew; they are then exposed to the action of pyroligneous acid, in the smoke of brushwood covered up with grass; and in this smoke they are turned and rubbed till the external coat comes off, after which, they are polished with oil obtained from the penguin or the mutton-bird.

When any of these people fall sick, in their native state, so as to be unable to accompany the others in their daily removals, they are furnished with a supply of such food as the party happens to have, and a bundle of the leaves of *Mesembryanthemum equilaterale*—a plant known in the Colony by the name of Pig-faces—which the natives use as a purgative; and they are left to perish, unless they recover in time to follow the others. This is done as a matter of necessity, and does not appear to arise out of a nature more cruel than is common to mankind generally.

In the course of a walk, along the margin of the woody land, adjoining the beach, we saw a Black Swan and some Ducks, upon a lagoon: several Spur-winged Plovers were feeding among the rocks on the coast, and we observed a number of interesting shells on the shore.

12th. The present site of the Settlement, being unfit for agriculture, and in other respects unfavourable for advancement in civilization, a project has been formed for removing it about 15 miles northward, to a place named by the sealers Pea Jacket Point. For this place, we set out in the afternoon, the weather having become fine after a wet morning. The company consisted of W. J. Darling, G. W. Walker, and myself, attended by four native men and two of their wives, with eight dogs. We had not proceeded far before a duck flew off her nest, and her numerous eggs quickly became the spoil of some of our attendants, who rushed to the spot, and each, seized as many as he could, but without quarrelling as to the division of them. Our way was sometimes along the beach, at others on the adjacent land, and sometimes through the scrub, in crossing projecting points. The dogs killed a Kangaroo Rat and some mice, rather larger than English Field-mice. The Kangaroo Rat was cooked during a halt, made till the tide ebbed sufficiently to allow us to cross a creek. The animal was thrown into the ashes till the hair was well singed off, and it became a little distended by the heat; it was then scraped, and cleared of the entrails, after which it was returned to the fire till roasted enough. This is the common mode of cooking practiced by the Aborigines, who find that, by thus roasting the meat in the skin, the gravy is more abundant. In eating, they reject the skin, and it forms the portion of their numerous dogs. These are generally very lean, but they are highly valued by their owners, who obtained them from Europeans, there being originally no wild dogs in V. D. Land. The flesh of the Kangaroo Rat is much like that of a rabbit. Near this creek some fine bushes of *Myoporum serratum* were beautifully in blossom. This shrub is like a

G 3

laurel, in size and general aspect, and is common along the coasts of V. D. Land, where it bears the name of Mangrove, which, in Australia, is given very promiscuously to shrubs and trees growing within the reach of salt-water. On the ebb of the tide, we crossed the creek, and proceeded till near dark. The dogs killed a Bandicoot. This animal like most other quadrupeds in this part of the world, carries its young in a pouch. The Bandicoot of V. D. Land, feeds chiefly on ants, but it gets the blame of much of the mischief done in gardens by the Kangaroo Rat. After passing over a remarkable, sloping point of granite, by following a projecting vein of quartz, that afforded hold for our feet, and collecting some limpets from the adjoining rocks, where four fine Pelicans passed over our heads, we turned into a well sheltered place, by a small streamlet, to remain for the night. A fire was quickly kindled, and the tea-kettle, which one of women brought suspended round her neck by a string, was set upon it. The Bandicoot and limpets were cooked, the latter being pitched by the natives, with great dexterity, into the glowing embers, with the points of the shells downward: their contents, when cooked enough, were taken out by means of a pointed stick. These, with provisions from the settlement, formed an ample meal, after which we laid down by the fire, in blankets, &c., brought by one of the men, and rested till morning.

13th. On the way to the place of our destination, the dogs killed a Wallaby, about the size of a lamb of three months old. Here we found two huts built of wattles and lined with grass, by an industrious soldier, who had also brought a plot of ground into cultivation. The site appeared much preferable for a settlement to the Lagoons, being a promontory with a considerable quantity of grass-land, sheltered by thick scrub toward the sea, and having access to the mountains behind; nevertheless fresh water was not so plentiful as was desirable, but sufficient for necessary purposes. Having surveyed the place, we returned to the Lagoons, with the addition to our company of a man carrying two young Cape Barren Geese, one of which died on the way, from the effect of cold and rain.

The Aborigines retained their cheerfulness all the way, and laughed when looked at, as the storm beat against them, notwithstanding, at first, they wished to stop when it rained. On being informed that people stopping in wet clothes would take cold, they were satisfied, and travelled on till the rain abated, when they dried their garments by holding them separately to the fire—a much safer and more expeditious plan, than drying them upon their backs.

We reached the Settlement again about six in the evening, well pleased with our excursion, but heartily tired; and had, as before, visits from some of the Aborigines; to whom both W. J. Darling and A. Mc'Lachlan are liberal, often encouraging good feeling, by giving them out of their own supplies, a panakin of tea, and a piece of biscuit or damper, which is a kind of bread made of flour, water and salt, and baked in the ashes, with which they are much pleased. They were also highly gratified by some coloured cotton handkerchiefs, which we distributed amongst them.

14th. This morning, the white population assembled in a place formed of branches, and used as a chapel: several of the Blacks were also present. I was particularly desirous of this opportunity, to point out to the Europeans, their responsibility to God, for being blessed with the knowledge of the Gospel, especially as it regarded their influence and example among these unenlightened people. By a paraphrase upon Romans 2nd, beginning with the 17th verse, and some comments upon the other parts of the same chapter, with the 1st and 3rd, which were also read, I endeavoured to point out the danger to some of them, through neglecting these things, of the unenlightened Blacks rising up with them in the judgment and condemning them; seeing that these people, like the Gentiles of old, having not the law, are a law unto themselves, when they do by nature the things contained in the law, showing the work of the law written in their hearts; their consciences also bearing witness, and their thoughts meanwhile accusing, or else excusing, one another.

Though able to understand little more than the general object for which we were assembled, and having scarcely

any ideas of a Deity, or a future state, the Aborigines behaved with great reverence and attention.—It was affecting
and humiliating to be cut off from communication with them
on these subjects, by the want of a knowledge of their
language; but there was a comfort in knowing, that "where
there is no law, there is no transgression;" and that "sin
is not imputed where there is no law;" and that they will
be judged only according to the measure of light, they have
received.

I am persuaded that this doctrine, which is held up in
the Holy Scriptures, in no way invalidates that of salvation
through Jesus Christ, nor diminishes the force of his injunction to his disciples, "Go ye into all the world and
preach the Gospel to every creature." The sins of those
who attain to peace with God, through attention to the law
written in their hearts by the Holy Spirit, are blotted out
through the blood of Christ, whether they know it or not;
for they are baptized by the Spirit unto him, and accepted
in him, the Beloved. Nevertheless, it is an unspeakable
blessing and comfort to have the understanding enlightened
upon this all-important subject, and to know Him in whom
we have believed, and to have this knowledge as a powerful
motive to induce us to comply with those indispensable
proofs of discipleship, self-denial and the bearing of the
cross daily. I cannot but fear that many who are great
sticklers for this knowledge, and are ready to limit salvation to the possession of it, are so far from living in accordance with it, as to fall under the condemnation spoken of by
the Apostle, when he says: "Shall not uncircumcision
which is by nature, if it fulfil the law, judge thee, who by
the letter and circumcision dost transgress the law?"

In the evening, a number of the Aborigines joined us,
when we were seated around some charcoal embers, contained in an old iron pot, by which the Commandant's hut
is warmed, and which might endanger the lives of the inhabitants, were it not for the free admission of air through
the crevices of the weatherboard walls. An elderly woman,
named Boatswain, by the sealers, to whom she had long
been in bondage, informed us, by means of signs, and a few

words in broken English, of the manner in which these men flogged the women who did not pluck Mutton-birds, or do other work to their satisfaction. She spread her hands to the wall, to shew the manner in which they were tied up, said a rope was used to flog them with, and cried out with a failing voice till she sank upon the ground, as if exhausted. The statements of this woman were confirmed by others, several of whom have escaped to the settlement. A M'Lachlan fell in with Boatswain and a New Holland woman, when they had been left on a distant part of the island to hunt, and they gladly availed themselves of the opportunity to obtain their liberty. The sealers got them back by false pretences, but Boatswain was afterwards found early in the morning, by the Commandant, on Guncarriage Island, where she stated, that herself and another woman were hid by the sealers, at a former time when one of these men assured him they were not there. The cutter's boat happened to go to Green Island about a year since, when two women, called Isaac and Judy, took the opportunity of escaping by it, while the sealers were asleep.—Two other women waded and swam from Green Island to the Settlement—a distance of three miles. Most of these women were originally kidnapped. Boatswain says, she got into a boat when a girl, and the sealers rowed away with her. These men teach the women to manage their boats, and often give them names ordinarily belonging the male sex—a circumstance small in itself, but connected with reckless depravity.

15th. Old Boatswain having understood that we wished to taste the inner portion of the upper part of the stem of the tree-fern, which is used by the natives as an article of diet, went several miles for some. It is in substance like a Swedish-turnip, but is too astringent in taste to be agreeable, and it is not much altered by cooking. They also use the root of *Pteris esculenta*—a fern, much like the common Brake of England, which they call Tara—a name given to other esculent roots, and to rice in the southern hemisphere. In hunting to-day, the people took several Wallabies, Porcupines, and Kangaroo-rats. The Porcupine of this land, *Echnida Hystrix*, is a squat species of ant-eater, with short quills among its hair : it conceals itself in the day-time among dead timber in the hilly forests.—An eruptive disease prevailed among the Aborigines at this period : it was attended with fever for about four days, and was supposed to have arisen from feeding too freely on young Mutton-birds. One of the men suffering under it, and covered with sores as large as a shilling, lay by a fire in one of the breakwinds, and was literally " wallowing in ashes," having covered himself with them from head to foot. This, we were informed, was one of their common remedies.

There being no hospital here, the surgeon took some of the sick people into his hut : one of them who recovered after being very ill, has shewn many demonstrations of gratitude. This virtue is often exhibited among these people. A romantic instance of it occurred in one of them, named Roomtya or Bet; she was addressed by a young man, named Trigoomi-poonenah or Jackey, who received a refusal; but on a certain occasion, the young woman was taken so ill when crossing a river, as to be in danger; Jackey was present, and availed himself of the opportunity of proving his attachment, he carried her out of the water, and thus saved her life. After this, she accepted his addresses and became his wife, and in her turn, she nursed him carefully when he was sick.—This woman excels in the chase; and once when the Commandant was detained for some days, in Kents Bay, by a storm, she and her husband, left a Wallaby at his house daily lest he should come home and not find a supply of food.

The chief instrument used in the chase by these people, is a Waddy, a short stick about an inch in thickness, brought suddenly to a conical point at each end, and at one end a little roughened, to keep it from slipping out of the hand. This, they throw with a rotatory motion, and with great precision. They also use spears made of simple sticks, having the thicker end sharpened, and hardened in the fire.

16th. After receiving a few waddies and some shell necklaces from the natives, and making them presents in return, we took leave of them, and went back to the cutter, at Green Island, where we went on shore. This island, like most, if not all others in this part of the straits, is of granite,

and like the majority of them, it is low. Its circumference
may be about three miles, and most of its surface is covered
with thick grass, which is knee-deep, and with nettles,
sow-thistles, and tree-mallows, breast high, or with spreading barilla-bushes of three feet. There are also upon it Yellow Everlastings, which attain to a large size. This luxuriance
of vegetation is attributable to the accumulation of the dung
of the Mutton-birds, which is mixed with the light soil that
is perforated in every direction by their burrows.

Where the barilla affords sufficient shelter, these birds do
not seem to consider it necessary to form holes, but they de-
posit their single eggs under the bushes, in hollows on the
bare ground. Perhaps no bird, except the American Migratory
Pigeon, is to be met with in flocks equal in magnitude to those
of the Mutton-bird; and the latter, like the former, lays only
a single egg. The Mutton-birds, or Sooty Petrels, are about
the size of the Wood Pigeon of England; they are of a dark
colour, and are called " Yola " by the natives. These birds
are often to be seen ranging over the surface of the Southern
Ocean, far from land: they visit several of the islands in Bass's
Straits, in the latter part of the 9th month, when they
scratch out their holes: they leave again in the beginning of
the 11th month, and return to lay near the end of the same.
Each burrow is occupied by a single pair: their egg is as
large as that of a duck, and is incubated in about a month.
They leave the islands with their young early in 5th month.
During the period of their resort to land, they become the
prey of men and of hawks, of crows and other ravenous birds,
and of black-snakes.

But notwithstanding the wholesale carnage committed
among the Mutton-birds, their number is not perceptibly
lessened. The greatest quantities are destroyed for the
sake of their feathers; two tons and a half of which are
said to have been sent from this part of the straits in a
season: these would be the produce of 112,000 birds, twenty
yielding one pound of feathers. From the great length of
their wings, these birds cannot rise from a level surface. The sealers take advantage of this, and enclose certain
portions of the islands at night, with converging lines of

bushes terminating at a pit, 6 feet long, 4 feet broad, and 3 feet deep, lined with boards or bark, and having a fence 2 feet, high at the further side, to prevent the birds taking flight, when they come to the edge of the pit. At sunrise, when the birds come out of their holes, they are driven toward the pit, into which they fall till it is full: a sail or thatched hurdle is then thrown over them, and the fences are removed, to allow the remainder of the birds to pass off to the sea. The birds in the pit are suffocated in a few minutes, and the native women are set to strip off their feathers, which are put into bags for exportation. The feathers have an unpleasant smell, but they bring about 6d. per pound, in Launceston.

When fresh, these birds are pretty good eating, at least as a substitute for salt meat. Great numbers of young ones are salted and dried, in which state they taste much like red-herrings. The eggs are also collected in great quantities; the Aborigines at the settlement have been supplied at the rate of six eggs a day, each, for upwards of two months together: as the young birds all leave the islands at the same time, it is not probable that the robbed birds lay a second time. The sealers make the young birds disgorge oil, by pressing their craws: this they use for their lamps, and for various other purposes.

We remained on the island till dusk, when the air seemed alive, with myriads of these birds returning to roost, so that in looking up, we were reminded of a shower of large flakes of snow. When once on the ground, they tried in vain to fly again: when alarmed they shuffled along, by the combined effort of their feet and wings, and tried to bite. They were easily taken by the point of the wing, being unable with their beaks to reach the hand that held them by that part. It was difficult to avoid treading upon them, and they were clucking in all directions among the Barilla, &c. W. J. Darling once laid down on his back when they were returning to roost, and killed twelve with a waddy, without moving from the spot. Flinders computed one of the flocks that he saw in these seas, to be forty miles long, and to contain as many birds as would require an area of sixteen square miles for their nests, at a yard asunder. From what is now known of their breeding places, they probably occupy a much larger extent of ground than sixteen square miles, in the various places of their resort.

18th. Yesterday was stormy, and the wind adverse : W. J. Darling brought four Aborigines on board, to accompany him to the Hunter Islands. The vessel remaining at anchor to-day, we went again upon Green Island, which has several small sandy bays.—When the Mutton-birds take flight, they either rise from elevated places, or from the edge of the cliff, or they run over the beach and upon the water, flapping their wings, till at length, after passing two or three considerable waves, they succeed in gaining sufficient elevation to enable them to mount into the air.

The four Aborigines took tea with us in the cabin: they were very cheerful, and used cups and saucers with dexterity.—When Jumbo first came on board, she was shown a musical box, constructed like a musical snuff-box. Having been brought up among Europeans, she did not feign inattention to novelties, as is common with her country people, but showed pleasure and astonishment, in a remarkable degree. Listening with intensity, her ears moved like those of a dog or horse, to catch the sound (a circumstance that J. Munro, with whom she had lived from childhood, said he had not before noticed) and at intervals she laughed immoderately.—When on the island one of the women threw some sticks at J. Thornloe, on his mentioning her son, who is at school at Newtown. The mention of an absent relative is considered offensive by them, and especially if deceased.

19th. We sailed from Green Island, and put J. Munro on shore on Preservation Island. The tide-ripple, which is occasioned by the meeting of different currents, is very strong in many parts of the straits ; it threatened to swallow up the boat in returning from Preservation. Many voices called to the man who was in it, not to be afraid, saying there was no danger, while the faces of the same parties betrayed their own fears : he, however, succeeded in reaching the vessel, amidst tremendous billows, which were so high that a green light shone through them in a remarkable manner.—Some Pelicans and a flock of Cape Barren Geese were on a rock called Rum Island, near which we passed.

20th. The night was boisterous, and many scenes occurred in it, calculated to excite laughter, even in the midst of much that was uncomfortable, and that would have been very trying, but for hope of a speedy change. At day light, we stood for the land, and soon descried it, near the heads of the Tamar or Port Dalrymple,—an estuary extending to Launceston,—and near to the mouth of which, George Town is situated. On reaching this place we "brought up," to take in some stores, and were kindly received by the Port Officer, Matthew Curling Friend, late of the Norval, in which vessel he brought us some boxes of clothing and tracts to Launceston, free of charge, on his own part, as a token of his approval of the cause in which we are engaged.

CHAPTER VIII.

GEORGE TOWN is a small assemblage of scattered houses, a
few of which are of stone, and the rest of weather-board.
This place was originally intended to be the chief port
in the north of V. D. Land; but Launceston took the precedence, having greater advantages, notwithstanding its distance
is forty miles from the sea; and the police, and other establishments were removed thither.   In the afternoon, the wind
and tide serving, we proceeded up the Tamar, which is
devious in its course, and opens out into many pretty bays.
The shores present traces of basalt.   The adjacent country is
hilly, and wooded down to the water, except in places where
the land has been cleared; on which corn and grass are
verdant.   Some of the habitations of the settlers look comfortable.   We completed the last few miles of our voyage in
the dark, in a boat, and met a hearty welcome at Launceston,
from Isaac and Katharine Sherwin, a thoughtful young
couple from whom we had received a previous invitation.

21st.   We visited a school that does not belong to any
particular denomination of Christians, but is supported by
several, and is in a thriving condition: we also had a meeting
in a small court-house, at which two hundred persons might be
present.   I went to this meeting feeling poor and empty, but

deriving some comfort from the expressions of the apostle Paul: " I was with you in weakness and in fear, and in much trembling." In this state, I found it my duty to attend to the injunction: " Thou, when thou fastest, anoint thine head, and wash thy face," and to put my trust in the Lord.— I had not sat long, before I apprehended it to be right for me to stand up, and explain briefly our views of worship, and to point out the necessity of sincerity, and of the sacrifice of our own wills, in order to being prepared to obtain the blessings of the Gospel. I was led also to speak on other points, connected with the glorious plan of redemption through faith in Jesus Christ, and on the necessity of good works, as the fruit of this faith; and on the benefit of frequent and fervent prayer, as well as on communing with our own hearts before the Lord, in order to feel our spiritual necessities, and to know what to pray for, &c. Thus, in condescending mercy, help was afforded to the weak, and the grain of faith that was exercised, was strengthened. There seemed to be an open ear in the congregation.

22nd. The population of Launceston is about 2,000. The streets are regularly laid out. Most of the houses are weather-boarded, but there are a few substantial ones, of brick. The Episcopal place of worship—the only one here— is a neat edifice of stone. The town is situated at the confluence of the North and South Esk, which here discharge themselves into the head of the Tamar. The South Esk rushes through a deep, narrow, picturesque, basaltic gorge, called The Cataract, distant about half a mile from the town, which is pleasantly situated, and has anchorage for ships of considerable burden near its quay.

W. J. Darling had the four natives that he brought with him from Flinders Island, dressed in decent clothes, and he took them into the town, where their cheerful, intelligent appearance excited a favourable impression in the minds of many who had known little of the Aborigines but as exasperated enemies, charged with treachery and implacable cruelty.— We called on Major Fairtlough, the Commandant, who received us politely. At his house we learned that the cutter was going to sail immediately; we therefore proceeded to the jetty, where we were requested to take seats in the Port Officer's boat. A dispute arose between the cockswain and the harbour-master, both of whom, we soon discovered, were intoxicated, and this proved also to be the case with several of the crew. The harbour-master remonstrated against the boat proceeding, but the cockswain persisted in putting off: he soon brought us alongside of a ship lying at anchor, where he took in two prisoners to assist in pulling the boat: they were not very expert hands; and when the cockswain recovered from the effects of his intemperance, he desired to know who they were, and from whence they came, and he turned them both on shore! Committing the steering of the boat to G. W. Walker, and himself taking an oar with the men, they brought us in safety to the cutter, which had proceeded some miles down the Tamar.—When the tide was spent, we dropped anchor and went on shore. The natives pursued some kangaroos, casting off all their clothes in the chase. —We supped at a public-house by the water-side, where we had some conversation with a settler, respecting the atrocities committed by some reckless individuals upon the Aborigines; these were of such character, as to remove any wonder at the determination of these injured people, to try to drive from their land a race of men, among whom were persons guilty of such deeds.—In our ramble this evening, as well as in one at the Cataract, this morning, we noticed several striking shrubs in blossom; among them were a *Prostanthera*, with long spike-like branches of beautiful, purple flowers. *Veronica formosa*—a myrtle-like bush with lovely, blue blossoms, and *Clematis blanda*, with a profusion of fragrant, white flowers, an inch across.—When out this evening, Jumbo turned up her heel, and with a laugh, asked what that was, pointing to a leech as large as a black snail, that was biting her: she plucked it off and threw it away. One of the men pointed to the ground, and said in broken English, "Two more crackne here," i. e. rest, remain, or are here. One of the Blacks got the Commandant's hat and decorated it with the twining branches of *Comesperma volubilis*, covered with bright blue flowers resembling those of Milkwort.

23rd. The tide not serving till noon, I took a walk alone,

and saw some Forester Kangaroos; these are a large species, which is gregarious. The Brush Kangaroo, the commonest kind in this island, is rather solitary in its habits.—In the evening we reached George Town, where we again received much kindness from M. C. Friend and his wife, and from a magistrate named John Clark, whose guest I became till the 29th.

In this interval we put to sea, but were driven back. This gave me an opportunity of speaking to the inhabitants of George Town, on their religious state. I also visited some prisoners, employed in quarrying and burning lime, up a branch of the Tamar, called Middle Arm. The limestone is accompanied by silicious sandstone, which, as well as the limestone, contains marine fossils, and is in connexion with micacious veins of a silvery appearance.

On the 29th, we got to sea, with a light breeze. At the mouth of the Tamar there was a tremendous tide-ripple, that occasioned the cutter to pitch violently, and seemed ready to swamp the pilot's boat; the men who were in it cried out through fear, notwithstanding the boat was made fast to the vessel by a rope.—The country on the north coast, between Port Dalrymple and Port Sorell is mountainous, that between Port Sorell and Port Frederick is low toward the shore, and has a gentle rise further inland, where there is some fine pasture.—On passing one part of the coast, two of the Aborigines shewed some uneasiness and fear. This, we afterwards found, resulted from circumstances connected with the destruction of two settlers, on account of which one of these men had been in prison, but had been discharged. The other had actually been of the party, who put the settlers to death; but it appeared, that their misconduct had been such as, in a civilized country, would have rendered the case one of what is termed in law, " Justifiable homicide:" but notwithstanding this, and without further evidence than that the parties had been killed by Blacks, a verdict of wilful murder was given at the inquest, and the whole Colony was thrown into excitement through fear of the barbarous Aborigines, so that few people thought of going from home without guns or pistols. This occurred about the time of our arrival in the Colony, when many persons expressed apprehension at our travelling without fire-arms.

30th. Some person having suggested that Proper—a native of the country near Circular Head—would probably run away if we put in there, W. J. Darling, who at the time was lying on a bed on the cabin floor, inquired what was his intention. Proper, with characteristic cheerfulness, answered this question by slipping into bed to Darling, and thus assuring him that he would not forsake him.—From this man, I learned, that the Aborigines of V. D. Land had no artificial method of obtaining fire, before their acquaintance with Europeans: they say, they obtained it first from the sky—probably meaning by lightning. They preserved fire by carrying ignited sticks, or bark, with them, and if these went out, they looked for the smoke of the fire of some other party, or of one of the fires that they had left, as these often continued to burn for several days.—In the afternoon we brought up under Circular-head, where a whale-boat belonging a sealer, residing on Stack Island, came along side the cutter. Seated at the stern, was a native young woman, of interesting appearance, neatly dressed, and having her hair cut off, according to the common custom among her sex in this Land. The mild expression of her features was beclouded by sadness. When she spoke, which was rarely, it was in a low tone. The sealers appeared to treat her kindly, but there was something in their manners that excited suspicion. On being asked, if she would like some soup, she replied in the affirmative, and was requested to come on board for it. Having finished the soup, she sat in silence: Jumbo was asked, if she knew the woman. She replied, Yes, she is my country woman. Jumbo was then inquired of, why she did not talk to her. She replied, She wont speak to me. W. J. Darling ordered the two women into the cabin, and desired Jumbo to ask Jackey—for this was the name that the sealers had given this woman—if she would go to Flinders Island, and live with her own people there. No, was her answer. He then requested, she might be informed, that if she wished to go, he had power to take her, and that the sealers should not hurt her.

Her countenance at once lost its gloom, and with a burst of joy, she said she would go. She now laughed heartily, and entered freely into conversation with Jumbo, and said the sealers had told her not to speak, and that she was afraid of them.—Another native woman, named Maria, was on the jetty much of the day, growling (as they term expressing displeasure) toward the cutter; but this also proved to be assumed by the direction of the sealers; and she likewise, with her baby, was rescued from them.

On landing at Circular Head, we met with G. A. Robinson, returning from a visit to the west coast, in which he had prevailed on more of the natives to join those on Flinders Island. We walked with him to the house of Edward Curr, the Superintendent of the V. D. Land Company's concerns; where we were received with much hospitality. At this place, the large garden, with a fine crop of vegetables, the well fenced fields, with luxuriant herbage of rye-grass and white-clover, and the beautiful cattle and horses, and almost every other object but the Gum-trees, resemble England.

31st. While W. J. Darling and myself were on shore this morning, the cutter broke from her mooring. By getting promptly under sail, those on board were able to beat off from the shore, and by the admonition of one of the rescued women, they escaped running on a reef. We joined them in the West Bay, where they brought up under the lee of the land, and where the luggage of G. W. Walker and myself, was speedily transferred into the Company's Cutter, the Fanny, which immediately sailed for Woolnorth, in company with the Charlotte. We passed northward of Robbin Island, and of the small islands between it and Three Hummock, or the East Hunter Island, and anchored on the west of Stack Island, upon which we heard some dogs, but saw no person. We afterwards learned, however, that a native woman was there, who had concealed herself by order of the sealers, notwithstanding she would have been glad to have escaped from them: they subsequently carried her off to Kangaroo Island.

11th mo. 1st. Leaving the Charlotte at anchor, to take

the natives, collected by G. A. Robinson, from Barren Island, where he had left them, we proceeded by an intricate channel, to Woolnorth, where we became the guests of Samuel Reeves, the Superintendent of this part of the establishment of the V. D. Land Company. Here we were welcomed also by their surgeon, James Richardson, who studied his profession under a friend of mine in Leeds; and who frequently accompanied us in our walks in this neighbourhood.

There are only a few weather-boarded buildings at Woolnorth, which is on the north coast, near Moandas Point, and not far from Cape Grim. Much of the country in this neighbourhood is basaltic, and some of the soil is a fine red loam. To the west, the land is low and swampy, but a considerable, grassy marsh is under drainage.—While walking over this marsh, a large leech crawled up my clothes, and bled me so quietly, that I was unconscious of its intrusion until it droped off. These animals live among the roots of long grass, &c. in moist ground: their mouths are oval, and they give much less pain in biting than the leeches of Europe.—There are some large rocks of white quartz in this direction; and on the coast, the clay-slate formation emerges in a form resembling Turkey-stone, and is useful for hones. The low ground near the coast is open, grassy forest, of small Gum-trees, Honey-suckles, &c. and on the sand-banks, there are large round bushes of a remarkable, oval-leaved *Corræa*.—Short bushes cover some parts of the interior land, and the hills of the west coast are grassy. On these some Merino sheep are fed, but the climate is rather too moist for them.

At Cape Grim, some of the upper portions of the cliffs, are soft sandstone, but their most striking portions are basalt, some of which is columnar. In these cliffs there are caves, formed of slender columns of basalt, of a bluish colour, converging to a sort of keel above and below.—At the foot of the cliff, there is a rugged flat, over which the sea breaks furiously, when the wind lays strong on the shore, which is often the case. The whole scenery is in harmony with the name of the place.

The Islands at this extremity of Bass's Straits are

numerous, but I only visited two, named Trefoil Island, and
Pelican Island, both of which are small. The V. D. Land
Company have some fine Merino sheep upon the former,
on which there are breeding places of the Mutton-bird.
Pelicans are said to breed on the latter, as well as some
smaller birds. The Stormy Petrel and the Blue Petrel,
colonize the Petrel Islands, and the Wandering Albatross
rears its young on Albatross Island, where it sits on its
eggs till knocked down by the sealers for the sake of its
feathers, which are sold for about 9d. a pound. A single bird
will yield about a pound of feathers. Nearly 1,000 Albatrosses
are said to have been killed on this island, last year. Sometimes the birds are stunned, plucked, and cruelly left to
linger; but often, the skin of the neck is taken, as well as the
feathers; the down on this part being nearly equal to that
of the swan. The colonization of many of the Islands in
Bass's Straits, by different kinds of sea-fowl, is a curious
subject, probably dependent upon circumstances of peculiar
character. One of these, is the absence of the carnivorous
quadrupeds of the larger islands, which, though not destructive to man, are so to birds. Another is the structure of
the coast. The Albatross and Mutton-bird requiring a
cliff, or sudden rise, to fly from, cannot take up with a
low, sloping shore. The Penguin, which cannot fly, requires
an easy ascent from the beach. Perhaps some of the other
species take up with islands that are unoccupied by the
myriads of those already named, merely because these Islands
are left vacant.

Some of the kelp or sea-weed, washed up on this shore, is
of gigantic magnitude; a palmate species has a stem thicker
than a man's arm, and proportionately long. The flat portion
between the stem and the ribbon-like appendages, is so large
as to be converted by the Blacks, into vessels for carrying
water. For this purpose, they either open an oblong piece,
so as to form a flat bag, or run a string through holes in the
margin of a circular piece, so as to form a round one. There
is also much kelp of smaller dimensions, near the shore:
among this, there are shells, in considerable variety; and adhering to the rocks, *Haliotis tuberculata* and *levigata*, called in

this country Mutton-fish, are met with abundantly.   These
are often taken in deep water by the native women, who dive
for them, and force them from the rocks by means of a
wooden chisel.   They put them into an oval bag, and bring
them up suspended round their necks.

While we were at Woolnorth, a party of the domesticated
Blacks, who had been with G. A. Robinson, on the west
coast, arrived from Barren Island, under charge of Anthony
Cottrell, G. A. Robinson's assistant.   A woman of this party
was the sole relick of a tribe that inhabited the western side
of the Huon River, on the south coast.   I enquired of her what
became of the people of her country.   She answered, They
all died.   I then asked what killed them.   An aged man of
the Bruny Island tribe, who is one of their doctors, and was
sitting by, replied, The Devil.   I desired to know how he
managed.   The woman began to cough violently, to show
me how they were affected, and she said, that when the rest
were all dead, she made a " catamoran," a sort of raft, and
crossed D'Entrecasteaux Channel to Bruny Island, and
joined a tribe there.

The old Doctor was smeared and streaked with red ochre
and grease, with which his beard was also dressed : he is
affected with fits of spasmodic contraction of the muscles of
one breast, which he attributes, as they do all other diseases,
to the devil ; and he is cunning enough to avail himself of
the singular effect produced upon him by this malady, to
impose upon his country people, under the idea of satanic
inspiration.   When it comes on, he seizes a stick out of the
fire, and brandishes it about him, in the manner that is
common under circumstances of rage among this people.
The Doctor had his instruments lying by him, consisting of
pieces of broken glass, picked up on the shore ; with these
he cuts deep gashes in any part affected with pain.

One day, when sitting by the fire of the natives, watching
a woman making the oval bags of open work, used in fishing, &c. of the leaves of a sedgy plant, which she split
with great dexterity, and after having divided them into
strips of proper width, softened by drawing through the fire,
I observed another woman looking carefully about among the

grass, and enquired what she was seeking. Her companions replied, to my surprise, A needle. To this I answered, that I had often heard hopeless search compared to "seeking a needle in a bottle of hay," and A. Cottrell, who sat by, said, You will see she will find it: you have no idea how keen sighted and persevering they are; and after some time she picked up her needle, which was one of English manufacture, and not of large size!

These people not only smear their bodies with red ochre and grease, but sometimes rouge the prominent parts tastefully with the former article, and they draw lines, that by no means improve their appearance, with a black, glittering, mineral, probably an ore of antimony, above and below their eyes.— One day we noticed a woman arranging several stones that were flat, oval, and about two inches wide, and marked in various directions with black and red lines. These we learned represented absent friends, and one larger than the rest, a corpulent woman on Flinders Island, known by the name of Mother Brown.—The arithmetic of the Aborigines is very limited, amounting only to one, two, plenty. As they cannot state in numbers the amount of persons present on any occasion, they give their names.—The west coast being very humid, those inhabiting it make huts for winter habitations, by clearing a circular area in a thicket of slender, young, Tea-tree, and drawing the tops of the surrounding bushes together, and thatching these with branches and grass. Sometimes for temporary shelter, they use large slabs of bark, from some of the Gum-trees.

Each tribe of the Aborigines is divided into several families, and each family, consisting of a few individuals, occupies its own fire. Though they rarely remain two days in a place, they seldom travel far at a time. Each tribe keeps much to its own district—a circumstance that may in some measure account for the variety of dialect. The tribe called by the settlers, the Ben Lomond tribe, occupied the north-east portion of V. D. Land; that called, the Oyster Bay tribe, the south-east; the Stony Creek tribe, the middle portion of the country; and the Western tribe, the west coast. Besides these, there were also a few smaller sections. Those on the west coast differed from those on the east, in some of their customs. The former did not mark their bodies with the same regularity as the latter: the scars upon those of the west coast appeared to have proceeded from irregular surgical cuts, and were principally upon the chest, which is very liable to be affected by inflammation, that often speedily issues in death. A large proportion of these people died from this cause, in the course of the late inclement season.

Lately, several of these people were sick upon the West Hunter or Barren Island, and one of the women died. The men formed a pile of logs, and at sunset, placed the body of the woman upon it, supported by small wood, which concealed her, and formed a pyramid. They then placed their sick people around the pile, at a short distance. On A. Cottrel, our informant, enquiring the reason of this, they told him that the dead woman would come in the night and take the devil out of them. At daybreak the pile was set on fire, and fresh wood added as any part of the body became exposed, till the whole was consumed. The ashes of the dead were collected in a piece of Kangaroo-skin, and every morning, before sunrise, till they were consumed, a portion of them was smeared over the faces of the survivors, and a death song sung, with great emotion, tears clearing away lines among the ashes. The store of ashes, in the mean time, was suspended about one of their necks. The child of the deceased was carefully nursed.

A few days after the decease of this woman, a man, who was ill at the time, stated, that he should die when the sun went down, and requested the other men would bring wood and form a pile. While the work was going forward, he rested against some logs that were to form part of it, to see them execute the work: he became worse as the day progressed, and died before night.

The practice of burning the dead, is said to have extended to the natives of Bruny Island; but those of the east coast put the deceased into hollow trees, and fenced them in with bushes.—They do not consider a person completely dead till the sun goes down !

The chiefs among these tribes are merely heads of families

of extraordinary prowess. One of these now here, belonging
an eastern tribe, has not the flattened nose common to his
countrymen, but is much more like a European in features.

In the course of our tarriance at Woolnorth, we twice had
meetings with such of the people as could be assembled.
These, with a few Aborigines, amounted to forty-five, on one
occasion, and to fifty-eight on another. The company were
reverent in their deportment, while we read to them from
the Scriptures, and spoke to them respecting the way of
salvation. This was strikingly the case with a few of the
natives who could understand a little English. The solemn
feeling that pervaded the mind, especially during intervals of
silence, was very comforting. The state of the people at
this settlement was such as greatly needed religious instruction.

We returned to Circular Head on the 13th of 11th mo.
by the Fanny, which had on board forty-eight young Merino
Rams, designed for sale at Launceston, and which had been
fed upon Trefoil Island.

CHAPTER IX.

On arriving at Circular Head, we found the Conch, bound for the Isle of France and the Cape of Good Hope, lying at the jetty, where she had taken shelter from adverse winds. On landing, a young man was waiting with assistants, to convey our luggage to a small cottage, which Edward Curr had kindly appropriated to our use, his large family fully occupying his own house : he received us kindly, and invited us to take our meals at his table during our stay here.

Circular Head is a basaltic peninsula, on a flat part of the coast : it takes its name from a large circular bluff, facing the east, and at the south side of which is the anchorage. Portions of the peninsula, which contains about 4,000 acres, are hilly and clothed with wood : much of the soil is good, and notwithstanding some of it is light, it is very productive. On the main land, the coast is sandy, or swampy, and further in, the forest is dense and lofty.

The whole grant of the V. D. Land Company here, is 20,000 acres. The dwellings of persons in their employment, are chiefly on the portion of the peninsula called Highfield Plain, which lies to the north-west of the bluff. We had several meetings with the work-people at this place, generally in the carpenter's shop. Their remote situation excited our sympathy, and we endeavoured to direct them to Christ, the Shepherd and Bishop of souls.—Many of the people who emigrated hither under the auspices of the V. D. Land Company, came out as their indentured servants; but these, finding they had agreed for less wages than they could readily obtain in the Colony, took every opportunity to run away; and the Company having in but few instances, agreed specifically what rations the people should receive, in addition to wages, this also became a fruitful source of dissatisfaction, so that, at present, they have few indentured servants left.

The people here have the advantage of being generally secluded from strong drink, but a Colonial vessel putting in at the jetty, a few of the prisoners, in defiance of admonition, obtained some. I was present when two of these received flagellation, to the amount of twenty-five lashes each, for this offence. Witnessing this punishment tended to confirm me in its inefficiency compared with solitary confinement.

Pelicans and other wild-fowl, resort to the bays adjacent to Circular Head. Eagles also are common here, as well as in other parts of the Island. One day, I saw a large Eagle sallying over my companion, while he was busily occupied in picking up shells. It approached nearer every time it swept over him, until, being afraid he should receive a stroke from its talons, I called to him, and on his resuming an erect posture, it flew away.—On the western shore of Circular Head, there is a remarkable bank of sponges, of several hundred yards long, and more than a yard thick. There are also some others of smaller dimensions. The species are numerous and curious. Sponges, as we see them in England, are merely skeletons. In their living state, those of this coast are filled with a scarlet, crimson, or bright yellow pulp, and covered with a thin skin; they are of great beauty, when seen in clear water.

Shells are also numerous here, we picked up more than a hundred species. The sand north of the bluff, was sometimes covered with myriads of globular crabs, about the size of a hazel-nut. On going among them, they made a noise like a shower of rain, and by a rotatory motion, in a few seconds, buried themselves in the sand, the surface of which they left covered with pellicles like peas.

Seals are not now frequent on this part of the coast; one of large size was killed on the beach during our stay; in the course of which the weather was occasionally inclement for a few days at a time. Rain was often attended by thunder: previous to it, the Ants were busy raising mounds around their holes, to prevent inundation.

12th mo. 13th. Accompanied by Edward Curr, and three assigned servants of the Company, we set out for the Hampshire Hills: the weather previously had rendered the rivers on the way impassable. We travelled on horseback, and were each equipped with a long bundle, formed by a blanket, containing sundry needful articles, and with a tin pot, and a tether-rope, attached to the fore part of the saddle. We crossed a muddy bay, and rode eight miles along a sandy beach, to the Black River, which we forded without difficulty, the tide being low.—On this river, there is blue slate, of good quality, limestone, and quartz-rock. Continuing on the beach five miles further, we crossed Crayfish River, and in four miles more, came to the Detention River, which we also passed on the bar. Here we halted, on a grassy place, where there was a small spring, and made tea, while the horses grazed; they being relieved from their burdens, and tethered to the bushes. When the horses were a little rested, we ascended the white quartz hills, of Rocky Cape, which were but thinly covered with sandy peat. A species of *Xanthorrhœa*, or Grass-tree, is scattered over them, having a root-stock of a few inches high, supporting a crest of stiff spreading rushy leaves, from the centre of which rises a stem from 2 to 5 feet high, thickly covered, excepting a few inches at the base, with rough buds, and with flowers resembling little white stars. A beautiful *Blandfordia* was also scattered in this district: its stems were $1\frac{1}{2}$ ft. high, and supported crests of from 10 to 20 pendulous, red blossoms, margined with yellow, $1\frac{1}{2}$ inch long, and $\frac{3}{4}$ inch wide, at the mouth.

Beyond these hills is a level, upon which, and on some

contiguous hills, *Banksia serratifolia* is the prevailing tree. This, so far as I know, is its only locality in V. D. Land. It is equal to a Pear-tree in size, has leaves 3 or 4 inches long, and ⅜ broad, and strongly toothed: its heads of flowers are 6 inches long, and 12 round; and the seeds are as large as almonds.

The ascent of some of the hills was as steep as a horse could climb, and in some places, little but bare rocks. Some whitening, human bones lay by the side of one of the paths through this dreadful country, in a situation likely for a person exhausted by fatigue, to sink down and die.—Sometimes, we had to lay hold of the manes of the horses, to retain our seats, sometimes to leap over logs, in awkward situations, and sometimes it was impracticable to ride. In some places, the scrub, of *Acacia verticellata*, was so thick that we could not see each other, and when we came upon Table Cape, a fern, *Pteris esculenta*, was so deep as to obscure us from the view of each other.

In the evening, we descended a steep place, at the foot of which, on the coast, there was a grassy level, watered by a clear spring. Here we took up our abode for the night, and formed beds of dry fern and branches, under the shelter of a tarpawling, and a Honey-suckle-tree; and after another meal, of which tea formed a refreshing part, retired to rest, two of our attendants having previously returned to Circular Head with some cattle.

14th. Early in the morning we mended our fire, and supplied ourselves with water for breakfast, from the roof of a cave, in compact silicious rock, imbedding a variety of shells, of similar species to the recent ones on the strand below. We made a hasty meal of tea with beef-pasties, which we took while walking about in the rain, and listening to loud peals of thunder. *Lotus australis,* a bushy plant with pretty, pink, pea-flowers, which also occurs at Cape Grim, was growing here.—The bones of a person supposed to have been a soldier, and some of his fishing tackle, &c. were some time since, found among the fern, by the sea side, at this place, by one of the Company's servants.

After ascending to the top of Table Cape, we passed over

some rich, red loam, clothed with luxuriant vegetation. Fern, Prickly Acacia, and Musky Aster, were so thick as to be passed with difficulty. Tree-ferns were numerous, and many lofty shrubs were overrun with Macquarie Harbour Vine and White Clematis. Above the shrubs, rose stately Stringy-barks and White Gums, attaining to about 200 feet in height. Here and there, a tree had fallen across the path, which was but indistinctly traced in places, and when left was not easy to find again.—Leaving Table Cape, we crossed the Inglis and Camm Rivers, upon the beach, on which we rode most of the way to Emu Bay; where the Company have a store, for the supply of their establishment, at the Hampshire and Surrey Hills. Goods are landed at this place, on the basaltic rocks, which rise perpendicularly out of the sea in pentagonal columns.

After a short rest, we set out for the Hampshire Hills, distant $20\frac{1}{2}$ miles, through one of the most magnificent of forests. For a few miles from the sea, it consists chiefly of White Gum and Stringy-bark, of about 200 feet in height, with straight trunks, clear of branches for from 100 to 150 feet; and resembling an assemblage of elegant columns, so irregularly placed as to intercept the view, at the distance of a few hundred yards. These are elegantly crowned with branching tops, of light, willow-like foliage, but at an elevation too great to allow the form of the leaves to be distinguished, yet throwing a gentle shade on the ground below, which is covered with splendid tree-ferns and large shrubs, and carpeted with smaller ferns. Some of the larger Stringy-barks exceed 200 feet, and rise nearly as high as " the Monument" before branching. Their trunks also will bear a comparison with that stately column, both in circumference and straightness.—The bark of these trees is brown and cracked: that of the White Gums is french-grey, and smooth.

The prostrate trunks of these sylvan giants, in various stages of decay, add greatly to the interest of the scene. Some of them, lately fallen, have vast masses of the rich red earth in which they grew, still clinging to their roots; others, that have been in a state of decay before they fell, present singular ruins of shattered limbs and broken boughs; others, that seem to have been in a state of decomposition for ages, have become overgrown with various ferns and shrubs.

As the distance from the sea increases, the Australian Myrtle and Sasafras, of dark dense foliage, become the prevailing trees. In these denser forests, tree-ferns form nearly the sole undergrowth, except thes mall, starry ferns, of low stature, of the genus *Lomaria*, that cover the ground thinly. Some of the tree-ferns have trunks 20 feet high. Their leaves are from 8 to 12 feet long, and the new ones, now forming, rise in the centre like elegant croziers.

This forest is an ascending, undulating ground, and is interrupted by a very few, small, grassy plains. One of these had recently been burnt by a few Aborigines still remaining in this neighbourhood. They burn off the old grass, in order that the Kangaroos may resort to that which springs up green and tender.

The road which has been cut through this forest, is so much shaded as to be kept constantly moist. It is impassable, except for pack-horses, for several months in the year; and many parts of it may be termed sloughs filled with tangled roots. Several brooks that pass through it, are crossed on bridges, formed of poles laid closely together, so as to make a compact platform.

On arriving at the Hampshire Hills, we received a warm greeting from G. W. Walker's relations, George and Mary Robson; who were rejoiced to see their relative in this sequestered spot, so far from their native land.

CHAPTER X.

THE settlement of the Van Diemens Land Company, at the Hampshire Hills, consisted of a few houses for the officers and servants, built of weather-board, upon a gentle eminence, among grassy and ferny hills, interspersed with forest, and watered by clear brooks, bordered with beautiful shrubs.— Here we remained seven weeks, using such opportunities as occurred for communicating religious instruction to the people. While my companion enjoyed the society of his relations, I often made excursions into the surrounding country; in company with Joseph Milligan, the surgeon of the Company's establishment at this place.

12th mo. 15th. In the course of a walk, we met with the V. D. Land Tulip-tree, *Telopea truncata,* a laurel-like shrub, bearing heads four inches across, of brilliant, scarlet, wiry, flowers; we also saw by the side of a brook, a large upright *Phebalium,* a shrub with silvery leaves and small white blossoms, and a white flowered Wood Sorrel, *Oxalis Lactea,* resembling the Wood Sorrel of England.

17th. When in the forest, a large Black Snake apprized me of its proximity by a loud hiss: I struck it, but

I

my stick breaking, it escaped. We set fire to some dead grass and fern, which burnt rapidly, and ignited some of the dead logs with which the ground was encumbered. In this way, the land is often advantageously cleared of unproductive vegetable matter; but it requires many burnings to destroy the logs, many of which, either partially consumed, or entire, are scattered in all directions over this Island. In the afternoon we accompanied E. Curr and G. Robson to Chilton, a farm house on the Surrey Hills, 19 miles distant. Three miles of the road is through dark Myrtle-forest, the rest over grassy hills, on which Stringy Bark trees are thinly scattererd. The numerous brooks of this part of the country are margined with Tea-tree, Sassafras, Blackwood, and Telopea; the flowers of the last abound in honey, which we found easy to extract by means of the slender tubular stems of grass.

19th. After visiting a pretty little opening in the forest, we returned to the Hampshire Hills, by a place called Long Lea, where there is a single hut.

20th. In company with E. Curr and G. Robson we visited an open place in the forest, called St. Marys Plain; not because of being level, but because it is clear of wood, except a few clumps of Silver Wattle, on the hills, and lines of Tea Tree, on the margins of the brooks by which it is intersected. It is bounded by a lofty forest, and is a spot of great beauty. One of the brooks tumbles over a basaltic rock, and forms a very pretty waterfall, about forty feet high, and thirty wide. It is decorated with Tea Tree, at the top and sides; and at the bottom, a shrubby *Aster*, with toothed leaves, is loaded so profusely with pure white blossoms as to bend gracefully in all directions. The grassy hills are besprinkled with Buttercups, Blue Speedwell, Flax, Stylidium, and little white flowers resembling English Daisies. Several Brush Kangaroos sprang from their hiding-places as we approached them.—The road to this place is through a succession of Myrtle and Stringy-bark forest. The track up an ascending portion of the former, may be compared to a staircase of wreathed roots.

21st. Edward Curr returning to Circular Head, J.

Milligan and I accompanied him as far as Emu Bay.—On an old road called the Lopham-road, a few miles from the Bay, we measured some Stringy-bark trees, taking their circumference at about 5 feet from the ground. One of these, which was rather hollow at the bottom, and broken at the top, was 49 feet round; another that was solid, and supposed to be 200 feet high, was 41 feet round; and a third, supposed to be 250 feet high, was 55½ feet round. As this tree spread much at the base, it would be nearly 70 feet in circumference at the surface of the ground. My companions spoke to each other, when at the opposite side of this tree to myself, and their voices sounded so distant that I concluded they had inadvertantly left me, to see some other object, and immediately called to them. They, in answer, remarked the distant sound of my voice, and inquired if I were behind the tree!—When the road through this forest was forming, a man who had only about 200 yards to go, from one company of the work-people to another, lost himself: he called, and was repeatedly answered; but getting further astray, his voice became more indistinct, till it ceased to be heard, and he perished. The largest trees do not always carry up their width in proportion to their height, but many that are mere spars, are 200 feet high.

The following measurement and enumeration of trees growing on two separate acres of ground in the Emu Bay forest, made by the late Henry Hellyer, the Surveyor to the V. D. Land Company, may give some idea of its density.

FIRST ACRE.

500	Trees under		12	inches in girth.
992	do. ..	1 to	2	feet	do.
716	do. ..	2 to	3	do.	do.
56	do. ..	3 to	6	do.	do.
20	do. ..	6 to	12	do.	do.
12	do. ..	12 to	21	do.	do.
4	do. ..		30	do.	do.
84	Tree Ferns.			

2,384 Total.

SECOND ACRE.

704 Trees under   12 inches in girth.
880   do.   ..   1 to 2 feet   do.
148   do.   ..   2 to 3 do.   do.
 56   do.   ..   3 to 6 do.   do.
 32   do.   ..   6 to 12 do.   do.
 28   do.   ..   12 to 21 do.   do.
  8   do.   ..   21 to 30 do.   do.
  8   do.   ..   30 feet and upwards.
112 Tree Ferns.

1,976 Total.

22nd. We spent the day with a young man who had charge of the Emu Bay Stores.—In walking on a hill in the forest, we fell in with the trunk of a White Gum, nearly 100 feet long, and of such even circumference that it was not easy to determine which end had grown uppermost: it was rather the thickest in the middle. It had been broken off at about 15 feet from its base, and precipitated upon its top, which had been broken to shivers, and the trunk making a somerset, and shooting forward down the hill, had made a vista through the scrub.—In the forest here, we found a curious epiphyte of the orchis tribe, afterwards named *Gunnia australis.* Epiphytes are so called because they grow upon other trees, without becoming incorporated with them. This was growing upon the branches of the larger shrubs, especially upon *Coprosma spinosa,* which last has small, red and rather insipid berries, that are sometimes preserved, under the name of Native Currants.

In the neighbourhood of Emu Bay, there are rocks of felspar, or of quartz, of a reddish colour, and there are traces of granite in this vicinity, as well as at the Hampshire Hills, but the country is chiefly basaltic.—Sometimes, when large trees are blown over, they bring up portions of slender, basaltic columns with their roots. Much of the earth in the forests is rich, red, basaltic loam.

23rd. We assembled the assigned servants, to whom J. Milligan read a portion of Scripture, after which I spoke to them on the importance of securing the salvation of their souls.—This proved an awakening time to a poor prisoner, who died some years after at Launceston, in a hopeful state of mind.

While here, we saw some fires, at a distance, to the eastward, along the coast, which were supposed to be those of lime-burners; but I felt no mental attraction toward them, at which I was surprised.   On afterwards ascertaining that they were the fires of a few natives, who showed hostility, by spearing one of the servants of the Company, I could not but regard this as a mercy from Him, who can keep his dependent children out of danger, as well as preserve them when in it.

24th. We returned to the Hampshire Hills. On the way I ascended the trunk of a prostrate Stringy-bark, by climbing a small Black-wood tree.   The Stringy-bark having laid long on the ground, was covered with moss and ferns: it measured 200 feet, to the first branches, where the trunk was about 12 feet in circumference. It was amusing to look down from the butt of this tree, upon my friend, who was on horseback below. We also measured some White Gums, supposed to be 180 feet high, which varied from 30 to 35 feet in circumference. While taking tea, our attention was arrested by a noise like a peal of thunder, which proved to have been occasioned by the fall of a lofty tree, at the distance of half a mile !

28th. We came to Chilton last night, and this morning ascended the mountain called St. Valentines Peak, which is probably 4,000 feet above the level of the sea, the Surrey Hills, from which it rises, being upwards of 2,000. It is of whitish, silicious conglomerate. The imbedded pebbles are small and rounded : some are translucent, and of various appearance, from that of semi-opal to flint; others are opaque, and white, red, or scarlet. The Myrtle forest extends part of the way up one side of the mountain, and is so thick and difficult to pass through, that though the distance is only six miles from the Hampshire Hills, the road taken to reach it, is sixteen. In the line between these places there are some scrubs, so tangled that to cross them, a person must travel among their branches at many feet above the ground. The sides of the Peak are clothed with shrubs, among which are, a low dense species of *Richea* and *Cystanthe sprengelloides.* The upper part is scantily covered with herbage, and is rocky : it commands a very extensive and remarkable view. The north coast is visible near Port Sorell. The Cradle Mountain, Barn Bluff, and lower parts of the Western Tier, bound the prospect on the east. Numerous mountains are visible to the south; and, on the west, the sea is seen, through a few openings among the hills. The whole, except the sea, the projecting rocks, and a few small, open tracts of land, such as the Hampshire Hills, Goderich Plains, &c. is one vast sombre forest; the open parts of which, having from 10 to 30 trees per acre, are not distinguishable from those that are denser, except in colour.—The dogs belonging to some of the company, killed a Black Opossum, and we destroyed two small snakes, with minute, venom-fangs. Two Wedge-tailed Eagles, called in the colony Eagle Hawks, shewed a disposition to carry off a little dog; but he kept close to us for safety. In approaching the Peak, we crossed some wet land, covered with Bog Moss, *Sphagnum,* of the same kind that occurs in England.

29th. Notwithstanding it is now midsummer, the weather is cold with hail and sleet. The climate here is much colder than that of the coast. We rode to a plain called, The Race Course; on which there is a hut, from whence one of the native Blacks was shot last year, by a young man who, when alone, observed one of them approaching slyly and beckoning to his fellows in the adjacent wood. A hut in the neighbourhood had been attacked by them a few days before, and a man killed; several others had also been speared. The young man that shot the Black became depressed, almost to derangement, at the idea of having prematurely terminated the existence of a fellow-creature.

30th. We remained at Chilton till to-day, for the purpose of having a meeting with the few servants of the Company. In the afternoon, we had also a religious interview with three men at a place named Wey-bridge; after which we returned to the Hampshire Hills.

1st mo. 1st. 1833. I measured a Tea Tree, *Leptospermum lanigerum*, 7 feet in circumference, and about 70 feet high. This is usually a shrub of about 10 feet in height. I afterwards met with one of these trees 80 feet high. A Silver Wattle, *Acacia mollis?* was 11 feet 2 inches round: the area of its branches and its height 60 feet. A Sasafras was 6 feet round and 140 feet high.—On a Myrtle, we met with a large fungus, such as is eaten by the natives in cases of extremity. It is known in the colony by the name of Punk, and is white and spongy; when dried it is commonly used instead of tinder. Another edible fungus grows upon the Myrtle, in these forests: it is produced in clusters, from swollen portions of the branches, and varies from the size of a marble to that of a walnut. When young, its colour is pale, and it is covered with a thin skin that is easily taken off. Its taste, in this state, is like cold cow-heel. When matured, the skin splits, and exhibits a net-work of a yellowish colour. It may be considered the best native esculent in V. D. Land.

A White Hawk, and some other birds of the Falcon tribe were observed here.—Among the few singing birds of this country there is one with a slender note, like that of a Red-breast; another has a protracted whistle, repeated at intervals.—The shrill chirp of the Mole-cricket has been heard during the two last days, and the harsh creaking note of a small *Tetagonia?* a kind of fly, called the Croaker, is every where to be heard among the grass and bushes.

2nd. Showery with thunder. I dug up a *Gastrodium sesamoides*, a plant of the orchis tribe, which is brown, leafless, and 1½ feet high, with dingy, whitish, tubular flowers. It grows among decaying vegetable matter, and has a root like a series of kidney potatoes, terminating in a branched, thick mass of coral-like fibres. It is eaten by the Aborigines, and is sometimes called Native Potato; but the tubers are watery and insipid.

3rd. In company with J. Milligan and Henry Stephenson, a servant of the Company, from near Richmond in Yorkshire, we visited a place in the forest, remarkable for an assemblage of gigantic Stringy Barks, and not far from the junction of the Emu River with the Loudwater; the latter of which takes its name from three falls over basaltic rock, at short intervals, the highest of which is 17 feet.—Within half a mile we measured standing trees as follows, at 4 feet from the ground. Several of them had one large excrescence at the base, and one or more far up the trunk.

No. 1—45 feet in circumference, supposed height 180 feet, the top was broken, as is the case with most large-trunked trees; the trunk was a little injured by decay, but not hollow. This tree had an excresence at the base, 12 feet across, and 6 feet high, protruding about 3 feet.

No. 2—37½ feet in circumference, tubercled.

No. 3—35 feet in circumference; distant from No. 2 about 80 yards.*

No. 4—38 feet in circumference; distant from No. 3 about fifty yards.*

No. 5—28 feet in circumference.

No. 6—30 feet in circumference.

No. 7—32 feet in circumference.

No. 8—55 feet in circumference; supposed to be upwards of 200 feet high; very little injured by decay; it carried up its breadth much better than the large tree on the Lopham Road, and did not spread so much at the base.

No. 9—40½ feet in circumference; sound and tall.

No. 10—48 feet in circumference; tubercled, tall, with some cavities at the base, and much of the top gone. A prostrate tree near to No. 1, was 35 feet in circumference at the base, 22 feet, at 66 feet up, 19 feet, at 110 feet up; there were two large branches at 120 feet; the general head branched off at 150 feet; the elevation of the tree, traceable by the branches on the ground, was 213 feet. We ascended this tree on an inclined plane, formed by one of its limbs, and walked four a breast, with ease, upon its trunk! In its fall, it had overturned another, 168 feet high, which had brought up with its roots, a ball of earth, 20 feet across. It was so much imbedded in the earth that I could not get a string round it

* These were fine sound trees, upwards of 200 feet high; they had large, single excrescences at the base.

to measure its girth.   This is often the case with fallen trees.
On our return, I measured two Stringy-barks, near the houses
at the Hampshire Hills, that had been felled for splitting
into rails, each 180 feet long.   Near to these, is a tree that
has been felled, which is so large that it could not be cut
into lengths for splitting, and a shed has been erected against
it; the tree serving for the back!

7th.   I accompanied J. Milligan in a visit to an open
plain, previously unexplored, which we had seen from an
eminence, and taken the bearing of, by the compass.   We set
out early and reached the place about noon.   It was covered
with long grass and tall fern, to which we set fire.   As evening
drew on, we made "a break-wind" of boughs, and thatched
it with fern, &c, of which we also prepared a bed.   Toward
night, rain fell, but not so as to extinguish our fire, though
it stopped the burning of the grass and fern.   We were
amused with the note of a little bird, in the wood near which
we had formed our shelter, that in a shrill whistle, seemed
to involve the words, "Who are you? who are you?   Are
you wet? are you?"— In passing through a woody hollow,
we saw many of the tree-ferns, with the upper portion of
the trunk split, and one half turned back.   This had
evidently been done by the Aborigines, to obtain the heart
for food, but how the process was effected, I could not discover; it must certainly have required considerable skill.
Many small branches of the bushes were broken and left
hanging: by this means these people had marked their way
through the untracked thicket.

8th.   The morning being wet, we concluded to return
to the Hampshire Hills, and having to pass over the burnt
ground on which the charred stems of the fern were
standing, we were blackened by them in a high degree;
but afterwards, on coming among wet scrub, we were as effectually washed.   We then passed $4\frac{1}{2}$ hours in traversing a
dreary Myrtle-forest, making frequent use of the compass,
and sometimes losing sight of each other, by the intervention
of tree-ferns.   We were much impeded by roots of trees
projecting above the grassless surface of the earth, and by
fallen and decaying timber.   In crossing some of the latter,

of large dimensions, a crack would sometimes inspire the idea of danger of incarceration, in the trunk of a rotten tree. The silence of the forest was only disturbed by a solitary Black Cockatoo and a parrot, and by the occasional creaking of boughs rubbing one against another. Near the Guide River, I measured two Myrtles of 32 and 45 feet round: these and many others appeared to be about 150 feet high. Few Myrtles exceed 30 feet in circumference, and they often diminish suddenly at about 10 feet from the ground, losing nearly as much in circumference.

12th. Part of the day was occupied in Natural History observations.—In the borders of the forest, which has here several trees from 35 to 40 feet in circumference, there are tree-ferns of unusual vigour: some of them have 32 old, and 26 new fronds, of 9 feet long: the most common number is 8 old and 4 new, exclusive of the dead ones. In some of the denser parts of the forest, the Celery-topped Pine occurs, and attains a stature adapted for masts: its fruit is somewhat like that of the Yew.—A laurel-like shrub of great beauty, with clusters of white blossoms, half an inch across, *Anopterus glandulosus*, grows by the sides of the Emu River, in shady places.

The Brush Kangaroo is common here, as well as in other parts of the Island: it is easily domesticated: one at the Hampshire Hills that is half-grown, embraces the hand that rubs its breast; it rambles away and returns at pleasure, feeds chiefly in the evening, and has a voice like a deer, but more complaining.—Dogs that have become wild, have multiplied greatly in this part of the Island, and are very destructive to sheep. The animal, called in this country the Hyena and the Tiger, but which differs greatly from both, also kills sheep: it is the size of a large dog, has a wolf-like head, is striped across the back, and carries its young in a pouch. This animal is said sometimes to have carried off the children of the natives, when left alone by the fire. One is said to have faced a man on horseback, on the Emu Bay Road, probably having had its young ones in the bush, too large for its pouch. Another animal of the same tribe, but black, with a few irregular white spots, having short legs, and being about the size of a terrier, is commonly known by the name of, the Devil, or the Bush-Devil: it is very destructive to lambs. Smaller species of an allied genus, but more resembling the Pole-cat in form, are known by the names of Tiger-cat and Native-cat. These are destructive to poultry. The whole group eats insects, particularly Grass-hoppers, which are extremely abundant in some parts of the Island. Some of the Owls also eat insects: a number were taken from the stomach of a small round-headed species, shot a few evenings ago. There is likewise here a beautiful owl, nearly allied to the Barn-Owl of England. The Land-lobster, noticed at Port Davey, throws up its chimneys also in wet ground at the Hampshire Hills.

14th. I walked with J. Milligan to some wet plains, covered with rushy herbage, and passed through some forest where a dense, wiry scrub of a white flowered Bauera greatly impeded our progress. We got turned round in it, and the day being cloudy, we could not correct our course by the sun. On discovering that the compass pointed the contrary way to what we expected, we had to summon all our resolution, to follow its guidance, especially as we had heard many tales of its being attracted by ironstone, in this country; but we had cause for thankfulness in being enabled to resolve to prove it, for an error here might have placed our lives in imminent peril. Though the compass, in some instances, may possibly have been attracted, so as not to point accurately, I suspect, that in a majority of cases in which this is alleged to have taken place, it was not so, but that the parties who had become bewildered, having lost their confidence in this useful instrument, had wandered at random, till by some accident, they discovered where they were; and then, without proving whether the compass was wrong or not, laid the blame upon it, rather than acknowledge that themselves had missed the way.

G. W. Walker and two of his nephews, felled a Stringybark, that had been burnt hollow, and on this account had been left by the sawyers: it was 10 feet 9 inches in circumference, at 3 feet up, and 4 feet 3 inches round, at the first branch, which was 143 feet from the ground. The extreme height was 215 feet. They brought down another, that was 12 feet 6 inches, at 3 feet from the ground; 4 feet, at 116 feet up, where the first branch was inserted; at 164 feet from the ground, the line of the trunk branched off, and the highest portions of the head were 216 feet.

18th. I again accompanied J. Milligan on an exploratory excursion. We visited the remains of a bark hut, in which a man who had been a prisoner, and was employed by the Aborigines Committee, to capture the natives, fired upon a party of them as they sat around their fire, with the recklessness that characterizes cowardice. One woman was killed, and others were made prisoners. There is reason to believe that this outrage, for which the man was discharged from his employment, led to increased animosity toward the white population, that resulted in loss of life on both sides. The Aborigines had robbed a hut on Three-brook Plain, two miles from the settlement at the Hampshire Hills, a short time before.—We were annoyed by leeches, when stopping to take our meals: they seem to have the power of perceiving persons at a distance, and may be seen making their way through the grass toward them, two or three yards off; we took about a dozen from our clothes, but more than that number eluded our vigilance, and obtained firm hold before being discovered.

19th. We slept near a brook last night, having previously burnt off the grass, and swept the place to clear it of leeches; early this morning, we proceeded further into the forest, which became extremely thick. On the slope of a hill J. Milligan felled a small tree, to make an opening, to see through, and we climbed about 30 feet, up the trunk of a Musky Aster, which had here become arboreous; but nothing was visible except tree tops spreading over hills and valleys. We became perplexed by missing a river that we expected to have come upon, but having confidence in our map and compass, pursued our way with more comfort than our prisoner attendant, who looked downcast, and said, it would be a bad set, if we did not get out of the bush to-morrow. When greatly fatigued, we heard the sound of a cataract, and determined to visit it. The water of what proved to be the union of our lost river with another, rushed down a rugged, basaltic channel, falling at intervals for about 300 yards; the whole elevation being about 100.—We had had some wine with us, and had taken it mixed with water; but it was exhausted some time before reaching this spot; and I was greatly surprised, on eating a morsel of food and drinking a draught of unadulterated water, to find my strength restored, in such a degree as to enable me, with comparative ease, to ascend a hill covered with forest, so thick as to resemble hop-poles, which often required to be pushed aside, to make a passage. After sunset, we discovered some Black-wood trees, and soon a few blades of grass; these were cheering as indications of the margin of the forest; and shortly after, to our great satisfaction, we emerged upon Three-brook Plain. The Myrtle forest was excessively dark, and the road through it so miry, that we had to use sticks to support ourselves, while feeling with our feet for roots to step upon; but patience and perseverance brought us safely to the Hampshire Hills by bed time. Some dogs that accompanied us, killed a Kangaroo and a Wombat, both of which supplied us with food. The latter is sometimes met with in the deepest recesses of the forest.

20th. We assembled for religious purposes, with the Officers and Prisoner-servants of the establishment. G. W. Walker read the Epistle to the Colossians, and I made a few remarks on the efficacy of Divine grace, and of faith in the Son of God, as shown in the conversion of Onesimus, whom the Apostle commends to the Colossian church, and in another epistle, also to Philemon, his master, from whom he had run away. I pressed upon the audience the necessity of seeking to know the same transforming power to operate in themselves, and to bring them from under the dominion of Satan, and into communion with God.—Few of the free servants have chosen to be present on such occasions: several of them were at work this afternoon, contrary to orders. Many of them are very reckless, and have little command over themselves. One of them, a short time since, set out with the overseer of the establishment, for

Launceston, to buy himself a saw, and obtain a work-mate, but he stopped at the first public-house he came to, spent £18 that he had saved, and ran into debt several pounds more. The overseer found him at this place, on his return, and brought him back without saw or mate; and from the effect of continued inebriation, he was in danger of perishing from cold which they had to endure on the way.—Cases similar to this are not uncommon in the Australian Colonies.

22nd. We took leave of our kind friends at the Hampshire Hills, and accompanied by G. Robson and J. Milligan, proceeded to Chilton.—Heavy rain fell, and the cold became so great, that we were glad to retire to bed early, for protection from the piercing wind.—By a register kept by my friend Joseph Milligan, of the quantity of rain that fell at the Hampshire Hills, from 1835, to 1839, the mean annual quantity appeared to be upwards of 67 inches. In 1837, it exceeded 80 inches. The greatest fall in one day in the five years, was upwards of 4 inches.

23rd. George Robson returned, and the rest of our company proceeded to Burleigh, another of the Company's stations. Notwithstanding it was summer, and large patches of ground were white with the blossoms of *Diplarhœna Morœa*—an Iris-like plant, common in the colony, the Barn Bluff and other mountains adjacent, were covered with fresh snow, and the tops of the potatoes at Chilton were touched with frost. The land here is high, with marshy flats and grassy forest. The trees of the open ground are chiefly Stringy-bark 20 to 30 feet in circumference, and 70 to 100 feet high. The country of the Hampshire and Surrey Hills, has proved unfavourable for sheep, but seems adapted for horned cattle.

24th. We crossed the Leven River, travelled through some open forest, and over the swampy Black Bluff Mountains, which are 3,381 feet high, and crossed a fine open country, called The Vale of Belvoir, in which there is a sheet of water named Patterdale-lake. This vale has numerous pits of water and streams, even with the grass, dividing and again uniting, so as to make travelling difficult. There are

also deep fissures in the earth, destitute of water.—We proceeded over the Middlesex Plains, one of the grants of the
V. D. Land Company, which is at present unoccupied, and
crossed the Iris River three times: we then entered an open
forest of White and Common Gum, that continued till we
reached Epping Forest, which is of Stringy-bark, where,
near a vacant stock yard, we encamped for the night.—
When crossing one of the brooks on the Vale of Belvoir, a
snake went into the water from the bank, and passed before
my horse, which became so much alarmed, that he was very
reluctant to leap over, or to cross any of the other brooks that
we came to, in the course of the day. The route we travelled
was upon what has been designated, The Great Western
Road; but in many places in the plains it was quite lost,
and could only be found again in the margins of the forest,
by seeking for the marked trees.

25th. The track was more distinct. On the descent
to the Forth, which, is about 2,000 feet, there are some
beautiful views of woody and mountain scenery. The river is wide and rapid, and the sound of the great fall,
called The Forths Gateway, is very distinguishable from
the road. Gads Hill lies between this river and the
Mersey: it is 2,588 feet high, very steep, and clothed with lofty forest, in which several of the larger
shrubs become small trees.—In ascending this hill, a large
Black Snake crossed the path, and I could not induce my
horse to pass the place where it had been without leading
him. On the top of the hill there are some pretty, grassy
openings, called the Emu Plains; to which, after resting, we
set fire, in order that the next travellers this way, might
have fresh grass.—The descent of Gads Hill is almost too
steep for horses: oxen have sometimes fallen over the side
of the path, and have been lost in the forest below.

On arriving at the Mersey we found it considerably
flooded. Here J. Milligan had some provisions deposited
in a hollow tree, for himself and his prisoner attendant
to return to.—After resting a little, we crossed this river,
which is also wide, and so deep that three out of four of our
horses, swam a short distance; but by keeping their heads a

little up the stream, they got footing again before reaching the dangerous rapids, towards which the stream impelled them. Passing over a few more hills, we came to some small, limestone plains, called the Circular Pond Marshes, from a number of circular basons, that seem to have been formed by the draining off of the waters, with which the whole are sometimes covered, into subterraneous channels. Some of these ponds are full of water, the outlets below being choked with mud, others are empty, and grassy to the perforated bottoms. There are also some cavernous places.— We fixed our quarters for the night under the shelter of a wood, and by the side of a place resembling the bed of a deep river, that commenced and terminated abruptly: the water, which at some seasons flows through it, evidently finds ingress and egress through a bed of loose gravel.

After burning off the grass, and sweeping the place, a fire was kindled against a log, that proved to be rotten inside, and became ignited; the fire spread, and catching the grass, soon extended into the forest, which was full of brushwood, that did not appear to have been burnt for many years. The conflagration was exceedingly grand; it brought down some considerable trees that had been nearly burnt through by former fires: such as were hollow, burnt out at the top like furnaces. This magnificent spectacle cost us, however, some labour, in beating out the fire of the grass, which we burnt off before us, to keep the fire of the forest from igniting it and coming round upon us in the night. We had also some anxiety from the tottering state of a tree that burnt furiously, and was not far enough from our encampment to clear us, if it fell in that direction. From this we were relieved, by its fall, before going to sleep; but our rest was nevertheless disturbed by the crash of others falling during the night.

26th. We explored a few of the caverns, the entrances of some of which resemble doorways, and open into a grassy hollow. At the end of a long subteraneous passage, into which I descended with a torch of burning bark, there was a fine, clear stream of water, three feet wide and equally deep, emerging from one rock and passing away under another. The limestone was of a bluish colour, imbedding iron pyrites.—Between the Circular-pond Marshes and the Moleside Marshes, some elevated land occurs. The latter takes its name from the Moleside River, which also becomes subterraneous in some places.—When we had passed this place, we began to see herds of cattle, and a few houses of settlers.—After taking a meal by the Lobster Rivulet, so called from producing a fresh-water lobster, six to twelve inches long, we parted from our kind guide and companion J. Milligan, who had devoted much time and labour to promote our comfort and accommodation: he and his prisoner attendant returned with three horses to the Hampshire Hills, and we pursued our route to Westbury, with one belonging to the Government, which we had undertaken to convey to Launceston. At a location on the Meander, we met with Ronald Campbell Gunn, the most industrious botanist in Van Diemens Land, who wished us to join him in a botanical excursion. This we declined, not for want of inclination, but because the way was now open for us to proceed with more important business, and we were desirous of having a meeting with the people of Westbury on the morrow.—We crossed the Meander or Western River, at Deloraine Bridge, near the first public-house in this direction, to which allusion has already been made.— Some of the country, passed through to-day, is named Dairy Plains, and is open grassy forest. Toward Westbury, where we arrived in the evening, the trees were all dead from some natural cause, for an extent of several miles. In cases of this kind, the trees may possibly have died from drought; the long grass or scrub amongst which they grow, having been burnt off, and kept from growing again by the browsing of cattle, and the roots having thus become more than formerly exposed to the action of the sun. Had the trees died from frost or from fire, the roots would have pushed up fresh shoots, but this is not the case; and the surrounding trees, not absolutely on the level ground, and consequently, not having been originally accustomed to much moisture, are still living.

27th. Westbury consists of a small number of weatherboard houses, two of which are inns: the others belong to the

K

military establishment. In one of these we found, as temporary residents, the family of George P. Ball, an officer
lately returned from service in India, with whom we had
previously become acquainted, and by whose assistance,
several of the inhabitants were collected at the military
barracks, where I preached to them the Gospel of peace
through Jesus Christ, and pointed out the necessity of
repentance, and the danger of impenitence.—Having been
long in a part of the Island where there are no public-
houses, and where the evils arising from strong drink are
little seen, we were forcibly struck with their exhibition at
Westbury, where intoxication, profane language, and depravity of countenance, bespoke in an appalling manner,
man led captive of the devil at his will.

28th. Our kind friend G. P. Ball accompanied us as
far as the settlement of P. Ashburner, a respectable magistrate, also returned from India, to whose family we paid
a pleasant visit.—Some of the locations of settlers in
this neighbourhood are upwards of 20,000 acres.—We
crossed the South Esk at Entally Ford, and when it
became dark, got involved among unfinished, post and
rail fences, which perplexed us greatly. This is a trial of
patience not unfrequent in a country in which enclosure
is commencing, and one which we generally avoided by
travelling on foot. It was late before we reached the town,
notwithstanding we had been long in sight of it. We found
comfortable accommodation for the night, at the Launceston
Hotel.—The distance from the Hampshire Hills to Launceston is 113 miles.

CHAPTER XI.

On calling upon our friends Isaac and Katharine Sherwin, they pressed us again to take up our quarters at their house, to which we consented: we continued their guests till the 21st of 3rd mo., making in the interval an excursion into the country, to the southward.

2nd mo. 1st. Washing is an expensive item in new colonies: here we are charged 5s. per dozen articles. To-day, our washerwoman laid out £3 in a coral necklace for herself, and a watchchain for her husband! forgetting, I suppose, that this foolish indulgence of pride would not alter her station in society.

2nd. The climate here is much warmer and drier than that to the westward; the harvest is ripe, and under the sickle, and the grass dry and brown upon the ground. Large Grasshoppers, with yellow underwings, margined with black, are very numerous, as are also several species of Lizard. In my walk this morning, I saw a lizard run into a hole with one of the grasshoppers in its mouth, and was induced to watch another, catching its more active prey. The lizard waited till a grasshopper alighted near it, and seized the insect with agility: it then broke off the wings, which it took up and eat; it afterwards laid hold of the grasshopper again, transversely, and by a few movements of the jaws, brought the head of the insect into its mouth, and

K 2

by continued efforts it swallowed the whole grasshopper. The lizard was 8 inches long: it did not use its feet in capturing the grasshopper, which was two inches long, nor in arranging it in its mouth.

3rd. Our kind friend I. Sherwin invited a few persons, whom he knew to be piously inclined, to meet us for worship at his house. After spending a considerable time with them in silence, I called their attention to the greater profitableness of feeling our own necessity before the Lord, in this state, and of putting up our petitions to him in secret, according to our feeling of need, than of having the time occupied continually in hearing. I stated that I did not despise true, gospel ministry, but wished people to learn the way to the fountain set open in the blood of Jesus, for themselves, and not to lean unduly upon their fellow men.— In the evening, we met a little company, in a very humble cottage: they were persons professing with the Wesleyans, who at that time had no congregation in Launceston. We recommended them to meet regularly for worship, though they might be without a preacher, and to seek to know the Lord to teach them himself.

5th. On the way to Perth, we visited a company of prisoners, who were very destitute of religious instruction.— The road to this place is through open forest, except where there are habitations of settlers. The town of Perth consists of ten houses, two of which are inns; it is prettily situated on the high banks of the South Esk River, which is about 60 yards across, at the ferry.

From the 6th to the 14th, we visited the settlers in the vicinity of Perth, as well as on Norfolk Plains, and on the Macquarie and Lake Rivers, and held some meetings among them. Many of these people are in good circumstances, and are living in substantial, brick houses.—Norfolk Plains is a fine agricultural district: the wheat crops are often self-sown, and continue for several years in succession, till the land becomes almost overrun with Wild Oats; but these form useful hay in this dry country. The average yearly crops of wheat, are estimated at from twelve to fifteen bushels per acre; but this is perhaps from mismanagement,

and there are places that yield much more abundantly.—
Many of the original settlers on Norfolk Plains, resided
previously on Norfolk Island : being generally intemperate,
many of them killed themselves, or came to ruin, and their
property has passed into other hands.—Some of the finest
land, on the Lake River, belongs to various branches of a
family of the name of Archer, who have been very successful, both in agriculture and sheep-farming.

At the house of Rowland R. Davies, the Episcopal Chaplain of Norfolk Plains, we met with a man who was transported from Wiltshire for rioting : he said that he was
thoughtful on religious subjects before he left home; that his
wife kept a little shop, and that he was a carrier; that he was
about his lawful concerns when a mob passed his residence,
and compelled him to accompany them; that he was seen
among them by some one who knew him, and who appeared
against him on his trial: he did not however say that he
was altogether clear of blame; but he thought he saw the
hand of the Lord in permitting him to be apprehended;
for in calling at public-houses, &c. in connexion with his
business, he had been gradually sliding into habits of intemperance, which he thought might have proved his ruin.
By means of his apprehension, this snare had been broken;
and he now enjoyed more comfort in his bondage, as the
Lord's free man, than he did when free in body, but
Satan's bond servant. He said also, that he was educated
in a Sabbath-school, and that he now found the benefit of such
an education, and was, with his master's leave, doing what
he could in assisting in the Sabbath-schools at Perth and
Norfolk Plains. Himself and a few others in the lower
walks of life, meet occasionally for mutual edification. A
short time ago this man was ill, and appeared as if near his
end, and his master told us that he often visited him, not
so much to give him counsel, as to be edified by his pious
remarks, to which it was delightful to him to listen.

The country along the Lake and Macquarie Rivers, is
generally open forest, except where it has been cleared.
To the west, it is bounded by a high mountain range, called
the Western Tier.

14th. We returned to Launceston, where we visited the prisoners in the jail, and penitentiary; the latter are about 170 in number; we also held a meeting for worship in the Court House, and distributed a considerable number of tracts.

17th. This morning the mountains visible from Launceston, to the north-east, were covered with snow. This was also the case in the south of the Island, down to 1,000 feet above the level of the sea. Snow is unusual in summer in this country, notwithstanding summer frosts are by no means of rare occurrence.

21st. We set out for Hobart Town, and had a religious opportunity with Nottmans Road-party, consisting of 130 prisoners, several of whom work in chains. They are lodged in huts of the humblest character; twenty-one to twenty-eight in each hut. They were very still and attentive while we revived among them the invitation, "Let the wicked forsake his way, and the unrighteous man his thoughts, and let him return unto the Lord and he will have mercy upon him; and to our God for he will abundantly pardon." We became the guests of Theodore B. Bartley, of Kerry Lodge, a pious man, who had previously invited us to resort to his house when in the neighbourhood.

22nd. On the way to the Eagle Inn, a solitary house in the forest, we passed through Perth, and round one end of the Hummocky Hills, which form the only striking exception to low country, in this part of the extensive vale of the South Esk and Macquarie Rivers.

23rd. We proceeded to breakfast to an inn, by the side of a rushy lagoon or pool, such as is common in this part of the Island, and were grieved on entering it, to hear a man cursing and using blasphemous language, because one of his horses had strayed, as they often do in a country so sparingly intersected by fences.—The conduct of a poor black native, who cut the feet of seven women, whom he attacked as they slept, because his wife had broken a bottle that he valued, has been referred to as a proof of savage character and want of intellect; but what is it when compared with the conduct of persons, who, because offended by a fellow-mortal, or perplexed by the straying of a beast, will insult the Majesty of Heaven?—After breakfast we pursued our route over a second Epping Forest, a sandy track more thickly timbered than the generality of this part of the country; and emerging from it near a good looking house called Wanstead, soon arrived at the dwelling of John Mc. Leod, a hospitable Scotchman, residing upon the Elizabeth River, near Campbell Town.

24th. In the forenoon, we had a meeting with about two hundred persons in the Court House at Campbell Town, a place consisting of a Court-house, a small wooden jail, and about a score of houses, some of which are of brick. Being helped on our way by J. Mc. Leod, who provided us with horses, we had a meeting in the evening at Ross, eight miles further from Launceston: this, like the one at Campbell Town, was a general assembly of the neighbouring settlers and their servants, to whom the Gospel was freely proclaimed.—We lodged at the house of George Parramore, a venerable and pious settler, whom we considered it a privilege to visit.

25th. We breakfasted at Mona Vale, with William Kermode, an opulent sheep-farmer, who accompanied us across Salt Pan Plains, an open grassy district, over which a low, drooping species of Gum-tree is thinly scattered. Upon W. Kermode's estate, near the junction of the Blackman River with the Macquarie, there is a piece of ground that yields about forty bushels of wheat per acre, but it is of small extent.—Salt Pan Plains are more valued as sheep pasture, than for agriculture. These plains are terminated southward by woody hills, among which is an opening called St. Peter's Pass, through which lies the road to Oatlands, a town of about twenty houses of freestone, adjoining a rushy lagoon, called Lake Frederick.—About eight miles further is a little scattered settlement named Jericho, upon a small periodical stream, designated The Jordan. Here we found comfortable accommodation at a respectable inn.

26th. We proceeded by another little settlement called The Lovely Banks, and by the Cross Marsh, to Green Ponds. The Cross Marsh is a rich flat, intersected by the Jordan, which in the drier seasons of the year, is reduced to a chain of pools. On the margin of this river, there is an elegant willow-like *Eucalyptus*, called the Black Gum, forming a tree of moderate size. Green Ponds is a scattered village, with an Episcopal place of worship, and a good inn.—In the evening we continued our walk, by moonlight, along a winding woody pass to Constitution Hill, where we lodged at an inn.

27th. Early in the morning, we visited a road-party of 120 men, and then pursued our route along the vale of Bagdad, much of which is enclosed with post and rail fences, and in which there are several decent houses, and a good inn. Soon after leaving this vale, the road crosses the Jordan, by a handsome wooden bridge, on stone pillars, over a deep ravine; it then continues over low woody hills till it reaches the Derwent, opposite to Bridgewater.—We crossed the Derwent in a small boat, to the Black Snake Inn, where, being very foot sore, we tried the experiment of drawing a double, unbleached, linen thread through the blisters, by means of a needle, and cutting off the thread so as to leave it protruding at each side. This allowed the water to pass out when the blister pressed the ground, by which means the pain was greatly alleviated, and the thread produced no inconvenience by remaining till the blister was healed. Sometimes a thread of white worsted is used for the purpose. Probably, so long as it is undyed, the material is not of much consequence, but the relief to foot-sore pedestrians is very great. We subsequently walked ten miles to Hobart Town, at the rate of a mile in sixteen and a half minutes.— On the way, we met several persons with whom we were acquainted, and passed two good stage coaches going to New Norfolk, which had an enlivening effect at the conclusion of this long journey.—There was at this time no coach to Launceston; but an open four-wheeled carriage performed the journey of 120 miles, in two days, not running at night: the fare was £5.—On reaching Hobart Town we found our friends T. J. and S. Crouch in a larger house, in Bathurst-street, where they willingly allowed us again to become their lodgers.

CHAPTER XII.

Soon after returning to Hobart Town, where we remained
nine weeks, we spent an evening with the Lieut. Governor
and his family, and renewed the Christian intercourse which
we had often enjoyed in their company. It was gratifying to
see the anxiety exhibited by Colonel Arthur, to rule on
Christian principles, and to prosecute the work of reformation among the prisoners, according to the same unerring
standard.—Mankind have too long striven to prevent crime
by visiting it with vengeance, under the delusive hope that
vengeance upon the criminal would deter others. The effect
of this system was unsuccessful, as the means is unauthorized
by the Gospel, which says, " Vengeance is mine, I will
repay, saith the Lord ; therefore if thine enemy hunger, feed
him ; if he thirst, give him drink ; for, in so doing, thou
shalt heap coals of fire upon his head. Be not overcome of
evil, but overcome evil with good." (Rom. xii. 19—21.) No
doubt but these principles, if acted upon, would promote
reformation and reduce crime, more than any others, whether
by individuals or by governments ; and they would not

prevent a salutary restraint being placed upon transgressors, till these kindly principles could be made to bear efficaciously upon them.

Several persons called upon us to obtain tracts: some of these were reformed prisoners, who were diligent in distributing them, sticking up in cottages the broad sheets containing the Ten Commandments, &c. and in other ways endeavouring to do good.—One of them said he had reason to bless God, day and night, for having caused him to be sent to this colony; for by this means he had been broken off from his evil associates: he attributed his change to the labours of Benjamin Carvosso, a Wesleyan minister, whom he heard preaching to condemned criminals in Hobart Town Jail; and he said he was much confirmed by reading religious tracts.—Another told us that he was distinguished as an audacious sinner, and a pugilist; he was awakened to a sense of his undone state about a year and a half ago; he is now distinguished among the Wesleyans for his great fervency in prayer.

Intemperance, and a disposition to embark in business beyond the capital of the parties engaging in it, are prevailing evils in V. D. Land. The consequences are such as might naturally be expected. In addition to premature death, and other awful effects of intemperance, distress and ruin in temporal concerns, are of frequent occurrence. Upwards of four hundred writs have passed through the Sheriffs Office within the last three months.

In a walk in the forest embosoming Mount Wellington, I was attracted to a timber-feller's hut, by the singing of two men, the father of one of whom was a Wesleyan class-leader. This young man said he was sure they were not singing because they were comfortable, but because, having finished their work, they had nothing to do; they had no books, and he assured me that he was very uncomfortable in his mind; he said he had been thinking in the night, how easily one of the trees, such as they are surrounded by, might have fallen upon their hut, and crushed them to death, and he was sure he was not prepared to die. The scrub was burning near to the place: their little bark hovel had narrowly escaped the flames, which had communicated to the lofty Stringy-bark trees, and charred them to the top. The fire had also burnt into the butts of some of them, and had loosened them, and in some instances, brought them down. The young man repeatedly pointed to these trees, which were a hundred and fifty feet high, and some of them nearly thirty feet in circumference, and said, "You see, sir, we cannot tell but at any hour of the day or night, one of these great trees may fall upon us, and crush us; but we are prisoners, sent here to work, and cannot help it:" he did not complain of this as an undue hardship, but spoke of it as giving a sense of the necessity of being prepared for death. He told me that he had slighted the counsel of his father, but said "Now I begin to think of what my father used to say to me." Sometimes his emotion almost choked his utterance. I encouraged him to cherish these feelings, and to be willing to understand his errors; to attend to the convictions of the Holy Spirit, by which he was given to see his unfitness to die, assuring him, that if he kept under this holy influence, he would be led to repentance toward God and faith toward the Lord Jesus, by which he would know his sin to be blotted out, and ability to be given, to walk in holiness before the Lord.

Our meetings for worship at Hobart Town, were often favoured with a solemn sense of divine influence, bowing our hearts before the Lord; and sometimes raising a vocal testimony to his goodness, both from ourselves and from pious persons who were casually present. The number who regularly met, became a little augmented. Among these were two persons from England, members of the Society of Friends; one of whom had been several years in the Colony. A man also became one of our congregation, who had had his education among Friends, but had committed a crime for which he was transported when young, and who in his old age had been stirred up to seek the Lord in earnest. With these we had a conference, on the subject of continuing to assemble regularly for worship when we were absent from the town; and they being desirous to do so, a room in a private house was hired for the purpose, as they united with us in the judgment, that they were not in a state to open a house for public worship, notwithstanding it might be to their edification to meet more retiredly. The room, hired for this purpose was in the upper part of Macquarie Street. The first meeting was held in it on the 7th of the 4th month. The congregation consisted of fifteen persons, including some children. On this occasion I had much to express in doctrine and exhortation; and especially to point out the necessity of the superstructure of a religious profession, being raised upon the solid foundation of repentance towards God and faith toward our Lord Jesus Christ.—In consequence of several of the children having had but little religious instruction, it was determined, temporarily to hold a meeting for religious reading in the afternoons; and on this day a chapter of "Tuke's Principles of Friends," a part of "Chalkley's Observations on Christ's Sermon on the Mount," and a portion of Scripture were read.

4th mo. 8th. We set out on another long journey among the settlers.—Crossing the Derwent to Kangaroo Point, we proceeded over a woody steep called Breakneck Hill, to Richmond, where we were again kindly welcomed by W. T. Parramore and J. H. Butcher.

9th. W. T. Parramore, furnished us with a guide, who took us through among the woody hills, by a narrow winding track, called Black Charleys Opening, to the Brushy Plains; where the path joined the cart track from Sorell Town. Here we parted from our guide, who was a prisoner in the field-police, and was anxiously looking forward toward restoration to liberty. This is indeed universally the case, except with such prisoners as are sentenced for life, or have become reckless. Our guide assured us that many of the latter class were infidels, and of this we afterwards had much proof.—Brushy Plains is an extensive flat of open forest, bearing grass and sedgy herbage, intermingled with scrub, and joining some swampy land, called The White Marsh. Here, we found a young prisoner, in charge of a settler's hut, who said he had seen it asserted in an English newspaper, that transportation was no punishment; but that he felt it to be a very severe one; that the best of his days were wasting, and he doing nothing for himself; that being sent out for life, it made him dull to think of liberty, as the time would be long before he could even obtain any such a mitigation of sentence, as in this country is called Indulgence; and that transportation had taught him a lesson, which would make him use his liberty very differently to what he had formerly done, if ever he had it again.—A track over a series of open, forest hills, brought us to Prossers Plains, an extensive grassy opening with a few settlers houses; in one of which, occupied by a person named Richard Crocker, we found a hospitable reception.

10th. We crossed the Thumbs Marsh, a grassy opening under the Three Thumbs Mountain, and met our friend Francis Cotton, who proved a most welcome guide in passing through the rugged, woody, ravine of the Prossers River, which is ironically called Paradise. We forded the River, at a rocky place, and travelled along the side of some very rough, steep hills, called the Devils Royals, to the sandy beach of Prossers Bay, on which there were the skeletons of two whales. On again entering the forest, the path lay by the side of a rushy lagoon, near which was a bushy species of *Conospermum*, a shrub with narrow, strap-shaped leaves, and small white flowers. This was the only place in which I met with a plant of this genus in V. D. Land. Passing a few grassy hills of open forest, we reached the habitation of Patrick M'Lean, at Spring Bay, by whom we were kindly received, and on whose land we viewed with satisfaction, the agricultural progress of one who had beaten his sword into a ploughshare.

11th. The country which we passed through was a continued series of open forest, abounding with Kangaroo-grass, *Anthistiria australis*, which affords the best pasturage of any of the native grasses of this island, and is less affected by drought than those from Europe; but as there is a tinge of brown upon it, even while growing, the grass lands of Tasmania do not, at any season of the year, present a lovely green like English pastures and meadows. There are a few settlers on the best pieces of land near Spring Bay, and we were hospitably entertained by one named John Hawkins, in Little Swan Port, who had also been brought up to a military life.

12th.   We visited a few huts on the side of the inlet opening into Oyster Bay, and called The Little Swan Port, which
is also the name of the district.   Upon this inlet there were
more than a dozen Pelicans.   We also walked over the cultivated land of J. Hawkins.   The ground adapted for cultivation is of limited extent, compared with the estate.   This is
generally the case throughout the Colony.   On the first
settlement of this place, the Aborigines killed one of the men
near the house.   Many other persons lost their lives by
them, in the Oyster Bay or Swan Port district.

13th.   We visited a free man, living in a miserable hut
near the Little Swan Port, who had been notorious for the
use of profane language and for cursing his eyes; and he
had become nearly blind, but seemed far from having pro-
fited by this judgment.   We then pursued our way through
the forest, and reached Kelvedon, the residence of Francis
and Anna Maria Cotton, and their large family, in which
George Fordyce Story, M.D., who fills the office of District
Surgeon, is an inmate.   The road, which is impassable for
carriages from Prossers Plains, lies along a soft salt-marsh at
the head of the Little Swan Port, and past the habitations of a
few distantly scattered settlers, and over the Rocky Hills—a
series of basaltic bluffs divided by deep ravines, and separating the districts of Little and Great Swan Port.   The forest
of this part of the country is distinguishable from that of
most others, by the prevalence of The Oyster Bay Pine,
Callitris pyramidalis, a cypress-like tree, attaining to seventy
feet in height, and affording narrow plank and small timber,
which is useful in building, but not easy to work, being
liable to splinter: it has an aromatic smell resembling that
of the Red Cedar of America.   The other trees of these
forests, are the Blue, the White, and the Black-butted Gum,
the Silver and the Black Wattle, and the She-Oak.   The
country is favourable for sheep and horned cattle, as well as
for agriculture; the proximity of the sea preventing summer
frosts; but it often suffers from drought.

The annexed etching, from a sketch by my friend George
Washington Walker, represents the dwelling of the family at
Kelvedon, which is more commodious than the houses of

most settlers in this colony. It is fronted by a good garden, separated from a field adjoining the sea bank, by a lagoon. On this bank there are grass, bushes, and small trees. One of the trees, a She-Oak, in a state of decay, is depicted standing by a post and rail fence, such as is common in this country. The woody, basaltic hills in the back ground form a general feature in a Tasmanian landscape. The sandstone of the coal formation occurs here between the hills and the sea.

In a gully among the Rocky Hills behind Kelvedon, *Gunnia australis* was growing upon a variety of trees and shrubs. This is the most southerly locality in which I have met with an epiphyte of the orchis tribe, growing upon the trunks of trees. *Gastrodium sesamoides*, supposed to grow from the decaying roots of Stringy-bark trees, is found near Hobart Town.

We remained at Kelvedon till the 26th, having, in the mean time, religious interviews with the family and assigned servants, and with some of the neighbouring settlers, and a meeting at Waterloo Point, a village where there are a jail, military barracks, and a few cottages.

We set out on the 26th, to visit the settlers at the head of Great Swan Port.—In a religious opportunity with the family of one of these, Francis Cotton, who accompanied us, made some observations, under much feeling: this proved the commencement of his ministerial labours, which were very comforting to us, and helpful in promoting the great object for which we left our native land,—that of spreading the knowledge of Christ and of his Gospel.

Several of the estates in this part of the country, contain above an average quantity of good land, nevertheless a settler does not find it easy to obtain much return for his labour in less than four years.—On receding from the sea, the wheat becomes liable to be blighted by summer frost.— Some of the best native pasture will keep more than an average of one sheep to an acre; but in many parts of the island that is esteemed good land which will maintain one sheep to three acres, throughout the year. This does not, however, arise altogether from defect in the quality of the land, but in a considerable measure, from the scarcity of rain on the eastern side of the Colony.

On the banks of the Swan River, the beautiful, blue, shrubby, *Veronica formosa*, and the gay, pink, *Bauera rubiæfolia*, were very abundant, along with some species of *Pomaderris, Melaleuca, Hakea, Hovea, Westringia,* and other interesting shrubs: here is also another species of *Callitris*, resembling a Red Cedar, and seldom attaining to ten feet in height.—On a branch of an inlet called Moulting Bay, Black Swans were very numerous; I counted nearly eighty, swimming in pairs. The large species of Kangaroo, called the Boomer, which, when it stretches itself upon its hind feet, is almost as tall as a man on horseback, has become scarce, but we saw one in passing through a bush. Though harmless when unmolested, it is said to be formidable when hunted, taking to the water, and endeavouring to drown its antagonists. The stroke of the hind claws, both of this and some other species, is destructive, and not unfrequently fatal to dogs.

On the 30th, we set out early from the house of William Lyne, who, with his sons, guided us through the forest for about ten miles, before the sun rose: his wife loaded us with provisions, lest we should suffer from hunger on the way, with a liberality, such as we often experienced in the Australian Colonies. We came upon the coast at a place to the north of a series of grey, granite hills, where a low species of *Xanthorrhœa* was plentiful. We then proceeded along the shore for eighteen miles, occasionally crossing points of land. Upon one part of the beach, sandstone and coal were visible; and in several places, we saw the footprints of the Tasmanian Tiger, and the Bush Devil, which had been in search of fish cast up by the sea. The mouths of the rivers were choked with sand, so that they did not impede our progress; sometimes they are dangerous to cross. A line of high, woody hills continued parallel with the shore, at a little distance inland, until it ran out upon the beach, toward the point, called St. Patricks Head. We travelled over these hills for about twelve miles further than this point, to Falmouth, a small settlement where one of our friends, named

David Stead, was overseer, on an estate belonging to a gentleman in India.

The dwelling occupied by D. Stead was superior to many of those in out-stations, but inferior to the houses of the generality of settlers: it was built of upright split timber, plastered inside, and divided to the height of the walls, into four apartments, a sitting-room, bed-room, kitchen, and store-room. The last only, was secured by a lock. The outer doors had no other fastenings than wooden latches, and the windows were of canvass stretched in frames in square openings. The kitchen was also the sleeping-place of the prisoner-servants. A hammock formed the sleeping accommodation of our friend. A wooden sofa in the parlour served a passing guest; and in case of more travellers having to be accommodated, the hospitality of a neighbour was claimed.

The timber on a piece of low ground here, was remarkably tall and slender. Trees had been felled, 140 feet of which were adapted to being cut into lengths for log-fencing: many of them were 200 feet high, and of very even thickness.—From Whales occasionally cast upon these shores, the settlers supply themselves with oil. This is not unfrequent on other parts of the coast. They are probably fish that escape after being struck by the people from the whaling vessels which are stationed in some of the bays, and which cruise about the Island.

After a meeting here, some of the people noticed, that it was the first time the Gospel had been preached at this place. While " neither is he that planteth any thing, neither he that watereth, but God that giveth the increase;" it is, nevertheless, an honour to bear his message of mercy through Christ Jesus, though it be but to a few, remotely scattered.

5th mo. 2nd. We crossed a series of lofty hills, to Break-o'-day Plains. The first of these are granite, and the succeeding ones, are argillaceous, and red sandstone. On the granite is a species of *Eucalyptus*, not frequent in Tasmania, called Iron-bark, which name is given to more than one species of this genus in N. S. Wales, on account of the bark being exceedingly coarse, hard, and iron-like. On the argillaceous hills, the Peppermint-tree attains a considerable

L

size: one on the ground was 147 feet long, another, standing was 26½ feet round. *Daviesia latifolia*, a low shrub
with bluish leaves, and axillary spikes of small, handsome,
pea-like flowers, of yellow, shaded into orange in the middle,
abounds on these hills. This kind of colouring is frequent
in the numerous little pea-flowered shrubs that decorate the
" scrubs," or bushy places of this land.

Open, grassy lands, watered by rivulets from the mountains, and thinly settled, succeed to these hills, and are
bounded on the north, by those of the Ben Lomond range,
and on the south, by those called the St. Pauls Tier, on
account of the dome-like appearance of one of them, which
also bears the name of Tasmans Peak.—At the farm of
Michael Bates we were kindly welcomed, and enjoyed a
meal of boiled mutton and tea, notwithstanding, in consequence of the distance from a shop, the latter had to be made
in a canister, and when the party became enlarged, in the
tea-kettle, which very generally supersedes the tea-pot in
this country. As tea is cheap, the chest, which often stands
under the table, is frequently resorted to in place of a tea-
caddy; and the refreshing beverage is sweetened with coarse
Mauritian sugar, conveyed from the bag into the kettle
with an iron spoon.

3rd. We proceeded down the Break-o'day Plains, and past
the township of Fingal, which is marked only by barracks,
occupied by five soldiers. We reached the house of a settler, by moonlight, and were glad of a shelter from the
frost.

4th. We continued our journey through a pass between
the hills, to Avoca, a small settlement at the confluence of
the Break-o'day and St. Pauls Rivers with the South Esk.
Here we became the guests of Major Grey, a retired military
man, who was formerly, for some time, in Western Africa.

In the course of the three following days we visited the
settlers on St. Pauls Plains, another series of grassy vales, running to the east.—In one part of this district, where the soil is
sandy, *Stenanthera pinifolia*, a pretty heath-like shrub, is
found: it is common in N. S. Wales, but this is the only
place in which we saw it in V. D. Land. In another part,

the soil is strong, and stands in remarkable ridges, called in this country, "Dead-mens-graves." These occur, also, on the Macquarie River and in other places, and are, beyond doubt, of natural origin; nevertheless, the manner in which they have been formed is not easy to determine.

On the 8th, we reached John Batman's, on Buffalo Plains, under Ben Lomond. These plains are so named from horned cattle, imported from India, which obtained the name of Buffaloes in V. D. Land, and were fed here. J. Batman was formerly employed by the Government to take the Aborigines, by capture, if practicable, but by destruction, where they could not be captured! This was at a time when they had killed many white people. Under these instructions, about thirty were destroyed, and eleven captured! Those captured became reconciled, and highly useful in the peaceable arrangements, successfully made of latter time, by George Augustus Robinson and Anthony Cottrell. The last time A. Cottrell passed down the west coast, he had a friendly interview with a tribe, near the Arthur River, that a few months prior, attempted the destruction of G. A. Robinson.

Previously to this, two white men, of A. Cottrell's party, were lost in crossing a river on a raft, before the tide was out. When some of the native women saw them in danger, they swam to the raft, and begged the men to get upon their backs, and they would convey them to the shore; but the poor men refused, being overcome by fear. These kind-hearted women were greatly affected by this accident.

9th. When walking with J. Batman, in his garden, he pointed out the grave of a child of one of the Blacks, that died at his house. When it expired, the mother and other native women made great lamentation, and the morning after it was buried, happening to walk round his garden before sun-rise, he found its mother weeping over its grave: yet it is asserted by some, that these people are without natural affection.

10th. We visited John Glover, a celebrated painter, who came to this country when advanced in life, to depict the novel scenery: his aged wife has been so tried with the convict, female servants, that she has herself undertaken the house-work. We generally find that females prefer England to Tasmania, on account of this annoyance.

13th. We reached Launceston, after visiting a few settlers on the Nile, and on the South Esk, into which the former flows.

At Launceston, we found an interesting letter from W. J. Darling, from Flinders Island, dated Establishment for the Aborigines, formerly Pea-Jacket, now Wybalenna, 6th April, 1833. The following are extracts from it:—

"We have been removed since the 1st February, down to this place, which is a paradise compared with the other, and which I have named Wybalenna, or Black Man's Houses, in honest English. We have abundance of water, an excellent garden, and every comfort a rational man can want. If you were gratified with the establishment before, you would be doubly so now, and would find a vast improvement among the people since your last visit: their habitations are in progress, four of them being nearly completed. I think you would approve of them. They consist of low cottages, twenty-eight feet by fourteen, with a double fire-place in the centre, and a partition; each apartment calculated to contain six persons. They are built of wattles, plastered and whitewashed; the wattles and grass for thatching,—of which a great quantity is required for each building, —have been brought in entirely by the natives, and the delight they show in the anticipation of their new houses, is highly gratifying. They are of course to be furnished with bed-places, tables, stools, &c. and each house will have a good-sized garden in front of it. By next spring there will not be a prettier, or more interesting place in the colony of V. D. Land. The women now wash their own clothes and those of their husbands, as well as any white women would do. We are not now half so naked as when you were last here, but have neat and substantial clothing."—In a letter of later date, after the Aborigines had got into their houses, W. J. Darling says, "Their houses are swept out every morning, their things all hung up and in order, and this is without a word being spoken to them. They all know, and make a distinction on the Sunday; the women having washed their clothes on the Saturday; this too springs entirely from themselves. The men dress every Sunday morning in clean, duck frocks and trowsers, and every one of them washes himself. "

We remained in Launceston a month; in the course of which we held some religious meetings with the inhabitants, and with the prisoners in the Penitentiary, and had also a meeting for the promotion of temperance. We likewise visited the inhabitants of Patersons Plains, an open grassy district, on the North Esk, to the eastward of Launceston.

During this period, the weather was frosty at night, the thermometer frequently falling to 25°. From the adjacent hills, the town, in a morning, often appeared as if it were based on clouds, as the fog, to which it is liable, dispersed. The days were generally clear and warm.

On the 11th of 6th month, we set out on a more extended visit than the former, to the settlers on Norfolk Plains and the Macquarie River, which occupied us till the 1st of 7th month, when we returned again to Launceston.

In the course of this journey, we visited an interesting boarding-school for girls, at Ellenthorpe Hall; and one for boys, on Norfolk Plains; and also inspected one of four Government day-schools, under the care of R. R. Davies, the Episcopal chaplain at Longford.

While in Launceston, we joined several other persons in organizing a Temperance Society, which was attended with good results, notwithstanding, several who originally united in it, relapsed into drinking practices, and one of them fell into the commission of a crime, through the influence of strong drink, for which he forfeited his life.—We also paid some attention to the state of the prisoners in the Penitentiary, and other places where they were under the charge of the Government. On one occasion, I saw fourteen men sent into the Penitentiary, from Nottmans Road Party, to be flogged, for not executing their full quota of work.

We left Launceston again on the 13th of 7th month, and went by Patersons Plains, the Cocked Hat Hill, Perth, the South Esk, Campbell Town, Ross, Oatlands, Jericho, the

Lovely Banks, Bothwell, Hamilton, the Dee River, and New
Norfolk to Hobart Town; where we arrived on the 9th
of 8th month; having held religious meetings, and meetings
for the promotion of temperance at the several towns; and
religious meetings almost every evening, at the houses of
the settlers, who kindly allowed us to invite the neighbouring
families to their dwellings.

The weather at this period was tolerably mild, and generally remarkably fine for the season; we had seldom to
use umbrellas as a defence against rain, and the tracked
roads were but little cut up. The tops of the mountains,
adjacent to the low country in which we were travelling,
were often covered with snow, and there, the weather seemed
to be wild and stormy. We felt that we had cause, gratefully to acknowledge the merciful guidance of the good Spirit
of our Lord and Master, by which we were led to visit the
interior this winter, during which it was pleasant travelling
on foot, and to go to places accessible by sea, last winter,
when the wet would have rendered travelling in the interior very unpleasant.

We found some families affected with a low fever, which
occasionally occurs in this country, but is seldom fatal. The
most direful diseases in the Colony, are the result of the
free use of intoxicating liquors. Delirium tremens, under
its varied forms of horror, is one of these. Apoplexy is
also common: an instance of it occurred in one of the
prisoners, that came out in the Science, who died lately in
a public-house at New Norfolk, in an awfully hopeless state.
He fell lifeless from his seat, as he declared, with a horrid
imprecation, that he would never forgive the landlady, because she refused to supply him with more rum, when his
money was spent.

While waiting in the Police Office at Campbell Town, for
a person, temporarily acting as Police or Paid Magistrate,
who kindly accompanied us in calling upon the neighbouring
settlers, some pensioners made application for the office of
constable, stating themselves to be from forty to fifty years of
age; but their appearance was more like that of men of from
sixty to seventy. This was attributable, in, great degree, to

the use of strong drink.—The police clerk spoke to us courteously: we were about to invite the people of the neighbourhood to a temperance meeting, and when we returned, he was ill, from the practice of dram drinking: he died in the night, and was a corpse upon the premises at the time the meeting was held!

In the houses of most of the prosperous settlers, from whatever rank they may have risen, piano-fortes are to be seen. Next to drinking and smoking, they seem to be resorted to, to relieve the mind from that sense of vacuity, which ought to lead it to seek to be filled with heavenly good; and thus these instruments of music are made a means of truly injurious dissipation.

Spring commences early in Tasmania, and is marked by the opening of many pretty flowers, and the blossoming of the trees and shrubs; but as the latter are universally evergreens, it is not marked by the change so striking in England, except in gardens, in which the fruit-trees from Europe, rest more regularly than in Great Britain, and do not appear to be disposed to grow till spring is fully set in. The advance of spring was, however, very pleasant on our journey; in which we had now and then, fine and extended views, that were rendered the more interesting by the continuity of the forest, generally limiting observation to a small space. One of the objects occasionally visible, from the South Esk to St. Peters Pass, was Ben Lomond, which presents a remarkably castellated bluff to the south, and is represented in the annexed sketch, taken near the residence of James Crear, on the South Esk. This mountain is said to be volcanic, and to have a lake, in an extinguished crater, at the top.

Considerable quantities of gum have been exported from V. D. Land. One kind resembling Kino, is the produce of various species of *Eucalyptus;* the best is from the White Gum, which is probably *E. resinifera:* it is collected for a shilling a pound in the colony. A species of Acacia, called the Black Wattle, probably *Acacia affinis,* produces, a gum inferior to Gum Arabic, but which is said to be used in sizing silk goods: it is collected for three-pence a pound. Sometimes we found the gum of the Acacia serviceable in allaying hunger.

When at Macquarie Plains, upon the Derwent, we visited a fossil tree, which is imbedded in basalt, in the point of a hill, near a cascade, in a creek that empties itself into the river. The tree is erect, and may possibly prove to be standing where it has grown. About ten feet of its height are laid bare by removing the basalt, which is here porous and cracked. The tree is about ten feet in circumference at the lowest part that is bare. Some of the exterior portion has become like horn-coloured flint: much of the internal part is opaque, white, and fibrous: some portions of it split like laths, others into pieces like matches, and others are reducible to a substance resembling fibrous asbestos. The grain of the wood and of the bark is very distinguishable. Fragments of limbs of the same kind, have been found contiguous to the tree; and pieces of petrified wood of similar appearance are abundantly scattered over the neighbourhood. The structure of this tree is such as is considered to belong to coniferous trees; the only one of which, now found in this Island, of size equal to this petrefaction, is the Huon Pine.

In the neighbourhood of Ross, as well as near Bothwell, there are salt springs; and in some of these places there is fresh water, nearer the surface than the salt. On Salt Pan Plains, there is a small, salt lagoon, that dries up in summer, when the salt is collected, by the shepherds in the vicinity, and sold for about a halfpenny a pound. Several marine plants grow around this lagoon. When visiting it, we saw five Eagles soaring over some flocks of sheep. We also fell in with a young lamb that had had its eyes picked out by a crow. This is a circumstance of common occurrence, and the eagles carry off the lambs that have been killed by this means, as well as living ones. Probably similar circumstances occurring in Palestine, might give rise to the denunciation in the book of Proverbs, "The eye that mocketh at his father, and despiseth to obey his mother, the ravens of the valley shall pick it out, and the young eagles shall eat it."

On speaking to one of our acquaintance, from near

Hamilton, of the ferocity of the Tasmanian eagles, she informed us, that she was once chased by one of these birds for some distance, and obliged to run to her house for shelter. A similar occurrence also happened to a person on Macquarie Plains, and the wife of a settler told us, that she one day observed a horse galloping backward and forward, whilst two eagles were chasing it; one of which was driving it in one direction, and the other in the other. At length the horse fell, and one of them pounced upon its head; she then called some of the men, who immediately drove off the ravenous birds: the poor beast soon regained its feet, and was thus delivered from its destroyers. The horse being in an enclosure, had not the opportunity of escaping.

Many shrubs and plants were in flower on the banks of the Derwent and the adjacent hills. The most striking were *Acacia mollis, verticillata* and *Melanoxylon, Aster dentatus, Banksia australis, Pomaderris elliptica, Goodenia ovata. Indigofera australis, Pimelia incana, Tetratheca glandulosa, Euphrasia speciosa,* and *Kennedia prostrata.*

A single Lemon tree exists in a garden at New Norfolk, and another at O'Briens Bridge, but the climate is not warm enough for them, and they are protected during the winter. Cape Pelargoniums (the Geraniums of English Greenhouses) endure the winter at Hobart Town, but they are killed by frost at New Norfolk, and at other places in the Interior.

During this journey, of two months, our wants were so hospitably supplied by the settlers, that we only spent twenty-five shillings, which were chiefly laid out in washing and postage.

CHAPTER XIII.

Meeting for Discipline Established.—Meetings for Worship.—Temperance Lecture.—Flagellation.—Causes of Crime.—Judicial Oaths. — Peculiarities of Friends.—Chain Gang.—Unsteady Emigrant.—Ascent of Mount Wellington. —Notice of a Pious Prisoner.

On returning to Hobart Town, we found the little congregation with which we had become associated, in a state requiring care: a conference was therefore held with the two persons, who, with ourselves, were members of the Society of Friends in England, and it was concluded to organize a meeting for discipline, for the purpose of preserving good order, keeping records, discharging regularly the expenses attendant upon the occupation of the room in which the meetings for worship were held, and maintaining a general care respecting such other matters, as might be connected with the welfare of those professing with the Society of Friends, in this Colony.

At the first of these meetings, which was held on the 20th of 9th month, 1833, the certificates of George Washington Walker and myself, sanctioning our visit to the Southern Hemisphere, were read.—Appendix A.—A certificate of the membership of another individual, who had brought this document with him from England, was also read, and a record was made of the membership of two other Friends, with a notice of the respective Monthly Meetings in England, to which they belonged. A list of the names of other persons attending the meetings of Friends in Hobart Town, and of those professing an attachment to the principles of the Society in other parts of the Island, was likewise entered on minute.

We continued in Hobart Town at this time for twelve weeks, in the course of which, a few more meetings for discipline were held, two persons were admitted into membership, and it was concluded to hold one of these meetings monthly, under the appellation of "Hobart Town Monthly Meeting of Friends."

Meetings for worship continued to be regularly held on First day mornings, and reading meetings in the afternoons. A meeting for worship was also settled on Fifth-day evenings, not because the evening was preferred, for the meetings held at that time were often heavy, from the exhausted state of those who composed them, but because we could only have the use of the room in which we met, in an evening, as it was used for a school, in the day-time, on week-days.

We also invited the inhabitants of Hobart Town to a meeting for Public Worship, and to another for the promotion of Temperance; both of these were held in the Court House, the use of which was kindly granted for these purposes, on various occasions. On going to the former of these meetings I felt a perfect blank, as regarded anything to communicate, but was preserved quiet, trusting in the Lord, in whose counsel, I apprehended, I had requested the meeting to be convened. The passage of Scripture, "It is a fearful thing to fall into the hands of the living God," impressed my mind soon after sitting down, along with the belief that it was my duty to rise, and quote it, and to make some comments upon the cause of this fearfulness, as well as upon the plan of salvation by Jesus Christ; inviting all to come unto God by him, and to abide in him, and to prove this abiding, by walking as he also walked. The congregation was attentive, and a preciously solemn feeling pervaded the meeting toward the close, in which prayer was put up for an increase in the knowledge of the things belonging to salvation, and of a disposition to practice them.

The Lieutenant Governor and several other persons of note attended the Temperance Lecture; in which, after explaining the origin and progress of Temperance Societies, and conveying much general information, I invited a more extensive co-operation with them. I was induced to give this lecture from a sense of duty; and I had great occasion to render God hearty thanks, for enabling me to unfold to the company something of the working of the mystery of iniquity, as connected with the use of strong drink, and to do it in such a way as to keep hold of their kindly feelings, whilst attacking unsparingly the habits and indulgences of many present.

10th mo. 4th. I read, "Three Months in Jamaica," by Henry Whitely. What a picture does it present of colonial slavery, and human depravity! Severe as is the discipline of the prisoners in this colony, it is not to be compared with the tyrannical barbarity exercised upon the poor Negroes; yet I think the vengeful part of the former, both degrading and demoralizing. A Magistrate who formerly thought the flagellation of prisoners necessary, said, a short time ago, when conversing with us on the subject, that he was now convinced that it was an ineffectual punishment, universally degrading in its consequences. This is an increasing conviction among men who have gained some degree of victory over themselves: those who are in bondage to their own evil passions are attached to the system, by which a man may receive far beyond "forty stripes save one,"—upon complaint before a magistrate. It may, however, generally be observed, that those who plead for flogging, practice swearing, whether magistrates or others: and their own overbearing manner is often the exciting cause of the insolence in the prisoner, which occasions him to be brought before a magistrate and to receive flagellation.

Had justice toward offenders been more duly considered the legislature would probably, long ere this, have been induced to inquire more seriously than it has done, into the causes of crime, with a view to remedying them. This consideration is especially due to prisoners, when it appears, that the use of ardent spirits is the chief cause of crime, and that, by legalizing the sale of this article, and by the countenance given to its use by the community, they and the Government are the chief patrons of crime.

Want of education being another fertile source of vice,

consideration ought to be had for those who are ignorant, and through this cause go astray. It is not generally with themselves that the fault of the want of better education lies. Again, the immoral example of persons of the upper and middle classes, and often of the professed teachers of religion, has, beyond a doubt, a great place in the encouragement of crime. By far the greater proportion of prisoners is from the lower class; and it will be found, that most of the crimes which they have committed, were committed under the excitement of ardent spirits; and that, apart from this excitement, they are not commonly more depraved than the generality of their countrymen. Also, that most of their robberies were committed to enable them to obtain money to pay for indulgence in vice; and that the example of similar indulgence by persons above them in circumstances, was a great means of destroying in their minds the barrier of that moral principle, which would have made them fear such indulgence. Those who expect the punishment of crime to prevent its commission, whilst such fertile sources of its propagation remain, will certainly be disappointed. The removal of persons who have become contaminated, will no doubt, prevent crime increasing as it would do, were their influence continued on the British population; but unless the incentives to crime be removed, punishing it will only be like trying to pump out a river that threatens inundation to a country, whilst the remedy of stopping the springs that supply it, is neglected.

About this time I wrote a small tract, entitled, " A Concise Apology for the Peculiarities of the Society of Friends, commonly called Quakers, in their Language, Costume, and Manners." These peculiarities having often been the subjects of so much inquiry and objection, as to limit our opportunities of explaining our views of the Gospel in regard to more fundamental points, and especially, to that immediate teaching of the Divine Spirit, which, when fully followed, we believe, leads into the practice we have adopted.—APPENDIX B.

In the 10th month, a young woman, professing with the Independents, refused to take an oath, as witness, in the

Supreme Court. She was called upon to state her reasons for this refusal, which she did in a clear and concise manner, urging the command of Christ as the ground of her objection. According to existing regulations, the Judge must have committed her to prison for contempt of court, had the matter been pressed! but to avoid this, the Counsel withdrew her evidence.

This circumstance increased an exercise that my mind had been under, respecting the practice of judicial swearing, and this feeling was further increased, by learning that a discourse had been delivered in the Independent chapel, attempting to defend the practice; and believing that it would conduce to my peace to throw something before the public on the subject, I wrote an essay, entitled, "The Question, are Judicial Oaths Lawful? answered; with some Observations on the Moral Influence of Oaths." In this tract the fallacy of the arguments brought forward in support of the practice of Judicial Swearing was proved on Scriptural grounds.—APPENDIX C.

10th mo. 16th. We had a religious interview with the Hulk Chain-gang, in a long shed, in which they regularly assemble for worship, on First and Fourth days. The discipline of this gang is very strict; and from its local situation, the men are effectually kept from strong drink. The hulks, on board of which they sleep, are kept clean, and are well ventilated: they are moored close alongside of the yard in which the men muster. These prisoners are employed in public works of improvement on the side of Sulivans Cove, and are kept constantly under an overseer and a military guard. This gang, which forms an important link in the chain of the prison-discipline of the colony, is depicted, in the annexed etching, copied from a work called "Ross's Hobart Town Annual."

10th mo. 24th. A young Irishman called upon me, who came to V. D. Land, a few months ago, with a small sum of money, and soon after his arrival got into a situation; but giving way to dissipated habits, and making a mock, as he said, of temperance, he found many of his own stamp, who were willing to seek his friendship while his

A Chain Gang

Convicts going to work nr Sidney N. S. Wales

B⟲L

money lasted. This was not long; and as he soon incapacitated himself by intemperance, he lost his situation. When his money was gone, his friends were gone also; and some that he had helped, were unwilling to help him in return, and he was at his wit's end to know what to do. Many young men who come out with fair prospects, ruin themselves in this way, and then find fault with the Colony. Without persons have capital, and conduct to take care of it, they should not emigrate to the Australian Colonies. If they have stability, and their capital be in their physical powers, and they have ability to employ it efficiently, in mechanical occupations, or in agricultural labour, it may be of good service.

10th mo. 25th. We ascended Mount Wellington. At the base, sandstone and limestone, form low hills; further up, compact argillaceous rock rises into higher hills, which abound in marine fossils. The height of the mountain is four thousand feet. Near the top, basalt shows itself in some places, in columnar cliffs. The trees, for two-thirds of its height, are Stringy-bark, White and Blue Gum, Peppermint, &c. A species of *Eucalyptus,* unknown in the lower part of the forest, is frequent at an elevation of three thousand feet. Another is found on the top of the mountain. The different species of *Eucalyptus* are very common, and form at least seven-eighths of the vast forests of Tasmania. In the middle region of the mountain, the climate and soil are humid. The Tasmanian Myrtle, *Fagus Cunninghamii,* here forms trees of moderate size; the Australian Pepper-tree, *Tasmania fragrans,* is frequent; the Broad-leaved Grass-tree, *Richea Dracophylla,* forms a striking object; it is very abundant, and on an average, from ten to fifteen feet high; it is much branched, and has broad, grassy foliage. The branches are terminated by spike-like panicles of white flowers, intermingled with broad, bracteal leaves, tinged with pink. *Culcitium salicifolium, Hakea lissosperma, Telopea truncata, Corræa ferruginea, Gaultheria hispida, Prostanthera lasianthos, Friesia peduncularis,* and many other shrubs, are met with in the middle region of the mountain. For a considerable part of the way up, we availed ourselves of a path that is nearly obliterated, which was used by the workmen, when laying a watercourse from the breast of the mountain, for the purpose of supplying Hobart Town with water. This path led through a forest of Tree-ferns, surmounted by Myrtle, &c. Nearer the top, we had to pass a large tract of tumbled basalt. The upper parts of many of the stones were split off, probably by the alternations of frost and heat. A few patches of snow were still remaining.

The top of the mountain is rather hollow, sloping toward Birches Bay, in the direction of which, a stream of excellent water flows. The ground is swampy, with rocks and stony hills. *Astelia alpina, Glichenia alpina, Drosera arcturi,* several remarkable shrubby *Asters,* a prostrate species of *Leptospermum, Exocarpos humifusus,* a dense bushy *Richea,* and several mountain shrubs, of the *Epacris* tribe, are scattered in the swamps, and among the rocks. Two Snipes flew up from a marsh, in which there was a frog with a voice much like that of the English Red Grouse.

We ascended the highest portions of the mountain on the west and south, from which the view is extremely fine. It commands the whole of the south-east portion of V. D. Land, with its numerous bays, peninsulas, and adjacent, small islands, the singular outlines of which may be seen upon one of the maps at the end of this volume. The ocean forms the horizon, from the westward of the mouth of D'Entrecasteaux Channel, and to the southward, and as far to the north-east as about St. Patricks Head. The atmosphere was rather milky to the north, so as not to leave the horizon very distinct in that direction. To the westward we thought we could recognise the Peak of Teneriffe, and some of the mountains near Macquarie Harbour, Port Davey, and the South Cape. Hobart Town, Sorell Town, and the cultivated lands, with the houses of the settlers about Richmond, New Norfolk, and Hamilton, along with the courses of the rivers Derwent and Huon, were striking objects. The green patches of cultivated land on Browns River, and in various other places, in the recesses of the " bush," proved interestingly, the powers of industry in subduing the forest.

In descending, we got into a thick part of the forest, through which we had sometimes to force our way among deep cutting-grass, and tangled *Bauera;* and sometimes we had to travel on fallen trees, at an elevation above "terra firma," much greater than was agreeable. We were glad to reach a known track, in the foot of the mountain while twilight lasted, having effected the descent in 3½ hours.

While we were at Hobart Town, at this time a prisoner, named Robert King, died in the Hospital. We had long felt much interest respecting him, on account of his simple piety. He gave me the following account of his life, which I have interspersed with a few remarks upon his situation as a prisoner, and his state as a practical Christian.

Robert King, was the son of persons in respectable circumstances, who resided in London : they gave him a good education, but at an early age he fell into much evil, under the influence of bad company : he became exceedingly intemperate, and immoral in other respects ; and at length, his conduct was unbearable to his relations, and they closed their doors against him, so that he became, in the true sense of the word, an Outcast. He joined himself to a gang of thieves in Tothill-fields ; who supported themselves in their profligacy, by picking pockets, and committing other kinds of robbery. He adopted infidel principles, on similar grounds to those on which, there is reason to believe, many other infidels have also adopted them ; and who are, nevertheless, very ready to ridicule the truths of Christianity, with a pretence of being very knowing about them : —"Not," said R. King, "because I had carefully examined the subject and found any reasonable objection to the truths of Holy Scripture ; but because I wished to be an infidel, and hoped there was no future state ; for, I knew, if there was, I had no prospect of happiness in it."

But though R. King had joined with those fools, who, in their folly, deny the being of a God, and who make a mock of sin, yet God, who is long-suffering, and rich in mercy, still followed him for good ; and, in the dispensation of his providence, the transgressor was arrested by the strong arm of the law, when sinning with a high hand,

M

and was tried, found guilty, and sentenced to be transported.

Having forfeited, by his crimes, that freedom to which, as an Englishman, he was born, his ankles were loaded with chains, and he was subjected to the rigid discipline of a convict, on a voyage of sixteen thousand miles from his native land—that land to which he was never more to return—and on arriving at Hobart Town, he, and his numerous shipmates, under like circumstances, were assigned into bond service. This service differs little from slavery, except that the prisoner remains the property of the Government, and consequently cannot be sold by his master. The master agrees with the Government to comply with certain terms in regard to the food, clothing, and labour of the assigned servant; and the servant may complain to a magistrate if his master fail to do justly in these respects. But the prisoner is liable, on the complaint of his master, to be flogged or sent to work in chains, for insubordination and other offences; and his insubordination may often be little more than irritation of temper, excited by an unreasonable master.

The convict, like a slave, may happen to be the servant of a kind or of a hard-hearted master; and if he should be the servant of a hard master, he must bear it, for he cannot change at pleasure, because he is in bondage—galling bondage! a state from which even those who have the best of masters, are glad to be delivered.

On arriving in Van Diemens Land, R. King saw several young men, whom he had known in England, such as himself, but who, in the day of their trouble had sought the Lord, and had come under the power of religion; and the change in them was so great, that he began to think there was more in religion than he had been willing to admit. Happily for him, he was assigned to a kind and pious master, whose wife was of similar character; and their example helped to deepen those favourable impressions which he had received, in regard to religion, at a time when his heart was softened by the affliction that he had brought upon himself by his sins. His mind now became open to the convictions of the Holy Spirit as a reprover of evil; he saw the sinfulness of sin, and felt the terror of the Lord in his soul, because of his transgression; and, in repentance, he began to cry for mercy, to that God whom he had despised; for he now no longer doubted the existence of that Almighty Being, whose hand lay heavy upon him in judgment. He lamented his folly, abhorring himself in deep humiliation; and the Lord was pleased to open his understanding, to look upon Jesus, as the Lamb of God, who taketh away the sin of the world; and to give him an evidence by the Spirit, of the pardon of his sins, through faith in that atoning blood which was shed upon the cross, for the redemption of sinners.

The sense of the love of God, who had been thus merciful to him, contrited him greatly, and he earnestly desired to live to his glory; but he found that the natural depravity of his own heart had been so greatly increased by indulgence in sin, that he was very easily ensnared. He now experimentally learned, that he could only stand against temptation by watchfulness and prayer to God, who alone was able to deliver him. In these exercises he persevered, and God was honoured by his upright conduct, which gained him also the favour of pious persons, who became acquainted with him, and who esteemed him as a brother in Christ, notwithstanding, he was still a prisoner. His master was interested in the management of "a Sabbath school;" and in this, R. King gladly rendered assistance, from a desire to do what he could, toward training up children in the fear of the Lord, in the hope that they might be preserved from the snares into which he had fallen.

As he grew in grace, he felt more strongly his own unworthiness and helplessness, and understood better than when he was first awakened from sleep in sin, that it is for Christ's sake alone, and through his intercession, that mankind have access to the throne of grace; and he became diligent in waiting upon God, with his mind stayed upon Him, and in lifting up his heart in prayer, according to the sense of his necessity, given him at the time.

After having maintained a Christian character for a

considerable period, he was attacked by a fever; and though he recovered from it so as to be able to walk out, and enjoy the fresh air, yet the effects of his former depravity upon his constitution prevented him from regaining his strength, and he died while yet but a young man. Disease, for a short time, rather beclouded his mind; and he expressed a fear respecting the sincerity of his love to God: but the fruits meet for repentance, that he had continued to bring forth from the time of his awakening, left no room to doubt his sincerity, but afforded ground to believe, that, as he had penitently sought the forgiveness of his sins, through Jesus Christ, and the help of God, to turn away from his wickedness, and to do that which was lawful and right, he was mercifully prepared to join the glorious company, "who have washed their robes and made them white in the blood of the Lamb."*

---

* This account of R. King, with a few additional remarks, is published by "The York Friends' Tract Association," under the title of "The Van Diemens Land Convict."

CHAPTER XIV.

SOME disagreement having arisen between a person employed as Catechist, at the Establishment for the Aborigines,
on Flinders Island, and the officers there, which the Commandant had suggested we might be helpful in reconciling,
the Lieut. Governor applied to us on the subject, and after
serious consideration, we believed it right to accept his
invitation again to visit the Island. The Shamrock cutter
was put under our direction for the voyage, and we sailed
from Hobart Town on the 22nd of 11th month, Richard H.
Davies, being in command of the vessel.

We had on board a party of sixteen Aborigines, who
had joined G. A. Robinson, on the west coast. When we
were first introduced to them, they were smeared from head
to foot with red ochre and grease; and, to add to their
adornment, some of them had blackened a space of about
a hand's breadth, on each side of their faces, their eyes
being nearly in the centre of each black mark! Some of
the elderly women were as far removed from handsome as
human beings could well be. As they sat naked upon the
ground, with their knees up, and their heads bare, their
resemblance to Oran-outangs was such as to afford some
apology for those who have represented them as allied to
those animals. Some of the younger women were of a

M 3

more agreeable appearance; a man in the company was
tall, and of features so patriarchal and Jewish, as strongly
to resemble pictures designed to represent Abraham. He
was blind of one eye, which we understood he had lost
some years ago, by a shot from a white man.

I am not aware of any custom of the Aborigines of V.
D. Land, common with the Jews, except it be of not eating
fat. This they so much abhor as even to reject bread, cut
with a buttery knife. On my companion offering some soup
to a poor emaciated woman, on board the cutter, who had a
baby that looked half-starved, she tried to take it, seeing it
was offered in good will; but having a little fat upon it, she
recoiled from it with nausea. John R. Bateman, master of
the brig Tamar, once had some soup made for a party of
these people, whom he was taking to Flinders Island: they
looked upon it complacently, skimmed off the floating fat
with their hands, and smeared their hair with it, but would
not drink the soup!

The wind being unfavourable, we anchored at the mouth
of D'Entrecasteaux Channel, where the Government brig
Isabella, with English emigrants for Launceston, and the
Adelaide, a vessel in the Sperm Whale fishery, were lying.
—A great number of emigrants have lately arrived from
England. Many of them are mechanics, who cannot find
employment in Hobart Town, in consequence of the number
that have preceded them. As this class of emigrants is
wanted in Launceston, the Government has undertaken to
convey them thither. Persons wanting places as clerks, find
great difficulty in obtaining situations in new colonies.—We
went on shore at Kelleys Farm, on Bruny Island; where
vessels are frequently furnished with potatoes, eggs, fowls,
&c. The land is of fair quality, but the adjacent hills are
sandy, and thin of soil and herbage. This island is nearly
covered with wood like that of the main land, and has a few
Austral Grass-trees interspersed among them.

11th mo. 23rd. Very wet; the wind contrary. The decks
were so leaky that it was difficult to find a dry place to sit in,
in the cabin; happily, no wet of any consequence came into
our berths. The poor Aborigines had to sleep under a tent,

formed of a sail, on deck, the hold being occupied with provisions, which it was hoped would have been delivered at
Port Arthur yesterday. They seemed, nevertheless, contented and cheerful.

25th. We reached Port Arthur, which is greatly improved
since we were here before, though much still requires to be
done before it can be fully effective for the purpose of a
Penal Settlement. A good penitentiary, and a place of
worship are much wanted. The Penitentiary in use consists
only of bark huts, surrounded with a high, stockade fence.
One hut is appropriated to educated prisoners, who are now,
in many instances, sent here on their arrival in the Colony,
being considered as having abused their advantages more
than the uneducated. This class of prisoners feel their
degradation greatly: they are occupied in manual labour in
the settlement gardens. The other prisoners are divided
into a chain-gang, and a first and second class, distinguished
by the kind of labour allotted them, by their clothing, and
by the second class having an allowance of tea and sugar.
This classification produces a good effect. Captain Charles
O'Hara Booth, the Commandant, has succeeded in establishing a more strict discipline than his predecessors, and in
some respects, than that pursued at Macquarie Harbour: he
has abolished the use of that great desideratum with prisoners—tobacco. The health of the prisoners is generally
good, though cases of scurvy have of late increased. In the
afternoon we walked with Capt. Booth to the signal-station,
two miles and a half distant, through forests of Stringy-bark,
Blue-gum, White-gum, Myrtle, Sasafras, Tree-fern, &c. an
assemblage proving the climate to be somewhat humid; it is,
however, much drier than that of Macquarie Harbour.

26th. We accompanied Captain Booth to Eagle Hawk
Neck, the isthmus separating Tasmans Peninsula, on which
Port Arthur is situated, from Foresticrs Peninsula, which is
connected with the main land. The distance, after leaving a
boat at the head of LongBay, was about eleven miles, which
we walked in a soaking rain.—A guard of soldiers is stationed
at Eagle Hawk Neck, which is only 120 yards across, at high
tide; and to make the barrier more secure, nine watch dogs

are placed at intervals, with nine lamps between them. Constables are also stationed at several outposts. By these means escape from the Penal Settlement is rendered very difficult. The dogs soon give notice of the approach of any person. Some of the hills on Tasmans Peninsula may be about 1,000 feet high, and much of the forest with which it is covered, is very dense.

28th. We visited a company of prisoner brick-makers, and proceeded to the coast, betwixt Cape Roaul and the entrance to Port Arthur, to see a remarkable chasm in the basalt. It is about 127 feet deep, and very narrow. The sea may be heard rushing up it. In the course of our walk, we had much conversation with Captain Booth, of a satisfactory character. From what we see and learn, we are disposed to consider that the punishment of Port Arthur, consists in its restraint, rather than in any excessive degree of labour that is exacted. The prisoners work with reluctance. The privations of liberty and society, with the vigilant superintendence, are keenly felt. The generality of prisoners look upon themselves as the aggrieved parties, which is much to be regretted: when they take an opposite view it is to be regarded as a token of reformation. No prisoners are now allowed private gardens; none but the boat's crew are allowed to fish, and none are allowed to hunt.

29th. We anchored in Safety Cove, the wind being contrary. G. W. Walker and myself went on shore, and walked to the coast, in the direction of Cape Roaul, on a steep sandy part of which, the white variety of *Helichrysum bracteatum* is found; also *Hierochloe australis*, a fragrant grass. In the afternoon we went on shore on a fishing excursion, and obtained a plentiful supply of Muttton-fish, *Haliotis lævigata*, from the rocks, at low-water. They were mostly under the kelp, immersed in the sea, and were dislodged by means of sharp-pointed sticks. Some of the women went into the water among the large sea-tangle, to take Cray-fish. These women seem quite at home in the water, and frequently immerse their faces to enable them to see objects at the bottom. When they discover the object of their search, they dive, often using the long stems of the kelp to enable them to reach the bottom; these they handle as dexterously in descending, as a sailor would a rope, in ascending.

We sailed from Port Arthur on the 30th of 11th mo. After rounding Cape Pillar, the swell, which had been left by a recent gale, was very trying. We passed to the eastward of Maria Island, and sighted Cape Barren Island, in Banks's Strait, at daylight, on the 2nd of 12th mo.—Sailing west of Preservation Island, we anchored under Green Island, at high tide; and a gale from the south-east occasioned the vessel to drive, so that it was left dry at low water, lying down to one side very uncomfortably, but without further damage.—In consequence of this accident, the Aborigines were put on shore on Green Island, where they had a feast of Mutton Birds and their eggs, and smeared themselves from head to foot with red ochre and grease. The multitude of birds returning to the island in the evening was so great that it was difficult to conceive how each pair would find a burrow. The Aborigines from Flinders Island had been here, and we learned that they had collected 8,000 eggs: countless numbers were, however, still left: they had also destroyed great numbers of birds, which were scattered in all directions over the island.

12th mo. 3rd. Being landed by a whale-boat, at the Lagoons, the site of the old settlement on Flinders Island, we made our way along the beach, and through the bush, to Wybalenna, where we received a hearty welcome from both the Black and the White Inhabitants; and were much pleased with the improvements, since we were here fourteen months ago. A number of neat huts have been erected, and some land has been converted into gardens. One piece, of more than an acre and a half, has been broken up, fenced, and planted with potatoes, by the Aborigines.

The Aborigines of V. D. Land soon learned to distinguish between free people and prisoners, and shewed a contempt for the latter. The prisoners have adopted the expression, "to plant" a thing, to signify, to hide or conceal it, especially in regard to things stolen. On a Black, on Flinders Island, being asked, if he would like to have some potatoes to plant, he replied, No, with disdain, supposing it was meant to

conceal dishonestly; but said he, I should like to have some
to put into the ground, that I might see them jump up.

4th. We had a conference with the parties at variance,
and endeavoured to soften down the asperities that had
arisen between them, in consequence of a conscientious man
having expected too much from others, not awakened like
himself to the importance of acting in all things on religious
principle, and having imbibed some prejudice against them,
which had excited disgust on their part.

A large company of the native women took tea with us, at
the Commandant's: they conducted themselves in a very
orderly manner, and after washing up the tea-things, put
them in their places, and showed other indications of advancement in civilization. They are gaining a taste for
European provisions, particularly for milk and mutton.

5th. Another party of Aborigines breakfasted with us.
We distributed among them some cotton handkerchiefs, and
some tobacco, an article of which they are exceedingly fond,
but the use of which they have learned from Europeans.
Some of the women immediately commenced hemming the
handkerchiefs, having learned this art from the wife of the
Catechist. They presented us with some spears and shell
necklaces in return. The Surgeon brought the new comers in
a boat from Green Island, having first successfully assisted
in getting the Shamrock off the sands, into deep water.—On
the arrival of the new party, it was found that the husband
of one, and the father of another, who had come hither
before them, were deceased; but this did not, in these
instances, produce much emotion.—Accompanied by the
Commandant of the Settlement, the Master of the Shamrock,
and an intelligent native, we visited the Grass-tree plains
that extend toward the east coast. The soil is sandy and
poor, and clothed with thin rigid herbage, and scattered, low
Gum-trees, low scrub, and large Grass-trees, *Xanthorrhœa australis?* Some of the last are from 5 to 7 feet high, and as many in
circumference; they have leaves 3 to 4 feet long, and flower-
spikes 5 to 10 feet high, thickly clothed with hard scales,
and small, white, star-like flowers, except for about $1\frac{1}{2}$ feet
at the base, which is bare. All the trunks are charred from

the burning off of the scrub. Abundance of red resin,
capable of being used in the manufacture of sealing wax and
French-polish, is exuded by them. This substance fills up
the places left by the decay of the flower-stems of former
years, and by injuries; it is also lodged abundantly around
the base of the trunk, which is thus defended from an excess
of moisture. The blanched base of the leaves, which our
swarthy companion obtained for us, by beating off the head
of a Grass-tree that had not thrown up a flower-stem, is
pleasant eating, and has a nutty flavour. A species of
Isopogon occurs on these plains. This is probably the most
southern locality of the genus.

The Grass-tree plains, which are represented in the accompanying etching, are separated from the west coast, by a
range of granite hills, covered with Common and Blue Gum-
trees, Oyster Bay Pine, &c.

The low ground about the Settlement, is clothed with
long grass, and with *Leucopogon Gnidium* and *Fabricia myrtifolia*, handsome, white-flowered shrubs, here attaining to
20 feet high, and with a few bushy species of *Acacia*, &c.
These are decorated by the lovely climbers *Clematis aristata*
and *Comesperma volubilis*; the former of delicate white and
the latter of lively blue.

6th. We visited Prime Seal Island, distant about eight
miles. This also is a granite island. Black fibrous Schorl,
here called Jet, is imbedded in the rock, in the cavities of
which, large crystals are also met with.—In the low part
of the Island, there were patches of an unrecorded species
of *Lasiopetalum*, with purple flowers. *Croton rosmarinifolium*,
a pretty, privet-like bush, forms thickets, both here and on
Flinders, where it is also interspersed with She-oak.—The
Wallaby abounds here. Several were killed by the natives
who accompanied us. Some of these people only eat the
male animals, others only the females. We were unable to
learn the reason of this, but they so strictly adhere to the
practice, that it is said, hunger will not drive them to de-
viate from it. This island did not prove favourable for
sheep. It was formerly the resort of vast herds of Fur
Seals; but they have nearly forsaken both it and many of

the neighbouring ones, in consequence of the slaughter committed among them by the sealers. We saw a few on an
adjacent rock.

7th. Some of the male Aborigines amused themselves
with throwing waddies and spears at grass-tree stems, set
up as marks, which they frequently hit. They still strip
off their clothes when engaged in this amusement; but in
wearing decent covering at other times, as well as in many
other respects, they shew decided marks of advancing civilization.—In dressing their spears, they use a sharp flint
or a knife: in using the latter for this purpose, they hold
it by the end of the blade. They straighten their spears
till they balance as accurately as a well prepared fishing-rod,
performing this operation with their teeth. The simplicity
of the weapons of these people, has been urged as a proof
of their defect of intellect, but it is much more a proof of their
dexterity, in being able, with such simple implements, to
procure game, &c. for food. A shower of their spears,
which they send through the air with a quivering motion,
would be terribly destructive.

The climbing of the lofty, smooth-trunked gum-trees, by
the women, to obtain opossums, which lodge in the hollows
of decayed branches, is one of the most remarkable feats
I ever witnessed. This is effected without making any holes
for the thumbs or great toes, as is common among the
natives of N. S. Wales, except where the bark is rough
and loose, at the base of the tree. In this a few notches
are cut by means of a sharp flint, or a hatchet; the latter
being preferred. A rope, twice as long as is necessary to
encompass the tree, is then thrown around it. In former
times, this was made of tough grass, or strips of Kangaroo
skin, but one of hemp is now generally used. The left
hand is twisted firmly into one end of the rope, the middle
of which is tightly grasped by the right, the hatchet is
placed on the bare, closely-cropped head, and the feet are
placed against the tree: a step or two is then advanced,
and the body, at the same time, is brought into a posture
so nearly erect as to admit the rope, by a compound motion,
to be slackened, and at the same moment hitched a little

further up the tree.—By this means a woman will ascend a lofty tree with a smooth trunk, almost as quickly as a man would go up a ladder. Should a piece of loose bark impede the ascent of the rope, the portion of the rope held in the right hand, is taken between the teeth, or swung behind the right leg, and caught between the great and the fore toe, and fixed against the tree. One hand is thus freed, to take the hatchet from the head, and with it to dislodge the loose bark.—On arriving at a large limb, the middle of the rope is also secured in the left hand, and the loose end is thrown over the limb by the right hand, by which also the end is caught, and the middle grasped, till the left hand is cleared. This is then wrapped into the middle of the rope, and the feet are brought up to the wrinkles of the bark, which exist below the large limbs. One end of the rope is then pulled downward, and this causes the other to ascend, so that, by an effort of the feet, the body is turned on to the upper side of the limb of the tree.—In descending, the woman places one arm on each side of the limb of the tree, and swings the rope with one hand till she catches it with the other: she then turns off the limb, and swings underneath it, till she succeeds in steadying herself with her feet against the trunk, around which she then throws the loose end of the rope. Having secured this, she lets go the portion by which she was sus-pended under the limb, and descends in the manner in which she ascended.—Although this is done with ease by women in vigour, one who had been out of health, but seemed recovered, could not get many steps off the ground, so that not only skill, but a considerable measure of strength, appears necessary to ascend the gigantic gum-trees.

After having seen something of the natives of V. D. Land, the conviction was forced upon my mind, that they ex-ceeded Europeans in skill, in those things to which their attention had been directed from childhood, just as much as Europeans exceeded them, in the points to which the attention of the former had been turned, under the culture of civilization. There is similar variety of talent and of temper among the Tasmanian Aborigines, to what is to be found among other branches of the human family; and it would not be more erroneous in one of these people, to look upon an English woman as defective in capacity, because she could neither dive into the deep and bring up cray-fish, nor ascend the lofty gum-trees to catch opossums for her family, than it would be for an English woman to look upon the Tasmanian as defective in capacity, because she could neither sew nor read, nor perform the duties of civil, domestic life. Were the two to change stations, it is not too much to assume, that the untutored native of the woods would much sooner learn to obtain her food, by acquiring the arts of civilization, than the woman from civilized society would, by acquiring the arts belonging to savage life.

8th. The Aborigines, having noticed that the few soldiers at this station, who were placed as a guard against the Sealers, were mustered on First-day mornings, to see that they had made themselves properly clean, voluntarily commenced mustering in a similar way: they also brought out the wares with which they had been entrusted, to have them inspected. The Commandant took advantage of this, and encouraged them to do so weekly. This morning they presented their tin pots and plates, knives and spoons, bright and clean, and except three men, were clean in their apparel. These men complained, that the women had not washed their clothes, and threatened to wash them themselves, if they should again be so neglected! The men were dressed in duck frocks and trowsers, and had handkerchiefs about their necks. The women had on stuff under-garments, and checked bedgowns, and had handkerchiefs on their heads and around their shoulders. Many of their countenances were fine and expressive. It was surprising to see how much improved some of the most unsightly of the women had become by being decently clad: they scarcely looked like the same race of beings. They afterwards assembled in a very orderly manner, with the white people, in the rude shelter of boughs, used as a chapel. On this occasion a portion of Scripture was read by G. W. Walker; after which I had a little to communicate in the line of ministry.— There was something peculiarly moving, in seeing nearly the whole of the remaining Aborigines of Van Diemens Land, now a mere handful of people, seated on the ground, listening with much attention to the truths of the gospel, however little they might be able to understand what was said, and conducting themselves with equal gravity in the times of silence.

9th. Several of the Aborigines were out hunting: they obtained little but a Tasmanian Porcupine. The Wallaby and Brush Kangaroo are become scarce on Flinders Island, in consequence of the improvidence of the people in killing all they can, when they have opportunity, and often more than their wants require. Snakes are common on these islands. Three kinds have come under our notice —the large black species, the one with red sides, *Coluber porphyryaceus*, and a smaller species called here, the Diamond Snake—all of which are dangerously venomous. Some large ticks were sticking to the sides of one of the red snakes.

10th. We dined with the Catechist, who has taken considerable pains to instruct the Aborigines, and to acquire their language: he has translated the first three chapters of Genesis into one of their dialects.—Finding that the cutter must proceed to Launceston for supplies, we concluded to accompany it, and sailed this evening.

11th. After a fine voyage, we entered the Tamar early, the eastern headland of which is rendered much more distinguishable by a newly-erected lighthouse. On bringing up at George Town, we found the inhabitants in great alarm: they had been keeping guard all night, in consequence of a party of bush-rangers having entered one of their houses, the preceding evening, and robbed it, after binding the master. Circumstances of this kind are of rare occurrence at the present day.

12th. We had a pleasant sail, with the help of the tide, to near Launceston, where we arrived in the course of the day, and met with warm greetings from our acquaintance.

CHAPTER XV.

SINCE our former visit to Launceston, considerable improvements have been made in the place. A bridge across the North Esk is in a considerable state of advancement, and a Penitentiary for females is nearly completed. The latter is to supersede one at George Town, which is in a ruinous state, and to which the transfer of the prisoner-women, in boats, is highly objectionable.

The Aborigines now residing on Flinders Island have a small flock of sheep, that were given them by a benevolent individual in the Colony. These are fed upon Green Island; and the wool which they have produced, was committed to my charge, to dispose of, for the owners. The proceeds were to be applied in the purchase of hardware and clothing; this was effected accordingly, and some of the inhabitants of Launceston, liberally added to the stock of goods, in a variety of useful articles that were not very saleable in their shops, and of partially worn garments, so that on returning to Flinders Island, we had some considerable packages of goods for the Blacks.

12th mo. 15th. We had two meetings in the Court-house, at Launceston, which were attended by a considerable number of people. To me, they were seasons of laborious exercise, under a sense of great weakness of flesh and of spirit: I was enabled, however, to hold up the standard of the Truth as it is in Jesus, and to show that the salvation proposed in the Gospel, is not only the forgiveness of past sins, through faith in the atoning blood of Christ, but deliverance from the power of Satan, by the effectual operation of the Holy Spirit; by which the sincere disciples of a crucified Lord are created in him unto good works, in which God hath ordained that we should walk. I had also to point out the great benefit of waiting on the Lord in silence, with the attention turned to the teaching of the Spirit, by which a true sense is given of the state of the soul, and thus a right preparation is received, to ask in the name of Jesus, the supply of our spiritual necessities. There was a degree of solemnity pervading my own mind in the times of silence, in which the creature, bowed before the Lord, felt its own nothingness, and was sensible that God was all in all; in which there was not only the silence of all flesh, but something also of a reverent silence of spirit.

16th. In a religious interview with a few persons, who have manifested an attachment to the principles of Friends, and three of whom have occasionally met on First-days, for the purpose of worshipping God unitedly, I expressed a few words, to encourage them not to be cast down, when in their silent waiting, they might be sensible, only of their own emptiness, and of the natural depravity of their own hearts. I also pointed out the importance of our learning these things, in order that we may be humbled, and be taught not to trust in ourselves, but in the Lord alone. After this, one of them, in a weighty manner, related a little of his own experience, both in his early life, before he came under the power of religion, and of his comforts and conflicts since that time. This was followed by similar communications from the rest. One of them mentioned, that the first recollection of condemnation which he had, was on an occasion on which his father had given him three half-pence, in mistake for a penny, when he was very young: he kept the whole sum, notwithstanding powerful convictions that he was doing wrong in not returning the half-penny; and, from that time, he added sin to sin, until it brought him under the sentence of the law.   He also noticed his awakening, when a prisoner; losing ground by unwatchfulness on his passage out, and giving way to the gratification of pride in his dress after his arrival in this country, by which he had been brought under great condemnation; his renewed convictions and conflicts; his sense of pardon through the atoning blood of Jesus, and his comfort under the remembrance of the declaration, that nothing should be able to separate us from the love of God.   He has adopted the plain language, habits, and manners common among Friends, and appears to maintain a deep exercise of soul before the Lord.

21st.   We embarked again on board the Shamrock, and drifted a few miles down the Tamar with the tide.   The settlements on the banks of the river, appear much improved within the last fourteen months, and present an enlivening interruption to the continuous forest.

22nd.   A favourable breeze brought us to George Town, early.   On arriving, we made arrangements to hold a meeting with the inhabitants, at five o'clock in the evening, and occupied the forenoon in giving notice to such people as were not at their place of worship, which is very thinly attended, except by persons, such as prisoners, who have no option in regard to staying away.   George Town is going fast to decay; the whole population now amounts to only a small number.   It was, however, a satisfaction to have this meeting with them, which was well attended.   I had been impressed with a belief that we should be with them to-day; but yesterday, when the wind was contrary, and we made little progress, I was ready to think this impression was only from the activity of my own imagination.

Contrary winds delayed the Shamrock a few days at George Town.—We had now added to our company James Allen, from Tyrone, in Ireland, who was on his way to Flinders Island, to succeed A. Mc. Lachlan in the office of Surgeon to the Establishment for the Aborigines.   We found this young man a pleasant companion in our rambles in the neighbourhood.—We visited the light-house, on the eastern head of the Tamar; near to which there is a lagoon of nearly fresh water, just within the shore, a circumstance common on low parts of these coasts.—In this direction *Corræa speciosa* is found, which though abundant in some parts of N. S. Wales, is scarcely known in V. D. Land. *Corræa alba*, the Cape Barren tea, becomes a large bush, and covers the sand hills of the western head of the Tamar. Shrubs of this genus, as well as of some others in this country, shed their seeds while the seed-vessels remain green, the seeds are consequently, difficult to collect.—We also visited the remains of York Town, which was one of the first settlements in this island. The country around it looked temptingly green, but this greenness proved to be rigid herbage, unfit for cattle, consisting chiefly of a stemless *Xanthorrhæa*, or Grass-tree; and the place was consequently abandoned, except one or two cottages, to which labour has added productive gardens, well stocked with apple, pear, and cherry trees, gooseberries and vegetables. The cherries and gooseberries were now ripe, the former sold at 1s. per pound, and the latter at 1s. 6d. per quart.—Near this place, a beautiful *Bauera*, with pink blossoms, as large as a shilling, was in flower.—The hills in this neighbourhood are very arid, but covered with wood; they abound in iron ore, and asbestos, which last is here called "Cotton Stone." Some of the pools near George Town produce a small speckled fish, which is named Trout, but is far inferior to the Trout of Europe; yet it is a pleasant fish for the table. Many European names have been given to things here, at the antipodes of Europe, which have very little resemblance to the originals.

On the 27th, we put to sea, but made little progress. At night we were off the seal rock, called Barren Joey, or Eleventh Island; and, on the night of the 28th, off Twenty-day Island. A westerly breeze sprung up before sunset. My mind had been under great exercise for the last two days, from a strong sense of temptation, and of the danger of falling away. The mercy of God in Christ Jesus was the ground of my hope, and my prayer was that he might cut the thread of my life rather than permit me to bring dishonour upon his holy cause. Still I felt an appalling sense of my own weakness and danger, and of the necessity

to watch and pray, lest I should enter into temptation.
My trust was in the Lord for strength, and my desire that
his strength might be made perfect in my weakness, and
that he alone might have the glory. So far as I could discover I was in my right place, and the Lord was pleased,
in great mercy, to confirm this feeling, by some precious
and clearly perceptible intimations of his Spirit.

29th. We were favoured again to come safely to anchor,
under Green Island, after a gale in the night, in which the
cutter was driven through a channel between two Islands,
the depth of which was unknown to those on board; but
the mate, by keeping a good look out from the mast head,
was enabled to direct the course of the vessel, so as to avoid
the shallows.

30th. The wind having moderated, we were again put
on shore on Flinders Island.—While waiting at a creek, for
the ebbing of the tide, we cooked some Mutton-birds for
dinner, and having no salt, dipped the morsels in salt water
as we eat them, which made them palatable. The fresh
water at the Lagoons, to the south of which we landed,
being dried up, we could obtain no drink till evening, but
we got a few Kangaroo-apples, which resemble potato-apples
in form, but are slightly acid, and rather mealy though not dry.
We reached Wybalenna soon after sunset. On approaching
this place, we were discovered by some women who were
cutting wood: they now recognized us as old acquaintance,
and gave us a clamorous greeting, which brought all the
people and dogs out of their huts, with such a noise as,
had we not known that it was the expression of friendship
on the part of the people, would have been truly appalling.

1st mo. 3rd, 1834. The weather having become moderate,
the Shamrock came to the settlement and discharged her
cargo; and we had the pleasure of distributing among the
Aborigines the various articles purchased with their wool,
and contributed by their friends at Launceston. The dressing of many of them in clothes, such as they had not been
accustomed to wear, was not a little amusing, but all were
made to fit. One of their chiefs took a great fancy to a
japanned comb, such as he saw a woman use, that had been

among the sealers; but when he obtained one, he was much disappointed to find that he could not get it through his tangled hair, which had among it, knots of dried ochre and grease, notwithstanding he had ceased for sometime to use these articles, and had tried to wash them out. In this dilemma he applied to me; and being desirous to please him, I did my best, but was obliged to hold the hair back with one hand, and pull with the comb with the other. From this he did not shrink, but encouraged me in my work, saying frequently, "Narra coopa"—very good. And when the work was accomplished, he looked at himself in a glass, with no small degree of pleasure. He was a man of an intelligent mind, who made rapid advances in civilization, and was very helpful in the preservation of good order at the Settlement. In former days, when the Aborigines committed depredations upon the settlers, he lost one hand by a steel trap that was concealed in a cask of flour, in a cottage, near Little Swan Port.

5th. In the forenoon, we had another religious interview with the people of the establishment, in their chapel of boughs. In the afternoon, we were occupied in assisting to extinguish a fire, that threatened the destruction of the Settlement, and which had caught the long grass on the adjacent hill. This fire burnt furiously before a strong wind, but was brought under, by beating it out with green, gum-tree boughs. In this work the Aborigines joined and shewed great dexterity.—These people have received a few faint ideas of the existence and superintending providence of God; but they still attribute the strong emotions of their minds to the devil, who, they say, tells them this or that, and to whom they attribute the power of prophetic communication. It is not clear that by the devil, they mean, anything more than a spirit; but they say, he lives in their breasts, on which account they shrink from having the breast touched. One of their names for a white man signifies, a white devil, or spirit; this has probably arisen from their mistaking white men at first for spiritual beings. They have also some vague ideas of a future existence, as may be inferred from their remarks respecting the deceased woman on the Hunter Islands, before noticed. They also say they suppose that when they die, they shall go to some of the islands in the Straits, and jump up white men ; but the latter notion may be of modern date.

6th. Having accomplished the object of our visit, so far as to effect a reconciliation between the parties, who were at variance, which did not, however, prevent the ultimate removal of the worthy Catechist, we again embarked on board the Shamrock. A large party of the Blacks accompanied us to the shore, and we took leave of them under feelings of much interest, excited by their kind, affectionate and cheerful dispositions, and by the circumstances under which they have left their native land for the convenience of strangers.

7th. We beat up to Green Island, through a narrow and shallow channel, among some small islands. Some of the men had got liquor clandestinely, and were excited by it. The mate became exasperated, and set them to some additional but unnecessary work, as a punishment. At this juncture, a current rendered the cutter unmanageable, and it drifted rapidly toward the rocks under Chapel Island. At length, an effort to put about, proved successful, and we again came to anchor under Green Island.

8th. The wind blew from the east, and increased into a gale, which soon raised a heavy sea. Our anchors dragged, and the cutter went on shore : she beat upon the sand from nine o'clock in the evening till two, in the morning, and then settled.

9th. The morning's tide again floated the Shamrock, but the storm continuing, she drove upon a bank of soft, calcareous rock, upon which she settled within a few yards of a place where this rock joins the granite. The rudder was hawled up to save it from injury, and the ebb of the tide left the vessel dry and uninjured, standing with her coppered keel imbedded in the soft rock. In the evening the wind shifted, and a heavy rain stilled the sea so quickly, that the effect was almost like awaking from dreaming of a storm and finding a calm. The same rain also extinguished the fire at the settlement on Flinders

Island, which by the columns of smoke, we could discover
had been rekindled.—After the rock had been cut away by
means of felling axes, so as to allow the rudder to be
restored to its place, a kedge anchor, with a warp, or slender
hempen cable was carried out by a boat, and fixed in a convenient place; and as soon as the rising tide began again
to float the vessel, the warp was plied, and we were favoured
by eleven in the evening, to be again riding at anchor in
deep and still water.

The time the vessel lay upon the rocks, was to me, one of
deep humiliation before the Lord, who condescended to
be very merciful to us. On the first night, being exhausted
and weary, and not seeing any immediate danger, I retired
to my berth, under the impression, that if anything were
to be done, I should be more equal to it after some rest;
and though I was sometimes awaked by a heavy shock of
the vessel on the sand, I could thankfully adopt the language
of the Psalmist: "I laid me down and slept: I awaked
for the Lord sustained me." During the following day,
we could pitch a stone from the deck upon the granite
rocks; the vessel was sure to break up, if she went upon
them, and the change of wind was in the direction to set
her that way, unless advantage could be taken by the
warp of every inch she floated. Under these circumstances,
it appeared a serious thing, when we were safe on land,
again to climb up the side of the cutter, and await the
rising of the tide; but feeling peaceful before the Lord,
on looking this way, and not equally so on looking the other,
I followed the direction of my own feelings, without making
any remark, even to my companion. All the rest of the
company returned on board, which proved to be for the
best, as we were thus able to help in pulling at the warp,
and were on board at a time when hands could have been ill
spared to bring us from the shore.—It was, however, awful,
in this season of suspense, to hear the seamen with reckless
thoughtlessness, swearing more than usual. My companion
watched an opportunity to remonstrate against this insult to
the Majesty of Heaven; and his rebuke was well received,
as from a well-intentioned man, but without any appearance

of humiliation before God. Circumstances like these often prove who are on the Lord's side and who are not: they are strong trials both of principle, and of faith.

10th. When off the Peaks of Cape Barren, and going about eight knots an hour, with the wind from the west, it changed for a few minutes, and blew so suddenly from the north, that it caught the cutter on her broad side, and bore her so much down, that it was necessary to let the square-sail fly, and drop the peak of the main sail, to allow her to right again. The lurch was so sudden as to occasion me to fall upon the top of the cabin, which was raised and had a gangway round it, and I was obliged to hold on with my face downward towards the sea, till the vessel righted again; for she was too far gone to allow me to recover myself, until her own side rose out of the water.

11th. Off the coast of V. D. Land. The wind was adverse, and the swell such as to occasion great sickness.

12th. A gentle and favourable breeze brought us through Schoutens Passage about noon; it then increased so as to bear us much down on one side, and to impel us rapidly across Oyster Bay, to Kelvedon, where our dear friends, Francis Cotton and his family, awaited our arrival on the beach. We gladly took leave of the Shamrock and were conveyed through the surf by the intrepid mate, who was soon after lost, by the upsetting of a small vessel in a gale of wind. In the haste, of our departure, the plug-hole of the boat was left open, and the state of the sea admitted of no delay, to remedy this inconvenience, I therefore stopped the hole with my thumb, and we were favoured to reach the land in safety, the men jumping out of the boat, and running it quickly through the surf.—Thus, through the mercy of our Heavenly Father, was this tedious voyage terminated, under feelings of thankfulness, in the remembrance of our many deliverances, and with the desire, that if any good had been effected, the Lord might have all the glory, for to him alone all glory belongeth.

CHAPTER XVI.

WE remained a few weeks with our friends at Kelvedon. In the course of this time, my strength, which had been much reduced by the previous exertion, excitement, and sea-sickness, was considerably restored.—In this neighbourhood we had several religious meetings, in some of which we were comforted by the exhortations of Dr. Story, who had yielded to the convictions of the Holy Spirit, and had seen it his place to adopt and advocate the principles of Friends.

While we were in Great Swan Port, a soldier at Waterloo Point received a serious injury, by swimming upon a log of wood, which is an accident that may easily occur in this country, where most of the timber is so heavy as to sink in water. When accompanying Dr. Story, in a visit to this man, I saw an Irish soldier doing penance, by kneeling with his bare knees on some rough gravel. It is lamentable to behold practices so repugnant to the spirit of the Gospel, imposed by any church upon those convinced of sin, and by which their attention is diverted from that "repentance toward God, and faith toward our Lord Jesus Christ," which the Apostle preached as the way of salvation.

At Kelvedon, my attention was called to the circumstance, of the flesh of cattle that had died in the bush, having become poisonous. Several pigs, geese, and fowls died, from having eaten of the flesh of a dead bullock, or pecked about the carcase. A person in this neighbourhood had boiled some of the flesh of a cow, found dead in the bush, and had given it to his dogs and pigs, which were made so sick that he thought they also would have died. It is possible that these cattle might have died from the bite of serpents, and that the poison might have become propagated in their carcases; but from whatever cause they may become poisonous, the instinct of wild animals protects them from suffering by it; for the carcases of such cattle often remain untouched either by birds or beasts of prey.

2nd mo. 17th. Accompanied by Francis Cotton, we set out to visit the central part of the Island, on our way back to Hobart Town, and proceeded to the mouth of the Little Swan Port River. Here a person was making an attempt to dry fish for distant markets. This we were satisfied could not succeed, because of the quantity of rum allowed to the men employed, and it was soon given up. The use of spirituous liquors, is equally injurious in whale-fishing, notwithstanding much is sometimes said in its favour. I once asked a seaman, a native of Sydney, who had been brought up in this occupation, what was his opinion on the subject: he replied, " I will tell you, sir, how we used to do when we went to catch sperm-whales. We always left Sydney with a good stock of spirits on board; and as soon as we got clear of the Heads of Port Jackson, we fell to work, the captain and all hands, to drink: we kept it up till the grog was done, and then we were ill two or three weeks, after which we began to catch whales ! Once, we came upon a shoal of sperm-whales, when we were all so drunk that we could hardly see, and we manned the boats and ran upon them in such a way, that it was a wonder we were not all lost. Now, sir, you may form your own judgment of the use of spirits in whaling."

18th. We crossed the Little Swan Port River, in which were a considerable number of poisonous, smooth-skinned

fish, the Toad-fish of this country.   Three persons in a family
near Hobart Town, in 1831, lost their lives, by eating fish of
this kind.—The evening was spent with a settler, who has
exercised a considerable degree of moral and religious care
over his assigned servants, with very satisfactory results.

19th.   Taking a westerly course, we travelled through
several miles of trackless forest, and over some lofty hills.
In one place, a deep, woody ravine is crossed by a remarkable
natural causeway; which, being a little depressed in the
middle, is called The Saddle: its breadth is scarcely more
than would admit a good road, and its sides are almost
perpendicular.   It is the only known pass out of the central
part of Oyster Bay.   Beyond the Saddle, the land joins the
side of a remarkable peak, called The Sugar Loaf, the further
side of which descends steeply to the Eastern Marshes.
The southern entrance to Oyster Bay is equally impassable
for carriages, and the northern one is exceedingly rugged,
but carts are dragged over it.   The district is only accessible
for goods, by sea.   On the Eastern Marshes, nearly all the
Gum-trees are dead.   We were hospitably entertained by a
settler, who was disposing of his cattle, and endeavouring to
let his farm, of 2,000 acres, 400 of which are enclosed, and
50 in cultivation, for £150 a-year.   There are upon it a
plain, stone house, and a few out-buildings.   Kangaroos are
numerous in this part of the country.

20th.   The country toward Oatlands, where we arrived in
the evening, is of hills, of small elevation, thinly wooded
with Black and Weeping Gum-trees, and interspersed with
level grounds, marshy in winter, but very dry in summer.—
We called upon a respectable settler, who, in consequence
of the dishonesty of his assigned servants, had been induced
to act as his own shepherd.   Though this is a great inconvenience to a person having all his other affairs to superintend, yet it has preserved his flocks from depredations, such
as have greatly reduced many others.—From Oatlands we
proceeded to Ansty Barton, the hospitable mansion of
Thomas and Mary Ansty, from whom, on a former visit,
as well as at the present time, we received great kindness.

The domain of Thomas Ansty, consists of upwards of

20,000 acres, much of which is of thinly wooded, grassy hills, adapted for sheep; but in the dry climate of this part of V. D. Land, it will not, on an average, maintain one sheep to two acres during the year.—Opossums are exceedingly numerous in this neighbourhood: they are to be seen in almost every gum-tree, by moonlight.

We remained at Ansty Barton till the 25th, and in the mean time, held religious meetings, and meetings for the promotion of temperance, at Oatlands and Jericho. At the latter place, William Pike, the Episcopal Chaplain, and his family, were kindly helpful to us. From their house, Francis Cotton returned to Swanport.

26th. We proceeded over some fine sheep-hills, to the house of John Bisdee, a prosperous settler, located in a pleasant vale, surrounded by fine, thinly-wooded sheep-hills: his estate which has the benefit of a few springs that supply water during this dry season, includes 5,000 acres, that, on an average, will maintain about two sheep to three acres: it extends to the Black Marsh, upon the Jordan, which is now a chain of large, deep pools. The Common Pheasant has been introduced upon this estate; and in order to preserve it, his men have been encouraged to destroy the Native Cats, by receiving eight-pence for each of their skins. These animals are so numerous, that at one time the people brought in six hundred skins.

3rd mo. 2nd. In the course of the last three days, we visited the settlers at the Lovely Banks, the Cross Marsh, the Hunting Ground, and Green Ponds, and held some meetings among them. At Green Ponds we called upon a respectable family, in which an aged woman, who had been remarkable for steady piety was declining under paralytic disease. On being enquired of, as to how she was, she replied, "Very happy in body and mind." How encouraging is the calm sunshine of the close of the day, in such persons!

3rd. Accompanied by George Gorringe, a medical man, filling also the office of Catechist, we proceeded to the Broad Marsh, and had a meeting with the neighbouring families, at the house of Peter Murdoch. This person has the finest dairy-farm, in V. D. Land. It is situated on a fertile level, on the Jordan, and is advantageously stocked with Alderney cows.

4th. We proceeded along the course of the Jordan, to the Black Brush, passing the houses and enclosures of several settlers. The vale of the Jordan, with its boundary of hills, reminded me of Bilsdale, in Yorkshire; but the climate is much milder than that of England, though liable to occasional summer frosts. Platypuses are not uncommon in the pools of the Jordan, in which, as well as in the other rivers of Tasmania, and on the sea-coast, Black Shaggs are often seen fishing.

At the Black Brush several young men, who emigrated from Birmingham, have opened a store, which has paid them well. They erected a house, in which they are residing, though it has yet only shutters to close the places intended for windows. In the evening, we collected the establishment, and some of their neighbours, and had a religious opportunity with them. An adjacent settler, who appeared to be a very decent man, was one of the congregation. He was formerly a prisoner, having been transported for seven years, for a very trifling offence.

5th. We passed round the end of a lofty tier of hills, into the vale of Bagdad, and went by the Tea-tree Brush, to Richmond. On the 6th we continued our journey to Sorell Town or Pitt Water, and on the 7th, proceeded to the Carlton, a small settlement on a creek opening into Frederick Henry Bay. Here the Government has placed a schoolmaster, a native of Scarborough, who has been most of his life a seafaring man, and who seems to be a man of much simple, religious feeling: he reads the prayers, &c. of the Episcopal Church every First day; but this sort of mechanical religious service does not seem to be very attractive to the people, either here or in other places. The old man was much pleased with our visit. We had a meeting with some of his neighbours and scholars; at the close of which, in the true spirit of a village school-master, he requested his pupils to repeat the Evening Hymn, and then pronounced the "Apostolic benediction." He appears to try to impress upon their minds the spiritual signification of the hymns which he teaches them.

The wife of a settler in this neighbourhood, to whom we made some remarks on the loneliness of their situation, said, that as there was no inn nearer than Sorell Town, they were seldom many days without visiters; and that, at one period, they were not more than three days at a time, for six months, without some person, who was travelling to look for land to settle upon, or under some other pretext claiming their hospitality. This is a common circumstance in all parts of the Colony.—Having become accustomed to travelling in the bush, and the evening being starlight, we made our way back to Sorell Town, though not without some difficulty.

8th. Arriving late last night, we went to an inn, kept by a person named Leigh, which we found remarkably clean and comfortable. Inns in this country are often rendered very uncomfortable by vermin. Part of the day was spent with our fellow-passenger from England, Frances Halls, at whose house a neighbouring settler called, who informed us, that when the views of the Temperance Society were first promulgated in this colony, he thought them foolish; but that he was now convinced of their soundness, and was astonished at their influence in discountenancing spirit drinking.

11th. On the 9th and 10th we had religious meetings with the inhabitants of Sorell Town and Richmond, and with about one hundred prisoners employed in the public works. Richmond is nearly doubled in size since we visited it a few months ago.—Accompanied by our kind friend J. H. Butcher, we again visited some of the settlers on the Coal River, and were hospitably entertained by one, who having capital, and paying attention to the improvement of his estate, has been remarkably prosperous.

12th. We proceeded to Jerusalem, ten miles further up the Coal River. Where we held a meeting with some free people, and a number of prisoners in the public works, who are at present employed in building a gaol. Drought has continued so long that most of the mills in the Island, are unable to grind. The family with whom we lodged were nearly out of bread, and had so little prospect of soon being able to renew their stock, that it was trying to us to think of partaking with them, notwithstanding they entertained us cheerfully.—Green Parrots are very numerous in this neighbourhood, a flock of about a hundred, flew up from a stubble, as we passed.

13th. Taking a westerly direction, from the upper part of Jerusalem, we passed over some lofty tiers of hills, to Green Ponds. Part of the way was very steep; the whole of it a trackless forest. Some of the thick scrub among these hills had lately been burnt. The ground in these places was covered with ashes and black sticks, that made travelling unpleasant. We crossed several deep gullies in our descent, and in five hours and a half from leaving Jerusalem, emerged from among the hills, close to the house of an elderly man, whom we much wished to see, and by whom we were courteously received. This person was formerly a prisoner, and came out with Governor Collins. Being industrious, and of more sober habits than many of his cotemporaries, he has prospered greatly since he became free: he is now possessed of five thousand acres of land, capable of maintaining two thousand sheep, and some horned cattle. He has taught himself to read and write, and his Bible has the appearance of being well read. His wife, who was also formerly a prisoner, prepared tea for us, and waited on us very kindly. They both seemed grateful for our visit; and for the religious instruction conveyed to their family.

17th. In the course of the last three days, we had meetings at Green Ponds, Constitution Hill, and Brighton; at the last two of which, a large number of prisoners were present. We became the guests of a settler, who had a value for religion, but like many others, enjoyed but little of clearness or comfort in it, for want of submitting to the baptisms of the Holy Spirit, by which the true disciples of Christ are crucified to the world and the world to them, and know that they abide in him, by the Spirit which he hath given them.—To-day, we had a religious interview with a road-party of the halt and maimed. Though

many of them were grown old in sin, there was a remarkable
sense of divine influence over our minds whilst assembled
with them, and we had no doubt but it was, to some of
them, a time of renewed, merciful visitation.—We afterwards
went along the north bank of the Derwent, to New Norfolk,
and coming opposite to the mill of John Terry, a boat was
sent across for us, and we spent the evening under his
hospitable roof.   This mill is now working night and day;
notwithstanding most of the mills to the northward and
westward are stopped for want of water.   Many families
have to send their corn more than fifty miles to grind.
J. Terry's mill is turned by a streamlet from the mountains,
called the Thames, a tributary of the Derwent.   The fall
accommodates three water-wheels, one above another.

19th.   We had a meeting in the hospital with the patients
and the prisoners in the public works; a few other persons also attended.   Most of the congregation stood, the
room being incapable of containing them if seated.   I felt
empty of all qualification to labour, till after entering the
room, but looked to the Lord for help to do his holy will.
A feeling of solemnity came over my mind, and under it, I
was enabled to extend the gospel message to sinners, to
repent and believe in Jesus, for the remission of sins, that
through him, they might receive the washing of regeneration,
and the renewing of the Holy Ghost, and thus be enabled
to work righteousness.   They were referred to the conviction
of sin in their own minds, as the drawing of the Father,
seeking to lead them to repentance, and to faith in Christ,
and to bring them to wait and pray, daily, for the help of
the Holy Spirit, to enable them to walk before God, and
be perfect.

20th.   We spent a little time at the bedside of a man
in the hospital, who had expressed a wish to see me, and who
was in a deplorable state, in consequence of early instability.
According to his own account, he had often called upon the
Lord in time of trouble, and again forgotten him when his
trouble ceased.   Now, when racked with pain, and without
hope of being raised up, he often feared that he was too
great a sinner to be pardoned.   I entreated him to cherish

the feeling of condemnation for sin, and to wait on the Lord in the way of his judgments, and to seek a true repentance and unfeigned faith in Christ, " who bore our sins in his own body on the tree:" remembering that God is almighty to save, both by pardoning sin for Christ's sake, and through him, working in us that which is well pleasing in his sight. Sin had a dreadful hold of this man, who seemed unable to keep his mind turned toward the Lord.

22nd. In the afternoon we visited a person, who was brought up in the Episcopal Church, with whom we had much conversation on the simplicity and the spirituality of the Gospel. She said, she perceived that religion was a very different thing from what she had been taught to think it; and that it did not consist in forms and ceremonies, but in an exercise of soul before God.

23rd. We had a large meeting in the forenoon, in the loft of a building erected for a store. In the afternoon another was held in a room in the hospital. Both were seasons of Divine favour, in which ability was afforded to warn sinners of their danger, and to invite them to turn to the Lord and live. The privilege of the true Christian, in holding communion with the Father and the Son, under the influence of the Holy Spirit, sensibly manifested as the Comforter, and the Spirit of Truth, was also pointed out.

26th. Our kind friend Robert Officer, in whose family we were inmates for a few days, drove us to the residence of an aged and pious man, of the name of Geiss, who had long served the Lord, and walked in peacefulness before him. The influence of his bright example of piety, is perceptible on those around him. From this place, we walked to Bridgewater, where we had an interview with the chain-gang, in a rude, dry-stone building. The Wesleyans have for some time past, gratuitously afforded religious instruction, every First-day, to these poor outcasts, and there seems a decided relaxation, in the ferocity of their countenances, since they have received this attention.

27th. We reached Hobart Town, and attended the little week-day meeting, of those in religious fellowship with us, with whom we sat in silence, but in the enjoyment of the fulfilment of that promise of Christ; "Where two or three are gathered together in my name, there am I in the midst of them."

On the way to Hobart Town at this time, I was attacked with an affection of the heart, by which my life seemed often in great jeopardy, but it did not confine me to the house, notwithstanding I suffered much from it for several weeks; when thus, continually admonished of the uncertainty of surviving from one day, and sometimes from one hour, to another, I was often favoured with such a sense of the divine presence, as was very confirming to my faith, and enabled me to speak more experimentally than before, on the benefit of holding communion in spirit with the Lord, and of neither neglecting the things that belong to salvation, nor resting in speculative opinions.

CHAPTER XVII.

Hobart Town.—Meeting Places.—Discontinuance of Reading Meetings.—Week-day Meetings.—Ministers.—Meetings to which the Public were invited.—Prayer.—Principles of Friends.—Base-line.—Perjury.—Prisoner Boy.—Grass-tree Hill.—Esculent Vegetables.—Silent Meetings.—Flagellation.—Monthly Meetings.—Reflections.—Report on Chain-gangs and Road Parties.—Traffic of the Blacks.—"Guide to True Peace."—Colonial Hospital.—J. Johnson.—Orphan School.—Penitentiary.

WE remained in Hobart Town, with little exception, from the 27th of 3rd month, to the 22nd of 8th month. During this period, and for some time afterwards, our meetings for worship were held in the cottage of William Holdship, on the Newtown Road. This individual had had his attention drawn to the principles of Friends, by reading a tract, on the Glory of the True Church, by Francis Howgill,* and another entitled "The Ancient Christian's Principle, &c." by Hugh Turford. Friends being under the necessity of removing their meetings from the house in which they had been held in Macquarie Street, in consequence of another tenant occupying it, they were held a few times in the houses of William Rayner and another individual, but neither of these proving convenient places, W. Holdship offered the use of a room in his cottage, saying he should count it a privilege to have the opportunity of sitting with Friends in their meetings, notwithstanding they were often held in silence.

At one of our Monthly Meetings for Discipline, it was

* A revised edition of this tract, has lately been printed by the York Friends' Tract Association, under the title of, "A Testimony against Ecclesiastical Corruptions."

concluded to discontinue the meeting for reading the Scriptures and the writings of Friends, on First-day afternoons,
and to hold meetings for worship instead. The persons who
attended our meetings being now in the practice of reading
their Bibles and religious biography, &c. diligently at home,
meetings for religious instruction by these means, appeared
to be no longer necessary. The room in which we now
met, being at liberty also on week-days, it was agreed to hold
a meeting for worship, at 10 o'clock, on fifth-day forenoons,
instead of at half-past six in the evening. This sacrifice
of a portion of the best part of a day, to the Lord in the
middle of the week, evidently received his blessing, as has
very universally been the case in the Society of Friends,
where the sacrifice has been made in sincerity. Several
fresh members were also added to our little company, and
two men, who had for some time spoken in our congregations,
to the edification of their brethren, were recorded as approved
ministers. The meeting also came to the settled judgment,
that the communications of another individual, were not
generally to edification, how well soever they might be intended; and in the spirit of love, he was requested to
withhold the expression of any mere cogitations of the
mind, such, not being accompanied by the baptizing power
of the Holy Spirit, without which no ministry can be of
any practically good effect.

When we first arrived in Hobart Town, the meeting-
houses of the Independents and Wesleyans were freely
offered for our use, in case we should wish to invite the
inhabitants to assemble with us At that time, it did not
appear to be our duty to enter upon such a service; but
now, believing it required of us, we held meetings for public
worship in both of these places, to which the inhabitants
generally, were invited. In one of the meetings in the
Independent chapel, some remarks were made upon the evil
resulting from the mind being kept in a state of excitement,
such as is common in the world, almost from the cradle
to the grave, and which is transferred also into performances
designed to be religious, often keeping the mind much
diverted from that attention to its own condition before

the Lord, which is essential to spiritual worship. The great benefit of retirement of mind from this excitement, and of communion of soul with the Most High in silence, was pointed out, and the people were directed to the teaching of the Holy Spirit, inwardly revealed, as essentially necessary to a saving knowledge of Christ.

After we had remained in silence about an hour, in the meeting, in the Wesleyan Chapel, a young man, originally sent to the colony as a convict, of whose repentance and reformation we had had many proofs, commended the attention of the audience, in a few sentences, to the inspeaking voice of Christ, the Good Shepherd; whose sheep know his voice and follow him, and receive of him eternal life. This opened my way to comment largely on the declaration, "The wages of sin is death; but the gift of God is eternal life through Jesus Christ our Lord."

We had likewise a meeting in the Supreme Court Room, in which silence prevailed for nearly an hour and a half, under a precious feeling of heavenly solemnity. The advantage of having the mind so stayed upon God, as to worship him in spirit and in truth, without being dependent on the stimulus of vocal exercises, was afterwards commented upon, as well as the loss sustained by many, who, after having attained to repentance, and to a sense of justification from past sin, through faith in Christ, instead of walking by faith according to the continued manifestations of the Holy Spirit, depend greatly upon the excitement of such vocal exercises as are popularly styled "means of grace," to enable them to hold on their heavenward course, and thus have their expectation divided between God, and these things; by which means they often fall away, or become weak and dwarfish in religious attainments. The desirableness of that state was shown, in which the mind, reverently bowed before God, is prepared either to be edified in silence, or by words spoken under the influence of the Holy Spirit, and which is nevertheless, not dependent on vocal teaching.

4th mo. 12th. We proceeded to the east side of the Derwent, by a steam-packet that has lately been established, to take passengers, &c. from Hobart Town to Kangaroo

Point, and by which the danger of this ferry is materially reduced, and the fare is lessened one-half. We afterwards walked to Lauderdale on Muddy Plains, making a few calls on the way. The evening was spent pleasantly in the family of a pious settler. After the reading of the Scriptures, a long silence ensued, which was concluded by my stating to the company, that I did not apprehend it was my place, at that time, to express any thing in the way of exhortation or prayer. On my doing this, the master of the house knelt down with his family, and uttered some petitions. We thought it our place, on this occasion, to keep our seats, and thus to bear a testimony against that disposition which determines, on such occasions, to utter something in the way of prayer, and which has, by this means, a strong tendency to draw the mind away from inward prayer, and to cherish a feeling, as if prayer must necessarily be vocal, and might be performed by proxy. We afterwards had some satisfactory conversation, on this subject, and on the advantage of cultivating in silence, an individual, inward exercise, and of not engaging vocally in prayer, except when the mind is brought under the feeling of duty in the matter. My mind was subsequently drawn towards the prisoner-servants, and we had an open opportunity with them, both in testimony and in prayer. A son of our host, who voluntarily accompanied us to visit the prisoners, became awakened to the importance of eternal things at this time: he, and most of the other members of the family, afterwards adopted the principles of Friends, under a conviction of their Scriptural soundness, and a clear perception, of the operation of divine power upon the mind, known in their practical adoption.

13th. We travelled to the Hollow-tree, where we had a small but satisfactory meeting. Much of the way to this place, lay through a narrow avenue of some miles in length, cut through the bush, for the purpose of measuring a base-line, for a trigonometrical survey, which is going forward in the Island.

14th. We visited a party, of a hundred and fifty prisoners, employed in cutting a road across Grass-tree Hill, by which the distance between Hobart Town and Richmond will be materially shortened.   In this company I recognized a man from York, transported on the charge of perjury. This crime, whether in this instance, well substantiated or not, is exceedingly common among the convict population. Another prisoner was a youth who was the cabin boy on board the Charlotte cutter, in our first voyage, in Bass's Straits : he had been trained in vice from infancy, and had passed from the milder to the severer form of punishment, in consequence of his waywardness, 'since he was transported. When on board the cutter, the following conversation passed between him and the mate :—Mate : " Tommy ! where do you come from ?"   Boy : " Liverpool, sir."   Mate : " What is your father ?"   Boy : " I have none, sir."   Mate : "What was he ?"   Boy : "Nothing, sir."   Mate : " What is your mother ?"   Boy : " She is dead, sir."   Mate : "Who do you live with, at home ?"   Boy : " My sister, sir."   Mate : " What is your sister ?"   Boy : " Nothing, sir."   Mate : " What did you do for a living ?"   Boy : " They used to put me in at the windows to open doors, sir."—In this way, it is to be feared, that many are trained to crime, and become the pests of society from the influence of an evil education ; and that the parties stated to be "nothing," which is a common description in such cases, have lived by vicious means.

The rocks that are cut through, in forming the road over Grass-tree Hill, are argillaceous, embedding shells. Sand-stone, with a calcareous admixture, also occurs in some places. The Grass-trees are not so large as those on Flinders Island, nor as some on the north end of Bruny Island, but they are of the same species.

15th. We returned to Hobart Town yesterday, and to-day, I spent some time in writing an account of the esculent, vegetable productions of this island for Dr. Ross, which was printed in his Annual for 1834. This article, amended by my friend, R. C. Gunn, is presented to the reader in Appendix D. In the evening we had a long conversation with a person of religious character, who admits that silent retirement in private, is a state most favourable to devotion, but he does not seem to be able to enter into the views of

Friends in regard to public worship, at least, as respects the silent part of it, and he cannot understand why meetings should sometimes be held wholly in silence. I believe these things are a mystery to many other good men; and unless the Lord open their understandings, to see the advantage of this united retirement of soul before him, I have no expectation that they will understand it by argument. Nevertheless, the matter is so plain to those who have felt the benefit of this mode of worship, that we rarely find they can be satisfied with any other. In dwelling under the baptizing influence of the Holy Spirit, in reverent stillness before the Lord, a sense is given us of our unworthiness, also of acceptance in the Beloved, who died for us: we feel that we become his adopted members, and are bowed in a reverent fear before him; so that we are brought to watch and wait before the Lord, in meetings and out of them, and to revert to this state of expectation from him alone, whenever we find ourselves carried away from a sense of his presence being with us.

30th. I witnessed the infliction of the punishment of flagellation, in the Penitentiary-yard, upon a prisoner belonging the Hulk Chain-gang, who was a very refractory man. The scars upon his back bore testimony to frequent previous inflictions of this degrading punishment. The Superintendent of Convicts said this man had been more frequently flogged, than almost any other in the Colony: he writhed and cried out greatly under the strokes of a "cat" of knotted cords, which raised red wheals, and drew some blood: his sentence was to receive fifty lashes.

5th mo. 1st. At our Monthly Meeting, it was proposed to hold these meetings alternately, at Hobart Town and Kelvedon, and to transmit the minutes from the one place to the other for confirmation, in order to secure the strength and judgment of the whole of the members of the little body, professing with Friends, in this land; the distance between Hobart Town and Kelvedon being too great to admit of the members at the one place, frequently meeting with those at the other. This proposition was subsequently adopted with advantage.

4th. In reflecting upon the command, " Go through the breadth of the land," which I believed to be of the Lord, when it was impressed on my mind, in the 3rd mo. 1832, and which we have now nearly fulfilled, I have felt much peace. As I have meditated upon this command, at various times, there has been a renewal of a measure of the feeling of sweetness and authority that accompanied it at the first. This I esteem a condescending mercy, to an unprofitable servant deeply sensible of many defects, who truly feels, that not unto himself, but to the Lord alone, belongs the glory of any good that may have been effected through his means.

7th. Occupied with a Report to the Lieut. Governor, on the state of the Chain-gangs and Road-parties of the Colony; nearly all of which we have now visited. Their state has claimed our sympathy, and we have thought it right to make several suggestions for the improvement of their discipline.— An extract from this Report is introduced into this volume, in APPENDIX. E.

8th. The upper and middle portions of Mount Wellington are covered with snow. This may be regarded as the commencement of winter in this region; and equivalent to the 8th of the 11th month in England.

9th. A hundred dried Brush Kangaroo skins were sent to my charge, by W. J. Darling, to dispose of for the Aborigines on Flinders Island. For these I obtained seven-pence each. With the money, several useful articles were purchased for the people who had collected them; and the stock returned was augmented by contributions from a number of benevolent persons in Hobart Town. The attempt to induce the Aborigines to preserve skins, and other articles of traffic, was afterwards carried out more extensively, and with success, by G. A. Robinson. A few more of the native Blacks lately joined this individual, on the west coast; and ultimately, they were all prevailed upon to leave the main land, and join their countrymen on Flinders Island.

11th. We had a meeting in the Wesleyan chapel at O'Briens Bridge, in which the people were reminded of the time, when, by attending to the convictions of the Holy Spirit upon their own consciences, they perceived their lost state, and that their hearts were occupied by sin, when they were also brought to repentance, and found peace, through faith in Christ, made a profession of religion, and brought forth fruits of righteousness. This process was then compared with that of their taking possession of the land they are occupying, and clearing it, by felling and burning off the timber and the scrub—the natural and unprofitable produce of the earth—and fencing and cultivating the land. They were then desired to reflect upon the condition to which such land soon returns, if neglected; and to consider how soon, according to their own knowledge, it again becomes covered with forest and scrub, so as only to be distinguishable from "the wild bush" by the remains of the fence. From this they were urged to remember, that without a constant care to keep their own hearts under the influence of the Holy Spirit, they, in a similar way, would soon again become unprofitable and overgrown with sin, notwithstanding they might retain the appearance of a fence against evil, in some remaining profession of religion. This appeal was not without effect. One man acknowledged to us, that he was already sensible of some measure of relapse, into the sinful state that had been spoken of.

17th. We revised a treatise entitled "A Guide to True Peace," which, we concluded to print as a tract, and to circulate chiefly among persons stirred up to some degree of religious feeling, but who do not get sufficiently deep in inward exercise, and in consequence remain weak Christians.

19th. In company with James Scott, the Colonial Surgeon, a man from whom we have received much kindness, and some other persons, we visited the Colonial Hospital, which seems to be a well-managed institution, and accommodates a hundred patients.—In the afternoon, accompanied by T. J. Crouch, we walked to Glenorchy, to see John Johnson, an aged man, who in 1800, was transported for seven years, from the vicinity of Leicester, for robbing a fish-pond. He told us that he was formerly a great poacher, and did not complain of the severity of his hard sentence, which separated him from his wife, who is since deceased, and from four children, then young. Since he became free, he has never had the means to return, so that transportation for seven years has been to him, as it has been to many others, exile for life. By his own account, the increased exposure to vice, to which he was subjected, in New South Wales, and subsequently on Norfolk Island, until his removal to Van Diemens Land, drove him further into sin. Notwithstanding this, he often remembered his degraded condition, and longed for deliverance. The ministry of a woman Friend, in England, appears to have been, under the divine blessing, the means of kindling these desires after salvation, which the floods of iniquity were never permitted entirely to extinguish.

About two years ago, a Wesleyan tract-distributor found this man "three-parts drunk," one First-day morning, in a room where several others were in bed, completely intoxicated. Some of them had been fighting in the night, and the floor was besmeared with their blood. Hopeless as this state of things was, the man left them some tracts, which Johnson was induced to read, and which inclined him to go to hear the Wesleyans, who began about that time, to preach in the neighbourhood. Himself and one of his companions, became deeply awakened to a sense of their sinful state, and groaned under its burden. In confidence in the declaration, that "the effectual fervent prayer of the righteous man availeth much," his burdened friend and he, set out to Hobart Town, one evening, and went to a Wesleyan meeting, where they stated the object of their coming, and desired the prayers of the congregation. By their own account and that of others, it appears to have been a time of great excitement; but the Lord, who condescends to the weakness of the upright in heart, was pleased to grant an answer of peace to their fervent and vociferous supplications; and these two pilgrims returned home under a sense of the pardoning mercy offered to mankind in and through Jesus the Saviour. Their subsequent walk has proved, that, great as was the excitement that prevailed on the occasion, it was not the mere illusion of a heated imagination, which made the difference that these two men felt in themselves; they remain established, quiet Christians. Through the continued labours of the Wesleyans, light has gradually diffused itself around them; so that, to these first-fruits, have been gathered from the drunken and dissolute, a number of others, who form the little congregation at O'Briens Bridge; whose influence, notwithstanding some grievous instances of backsliding, has greatly altered for the better, the population of the neighbourhood.

27th. We accompanied George Everitt, the Secretary of the Orphan School at New Town, in a visit to that large and useful establishment, which is now removed to a commodious new building. Some of the boys are instructed in tailoring, shoe mending, and other handicraft occupations, as well as in the common branches of school education. Among the pupils are five sons of the Aborigines, who are making as good progress in their learning, as boys of European extraction.

29th. We visited the Penitentiary for Females, which has lately received the addition of another court-yard, and two double tiers of cells. There is much difficulty in finding employment for the prisoners, notwithstanding they wash for the Hospital, and some other public establishments. There has not been sufficient religious interest excited on behalf of this class of prisoners, in any place in this country, to maintain a visiting committee of their own sex.

CHAPTER XVIII.

5th mo. 30th. WE walked to Browns River, a small settlement on the side of the Derwent. It is accessible by carts, but
sends sawn and split timber and potatoes, by water, to Hobart
Town, which is seven miles distant. Potatoes grow here to
great perfection, on light loam bordering a rivulet, which rises
on Mount Wellington.—*Sprengellia incarnata,* a heath-like
shrub, was in flower in some marshy ground on the road ; and
in the gullies about Sandy Bay, *Plagianthus discolor,* a shrub
of the Mallow tribe, bearing clusters of small, white blossoms, was beautifully in flower. There are other species of
this genus in the colony, all of which are called Curri-
jong. This name is also given in the Australian territories,
to all other shrubs, having bark sufficiently tenacious to be
used instead of cordage.

31st. We accompanied Thomas Bannister, the Sheriff,
over the Jail at Hobart Town, which is a very defective
building, and often much crowded, but it is kept clean, and
appears to be made the best of.

6th mo. 1st. We returned to Browns River, where, in
a tidy, weather-boarded barn, we met a decent-looking congregation of about thirty persons. After spending some

time in silence, I had a little to say to them, but there did
not seem to be much way open for expression, nor was there
much before my mind to communicate. Nevertheless, I
thought there was with us, a comforting sense of the Lord's
presence. We left this hitherto much-neglected spot, with
the hope that an interest on religious subjects, that seemed to
be awakened in several minds, was an omen for good. We
returned along the ridge of a tier of woody hills, of which
Mount Nelson is one, on which there is a signal station,
answering to that at Hobart Town. From this station we
again enjoyed a fine view of the latter place, and of the extensive bays of the Derwent, as well as of the surrounding
country, which rises in almost every direction, into hills,
covered with sombre forest, here and there invaded by
the hand of culture, which has introduced green fields,
that make a lively contrast with the dark olive of the
widely-spread bush.—From Mount Nelson, we descended
to Sandy Bay, and met another congregation, of about forty
persons. After a season of silence, I was enabled clearly to
point out the evil of sin, and the way to escape from
it, through repentance towards God and faith towards
our Lord Jesus Christ. We parted under solemn feeling,
after prayer had been vocally put up, on behalf of this
company.

3rd. We had a long discussion with some of our acquaintance, on water-baptism, a subject upon which we are
often called to explain our views. We rarely meet with
people so free from educational prejudice, as to be willing
to look upon the commands of Christ to his disciples, to
baptize, as separable from the idea of water, and in their
proper connexion with spiritual influence; or who are sufficiently enlightened, to discern the liberty of Christians to
abandon all those things, that in their nature accord with
the dispensation of types and shadows, rather than with the
spirituality of the Gospel.

Persons often tell us, that they see the accordance of the
principles of Friends with the Gospel, except in regard to
Baptism, and what is called the Lord's Supper; but that
on account of our disuse of these, they cannot join us. I

believe, however, that most of these persons deceive themselves, as to their reason for not joining us; and that the truth of the matter is, that they have not yet apprehended the nature of the simple teaching of the Divine Spirit, as true Friends have been privileged experimentally to receive it. The cross of sitting down in silence to wait upon the Lord, in order to be taught of him, and of bearing to be humbled under a sense of helplessness, is also too great for this description of people. We have noticed, that when any attain to this humbled, teachable, state, they generally become satisfied of the propriety of ceasing to use ceremonial rites, and feel the importance of bearing those testimonies to the simplicity, peaceableness, and spirituality of the Gospel, which Friends maintain to be its true characteristics, and in which, the faithful among them, endeavour to walk; and in so walking, know their communion to be with the Father and with his Son Jesus Christ, under the baptizing influence of the Holy Spirit.

8th. Our meetings were not particularly lively; but I had a few words to express, near the close of that in the afternoon; at which nineteen persons were present. An individual who, when resident in London, occasionally attended Gracechurch Street Meeting, now frequently meets with us: he acknowledges himself to be more fully convinced of the accordance of the principles of Friends with the Gospel, than formerly; especially in regard to the doctrines of the universal offer of Divine grace to man, and of the perceptible teaching of the Holy Spirit to the attentive mind.

15th. After dinner Abraham C. Flower came to our lodging, and signified that he felt an impression of duty to visit three men in gaol, ordered to be executed, to-morrow, for murder. G. W. Walker conferred with William Bedford, the Colonial Chaplain, on the subject, who said that he had no objection whatever to the visit being paid. Observing, from the Act, that the Sheriff possessed power to grant liberty for such a visit, we went to him, and he, with his wonted benevolence and urbanity, immediately granted this liberty, subject only to its being agreeable to the poor culprits to see us. The keeper of the gaol accompanied us into the cell, where there

was also a fourth prisoner, under similar sentence. Though
the murder, to which these men confess, was one of the most
deliberate kind, the bond of hardness of heart under which
it was committed, now appeared to be broken, and they
seemed to be in a tender frame of mind. They were far
from being men of ferocious countenances. We each had a
little to communicate to them, encouraging them to yield to
their convictions of sin, and to seek pardon, in unfeigned
repentance, through faith in the atoning blood of Christ, in
the hope that they might find mercy with God, with whom
" one day is as a thousand years," and who will forgive the
sincerely penitent. The poor men expressed much thankfulness for our visit; toward the conclusion of which, prayer
was put up on their behalf.

20th. The Lieutenant Governor having invited us to
prepare a report upon the state of the Prisoners and Penal
Discipline, of Van Diemens Land; with observations on the
general state of the Colony, we drew one up, and presented
it to him.—This document is introduced to the reader in
APPENDIX. F.

7th mo. 3rd. Our week-day meeting was small, but it
was one of remarkable exercise. A well-disposed young man
was present, who had come from the country to endeavour
to obtain an appointment to the office of Catechist. A
Friend, who was quite ignorant of such a person being in
town, was led, in commenting upon some passages of Scripture, to point out with remarkable clearness, the mistakes of
those who thought themselves advancing the Lord's work,
by entering in their own wills, upon formal services, and thus
holding up imitations of religion, in the place of religion
itself. He also showed how, in this way, they wasted their
own strength, when, if they would have remained patiently
under the baptizing power of the Holy Spirit, self would
have been subdued in them, and a concern on behalf of others
excited by this holy influence; which concern, as it was given
way to in simplicity, would have edified others, and have
been attended with peace to the labourers, even though they
might appear to themselves to do but little. More to the
same import was added by G. W. Walker and myself, under

what we apprehended to be a right exercise, but which might have been more liable to be called in question, as we were aware of the views of the individual. He received the whole well, and appeared thankful that he had been placed in the way of such counsel.—In our meetings, we have of late had much evidence, that the simple-hearted are often baptized one for another.—Circumstances needing religious counsel, have in this way been spoken to, by parties who had no outward knowledge of them, but who gave way to express the exercises that settled upon their own minds, often in the feeling of much weakness and fear.

4th. In referring to the circumstance of an individual, formerly a prisoner at Macquarie Harbour, having been lately recorded as an approved minister, by Hobart Town Monthly Meeting of Friends, a person of our acquaintance, belonging to another body of Christians, writes:—"The intelligence conveyed in yours, is exceedingly gratifying to me. That one of the despised, hated, and persecuted little band at Macquarie Harbour, should become an accredited minister of a body of Christians, whose steady piety and arduous labours are heard of through the world, and acknowledged as extensively as they are known, cannot but be considered as one of those glorious triumphs of grace, which cause the saints to rejoice, to adore, and to love the Saviour with increasing ardour. To me, who have seen something of the trials and difficulties of that penal abode, it appears truly wonderful. But why should I wonder? Does it not often please the Great Disposer of events, to prepare his choicest instruments in the hottest fire? I fervently pray that * * * may continue a faithful standard-bearer in the cause of Truth, until his earthly pilgrimage shall close."

6th. In reading the book of Genesis lately, I have been much struck with the similarity of character exhibited among the sons of Jacob, to that which is to be found among the stock-keepers of Tasmania, and among some of the settlers. Similar occasions of "evil report," and exhibitions of hardness of heart, such as induced them to deal hardly with Joseph their brother, and other descriptions of

profligacy, are here found to prevail, and are reported to
have prevailed formerly, in a much greater degree, especially
where, from remoteness of situation, there was not much
probability that the hand of justice would interfere. This
seems to prove human nature to be the same in this age,
as it was in that of the patriarchs, by showing its similarity
under similar circumstances. It is true that its malignant
features are aggravated in this day, by the use of spirituous
liquors; but this evil is now becoming generally acknowledged, and is likely to be abandoned. Appalling as the
picture is, to me, there is some encouragement in it, for the
sons of Jacob, when brought under the government of
Joseph, and influenced increasingly, as they advanced in
years, by the example of their pious father, appear to have
become greatly improved, and similar effects are visible from
similar causes, in this land. The improved government of
the last nine years, and the increase of moral and religious
example and instruction, are universally admitted to have
restrained much of the evil propensity of human nature,
which was formerly given way to, and to have drawn out
some of the better feelings of the human heart. Much,
however, remains to be done, but the improvement already
visible, ought to operate as an encouragement to the use of
such efficacious means.

7th. In a walk, I observed some of the early indications
of Spring. *Acacia Oxycedrus, Boronia variabilis, Epacris
impressa, Eriostemon obovatum,* and a few other pretty shrubs
are in flower. I have lately obtained skins of several of the
birds of this Colony, among them are species of Bittern,
Coot and Duck, and a little bird with open feathers, like
those of the Emu, in its tail, whence it has obtained the
name of the Emu Wren. I also got specimens of the Wandering Albatross, which were taken at sea, off Storm Bay.
The skin of this bird is so oily that the only mode of preserving it seems to be, by filling it repeatedly with wood-ashes
until dried. I have likewise obtained skins of the Wombat,
and of a small animal inhabiting the shores of rivers, and
some parts of the coast, and having the habits of a Water Rat:
its hind feet are webbed, and its tail is tipped with white.

It is called in the Colony, the Musk Rat, in consequence of a skin having been, at an early period, packed with one of a Musk Duck, by which means it acquired a musky smell, and not from any natural smell of musk in the animal.

7th. The Monthly Meeting received an application for membership, from an individual who has lately adopted the principles of Friends, on conscientious grounds. The father of this person has also become convinced of the accordance of the principles of Friends with the Gospel, in consequence of reading a copy of "Barclay's Apology," that he purchased in London, of Isaac Veale, who seized it from Edmund Fry, for an ecclesiastical demand.

10th. The week-day meeting was small. A pious man, formerly a prisoner, attended, and spoke a few words, apparently with great sincerity; but clearly not from the description of exercise, which Friends recognize as the spring of Gospel ministry. Something was afterwards communicated by two Friends, on the nature of such exercises, and on the benefit of suffering the Lord to work in us and by us, rather than of setting ourselves to work. After meeting this person acknowledged himself to have been instructed.

15th. We had satisfactory letters from two of our friends; both indicative of a growth in the root of religion, as well as of some enlargement in its fruit: one of them holds a meeting in his own lodgings. He is a clerk in a Government-office, and being allowed a small sum to procure himself lodging and clothing, he has this advantage over many other prisoners. He often sits alone to worship the Lord, but sometimes one or two others join him, and on some of these occasions, he says, " In obedience to what I believed to be required of me, I have given expression to what, for dread, I dared not to suppress, though in much backwardness and brokenness. I have experienced the terrors of the Lord in not freely giving up; and once for going beyond the word of life." Like one of our friends here, he is another Onesimus. Some of the free population of respectable rank, and of some degree of religious thoughtfulness, regard him as a shining light, in a dark place, very humble, but full of faith, and abundant in good works.

On the 18th we again went to Muddy Plains, where we held two meetings, on the 20th. Many of the inhabitants of this district still retain a very low and immoral character, but there is some willingness among them to listen to counsel. Many of the assigned servants are far from what they ought to be; but we always find they receive plain dealing well, when it is administered in love.

21st. We visited Hugh and Mary Germain, in their neat cottage. Hugh Germain came to V. D. Land with Colonel Collins, at the first settlement of the colony. He was a private in the Marines, and was for many years employed in hunting Kangaroos and Emus for provisions, which the officer, whose servant he was, received from him, and sold to the Government, at 1s. 6d. per pound. Germain, assisted by two prisoners, returned 1,000 pounds per month, on an average. Though Emus are now rarely seen on the island, at that time they were frequently met with about New Norfolk, Salt Pan Plains, the Coal River, and Kangaroo Point. The Kangaroo was also very plentiful in places where it is now rarely seen: one of the largest Foresters that Germain killed, was on the spot where Hobart Town Barracks now stand: the hind quarters weighed 130 lbs. and it measured nine feet from the tip of the nose to that of the hind feet. At this period, these animals were usually taken by dogs. H. Germain says, he rarely carried a gun, though he often fell in with parties of Aborigines, "in whom there was then no harm." He thinks they hurt nobody till two white men, charged with murder, escaped from Port Dalrymple, and got among them. He pursued this mode of life so closely, as to be at one time, five years without sleeping on a bed; and sometimes, in very wet weather, he was driven to take refuge from floods, in a tree; where he has had to remain all night, covered with a large kangaroo's skin, to keep off the rain. He was the first white man who penetrated into several parts of the colony, and a principal in conferring upon them such names as Jericho,

Bagdad, Abyssinia, &c. Only one of the party could read; and his only books were a Bible, and the Arabian Nights' Entertainment; out of which books the places were successively named. He considers his health to have been preserved through these hardships, chiefly, by washing himself well every morning and evening.

22nd. Was very showery. We returned to Hobart Town, crossing at Kangaroo Point, in a whale-boat. It was rough on the Derwent, near the middle of which, we passed several Jackass Penguins. I had often before, heard the cries of these birds on the river.

23rd. A person of my acquaintance furnished me with a living Albatross, but as I could not conveniently accommodate a large, living bird, I killed it, being desirous of preserving its skin. The stomach contained a green substance resembling Barilla, and a large quantity of pure, whale oil; about a quart of which ran out of the bird's mouth. Probably the Albatross may eat Barilla and other vegetables containing soda, to enable it to digest the oil. Like many others of the gull tribe, it feeds greedily on blubber, which is often to be had in these seas, in the whaling season. The oil from the stomach remained limpid, but that from the skin, which was so abundant as to require to be removed with a spoon, became opaque, white, and almost solid, on cooling.

The adaptation of animals to their station, is one of the subjects in which the wisdom and skill of the Creator, is remarkably exemplified. Thus the eye of the Morepork or Greater Night Jarr, which I lately had the opportunity of examining, is wonderfully adapted for enabling it to see the insects in the dark, on which it feeds. The eye is large and stretched by a bony ring, of one piece; and when recently removed, it forms a fine camera-obscura, transmitting the images of objects facing it, through the integuments at the back of the retina. The tongue of the Wattle-bird and the Honey-eater being pencilled with hairs, is as remarkably adapted to enable them to obtain the honey which forms their food, from flowers.

25th. G. W. Walker wrote to Sydney, to request our

letters still to be forwarded to us here. In some respects, it is trying to us to remain so long in this land, and when way opens, we shall be glad to proceed to New South Wales; but we must wait with patience the will of Him who knoweth the end from the beginning; who hath condescended to lead us about and to instruct us; and whose time is the best time. The little company here, who have been gathered to Friends, is becoming more organized, and is, I trust, deepening in the root of religion: this also appears to be the case with some others.

31st. The week-day meeting was small. It was a season to be remembered with comfort, by those who were brought to wait for the revelation of Jesus, by the Spirit, sent to them of the Father, in order that they might feel his power raised into dominion in themselves, over all the powers of darkness, and know the true Shepherd to put them forth and go before them. Thus such become built up in Him, members of that church of God, against which the gates of hell shall not prevail; whilst all systems that are mixed up with the short-sighted views of human expediency, must ultimately have the unsound mixture rooted out of them, or otherwise they must become disorganized, how much soever they may enlarge their borders for a season.

8th mo. 7th. The propriety of recording my dear Companion as an approved minister, came under the consideration of the Monthly Meeting; and it concluded, under the feeling of unity with his Gospel labours, to take this step, subject to the confirmation of the next Monthly Meeting, to be held at Kelvedon, in Great Swan Port.—A communication was received by the Monthly Meeting, from a young man, who is an assigned prisoner servant in the Colony, desiring to be commended to the notice of Friends. The meeting being interested by his expressions of penitence, recorded its feeling of Christian interest for him, and its wish to hear from him, from time to time, that it might know the state of his religious progress. The following extracts are from a letter from this young man, in reply to one written a few weeks since: " I am thankful to say, that I feel rather more comfortable in my mind than I did when I wrote to you before. Your kind advice respecting the Temperance Society has claimed my close consideration; for I now believe it right, well to consider before I engage in any matter, under a sense, that if I had done that before, I should have been preserved from falling into many snares, amongst which strong drink was one. I may say, it was the first of my going astray: this led me to company, by which it increased on me, together with going to places of amusement; and being under many engagements of this abominable nature, it caused me to neglect my business; so at last, I became a thief, a disgrace to my relatives, my friends, and my country. I have now come to forsake such abominations, through the Lord's assistance, who strictly commands to go 'out from among them, and touch not the unclean things.' Tell the young men at home, how strong drink, and what the world calls pleasure, bring destruction and misery, upon both soul and body: encourage them in a particular manner to strive against such evils." In the same letter he speaks of his parents, in terms of affection, and laments with much bitterness, that he behaved so wickedly towards them, and neglected their pious advice, which, if he had attended to it, would have preserved him from coming into such a state, as that in which he is now placed. He then expresses thankfulness, that the Lord was merciful toward him, both at the hulks, and on his voyage, and that he is so now, in the colony, also that he has a good master and mistress. In speaking of his wish to have some tracts, &c. he says, "A Bible would be a very great treasure to me, for it is very seldom I can get the loan of one." In a former letter he says: "I resigned my membership with Friends, not on any religious point of view, far from it; it was to prevent my vile and evil conduct being discovered." In his last letter, after requesting to be commended to the love and notice of Friends here, he says, "I have a great desire once more to join that Society; for it is the only one that my conscience would allow me to join: their belief and principles I love, and I prize them more now than ever I did; and through the Lord's assistance I shall practise them more than ever I have done. I have been highly favoured, at different times, in silent waiting on the Lord, when seated upon an old, fallen tree, under a rock, at the back of the hill, where the trampling of human feet is seldom heard."

15th. We have regretted of late, to see in some well disposed persons, a disposition to calumniate Friends, and to try to make out that Quakerism is not accordant with the Gospel. The occasion of this has been, that a few persons have adopted the principles of Friends, from a conviction of their more complete accordance with the Gospel, than those of the communities with whom they were before associated. This has also led to the exhibition of a very different spirit toward us, on the part of some persons, from that which we have endeavoured to entertain toward those who conscientiously differed from us; and which we hope ever to be enabled to maintain toward such: it has also sometimes drawn us into discussions, much against our inclination, which have, however, been overruled for good. Inquiry into our principles has been excited, and we have been willing to give an answer in meekness, to those who have sought information respecting them.

On the 22nd we commenced another journey, and proceeded in company with Robert Mather and Francis Cotton, to Lauderdale; where, on the 24th, we held another meeting with the neighbouring inhabitants.

25th. On arriving at the Bluff-ferry, on the Pitt Water, there was no boat-man, we therefore walked along the Seven-mile Beach, to the Lower-ferry, where we had to wade a considerable distance to the boat. I do not remember to have suffered so much before, from the coldness of the water. A heavy surf from the Southern Ocean, breaks upon this beach; upon which a number of remarkable marine animals were cast. One among them, of about a foot in length, belonged to the order of Holothuridæ or Sea Cucumbers. We quartered for the night at the hospitable dwelling of James and E. Gordon.

26th. We pursued our way through the long and dreary Cherry-tree Opening, over the Brushy Plains, the White Marsh, and Burst-my-gall Hill, to Prossers Plains. Here we designed to visit a settler, and turned aside, at the

close of day, along a track leading toward his house. About
two miles on the road, we found it intersected by a new fence,
a common difficulty in a newly settled country; and being unable to find our way further, as it was dark and rainy, we returned three miles, to a little inn. At this place about half-a-
score men were intoxicated, whom we judged, from their
appearance, to be soldiers and assigned prisoner-servants :
they remained drinking and using bad language, till midnight.
In other respects our accommodation was tolerably good for
such a place. There is reason to believe that much drunkenness exists in secluded situations, among prisoners, as well
as among free people, and that the former often pilfer to
obtain the means of paying for liquor.

27th. Being at this time in poor health, my friend
Francis Cotton had mounted me on his mare, it being
necessary that one person should ride, to keep a sack
containing some of his goods, from falling off, as he had no
means o fastening it to the saddle. The road through
Paradise was too rough and precipitous to be pleasant
for riding, and it had the appearance of danger. The
scrub was also difficult to get through, in some places,
and care was necessary, as the way is a mere foot-track,
to avoid being carried against trees, or amongst branches.
However, having the sack to take care of, I rode at a
foot's pace over the whole, except one hill, and the river.
The rocky bed of the latter is slippery, and has narrow
chasms in it, dangerous to the legs of horses. Sometimes I found it necessary to twist one hand into the
mane, and with the other to lay hold upon the sack, to keep
it from slipping off behind. Horses accustomed to this
kind of country, descend the stony hills best, with the bridle
quite slack; taking care of themselves, they take care also
of their riders. On this journey we tried carrying our own
luggage in knapsacks, but did not find it so convenient to
persons unencumbered with guns, as having each a parcel
to carry by a strap in the hand. We reached the habitation
of some kind friends, a little after dark, having had to use
a compass, observe a star, and listen to the direction of the
roaring of the surf, on a neighbouring, sandy beach, to

enable us to keep in the right direction, which, here and there, was not distinguishable by a track.

28th. Early in the afternoon, we reached the dwelling of Thomas Buxton, whose family are noted for their hospitality, and were soon supplied with what was needful for our wants. Leaving my companions to follow on foot, I rode at a gentle pace over the Rocky Hills. We all arrived at Kelvedon in the evening, and were again refreshed together in waiting upon the Lord.

29th. Was occupied in assisting F. Cotton to plant some fruit-trees, and to engraft others. He had brought the trees and scions upon his back, more than eighty miles, to preserve them from injury. Fruit trees are valuable in a newly-settled country. Some of the scions were obtained from the Government Garden at Hobart Town, where there is a valuable collection of fruit-trees, from which scions may be had, on application to the Aide-de-Camp of the Lieut. Governor. The others were from the capital garden of James Gordon, of Pitt-water.

31st. We assembled twice for worship, with F. Cotton's large family, the assigned servants being also present, and were favoured with a sense of divine overshadowing. A portion of Penn's "No Cross no Crown," and a Psalm, were read at the commencement of the opportunity in the evening. The chapter on the use of flattering titles was the one falling in course; and I had some remarks to make on this subject, which possesses more importance than is usually attributed to it. As my understanding has been opened to it, I have had perfect unity with our early Friends, in their testimony against these titles, and also against complimentary forms of speech; and a strong apprehension has rested on my mind, that if Friends should abandon these testimonies, the Lord would soon take them away from being a people. To cherish pride, which is an abomination to the Lord, in others, is diametrically opposed to the principles of the Gospel; and though it is often argued that these things are now so common, that pride is but little, if at all, flattered by them, it requires but a small degree of penetration to perceive that they are very gratifying to unregenerate men;

and that the remains of pride, even in persons of some degree of spirituality, are mortified by the omission of these titles and addresses.

9th mo. 4th. The Monthly Meeting was held at Kelvedon, and the judgment of that held in the 8th month, at Hobart Town, was confirmed, respecting recording my companion, as an approved minister, and sanctioning his proceeding with me in that capacity.

Between the 12th and 17th, we again visited the settlers in the upper part of Great Swan Port, holding several religious meetings among them.

When at Moulting Bay, close to the house of a settler, we counted fifty-six Black Swans, in pairs: their nests had been carried away by floods. This is often the case, and at other times they are extensively robbed of their eggs. One family, at whose house we lodged, had sometimes taken as many as five hundred eggs at a time. Formerly a tribe of Aborigines resorted regularly to this neighbourhood, at this season of the year, to collect swans' eggs.

Happening to take up the Hobart Town Courier, at Belmont, on the 17th, we saw, with much interest and satisfaction, a notice of the safe arrival of our dear friends Daniel and Charles Wheeler, in Hobart Town. They landed from the Henry Freeling, on the 10th inst.; being on a religious visit, to some parts of the Australian Colonies, and to the Islands of the South Seas.—Dr. Ross, the editor of this newspaper, had kindly inserted a special notice of their arrival, hoping that the tidings would reach us through this medium.

On the 22nd, we set out to return to Hobart Town, in company with Francis and Anna Maria Cotton. Several of their children, with Dr. Story, accompanied us a few miles on the way. On the beach, near T. Buxton's, the Doctor and I turned over some flat, basaltic stones, in a pool of salt water, that did not become empty by the recession of the tide, and were gratified with the sight of several species of coralline, alcyonite, sponge, and others of the lower tribes of animals, of curious and singular structure, but of which we had not the means of preserving specimens.

On the beach of Prossers Bay, we saw two beautiful White Cranes; a bluish, lead-coloured species is not uncommon; several species of Duck are also met with in this Colony.

Some parts of our journey to Spring Bay, were very uncomfortable to those on horseback. A slight mistake in regard to a track, occasioned us a trackless journey for several miles. This is a common circumstance in Van Diemens Land, where, except in a very few places, naturally clear, and in the immediate vicinity of settlers' houses, the way is through forests, bounded only by the sea that surrounds the island, and which are full of dead logs, and fragments of the limbs of trees, scattered in all directions; these continually turn travellers from a straight line, except where a path has been cleared. On our way, we had conversation with some prisoner-guides, confirming the belief that there are many of this class, far from being destitute of religious sensibility.

On the 27th, we crossed the Derwent, in a whale-boat, to Hobart Town; where we had a mutually pleasant meeting with our friends D. and C. Wheeler; who, within a few months, had been in company with our dear connexions in England. Although we hear of these frequently by letter, yet there is a satisfaction in hearing of beloved relatives, from the lips of those that have lately seen them, which none can fully understand but by experience.

In reviewing our late journey, and the many blessings, and mercies we have been made partakers of, among which is the improvement of my own health, and now, in having the comfort of meeting our dear friends, we felt that there was great reason for us to adopt the language, "What shall we render to the Lord for all his benefits?"

CHAPTER XIX.

8th mo. 29th. In company with G. W. Walker, F. Cotton, and T. J. Crouch, I walked to Glenorchy, to see old John Johnson, who has been very ill, and is still so feeble that he compares himself to a cracked earthen vessel, bound about to keep it together. He is full of thankfulness for the mercies he receives, often saying, " What am I, a poor bit of dust, that the Lord should regard me ; I, who have lived so long in rebellion against God ? He has had mercy upon me, but I can never forgive myself, nor love him sufficiently. What am I, or what are we all, that the Lord should thus regard us ?"—In his illness, he said, he felt quite willing to die, that he cast himself upon his Saviour, and was quite willing to go. When his pain was excessive, he prayed, that if consistent with the divine will, he might be eased of his pain, and permitted to speak a few words of the Lord's goodness before he was taken away : his prayer was immediately answered, and the violence of his pain assuaged. The old man made many inquiries of us, on the nature of prayer. He said, he had been taught to think his petitions would not be accepted, unless offered upon bended knees ; and that, for four years, he had not

missed a night in getting out of bed to pray, in addition to
praying before going to bed, and on rising; but that he
began to think, it was perhaps unnecessary for him to get
out of bed for this purpose, and that he was nearly unable
to do so. We explained to him, that God is only worshipped in spirit and in truth ; that if the heart be
but bowed before him, he will accept its offerings, whether from persons in bed, or out of bed, on bended knees,
or at their daily occupations ; and whether their petitions
be uttered or unexpressed : that if people be bowed in
reverent stillness of soul, under the sense of the Lord's
presence, though no words may be formed in the mind,
he will still regard and bless them.   The old man said he
was comforted, and saw the matter more clearly than he
had done before, but that when he was first awakened, he was
so ignorant as to think that he must go into " the bush "
to pray, where he could make a great noise.

In the course of a walk, with a serious person, about this
time, he told me, that he thought he had sustained loss, by
regarding the feeling of his own weakness and emptiness, as
a state of desertion, and by trying to turn from it, instead of
regarding it as the teaching of the Holy Spirit, designed to
humble him, and to bring him into a more simple trust in
the Lord, and a closer communion of soul with God.   I
believe this is the case with many, who thus flinch from
humiliating baptisms, and regard them as the withdrawing of
the Lord's Spirit; not recollecting, that the presence and
light of the Holy Spirit, are as necessary to enable us to
behold our own weakness and emptiness, and even our sinfulness, as they are, to give us a perception of the Divine
fulness; nor considering that we can never properly seek
reconciliation with the Father, until we are given to see our
alienation from him by sin; nor come unto Christ, as those
who feel that they need a physician, until we feel our
spiritual diseases; nor can we seek to know the Lord to
be our fulness, till we are made sensible of our own emptiness; nor shall we know him to be our strength, till we be
made sensible of our own weakness.   But, blessed for ever
be his holy name, he is still known, by his dependent chil-

dren, to be riches in poverty, strength in weakness, and a very present help in trouble.

On the 3rd of 10th month, the first Yearly Meeting, of the persons professing with the Society of Friends, in Van Diemens Land, commenced; it was continued by adjournments to the ninth, inclusive. The principal subjects that occupied its attention, were, the reading and recording of the certificates from Friends in England, respecting Daniel and Charles Wheeler, and George W. Walker, and myself; the granting of an additional certificate to G. W. Walker, to authorize his proceeding with me to New South Wales and South Africa, in the character of a minister of the Gospel, (APPENDIX. G.); the making of a record of our labours in V. D. Land; the investigating into the state of the little community professing with Friends in this Colony, and agreeing upon regulations for preserving good order among them; and the addressing of an Epistle to the Meeting for Sufferings, of Friends, in Great Britain, proposing a correspondence with them. The meeting was favoured to be able to adopt the following minute at its termination :—

"In conclusion, we believe it our duty to record, under feelings of reverent thankfulness, that, in the sittings of this our first Yearly Meeting, the sensible presence of the great Head of the Church, has been mercifully felt among us, enabling us to transact the business that has come before us, in much love, and in unity one with another."

On the 25th of 10th month, G. W. Walker and I, went again to New Norfolk, where, on the following day we held two meetings. In one of them a man, who is attached to the principles of Friends, reproved some persons for whispering; and afterwards remarked, that our sitting in silence might appear strange to some, who had not considered the matter, but that, for his own part, he could bear testimony to the benefit of the practice; that before leaving England, he had for some time, attended a little meeting of Friends, in which, often, not a word was spoken; that when these meetings had been held in silence, he had been more edified, as his mind was turned to the light of Christ, than ever he had been under the most learned, studied discourses; and that he was convinced, others would also be thus edified, even in silence, if their minds were turned to the inward manifestation of that light, which is given us, through Jesus Christ.

On returning to Hobart Town, we found Daniel Wheeler very ill, in the influenza, which had been prevalent, and in many cases, fatal.

11th mo. 11th. In company with two young surgeons, I again ascended Mount Wellington, and collected specimens of various plants. Though the summer is advancing, snow fell dry on the top of the mountain, and the cold, with a high wind, was so intense, that I was unable to restore circulation in my hands, by rubbing them with snow: some of my fingers were consequently numb for several days after. Another of our company became violently affected with cramp, from which we all suffered in some degree. Though the snow was insufficient to protect vegetation from the frost, many plants which were in flower, did not seem to be injured by it; yet they cannot endure the continued cold of an English winter.

Insects are now numerous, some species of the remarkable genus *Mantis,* are found in Tasmania; they have obtained the name of the Praying Mantis, from the remarkable posture in which they stand to catch flies, which they eat with great voracity. The species, common at this season, in the gardens here, is of a light pea-green, an inch and a half long, and three-tenths wide in the broadest part of the body, which is covered with wings, an inch long, of an elliptic form, overlaying each other.

Colonel Arthur having invited us to express freely any thing we wished to say connected with the welfare of the Colony, we presented to him on the 15th a paper entitled, "Observations on the Distillation, Importation, and Sale of Ardent Spirits, as sanctioned by the Government." He informed us that he approved of the suggestions contained in this document, but felt a difficulty in regard to acting upon it, on account of the revenue. The state of a Government which depends upon the continuance of the sins of the people for the support of its revenue, is truly an awful state. A copy of this paper is inserted in APPENDIX. H.

Some notice having been taken, in the Sydney papers, of our Report on the state of the penal settlement at Macquarie Harbour, which had been printed among some parliamentary papers on Penal Discipline, the editor of the "Hobart Town Tasmanian" denounced us as Government Spies, and took much pains to bring us into discredit, and the Gospel through us. One of the Launceston papers also followed, in some degree, in the same steps. The "Colonist" and "Courier," of Hobart Town, of their own accord, defended us. We believed it our place not to interfere in this matter, and were preserved in calm dependence upon the Lord, to make our sincerity manifest, if such should be his will; and "the shield of faith" was made effectual to "quench the fiery darts of the wicked."

The Lieutenant Governor having expressed a wish, that we should again visit the Penal Settlement, on Tasmans Peninsula, we took the subject under serious consideration, and came to the conclusion, that it would be right for us to comply with his wish. A whale-boat was provided for us, in which we proceeded, on the 17th of 11th month, to the north-east extremity of Ralphs Bay, and lodged at the house of our friends, the Mathers, at Lauderdale. On the following morning, the men dragged the boat across Ralphs Bay Neck, and rowed us over Frederick Henry Bay. We landed on a small basaltic island, off the Carlton, called Dumpling, or Doughboy Island, which is a favourite name for a small island among sailors; here, in a short time, our boat's crew collected about twelve dozen of the eggs of the Black-backed Gull. This Gull makes no nest, except a slight hollow among the grass, or in the light earth, in which it lays about three eggs, nearly as large as those of a Common Fowl, but more conical, and of a dirty green colour, speckled with irregular, dark spots.

This Island produces a Tree Mallow, *Lavatera plebia*, and the other maritime plants of this part of the world. From hence, we proceeded to the southern extremity of Norfolk Bay, and walked from thence to Port Arthur; where we occupied the house of the Commandant, who was absent during our stay. He had gone to visit the signal stations, and had lost his way in the intricate forest: his life was thus endangered more than once, on similar excursions.

The Settlement was greatly improved since our former visits, but was still incomplete in accommodation, for the separation and instruction of the prisoners, who were now, 887 in number. The association of men of this description, in common day-yards, and sleeping-places, is fraught with much evil, that is very difficult to obviate.

In consequence of the prisoners living on salt meat, and being defectively supplied with vegetables, a large number were suffering from scurvy. Nineteen, who were in the Hospital, chiefly from this disease, presented as appalling a picture of human wretchedness, as I recollect ever to have witnessed.—This defect, on being represented to the Government, was speedily remedied, by the cultivation of more land with vegetables, and an occasional supply of fresh meat.

The general discipline of the Settlement was improved, but we found very little reformation on religious principle; and very few of the educated prisoners showed any disposition to assist in the instruction of the others, in the evening school, which was held twice a week. The few books to which the prisoners had access, were diligently read, but the number of these was small.

The prisoners were employed in ship-building, shoe-making, breaking stones, cutting timber, brick-making, &c. and many of them were working reluctantly, as is always the case where labour is compulsory, and without reward.—A few men, employed in making bread, were locked up in the bakehouse till the bread was delivered to the Commissariat Officer, to prevent pilfering, which is sometimes attempted here, very artfully.

An interesting addition has lately been made to this Settlement, in an establishment for convict boys, on a point of land, now called Point Puer, access from which to the main land is cut off by a military guard. 157 of these boys, formerly kept on board the hulks, on the Thames, are here placed under restraint and coercive labour, as a punishment. By these means, combined with attention to education, they are

acquiring habits, calculated to enable them to maintain themselves honestly.   The restraint is irksome, but upon the
whole, the boys seem pleased with the idea of being put in
the way of obtaining a livelihood.—Considerable difficulty
has been found, as might be expected, in raising the morals
of these juvenile delinquents, from a most degraded state.

On the 21st, attended by a prisoner constable, we returned
to Norfolk Bay, and proceeded to Eagle Hawk Neck, and
from thence down Eagle Hawk Bay, to Woody Island, where,
as well as at many other places, constables are stationed.
From Woody Island, we were rowed to a coal mine, lately
opened, on Sloping Main, a point of Tasmans Peninsula:
we crossed this point to a hut, where we took up our quarters for the night.   Here we read a portion of Scripture, to a
few constables and soldiers, and addressed them on the importance of attending to their eternal interests.

When passing through the forest between Long Bay and
Norfolk Bay, a large Black Snake met us on the path, which
we, of course, left to make way for the snake: it passed us with
its head a little raised, and with an air of boldness that was
rather appalling.   Stout switches being plentiful in the bush,
G. W. Walker immediately cut one, and following the
venomous reptile, despatched it with a single blow.

On the 22nd, we returned to the coal mine, and mustered
the prisoners employed in it; with whom we had a religious
interview, as we had also had, with the different groups at
Port Arthur.   The coal from this place makes hot fires, but
scarcely changes its form in burning: it finds a market in Hobart Town, for about ten shillings a ton.   Only the top seam
has yet been worked.   Access is gained to it by a level, that
is very little above the high water mark.

Having completed our visit, we returned across Frederick Henry Bay, and landed near Lauderdale, where I left
my companion, and proceeded by Clarence Plains and
Kangaroo Point, to Hobart Town, which place I was favoured to reach in safety, thankful in having been privileged
with fine weather, in a deeply interesting excursion, in which
storms would have exposed us to great risk.

Anguillaria uniflora, Anopterus glandulosus, and several

other interesting plants, were in flower, on Tasmans Peninsula, as was also *Thysanotus Patersonii,* on Clarence Plains. The last is a low, twining plant, with fringed, purple blossoms, delightfully fragrant.

On returning to Hobart Town, I had the satisfaction to find my friend Daniel Wheeler restored to health, and proposing soon to depart for Sydney; whither G. W. Walker and myself had, for some time, believed it would be right for us to accompany him and his son.

24th. George W. Walker rejoined me in Hobart Town, where we made up a report, of our visit to Port Arthur, containing the substance of the foregoing remarks, and presented it to the Lieutenant Governor.—Feeling much interested for the prisoners, and for the Catechist who had lately come into office at the Penal Settlement, but who was absent during our visit, I addressed a letter to him, of which an extract is inserted in APPENDIX. I.

30th. Our meetings were largely attended, and were seasons of comfort. D. Wheeler and myself had to inculcate in them, the necessity of a more full submission to the inward dominion of Christ, as the leader and governor of his people; testifying, that, without submission to his Spirit, we can never truly assure ourselves of the pardon of our sins, even through faith in his blood; as he said, " Not every one that saith unto me, Lord, Lord, shall enter the kingdom of heaven; but he that doeth the will of my Father, which is in heaven."

12th mo. 1st. I had a conference with a person respecting the settlement of his affairs, and took some memorandums, from which the draft of his will was prepared, which was read to him, in the company of his wife and sons. It is to be regretted that the Laws of Primogeniture and Entail, which are of prejudicial influence in Great Britain, should be in force in a new Colony like this. Their direct tendency is, to preserve influence in the hands of persons who may have nothing to qualify them to use it aright, and thus to prevent the influence of others, who may have every necessary qualification to benefit the public, but may not be possessed of great property; and this is but a small part of the evil connected with these laws. My attention has long been attracted to their pernicious effect upon the progress of civil and religious improvement in my native land, the prosperity of which lies near to my heart.

4th. We have lately met with several of the Pensioners who came out with us in the Science. Many of them, and of other persons of the lowest class, find difficulty in obtaining employment. Some of the steadier ones are employed as police-constables, at the wage of one shilling and nine pence a day. Several have died, and others have been brought into circumstances of degradation, through intemperance.

10th. We completed the shipment of our luggage, and embarked on board the Henry Freeling, after taking leave of our friends; from many of whom it was a trial to part.

11th. The wind being unfavourable, we went on shore, to meeting. To myself it was a season of poverty, but not without consolation. My work being done here, at least for the present, it has pleased my Heavenly Father to permit me to feel much of my own emptiness, but in something of true stillness, in which I desire to give all glory to the Lord, in the acknowledgment of being an unprofitable servant.—We took tea with Philip Palmer, who was at this time holding the office of Rural Dean, and from whom we had received much kindness. Several other persons were also of the company, among whom was William Marshall, the surgeon of the Alligator, ship-of-war, with whom we had, at various times, much pleasant intercourse. He took no active part in fighting, but laboured diligently to promote the spread of the Gospel of Peace; often reasoning also with the people, on temperance, righteousness and judgment to come. In many respects, we felt much unity of spirit with him, notwithstanding we considered his position on board a ship-of-war, a very doubtful one for a vital Christian.—[This valuable individual lost his life in the Niger expedition, in 1841.]

After this visit we returned on board the Henry Freeling, accompanied by our kind friend T. J. Crouch, who took leave of us at a late hour, when the ketch was preparing for sea.

Q 3

CHAPTER XX.

12th mo. 12th. THE weather was beautifully clear, and the moon was shining brightly, when we came on board the Henry Freeling, last night. The ketch was soon got under weigh, and it was proceeding smoothly down the Derwent when we retired to rest; but we had scarcely cleared Storm Bay, before our gentle breeze increased into a gale. At an early hour we were roused by the rolling of the vessel, on a heavy sea: it frequently washed over the deck, the seams of which had opened under the influence of the dry atmosphere of Tasmania, so that some of us were soon compelled, from the dripping in, of the salt-water, to leave our berths, and take to the sofas.

17th. At sun-set, we were off Cape Howe, the south-east point of New South Wales: the cape and adjacent coast were faintly visible. The sea had been rough much of the time since we left Hobart Town. The roll of the vessel was so great after rounding Cape Pillar, as to make some of the oldest sailors on board, sick. Birds have been numerous, and we have seen a few whales.

18th. The weather was fine in the forenoon. In the course

of the day we passed Montagu Island, Mount Dromedary, and Point Dromedary.—In perusing the Journal of the visit of my friends, John and Martha Yeardley, in Greece, &c. I was led to admire the goodness of the Lord, in preparing instruments for the particular fields of labour, into which he calls them. Thus, these dear friends have been prepared for service among the dense population of an old continent; our dear Daniel and Charles Wheeler for a course of voyaging among the islands of the Pacific; and G. W. Walker and myself, as a sort of pioneers, in the bush of Tasmania. Each party would, I suppose, have found the path of the other more trying than the one in which himself was sent; the diversified gifts of each have been adapted by the Lord of all, to the respective services in which he has required them to be exercised.

19th. The forenoon was beautifully fine. We dried our wet bedding in the sun, and got a leak in the deck stopped. Shoals of small fish were frequently passing, and numbers of larger ones, rising out of the water among them, probably, taking the small ones as their prey. A few Albatrosses and Mutton-birds were swimming on the smooth surface of the sea. In the afternoon, we had thunder, lightning, rain, and a brisk wind. The evening was wet and dark, and the current had carried us so close in shore, that when near Cape George, at the entrance to Jervis Bay, it was discovered, by some lights of the natives on the land, that a few minutes' continuance in the same course, would have run us upon the rocky coast. Alarm was excited among the seamen, and I do not doubt but our situation was a perilous one; yet on turning my mind to the Lord, as I continued writing, I felt a peaceful calm, and sufficient evidence to satisfy me, that no harm should befall us.— Blessed for ever be the name of the Shepherd of Israel, who neither slumbereth nor sleepeth, but who, at times, permits us to see danger, under such circumstances, as that we may know that it is he who delivereth us. The vessel was got round in time to clear the inhospitable shore, and we proceeded in safety on our voyage.

20th. We passed Botany Bay this morning, and about

noon, entered Port Jackson. The coast of this part of New South Wales, is bold, and in many places, perpendicular. The cliffs, which are of sand-stone, are interrupted by small sandy bays. Port Jackson is a considerable estuary. The entrance, with the Henry Freeling, is represented in the annexed etching, from a sketch by my friend Charles Wheeler. A light-house marks the South Head, which is about a mile from the North Head. The estuary branches into numerous bays; some of which have sandy beaches, others are very rugged, as are also some of the low hills behind them. The hills, in many places, are covered with Gum-trees and different species of Banksia, and other trees and shrubs, such as are peculiar to this part of the world. Some of the more even places have been cleared, and have houses erected upon them. A few of these are of imposing appearance.—A pilot boarded us at the Heads, and brought us safely to anchor in Sydney Cove. Thus, through the mercy of him whose providential care is over us, we are at the end of another voyage, and advanced another step on our way.

After dinner, I went on shore with George W. Walker. We called on Joseph Orton, the superintendent of the Wesleyan Mission, in these parts, for whom we had despatches from Hobart Town, and after spending an hour pleasantly with him, returned on board the Henry Freeling. In point of building, Sydney strikes us as being more like a large English town, than Hobart Town. Many of the houses are in contact: the shops are quite English. In general appearance, the buildings are like those of towns within thirty miles of London. In the court-yards and the gardens of the more retired streets, Peach, Orange, and Loquat trees, Grape-vines, and many singular and beautiful shrubs are growing luxuriantly; here and there, towering Norfolk Island Pines also mark the difference from the climate of England. White Mulberry forms a common screen round the gardens, and a small tree, called here White Cedar, *Melia Azederach*, is often planted between the houses and the outer fence of the premises. In our walk, we saw no person that we knew. We are again strangers, in a strange land.

21st. We remained on board, and twice assembled with
the crew, for what might more properly be called religious
instruction than public worship. After a solemn pause, a
portion of Holy Scripture was read; another pause ensued,
then a few Psalms were read, after which a considerable
time was spent in silence. In the morning the silence was
broken also, by the ministerial labours of George W. Walker
and myself.   In assembling with the crew of the vessel,
who have not been brought to the same views with Friends,
and few of them to clear religious principles, our friends
Daniel and Charles Wheeler have adopted the practice of
spending a portion of time in reading the Scriptures, as we
have done on like occasions.

22nd. We received a friendly call from John Saunders,
the Baptist minister, and made acquaintance with a few
persons attached on principle to the Society of Friends.

23rd. We called at the Government House, and entered
our names for an audience with General Bourke, who at
this season of the year, resides at Parramatta. We also
waited on Alexander Mc. Leay, the Colonial Secretary, and
on Thomas C. Harington, the Under Secretary, to each of
whom we had letters of introduction, and by whom we were
politely received.—From these individuals and their family
connexions, we received unvarying kindness during our
sojourn in this Colony.

After dinner we crossed to the north shore of Port Jackson, and had a walk in the bush. Though Gum-trees and
Acacias are prominent productions of the vegetable kingdom
here, as well as in Tasmania, yet there is so great a variety
of other trees and shrubs, not found in that island, as to
give this country a different aspect, in many places. Insects
are more numerous here than in V. D. Land. The *Tetti-
gonicæ*, here called Locusts, of which there are several
species, keep up a constant rattle, like that of a cotton-mill,
both in the town and out of it. They are generally stationed
on the upper portion of the trunks of trees, or on the larger
branches: some of the kinds attain to four inches in length.
Moschettos are abundant, and are very annoying to some
persons. On returning, we passed a family of Aborigines,

sitting round a small fire: two women had blankets thrown around them, and one of them had a dirty piece of flannel about her neck: she said she had been very ill. They had three children, that seemed from five to eight years old; one of which, at least, was a half-caste. They had also several dogs and a cat. Some men belonging to them were fishing; and three fish were lying near their fire. They said, one of the men had gone to the town to buy bread, but they were afraid he would spend the money in drink. In features an old woman reminded us of some of the least personable of our acquaintance among the Tasmanian Aborigines: a younger woman was of less forbidding aspect; and the childrn were of fine lively countenance, and by no means of unpleasant features. They spoke English tolerably, and gladly accepted a few pence to buy bread. Their whole appearance was degraded and very forlorn.

imposing his own agenda?

The Sandstone rocks on the shores of Port Jackson, are covered with Rock Oysters: these are of small size, and have undulating shells; one of which is convex and fixed to the rock. The upper shell is nearly flat, and is easily struck off by means of a horizontal blow. The fish is of good flavour, and is sold in Sydney, clear of the shell, at 6d. a pint. The Aborigines had been eating Rock Oysters, and another shell-fish that resembled a Cockle.

24th. The evening was illuminated by lightning; in the town, the air, after sunset, was perfumed by the blossoms of *Brugmansia suaveolens*, a large South American shrub, cultivated in almost every garden, and bearing pendulous, whitish, trumpet-shaped blossoms, seven inches in length.

27th. Daniel and Charles Wheeler, and George W. Walker, and myself, proceeded to the office of the Colonial Secretary, who accompanied us to the Government-house, and introduced us to Major General Richard Bourke, the Governor, by whom we were courteously received. Daniel Wheeler presented his certificate, from the Morning Meeting of Ministers and Elders of the Society of Friends, in London, and a letter from the Secretary for the Colonies. The Governor alluded to some interviews I had had with him in London, in 1831, when he read my certificates, from our own religious

society. I now presented a letter to him from Viscount Goderich, recommending G. W. Walker and myself, and the object
of our visit to these Colonies, to his notice; also a letter from
Colonel Arthur, written with a view to forward our desire to
visit Norfolk Island, and to attend to similar services in this
Colony generally; and one from Joseph Massey Harvey, of
which the Governor was furnished with a copy, by the writer,
when in Ireland. On my expressing a desire to be permitted
to fulfil an apprehended duty, in visiting the Penal Settlement on Norfolk Island, in company with G. W. Walker,
the Governor informed us, that care was exercised to prevent persons, under ordinary circumstances, from landing
there, but he readily consented to our going thither, under
an apprehension of religious duty; and to our being put on
shore there by the Henry Freeling, on her way to Tahiti,
and being left to be brought back by a Government vessel.
Thus, through the over-ruling of the Most High, another
important object was put in train to be accomplished, by our
friends coming out in the Henry Freeling, in this direction,
and, for the accomplishment of which, way opened in such
a manner, as to afford to my own mind satisfactory evidence
that the means for its accomplishment, as well as the sense
of duty with respect to the visit, were of the Lord.

28th. We assembled twice on deck, for public worship,
having "rigged a chapel," by putting up the awning, and
fixing a number of the colours along the sides and ends.
A small congregation, consisting of persons somewhat connected with the Society of Friends assembled with our ship's
company. A considerable time was spent in solemn silence,
in which there was a sense of the presence of the Lord;
whose presence gives life and consolation to those who wait
upon him in sincerity and in truth, and to whose goodness
and mercy both Daniel Wheeler and myself bore testimony
on these occasions.

30th. The forenoon was occupied in conversation with
Samuel Marsden, the intelligent, aged, episcopal clergyman,
of Parramatta; whose heart has long been open to encourage,
the improvement and civilization of this part of the world,
and especially the introduction of Christianity among the

inhabitants of the isles of the Pacific. He dined with us, and gave us much interesting information respecting his visits to New Zealand, &c.

1st mo. 1st. 1835. Our week-day meeting was held on board. Several persons attended it. Daniel Wheeler alluded to the commencement of the new year, and exhorted us to examine what progress we had made toward the kingdom of heaven, since we first believed. It was a season of comfort under a sense of the pardoning and sanctifying mercy of the Most High.

We took a walk near the town in the evening. Many beautiful native shrubs are in flower : among them are *Lambertia formosa, Grevillea buxifolia* and *sericia, Epacris grandiflora,* &c. which grow in heathy soil, on the bushy ground, covering the sandstone.

3rd. The early part of the day was calm : the thermometer rose to 100° in the shade. About two o'clock the wind arose, with violence, from the south east, and the thermometer fell to 70°. It rained in the evening. This kind of wind has occurred a few times before, since our arrival : it is frequent in the summer, and coming upon the town from the direction of some old brick-fields, has obtained the name of a Brick-fielder. It brings small pebbles pelting like rain, and clouds of red dust, formed, not however, entirely from the brick-fields, but also from the reddish sand and soil in the neighbourhood. This dust penetrates the houses, in spite of closed doors and windows, till it is seen upon everything, and may be felt grating between the teeth.

4th. A meeting was held in our cabin, this morning : it was a season preciously owned of the Lord; the influence of whose Spirit brought us into the feeling of solemn reverence. The like blessing was also showered down upon us, even more abundantly, at the first meeting of Friends held on land, in N. S. Wales, at John Tawell's, at six o'clock this evening. Twenty-two persons were present. On both occasions I was engaged in testimony and prayer; in the evening, Daniel Wheeler spoke also in testimony, and at the close of the meeting exhorted us to endeavour to keep close to the sense of the divine presence, which had been so mercifully granted us, through Jesus Christ our Lord.

5th. In the evening, we were present at a public meeting of the Temperance Society, in a large school-room, formerly used as a court-house. It was numerously attended, and many respectable females were of the company. Richard Jones, one of the vice-presidents, was in the chair; and Richard Hill was secretary. Some resolutions, which time did not admit of being brought forward at a former meeting, were now proposed, and carried: and the meeting was addressed by William P. Crook, Dr. Laing, John Saunders, William Jarratt, George W. Walker, myself, and a number of persons, whose names I do not recollect. I have no doubt but the cause of temperance was promoted. This was the first meeting of the kind at which D. and C. Wheeler were ever present, their residence having long been in Russia. They were agreeably interested. They, with G. W. Walker and myself, were kindly and publicly welcomed to the Colony at this meeting.

6th. Having been prevented taking exercise for some days, we went on shore, in the evening, on the north side of Port Jackson, and collected a few specimens of plants and insects: some of the latter, as well as many of the former, are very beautiful, and all display the power and wisdom of the Creator. The more the works of creation are understood, the more the evidence of infinite wisdom and power in the Creator is seen. If it were designed that the display of these, in every part of creation, should be among the incitements to adoration and praise, in the mind of man, how greatly is his fallen state exhibited in this connexion! Instead of being able to name them according to their qualities, as Adam was, before the fall, most persons pass them unheeded by; many are disgusted at the properties which render them fit for the places they are designed to fill; and among those who study them, too many make them their idols, instead of giving God the glory.

11th. Having obtained leave to hold a meeting for public worship with the Inhabitants of Sydney, in the Old Court House, and extended an invitation to them, a congregation of from four to five hundred people assembled with us. Among them were several persons of influence. It was a season to be remembered with gratitude to Almighty God; who strengthened Daniel Wheeler and myself to preach Jesus Christ, and him crucified, and to direct our auditors to the teaching of the Holy Spirit, manifested as the light and grace of Christ, in the secret of the heart; and leading to repentance and to faith in him, and to a humble dependence upon God for ability to work righteousness.

13th. The Governor having invited Daniel Wheeler and myself to visit him at Parramatta, the Private Secretary came on board the Henry Freeling, yesterday, and made arrangements for conveying us thither. This morning a government-boat took us up to Parramatta, which is distant, by water, fifteen miles, up the estuary of Port Jackson; which for the greater part of the way, runs into bays on both sides. For about half the distance from Sydney, the bays are formed by woody hills of low elevation, running into rocky, sand-stone points. Toward Parramatta, the shores are low and muddy, and the contiguous lands cleared and cultivated. Houses are interspersed at moderate distances; some of them are inhabited by prosperous settlers, and have the aspect of those of English gentlemen. Many of the gardens are well stocked with Peach, Orange, Mulberry, Fig, and Loquat-trees, and Grape-vines. The grass lands are green from the abundance of *Cynodon dactylon*, a grass that resists the drought more than most other kinds. It not only abounds in pastures in this country, but takes the place occupied by *Poa annua* in England, at the roots of walls, by the sides of foot-paths, &c.

Conversation on various subjects passed at the Government House, in the course of the afternoon and evening, and among them, on lunatic asylums. The Governor remarked that an institution of this kind was greatly wanted in N. S. Wales, and seemed pleased with a proposition to supply him with the "Sketch of the Retreat," and "Hints on the Construction, &c. of Pauper Lunatic Asylums;" with which I afterwards furnished him. Tea was introduced at eight o'clock, and after it, cards, with which some of the company amused themselves. One who declined joining them, said he had not played for so long, that he had forgotten how, and that his recollections of card-playing were painful. On behalf of Daniel Wheeler and myself, I stated the objections of the Society of Friends to the practice, on account of its dissipating effect upon the mind, and its tendency to draw into an immoral risking of property. This elicited the remark, that the present company only played for nominal stakes. The same objection, however, lies against playing for nominal stakes in gaming, as that which lies against what is called moderate drinking, in the use of intoxicating liquors. It gives a sanction to the practice, and opens the door for the greatest excesses. Where money is risked in gaming, to take it one from another on such a ground, seems to me, not only objectionable for the reasons already stated, but as a breach of that consideration one for another, which is an essential ingredient in true politeness. And I have remarked, that the inconsistency of the characteristics of card-playing, forces itself so quickly upon the minds of persons, on their coming decidedly under religious conviction, that they soon discontinue the practice.

14th. On returning from Parramatta, a large Black Snake crossed the road close before the carriage; it alarmed the horses, so as to make them start to one side, and become difficult to manage.

15th. We walked to Elizabeth Bay, and met the Colonial Secretary, at his beautiful garden, which is formed on a rocky slope, on the margin of Port Jackson, of which it commands a fine view.—Here are cultivated, specimens of many of the interesting trees and shrubs, of this Colony, along with others from various parts of the world, intermixed with some growing in their native localities. Among the last, is a fine old Rusty-leaved Fig-tree, *Ficus ferruginea*, which is an evergreen, and has laurel-like leaves. A noble specimen of *Acrosticum grande*, a fern of very remarkable structure, from Moreton Bay, is attached to a log of wood, and secured by a chain to a limb of this Fig-tree. The walks at this place are judiciously accommodated to the inequalities of the sinuous bay, and are continued round a point covered with native bush. Peaches are ripe in the open ground in abundance, and liberty to partake of them freely, was kindly given, by the open-hearted proprietor.—*Dendrobium speciosum* and *linguiforme,* remarkable plants of the Orchis tribe, are wild here, upon the rocks, and *D. tetragonum* is naturalized on a branch of *Avicennia tomentosa,* covered with Rock-oyster shells, and suspended in a tree near the shore. A fine patch of the Elks-horn Fern, *Acrosticum alcicorne,* retains its native station on a rocky point in the garden.

18th. Our meetings to-day were seasons of renewed favour and mercy. Several persons were present in the morning, who had not before met with us: at the conclusion of that in the evening, D. Wheeler alluded to the sense of divine influence that had prevailed over us, until it might rightly be said, "The Lord God omnipotent reigneth."

19th. A meeting was held for the organization of an Australian School Society, auxiliary to the British and Foreign School Society. Some opposition was exhibited, but ultimately this was overruled, and measures were adopted for carrying the object into effect.

20th. In the evening, we went to the north shore, and again fell in with a group of the Aborigines, that we met with there a few days since. They were now sitting around a fire and smoking, not excepting a little, naked boy, about two years old, who seemed as busy with his short pipe as any of the company. They often obtain in Sydney, the washings of rum-casks, which they call " Bull," and get intoxicated with it. In this state they quarrel among themselves, notwithstanding they are very peaceable toward the white population.—A group of these people, as they are seen, degraded by contact with a population of European extraction, is represented in the accompanying etching from the pencil of Charles Wheeler.

27th. At the request of the Governor, we waited upon him, and he kindly desired to be informed, if he could do anything further to assist us in our anticipated voyages.—In the afternoon we joined a company of pious persons, of various denominations, at the house of George

Allen, a short distance from Sydney. Conversation took place, on the views and practices which distinguish the Society of Friends. These we had in some measure to exemplify, in a religious opportunity, which commenced with the reading of the first epistle to the Thessalonians. I made some comments on this occasion, upon the text, "Pray without ceasing;" shewing, that the fulfilment of this injunction, depended upon a close attention to the teaching of the Holy Spirit, by which we are made quick of understanding in the fear of the Lord; and are enabled to discern our wants, so as continually to breathe our petitions in secret, to our Father who seeth in secret. Daniel Wheeler was also engaged in the same line of service.

In an evening walk, on the North Shore, we saw a large, old, bushy Fig-tree, *Ficus ferruginea*, overhanging the water; some of its limbs were almost covered with *Acrosticum alcicorne* and *Dendrobium linguiforme*. A broad-leaved *Loranthus*, a parasite of the same tribe as the Mistletoe, but with much finer blossoms, was growing upon some of the branches. Plants of this genus are of frequent occurrence in this Colony. Some of them incorporate themselves with the wood of the foster tree, and others adhere to the bark by an external root.

2nd mo. 1st. We held our meeting, in the forenoon, on board the Henry Freeling. It was attended by most of the persons who generally assemble with us. Silence was only interrupted by a few words, near the conclusion, expressed by myself, on the doctrine of Christian love, as set forth by our Saviour and the apostle John, and a short addition on the same subject by Daniel Wheeler.

In the evening, we had a large meeting in the Old Court-house, the use of which was granted us for the purpose. It was an exercise of faith, to invite people to such a meeting, under an apprehension of religious duty. But I was enabled to believe, that whether it should be best for us to set an example of waiting on God in silence, or to speak in his holy name, qualification would be given at the time; and in this confidence, to fulfil the injunction, "Cast thy burden upon the Lord, and he shall

R

sustain thee." I was preserved in great mental quietude, through almost half the meeting, though feeling much of a blank in mind, except as regarded this sense of dependence. When, at length, the passage, "Why do the disciples of John and of the Pharisees fast, but thy disciples fast not?" was presented to my view, with an apprehension that it was my duty to express it.—I saw but little of the scope of these subjects, to what opened, as I gave utterance to them, and by which I was enabled to preach the new birth, Christ crucified, &c. Daniel Wheeler added a few sentences in the same strain. After I had given utterance also to prayer, on bended knees, the meeting separated. We felt thankful to Him who continues to be, to his dependent children, a present help in time of need, and who qualifies them for the labour to which he calls them, in such a manner as to prove, both to themselves and to others, that all the glory belongs unto Himself, and to Himself alone.

On returning to the Henry Freeling, the water was beautifully luminous, wherever it was agitated. This is often the case in calm nights. A train, like the tail of a comet, followed the boat; and each oar, as it dipped, became surrounded by a luminous patch, which became fainter for some time after the oar left the water, and at length died away. Sometimes brilliant shining points adhere to the oars, which may possibly be phosphorescent animalcules. The light, in the wake of the boat, and on the dip of the oars, is also probably occasioned by this race of minute, animated beings, or by phosphorescent matter disengaged from the water; and which may be formed by decomposing animal and vegetable substances.

4th. I had some conversation with Samuel Marsden, and with the Colonial Secretary, on the case of a New Zealander, who was on board the Henry Freeling a few days ago; he, and his wife and child, were brought away from their own country, as hostages, by a house in Sydney, that has a whaling establishment on that part of the coast of New Zealand, to which these people belong, and of which, this man is said to be a chief. The lives of the persons employed by this house were thought to be in danger, and this

expedient was adopted for their protection.   There is reason
to believe, it was with the consent of the man and his countrymen, that he and his wife became hostages, but they seem to
have had no idea of being so long detained.   The chief com-
plains of the detention, and says, that, if an Englishman had
been detained in like manner in his country, a man-of-war
would have been sent to demand him.   It is an important
question, how far it is proper to allow of acts of this character, and one which merits the consideration of the British
Legislature.—In the evening George W. Walker and myself
attended the committee of the Temperance Society.   About
a dozen persons were present.   The cause of temperance appears to be gaining ground.

   5th.   We had a visit from a young physician, who was
prevailed upon to join a ship at Liverpool, as the medical
officer, with the understanding, that for his passage out, he
was only expected to attend to the state of the crew ; and
that if his services were required by the passengers, they
would pay him on their own private account.   But he afterwards found, that the contract of the owners with the passengers, included medical attendance ; and of this, the owners
took care to apprize him, when the ship was on the point of
sailing.   Thus they availed themselves of his services for the
whole ship's company, when he was unable to make a stand
against their imposition.—This is the second instance we
have met with, of medical men being imposed upon, in connexion with voyages to these colonies.   In the other case,
the surgeon was invited to see the ship, when at Gravesend,
and to sleep on board, and in the morning he found himself
at sea!

   Having believed it would be right for us, before proceeding
to Norfolk Island, to hold a meeting with such of the crews
of the numerous vessels, now lying in Port Jackson, as could
be collected, application was made to John Hart, the master
of the Henry Porcher, for the use of the deck of his vessel,
for this purpose.   This was readily granted, and arrangements were made accordingly.

   8th.   Notice of our intended meeting having been given
on board all the ships, in the port, about a hundred and fifty

persons, chiefly masters of vessels and officers, assembled on board the Henry Porcher, this morning. It was a season in which Divine Mercy brought us under solemn feeling, and gave ability to preach the Gospel freely, without any compromise of principle, to the practices of men. When constrained by the love of Christ, to preach, it is a favour to be enabled to preach the Gospel fully, both with regard to faith and practice, even when we ourselves may feel, that we have not attained to the full measure of that which the Gospel requires; a feeling that ought to prompt to an increase of diligence, in making our calling and election sure. After the meeting, we distributed a number of tracts, confining ourselves, on this occasion, to those published by Friends, and those of the Temperance Society.—At our meeting on shore, in the evening, a long time of silence, preceded a lively testimony from Daniel Wheeler; I also addressed the company, and afterwards gave utterance to prayer, in the prospect of departing for a season from this land.

CHAPTER XXI.

Arrangements for visiting Norfolk Island.—Departure.—Adverse Winds.—Shark and Pilot-fish.—Seamen.—Spiritual Navigation.—Jelly-fish.—"The Elizabeth" Whaler.—Tropic Bird.—Norfolk Island.—Departure of D. and C. Wheeler.—Orange Vale.—Oak.—Geology.—Features of the Island.—Norfolk Island Pine and Tree-fern.—Fruits.—Description of Prisoners.—Assemblies for Worship.—Jail.

2nd mo. 12th. At the request of the Governor, we again waited upon him, to receive further instructions respecting our visit to Norfolk Island; and, by his order, the Colonial Secretary furnished us with the documents needful to secure us a reception, addressed to the Commandant. In order to be ready for sailing, the Henry Freeling was yesterday removed from her mooring, into the stream, where she lay close by the Government schooner, Isabella, also bound for Norfolk Island, with soldiers and prisoners. In the evening we took leave of our friends in the town, and returned on board the little vessel, which had been our dwelling-place during our sojourn, at this time, in N. S. Wales.

13th. The Isabella sailed early in the morning; and we took a pilot on board, who brought us to the Heads of Port Jackson, by noon. We had not been long at sea before we all fell sick. Though the distance to Norfolk Island is only about a thousand miles, this voyage occupied nineteen days. Adverse winds drove us far eastward, toward New Zealand, and we were much delayed by calms.

17th. Being pretty well recovered, we were able to read, and to take exercise on deck. A Shark, about seven feet long, followed at our stern, most of the day. It had been attracted by the offal of a sheep that was killed in the morning. Having had its hunger appeased, it could not be tempted to take a nice piece of pork that concealed a large hook. Two little Pilot-fish were swimming fearlessly before the nose of this rapacious animal, and three larger ones in advance of the bow of the vessel, often almost in contact with it; but they darted nimbly forward, so as always to avoid a blow. To have the precedence of something larger than themselves, seems a pleasure to them; but I could not discover their inducement.

21st. We have lately spent a little time in reading, notwithstanding the motion of the vessel renders the head incapable of bearing much effort at one time, either in this exercise, or in writing.—It is pleasant to see the seamen instructing one another in nautical observations and calculations. The carpenter is a good navigator; he became awakened to the importance of eternal things on his voyage from England; since he became a steady man, he has taken pleasure in instructing the other sailors, who are improving in knowledge and conduct. On board the Henry Freeling, there is a happy exemption from the foolish mystery that prevails on board many other ships, respecting the course of the vessel, by which the sailors are kept in ignorance, to no good purpose.

22nd. We assembled twice on deck, with the crew. Some portions of Holy Scripture were read, and a considerable time was spent in silence. In the morning, I spoke to the seamen on the importance of having the attention constantly alive to the pointings of the Spirit, and on the necessity of daily, close self-examination, in order to maintain a steady course heavenward; illustrating these subjects, by comparing them with the necessity of attention to the compass, in steering the vessel, and with making daily observations of the sun's altitude, &c. by means of nautical instruments, to ascertain the exact place to which the vessel had attained in her course.

25th. The wind has generally been adverse, since we left Sydney; to-day it is light, and the swell is high from the opposite direction. A shoal of Black-fish passed us this morning. A Dolphin threw itself out of the water several times at our bow, being probably in pursuit of small fish.

It resembles a Pike in figure, much more than the strange-looking thing that is represented on signs in England. Sometimes, however, it gives itself remarkable twists, when playing on the water. Its colour is brilliant blue, and gold bronze, on the back, and silvery, underneath. Jelly-fish were very numerous; sometimes the sea seemed almost full of them.

 The most common species, represented at Figure 1, consisted of from five to fourteen transparent tubes, about three inches in length, and one inch in diameter, united laterally, so as to form a truncated cone, of about twelve inches in circumference. These tubes had angular openings at their upper extremities: the lower ends were closed by membranes, that the animal drew in and projected at pleasure, and which, in connexion with the alternate expansion and contraction of the tubes, served to take in and eject water. By this means the animal was also propelled along in the ocean. In the upper part of each tube, there was a brown, horse-shoe-shaped line, under which a small, white body was situated as in Fig. 4. A smaller conical body was enclosed within the circle of the external tubes. The complete tubes ultimately become separated, and are to be met with swimming about separately, without any apparent diminution of vital power. In these, the coloured line was perfectly straight. Fine, transverse striæ were visible in some portions of the tubes. At night, numerous animals of another species, of this tribe, represented at Fig. 2, were floating about the vessel, and emitting a brilliant light.

These were conical tubes, open at one end, without any intersecting membrane, transparent, colourless, or slightly green or brown, five to seven inches long, and an inch wide, covered with small tubercles, among which were short, thick, transparent, hooked protuberances, pointing upward. The light emitted, was visible from a considerable depth below the

surface of the ocean, but it was more brilliantly phosphorescent when the animals were on the surface. When
taken out of the water, these animals, which have a slight
motion, continued to emit light, for a short time, and
then shone only at intervals, particularly on being irritated by rubbing. The shining re-commences at the part
rubbed, and soon spreads over the whole animal. There
were also other molluscous bodies taken out of the sea,
emitting light, like brilliant sparks, but they were so minute,
that I could not trace any distinct form.

Another Jelly-fish resembled the cap of a mushroom,
about two inches in diameter. It was entirely colourless,
but was marked by about thirty short, worm-like tentaculæ,
attached, a little above the margin, alternately with patches
of a few fine lines. It had also a bundle of colourless fibres
in the centre, internally. This animal is represented in
Figure 3.

3

The wood-cuts of this curious race of
animals, interspersed in this volume, will
give the reader a good general idea of
some of their remarkable forms.

27th. We spoke the Elizabeth, of
Sydney, a whaler, that had been out eight
months, and had got twelve hundred
barrels of oil. Some potatoes and onions were exchanged
for oil, for our lamps. The people seemed glad to obtain
fresh vegetables, and they accepted a few tracts gratefully.

4

28th. More Jelly-fish were examined.
One was somewhat similar to those noticed yesterday, see Fig. 4, though of only
five tubes, but it also formed a truncated
cone of a perfect form. The tubes were
open at the base, and the animal propelled
itself by the force of the water expelled from them. Another
species represented at Figure 5, consisted of about twenty
associated, inflated, transparent tubes, an inch in length, and
a quarter of an inch in diameter, slightly attached side
by side, in a line, with about every third standing out
of the line, or, the whole mass was joined together so

as to form a compact body. Each of these tubes had a red, forked line, extending from the open end to the base, intersecting the tube diagonally, and terminating at the lower end, by a deep-red, spherical body, not larger than a pin's head. The opposite end of the tube was opened or closed, by two transparent, projecting lips. The whole animal seemed little more than a delicate, gelatinous membrane.

We observed animals of this tribe, in the 2nd mo. 1832, off Port Davey; some of which resembled the single tubes of the last, but were several inches in length and breadth; others were concave, pellucid bodies, tinged with pink or crimson, and having fringed margins. In the 5th mo. of the same year, myriads of pellucid bodies were swimming just below the surface of the sea, off the Mew-Stone, of V. D. Land: they were about the size of horse-beans: most of them were oval, and resembled beads of cut glass: others were round and encircled by small oval excavations. Whales are said to feed on these. In the Tamar, in the 12th mo. 1833, the Jelly-fish, Fig. 6, was numerous. It had a mushroom-like cap; the

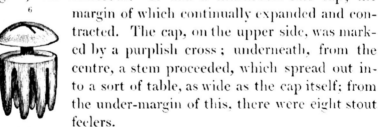

margin of which continually expanded and contracted. The cap, on the upper side, was marked by a purplish cross; underneath, from the centre, a stem proceeded, which spread out into a sort of table, as wide as the cap itself; from the under-margin of this, there were eight stout feelers.

Animals of this tribe seem little more than organized water, yet in the beauty of their structure, as seen in their native element, they exhibit the inimitable skill of their great Creator, and surely ought, with the rest of his wonderous works, to incite to his praise.

3rd mo. 4th. Yesterday and to-day, many Tropic Birds

were flying about; they are called Boatswains, by seamen, from a fancied resemblance of the two long feathers of the tail, to a marline-spike, an implement used on ship-board, in splicing ropes, and kept with others, under charge of the boatswain. These birds, with Gannets and Terns, indicated the proximity of land; and early in the morning, Phillip Island, which is high land, with a bold peak to the south, was in view; and close beyond it, the lower hills of Norfolk Island, clothed with lofty pines, towering like spires, and giving it a very remarkable appearance. Nepean Island, which is small, and very sterile, lies between these islands. Two government vessels, the Governor Phillip, and the Isabella, were standing to and fro, off these islands, none of which have harbours. The sea was breaking heavily on a low reef, fronting the little bay, on which the settlement on Norfolk Island is situated. The commander of the Governor Phillip came along-side, and gave us some instructions; he kindly presented Daniel Wheeler with some Trumpeter-fish which are much esteemed. The Commander of the Isabella also came on board, and with him, an officer, who brought us a letter from Major Anderson, the Commandant. We took a hasty leave of our dear friends, D. and C. Wheeler, and their ship's company, and went on shore. In passing through a narrow opening in a reef that fronts the island, a surf caught the boat, and threw its bow on the rocks; but we quickly got into deep water again. Being delivered from the momentary danger, by the merciful providence of our Heavenly Father, we soon stood again on dry land, thankful for our preservation. On landing on Norfolk Island, we received a very kind welcome from the Commandant, who ordered a boat off to bring our luggage on shore immediately; but the surf became too heavy to allow the boat to proceed. Having taken a very hasty leave of our dear friends, we wrote a parting letter to them, to go by a boat that was to convey to them, a few refreshments from Major Anderson, and to bring our luggage on shore, in the morning.

5th. By the return of the boat, at an early hour, we welcomed a feeling reply to our parting letter, from our dear

companions. They soon made sail, and before noon the Henry Freeling was out of sight, on her voyage for Tahiti, &c. In the afternoon, we accompanied the wife of Major Anderson, and some other persons, to the Commandant's garden, which is situated in a beautiful hollow, called Orange Vale. The Commandant joined us, at four o'clock, at dinner, under a spreading English Oak, that must have been planted at the earliest settlement of the Island, about fifty years ago, as it is as large as an oak would ordinarily be, in a century, in England.

Norfolk Island is about seven miles long and four broad. A small portion of its southern side, is limestone; to the east of this there is a still smaller portion, of coarse, silicious sandstone. The remainder of the island is basaltic, and rises into hills, covered with grass and forest. The highest hill is Mount Pitt, which is on the north side of the island, and about 1,200 feet above the level of the sea. The upper portions of the vallies, and the higher parts of the hills, are covered with wood. The Norfolk Island Pine, *Altingia excelsa*, towers a hundred feet above the rest of the forest; it also grows in clumps, and singly, on the grassy parts of the island, to the very verge, where its roots are washed by the sea, in high tides. In figure, this tree resembles the Norway Spruce, but the tiers of its branches are more distant. Its appearance is remarkably different, in its native soil, from what it is in the fine collection of trees, at Kew; where it nevertheless exhibits many of its striking and beautiful features. Where the wood of Norfolk Island, merges into open grassy valley, a remarkable tree-fern, *Alsophila excelsa*, exhibits its rich crests, among the surrounding verdure. The fronds are from seven to twelve feet long; they resemble those of *Aspidium Filix mas*, and are produced in such a quantity, as to make this noble fern excel the princely palm-tree, in beauty. It usually has its root near the course of some rain-stream, but as its trunk rises to fifty feet in height, and its top does not affect the shade, like many of its congeners, it forms a striking object in the landscape.

Much of the land was formerly cultivated, but this is now

over-run with the Apple-fruited Guava, and the Lemon, which were introduced many years ago, when the Island was settled, with a view to its becoming a granary to New South Wales. Grape Vines, Figs, and some other fruits have also become naturalized. In the garden at Orange Vale, Coffee, Bananas, Guavas, Grapes, Figs, Olives, Pomegranates, Strawberries, Loquats, and Melons, are cultivated successfully. Apples are also grown here, but they are poor and will not keep.

This Island being inaccessible, except at the opening in the reef, before noticed, and very remote from all other inhabited lands, has been selected for a penal settlement, for the worst description of prisoners. Most of those now here, have been transported from New South Wales or Van Diemens Land, on account of crimes committed in those Colonies, after the parties had been transported from Great Britain or Ireland.

3rd mo. 8th. At ten o'clock, we accompanied Major Anderson to the congregation of Protestant prisoners, which meets in a room, called The Court-House, within the yard of the prisoners' barracks. This room is capable of containing about two hundred and fifty prisoners; those who cannot be accommodated within it, sit outside. The Protestant prisoners meet here on First-days, at ten and two, for public worship; and from twenty to thirty of them, assemble at one end of the room, at eight, and half-past twelve, as an adult school; at the same time, for the same purpose, about the like number of Roman Catholics, meet at the other end. The prayers, &c. of the Episcopal Church were read by a prisoner, said to have been brought up as a minister of that denomination of Christians. He delivered an appropriate address, or sermon, including an uncompromising denunciation of sin, and an exhibition of the hopes of the gospel. Had his own life been an exemplification of the efficacy of the doctrines he preached, and his mind so kept under the influence of the Holy Spirit, that the baptizing power thereof might have freely accompanied his ministry, much good might have been expected from his labours. I would not be understood to intimate that no benefit resulted from them, nor yet that the man did not in some degree, feel what he preached; but in the course of his address, he honestly acknowledged, his own want of conformity to what he so strongly urged as necessary for himself and others. This individual also reads prayers, in the Jail, and in the Hospital, on First-days, and attended to the opening of the Protestant Adult-school. After his service was concluded, a short pause ensued, when I briefly addressed the prisoners, as did also George W. Walker.

At two o'clock, we went with Major Anderson to the public worship of the Roman Catholic prisoners, which commences at the same hours as that of the Protestants, in a mess-room, in what is designated a Lumber-yard. The prayers were read by a prisoner, in English, except one, near the close, in Latin. This man is also said to have been educated for the ministry; he seems likewise to have some practical knowledge of the inward work of grace. He also read a well-arranged address, of his own preparing, inciting to practical piety; and which, in point of doctrine, would not, I suppose, have been considered faulty, by any Protestant congregation.

At the conclusion, I stood up, and remarked, that having come among them in the love of Christ, I would take the liberty of expressing what was in my heart toward them. They were very attentive, while I referred them to their own convictions of sin, as the reproofs of the Holy Spirit, by which the Father sought to draw them to his beloved Son, in order that they might obtain eternal life through him. When I had concluded, my companion also addressed a few words of Christian counsel to them, to which they listened with like attention. The prisoners officiating as the ministers to these congregations, had been selected as the most suitable persons on the island for this office. Some free persons were, however, always present, to see that good order was kept, and nothing improper communicated. The free Protestants met at ten o'clock, in a room, at the military barracks, and the free Roman Catholics in another. The Episcopal service, and a sermon, were read by one of the officers, and that of the Roman Catholics by a sergeant. The First-day of the week is now spent in a very orderly

manner upon this island; where, in former days, it is said
to have been far otherwise.   Before the present arrangement
was made, the only apology for public worship attempted,
consisted in assembling the whole of the prisoners in a little
square, in the front of the military barracks, with the military
opposite to them, under arms, while a few prayers were
hastily read by an officer.   The whole of this was concluded
in the space of little more than ten minutes.   The effect
was such, that to this day, the prisoners say they formerly
never heard the Divine name on Norfolk Island, except
when it was blasphemed.

9th.   We visited the Jail, an inadequate building for
the purpose for which it is used.   In one room, about
30 men were confined, who had formed a plot to take the
Governor Phillip, on her last voyage to this Island.   They
had chains from one ankle to the other; through these, a
long chain was reefed, which was secured outside.   The
place was so hot and close, that many of the prisoners had
stripped off their clothes for relief.   They were very attentive while we read to them from the Scriptures, and
imparted to them religious counsel; comparing the misery
produced by sin, with the peace resulting from righteousness,
and exhorting them to flee from the former, and follow
after the latter.   We assured them of the willingness of
God to enable them to serve him, if they would only seek
help from him; seeing he gave his beloved Son to die for
all men, and has exalted him to his own right hand, to be
a Prince and a Saviour, to give repentance and the remission of sins.

CHAPTER XXII.

THE Settlement on Norfolk Island was formerly called Sydney, but in order to avoid confusion with the capital of N. S. Wales, its name has been changed to Kings Town. It consists of the Commandant's Residence, which is a commodious and substantial dwelling, the Military Barracks, the Penitentiary, the Commissariat Stores, the Jail, the Hospital, and a few other buildings, of stone, and some small dwellings, of weather-board, and a few thatched cottages, of dried grass. These are situated on the narrow flat of the limestone, which is on the south side of the island, and but little above the level of the sea. There are also some weather-board, farm buildings, at a place called Longridge, a mile from the Settlement. Many of the prisoners are employed in quarrying stone, and in building a new Commissariat Store. As no gunpowder is used in blasting the rock, and the stone is raised by means of levers, there is great waste of labour. This is also the case where persons in heavy irons are put to work with those in light ones, or entirely without; the latter having to wait for the tardy movements of the former. Prisoners, generally, are indisposed to industry, and circumstances like

these are taken advantage of by them.   The practice of
confining them in jails, without work, tends to inure them
to idle habits, and is a great evil.

3rd mo. 10th.   The Isabella sailed for Sydney, taking back
some prisoners, whose time here had expired, and others who
had had their sentence shortened, on account of good conduct.   Mitigation of sentence of this kind, has been attended with very happy results.   When no hope was held
out, the prisoners were reckless.

12th.   We had an interesting religious interview with
the prisoners employed in agriculture, at Longridge, where
they were assembled in a thatched building used for a
mess-room.   The feeling of solemnity was striking, both
while we sat in silence, and while we read the Scriptures,
and addressed them.

13th.   After visiting the patients in the Hospital, we
walked into the forest.—One of the remarkable vegetable
productions of this island is *Freycinetia Baueriana*, or the
N. I. Grass Tree.   It belongs to the tribe of *Pandaneæ*, or
Screw Pines.   Its stem is marked by rings, where the old
leaves have fallen off, and is an inch and a half in diameter;   it lies on the ground, or climbs like Ivy, or winds
round the trunks of trees.   The branches are crowned with
crests of broad, sedge-like leaves.   From the centre of these,
arise clusters of three or four oblong, red, pulpy fruit, four
inches in length, and as much in circumference.   When
the plant is in flower, the centre leaves are scarlet, giving
a splendid appearance to the plant, which sometimes is seen
twining round the trunk of the princely Tree-fern.   The
New Zealand Flax, *Phormium tenax*, a large, handsome
plant, with sedgy leaves, covers the steep declivities of
many parts of this Island, particularly at the tops of the
cliffs of the coast.   It is suffered to grow to waste, except
a little that is converted into small nets and cordage, by the
prisoners, for their own use.   Two New Zealanders were
once introduced, to teach the prisoners to prepare it; but
their process was so tedious, that the scheme was abandoned.

14th.   All the agricultural labour here is performed by

the hoe, under the idea of making the work of the prisoners laborious ; but they work so idly as to counteract the intention. They are now harvesting a crop of Maize. Scarcely enough of this grain is raised for the settlement, where the supply might be very ample. They are usually separated into gangs of from ten to fifteen men, to prevent combination, but a much larger number are now together. After having a meeting with those employed in agriculture, we joined a company of the officers, who were taking a rustic dinner, on the west coast, at a place adjacent. The cliffs here were high and steep, so that it was difficult to reach the sea, which washes perpetually against the lower rocks. The Domestic Pigeon has become naturalized, and breeds abundantly in these cliffs ; as does also the Domestic Cat, under like circumstances, feeding on the Pigeons, Tropic-birds, Gannets, and other birds, and on Rats, which are very numerous. As no gun is allowed to be fired within a mile of the Settlement, many birds are very tame ; some here appear naturally fearless. The Flycatcher will come so close, that I have seen it take flies off a persons hat, or off his hands, as he has stood with them behind him. A small green Parrot, with a red ring around the base of its beak, is remarkably tame. I missed my way, in rambling from my companions, and in the evening, saw a pair of these birds fly into a bush, which I opened where they were sitting : they did not seem disturbed at my presence, but kept chattering one to the other. When I imitated their noise, they took no notice, and did not fly, till my hand was within a few inches of their feet. The Lory Parrot, *Psittacus Pennantii*, which is crimson and blue, is common here, but it is rather shy.

15th. We visited the free Protestant congregation, which consists entirely of the Civil and Military Officers, and their families ; no other free persons being allowed to reside on the Island.

16th. We met with a man, who was in the hospital, sinking, from an old chronic disease of the chest : he seemed in a dark state of mind, but not without some glimmerings of light. We encouraged him to give way to his convictions for

s

sin, and to pray for ability to look upon Jesus, as the Lamb of God that taketh away the sin of the world. It is awful to see repentance deferred to a death-bed, when the powers of the mind, as well as those of the body, are weakened by disease.

I rode with Major Anderson to Ansons Bay, on the north side of the Island. This was formerly a landing place, but the sand has been washed away, and large stones remain, too rough for boats to venture upon. The road was chiefly through thick forest, overrun with luxuriant climbers. Among them was a *Wistaria*, with pea-flowers, of purple and green, and leaves something like those of the Ash. It hangs in festoons of twenty or thirty feet, from the limbs of the trees that support it. One of the most beautiful climbers of the Island, is *Ipomœa pendula,* which has handsome, fingered foliage, and flowers like those of the Major Convolvulus, but of a rosy pink, with a darker tube. The remains of two Pines, which were noted for their magnitude, and were blown down in a storm, were lying by the side of the road. These were called "The Sisters;" they were nearly 200 feet in height.

While on Norfolk Island, I usually took a walk before breakfast, and explored some of the beautiful hills and valleys, many of which are thickly wooded. In the borders of the woods, there is a great variety of beautiful shrubs. Among these is the Slender Jasmine, *Jasminum gracile,* known in England, as a delicate, green-house plant. Here it climbs over the bushes, or with twisted stems, as thick as a man's wrist, reaches the branches of lofty trees, at fifty feet from the ground, and climbs in their heads. In these cases, it has probably grown up with the trees, the lower branches of which have progressively died away, and left the wreathed stems of the Jasmine, like ropes, hanging from the upper boughs. Scattered on the grassy hills, is *Hibiscus* or *Lagunea Patersonii,* which forms a spreading tree of forty feet in height: it is here called White Oak: its leaves are of a whitish green, and its flowers pink, fading to white, the size of a wine-glass. It is perhaps the largest plant known to exist, belonging the Mallow tribe. In a thick wood, I met with it eighty feet high, and with a trunk sixteen and a half feet round.

18th. I attended the interment of the prisoner, before alluded to, who died yesterday. After the "Burial service," of the Episcopal Church had been read, I spoke a few words to those assembled on the occasion, I was never more struck with the inappropriateness of much of this service, and of its danger of misleading the ignorant, and of lulling them into a state of ease, by holding out the idea, that all would be well with them at last, without distinction as to their past lives. We afterwards had an interview with a considerable number of the prisoners, in the Court-house, in which much openness was felt in preaching the Gospel.

19th. The dryness of the weather having stopped the mill stream, a number of men are employed in grinding Maize, or Indian Corn, in hand mills. This is hard work, in this climate, where the thermometer is usually at about 80°, at this season of the year. We had a religious interview with these men, and were sensible of the love of our Heavenly Father bringing a feeling of sweet solemnity over our minds. This we could not but regard as an evidence of the continued extension of divine mercy to our auditors, and we esteem this feeling as one of the greatest of comforts to ourselves; we had also a religious interview with the agricultural gangs at Longridge. On speaking to an overseer, who had been long on the island, he informed us, that there had been a progressive improvement among the prisoners for some time past; especially, since Major Anderson had availed himself of the means within his reach, for their religious instruction, and had regulated the appropriation of punishments to the nature of the offences committed.

A man spoke to us of the defective quality of their provisions, and complained of the dryness of the maize bread, and the hardness of the salt meat. To be restricted to such diet is felt to be a privation, but the state of the health of the prisoners, shews that it is not unwholesome; and they are not designed to be pampered by indulgence. The supply of vegetables and wild fruits, keeps off scurvy, at this settlement.

The more orderly prisoners are allowed to cultivate small portions of ground as gardens. They grow chiefly the Sweet Potato, *Batatas edulis*, a plant of the Convolvulus tribe, producing large, tuberous roots, which are excellent for food, either roasted, boiled, or fried in slices. When prepared by frying, this root resembles sweetish cake, and sometimes supplies the place of toast at breakfast.

20th. Visited the hospital and jail. In the former, one of the patients was a man whose ankles had become chafed by his chains. In the latter, a man confined for indolence, and awfully blasphemous language, complained of his sentence, for what he termed, a frivolous offence. No person can be long on Norfolk Island without discovering, that he is indeed, amongst a people, extremely depraved. His ears are assailed by dreadfully profane language, especially if the prisoners are not aware of his presence. Other crimes, most degrading in their character, are not unfrequent; and to avoid punishment for offences, perjury is committed with the most hardened recklessness.

21st. I spent much of the day on the east coast; where, in some pools, among the rocks, there were several species of Madrapore, of the kinds called Corals, and of those which, when fossilized, are called Brainstones. One deep bason was lined with them, and presented a scene of uncommon beauty. A kind of Coral stood up in broad, thin, leaf-like tables, rising one above another on a common stalk. Some, on the sides, were variously branched and diversified. Their colours were white, light-blue, and olive. There were holes through those on the sides, that would admit a finger, out of which tubular Polyps, of the Sea Anemone tribe were protruded, displaying in the sunny water, their crests of variegated feelers, of the richest hues, resembling gorgeous flowers.

22nd. In the morning, we visited the congregation of free Roman Catholics, consisting chiefly of soldiers and their families, with a few officers. The service was conducted by a sergeant. The order and attention of the people was exemplary, but it was sorrowful to hear some of their prayers addressed to the Virgin Mary and other "saints;" especially when remembering, that they had been trained in this delusion, by those who were not content with the one Mediator between God and poor fallen man, provided of the Father, in his mercy and wisdom, even the Lord Jesus, who ever liveth to make intercession for us. We did not, however, feel it our business, to point out to them their errors of doctrine; but rather, in connexion with those points in which their profession of faith is sound, to lead them to a practical attention to the teaching of the Holy Spirit, the Spirit of Truth, which, when implicitly obeyed, leads out of error, and into all truth. In the afternoon, we visited the adult-schools, and the congregation of the Protestant prisoners. At the conclusion of their service also, I had something to communicate, of the same tendency. How lamentably has the teaching of the Holy Spirit been neglected by professing Christians, notwithstanding the promise respecting this Spirit as the Comforter, that He should take of the things of Christ and show them unto his disciples. —From this neglect arose the apostacy of the Christian church, in early days, both in faith and practice; and from the same source, arises in the present day, the unscriptural provision of most churches, in regard to ministry, and various other subjects, by which the people are drawn to lean unduly upon man, instead of being instructed to seek, to know the Lord to be their teacher, and to trust in him alone. The professors of Christianity, are consequently very generally, kept in great weakness, and in great shallowness of Christian experience.

24th. In a gang which we visited, at an out-station, there was a man, who was under sentence of death, and expecting to be executed, at a time when we had an interview with the prisoners in the Jail, at Launceston, in V. D. Land. This man referred to the meeting we had, at that time, with the prisoners, with expressions of gratitude, and seemed thankful to receive another visit.

CHAPTER XXIII.

3rd mo. 25th. Major Anderson allowed such of the prisoners
as were inclined to meet with us, for the purpose of hearing
the Scriptures read, and of receiving such counsel as we
might have to impart, to remain behind, when the bell rung
for work, at noon. This was designed to prevent any unpleasant feeling respecting encroachment upon their leisure.
The number who chose to remain was, however, small.

26th. We visited the Prisoners' Barracks, which form
a large tier of buildings, of three stories. They are kept
very clean, and are frequently whitewashed. The wards are
large, which is disadvantageous. Opportunity is thus afforded to considerable numbers of men, to unite in plotting
mischief. The prisoners are lodged in hammocks, suspended
in two tiers, to wooden frames. The bedding is kept perfectly
free from vermin, by being not only washed, but baked in
an oven. For this purpose it is placed on bars of wood,
which are kept clear of the sides of the oven to prevent its
burning.

27th. The case of a prisoner, who complained of rigorous
treatment, underwent examination by the Commandant.
The man was formerly a soldier: he had been sentenced
to wear irons for life. Good conduct would have entitled
him to have had the irons only on one leg, at the expiration

of twelve months; but he had been concerned in a mutiny
and had conducted himself improperly in other respects;
his irons were therefore heavy, and attached to both legs;
and it did not appear that he had any just cause of complaint.

Flagellation is now but seldom resorted to here; when
it was frequently inflicted, some of the more callous prisoners said, they would stand a hundred lashes for a small
piece of tobacco; and the recklessness with which they
committed offences, to which this punishment was attached,
accorded with their declaration. It was accounted a mark
of bravery among them, to bear the punishment unmoved.

Overseers, selected from among the first-class men, have
the time of their sentence reduced, by every two years
counting for three; but if they misconduct themselves, and
be removed from office in consequence, they lose the benefit of the previously reduced time. Two of the overseers
on Norfolk Island are free men. A number who are called
Volunteer-overseers, are prisoners, of New South Wales,
holding tickets-of-leave, who have volunteered to become
overseers on Norfolk Island, for salaries of from 1s. to 2s. 3d.
a day, with the hope of obtaining free or conditional pardons, as a reward for the faithful discharge of their duty.
The time spent on Norfolk Island, under a colonial sentence, is not reckoned as any part of an original sentence.
Thus, a man transported from England, or from Van Diemens Land, to New South Wales, for seven years, committing an offence at the expiration of three years, and
being sentenced to Norfolk Island for seven years, will have,
at the expiration of that period, to serve the four years remaining of his original sentence, in New South Wales, on
being returned thither.

We had an interview with the prisoners, in the Jail and
Hospital. In the latter, there was an aged man, who said
he had lived so wicked a life, that there was no hope for
him! How awful is such a reflection on a sick bed! Yet we
were glad to find, even so much reflection as this, hoping,
even against hope, that it might lead the man to seek for
divine mercy. Another man, who was suffering severely

from the effect of his own sin, professed to have found mercy through Christ, in the day of his trouble: he acknowledged himself to be among the chief of sinners, and said, he sometimes felt very fearful, but at other times was peaceful.

28th. Accompanied by the Agricultural Superintendent, we walked to a stock-station, called Cheeses Gully, on the north side of the Island; where three men are placed in charge of some cattle, feeding on grassy hills, embosomed. in wood, and partially overgrown with Lemon and Guava-trees. On the coast, there are two remarkable arches, in the basaltic rock, one of these is between the cliff, some portions of which are columnar basalt, and an inaccessible, little islet, inhabited by Gannets and Tropic Birds. The latter, with their speckled young, and Common Pigeons are to be seen, in many places on the ledges of the cliffs.

Many old roads, formerly used for bringing timber out of the woods, are grown up with the Cape Gooseberry, *Physalis edulis*, which produces abundance of pleasant, small, round fruit, in a bladder-like calyx. This is eaten by the prisoners, who also collect and cook the berries of the Black Night-shade, *Solanum nigrum*. These berries, are accounted virulently poisonous, in England, but their character may possibly be changed by the warmer climate of Norfolk Island.

In the woody gullies, the Norfolk Island Cabbage-tree, *Areca sapida*, abounds. It is a handsome palm, with a trunk about twenty feet in height, and from one and a half to two feet in circumference, green and smooth, with annular scars, left by the fallen leaves. The leaves or fronds form a princely crest, at the top of this elegant column; they are pectinate, or formed like a feather, and are sometimes nineteen feet in length; they vary from nine to fifteen in number. The apex of the trunk is enclosed in the sheathing bases of the leaf-stalks, along with the flower-buds, · and young leaves. When the leaves fall they discover double compressed sheaths, pointed at the upper extremity, which split open indiscriminately, on the upper or under side, and fall off, leaving a branched spadix, or flower-stem, which is the colour of ivory, and attached by a broad base to the

trunk. The flowers are produced upon this spadix: they are very small, and are succeeded by round seeds, red externally, but white, and as hard as horn, internally. As the seeds advance toward maturity, the spadix becomes green. The young, unfolded leaves of this Cabbage-tree, rise perpendicularly, in the centre of the crest. In this state, they are used for making brooms; those still unprotruded, and remaining enclosed within the sheaths of the older leaves, form a white mass, as thick as a man's arm; they are eaten raw, boiled or pickled. In a raw state, they taste like a nut, and boiled, they resemble artichoke-bottoms. The seeds furnish food for the Wood-quest, a large species of pigeon, which has a bronzed head and breast, and is white underneath, and principally, slate-coloured, on the back and wings. This bird is so unconscious of danger, as to sit till taken by a noose at the end of a stick; when one is shot, another will sometimes remain on the same bough, till itself also is fired at. We measured a Norfolk Island Pine, twenty-three feet, and another twenty-seven feet, in circumference. Some of them are nearly two hundred feet high. The timber is not of good quality, but it is used in building; it soon perishes when exposed to the weather. This is said to be the case with all the other kinds of wood on the Island. Norfolk Island Iron-wood, *Olea apetala*, is the only other sort, reputed to be worth using. No fences of wood are expected to stand above three years. Vegetation is rapid, in this fine climate, but decay is also rapid. There are very few dead logs lying in the bush. A group of the remarkable trees of this Island, are represented in the annexed sketch.

In the course of our walk, we had some conversation with two prisoner stock-keepers, who were Roman Catholics; to whom we offered a bible and some tracts, to instruct them in their solitude. One of them declined accepting them, saying that, according to their church, he had been instructed by his parents and their priests, from a child, not to read the Bible! The other said he was not against reading the Bible, but that it was the most dangerous book that could be put into the hands of an illiterate man! However, on reflection, they both concluded, that they would read the

Bible, as they were not able to attend public worship at the Settlement, on account of the nature of their occupation.

29th. We visited the congregations of the Protestant and Roman Catholic prisoners; and before they separated, availed ourselves of the opportunities, freely granted us, to express what we had to say to them. This being the last First-day in the month, the prisoners were mustered, and inspected by the civil surgeon, after the morning service. Their state of health is good; great attention is paid to cleanliness: they are not only required to wash themselves regularly, but every First-day morning, they all bathe in the sea, within the reef, opposite their barracks, and many of them bathe also in the course of the week.

30th. The weather has become stormy and wet. The temperature has lowered to 75°. From 65° to 85° in the shade, may be considered the usual range of the thermometer here: it rarely falls below 65° in winter, or rises above 85° in summer; and the night is but little cooler than the shade is in the day. The temperature is registered three times in the day, at the Hospital.

In a visit to the Jail, we had conversation with a man of great recklessness; of such, there are several on this Island. He was confined in a cell, for misdemeanour, and was chafed in his mind, and ready to blame any one rather than himself, for his sufferings. He said, he doubted the being of a Deity, but wished, if there were a God in heaven, that he would deprive him of life, he was so miserable: also, that he had only five years to serve as a prisoner, but he knew he should not live out half his time; for before it was half expired, he should die upon the drop. He told us likewise, that when out of prison, he was miserable still, and said, that if the officers took as much pains to annoy the prisoners, as many of the prisoners took to annoy one another, the place would be worse than hell itself. We endeavoured to direct the poor infatuated man, to the proof, afforded by himself, and by others of such character, of the overruling of the Most High, in the misery dispensed to them for their perverseness and wickedness.

Awful is the state of those who are in the gall of bitterness, and the bond of iniquity! This Island, beautiful by nature, and comparable to the Garden of Eden, is rendered, not only a moral wilderness, but a place of torment to these men, not so much by the punishments of the law, as by their conduct one to another. They form schemes of mischief, and betray one another; and being idly disposed, they are very generally chafed, by the exertions of the prisoner-overseers, to keep them at work. Being surrounded by the ocean, and all other lands being so distant, the hope of escape is precluded. This renders the wicked, very wretched, particularly men of bad conduct, sentenced for life. Those of reformed character might be moderately comfortable, were it not for the society of the depraved.

4th mo. 2nd. We walked to the north side of the Island, to visit a "felling-gang," whom we found busy, rolling the trunk of a large Pine, to a saw-pit. While they were thus engaged, we explored an adjacent gulley, shaded by dense forest, and abounding with ferns, and young palms. On the upper branches of the trees four epiphytes of the orchis tribe, and some ferns and Peperomias were plentiful. The Peperomias, which are spreading, green plants, allied to Pepper, grow also on moist rocks, on the dark sides of which, *Trichomanes Bauerianum*, a membranaceous fern, of great beauty, forms tufts exceeding a foot in height.

Having had a religious interview with the men, we proceeded to visit some others, near Ansons Bay, who have charge of a flock of sheep, kept for supplying the officers with fresh meat: of this privilege the well-conducted prisoners also, are occasionally permitted to partake. Some cows and pigs are likewise kept on the Island, and each free person is allowed a small quantity of milk, daily.

On the rocks of the south coast, *Asplenium diforme*, a fern resembling the Sea Spleenwort, *Asplenium marinum*, of England, is found. At a short distance from the shore, its leaves become more divided, and in the woods, in the interior of the Island, they are separated into such narrow segments, that the lines of fructification are thrown upon their margins. It then becomes *Cænopteris odontites*. But every possible gradation is to be met with between this state and that in which it grows, on rocks washed by the sea.

4th.   After visiting a gang of invalids, employed in breaking stones, I walked to a place called The Cascade, on the north-west side of the Island.   A little brook descends from the woody hills, and winds among the grassy ones, bordered, in many places, with copses, and straggling tree-ferns, till it reaches an open valley, formerly inhabited by settlers, where their old chimneys are still standing, and their orchards have run wild, and have spread Grape Vines, Lemons, Figs, and Guavas, all around.   Their Sugar-canes have also become naturalized, and border the streamlet thickly, till it falls over a basaltic rock, about twenty feet high, decorated with ferns, and a variety of other plants. Here the brook is again narrowed by woody hills, and margined by luxuriant plants, of the broad, sedgy-leafed New Zealand Flax, and Water Cress, till it emerges on an open, flat, basaltic promontory, from the very point of which, it falls, about twenty feet, to the sea beach, where it is lost among the large, rounded, tumbled stones.—Among the Sugar-cane and scrub at this point, a beautiful convolvulus-like plant, *Ipomœa cataractæ*, is entwined, and exhibits its large, purple flowers, shot with red.   It was named from this place, by Bauer, a celebrated botanist, who accompanied one of the earliest navigators of these seas, and whose Flora of Norfolk Island, has lately been published by a person named Endlicher.

Ipomœa carinata, a large plant of the Convolvulus tribe, having white flowers, with long tubes, that open at night, climbs among the trees, in the borders of the woods.   Among the bushes there are two pretty species of Passion flower, *Disemma adiantifolia* and *D. Baueriana*, with copper-coloured blossoms.

From the Sugar-cane, the old settlers of Norfolk Island succeeded in making molasses, but they failed in obtaining sugar, not being aware, that the addition of a little lime, or potash, was needful to make it crystallize.   They also distilled rum, and injured themselves greatly by drinking it; but they imagined the pernicious effects of the rum were produced by the lead of the worms, used in the distillation. They never seemed to dream, that they were suffering from the deleterious property of the "balmy spirit of the cane;" under which, many of them sank prematurely to the grave; and others became so enthralled, that the love of strong drink has gone with them, as a curse, into other lands, blighting their prospects of temporal prosperity, and bringing them hopeless and unhonoured to the end of their days.

Near the foot of the Cascade, there is a rock, forming a natural jetty, from which boats are hauled up out of the sea, when they are unable to land on the south side of the island.

5th. We visited the congregation of free and military Protestants, to which the Commandant's Clerk read the prayers of the Episcopal Church, and a sermon. The sermon was a very pointed one, on 2 Peter iii. 3. At the conclusion, my dear companion and myself, again availed ourselves of the opportunity afforded us, to bear a plain testimony to the necessity of becoming the servants of Christ, in order to obtain salvation, and to the impossibility of being saved whilst remaining servants of the devil, through sin. We also directed the attention of the congregation, to the convictions of the Spirit of Truth, making sin manifest in the conscience, as the drawing of the Father leading to the Son, in order that mankind may obtain repentance, and remission of sins through him, and know, through him, a capacity wrought in them, to will and to do the good pleasure of God.

CHAPTER XXIV.

4th mo. 6th. WE went to see a singular little cave, not far from the Commandant's house. In this place, two men who absconded, a few months since, concealed themselves in the day-time, and for a considerable period, eluded detection. The cave is in the rugged limestone, that forms two low hills, the flat, and the reef on the south of the Island. Nepean Island, and a rock that resembles a ship under sail, off the north of Phillip Island, are of the same formation of limestone. The cave was near to a lime-kiln, and was concealed by a stone, drawn over its mouth. The Sandstone, adjoining this limestone, is very hard and sonorous: it is valued for making filtering stones.

The rocky shore of this Island is accessible from the land, in some places, on the south-west. In a few of the valleys, near the sea, in this direction *Euphorbia obliqua,* a remarkable shrub, forms copses, attaining, when shaded by trees, to 15 feet in height, and 2 feet in circumference. Here also, as well as in most of the other shady woods throughout the island, *Botryodendron latifolium,* a shrub of singular form, allied to the Ivy, but of a very different appearance, prevails. Its figure may be compared to that of a long-leaved cabbage, mounted on a broom-stick. Its stem is about five feet high, and five inches round; its largest leaves are about two feet long, and one foot broad. The prisoners in the out-stations, wrap their bread in these leaves, and bake it in the ashes. The fruit is a dense cluster, of greenish, purple berries, not edible, produced in the centre of the crown of leaves.

8th. In company with Major Anderson, and the military surgeon, we ascended Mount Pitt. The vegetation is of the same general character, as on other parts of the north of the Island. Lemon trees grow at the very top. On the northern ascent, a Pine was measured, 29½ feet in circumference, and a Norfolk Island Bread-fruit, *Cordyline australis*, 2 feet 9 inches. The last, sometimes attains 20 feet in height: it branches from within a few feet of the ground, and forms several heads, with flag-like leaves, and long, branched spikes of greenish, star flowers, succeeded by whitish, or bluish-purple berries, that are eaten by parrots. It often forms a striking object, where a woody valley runs out into grass, growing at the extreme margin of the wood.

Niphobolus serpens and *Polypodium tenellum*, two climbing ferns, ascend the trunks of trees, in the northern portion of the Island; and the Norfolk Island Pepper, *Piper psittacorum*, which produces a yellow, pulpy, pendent, cylindrical fruit, of a spicy, sweetish taste, is every where plentiful, in the woods. It rises, with a few, jointed, cane-like, green stems, to from four to ten feet high, bearing large, heart-shaped leaves.

From the top of Mount Pitt, by ascending a tree, we could see the whole circuit of the Island, which approaches a triangle in form; it is rendered very beautiful, by the variety of hill and dale, wood and open land. Nepean and Phillip Island are also included in the view; the former being very small, and rising only a few feet out of the ocean, and the latter, about five miles in circumference, steep and lofty, and varied by thick wood, and bare, red peaks. These three islands form the whole of this remote group. Norfolk Island is the only one inhabited.

9th. The gangs being too busily occupied in harvesting Maize, to allow us to have interviews with them, I made another excursion into the bush, having as guide, a prisoner who was sent here, from New South Wales, for bush-ranging, or in other words, for breaking away from the restraint of penal discipline, and becoming a robber. This course of life he informed me, he should never have taken to, had he not fallen into the hands of a bad master. In the course of our walk, one of the Orange-faced, Green Parrots, alighted on a bush near us. The prisoner broke a long stick, so near to the bird, that I expected it would fly away at the noise, but it sat still; with a shoe-string, he made a noose, which he fastened to the end of the stick; this he reached to the bird. After a few unsuccessful attempts, which only occasioned the parrot to move a little from its place, he passed the noose over its head, and captured it.—The most remarkable object that arrested our attention was *Marattia elegans,* a fern of great beauty, having fronds 14 feet in length, 7 feet of which were destitute of branches; of these, it had 8½ pair, which were again branched, and clothed with leaflets, five inches long, and three-quarters of an inch broad.

13th. The petty sessions were held: they occur twice a week. Several prisoners received reprimands, or sentence to sleep in Jail, to solitary confinement, or to wear chains, for neglect of work, or for insolence to overseers. A circumstance of improper conduct in a military officer, lately removed from the Island, came to light, in the examination of a prisoner, such as shewed the pernicious effects of the bad example, by which the penal discipline is too often let down. It is awful to see the unmoved hardness with which prisoners make oath, most solemnly, to the truth of what they state, on both sides, when it is obvious, that on one side there must be perjury. Truly oaths are insufficient to secure correct testimony, where the moral standard of truth is low; where it is gone, they only add to crime; and where this standard is properly maintained, they are useless, yea being yea, and nay, nay.

The tide being low in the afternoon, I walked among the rocks, and detached a few pieces of Coral, of different sorts. Some species of *Alcyonium,* that are met with here, so much resemble the Corals, that it is difficult to distinguish them, except by the former being soft. Some long-spined

Echini or Sea Urchins are found here, and two remarkable, sea Slugs. One of them is about three inches long, black, and covered with spine-like projections: it exudes a milky slime, on being alarmed. The other is as large as a rabbit, of a week old: it is drab, netted with dark lines, and has folds on its back and head. When irritated, it exudes a large quantity of purple fluid.

14th. In company with Robert Ellson, the military surgeon, and attended by William Percival, a reformed prisoner, as our guide, I explored some of the gullies, on the south of Mount Pitt. Here two tree-ferns, *Alsophila excelsa* and *Cyathea medularis*, were very fine; the former measured 40 feet, and the latter 20 feet, in height; both had magnificent, circular crests of fronds: those of the *Cyathea*, were 11 feet in length.

When Norfolk Island was first discovered, it was uninhabited, and white Guinea-fowl were numerous upon it; they are now quite extinct. When the Island was re-occupied, for a penal settlement, Pigs, Goats, Barn-door-fowl, Pigeons, Cats, Rats, and Mice, had become very numerous. Percival, who was sent here soon after the penal settlement was established, told us, that the pigs and goats were chiefly destroyed in the first two years, in which time, from the irregular supply of provisions from Sydney, the settlement was sometimes dependent upon these animals for food, and the people had to catch them in a morning, before they could get anything to eat. Pigs and goats, in a wild state, consequently, soon became extinct; but they are still numerous on Phillip Island. Barn-door-fowl are also now extinct, or nearly so, in a wild state. Pigeons are very abundant, breeding in inaccessible places among the cliffs. Wild-cats resort to the cliffs in summer, and in winter make incursions on the poultry-yards; when they also feed on birds, rats, and mice; the two latter of which are very numerous at certain seasons of the year. There are neither snakes nor lizards on Norfolk Island; but lizards are said to be found on a small, rocky, detached portion of Phillip Island.

Two young officers pressed me much, this morning, to accompany them to Phillip Island; but I did not feel

T

satisfied to go, as there was uncertainty in regard to being
delayed there, and there are no human inhabitants upon it.
They shot thirteen Goats, which they sent back by the boat,
on its return; it brought also a supply of fine fish, of the
kinds known here as the Trumpeter, King-fish, and Rock
Cod. The last is very different from the one called by the
same name in V. D. Land.

Guavas are now ripe; they are so abundant on various
parts of the Island, that the supply is more than sufficient,
for man, pigs and birds, all of which consume great quantities of them. They are the size of small apples, and have a
thick coat, enclosing a pink, sweet, seedy mass, that is
agreeable to eat, either raw or cooked.

15th. We met a number of the prisoners, in the Court-
house, and after reading a chapter in the Bible to them,
were again strengthened to urge upon them, the importance
of attention to the teaching of the Lord's Spirit; without
which no profession of religion can avail anything; for all
the members of the true church, are taught of the Lord, and
great is their peace, and in righteousness they are established, according to the declaration of his prophet, whatsoever may be their name among men; or how much
soever the influence of education may have led them to
esteem as important, things that are unimportant, or even
encumbering. Without this teaching, none can come to
repentance toward God, or to faith in Christ, or persevere
in perfecting holiness in the fear of the Lord; for all the
children of the Lord are taught of him, even though they
may not clearly apprehend the nature of this teaching, so as
to acknowledge it in words.

20th. The weather has become fine, after being stormy
and wet since the 15th. Two boats were sent to Phillip
Island, to-day: they succeeded in bringing off the two
young officers, and all their attendants, except a prisoner,
who was too remote to reach the boats before they were
under the necessity of putting off, on account of the rising
surf, and he remained till the 24th. A soldier was washed
off the rocks, while they were embarking, and was saved
with difficulty.

While the party was on Phillip Island, the prisoner who, is left behind, was attacked by a Wild-boar; he faced the ferocious animal with a long stick, that he happened to have in his hand, and with which he parried off the boar, at the same time advancing upon it, till it was on the edge of a lofty cliff; he then made a sudden rush, which occasioned the boar as suddenly to recede, and it fell backward, over the precipice, and was killed. This man once made his escape from Norfolk Island to Phillip Island, where he eluded pursuit, among the peaks, for three months: he supported himself on wild animals and fruits; but solitude became so irksome to him, that he gave himself up, and has since been a well-conducted man. I have felt thankful to the Lord, who restrained me from going to Phillip Island, where the party have had a miserable time, in the rain, and from whence no boat could have brought me on the following day, as was kindly proposed.

21st. We went about two miles into the bush, to visit some working gangs, with whom we had a religious interview: they were seated, as has been usual on such occasions, on logs of wood, or on the ground, in a sheltered place; and we were kindly provided with a wheelbarrow, leaned against a tree, and covered with a sack, as a seat. In our visits to these men, we have generally read a chapter from the Holy Scriptures, then made a pause, and subsequently, given expression to such impressions as were made upon our minds, either in testimony or prayer. We crossed to Longridge in the evening, and had an interview of a similar kind, with about two hundred of the men who are employed in agriculture. Two men, under religious convictions, spoke to George W. Walker, and he encouraged them to keep under these impressions, hoping that it might please the Lord to give them a sense of the pardon of their sins, and to lead them in the way of salvation.

Being out after dark, we were interested by seeing numbers of a small species of agaric, or mushroom, so luminous as to reflect a shadow on substances near them. When held near a watch, the hour might be distinctly seen, or on being put near the face, the features might be discovered

This remarkable fungus has obtained the name of Blue-light, though its radiance is rather green than blue: it grows from decaying sticks or straw, and is very abundant amongst the sugar-canes, as well as in the bush. Its cap is rather convex, covered with mucilaginous matter, and is less than an inch across; the stalk is slender, two or three often grow together; the whole plant is very watery. The brilliancy is greatest in the cap, which shines most on the under side.

23rd. At an early hour, the Government-schooner, Isabella, was descried; but as the wind was against her, she did not get near enough to land her despatches. I took a long walk, to a wood-cutting gang, to collect some transverse sections of the wood of the Island, for my kind friend Alexander M'Leay. A prisoner who was my guide, gave me several particulars of his life. He said, he was carefully brought up by his mother, who made him "attend church, and repeat the text;" and who sent him to a school, where he often got passages of Scripture off, by heart. He was afterwards errand-boy to a common-councilman of London, for whose convenience, he waited at a neighbouring public-house, to be ready to run errands. This public-house was the resort of thieves, and women of loose character, with whom he became entangled; at length, he joined some of them in robbing his master's premises. By the vigilance of a watchman, the party was detected, and he was tried, and transported to Bermuda. Charged with mutiny there, along with many others, he was sent back to England, and from thence to New South Wales, where he was assigned to a master who, he then thought, pinched him in his rations, and from whom he consequently pilfered. He was afterwards removed into the public works, where, through bribing an under-overseer, he earned money by occasionally working for a settler. He afterwards resolved to leave off all his dishonest tricks, calling to mind how much he used to hate the character of a thief, when a child. But being sent into Sydney one day, while he yet had money in his pocket, he met an old acquaintance, who was pennyless, and took him to a public-house, to refresh him. Here he took a glass of spirits with the man, out of the idea of good-fellowship; this excited an old appetite for strong drink, and he and his companion concluded to have a second glass. This destroyed their resolution to keep sober, and they continued drinking, until the whole of his money was gone, and with it, his resolution to keep from thieving. On reflecting upon this, he marvelled to think how soon strong drink destroyed strong resolution to keep from sin!

He fell completely back into his old habits, was apprehended, transported to a penal settlement for life, and sent to Norfolk Island. He had cherished a strong desire again to see his parents; but now, had no hope of ever effecting this, unless he could escape from the settlement; he therefore joined some others in taking off a boat. They were pursued, one of the party was shot dead, another dangerously wounded, and the whole recaptured. He had indulged in infidel principles, but the sight of the dead man had a powerful effect upon him, and he could not help looking upon him as lost for ever. He was committed to jail in irons, with the rest of his fellows, and they were put upon the chain, that is, they had a chain passed within their irons, and fixed outside of their prison, to render them more secure. Here he felt his situation keenly. Passages of Scripture were brought to his recollection, and he obtained the use of a Bible, which he read diligently, determining, if through the mercy of God, he should get over this offence, so as again to be liberated from the jail, he would lead a different life. He also began to pray to God for help. The party were tried for attempting to take away the boat, found guilty, and sentenced to death; but as they had used no personal violence, they were ultimately reprieved, and after lying long in prison, they were returned to their work. This was only a short time before the mutiny of 1834, in which, an attempt was made by the prisoners to take possession of Norfolk Island; having a bad name, he was charged as being one of the party, and sent to prison, but was afterwards dismissed.

While in prison, on this occasion, he became privy to a plot, for rescuing some men, sentenced to death, which he was not comfortable till he had disclosed. His comrades suspected that he had communicated their plans, they marked also his altered conduct, for he could no longer join in many of the evil practices in which they indulged, and he became in their estimation and language, " A bad fellow." Before, when he ran with them into the depths of iniquity, he passed among them as a "good fellow"; for thus, among this depraved portion of our race, is good too generally called evil, and evil good! and a man, who in any measure becomes reformed, is liable to much persecution. This man, and others of reflection, say, such is the wickedness of this place, that they often marvel that God, in wrath, does not cause it to be swallowed up, or destroy it, as he did Sodom of old; for some of the sins of that ancient city are awfully prevalent here. "And the time was," said the prisoner, " when there was not half-a-dozen righteous persons to be found on the Island," though there is reason to believe the number is now increased.

24th. By the mail of the Isabella, we received intelligence of our dear friends in England, by a letter dated the 29th of 9th month, 1834. I had also a letter from Alexander M'Leay, informing us, that the Friendship would call here, for Coffee Plants, on her way to Tahiti, and that by her, we might convey letters to our late dear companions, D. and C. Wheeler.—We had also tidings of the fall of an individual in V. D. Land; for whose friends as well as for himself, we felt much sorrow. He was one who, through repentance and reformation, had been raised from a low state, into which he had brought himself by transgression. But old, sinful habits are hard indeed to root out. When they are overcome, close walking with God is required, to keep them down. If carelessness be given way to, they easily revive: and like the old inhabitants of Canaan, who were driven to the hills, they again invade their old domain. In countries like these, where a large part of the population, free and bond, have become exiles from their native land, through habitual misconduct, relapses may reasonably be expected, in many cases in which hope has been excited; and care is required, not to be too much discouraged by them.

26th. In the morning we visited the congregation of free Protestants. Their service being short, we had an opportu-

nity again to testify our Christian concern, for their present
and eternal welfare. On taking leave of them, we went to
the prisoner Protestants, in time also to take leave of them.

In the afternoon, we visited the prisoner Roman Catholics,
and took leave of them likewise. On all these occasions, we
were enabled to bear an uncompromising testimony against
sin, and to hold up the necessity of repentance toward God,
and faith toward our Lord Jesus Christ, in order to obtain the
pardon of past sins, and to inculcate a humble, as well as
watchful walking in the Spirit, as necessary, to being preserved from fulfilling the lusts of the flesh.

A sense of the divine presence, has often pervaded our
minds, in a remarkable degree, when labouring among the
outcasts of human society, in this Island, inspiring the hope,
that some of them may yet come under the power of the
Gospel. Though abundance of the worst of crimes are to be
found among the prisoners on Norfolk Island, there are, even
among them, a small number, who are not insensible of the
operations of divine grace.

One man, who now mourns because of his past sins, told
us, that he had been twice sentenced to death, and a third
time, had narrowly escaped the gallows, when he had been
concerned in a robbery, with attempt at murder. He was
formerly in high esteem with his fellow prisoners, for his
boldness; but this boldness was then exercised in the practice
of iniquity. He was brought to reflect upon his sinful state,
under the divine blessing, upon the labours of William Marshall, the Surgeon of the Alligator, who, when that vessel
was here, a few months ago, during the time that a number
of men were tried for mutiny, frequently visited the prisoners, and endeavoured to turn them from darkness to light,
and from the power of Satan to God.—This prisoner was
scarcely known to flinch under the lash, of which he received
at one time, three hundred strokes, nor did he weep under the
sentence of death; but now, the tears steal down his cheeks,
while he lifts up his heart in prayer to God, against whom he
has so greatly revolted, and implores the pardon of his sins
for Jesus' sake. In remarking upon the contriting influence
of the love of God, he told us, that he sometimes heard

the prisoner who slept next him, and who had also been very hardened, weeping under its influence, while others slept.

28th.   We had a satisfactory interview with two prisoners, lately awakened : they made some feeling acknowledgments respecting their past vicious lives, and said, they fully merited all the punishment they had received. Such acknowledgments are rarely made by prisoners, except in an awakened state.

29th.   A number of the prisoners having expressed a wish to see us again, before we left the Island, we met them in the Court-house, at their dinner-hour.   There were about forty of them, and they desired us to consider them as the representatives of a much larger number, who being out at work, on the farm, and in the gangs, could not then be present.   They presented us with the following address, which one of them first read :—

"Norfolk Island, 29th April, 1835.

" GENTLEMEN,

"We, the prisoners of the crown, embracing the tenets of the Prostestant faith, cannot, from pure motives of unfeigned gratitude, allow you to quit this Island, without thus, publicly, expressing our sentiments for your unwearied zeal, and attention to our best interests, since you came amongst us, viz. the salvation of our immortal souls.

"Permit us to implore, that you would convey to Major Anderson, our Commandant, the deep sense we entertain of his great anxiety, since he assumed the command, for our well-being, here and hereafter.

"That a kind Providence may conduct you both, in safety, through the trackless deep, to the haven where you would wish to be, is,

"Gentlemen,
"The ardent wish of
"THIS CONGREGATION."

"Messrs. Backhouse and Walker,
"Members of the Society of Friends."

We acknowledged the kind intention of the prisoners, imparted to them a few more words of Christian counsel, commended them again to God, and to the word of his grace, and took a final leave of them.

An early dinner was provided for us, after which Major Anderson and his wife, and several other individuals, who had shown us much kindness, accompanied us to the landing place, where we took leave of them, and went on board a whale-boat, along with Ensign Wyatt, who returned with us to New South Wales. A boat, coming from the Isabella, a short time before, was overtaken by a heavy surf, and driven upon the rocks, to the imminent peril of all on board; but it was got off again with little damage.— A police-runner, on this Island, formerly a notorious bushranger, in New South Wales, was sent out upon the point of the reef, the tide being low, to give notice of approaching surges, and we were favoured, through this precaution, to escape some, such as might have swamped the boat. Being apprized of their approach, we kept under the shelter of a point of rocks, till they had passed. Our intrepid boat's crew then pulled briskly out, and we passed the broken water safely, though not without meeting some heavy surfs, that wet us a little; within a few minutes, we passed some high swells, that would break with awful force in the passage that we had but just left. Thus being again favoured to escape the dangers of this shore, we soon reached the Isabella, which had remained attached to a buoy, laid down for the purpose, in eight fathoms water, to which vessels are made fast in fine weather. If it come on to blow, vessels are obliged to stand off and on, till it be fine again. In such cases, communication with the shore is sometimes cut off for many days. We loosed from the buoy about four o'clock in the evening, with a southerly breeze, that became so light, as to place us in doubt for some time, as to whether we should drift with the tide, upon the rocks, or clear the south-west point of the Island, which we were favoured to pass before night.

Before we sailed, several prisoners requested leave of the Commandant, to send letters by us to Sydney, to be forwarded to their relations, under the idea, that they would be despatched from the Colony with more certainty, in this way, than if sent by the regular packet, to the Government Office. This was readily granted, on condition that the letters should be open, and that we should inspect them, to see that nothing improper was communicated. As some of these letters contained expressions illustrative of the feelings of the writers, with regard to their situation as Convicts at a Penal Settlement, and the causes of crime, I ventured to make a few extracts from them; which are introduced at APPENDIX. J.

The voyage from Norfolk Island to Sydney, occupied three weeks, in consequence of calms and adverse winds.—The company on board the vessel, were Ensign Wyatt, G. W. Walker, and myself, twenty-five soldiers, ten prisoners, a free overseer, a store-keeper and his wife, and sixteen seamen, inclusive of the captain and mate.

5th mo. 6th. A storm came on in the night; in which, on reflecting upon the many snares that are in the world, and the many persons that have fallen away from righteousness, after having witnessed a precious state of divine favour, I felt willing to perish, rather than that I should be permitted to falsify the testimony which the Lord has given me to bear, to the truth as it is in Jesus. Unworthy as I felt myself to be, of the least of the Lord's mercies, I prayed to him, if he saw meet to continue my life, to continue also the baptisms of his Holy Spirit, until the very root of sin should perish; and to enable me so to watch, as that the seeds of sin might not be suffered to vegetate, but their smallest buddings be destroyed, by the power of the Spirit. While thus meditating and praying in the storm, with thanksgiving, for the accommodation of a good berth, and many other blessings, I was preserved very peaceful, under a sense of the divine presence. Thus, as in days of old, and as on many former occasions, in my own experience, the Lord proved himself to be "a very present help in time of trouble;" and I could adopt the language, "Therefore we will not fear, though the waters roar and be troubled, though the mountains shake with the swelling thereof: for the Lord of hosts is with us, the God of Jacob is our refuge, and blessed be his holy name for ever."

10th. Balls Pyramid was seen at sun-rise, and a high bluff, of Lord Howes Island, towards sunset. The distance was only about thirty miles, but there was so much fog in the horizon, that the island was obscured most of the day. In the forenoon, the whole of the ship's company, including prisoners, assembled on deck, and we had a satisfactory religious interview with them. George W. Walker read a portion of Scripture; after which, we both addressed them, on the danger of deceiving themselves, and imagining themselves the servants of God, while worshipping the devil by habitual and careless sin. The practise of cursing and swearing, awfully prevalent, was noticed, as one of these habitual sins; and others were also denounced. The test pointed out by the Saviour of men, " By their fruits ye shall know them," was appealed to, and the doctrines and invitations, as well as the denunciations of the Gospel were set forth, the Lord helping us. The folly of neglecting the guidance of the Holy Spirit was illustrated, by the folly which it would be accounted in a mariner, to neglect the Compass, in steering a vessel, and the almost certain wreck, to which such neglect must lead. The mercy that had preserved us in the late gales, and spared us till the present hour, was magnified; and all were exhorted to flee from the wrath to come, and to seek, in repentance, to be reconciled to God, through the death of his Son, and to be enabled, by his grace, to serve him in holiness. The people conducted themselves more properly afterwards, and spent much of the day in reading some tracts, with which we supplied them.

14th. A dead calm. The sea was covered with minute, red animalculæ, like tadpoles, with transparent tails. Jellyfish, and Portuguese Men-of-War, also a blue slug, half an inch long, with a silvery back, and palmate appendages, like fore fins, and posterior ones of a trilobed form, with a shark, sailing about with its dorsal fin above water, and a few birds, varied the smooth, circular expanse of blue ocean, bounded only by the sky.

15th. Stood for land in latitude 31°. 9'. S., and descried some hills on the coast of N. S. Wales.

16th. The Heads of Port Stephens were in sight, at noon. The weather was so rough as again to make me sick: this has often been the case in the course of the voyage. The vessel leaks greatly on one tack, as the wind lays her over to that side. Some of our company, at times get alarmed, but I have been favoured to feel peaceful and content, yet pitying the seamen who have to work hard at the pumps.

18th. The wind still adverse. We are out of sugar and coals, and are using the last bag of biscuit, but have plenty of salt beef and flour. A spar has been cut up for fuel. The biscuit has long been full of Weevils, but we have made the best of it, by putting it into the oven.

19th. Off the Heads of Port Jackson. The wind still against us. We remembered that this was the time of the Yearly Meeting of Friends, in London, where many of those who bear the care and burden of the Society, would be assembled, and would feel the loss of those who have been removed from the church militant to the church triumphant. The prayer of our hearts was, that the Lord might support the burden-bearers, strengthen their hands, add to their numbers, give them sound judgment and clear discernment, and clothe them with the love of Christ: and that he might yet cause his truth to be exalted among the nations, to the praise of his own everlastingly great and glorious name.

20th. A gentle breeze sprung up about midnight. At break of day, we were favoured again to enter the Heads of Port Jackson, in safety. A calm soon ensued, but the tide, and a light air that arose about noon, brought us into Sydney Cove. G. W. Walker and myself went on shore by a boat from the Government dock-yard, and found eighteen letters for us at the Post-office, eleven of which were from our friends in England.

While becalmed in Port Jackson, a number of Venus's Girdles, passed the vessel, swimming a little below the surface of the water. These remarkable animals belong the same order as the Jelly-fish, but they resemble a long semi-pellucid, horn shaving. There were also in the water, atoms glittering in the sun, and exhibiting prismatic colours, the precise nature of which, we were unable to ascertain.

21st. We engaged a lodging in the town, but as it was not ready for our reception, we returned on board the Isabella, for the night. The excitement of landing, in connexion with the squeaking of rats, in the pantry, the bleating of goats, and the crowing of cocks, on the deck, together with the quarrelling of drunken soldiers, in the hold, allowed us but little sleep. The prisoners had been safely delivered on board of a hulk, and the Isabella had been brought close up to the Dock-yard. Many of the soldiers had been on shore, and had returned in a state of intoxication, and appalling excitement. They were very quarrelsome. I went to them at midnight, fearing lest they should injure one another with their fire-arms, which they had with them, loaded. After labouring in vain, for some time, to get them quiet, I requested one of the most moderate, to hand me their lantern, which I blew out, and sent away. They became a little quieter, when unable to see each other, and then were soon overcome by exhaustion, and fell asleep, to awake in the morning, in shame, at the testimony which their black eyes, and bruised faces, bore to their misconduct.

CHAPTER XXV.

Sydney.—Penal Discipline of Norfolk Island re-modelled.—Epistle to Friends in Hobart Town.—Meetings.—Unclaimed Property of Deceased Persons.—Drought.—Shrubs.—Thoughtless Young Men.—Conceited Woman.—Prayer in Spirit.—Australian School Society.—Unworthy Descendants of Friends.—Blacks Fishing.—Species of Callitris.—Ministry.—Shrubs.—Friends' Books. D. and C. Wheeler.—J. Leach.—Consumption.—Meeting at Cooks River.—Travelling in New South Wales.—Mounted Police.—Meeting at the North Shore.—Botany Bay.—Dye-woods, &c.—Grass-tree.—Sweet Tea.—Miasmal Fever.

AFTER returning from Norfolk Island, we remained in Sydney nearly fifteen weeks. In the course of this time, at the request of the Governor, we presented him a Report, on the state of the Penal Settlement, on Norfolk Island, containing the substance of the preceding remarks, and some observations of temporary interest, not needful to be introduced here; especially, as the penal discipline, at that station, has been completely re-modelled, in order to afford Captain Maconochie the opportunity of trying to carry out his enlightened views, respecting the treatment of criminals. Some notice of these views will be found in this volume, under date of the 19th of 8th mo., 1837.

The few persons professing with Friends, in Sydney, had kept up a meeting for worship, during our absence, both on First-days, and in the forenoon of one other day in the week. The little congregation in Hobart Town, who had lately been placed in circumstances of trial, excited our sympathy; and soon after landing, we addressed an epistle to them, a copy of which is inserted in APPENDIX. K.

5th mo. 24th. The meetings were owned of the Good Shepherd, by a measure of heavenly solemnity. They were held in silence, except that G. W. Walker expressed a few sentences near the close of that in the afternoon. The effects of our late voyage, upon my own health, have been such, as to render it difficult for me to keep my mind properly settled, on these occasions; but divine mercy has condescended to my weakness, so that I have still been permitted to feel the sensible influence of the Holy Spirit.

26th. I consulted the Colonial Secretary, respecting the inquiries of a friend, in England, on behalf of one of his neighbours, whose brother died in this country, leaving some property. This, according to a good regulation in the Colony, was taken possession of by the Registrar of the Supreme Court, and advertised, to enable the relatives of the deceased to claim it. The Secretary kindly offered to obtain the desired information, if I would address a letter to him on the subject, which was done accordingly.

28th. Very little rain has fallen for many months. Wheat is ten shillings a bushel. Oranges and late Peaches are beginning to ripen. Apples from Van Diemens Land are in the market. Several fine shrubs are in blossom, in the woods and bushy places, on the borders of Port Jackson. Among them are *Banksia ericifolia, integrifolia* and *spinulosa, Crowea saligna, Styphelia tubiflora, Acacia suaveolens, Hakea gibbosa,* and *Epacris grandiflora.* Several of these are well known in English greenhouses.

31st. A few young men who have been brought up among Friends, but have not retained their membership among them, have lately attended our meetings for worship. Like too many others, they seem never to have given due thought to their eternal interests: they have evidently the first principles of religion to learn, before they can know "the way of peace," either as regards this world, or the next.

6th mo. 3rd. I called upon an aged woman, who was sent to this Colony many years since, to conduct a school, under the auspices of the Government. She possessed considerable abilities, but overrated them, and assumed a degree of consequence, and expectation, beyond her proper sphere. This has stood greatly in the way of her prosperity;

she is now very infirm, and in a dependent state, a monument of the folly of being " heady and high-minded."

4th. In our little week-day meeting, I was very sensible of the spirit of supplication, and many secret petitions ascended from the altar of my heart, both on my own account, and on account of others; but nothing of constraining influence was felt, indicating it to be my place to lift up my voice on behalf of the assembled company; who, I believe, were also sensible of the overshadowing of the Holy Spirit, and had access for themselves to the Throne of Grace.

5th. We attended the Committee of the Australian School Society; which is ready to open its first school, on the 8th.

9th. We visited some persons descended from Friends; but though they received us kindly, they neither appeared to understand the principles of the Society, nor the first principles of the Gospel, and consequently could not be expected to have much value for the example of their predecessors.

We walked to Cooks River, which empties itself into Botany Bay, and fell in with a party of Blacks, who were fishing. One of them had a canoe, made of a large sheet of bark, stretched open with sticks, and drawn together in folds at the ends. This process they effect, by first warming the bark in the fire. The man and his wife were seated on their knees in the canoe, in which they had a fire, on a flat stone. The man propelled the canoe by means of a paddle, that he applied first on one side and then on the other. He used a spear in fishing, made of a long stick, with four, long, wooden prongs, attached to it, by means of string and Grass-tree Gum. This he brought slowly, almost into contact with the fish, before striking. While fishing, he kept up a noise like the blowing of a Porpoise, and accompanied it by showers of saliva, that disturbed the surface of the water, like small rain. He seldom failed in transfixing his finny prey. Another man, who stood on a log that extended into the river, was equally successful, by a similar process.

14th. A person spoke in the meeting this morning, but

got into a state of excitement, and exceeded the measure of his exercise, and thus became confused. This gave rise to some observations, after meeting, on the advantage of being deliberate, and of avoiding excitement, and the consequent risk of going too far in expression. A few remarks were also made on the views of Friends, in regard to the liberty of speaking in assemblies for worship, as some of the persons who met with us needed information on this head. They were reminded, that though Friends admitted this liberty, in subjection to the judgment of the church, according to Scripture, they were careful that none should exercise it, but in the fear of the Lord, and under the belief, that it was in the counsel of his will, that they spoke.

15th. We committed a few books, the writings of Friends, of which we apprehend the religious world, generally, know but little, to a gentleman, in the East India Company's service, to be placed in a public library, at Madras, or disposed of in such other way, as he may think likely, to make their valuable contents the most useful. The weather of a Sydney winter is fine, clear, and remarkably agreeable; the thermometer varying from 46° to 66°, in the shade. Among the many beautiful shrubs, now in blossom, are *Acacia pungens, Bossiœa heterophylla, Dillwynia ericoides, Boronia pilonema* and *tetrathecoides, Eriostemon salicifolius, Lambertia formosa, Banksia collina,* and *Leptospermum baccatum.*

19th. Yesterday, we had the satisfaction of learning, from Captain Blackwood, of the Hyacinth, sloop-of-war, just arrived from Tahiti, that the Henry Freeling, with our friends, D. and C. Wheeler, had reached that island, in safety. To-day, we received satisfactory letters from them, mentioning the cordial reception they met with from the Missionaries and the Natives.

20th. We took leave of John Leach and his wife, on board the Governor Phillip, bound for Norfolk Island. They left V. D. Land, in consequence of the increased indisposition of John Leach, who has had consumptive symptoms for several years. General Bourke has appointed him to the office of Catechist, to the penal settlement, on Norfolk Island, in the hope, that the mild climate may conduce to lengthen his life, and that he may be made serviceable to the prisoners there, as he has been, in an eminent degree, to those in V. D. Land.—We parted from them in Christian love, under a precious sense of the divine presence overshadowing our minds.

Consumption is not of frequent occurrence, among emigrants from Europe, but children born in Australia, of European parents, sometimes die of this disease. Where it occurs amongst emigrants from Europe, it is generally as many years in running its course, as it would be months, in England.

21st. We had a satisfactory meeting, on the premises of a settler, at Cooks River, seven miles from Sydney, where, by the zeal of a Wesleyan, a small congregation has been collected, which assembles on First-day mornings. The congregation consisted of about twenty persons. They assembled in a small hut, of split timber, placed perpendicularly into the ground, having interstices between the timbers, so open as to admit more cold air than was comfortable, at this season of the year. The pulpit and seats were all very rustic. The appropriation of such a place to the purpose of divine worship, in this neighbourhood, is a token for good, not to be despised. Our kind friend, J. Tawell, conveyed us to the place, in a glass-coach. A few vehicles of this kind are kept in Sydney, to let out for hire; but there is no regular system of posting, yet established in any part of N. S. Wales, though coaches run daily to Parramatta, Liverpool, &c.

We passed some of the Mounted-police, who are scouring the neighbourhood, in search of bush-rangers; a party of whom robbed a cottage, at the angle of the road to Cooks River, last week. One of them was shot in the act. They were prisoners who had escaped from a neighbouring ironed-gang.

28th. We had an interesting meeting with the inhabitants of the North Shore of Port Jackson, at the house of John Parker, a gardener, from Norfolk, who emigrated to the Cape of Good Hope, in 1819, and subsequently to this Colony. The Divine Presence was sensibly felt, and ability was afforded us, to direct the congregation, to the teaching of the Lord, by his Spirit, manifested to the attentive mind, as a witness against sin, and as a guide, a counsellor, and a comforter. The nature of true worship was explained, as well as the advantage of waiting upon the Lord in silence, to receive a knowledge of our states, and thus to become prepared to pray in spirit for the supply of our wants, and to give thanks in the name of Jesus, for the mercies received. The example of our holy Redeemer was held up to view, in rejecting the temptation of Satan, to worship him, for the purpose of obtaining the glories of the world. The contrariety to this example, was pointed out, in those, who, for the sake of a share of these glories, sacrifice truth, honesty, and justice, or immerse themselves in the love of the world. These, and all others who live in transgression against God, and in the gratification of their own corrupt propensities, were shown to be, through such things, falling down to Satan in spirit, and worshipping him. From the feeling that prevailed, I have no doubt, but that the Holy Spirit was felt to bear witness to the same truths, in the minds of many of the congregation. G. W. Walker had a large part in the vocal labour of this meeting, much to my comfort.

7th mo. 4th. Wishing to hold a meeting with the few settlers, on the shores of Botany Bay, we walked thither, and called at their dwellings. These are chiefly small huts, on the edge of a marsh, built by some veteran soldiers, who were located there, a few years since. The soil being of a nature requiring to be turned over, and exposed to the action of the air, for two or three years before it becomes fertile, and these men having no capital, and not being generally industrious, many of their cottages have been deserted, and their lands have passed into other hands. Botany Bay, with its gay shrubs, might wear an imposing aspect, to the first navigators of these seas, after a tedious voyage; but its shores are shallow, and not convenient for landing, and most of the land on the north side, is dreary sand and marsh, of little, real value. The pieces that are worth anything, are of very limited extent, and are in few hands. One of the proprietors has established a woollen manufactory, which, from the price of labour in this country, is not likely to pay. He told us, that the leaves of the Wooden-pear, *Xylomelum pyriforme*, dye wool yellow, and that the branches of *Leptospermum scoparium*, answer the purposes of Fustic-wood, and dye fawn-colour. A handsome species of Grass-tree, *Xanthorrhœa arborea*, was in flower, in some of the sandy grounds : its root-stocks were surmounted by an elegant crest, of rush-like leaves; from the centre of which, the flower stem arose to ten feet in height; somewhat less than the upper half of this, was densely covered with brown scales, giving it an appearance, something like a Bull-rush. From amongst these scales the small, white, star-like flowers emerged, as in the other species of this genus. The plants with large root-stocks had been destroyed, for fuel, for which purpose they are much valued. In this neighbourhood, as well as at Port Jackson, the Sweet Tea, *Smilax glyciphylla*, abounds. It is a low, climbing plant, with narrow, heart-shaped leaves, having a taste something like Spanish Liquorice. It was used instead of tea, by the early settlers, and formed the chief ingredient in their drink, on occasions of rejoicing.

5th. Slight frost has occurred in some nights lately, so as to produce thin ice. Heavy rain fell last night, which was truly acceptable after the long drought. We lodged with a settler from Ireland, and had a meeting with about forty persons, at the house of his neighbour; where the Wesleyans, from Sydney, usually hold a meeting, on First-days.

6th. The rain continued, with little intermission, but we returned to Sydney; G. W. Walker became affected with low fever, from miasmata, raised by the wet on the parched marshes.

CHAPTER XXVI.

7th mo. 9th. Six persons, including G. W. Walker and myself, were present at the week-day meeting. It was a season
in which ability was granted, to point out the necessity
of being willing, to have "judgment laid to the line, and
righteousness to the plummet," in order that, not only the
pardon of past sin might be obtained, through faith in the
sacrifice of Christ, but also ability to do the will of God,
by the help of the Spirit, which is freely offered us, if we
do but ask it. The congregation was also shown, that we
cannot ask this help acceptably, unless we keep under the
operation of the Holy Spirit, so as to be preserved sensible
of our need of help ; and that without continued help, man
is sure to go astray, in one way or other, and to try to reconcile himself to an imperfect and sinful state.

We dined, and spent the evening, with some of our
friends, and were again refreshed by reading some extracts
from the journal of J. and M. Yeardley. The state of
society seems to be widely different, in the thickly-peopled
parts of Europe, from what it is in the thinly-inhabited regions
of Australia. In the latter, few persons are to be found, willing
to devote their time and energies to endeavouring to raise
the moral and religious tone of the population. Most of
the settlers, who rank above the lowest class, have come
hither, to try to better their fortunes ; this object they seem

chiefly to pursue; and where they are successful, pleasure, and a measure of display, are, with most of them, the chief additional objects, combined with the original pursuit.

12th. Our meetings were seasons of comfort. The sense of divine favour was not only granted, but also ability to labour, to bring the little congregation to a more steady attention to the impressions and operations of the Holy Spirit; in order that they may become more thoroughly engrafted into Christ, the True Vine, and be lively branches in him, bringing forth fruit to the glory of their Heavenly Father.

18th. Several days, lately, have been very wet. To-day, in a fine interval, we walked a few miles, to the east of Sydney. In a bushy hollow, we met with *Zamia spiralis*, a singular, Palm-like plant, in fruit. The whole fruit has some resemblance to a Pine-apple; but large nuts, in red coats, are fixed under the scales forming the outside. The Blacks, place these nuts under stones, at the bottom of water, in order to extract some noxious principle from them; they are afterwards converted into food. In wet weather, an insipid, jelly-like gum, which is wholesome, and not unpalatable, exudes from the plant.

20th. Three species of the genus *Loranthus*, which consists of plants, allied to Mistletoe, grow parasitically on trees in this neighbourhood. They have handsome blossoms, a little like Honey-suckle, but with more green, than yellow or red in them. Two of them have external roots, adhering to the bark of the trees that support them, and incorporating themselves with it; but occasionally, one of these species happens to grow upon the other, and then it emits no external root! This is a striking instance of that power, sometimes exhibited by a plant, to adapt itself to circumstances, and which is called Vegetable Instinct.

21st. We attended the anniversary meeting of the Benevolent Society, an interesting institution, for the relief of the infirm poor, many of whom are supported in its Asylum. The funds of this society are raised, to a considerable extent, by voluntary subscription; but as many of the objects of relief, and support, are persons who have come to the Colony as prisoners, the Government makes up the deficiencies in the funds.

23rd. I met a large group of Aborigines, in the street, several of whom appeared to be intoxicated. Some of them were dressed in dirty blankets. A few of the women had on skin garments, with the fur outside. Though some of the younger ones were not of unpleasing features, making allowance for their national outline, they looked meagre, and miserably degraded.

26th. The meetings were seasons of much conflict to my mind, under a feeling of the power of temptation, perhaps in sympathy with others, under that power, but I was mercifully enabled to trust in the Lord, and if not to stay my mind upon my God, yet to keep him in remembrance, in the sense that help was in him alone. In seeking this help, through faith in the blessed Mediator, I found it my place, out of my own weakness, to call others to the source of strength, and to testify to the stability of that Foundation laid in Zion, which whosoever builds upon, shall not be confounded.

28th. In the evening, we attended the committees of the Bible Society and Religious Tract Society, which were interesting. It is comforting to find a few persons, in this Colony, labouring, according to their various measures of spiritual light, to promote the spread of the Gospel. These are chiefly, individuals who left their native land as missionaries, or religious teachers; but some of them have found it necessary to enter into business, for the support of their families.

Having believed that advantage might arise from giving a few lectures on Temperance, and the matter having pressed upon me as a duty, we obtained the use of the Old Court House, for this purpose. I was enabled to get through the first, which took place this evening, with more comfort than I anticipated. The audience was pretty large, and I trust, there was left upon their minds, an increased conviction of the evils of spirit-drinking, and of the importance of persons, of respectable character, abstaining altogether from this great source of temporal and moral evil, in order to promote, by their example, a reformation among the population at large.

8th mo. 3rd.   We attended a meeting at Liverpool, twenty miles from Sydney, for the re-organization of an Auxiliary Bible Society. The one formerly existing there, having become extinct. It is difficult to keep up institutions of this kind, in a newly settled country, where they are more dependent for maintenance, upon excitement, than upon principle. The attendance was not large for the town, which contains about 600 inhabitants. The Colonial Hospital, at Liverpool, is a fine building, of brick; and there are a few good houses in the place, of the same material. The road from Sydney to Liverpool is good; it has two turnpike gates, and lies through a low forest of *Eucalyptus, Acacia,* and *Melaleuca:* it crosses Georges River, by a rude bridge; but a handsome one, of stone, with one elliptical arch, is in the course of erection.

4th. I called upon a young man, from whom I had received a letter, imploring assistance: he came to the Colony two years since, and has been sinking in the scale of society, till he has got very low. To send young men, who are unsteady, to a distant land, is a dangerous expedient. They meet with numerous temptations, and usually give way to them, till they are brought into the depth of wretchedness. In this state, some of them commit suicide, others take to thieving or forgery, and become convicts; others get berths among the lowest grade of sailors; and but few reform, or obtain situations in which they can retrieve their characters.

5th. We again crossed to the North Shore of Port Jackson, and invited the inhabitants to a meeting, to be held at the house of a settler. A young man accompanied us, from a family, who have become deeply interested respecting the principles of Friends, and are carefully reading "Barclay's Apology." We had a long ramble, and becoming hungry, regaled ourselves with Oysters, from the rocks.

9th. We returned to the North Shore of Port Jackson, in a boat, kindly sent for us, by the person at whose house the meeting was appointed. The congregation amounted to fifty-four persons. I was enabled to extend to them the invitations of the Gospel, and to show, from many passages of Scripture, the necessity of being led by the Spirit of God, if we would become the children of God; and that, without this Spirit, we have neither inclination nor ability to take one step in the way of holiness. But by the assistance of this Spirit, which is freely offered to all, and which works in all who do not resist it, we are enabled to perform the will of God; for his Spirit excites us to repentance, to faith in Christ, and to obedience to his words, and leads those into all truth, who yield themselves freely to its blessed dominion.

13th. The week-day meeting was a low season. Near the conclusion, I had to encourage those who felt themselves in any degree, in bondage to sin, to commit themselves in prayer to the Most High, and to beg, in the name of Jesus, under the sense of their unworthiness, that God would take unto himself his own great power, and reign in them; that he would render every thing, contrary to his will, so burdensome to them, as to make them seek his help to put it away; and that he would thus wean them from the things that keep the soul in bondage, from which none can deliver themselves, by their own power. The happy results of such exercise of mind before the Lord, I could testify to, from my own experience; when, out of the depths of humiliation, I had cried unto the Most High, and waited upon him, from day to day, for an answer to my petitions, which were often repeated, under the fresh feeling of the state of necessity, to which my soul was made alive, by the in-shining of the light of Christ, or the manifestation of the Holy Spirit; and which were, therefore, not vain repetitions; but in accordance with the instruction, that "men ought always to pray and not to faint."

14th. I gave my concluding lecture on Temperance, and felt thankful, in having been enabled to accomplish what, for the present, may be my duty, with regard to the promotion of temperance in this place; where iniquity has flowed as a torrent, through the medium of strong drink, which is still a most formidable barrier to moral and religious improvement.

15th.   Lancelot E. Threlkeld, the Government Missionary to the Aborigines, on Lake Macquarie, breakfasted with us: he has come to Sydney, to interpret for one of the Blacks, who is charged with the murder of a white man.   Threlkeld has written a grammar of the language of the Aborigines, which has been printed by the Government.

17th.   We took tea with two pious persons, from India. Before parting from them, the 50th chapter of Isaiah was read, and we spent a little time, in silently waiting upon the Lord, greatly to our comfort.   It is indeed a privilege, to take sweet counsel with those whose hearts are turned to the Lord, in these regions, that may be called, spiritually desolate, notwithstanding, such persons may not see many things belonging to the Gospel, in the same point of view with ourselves.   Many invalids from India, come to these Colonies, on account of their health, which they frequently recruit, in the drier atmosphere and cooler winters of Australia and V. D. Land.

18th.   The Committee of the Temperance Society was well attended.   The important moral reformation, in abstinence from spirituous liquors, is gaining ground in the public mind.   Some additional restrictions have lately been placed on the sale of spirits, by the Government; forbidding the payment of wages in them, beyond a third part, and interdicting the sale of them to prisoners, &c.   But while any portion of wages is allowed to be paid in them, and houses are very numerously licensed for their sale, and the example of free persons encourages their use, prisoners will continue to obtain them.   Sydney is still an awfully drunken place.

25th.   The anniversary meeting of the New South Wales Auxiliary Bible Society, was held in a large room, at the Pulteney Hotel, granted gratuitously by the landlord, who is a Jew!   The Colonial Secretary was in the chair.   The meeting was not very numerously attended, but was addressed by several persons, who ably set forth the privilege and importance of promoting the circulation of the Holy Scriptures.

29th. The weather has become much warmer. There was some lightning this evening. Peach-trees are in blossom, and Vines and Weeping Willows are beginning to vegetate. Oranges are in perfection, and Loquats are beginning to ripen. The last are the produce of a large, bushy, evergreen, Japanese tree. They grow in clusters, at the extremity of the branches, and are yellow; they are about the size of a large acorn, and contain one or two large seeds. Some of the varieties combine an agreeable acidity and sweetness, others are austere, and only fit for baking. Deciduous trees, from the northern hemisphere, rest in the mild winters of this part of the world, with remarkable regularity. Though the weather is as warm throughout the winter, as in the finest part of an English spring, these trees do not begin to vegetate prematurely, as they often do in their native country, after a time of severe cold.

Though all the native trees and shrubs of V. D. Land are evergreens, and the climate is cooler than that of N. S. Wales, there are a very few trees, natives of the latter country, that are deciduous. The chief of these are, *Melia Azedarach*, the White Cedar, which produces clusters of flowers, at the extremities of its branches, having the colour and smell of Lilac, just as its foliage begins to appear; *Sterculia acerifolia*, a tree resembling the Sycamore, but producing large quantities of flame-coloured blossoms, before its leaves unfold in spring; and *Cedrela Toona?* the Australian Cedar, a large tree, somewhat like an Ash, which casts its leaves in winter, at least in the cooler parts of N. S. Wales.

CHAPTER XXVII.

9th mo. 1st. HAVING made application for leave to visit
the prisoners, in the Jails, Penitentiaries, Ironed-gangs, &c.
in the Colony, we received a document to-day, signed by
the Colonial Secretary, on behalf of the Governor, granting
us this permission. An introduction to the Missionaries at
Wellington Valley, was also given to us, by Richard Hill, a
pious, and laborious Colonial Chaplain, and the Secretary
to "the Church Missionary Society." We likewise made
other preparations for a journey to Wellington Valley, believing that the right time was come, for us to proceed
in that direction.

2nd. We went to Parramatta, by a steamer, and took
up our quarters at a respectable inn. This town is the
second in size in N. S. Wales. In the census taken in
1833, it contained 2,637 inhabitants. Its population, at
this time, will probably be about 4,000.

3rd. We breakfasted with Samuel Marsden and his family, at the parsonage. After breakfast, he drove us to
the Female Factory, and the Female Orphan School. The

former is a large stone building, enclosed within a wall, sixteen feet high, divided into a number of wards, and having distinct yards, for assignable prisoners, and for those under sentence. There are sixteen solitary cells, in all of which prisoners were suffering punishment, chiefly for drunkenness and insolence. The number of females sentenced to confinement in this Factory, exclusive of those assignable, is about 250; who, it is to be regretted, are nearly destitute of employment. Formerly, women of this character were employed in spinning, and in weaving coarse, woollen cloth, but this occupation has been abandoned. The rooms where it was carried on, are empty, and like those of other parts of the building, have the glass of the windows much broken. This is said to have been done by some of the women, in unruly fits, which they occasionally take, one exciting another. This is not to be wondered at, among so large a number of the worst portion of the females of Great Britain and Ireland, confined, but unemployed. The assignable women were occupied with needlework, and the place they were in was clean. The Female Orphan School is a good brick building, kept neat and clean: it contains 150 children; who are generally healthy, and much like others of the same age.

On returning from the Orphan School, we called upon the Governor, and at his request, accompanied him to inspect the site of a projected Lunatic Asylum, at Tarban Creek. The situation is a little elevated, on the north shore of Port Jackson, or the Parramatta River, which, at this point, spreads, so as to have the appearance of a fine lake. The view is delightful, extending eastward to beyond Sydney, which is seven miles off; it also takes in Parramatta, to the westward, distant ten miles; and is bounded, in that direction, by the Blue Mountains, to the foot of which, is about thirty miles. There is good fresh water upon the spot, which, at present, is occupied by Gum-trees and scrub. Betwixt this place and Parramatta, there is a little settlement, called Kissing Point, with a neat Episcopal chapel. Not far from it, a fire in the bush had extended to a wooden bridge, and burnt it down. In several places along the road, fires had not only "consumed the thickets of the forest," and despoiled the trees, but had burnt considerable lengths of post and rail fencing. In some parts of the ride, tracts of clear ground were visible, bounded and interspersed with wood, giving the country the appearance of a large park; but every thing looks brown and withering, from the drought, which has now continued about nine months. The rains that have reached Sydney, have not extended many miles from the coast. There are some small Orange-grounds, about Kissing Point, and many of the settlers' gardens are furnished with Orange-trees, but they are losing their leaves for want of moisture.

4th. We called upon two thoughtful families, and then went again to the Female Factory; where we had interviews, first, with the third-class prisoners, and next with those of the first and second classes, jointly. Much Christian counsel was imparted to them, and supplication was put up, on their behalf, to Him who regards with compassion, the poor outcasts of our race, and who enabled us to point out the blessed effects of attention to the teaching of his good Spirit, leading to repentance, to faith in Christ, and to a holy, self-denying life, and who gave us some sense of his good presence, in the engagement.

The Episcopal congregation, at Parramatta, is attended by from 500 to 600 persons, on a First-day morning, inclusive of the military and prisoners. These have no choice in regard to being present. The Wesleyan congregation, on First-day evenings, amounts to about 150 persons; and there is also a small Presbyterian congregation. There are two schools in Parramatta, to each of which the Government contributes £100 per annum, furnishing also the school-houses. There is likewise an infant school, similarly supported, the parents of the children contributing something, by payments for the pupils. In addition to these, there are likewise some private schools in the town.

5th. We had an interview with an ironed-gang, of from two to three hundred prisoners, in their barracks, at six o'clock in the morning. They were very quiet and attentive;

and there was a measure of that solemn feeling over us, which we esteem to be an evidence of the divine presence, and a proof of the continued extension of the mercy of our Heavenly Father, both to ourselves, and to those who are straying from the paths of righteousness, whom he is inviting to return, repent, and live.

6th. Having believed it our duty to invite the Inhabitants to a religious meeting, we engaged a large room belonging the inn, where only a small company assembled this morning. We had but little to express among them: that little was, however, illustrative of the nature of true worship; and access was granted to the throne of Grace, in prayer, near the conclusion. Another meeting, held in the evening, was larger. The overshadowing of the divine presence was more perceptibly felt, and the doctrines of the Gospel were more largely preached, than in the former. After the state of the country, from drought, had been noticed, and the passage, "He turneth a fruitful land into barrenness, for the wickedness of them that dwell therein;" and some others, relating to such dispensations of the Almighty, had been commented upon, the benefits of silence before the Lord, were also spoken of, and prayer was vocally offered; after which, a solemn pause concluded the meeting.

7th. Samuel Marsden provided us with a guide to South Creek: he was a Black, of that place, named Johnny, an intelligent man, speaking English very fairly, and wearing a hat, jacket, trowsers, and shoes. He carried our bundles, and was very attentive, and by no means meriting the character given to us this morning, of their race, by a settler from Wollongong: "That nothing could be given to these fellows that they valued a straw." I could not think the person who made the remark, had attained to much knowledge of human nature. It is quite true, that the Blacks have not learned to place the same value upon many things, that the Whites place upon them. It is amusing to see the disappointment of many of the Whites, at the proofs they meet with of this fact; especially, when they think to hold out temptations to the Blacks, to work for less than their labour is worth. Few white people seem to reflect upon the fact, that our notions of the value of things, depend upon our habits, and are, in many instances, merely ideal. It is, however, to be regretted, when benevolent men adopt the notion, that the circumstance of the Blacks not estimating things by the same standard as the Whites, is owing to some invincible peculiarity in them; because such an opinion paralyzes their efforts for the civilization of this untutored race.

On the way from Parramatta, we stepped into several cottages, conversed with the inhabitants, and gave them tracts. We had also many conversations with persons travelling on the road, on foot, in carts, &c. We were kindly received by Charles Marsden, and his family, at the South Creek, sixteen miles from Parramatta, and in the evening had a satisfactory religious interview with them and their servants. Before dark, we walked to the side of the Creek, to see the Black Natives, who resort thither. In comparison with some other tribes, the South Creek Natives may be considered as half-domesticated, and they often assist in the agricultural operations of the settlers. The wife of our guide can read, she is a. half-cast, who was educated in a school, formerly kept for the Natives, at Parramatta. It is to be regretted that this school was abandoned; for though many who were educated in it, returned into the woods, yet an impression was made upon them, favourable to their further progress in civilization.

A few of the Natives were, at one time, located upon a piece of the worst land in this part of the country, at a place, called Black Town. Here some of them raised grain, in spite of the sterility of the soil, at a time when they were unable to dispose of it; and to add to their discouragement, at this juncture, the Missionary, who had been a short time among them, was withdrawn. The want of success, in this unfair experiment, is sometimes brought forward, as a proof that nothing can be done for these injured and neglected people.

8th. We set out, at an early hour, to Penrith, a small, scattered town, on the Nepean River. Our guide was another South Creek Black, named Simeon. His wife was killed, about two years ago, by some of those whom he

termed "Wild Natives:" he had one little boy, for whom
he shewed great affection. We tried in vain, to persuade
this man to accompany us to Wellington Valley; he did
not like to go to so great a distance. These people are
afraid of other tribes of their own race.

After breakfasting at a respectable inn, we proceeded to the
station of the Stockade Ironed-gang, on Emu Plains. The
huts, in which they are lodged, are but temporary structures
and the gang, which was large, is now reduced to seventy.
The Superintendent, a young man from Inverness-shire,
accompanied us to the gang, with whom we had a religious
interview. They have been employed in cutting a new road,
up Lapstone Hill, the ascent of the Blue Mountains, and are
now completing it with a bridge, across a deep gully.

On leaving the Ironed-gang, we proceeded along dusty,
mountain roads, through forests of Gum and Stringy-bark,
in some parts of which, fire was raging with fury; it had
burnt the scrub off other parts, and left it black. On
reaching a place, called The Valley, where there is a plain,
country inn, with the sign of The Woolpack, having moderate accommodation, we gladly rested for the night.

9th. About five miles from our lodging place, we visited
another Ironed-gang, and three miles further, a third; in
each, there were about sixty men, and both were under the
charge of a young military officer. The prisoners were
lodged in huts, upon large, open areas, by the road-side,
without any stockade. When not at work, they are kept
on the spot, by a guard of soldiers, who are ordered to fire
upon any that may attempt to escape, and who will not
stop when called to. We were informed, that they had no
Bibles, or other books, and that their only religious instruction consisted in the reading of prayers by the officer, or
sergeant in charge, on First-days. A few of the prisoners
lodge in moveable caravans, which have doors, and iron-
barred windows, on one side. Four or five men sleep in
each end of them, on the floor, and as many more, on platforms. They are not less crowded than the huts, and are
unwholesome dormitories. Many of the men sleeping in
them, become affected with the scurvy.

W

After travelling eighteen miles, we arrived at the Weather-board Hut, where we had intended to lodge; but the
only good room was occupied.   One, in which we had an
excellent meal of beef and bread, with tea, was without
glass in the windows, and could not have the door shut,
for the smoking of the wood fire.   This, as is common in
this land of trees, was a very large one, and it was acted
upon by a fierce and piercing wind; we therefore determined on making another stage.   The former part of our
journey through the forest, had been cheered, at intervals,
by remarkable views.   Some of these, opened to a great
distance, exhibiting the singularly winding cliffs of sandstone, which seemed as if it had decomposed, till ferru-
ginous veins had bid defiance to the weather.   We now set
out again, as daylight was departing, to make our way in
the dark.   We were informed, that there was but one road
through the woods, yet we sometimes felt a little perplexed
by this road dividing, for a short distance.   But notwithstanding these difficulties, we found our previously exhausted vigour to increase as we proceeded, in consequence
of the bracing effects of the cold wind; and we reached
the "Scotch Thistle," a solitary inn, at Black Heath, on
the top of the mountains, earlier than we expected.   The
road over the Blue Mountains, winds nearly forty miles,
along their ridge, which ascends and descends a little, at
intervals.   Some parts of it have been cut with much labour, by prisoners, and others are sandy or rocky, but
most of it is now good for carriages.   There are a few
miserable, solitary public-houses, by its side, in addition
to the better ones, already mentioned, and another, of decent character.   Along its whole course, there are no grassy
openings to afford pasturage for cattle.   At the present
time, the little rigid herbage, in the forest, is dried up.
The bullocks travelling with settlers' drays, are "ill favoured
and lean fleshed," from the scarcity of grass in the
countries below.   Dead bullocks were numerous by the
road side.   Wedge-tailed Eagles were frequently to be seen,
feeding upon the fresh ones.

10th.   The night was very cold, rendering the good

fires, the soft, clean beds, and excellent provision of this homely-looking inn, very acceptable. In the morning, the ice was as thick as a half-crown. In this cold region, there is a low species of *Eucalyptus*, that I have not before seen; there are also some other remarkable shrubs.—Our road continued to wind over the sand-stone mountains, to the pass of Mount Victoria, on the descent of which there was granite. The pass is carried, in two places, on causeways of mason-work, as wide as bridges, raised on narrow saddles, uniting the hills; in other places it is cut through the rock. This great work has been effected by the labour of prisoners, a small party of whom are still at work. We had an interview with twenty-eight of them, several of whom were of desperate appearance. They are under the charge of an overseer, have no Bibles, and no religious instruction.

At the foot of these mountains, there is a granite vale, called The Vale of Clywd, were there are two houses, one of which was lately deprived of its license to sell spirits. Further along the road, there is a brook, crossed by a wooden bridge. This brook was formerly called The Rivulet; but this name is now corrupted into, The River Lett! The country here is open and grassy, and has a few White and Weeping Gum-trees, and a Banksia resembling *Banksia australis*, scattered upon it. It will maintain a sheep to four or five acres. We turned a little from the road, to Helvellyn, the residence of two young settlers, by whom we had been kindly invited to such accommodation as they were able to furnish. On the margin of the brook, there are some fine specimens of the species of *Casuarina*, called River-oak: they are about seventy feet high, irregularly branched, and densely clothed with green, leafless shoots, resembling slender Horse-tail-weed.

11th. Last evening, we had a religious interview with the family, and a few other persons, who had called to beg a night's lodging. This morning, one of our young friends accompanied us over some of the grassy, forest hills, to the road leading to the Junction Stockade, where an ironed-gang, of upwards of 150 prisoners, is employed, under the charge of a military officer. These men were at work,

w 2

cutting a road, about three miles from the barracks, under
a guard of soldiers, some of whom returned from Norfolk
Island, in the Isabella, at the same time with ourselves.
We assembled the men by the road-side, and extended
some religious counsel to them; the guard standing, at the
time, as they generally do, in a position to prevent any of the
prisoners running away. The soldiers often use irritating language, mixed with curses, in speaking to the prisoners, which
is of bad influence, in hardening them, when they greatly
need to be rendered more susceptible of good. While in the
act of assembling, one man picked the pocket of another, of
a tobacco-box : he was seen, and knocked down by one of
the guard, near to the place where I was standing. This
circumstance occasioned no perceptible disturbance among
the others; and I trust there were some present who, at
least, for the time, were brought to think on eternal things.

Near the barracks, we saluted a native Black and his wife,
and they returned our tokens of notice. They were the first
we had seen in their wild state. We took some refreshment
at a decent public-house, at Solitary Creek, and afterwards
visited a small road-party, on the way to an inn, at Honey-
suckle Hill. As we approached this place in the dark,
we heard the cries of a female, and on arriving, found
that the landlord, in a state of intoxication, had struck his
wife to the ground, with a child in her arms; and such
was his phrenzy, that it was difficult to restrain him from
further mischief.

12th. We visited a small road-party, near the foot
of the Stony Ridge, and another betwixt that place and
Bathurst. It was past their work-hours, on seventh-day
afternoon, before we reached the last party, and several of
the men pleaded, that they were Roman Catholics, and did
not wish to come " to prayers," as they style all kinds of
religious interviews. With some difficulty, we got them to
understand our object, and most of them assembled in a
rude blacksmith's shop, in which we were glad of a shelter
from the cold. The message of love and mercy made a
softening impression upon these prisoners, and we separated
under different feelings, on their part, from those with which

they met us. This we find generally the case. The baptizing power of the Holy Spirit is felt, and their attention turned to their own convictions of sin, as the work of this blessed Spirit, and as the message of the mercy of their Heavenly Father, seeking to lead them to repentance, in order that they may obtain salvation through his beloved Son. When we stop them during their work-hours, which we have liberty from the Governor to do, few plead excuses; and as we do not enjoin any forms of worship, but simply, after a pause, say what is upon our minds, or pray for them, none seem to take it amiss. If it can be done, we always desire them to sit down, in order that they may rest at the same time; and if exposed to the sun, we request them to keep on their hats or caps. These little considerations for their personal comfort, often prepare the way for the reception of our counsel.

As we ascended the hills, Bathurst Plains opened to our view, relieving the eye after a long incarceration, in thick, or in open forest, by a fine, undulating expanse, fifteen miles in length, and ten in breadth, watered by the Macquarie, formed here, by the junction of the Campbell and Fish Rivers, all running westward, and margined by a line of River-oaks, which are almost the only trees upon the Plain. Toward the western side of this open country, the rising town of Bathurst is situated, and settlers houses, of respectable figure, are scattered here and there on all sides. Much of the land is enclosed with post-and-rail fences; but at present, it is one unvaried surface of brown, dried, short grass. We took up our quarters at an inn; and notwithstanding the contentions of some drunken people at the door, and the appearance of disorder in the house, we found good accommodation in a quiet, well-fitted-up room, in a square area, at the back. Bathurst consists of a number of inns and cottages, scattered along the sides of a projected street, for more than a mile, with an Episcopal place of worship, of brick, on a hill near the parsonage, and some scattered huts on one side of the river: there are also a place of worship, of the Scotch church, and several inns and other houses, a jail, military barrack, hospital, factory for female prisoners, police-office, bank, &c. on the other side of the river; where the buildings are nearer one to another.

13th. The night was very frosty. Bathurst is said to be about two thousand feet above the level of the sea; which accounts for the coolness of its climate. We breakfasted at the Parsonage; and wishing to have a meeting with the inhabitants in the evening, spent the forenoon in inviting them to assemble with us in a school-room, kindly granted us by John Espie Keane, the Episcopal Minister. It was pleasant, in the forenoon, at the hour of public worship, to see a number of the carriages of settlers driving in; many of them coming from a distance of several miles. The piety and diligence of J. E. Keane has been greatly blessed, in drawing the attention of people of this class, to the obligations of religion, at least, as regards the outward acknowledgment of them; and there are a few in his congregation who are considered spiritually-minded. Our meeting was not large, but it was owned by a comforting measure of divine influence.

15th. G. W. Walker having taken cold, we were constrained by J. E. Keane and his estimable wife, to become their guests, in order that he might be nursed. In the mean time, preparation was made for the continuance of our journey.

While at Bathurst, I saw much drunkenness, such as is common in remote situations in these Colonies. Many men, and some women, who appeared to be servants of settlers, were drinking at public-houses. It is common, with the men, many of whom have been prisoners, but have served out their sentence, to engage themselves as sawyers, shepherds, &c. in distant places, and to come into the town, when they have earned a few pounds, for the sole purpose of spending it in drunkenness and debauchery. When their money is gone, they return again to their labour. But for this, many of them might have been in easy circumstances, for they get good wages, and a little sets a man up in this part of the world. They prove the truth of the proverb, "The workman that is a drunkard will never be rich."

16th. We set forward for Wellington Valley. At a

short distance from Bathurst, a man was feeding a bullock, by the road-side, which had fallen from exhaustion. The continued drought has made " the famine wax sore " to these useful animals; and should there be no rain for a few weeks longer, it will be keenly felt, both by man and beast. In many places the ewes are so weak as to be unable to rear their lambs; and to the southward, the Influenza, a destructive disease, is prevailing among the sheep. We travelled about twenty-four miles along a well-tracked road, through open forest, and stopped, about noon, by the side of a pool, at a place called The Rocks, on account of the large masses of granite that project above the surface. Here we kindled a fire, and made tea, the common beverage with every meal, in travelling in this country. Among the rocks are some large Banksias, which are the last trees of this genus, in this direction, toward the interior. On our road, we passed two or three rude huts, at which we were informed that spirits were illicitly sold, and about sunset, reached a hut, called Kyongs, of late kept, as a public-house, by a man known by the name of " Charley Booth," who has been deprived of his license, and has retired into "the bush." It is now occupied as a stock-station, by the overseer and assigned servants of a settler. One of the men conducted us down the side of a creek, oozing from among some low, basaltic rocks, and opening into pools, called Lewis's Ponds, and put us into the way to Newton, where we were received with much kindness, by some pious, Cornish Wesleyans. In this neighbourhood, *Acacia dealbata* is richly laden with its golden blossoms, and *A. melanoxylon* is a frequent tree by the brooks.

17th. We travelled nearly forty miles, chiefly over low hills of granite, or argillaceous rock. At Broken-shaft Creek, there was the cottage of a blacksmith, and in other places, there were a few sheep-stations. We met some shepherds driving their flocks towards Bathurst, against the shearing time. Sheep are folded, in this Colony, at night, to preserve them from the Wild Dogs, which are said to be numerous; but they hide themselves in the day-time, and do not attack men. About noon, we stopped at a place where

there was water; and near sunset, at the side of the Molong River, which, at this season, is a small stream, widen-
ing here and there into pools. My companion was so
much exhausted by thirst, that he lay helpless upon the
ground, till I prepared tea, which revived him. We afterwards proceeded, at a pretty good pace, to a stock-station,
belonging to one of our acquaintance, further down the
river; to which we found our way with some difficulty, in
the dark. After making a hearty meal, we extended some
religious counsel to the men, but there did not seem to be
so much openness among them as we often meet with,
among men of this class.

In the course of our day's journey, the places that we
passed through that were clear of trees, were few and of
small extent. On one of these a flock, of a species of Ibis,
as large as a goose, was feeding; and on another there were
some birds resembling the Thick-kneed Bustard, which is
the Curlew of this country. Till to-day, we have seen
few birds except eagles, attracted by dead bullocks, and a
few Parrots, and White Cockatoos. We had some soup
at Bathurst, made from the latter bird, which was pretty
good. A Bandicoot is the only wild beast we have seen,
since leaving Sydney. Near the Molong River, we came
upon a limestone country.

18th. Our road continued to be distinctly tracked in
most places, though in some a little obscure, some of it
was over basaltic country, and some over argillaceous: the
soil of the latter was poor, with sharp gravel. In the forenoon we rested on a log, by a shepherd who was watching
his flock, with whom we conversed on the way of holiness,
and work of redemption. The young man's heart was
open to understand the things that were spoken, which he
frankly acknowledged had not had sufficient place in his
thoughts. Being much fatigued in the evening, with our
walk of thirty-two miles, we had concluded to make a fire,
and sleep in the bush, when it began to rain, lighten, and
thunder. We therefore made our way, which was now
become difficult to find in the dark, to a mean, dirty hut,
at a place called Newry, belonging to a settler, and occupied

by a ticket-of-leave stock-keeper, and an assigned prisoner-servant. These men entertained us hospitably with milk and damper, fare such as was offered to us at every station at which we called, on our way, and sometimes with the addition of tea and meat. There were two black youths residing in the hut with the stock-men; we were informed that they made themselves useful in minding the sheep, milking the cows, &c. The stock-keeper observed that these Blacks stopped with them better than their country-men generally do with white people, because they treated them more like companions, and gave them a part of such provision as they themselves eat, instead of throwing scraps to them, as if to dogs.

19th. Our accommodation last night, though the best the place afforded, was such as we but seldom have had to put up with. Our bed was more sombre than would be found in the meanest, mendicant lodging-house, in England; it was only outdone by a blanket, generally used by one of the Aborigines, which was folded to add to the width of the bed. Another such bed, spread on the uneven clay floor, served our hosts; the two Blacks coiled themselves up on some sheep-skins, near the fire, pulling a blanket over them. My companion was driven from his resting-place, by bugs, which were very numerous. He tried to rouse the Blacks, in order to obtain more fuel, to revive the fire, but his efforts proved in vain; he therefore sat down on the best seat he could find: it was an uneasy, narrow stool, which did not stand level. At length, he was obliged to return to bed, by cold and faintness, which overcame all obstacles, and he fell asleep.

These stations, as they are called, usually belong to opulent settlers, living in or near towns, who derive a great part of their wealth from their large flocks of sheep, and herds of cattle. These are tended by their servants, many of whom are prisoners, on their extensive locations, or on unoccupied, contiguous lands, in the interior of the Colony. Many of them also send flocks beyond the boundaries of the located part of the Colony, which is, in many directions for a great distance, low, open, grassy, forest hills, with here and there clear flats, or plains. In such situations, some of the less wealthy settlers feed their own flocks, foregoing, for a few years, most of the comforts of life. Three men called at the hut where we lodged, and after breakfast, we read a Psalm, and gave expression to the exercise of our minds on their account; pointing out the terrible consequences of remaining in sin, and directing their attention to the grace of God which bringeth salvation, and to the mercy offered us in Jesus Christ.

On the way toward Wellington, we passed a neat, but humble cottage, belonging to another settler. Most of the cottages in this part of the country, are of split timber, placed endwise into the ground, or of large sheets of Gum-tree bark, fastened to a frame work of poles; the roof being also of this material. A few of the timber cottages, are plastered inside and out, and are whitewashed. After re-crossing the Bell River, which we crossed thrice, yesterday, we again came upon Limestone. One of the trees upon this formation, is *Sterculia diversifolia;* it resembles the Oak in form, and the Poplar in foliage; and is like an English tree, in verdure. It attains to forty feet in height, and its bark is so tenacious as to be convertible into cordage; whence it also, is called Corrijong. Its roots are thick and soft, so as to be cooked for food by the natives. The trunk of the young tree is remarkably thick and green. It grows intermingled with various species of *Eucalyptus,* some of which are distinct from any we have before seen, and are about the size of the Willows and Birches of England.—On the side of the Bell River, we met a Black, with a blanket thrown loosely around him, driving a team of bullocks : he was the first we had seen, except the two boys last night, since the 11th. On arriving at the Missionary Station, at Wellington Valley, we received a kind welcome from John Christian Simon Handt and his wife, and from Ann Watson, whose husband was from home; and we felt thankful, that we had reached this extreme point of our journey.

CHAPTER XXVIII.

WELLINGTON VALLEY was formerly a Penal Settlement
for educated prisoners. The houses and barracks are of
brick; most of them are whitewashed. The best is occupied by the two missionary families; another, temporarily,
by two young settlers, and a third by four soldiers. The
number of Blacks at present on the settlement, is very
small: thirty were here lately, but most of them have
gone away for a short time, it is conjectured, on account
of the death of one of their countrymen. Two native
girls only, sleep in the house, the others preferring to be
out of doors, by their fires.

20th. G. W. Walker was confined to the house by
indisposition. At eleven o'clock, there was public worship. Some of the neighbouring settlers, and the few
soldiers stationed here, as a guard against bush-rangers, &c.
were present, in addition to the persons belonging to the
missionary establishment. I remained as a devout spectator,
while two hymns were sung, and J. C. S. Handt read the
prayers of the Episcopal Church. He then addressed the
congregation, informing them that, as I was present, he
designed to forego preaching. Then turning to me, he said,
if I had anything to say to them in love, they should be glad

to hear me. My mind had been under much exercise, and after a short pause, I stood up, and gave utterance to what was before me ; alluding to what was said by the apostle Paul, when he preached to the Athenians; and showing, that the superstitions of the present day, do not consist in worshipping idols of wood and of stone, graven by art, and man's device, but in imagining that we are doing God service, by going through certain forms and rituals, devised by man, in imitation of the expressions of spiritual devotion. These things I had to contrast with that worship which is in spirit and in truth; showing their inferiority, and that the Lord, to many who use them, is an unknown God. In commenting on the words, " whom ye ignorantly worship, Him declare I unto you," &c. I had to direct them to the working of the Holy Spirit, felt by all men as a witness in themselves against sin, and to declare, that this is the drawing of the Father, whose goodness seeks to lead us to repentance, in order to bring us unto the Son, that we may find life in him, and for his sake, receive the remission of sins that are past, and through him be enabled to perfect holiness in the fear of the Lord. That thus, we may come to the knowledge of God, who made heaven and earth, and all things that are therein, who is not worshipped by men's hands, neither dwelleth in temples made with hands ; but who is worshipped in spirit and in truth, by those whose hearts are turned unto him, and who are led by his Spirit; and who walk in his fear, and live to his glory. These regard his law, as it is recorded in the Holy Scriptures, and as it is put into their inward parts, and written in their hearts; their whole lives are an act of worship, both when assembled especially for the purpose, and when engaged in their daily avocations. Of such, the Lord is truly their God, and they are truly his people.

21st. I walked with J. C. S. Handt to see a flock of about five hundred sheep belonging to the mission, which has also a herd of about one hundred cattle, and a few pigs and horses; the sheep are said to be in the best state of any in this country. The harvest of last year was so plentiful that the surplus wheat is sufficient for the supply of the present season. This is a great blessing, as the drought has prevented the raising of an adequate crop for the present year, and the supply of food is a principal attraction to draw the Blacks to the place. These people are not numerous here ; a hundred is the greatest number that has been seen at the Station, at any one time, since its establishment, and several of these were from a distance. About thirty is the usual number resorting hither. They are said to be very capricious, and by no means desirous to learn, further than they are tempted by a supply of food. This is what may reasonably be expected, from a people who are not yet aware of what they are to gain, by learning to read. They are contented with food of the plainest kind, and like other races of men, are not disposed to work, beyond what they find necessary for obtaining the supply they require. They often prefer eating boiled wheat, to being at the trouble of grinding their corn in hand-mills, and making bread. Their moral state is represented as of the lowest grade. Immoralities of the grossest kinds are reported to be practised amongst them, but these are, in some measure, traceable to the influence of the prisoner stock-keepers.

The Blacks of N. S. Wales are a decreasing race: they do not, however, appear to be inferior in intellect to other nations; but man, when from under the influence of the restraints of religion, and of civil institutions, seems to be the same degraded being, all the world over. In N. S. Wales, he is far indeed, removed from the dreams of natural innocence, of those who do not see the effects of the fall in themselves, or believe that these effects exist in others. The N. S. Wales Aborigines do not openly make feasts upon human subjects, like the natives of New Zealand, and of some other islands of the Pacific; but there are pretty well authenticated instances of cannibalism among them.

The missionaries at Wellington have acquired a tolerably competent knowledge of the language spoken among the Natives of this part of the country; it differs considerably from that of the eastern coast; they are teaching two half-domesticated girls, and three boys to read, both in

their own language and in English. In the evening, all
the boys left the establishment, being offended because one
of them was refused a new pipe, as he had had one within
a few days. The oldest of the boys may be about sixteen,
the youngest about twelve; the intermediate one is about
fourteen. After the custom of many others of his race, he
wears a reed, about four inches long, through the cartilage
of his nose, as an ornament.

In the margins of the pools of the Bell River, there are
Reeds, *Arundo Phragmites*, Bull-rushes, *Typha latifolia*,
and some other aquatic plants, similar to those of England.
The surface of the water is, in many places, covered with
Azolla rubra, a beautiful, mossy-looking plant, occupying
the place that Duck-weed does in England.

22nd. Accompanied by J. C. S. Handt and a black
youth, who, with a man and a woman, returned to the
settlement this morning, we walked to Myami, two miles
distant, on the banks of the Macquarie River. This river
is now reduced to an inconsiderable stream, with large
pools at intervals. The rocks, where we crossed it, are
basaltic. At Myami, a Sydney merchant, has erected some
good, wooden buildings; consisting of a dwelling-house,
prisoners' huts, a large wool-shed, &c. Most of them are
weatherboard, of the Pine of this neighbourhood, which
is a species of *Callitris:* the wood is fragrant, but liable to
split. The prisoners' huts are of logs, of gum-tree; and
the shingles with which the whole are covered, instead of
slates, are of the Forest-oak, *Casuarina torulosa*. The
noble tree of the same genus, called the River-oak, grows
here to a large size, just within the banks of the rivers,
greatly ornamenting the country. Myami is a large location, of roughish, basaltic, open, grassy, forest sheep-hills,
with the advantage of an extensive back-run, beyond the
boundaries of the located portion of the Colony.

Our black companion was clad in a blanket, fastened
round his shoulders; under it he had a bag suspended,
in which he kept two pence, that he several times showed
me, with a pleased countenance, though he did not seem
to understand their value, except as pretty things to look

at. He amused himself as he went along, by throwing the flat, crooked, wooden weapon, called by the Whites a Boomring, but by the Blacks of this part, Barragan: he threw it at anything that took his fancy, not unfrequently missing his object. He informed us, that there was plenty of honey in the neighbourhood. It is the produce of small, stingless bees, that inhabit the hollow limbs of trees: these, the Blacks cut down with small tomahawks, obtained from the white people, and thus possess themselves of the honey, which they drink when mixed with water. The Blacks here climb trees, by cutting little notches in them, into which they fix their hands or feet, as occasion requires.

In the afternoon, I walked a considerable distance along the course of the Bell River, which was dry in some places, and running in others. In the pools, there were large flocks of Wild Ducks, of two sorts, and a few of the two species of the Shag or Diver, common in these Colonies. The Platypus, or Water Mole, and a small kind of Tortoise, are frequent in these rivers. The black youth, before alluded to, assured me, that the Platypus brings forth its young alive, several at a time, in holes, in the banks of the river: he also informed me, that the Tortoise came to warm itself in the sun, on logs that lay in the water, and that "Black fellows catch him by the leg, and eat him." The Natives roast their food lightly: they eat almost all kinds of living creatures that they can catch, including the Platypus, the River-muscle, which is a species of *Unio*, grubs, moths, ants' eggs, the larger lizards, and snakes, provided the last have not bitten themselves in the agonies of death. One of them informed me, that the ants' eggs tasted like fowls' eggs; and I have been told, that the large moths, roasted, are not unlike new bread. On inquiring of one of the boys, how he had taken a White Cockatoo that he was eating, he said, he had buried himself under the straw, near the corn-stacks, and when the birds came, he caught one by the leg. Scarcity of food, from the long drought, causes them to come in large flocks, into the stack-yards, along with Crows and Parrots.

24th. There was a fine rain, with much thunder and

lightning. Accompanied by J. C. S. Handt, and the black youth before mentioned, we visited the large cavern in the limestone, about three miles eastward of the settlement. The entrance is contracted and steep, opening among numerous small rocky projections: within there are a number of irregular chambers, some of which are very large. The sides and roof are formed of irregular, sub-hemispherical cavities, the surfaces of which, as well as the floor of the cave, are covered with dust, formed by the decomposing stone. In a few places there are sparry projections from the sides: stalactites, resembling icicles, depend from the roof, in several parts. In some places, the stalactites from the top have joined the stalagmites on the floor, and in one place the mass has become stupendous, and remarkably beautiful. The base is an ascent of irregular undulating narrow ledges, forming a series of perpendicular hollows, rising gradually for six or eight feet: the stalactites are slender columns, from fifteen to twenty feet in height, laterally united into a mass of irregular outline, which may be forty feet in circumference. But these dimensions not being from measurement, nor from memorandums made at the time, may be far from correct: they will, however, give some idea of this remarkable petrifaction, which by some has been compared to a great organ, to which it has a faint resemblance. The furthest extremity of the cave may be a hundred yards from the entrance: it is terminated by a sudden and almost perpendicular descent to water; which may be perceived by throwing stones down the opening. The top of one of the smaller chambers in the side, was dripping, and covered with short stalactites; another was dry, and inhabited by small bats, that were greatly disturbed by our flambeaux. Some bones are said to have been found in this cave, but I saw none, neither did I perceive any traces of fossil remains in the limestone, which is of a dove-colour, intersected with white veins, and of compact texture: possibly it may be transition limestone; but it is contiguous to basalt, and to hills of very hard, compact, reddish stone, traversed by white veins, possibly silicious. In the neighbourhood there are several smaller cavities; but I do not learn that they had been explored. Our black companion seemed a little fearful of entering the cavern, but he was pleased with exploring it. He enquired, as we returned toward daylight, who made it; and on being told, God, who made heaven, and earth, and all things, a momentary awe seemed to occupy his mind, as he repeated the answer. On the way to the cave, we saw a native black man, quite naked, (according to the common custom of these people,) walking with his blanket folded up in his hand. He stopped, and commenced cutting away the decayed bark of a tree, with his tomahawk, to get out grubs. When the aperture is cleared, the Blacks introduce a long reed, terminated by a hook of hard wood, pointed at the bend: this they force into the grub, and by this means draw it out of its hiding-place. On returning, we fell in with another, who had his head bound round with a fillet of netting, made of the bark of the Currajong, of this neighbourhood, and a strip of Kangaroo skin about his loins: he had in his hand, one of the hooks described, also a wooden paddle for digging up grubs and roots, a small club, and two opossums. These animals he had taken out of the hollow limb of a tree: they form a chief part of the subsistence of the native Blacks. At a short distance, his son joined us; he was one of the youths who left the settlement a few days ago. The man had curly hair: some of the Blacks here have straight hair: they rub themselves with grease, red ochre, yellow ochre, pipe-clay, &c. but I have not seen them with their hair matted with ochre and grease, like the Tasmanian Blacks. The rain of yesterday has greatly refreshed the country: already the grass is beginning to put forth greenness.

25th. A few more Blacks came to the Station, and two, who had been there, went away, saying there was going to be a fight, at a short distance. These fights generally arise about their women, and are seldom fatal; but occasionally, a few of the men get wounded. Among those who came to the station, were a woman and two little boys, the younger of which might be four years old.—In the afternoon, we walked to Mount Arthur, a hill about 500 feet high, near the junction of the Bell and Macquarie Rivers. From this point, there is an extensive view of the adjacent country, which seems to be a continuation of open, forest hills. Many of them look black, and very bare, from fire, which has "devoured the pastures of the wilderness." This hill is of compact, rufous stone, probably sandstone; near the top, its grain is coarse, and it imbeds larger pieces, forming a sort of Pudding-stone. On the upper portion, there were She-oak, *Casuarina quadrivalvis* and *Grammitis rutæ-folius*, a small fern, both of which are common in V. D. Land, also a *Cycas?* a remarkable *Eucalyptus*, and *Sterculia diversifolia*. Upon the last, there was a remarkable *Viscum*, or Mistletoe. Lower down the hill, the beautiful *Acacia venusta*, formed a bush, about six feet high; it bears heads of small, globular, golden blossoms.

26th. We went to see the grave of a native Black. We were accompanied by J. C. S. Handt, who informed us, that the legs of the deceased were bound up, so as to bring the knees to the chin: that in this posture, the body was thrust into a shallow, round hole, and covered with leaves and boughs, over which, a mound of earth, like a potato-heap, was raised up. On one side of this mound, and extending a third part of the way round it, there was a trench, formed of two low banks of earth. On the same side, some undulating lines, and others forming imperfect ovals, were inscribed on the trunks of adjacent trees.

27th. The public worship, this morning, was attended by some of the settlers, from beyond the Boundary. One of them informed us, that he was at a meeting which we had on the north shore of Port Jackson, a few weeks ago. He expressed, in very decided terms, his preference for the simple proceedings of Friends in regard to worship, over those of other communities of Christians. We find many prepared to see thus far, the beautiful simplicity of what we deem to be the Truth; but alas! how few are willing to take up the cross, and to put it into practice! There were also present this morning, of the Blacks, an aged man and three women, attired in clean blankets, two girls, and six or eight boys, some of whom reside with neigh-

bouring settlers, and make themselves useful. After the
Episcopal prayers had been read, we had an opportunity
of communicating what was on our minds, of which we
availed ourselves.   I was also engaged in vocal supplication.
—On a few occasions, when assembled with the persons
of the Mission Establishment, we have not found it our
place to say anything, after simply reading a chapter in
the Bible, but more frequently, have had something to express in exhortation, or prayer.—William Watson returned
this evening, from an unsuccessful expedition to endeavour
to gain an interview with some Blacks, who had killed
some cattle belonging a settler, in consequence of having
been exasperated, by the profligate conduct of a ticket-of-
leave stock-keeper, toward one of their wives.

28th. The forenoon was showery, but we took a walk
with the Missionaries, who are both much to be felt for.
I was never more fully convinced of the importance of
attending to divine qualification and direction, in missionary
concerns, than since we came hither; and though I heartily
desire, and earnestly hope, that good may result from this
mission, and I consider the example of such persons as the
Missionaries, and their wives, as a barrier against the over-
whelming, evil influence of a large proportion of the white
population of the neighbourhood, and a strength to those
who desire to walk uprightly; yet, should this mission not
succeed, as regards any perceptible fruits among the Blacks,
it will not be, to my mind, any proof that they are not
within the influence of the beneficial effects of rightly directed religious labours. The Missionaries themselves do
not think that they have yet effected anything, in the way
of the introduction of religious principle into the minds of
the Natives; though they have attempted preaching to the
Blacks, in their own tongue, and they occasionally read to
them, portions of Scripture, rendered into the dialect of
Australia. There is some ground to apprehend, that the
Blacks of Wellington may have been rendered more vicious
than some of the other tribes, by the Europeans sent
here, when Wellington was a penal settlement, and they
certainly are still demoralized by some of those residing in

the vicinity. The tribes are said to be more numerous, fifty miles northward and southward. Two half-civilized men, named Frederick and Jemmy, returned with W. Watson, whom they had accompanied on the expedition: they make themselves useful in the agricultural and other occupations of the Establishment. Frederick went lately to Liverpool; he says, before he went, the stock-keepers told him that what the Missionaries were trying to teach them, was all "gammon," or deceit, but now he knows better. —On visiting some of the Natives, at their fire, I saw the little, black boy, before noticed, after filling his pipe and smoking with the rest of his country people, lay it down, and kneel in his mother's lap, and suck! This was a combination of circumstances such as I had never imagined; and one that quite overpowered the feelings of gravity, excited by the degraded condition of the people.

The afternoon being fine, I walked to a distance, among some hills, on which there were fine, small trees, of the *Callitris* of this neighbourhood; which, like other species of the genus, resembles the Cypress and Red Cedar. In some of the vallies, dry Kangaroo-grass was ankle deep upon the ground; and thicker than I had seen it in any other place.

29th. After an early breakfast with the two mission families, we set out, to return to Bathurst. J. C. S. Handt accompanied us to Newry. We had much conversation with him, respecting the discouragements attendant upon their engagements as missionaries, and parted from him under a more than common degree of interest.

At Newry, there were four black men, at the hut where we lodged on the 18th. The hut-keeper expressed regret, at one of their kings having come to take away the two youths, who had become so useful, in order to make them young men; that is, to initiate them as young men in the tribe to which they belong, by knocking out a front tooth, and putting them under certain restrictions as to diet and conduct.

We also called at another station, where now, as well as on our way to Wellington, we were hospitably entertained with beef, damper, and tea. There were four black women and a little boy sitting before the fire, in a state of complete nudity, except having skin rugs thrown over their backs. The principal use of these skin rugs, which they usually carry with them, is, to draw over themselves at night, when they sleep on the ground, by their little fires. The dews of N. S. Wales, are often very heavy, and the nights chilly, rendering this kind of protection needful. The flesh side of the rug is turned outward, and is ornamented by a number of lines, forming oblong compartments and undulations, cut into the skin, and marked with a red pigment. They likewise carry with them, skin bags, with the fur outside, containing a few wooden implements for digging up roots, and taking grubs, also vessels for water, made of the large, tubercular excrescences of the gum-tree, hollowed out, which are here called Calabashes. These women were smoking and drinking tea; they said, the men they belonged to were gone up the creek. Though prisoner-servants are generally without religious principle, and are so degraded, that in situations of this kind, they are little above the Aborigines, in point of cleanliness and manner of living, they are to be pitied, in being exposed to the company of such as were now here.

On proceeding, we traced the foot-marks of the Natives, as far as the Three Rivers, where we again halted, made a fire, and prepared tea; we also cooked some Mushrooms, which are springing up abundantly, since the rain.

The day was showery. The ground being soft toward the conclusion of our day's journey, made it very fatiguing, and a slight error in regard to the road, lengthened thirty-eight miles to Molong, to forty. My companion was so much affected by the wet, cold, and fatigue, that he was seized with cramp in his legs, and was obliged to go to bed, where rest and warmth restored him. Two young men, also on their way from Wellington, reached this station before us, on horseback, and were kindly attentive. The overseer was from home: the men had got some spirits, from a dray that had stopped here for the night, and were in a state of excitement and disorder. One man, however,

X 3

was prompt in furnishing us with such things as we needed; and we were thankful to have reached a place of shelter before the rain set in, though it was one without glass in the windows, which were closed with shutters, and where the plaster had fallen from between the logs, till a hand might be put through in many places. On the way, we passed two drays, encamped for the night, by a large fire. They were conveying stores from Sydney, to a settler further into the interior. The poor draymen often spend very uncomfortable nights on these weary journeys, that take them many weeks; and in a morning, they have often to wander far after their bullocks, which stray in search of pasturage.

A short time after our visit to Molong, one of the men, went off the road, with a cart, toward a house, where (spirits) were sold illicitly. On the way, he upset the cart, which fell across his breast: he had cut away part of the side of the cart, with a pocket knife, but had died before he could extricate himself. When he was found, a wild dog was eating his head, and his own dog was eating the horse.—Accidents from the use of intoxicating drinks are not unfrequent in this land, where the quantity of spirituous liquors consumed is very great, in proportion to the population. We lately heard of a man falling, in a state of helpless drunkenness, on one of the large, flat, loose, ant-hills, that are common in the bush. When found, he was lifeless, the exasperated ants having eaten the interior of his nostrils and throat.

30th. The night was very wet, and the rain continued to fall heavily in the morning. Four black women arrived here, with two half-cast female children. The males of the mixed race are almost universally destroyed in infancy. This is more particularly the case in the remote parts of N. S. Wales; where we only met with two or three instances, in which their lives had been preserved. A person of our acquaintance expostulated with a woman, who had killed her child, but she only laughed; and when he appealed to another, as to the wickedness of the act, she said, " It was not a pretty baby."

The women who visited Molong this morning, were much pleased on being presented with an emptied sugar-bag. They soaked it in a bucket of water, and drank the muddy infusion, with avidity. One of them folded portions of the bag, took them into her capacious mouth, and sucked them, to extract the sweetness. They did not appear in the least degree intoxicated with their ample potations of the liquor; which, in common with the washings of rum casks, is called "Bull." The Blacks of Sydney reel after drinking the infusion of sugar-bags, and put on the appearance of intoxication so well, that it has generally been supposed, that the liquor really made them drunk. The following circumstances satisfied an acquaintance of ours, that this appearance of intoxication was feigned, and our own observation has confirmed this view :—The son of this person was, on a certain occasion, boiling down brine, to make salt, when a black man came in, and asked, if the liquor were rum. The young man, instead of answering the question, asked the Black, if he would have some: he answered in the affirmative, and took a tin-pot full, which he drank off. He then began to throw about his arms, and to stagger. The young man derided him, saying he surely did not mean to pretend to be drunk. The man replied—"Me murry (very) drunk like a gentleman." This circumstance induced our informant to remonstrate with some Blacks, who were making the same pretence in Sydney, and they made similar replies; certainly not much to the credit of some of the gentlemen of N. S. Wales, but strongly illustrating the force of example.

Towards noon the rain ceased. Our young friends commenced their journey, and kindly offered to mark the road for us, to Kangaroo Bay. We soon followed, and found they had done this effectually, by detaching bark from a tree, at the place of turning off, and scattering branches of a species of *Acacia*, with striking flowers, as they went along.

Kangaroo Bay is a beautiful, sequestered, grassy cove, among the hills, fertilized by a streamlet, now reduced to a chain of pools; by the side of which we saw one of the large Bustards, called here Wild Turkeys. At this place, we received a hearty welcome, from a warm-hearted Irish couple, who told us, that they had heard of our passing along the other side of the hills, on the way to Wellington, in consequence of our having given tracts to some shepherds, and had been regretting that they should not be likely to receive a visit from us.—An old Irishman, who was also a sojourner in the family for the night, informed us, that he could trace many points of resemblance to the ancient Irish language, in the language of the Blacks of this Colony. There were here two black boys; one of whom, named Dickey, said he was an orphan, belonging a tribe to the southward, on the Lachlan River. They were clothed in some old garments of the stock-men; which, though they fit badly, made them more decent than usual. Dickey, who appeared to be about twelve years of age, had become useful in the house, in the work of which, his mistress instructed him with motherly kindness: she also gave him his meals in the same room with themselves, and of the same kind of victuals as themselves eat. Being thus raised to the same grade with the family, in many points, the boy was making more progress in civilization than most of his race.

A rational attention to points of this kind, in labours to improve the condition of the Aborigines, is of more consequence than many well-intentioned Christians imagine. A line of consideration and conduct, such as Christian principles, fully carried into practice, would lead to, is of the utmost importance, in preparing the mind to receive the doctrines of the gospel. I now see more clearly than before, how much the Tasmanian Blacks on Flinders Island, were indebted to the rational, and well-directed endeavours of W. J. Darling and A. M'Lachlan, in raising them in the scale of civilization. Though neither of these men could be looked upon as religious missionaries, their labours materially advanced the Blacks toward a state, in which they might have been benefited by well-directed religious labours; not by teaching them to use forms of religion, without the power, or to go through formal repetitions

of devotional compositions; but by simply reading the
Scriptures to them, and turning their attention to the
convictions of the Holy Spirit upon their own minds,
as the drawing of the love of their Heavenly Father,
seeking to bring them to his beloved Son, in order that
they may find the pardon of sin, and help to work righteousness, through him. To these exercises, devout conversations, and the reading of religious biography, and other
practical works, might be usefully added, as the instructors
became able to engage in such communication, and way
opened for it. O, that many would give way to a right
exercise of soul before the Lord! who would then raise up,
both ministers and missionaries, qualified for their work to
his own glory.

10th mo. 1st. We left Kangaroo Bay, accompanied by
the two black boys, as guides. Soon after they left us, we
missed our road, taking a sawyer's track, which was more
strongly marked than the one along which we ought to
have gone, a common circumstance in Australia. This
lengthened our journey a few miles, and brought us across
some rough hills of white quartz, covered with trees and
scrub. At length we came out, upon a verdant tract, called
Fredericks Valley, where a man, who was making cheese, in
a solitary hut, kindly gave us some milk. This article,
which is scarce in V. D. Land, is abundant in this part of
N. S. Wales; and constitutes a part of the provision for the
servants of many of the pastoral establishments.

From over-exertion on the 29th ult. I became affected
with violent pain in one leg; and when, becoming so lame
as scarcely to be able to get along, one of our acquaintance,
from Newton, came up, with a spare horse ready saddled,
on which he invited me to ride. This circumstance might
be regarded by some as a mere casualty; but I could not
but consider it, as one of the many cases, in which relief
was sent by the overruling of Him, who cares for the spar-
rows, and much more for those who put their trust in
Him, unworthy of his notice as they may feel themselves
to be; and who, in his providence, often causes, circumstances, casual in appearance, so to meet, as to bring about

important ends. By this help we reached Newton in the evening; and spent a little time with comfort, among the little company of Wesleyans there.

2nd. We proceeded to Bathurst, in company with a pious man from the north of Ireland, who has known something of the power of religion for many years, and is more clear than many, in his views of the teaching of the Holy Spirit, and attentive to this guidance, in many respects. His conversation was cheering and edifying. Among many other things, he mentioned, that on asking a poor, bare-footed, Irish girl, a pupil in a Sabbath-school that he attended in his native land, to explain the meaning of love, the word having occurred in one of their Scripture lessons, she replied: " It is the union of all the powers of the mind, in one strong desire to please." This lucid and concise definition, from a child of drunken parents, greatly surprised him, but it tended to confirm him in his view of the benefits of such instruction. On arriving at Bathurst we again met a hearty welcome from John Espie and Mary Keane. Instead of the brownness of the country that existed on our first arrival in this part of the Colony, a fine verdure now covers the surface of the earth. The late, bountiful rain has caused both the people and the cattle to rejoice.

CHAPTER XXIX.

10th mo. 3rd. THE climate of Newton and Bathurst, is
much cooler than that of Wellington Valley, or of Sydney. At Newton there was hoar frost yesterday morning. At Bathurst and Newton, Apples and Gooseberries
succeed, but not Grapes. At Wellington and Sydney, the
heat is too great for the fruits of the cooler climates, and the
winter of Wellington and Bathurst, is too cold for Oranges,
and some other fruits, from the warmer parts of Europe.

4th. We had two meetings in the school-house. The
Episcopal Minister being at one of the out-stations, there
was no congregation in his place of worship to-day, and
many of the people, usually assembling there for devotional
purposes, met with the Presbyterians. I cannot but greatly
esteem the privilege, of having been trained to the practice of
meeting, to wait upon the Lord, independently of the intervention of a minister. The common custom, of no minister, no
public worship, ill accords with the precept, " Not forsaking
the assembling of yourselves together, as the manner of some
is." Indeed, I know of no people but Friends, who, exer-
cising faith in the Redeemer's declaration, " Wheresoever

two or three are met together in my name, there am I in the midst of them," act upon the Apostle's precept fully, by meeting when there is no preacher present. Much as I esteem Gospel Ministry as a gift of God, conferred for the edification of his church, I cannot but look upon those views of public worship, which render it dependent upon the intervention of a priest or a minister, as belonging rather to the dispensation of the law of Moses, than to the Gospel of Christ.

5th. I spent some time in the school, under the care of J. E. Keane, in which there are about thirty pupils, who are trained with much Christian care, and are diligently instructed in the Holy Scriptures. I could not, however, but lament to hear them taught such palpable error as is conveyed in the Catechism of the Episcopal Church, by which they are instructed to say, that they become members of Christ, and children of God, by baptism, clearly implying by baptism with water. I know this fallacy is attempted to be explained away, by various arguments; but it is quite in vain to try to twist the plain meaning of the words. It remains palpably untrue, that any infant, by water-baptism, becomes a member of Christ, or a child of God; and the direct tendency of such instruction, as teaches them to say that this is the case, is to deceive the young, with regard to their own religious state, and to lead them to attach to this rite, the imaginary effect of a mystical charm, and to divert their attention from the baptism of the Holy Ghost, received only through the mediation of Christ, by which alone they can become members of Christ, children of God, and heirs of eternal life.

6th. In company with J. E. Keane, we visited several of the settlers on Bathurst Plains, who generally live a mile or two from each other. Their houses are comfortable and well furnished, and more like those of England, than most we have seen in country situations, in this part of the world.

7th. A Branch Bible Association and an Auxiliary Temperance Association were organized. A number of the respectable settlers were present. These came from various distances, within nine miles. Several of them are in stations in life, similar to those of the more opulent of the middle class, in England. Among them, there is a pleasing attention to spiritual things: they generally assemble their whole families, including prisoner-servants, daily: for reading the Scriptures, and other devotional exercises. At the suggestion of the zealous, Episcopal Minister, they have established a Bank, in which they take small deposits, with the view of encouraging the labouring classes to save their money. This has already succeeded, in an encouraging degree, in regard to this object; it has considerably restrained the spending of money in strong drink, and, in other respects, has proved very useful in the district.

9th. We visited the Jail, Factory, and Hospital. The first of these, generally contains about fifty prisoners, convicts and others, under charges and sentences, all mixed together, and without employment; eating and sleeping in the same room. It has also five cells, and two rooms for debtors; all without airing courts. The Factory, which is occupied by female prisoners, and the Hospital, have better accommodations; but the latter is without enclosure, which is a great defect, especially, as many of its inmates are prisoners. These places are regularly visited by the Episcopal Minister, whose care for the prisoner, as well as the free population of the district, is exemplary.

Having concluded our labours at Bathurst, we accompanied a respectable settler, residing at Woodlands, at the junction of the Campbell and Fish Rivers, to his comfortable residence.

10th. The country about Woodlands is fine: the soil is a mixture of decomposed basaltic and granitic rocks, with pieces of rolled Jasper scattered on the surface. In a well, of seventy feet deep, in which water has not yet been obtained, a substance resembling soap-stone occurs, under the decomposed granite.—Several of the neighbouring settlers dined with us. Considering the shortness of the time since the Blue Mountains were first crossed by Europeans, the respectability of the population in this district is remarkable. They are placed under inconvenience at present,

by the difficulties of obtaining necessaries, from the long
drought, which has weakened the cattle, and has caused the
expense of carriage over the mountains, to be very great.

11th.   We had a meeting at O'Connell Plains, in a
chapel, built by a private individual.   The perceptible
influence of our Heavenly Father's love was with us, both
in time of silence, and when we were engaged in vocal
labour.   Ability was afforded us, to show clearly, the difference between formal and spiritual worship, and to illustrate the delusion and unprofitableness of the former, and
the validity and profitableness of the latter ; proving, that
it extended, not only to the right ordering of the mind
and conduct, in public and private devotion, but, having
its root in the fear of God, to a consequent regard to his
law, in all our public and private actions, as well as to our
words and thoughts ; so as to render the whole life of the
spiritually-minded Christian, a continued act of worship.

12th.   We took leave of our hospitable friends, at Woodlands, who kindly lent us their gig for the day, and proceeding by O'Connell Plains, we traversed several miles of
grassy and herby, open forest hills, affording pasturage for
sheep and cattle, till we came to the dwelling of a settler,
on the Fish River.   This person rented a section of land,
probably six hundred and forty acres, of the Government,
for £2 per annum.

13th.   Our route lay along the Fish River, which here
has a granite bed, and except in rainy weather, is a slender
stream.   It takes its name from a fish, about the size of a
Cod, that inhabits its waters.   We passed over a ridge of
granite and compact sandstone, the highest point of which
is called, Evans's Crown.   *Exarrhena suaveolens*, a plant
resembling Forget-me-not, but having large, white, fragrant
flowers, and some others, common also in V. D. Land, but
rare in N. S. Wales, were growing here.   The mid-day sun
was very hot, and Snakes, basking in its rays, were numerous.
Two young dogs belonging one of our friends from Helvellyn,
who accompanied us from O'Connell Plains, killed four.   One
of the dogs barked in front of the snake, while the other
seized it in its mouth, gave it a violent shake, and dropped

it. The other then barked, while his fellow attacked the reptile. This they continued, at the risk of their lives, till one of our party finished the destruction of the snakes with a stick. At Antonios Creek, we were refreshed with milk and damper, by a man formerly a prisoner. Milk is now so plentiful at many stations, that where they have not pigs to consume it, much of it is thrown away, after the cream is taken off.

14th. One of the prisoners, at the house where we lodged, having been flogged by order of a magistrate, for allowing the sheep to ramble over a piece of marshy ground, the whole of those at the establishment refused to come to the reading of the Scriptures, last evening. I went to them this morning, and gave them some counsel, which was well received.

We pursued our way to Black Heath. The advance of spring has decorated the Vale of Clywd, as well as the Blue Mountains, with many pretty blossoms. Among these, may be enumerated several species of *Grevillea,* a genus, including shrubs, with handsome flowers, but of very various foliage, aspect, and altitude; some of them are creepers on the ground, others are lofty trees.

Arriving at Black Heath, early, and not thinking it prudent to proceed further to day, we turned aside, to visit Govetts Leap; where, at an interval of a few hundred yards, two small streams fall over a precipice, at the opposite sides of a cove, in a sandstone cliff. The cove is half a mile, or more, in width, extending beyond the falls; and having ledges, upon which shrubs are growing; notwithstanding that to the eye it appears perpendicular. The perpendicular fall of one of the streams, is calculated, at 600 feet. The water is diffused into a shower of drops, before it reaches a mound of moss, that has grown up from below, to meet it, The other fall, is somewhat less in height. The course of the water, from the foot of the cliff, is traceable, in the dense forest of "the inaccessible valley," where it joins the Grose River, by the darker verdure, and the tree-ferns, on the margins of the streams. The cliffs, on the opposite side of this dark glen, are of similar character, forming a long series of coves. Above them, rise some considerable woody eminences, on which the snow lies in winter. Among these, are King Georges Mount, Mount Hay, and Mount Tomah; some of which, are visible from Sydney. The access to the point, from whence the waterfalls were seen, was difficult, but the magnificence of the scene, amply repaid for the trouble, in reaching it. The lofty, sinuous, sandstone cliffs, of this neighbourhood, have given it the name, of Hassans Walls.

15th. We set out in a smart snow-storm, dined at t^h Weatherboard-hut, and reached the Valley in the e^ ...ng. Several showers of hail and rain fell, in the co ...se of the day. In the lower altitudes of the mountains, the advance of spring was more striking. *Telopea speciosissima*, forming low bushes, with heads of flowers as large as small Peonies, was in full blossom. The Blue Mountain Parrot, partly blue, and with a breast of crimson, as brilliant as the flowers, was drinking nectar out of the blossoms of this splendid shrub; and a brown Honey-eater was darting its tongue, like a slender pencil of hair, into the elegant pink flowers of *Grevillea linearis*. *Gompholobium, grandiflorum*, a large, yellow, pea-flowered shrub, of great beauty, and several species of *Platylobium, Daviesia, Boronia*, and *Eriostemon*, enlivened the solitude, and beguiled the walk, of thirty-one miles, through this dreary forest, which we accomplished in ten hours. This kind of exercise, in such a climate, gives vigour to the digestive powers, and cheerfulness to the spirits. The number of dead bullocks had increased considerably, since we last crossed the mountains. We fell in with several parties of men with drays, conveying supplies for the settlers to the westward. Some of them were resting, others pursuing their way with cattle, so weak, that many of them appeared likely to die before reaching the other side. Notwithstanding the late rains have caused the grass again to grow, it is still very scarce in the little mountain glens, where it is not of a nutritious quality; and the cattle, in the low countries, have not yet had time, since the rain fell, to get into such condition, as is necessary to enable them to endure such a journey.

16th. Toward the close of the day, we overtook a magistrate, returning from an inquest, on the remains of a woman, who had hung herself, in a state of excitement from drinking. Her husband had been committed to prison, on the charge of wilful murder, for having assisted his wife, in the accomplishment of this rash and wicked act! —The man was afterwards tried, found guilty, and sentenced to death; but was respited till the opinion of the English Judges could be had, upon the before unheard of case; and this opinion had not been received, when I left N. S. Wales.

Our walk to Penrith was pleasant. As we descended from the mountains, the grass, on Emu Plains, looked beautifully green. It is of the kind, called here, Couch-grass, *Cynodon dactylon*, which creeps deep in the ground, and spreads over the cultivated lands, of this part of N. S. Wales. It is a widely diffused species, occurring also on the south coast of England, and in India, &c.

On visiting the Police-office at Penrith, to apply for leave to hold a meeting in it, we witnessed the infliction of the degrading punishment of flagellation, on two prisoners, to the amount of one hundred lashes each. One of them bore his punishment without complaint; the other writhed much under it, complained piteously, and was so faint, as to require to be frequently supplied with water. Yet I saw this man, a few minutes after, putting on his clothes, behind the jail, and jeering with a woman, in a way that proved that his mind was not beneficially operated upon, though in body, he must have suffered severely, unless the torpor of the mutilated flesh, rendered him temporarily insensible. I believe the disposition of mind, of those who think to keep mankind in subjection by severity, is much the same as it was in Rehoboam, when he took the counsel of the young men; and that it will, in one way or other, lead to similar results.—See 2 Chron. x.

At Penrith, a Jew, professing Christianity, the father-in-law of the landlord of the inn, told us, that as we had come among them to preach the gospel, we should be free of all charges. We acknowledged his kindness, and explained

Y

how our expenses were paid, to which he replied, he hoped
we would not debar him of this privilege.

18th. At ten o'clock, a small congregation met us at
the Police-office, at Penrith, where religion and morality
are at a low ebb. In the afternoon, we had a meeting at
Nepean, which was well attended. The Wesleyans preach
here occasionally, but the tone of religious feeling is low.
The message we have generally to proclaim is, that all unrighteousness is sin, and all sin the service of the devil;
that none can be saved in the service of the devil, for he
is the enemy of God, and so are all his servants. We
find it also our place, to state the fundamental doctrines of
the Gospel, and to urge the importance of attention to the
convictions of the Holy Spirit upon the mind, discovering
sin, condemning it, and leading to repentance, as being the
only way by which we can come to a true faith in Christ,
and a holy walk with God. These doctrines we are engaged
to press, with a variety of Scripture illustrations, and with
appeals to the convictions of their truth, in the minds of our
hearers, and with exhortations to seek after an experimental
knowledge of them.—After meeting, we called to see an
aged man, who had been confined to bed with palsy, for
several years, and was in a state of great suffering. He
was formerly a prisoner, became thoughtful without instru-
mental means, got a little forward in his circumstances,
gave the land where the school-house is built, and reared
a large family, by some of whom, he has been in danger of
being again led away from righteousness, by their joining
a medical man, in recommending him to take spirits as a
medicine.

19th. We breakfasted at Regentville, the hospitable
owner of which, has a large vineyard on his fine property,
but the promise for fruit this season is not great, in consequence of the late drought, during many weeks of which,
the sky was clear, and there was " neither rain nor dew,"
a circumstance not uncommon in these regions. During
the drought, the proprietor of Regentville, had a herd of
sixteen horses, which strayed to a peninsula, on the mountains, where they could hear the fall of water, but could

not reach it. As if enchanted by the sound, they had continued to pace round the spot, till they all perished by thirst.

20th. We called upon some of the neighbouring settlers, and visited Glen Brook, a romantic valley, through which a branch of the Nepean River flows, between high, woody cliffs, of the same character as those forming the inaccessible vallies of this part of the country. It contained several remarkable trees and shrubs; among which were a wild fig-tree, and *Hibiscus heterophyllus*, the flowers of which resemble the Hollyhock, and are of a delicate white, with a deep, purple eye.

21st. We walked by way of the little village of Castle-reagh, to Windsor, a town of about 1,500 inhabitants, beautifully situated, upon the Hawkesbury, and of very English appearance, where we found pretty good accommodation at an inn.

22nd. We called upon some of the Inhabitants, and made arrangements, for holding some meetings, in which, we were kindly assisted by the Wesleyan Minister.

23rd. We went to Richmond, another little town on the Hawkesbury, four miles distant from Windsor. The country here is very fine, and productive, with extensive grassy flats, along the sides of the river. On these, people continue to build and reside, notwithstanding there have been floods, at intervals of a few years, that have risen far above the tops of their houses.

A respectable Wesleyan, at Richmond, told us, that he had heard of our visit to Wellington Valley, several days ago, from a Native, who had had the particulars detailed to him, by a Black from that country. Our persons, costume, and many other particulars, including our manner of communicating religious instruction, had been minutely described. And on our Wesleyan friend inquiring what the Black supposed all this meant, he replied, " God Almighty come and sit down at Wellington;" implying, that the Most High would be worshipped there. The scattered natives of Australia, communicate information rapidly; messengers being often sent from tribe to tribe, for great distances. In the evening we returned to Windsor.

24th. Accompanied by a thoughtful, military officer, we walked to the villages of Pitt Town, and Wilberforce. At Pitt Town, we were helped, in obtaining a place to hold a meeting in, by the Episcopal Minister.

25th. We had meetings at Richmond, in the forenoon, and at Windsor, in the afternoon. There was a painful feeling in both meetings, on behalf of such as profess to be awakened, but do not maintain an inward exercise of soul before the Lord; and who try to feed upon external excitements, instead of upon "the true Bread," "which cometh down from heaven, and giveth life unto the world."

26th. We had some conversation with an unfaithful professor of religion; with whom we expostulated, on his inconsistency, in endeavouring to add to his income, by distilling spirits, both to his own injury, and to that of those who consumed them. This man tried to vindicate his practice, but himself became gradually ensnared by the insidious poison; he ultimately died of delirium tremens, declaring that the pains of hell were already his portion. We also visited some thoughtful people, not professing with any associated body of Christians; one of whom left the army on half-pay, when he became religiously awakened, finding military associations inimical to his religious progress.—In the evening, a Temperance Meeting was held in the government school-room, when we gave the company some information, on the progress of Temperance Societies. There are about ninety members here, many of whom are soldiers: one of their officers is a diligent labourer in this good cause.

27th. After breakfast, we went to see the jail; and were scarcely in the yard, before the prisoners, of their own accord, arranged themselves, to afford us the opportunity of addressing them, standing in the scorching sunshine, and leaving us the shade. We inquired, if we could not have an interview with them, in one of the rooms of the prison, and being answered in the affirmative, they were soon assembled and seated, and we had a memorable time with them. The sense of divine overshadowing prevailed in a remarkable degree, the message of mercy was freely proclaimed among them, and they were invited to turn to the Lord, against whom they had deeply revolted; with the assurance, that if they would submit to the government of his good Spirit, he would be their God, and pardon their past transgressions for Jesus' sake.—We afterwards walked again to Wilberforce, where we had a meeting in the school-house, with a congregation consisting chiefly of Australians, of European extraction, with whom I had an open time, in preaching the Gospel; to which, as regards its power, the auditors seemed much of strangers.—It is to be regretted, that in public preaching, a theoretical knowledge of the blessed doctrine of the atonement, should so much take the place, as it generally does, of the practical application of the Gospel, spiritually. There is ground to believe, that this is one great cause, why so few come to true repentance, such as is wrought by attention to the convictions of the Spirit of Truth, and leads to the practical and saving application of the atoning sacrifice of Christ.

28th. At six o'clock this morning, we had a religious interview with a road-party, of twenty-four prisoners, employed in replacing a wooden bridge, over the South Creek, close to Windsor. In the afternoon, we visited the hospital, and had a meeting with about forty patients, who were assembled in one of the four wards, of which this building consists. In the evening, we met about one hundred and twenty persons, in the school-room, at Pitt Town, to whom much Christian counsel, and warning were extended. The district of Pitt Town, contains about seven hundred inhabitants; many of whom have been prisoners, and are notorious for their drunkenness, profligacy, and neglect of public worship.

29th. We returned to Richmond, and made calls upon several persons, for the purpose of furnishing them with tracts. In the afternoon we held a meeting at Currajong, a scattered settlement, on the ascent of the mountains, near the confluence of the Nepean and Grose Rivers; which, uniting, form the Hawkesbury. The land here has been cleared, and numerous cottages have been erected; but the inhabitants, who are chiefly Anglo-Australians, seem very uncultivated.

In the evening we returned again to Windsor. The country in this neighbourhood, was settled at an early period of the Colony. Some of the alluvial flats on the Hawkesbury, which is navigable to this point, for small craft, are very rich; and the people are now busy planting Maize or Indian Corn. Crops of this useful grain are often obtained, after Wheat has failed from frost, drought, or hot winds.

30th. At six o'clock in the morning, we mounted a four-horse coach, which stopped for breakfast, at Parramatta, and arrived at Sydney, in four hours and a half, the distance being thirty-eight miles.—Between Windsor and Parramatta, there are a few large Orange-orchards, which are said to yield a very profitable produce to their owners.

CHAPTER XXX.

On the 1st of 11th month, we had the privilege of assembling, for the first time, in a neat meeting-house, in Macquarie Street, built by John Tawell, for the accommodation of persons professing with Friends. Several strangers met with us, on the occasion. Some of them seemed disappointed, that we did not dedicate this house for worship, by some vocal communication. We were willing to have spoken, had anything been given us to communicate, but this not being the case, we bore a plain testimony, by our silence, to our conviction, of the advantage of attending to the injunction, "Cease ye from man, whose breath is in his nostrils," and of trusting in the Lord alone. Our silence was also calculated to encourage those who might meet in our absence, to bear this testimony faithfully.

Having believed that it would be right for us, to join our friends in Van Diemens Land, at their Yearly Meeting, in the 12th mo. we engaged berths, in the cabin of the brig, Maria, for £10 each, and sailed on the 13th of the 11th month, for Hobart Town. In leaving Port Jackson, we narrowly escaped drifting upon the South Head. We were delivered from this danger, by the springing up of a breeze,

when all human efforts appeared to be unavailing. Being
affected with sea-sickness, I had "gone down into the sides
of the ship," and was fast asleep, I did not awake till the
danger was past; from which we thus escaped, by the intervention of the almighty power of Him, "who maketh the
wind his messenger," and watcheth over us when we are
asleep, as well as when we are awake, and "suffereth not
the briny wave to prevail against us," though, at seasons,
he permits the billows to assume a threatening aspect, in
order that we may know, that it is indeed himself who
protects us, and thus may be stirred up, to give to him
the glory, due unto his holy name.

On the 18th, we were off the point of Van Diemens
Land, called St. Patricks Head, and observed much snow
on the ridge of Ben Lomond. The Aurora australis was
remarkably brilliant, this evening, forming faint columns of
light, like the Aurora borealis. In New South Wales, there
is an electric phenomenon, somewhat allied to this. It
occurs in warm, summer evenings, when no clouds are to
be seen; and it is a diffuse, flickering light, differing from
lightening, in not being discharged from any perceptible
clouds, and in its want of density: it generally appears to
the eastward.

On the 20th, we landed, at Hobart Town; where we received a cordial welcome from many of our former acquaintance, including the Lieutenant Governor and his family.

During our absence in New South Wales, the little congregation professing with Friends, had been enabled to
maintain their ground, and some of them appeared to have
grown in grace, notwithstanding they had had to mourn over
the departure of one of their number, from the paths of
rectitude. His deviations had so offended another, that he
had ceased to assemble with the rest, for divine worship,
notwithstanding they had faithfully testified their disunity
with the offender, and after endeavouring in vain to restore
him, in the spirit of meekness, had disowned him as a member of the Society.

The Yearly Meeting commenced, on the 4th of 12th
month, and continued, by adjournments, to the 10th; on

the evening of which day, it concluded, after recording the following minute:

"In reviewing the several sittings of this Meeting, we feel it incumbent upon us, to record, that though we have met in much weakness, yet, through the unmerited mercy and condescension of our Heavenly Father, we have been made sensible; that 'the Everlasting Arms were underneath;' and strength has been afforded us, to conduct the business that has come before us, in unity and brotherly love; for which we feel humbly thankful; and reverently acknowledge, that 'hitherto, the Lord hath helped us.'"

12th mo. 16th.   Having purchased two horses, one for £21, and the other for £30, we commenced a journey, in company with Francis and Anna Maria Cotton. Crossing the Derwent, in a steamer we proceeded to Lauderdale, where we paid a visit to our friends, the Mathers.

On the 17th, we rode, by way of the Hollow Tree, to the Coal River, and from thence, on the 18th, to the Eastern Marshes. The road between Jerusalem and this place, is undergoing improvement, by a long cut, in the side of a steep hill. It is formed by prisoner labour, and is a great accommodation, though it is yet only passable for horses, and requires some nerve to ride along it. From the Eastern Marshes, we travelled by a road, lately cut, which winds up the Sugar-loaf Hill; and by which, Little Swan Port is rendered accessible for carriages.

On the 19th, we reached the peaceful dwelling of our friends, at Kelvedon. On the way from Hobart Town, we visited several of the families of the settlers; many of whom appeared to be prospering in temporal things. We were received with much cordiality, by an aged woman, who was slowly recovering from an apoplectick attack. She expressed great thankfulness, that she was not cut off at once, by the disease, but allowed time to repent. We were glad to see her in such a state of mind, but were confirmed in the conviction, that it is a dangerous thing to defer repentance to such a time. Well might the prophet exclaim, "O, that my people were wise, that they understood this, that they would consider their latter end!"

On the 28th, we left Kelvedon, being accompanied by
Francis Cotton ; and after visiting some of the settlers in
Great Swan Port, who also appeared to be in improving
circumstances, reached Moulting Bay, in the evening. On
the following day we arrived at Falmouth. Our chief object
in taking this route, was to visit our friend David Stead,
who was still residing here. My horse proved a very untractable one, and several times exposed me to danger, on
the way through the forests. To-day, he ran off with me,
and when passing under some low trees, close to the shore,
a short stump, projecting from one of them, caught my coat
by the shoulder, and took me off his back ; but when I fell,
he stopped, and I was mercifully preserved from injury.
The manner in which a skilful rider, on a tractable horse,
avoids the branches of trees, clears logs upon the ground,
rocks, and other impediments, in riding at full speed,
through the continuous, and hilly forests of this country,
is very remarkable ; particularly when hunting cattle out
of the bush. As these cattle are brought into the fold, in
some instances, only once a year, when the young ones are
branded, in order that they may be identified by their
owners, they are consequently, almost as wild as those that
have never been under human control. But the ferocity
observed in bulls, in England, may be said to be unknown
in them, in the Australian Colonies. Whether this arises
from the climate, or from some other cause, is doubtful.

On the 30th, we crossed the hills, and traversed the
Break-o'-day Plains, which being less parched than the land
on the coast, were more verdant than most of the country
that we had seen, since returning to V. D. Land. We
continued our journey by Avoca, and the Buffalo Plains, to
Launceston, where we arrived on the 1st of 1st mo. 1836 ;
having renewed our acquaintance with several estimable
families, on the way.

My horse fell, as if shot, when near the Nile-bridge, and
going at a smart pace. I received a severe bruise on my
right side, from which I was not fully restored for many
weeks.

On the 5th, we had a meeting with many of the inhabitants

of Launceston, in a large chapel, lately erected by the Wesleyans, who have become a numerous and influential body in the place, which is remarkably improved, both as a town, and in moral and religious character. In the course of the day, we visited a person in the chain-gang, who was brought up among Friends, but who sacrificed all his advantages to the love of strong drink, and through its influence became a prisoner. Having been respectably connected, he was treated with more than ordinary lenity, but he abused his privilege, received the addition of a year to his original sentence, and is now wearing party-coloured garments, and double irons. O that young men would take warning, and neither touch, taste, nor handle this accursed thing! and that they would beware of despising the counsel of their friends, and the reproofs of the Holy Spirit! for, after having suffered themselves to be carried, by almost imperceptible degrees, into evil habits, it is hard indeed for them to learn to do well.

We left Launceston on the 7th, and reached Kelvedon again on the 9th, having again visited some thoughtful families, with whom we were acquainted, upon the way. It was truly pleasant to see among them, the tokens of advancing religious character; yet I could not but lament that the immediate teaching of the Holy Spirit seemed to be so little understood. The consequence of this is, that it is not waited for, and little, if any, of its baptizing influence is to be felt, in the generality of the devotional exercises, of many truly estimable characters, who know something of the evidence of their past sins being blotted out, through faith in the blood of Jesus, and cherish a desire to conform themselves to the will of God, so far as they understand it. These have witnessed so much of the work of the new birth, as makes them very distinguishable from those whose minds are not yet, in any degree, brought under divine influence. They have a religious understanding also, according to the measure of their faith; but not having faith in the perceptible guidance of the Spirit, they do not so walk, as to perceive things clearly, by its light, and much of their religious exercise is, consequently, the produce of their own natural powers, with little, or, often, with nothing, of the Spirit of Life. In one family, in which we again proclaimed the Gospel message, I had to point out to the company, that, to the humble mind, the way of salvation is opened, not by deductions of the reasoning powers, but by the light of Christ shining into the mind, and giving a perception of the mercy of God in his beloved Son, and of the state of the soul before him, and of other truths, progressively, as there is a preparation of heart to receive them. How favoured are those, who, becoming humble and teachable, as little children, come to Christ, and know him to baptize them with the Holy Ghost, to open their eyes, to unstop their ears, and to bring them into the state of his disciples of old, to whom he said, "Blessed are your eyes, for they see, and your ears, for they hear!"

We left Kelvedon on the 19th, and again reached Hobart Town on the 25th, having travelled by way of Little Swan Port, Spring Bay, Richmond, and Lauderdale.

At Little Swan Port, we visited the mounds of Oyster shells, left by the Aborigines, who formerly inhabited this country. These shells are now dug out and burnt for lime; they must have been the accumulation of ages.

The tide was very high, in Spring Bay, on the forenoon of the 21st. It flowed four times in the course of the day! This might possibly be the effect of conflicting winds on the Pacific, or of a volcanic eruption somewhere, at sea.

While in Hobart Town, we took a room, at the rate of £10 a-year, for a meeting-place, for those professing with Friends; the one they had lately occupied, being wanted for another purpose. Rents are very high in V. D. Land.

On the 1st of 2nd month, I went with F. Cotton to New Norfolk, to pay a parting visit to my friends at that place, and returned by coach the following day. The Hospital there, as well as that in Hobart Town, is much crowded. In the one at New Norfolk, there are now about 300 inmates, 50 of whom are lunatics, and several others are aged, infirm persons. A successful experiment has lately been tried, in the irrigation of some land, near the town of New Norfolk, by which its produce, in this dry climate, is greatly augmented. Though the places capable of being irrigated, in this country, are comparatively few, yet the effect of irrigation is so decidedly beneficial, that it will probably be carried on hereafter, to a considerable extent.

The Wesleyans are building a meeting-house, at New Norfolk, and another at the Back-river. They are an industrious people, and are making way in V. D. Land, in spite of many cases of halting and relapse among their converts.

The anniversary meeting of the Temperance Society, was held on the 8th, when the cause was ably advocated by several persons of influence. The practice of spirit-drinking is materially diminished, in respectable society, in this Colony.

Having, for the present, concluded our labours in V. D. Land, we engaged berths on board the Ellen, an American-built ship, bound for Sydney, and embarked on the 10th; having, among our fellow-passengers, a medical man and his wife, from India, a pious couple, whom it was a comfort to us to meet, in various places.

On the 11th, we proceeded on our voyage, and had a fine view of the stupendous, projecting cliff, of columnar basalt, called Cape Raoul, passing very near it. Cape Pillar was involved in clouds; and a long bank of fog, stretched to the S.E. indicating an adverse wind, of which we soon felt the influence. The wind, however, became fair, on the following day; and after a succession of calms and thunder showers, we came safely to anchor, in Sydney Cove, on the 21st.

CHAPTER XXXI.

2nd mo. 22nd. On returning to Sydney, we found several letters from England, the perusal of which brought my mind renewedly into sympathy with my friends there, and into fervent desires that they might watch against that spirit, which would lead them from waiting upon God, with their attention directed to the Light; or, in other words, to the Holy Spirit, the Comforter, who takes of the things of Christ, and showeth them to his followers; to which our early Friends, following the example of Christ and his apostles, directed the attention of the people. There is a delusion, which requires to be guarded against, that is couched under denunciations against a "religion of feelings;" as though conviction, repentance, faith in Christ, peace in him, dependence on God, and every other impression, made upon the mind by the Holy Spirit, were not feelings. A religion without feelings, would be like a body without a soul.

24th. I spent a few hours with Alexander M'Leay, Chief Justice Francis Forbes, Sir John Jamison, William Macarthur, and some other gentlemen, who requested me to join them in examining the fruit of the Vines, of which they have a collection, amounting to about three hundred varieties; they were brought to the Colony, by James Busby, from Luxemburgh, Montpelier, &c. Among them, under their

French names, are most of the varieties cultivated for the table in England. Many parts of N. S. Wales are favourable to the production of Grapes, and for the drying of fruits.

The Sydney Botanic Garden is a fine institution; it is furnished with a good collection of native and foreign plants. Some of its Curators, have ranked highly as men of science.

28th. In our little meeting, I had to labour to turn the attention of the congregation, to the importance of self-examination; lest, by any means, after having known reconciliation with the Father, through repentance, and faith in his beloved Son, they should have forsaken their first love, and have suffered other things, so to have occupied their minds, and entangled their affections, as to have taken precedence of the love of God. They were also reminded, that though the deeds of a good man, will bear the light of open day, in the sight of his fellow-men, yet, as things may look well to the eye of man, while the heart is, nevertheless, far from right before God, it is necessary to bring our deeds to that Light, which manifests whatsoever is reprovable, which is spoken of by the apostle Paul, in his Epistle to the Ephesians, (chap. v. 13, 14,) and which is the same, as that treated of by the evangelist John, when, in speaking of Christ, he says, "in him was life, and the life was the Light of men." I had also to point out that if, in bringing our deeds to this test, we should find, that any thing has gained an undue place in our affections, or that, through unwatchfulness, and the evil propensity of our nature, the enemy of our souls has betrayed us into sin, it is necessary that we humble ourselves, repent, and do our first works, that we renew our attention, to the convictions of the Holy Spirit, and afresh seek the pardon of our transgressions, through faith in Christ, our Mediator and Advocate with the Father, and "the propitiation for our sins;" and that we abide in humble dependence upon God, waiting upon him, in watchfulness and prayer, for the renewal of our strength; in order that we may run in the way of holiness, and not be weary, and walk therein, and not faint. I had also to assure those, who were thus exercised, in the fear of the Lord, that how much soever they might have been cast down, God would restore unto them, the joys of his salvation, uphold them by his free Spirit, and enable them to walk in his love, and in the comfort of the Holy Ghost; that such should feel his presence to be with them, in their daily course, and when assembled, to wait upon him, and to worship him, to their own peace, and to his praise.

3rd mo. 3rd. A quantity of books, illustrative of the principles and practice, of the Society of Friends, were deposited in a room attached to the Meeting House, as a library, as is customary in England, for loan to persons frequenting our meetings, or inquiring into these subjects.

5th. We had the satisfaction of witnessing the destruction of five puncheons of Rum, containing four hundred and ninety-two gallons, and two hogsheads of Geneva, containing one hundred and sixteen gallons. They were the property of one of our friends, who had received them as part of an investment, from his agent in England, who had not been apprized of a change in the views of his correspondent, respecting the use and sale of spirits, in which he cannot now, conscientiously, be concerned. He therefore represented the case to the Governor, who allowed them to be taken out of bond, free of duty, under the same circumstances as if for export, and under the charge of an officer of Customs, placed on board a staged boat, which took them out into the Cove, where the heads of the casks were removed, and the contents poured into the sea. A few friends of the owner accompanied him, to witness this "new thing under the sun," in this Colony. We were much pleased with the hearty manner in which the custom-house officer superintended this sacrifice of property to principle. Some persons, from neighbouring vessels, looked on with approval, others with surprise, and others, not yet awake to the evils of spirit-drinking, expressed regret. A man, from a little vessel, cried out, "That's real murder." One of the puncheons, being too near the edge of the boat, went overboard, and brought its top above the surface of the water, with much rum in it. It floated close by the same little vessel, and a man dipped a horn into it, to try to get a drink of the devoted fluid. It was now rum and water; but happily for the man, it was rum and salt-water! even his vitiated palate rejected it, and he poured it back to the rest, which was soon mingled with the briny flood.

7th. Some discord having arisen among a few, of the little company who meet with us for public worship, we had an interview with them. An explanation shewed, that some things, innocent in themselves, that had been said, having been reported, had been made to appear very malicious: and that others, that had not been spoken with proper consideration, had been made to appear much worse than they originally were. The mischief of talebearing and detraction, which are common evils in these Colonies, were pointed out, as well as the necessity for those who desire to be found among the disciples of Christ, to maintain the spirit of love and forgiveness. Our admonitions were confirmed by the recital of the following passages of Scripture, with many others, as the Lord, in his goodness, brought them to our remembrance. "Thou shalt not go up and down as a talebearer among thy people." "Where there is no talebearer strife ceaseth." "The Lord hateth him that soweth discord among brethren." "So likewise shall my heavenly Father do unto you, if ye, from your hearts, forgive not every one his brother his trespasses."—(Mat. xviii. 35.) "By this shall all men know that ye are my disciples, if ye have love one to another." "If ye have bitter envying and strife in your hearts, glory not, and lie not against the truth. This wisdom cometh not from above, but is earthly, sensual, devilish: for where envying and strife is, there is confusion and every evil work." "Be ye kind one to another, tender-hearted, forgiving one another, even as God, for Christ's sake, hath forgiven you." Before we parted, a comfortable sense of the influence of the divine Spirit overshadowed us, exciting the hope, that this labour might not be in vain in the Lord.

9th. We attended a lecture on the manufacture and sale of spirits. The lecturer faithfully denounced the production and sale of these pernicious fluids; and by cogent argument, proved, that when informed upon the subject, no one could continue to circulate such pestilential beverage, for the sake of gain, and be guiltless.

15th. We presented copies of the Scripture Lessons, of the British and Foreign School Society, to some Missionaries, going to New Zealand, and Tonga. This work is invaluable to persons attempting the translation of the Holy Scriptures, into foreign languages. It may be considered an epitome of the Sacred Volume, which may be usefully put into the hands of those, who have not the whole Scriptures; and being in the words of the text, a translation of it, is so much, effected toward that of the whole of the Bible.

22nd. The Governor having granted us liberty to proceed to the Penal Settlement, at Moreton Bay, and being furnished with a letter of introduction from the Colonial Secretary, to the Commandant, we embarked on board the Isabella schooner, of 126 tons. The company on board, consisted of forty-four prisoners, a guard of fifteen soldiers, inclusive of a sergeant in charge, and two corporals, a soldier's wife, the crew of the vessel, sixteen in number, including the master and mate, with G. W. Walker and myself; in all seventy-eight souls. The prisoners were chiefly men under short sentences, for crimes committed in N. S. Wales, while under sentence of transportation to the Colony. A few of them had been at Moreton Bay before, under similar circumstances. They were secured in a fore-hold, by chains from ankle to ankle; within which, a long chain was passed, and bolted at each end to the deck, so as only to allow them to move a few feet. They were very clean, when they came on board; and their prison was fresh white-washed, so as to make it as comfortable as such a place could be, to men so secured, who were lodged, without blanket or other bedding, on the bare boards.

23rd. We got to sea yesterday. Most of the prisoners look pale, from sea-sickness, not being allowed to come on deck. Since an attempt at mutiny, on board the Governor Phillip, about a year ago, which occurred when a chain of the kind described, was opened for the purpose of taking off a few prisoners, to let them have air, the captains of these vessels, for their own safety, have kept the prisoners constantly below.

24th. The wind was adverse. It set up a high sea, and a curling billow pitched its white crest on the quarter deck, and sent us dripping below. Three of the crew were sick, from hepatic diseases, the result of hard drinking. The Government vessels of New South Wales, sail on Temperance principles. The seamen on board, acknowledge that this is much to their comfort. Nevertheless, not abstaining on principle, they have not resolution to abstain when on shore. One of those, now sick, is a hardy, old tar, a pensioner, in consequence of having lost an arm, in firing a salute; he is so skilful, that he is stationed at the helm, on all critical occasions. This man is now threatened with apoplexy, the result of his late inebriety. Another, is a man, lately returned from a whaling voyage. Two of his comrades died in Sydney, within the last three weeks, of inflammation of the liver, brought on by hard drinking; and this man is now suffering from the complicated effects of the same disease, with the fear of death! The soldiers on board, are allowed a ration of spirits, greatly to their injury. It keeps alive an appetite for drink, which leads them into all sorts of disorder.

25th. My companion, who had been sea-sick, was able to accompany me in visiting the prisoners, many of whom were so much affected by the rolling of the vessel, and the warmth of the weather, that they hardly attempted to sit up. We read a portion of Scripture to them, and made some remarks on the design of our Heavenly Father, in creating man liable to affliction, and in sometimes permitting his creatures to bring themselves under suffering. This design was shown to be, that they might consider their ways, and turn to the Lord. In the evening, we were off Shoal Bay. The weather was clear, with lightning in the horizon in the south and east.

26th. A brisk breeze in the night, brought us to Cape Byron by morning, and we made good progress during part of the day. Toward night, we had a light sea-breeze, and stood off the land. There were many of the fires of the

native Blacks, on this part of the coast, as well as on that
we have passed. A long sandy beach extends from Cape
Byron to Point Danger, behind which are low, woody hills,
some of which are pointed. Further back, there are woody
mountains; some of them of remarkable appearance, particularly Mount Warning, which also has trees to its summit.
This mountain, with the adjacent hills and coast, is represented in the accompanying etching; in the foreground of
which, two Wandering Albatrosses and some Gulls are
placed.

28th. Before noon, we were within sight of the pilot's
station, at Amity Point, Moreton Bay, and passed between
two rocks above water, with a light breeze. While in the
part of the bay, open to the sea, a large Turtle was seen
swimming, not far from us. Three species of turtle are
met with here, one of which is black and unwholesome.
We took the pilot on board, who conducted our little vessel
through the intricate channels, among the sand-banks; the
depth of water in some places did not exceed two fathoms
and three quarters. The pilot's dwelling is a neat building, with red walls, that look like brick: but he told
us, that it was of wood, and greatly infested with Scorpions,
Centipedes, and such-like vermin. The land about the entrance of Moreton Bay is low and sandy, and generally
covered with scrub. When the Isabella got into smooth
water, we took the opportunity of reading to the prisoners
and of conversing with them respecting their voyage, during
which they were not even furnished with salt water to wash
themselves. The tide serving, the vessel proceeded toward
the west side of the bay, which, within Moreton Island, is
about sixty miles long and twenty-five broad, and is full of
sand-banks and small Islands, that are covered with Mangroves, particularly to the southward; over most of these
the water flows, at spring-tides. At ten o'clock at night,
a part of our luggage was put into the pilot's boat, along
with a number of small packages; and with a soldier, as
guard of the despatches, we proceeded toward our point
of destination, on the Brisbane River, the mouth of which
was distant about twenty miles. The night was fine and

moonlight, but the temperature so low as to render the protection of some of our warmer sea-clothing, very agreeable. About midnight, we came upon some shoals, on which the boat was often aground; but after shoving her backward and forward, she was at length got into deeper water. The recollection, that we were now on the utmost verge of that part of the British dominions, inhabited by its white subjects, and that these were the very outcasts of civilized society, and that we were surrounded by uncivilized tribes of Blacks, often passed my mind, with a feeling I can hardly describe. But believing we were here in the allotment of religious duty, I could not desire to be in any other place; and though deeply sensible of my own unworthiness of the least of the mercies of the Most High, I had a sense of his power sustaining me, such as is to be accounted among the greatest of blessings.

29th. About two o'clock in the morning, the moon having set, and the tide being against us, we landed on one of the islands, on which the Mangroves were thick. Small Oysters were attached to the branches and trunks of those that were within the high-water-mark. This is commonly the case within the mouths of rivers, on this coast. Here we rested, on a little elevation, scarcely above the reach of high-water, and lighted a fire; by the side of which, our boat's crew refreshed themselves with their homely fare, of maize-meal-bread, and water; to which some of them added a smoke of tobacco. They were very attentive, carrying us from and to the boat, and in other ways showing their good-will. After some of them had taken a nap on the ground, and we had amused ourselves, by listening to the voices of Grasshoppers, and of Red-bills and other birds that cry in the night, one of which almost said " Cuckoo," we re-embarked, and proceeded up the river, twelve miles, to the Settlement, where we landed, early in the morning, on a wooden-jetty, near to the quarters of the Commandant, Captain Foster Fyans; who received us with much kindness, and afforded us all the attention and accommodation that our circumstances required.

CHAPTER XXXII.

Moreton Bay.—Brisbane Town.—Gardens.—Tread-mill.—Swearing.—Plants, &c.—Natives.—Prisoners.—Family Worship.—Trees, &c.—Plants, and Animals.—Female Prisoners.—Wood.—Destruction of Spirits.—Teredo.—Kangaroos, &c.—Birds.—Want of Bibles.—Absconders.—Aborigines.

3rd mo. 29th. AFTER making a hearty breakfast, we set out to inspect the settlement, which is called Brisbane Town: it consists of the houses of the Commandant, and other officers, the barracks for the military, and those for the male prisoners, a penetentiary for the female prisoners, a treadmill, stores, &c. It is prettily situated, on the rising, north bank of the Brisbane River, which is navigable fifty miles further up, for small sloops, and has some fine cleared, and cultivated land, on the south bank, opposite the town. Adjacent to the Government-house, are the Commandant's garden, and twenty-two acres of Government-garden, for the growth of Sweet-potatoes, Pumpkins, Cabbages, and other vegetables, for the prisoners. Bananas, Grapes, Guavas, Pine-apples, Citrons, Lemons, Shaddocks, &c. thrive luxuriantly in the open ground, the climate being nearly tropical. Sugar-cane is grown for fencing, and there are a few thriving Coffee-plants, not old enough to bear fruit. The Bamboo, and Spanish Reed have been introduced. The former, attains to about seventy feet in height, and bears numerous branches, with short, grassy leaves, the upper twenty feet bending down with a graceful curve. It is one of the most elegant objects, in the vegetable world. Coffee and sugar, will probably at some period, be cultivated here, as crops. The surrounding country is undulating, and covered with trees. To the west, there is a range of high, woody hills, distant, in a direct line, five miles.

The tread-mill, is generally worked by twenty-five prisoners at a time; but when it is used as a special punishment, sixteen are kept upon it, for fourteen hours, with only the interval of release, afforded, by four being off at a time, in succession. They feel this extremely irksome, at first; but notwithstanding the warmth of the climate, they become so far accustomed to the labour, by long practice, as to leave the tread-mill, with comparatively little disgust, after working upon it, for a considerable number of days. Many of the prisoners were occupied, in landing cargoes of Maize, or Indian-corn, from a field down the river; and others, in divesting it of the husk. To our regret, we heard an officer swearing at the men, and using other improper, and exasperating language. This practice is forbidden by the Commandant; but it is not uncommon, and in its effects, is perhaps equally hardening to those, who are guilty of it, and to those who are under them.

Whilst walking a few miles down the river, toward a brook, called Breakfast Creek, the waters of which are generally brackish, at high tide, we saw a number of remarkable plants, &c. On the margins of the brook, *Acrostichum fraxinifolium*, a large, ash-leaved fern, was growing, along with *Crinum pedunculatum*, a great bulbous-rooted plant, with white, tubular, lily-like flowers. *Hellenia cærulea*, a reedy-looking plant, with broad leaves, and blue berries, and a species of *Phytolacca*, with pretty, pink blossoms, were among the brushwood. By the sides of fresh-water ditches there were a *Jussieua*, resembling an Evening Primrose, with small yellow blossoms, and a blue-flowered plant, in figure like a *Pentstemon*. On the grassy slope of the hills, near the river, *Hibiscus Fraseri*, with yellow blossoms, like those of the Hollyhock, but having a deep purple eye, was in flower. Among the Mangroves, the Moschettos were so numerous, that we could not proceed many yards for them, notwithstanding we wiped them continually, off our hands and faces. Several striking butterflies were fluttering from flower to flower; some of them having considerable portions of the wings transparent. In returning, we fell in with half-a-dozen native youths, who, like the rest of their countrymen, in places uninfluenced by civilized society, were quite naked. As we could not converse with them, we shook hands with them, and they seemed pleased with this token of good-will. Having dressed their ebon skins afresh, with charcoal and grease, they communicated to us a little of their colour. Circumstances of this kind, we never regarded as important, compared with securing their friendship. We also met some older Natives, who afterwards came to the Settlement, having their hair filled with small, white and yellow feathers, and their bodies tastefully decorated, with broad lines of the same, stuck on with gum.

30th. We visited the Prisoners' Barracks, a large stone building, calculated to accommodate 1,000 men; but now occupied by 311. We also visited the Penitentiary for Female prisoners, 71 of whom are here. Most of these, as well as of the men, have been re-transported for crimes that have been nurtured by strong drink. The women were employed in washing, needle-work, picking oakum, and nursing. A few of them were very young. Many of them seemed far from being properly sensible of their miserable condition. We had, however, to convey to them, the message of mercy, through a crucified Redeemer.

31st. Was very rainy. We dined at the table of a pious Commissariat Officer, who is remarkable for his firmness, in what he believes to be his religious duty, and for his regularity in his family devotions, which he does not allow to be interrupted by visiters being present. After tea, the servants were called in, as usual. At the request of our worthy host, I read a portion of Scripture, but felt restrained from further vocal service. This led to conversation upon our view of waiting to feel, what we believe to be the putting forth, and guidance of the Good Shepherd, in these services, and to some comments, that appeared to be understood, on the frequency of no further vocal exercise than the reading of the Scriptures, occurring in the family devotions of Friends, the rest of the time being generally occupied in reverent, silent waiting on God, often, under a precious sense of the overshadowing of his love, or in the lifting up of the heart to him, in secret prayer. This exercise is known to be greatly blessed to the spiritually minded; and to be one, which often contributes much to the spiritual edification of their families.

4th mo. 1st. Being the day called "Good Friday," no work was exacted from the prisoners; but they, with the military and civil officers, whether Protestant or Roman Catholic, assembled, as on First-days, in the chapel; where the prayers and lessons of the Episcopal Church, with a few omissions, in deference to the Roman Catholics, were read, in a becoming manner, by the Superintendent of Convicts. After the service was gone through, I had a good deal to communicate; directing the audience to the convictions of the Holy Spirit, by which alone, man can be brought, savingly, to exercise faith in Christ, and to know him as his Mediator and Advocate with the Father, and the propitiation for his sins, and through him receive strength to walk in holiness. Prayer was also put up, in the name of Jesus, for an enlightened understanding of these truths. At three o'clock, we again met the male prisoners. G. W. Walker read the seventeenth of Acts; after which I addressed them on the importance of considering their latter end, and constantly bearing in mind, that we must all stand before the judgment-seat of Christ.

2nd. Accompanied by the surgeon, two prisoners, and a native Black, we visited a forest, called the Three-mile Scrub, on a low, alluvial soil, through which there is a small stream. Some of the trees far exceed 100 feet in height, a few may be 150. Among the lofty ones, may be enumerated some *Eucalypti*, called Iron-bark, Forest-mahogany, &c. and three species of Fig, with leaves resembling those of Laurel or Magnolia. One of these, *Ficus macrophylla*, was forty feet in circumference, at the greatest height that I could reach: its roots formed wall-like abutments, extending from the tree, over an area, thirty feet across. These Fig-trees are very remarkable in their growth: they often spring from seeds, deposited by birds, in cavities of other trees, at elevations of, perhaps, fifty feet, or more. From these situations, they send roots down to the ground, which, in their course, adhere to the tree: these again emit transverse, or diagonal roots, that fix themselves to others, in their course downward. Those that reach the ground thicken rapidly, still spreading themselves upon the face of the foster-tree, which, at length, is completely encased. These gigantic parasites rear their towering heads above all the other trees of the forest, sending out vast limbs, and spreading their own roots in the earth, from which also, they sometimes grow without the aid of other trees to sustain them.

The trunks and limbs of these, and other trees, support several species of fern, and some epiphytes of the Orchis tribe, with fleshy leaves, and singular stems and flowers. Numerous climbing plants, with stems varying in thickness, from that of pack-thread, to that of a man's body, ascend into their tops, and send down their branches in graceful festoons. Among the slenderer climbers were two species of Passion-flower, and one of Jasmine. The most gigantic climber, which might properly be called a climbing tree, belonged to a race of plants, called *Apocyneæ :* it had rugged bark, and sometimes formed a few serpent-like wreathes upon the ground, before ascending, and spreading itself among the tops of the other trees. There were also three species of *Cissus;* one of them with simple, and the other two with trifoliate leaves; these are kinds of Vine, bearing Grapes, about equal in size to English Sloes, but sweeter. The fruit of the figs is rather dry, but it is eaten by the native Blacks, and by numerous birds. The Moreton Bay Chestnut, *Castanospermum australe,* is a fine tree, with a profusion of flame-coloured blossom, and with leaves like those of the European Walnut. Some of its pods are ten inches long and eight round; they contain several seeds, in size and colour resembling Horse Chestnuts, but, in flavour, between a Spanish Chestnut and a fresh-ripened Bean, with a slight degree of bitterness. The Blacks roast them, and soak them in water, to prepare them for food. *Acrosticum grande,* one of the ferns that grow on the trees, is as large as a full-grown Scotch Cabbage, and is remarkably beautiful.

Caladium glychirhizon, a plant allied to the Arum, and one of
the race called Tara, the roots of which afford food to the
islanders of the Pacific, abounds in these woods. The root
is beaten and roasted by the Aborigines, till it is deprived
of its acrimony; it is then eaten, and is said to be pleasant to the taste. In the margins of the woods, and on
the banks of the rivers, the climbers are also numerous, and
very beautiful. Among them, are *Tecoma jasminoides*, a
large, white Trumpet-flower, with a rosy, pink tube and *Ipomœa
pendula*, before noticed, as bearing elegant, pink, convolvulus-
like blossoms. In the grass of the open ground, is a remarkable climbing Nettle, and in the forests, the Giant Nettle, *Urtica gigas*, forms a large tree. Many of the hills in this
neighbourhood are dry, and covered with quartzose gravel.
On these, the trees are chiefly of the genera, *Eucalyptus*, *Tristania*, *Casuarina*, and *Acacia*. In the basaltic soils *Altingia
Cunninghamii*, the Moreton Bay Pine, is interspersed; and
in some places, further into the interior, it forms large
woods.

One of the men who accompanied us, shot a Cockatoo
Pigeon; it is of a lead colour, with a reddish-brown crest, and
about the size of the English Wood Pigeon. Some of the
pigeons here, vie with the parrots in the gaiety of their plumage. Butterflies are numerous, large, and gay. Snakes are
frequent. The largest species, called the Carpet-snake, is
harmless; its skin is sometimes prepared for making into
slippers, &c. There are also several species of Lizard, some
of them very large, and prettily marked; they are eaten by the
Natives. One kind, of a moderate size, has a pouch, like a
large toothed, tippet, which it spreads when irritated: its
colour is blackish brown, with lighter markings.

3rd. This being the first First-day in the month, was
muster-day; when, after the service of the Episcopal Church
has been read to the prisoners, the regulations for their conduct, are also read, and subsequently, such men as think their
continuance of good conduct entitles them to any indulgence, or relaxation of the severity of their sentence, prefer
their petitions to the Commandant. We visited the prisoners in the Penitentiary, in the morning, and those in the

Barracks in the afternoon. A few Blacks came into the Barracks, and seemed desirous to understand what was going forward; but no one could interpret into their language on religious subjects.

4th. We visited the establishment at Eagle Farm, six miles from Brisbane Town, toward the mouth of the river: It is under the direction of a Superintendent who, with his wife, resides in a small cottage, close by some huts, formerly occupied by the male prisoners; by whose labour seven hundred acres of land were formerly cultivated, chiefly in maize. At present, there are no male prisoners here; but forty females, who are employed in field-labour: they are kept in close confinement during the night, and strictly watched in the day time, yet it is found very difficult to keep them in order. Some of them wear chains, to prevent their absconding, which they have frequently done, under covert of the long grass. Though these women are twice convicted, and among them, there are, no doubt, some of the most depraved of their sex, yet they received a religious visit with gladness; and the sense of the divine presence was with us, strengthening us to proclaim the message of mercy, through Him, who came "to seek and to save that which was lost," and in declaring the day of the vengeance of God, on those who continue in sin.

On the way to Eagle Farm, there are a few small trees of *Erythrina indica?* a species of Coral-tree, out of which, the natives to the north, are said to form canoes. The beautiful, blue *Ipomœa hederacea*, was in blossom, in the thickets, in which a *Wistaria*, not in flower, formed a luxuriant climber. In the margins of the woods, there was a white-flowered *Grewia*, with a thin, sweetish covering to the seeds, for which, it is valued by the natives. We saw several of the male Blacks, but none of the females; the latter are said, seldom to shew themselves, in this neighbourhood.

6th. In a wood, on the margin of the river, a few miles above Brisbane Town, I met with a species of Lime, *Citrus*, having small diversified leaves, and fruit, the size of a walnut; it formed a tree 15 feet high. *Flindersia australis*,

Oxleya zanthoxyla, and *Cedrella Toona,?* trees, of the
same tribe as the Mahogany, attain to a large size, in these
forests. *Oxleya zanthoxyla,* is the yellow wood, of Moreton
Bay: one I measured, was forty feet round, at about five
feet up: it was supposed to be one hundred feet high. The
Cedrella, is the Cedar of N. S. Wales; the wood of which
resembles Mahogany, but is not so heavy. The Silk Oak,
Grevillea robusta, also forms a large tree: its foliage is
divided, like that of some umbelliferous plants; its flowers
are somewhat like branched combs, of crooked, yellow
wire, shaded into orange, and are very handsome. *Hoya
Brownii,* and *Jasminum gracile?* were abundant, on the
bank of the river, along with *Tecoma jasminoides,* and many
other curious and beautiful, climbing shrubs. Eleven epiphytes, of the orchis tribe, were growing on the trunks of
the trees, in the forest. Most of these, were of the genera
Dendrobium, Cymbidium, and *Gunnia.* Some Bananas,
which had been washed from a place, in the Limestone
Country above, where sheep, for the provision of the
settlement, are kept, had established themselves on the
borders of a creek. Pumpkins were growing among the
brush-wood, in great luxuriance. The last were observed,
with evident pleasure, by my boats' crew of prisoners, who
anticipated making a meal of them, at a future day. They
are much used as a table vegetable, in New South Wales,
and are certainly to be valued as such, in this climate; they
keep well, and are a good substitute for potatoes, or for
turnips, by land, or by sea.

7th. We dined, in company with some other persons,
at the table of the Commissariat Officer. In the evening,
he desired the company, to witness the destruction of his
private stock of brandy, which he poured out in the yard,
having resolved to join the Temperance Society, and thus,
by his example, to throw his influence into the scale,
against one of the greatest of moral evils, and one, that
has brought a majority of the prisoners, to this place, and
has been the bane of a large proportion of the officers, and
military, who have had the charge of them. One of the
young men of the company, told us, that, on a certain

occasion, when lost in the bush, he was driven by hunger, to eat a species of *Teredo*, or Augur-worm, called by the Blacks, Cobra, which he found very palatable. In this part of the country, within the reach of the salt water, this animal is abundant in logs, which it perforates, till they resemble honeycomb.

8th. We visited the Hospital, which is in a dilapidated state. There being some prospect of opening this fine country to settlers, and the penal establishment being, consequently, reduced, many of the buildings have been suffered to get a little out of repair. The prevailing diseases here are Ophthalmia, Chronic Rheumatism and Dysentery; for-formerly Ague was frequent, but it has rarely occurred since the prisoners were properly fed, clothed and lodged. The surgeon, is an intelligent man, who has paid great attention to the anatomy of the curious tribe of animals, that inhabit this part of the world, and which, in Australia, generally, with the exception of the Native Dog, and a few others, are marsupial. They rear their young, from a very minute size, in pouches. Some species of Kangaroos, are met with here, that we have not seen before; also many birds, that are new to us; among them, are several splendid Parrots.

9th. On the way to Eagle Farm, we noticed a beautiful *Pavonia*, with a rosy, purple blossom, shaded deeply toward the centre. Here also, growing parasitically upon the climbers, was a splendid *Loranthus*, with foliage like that of a Lemon, and clusters of crimson, tubular blossoms, tipped with yellow. Several other fine species of this genus, grow on the branches of the *Eucalypti* and other trees, in the various parts of Australia. At Eagle Farm, we again visited the female prisoners, for whom a selection of tracts was left, with their Superintendent; they expressed thankfulness for them, being very destitue of books, even of Bibles, which the prisoners generally, have not access to, even on First-days.

On the way back to Brisbane Town, a prisoner constable was our guide. He gave us some account of his sufferings, when, on one occasion, he absconded, and was

in the bush for three months.   His companion died from
the hardships he met with.   In one place they found
the remains of two men, and in another of three, who
were supposed to have run away from Port Macquarie,
and to have been unable to sustain the fatigues and privations to which they had subjected themselves.   Instances
have occurred, in which men have run away, and lived for
some years among the Natives ; but at length, they have become so tired of savage life, as to return and give themselves
up.   In general, the Blacks bring back runaways, but a few are
supposed still to be out among them, to the northward.
Absconding is not now common among the prisoners.
This is attributable to the encouragement given to good
conduct, by relaxation of sentence, and to the regulation,
which requires the time spent in the bush, to be made up,
before any indulgence, or freedom, by expiration of sentence,
is allowed.

10th.   We again had religious interviews with the prisoners and officers.   Sixteen Blacks came to the Settlement, and we presented them with some cotton handkerchiefs, with which they seemed much pleased, and not less
so, with some Bananas, given them by the Commandant.
The Blacks here show less value for articles of European
manufacture, than those of some other parts of the Colony;
and though less contaminated by intercourse with white
people, they are evidently less civilized; they, however,
find Sweet-potatoes, Maize, and other food, such as they
obtain from the military and officers, so much superior to
the roots they generally feed upon, in their native haunts, that
some of the males visit the settlement daily, to obtain
them.

CHAPTER XXXIII.

4th mo. 11th. WE took a final leave of the Officers of
the Penal Settlement, and embarked on board the Commandant's gig, a fine boat of eight oars, to return to the
Isabella.

At the Lower Wharf, we took in two military officers,
one of whom was returning to Sydney. While waiting
for them, I went on shore, and saw, in the bush, a beautiful, blue *Plumbago*, possibly *P. capensis*, which I believe
is not known as a native of N. S. Wales. As we crossed
the Bay, we saw great numbers of Pelicans, standing in a
line, at the water's edge, on a sand-bank. One was also
fishing among shoals of Mullet, a migratory fish, probably
not the Mullet of the Northern Hemisphere, that is just
coming in from the sea, so thick, as to darken the water;
out of which, they are so continually jumping, as to give
the idea, of a dance among the fishes! but it is probably
a dance of terror, to elude the pursuit of their enemies,
the Porpoises and Sharks. The Blacks do not kill the
Porpoises, because they shew where there are fish to be
caught; but they value the flesh of another cetaceous animal, called here Youngon, the Dugong of India, *Halicore
Dugong*. This animal feeds on marine vegetables; and is

taken when it goes up narrow creeks, by means of nets, skilfully made of the bark of various species of *Hibiscus*.

Moreton Bay is shut in from the sea, by three islands, the northermost of which, is called Moreton Island, and the middle one, Amity or Stradbroke Island. On the north point of the latter is the Pilot's station. The forest about this point, is formed of some species of *Eucalyptus, Melaleuca,* and *Banksia,* with the Cypress-Pine, *Callitris arenosa,* which forms a spreading tree, forty feet high, and eight feet round. On the sandy flats, by the shore, *Ipomœa maritima,* sends out long, straight shoots, to the extent of many yards: it has large, pink, convolvulus-like blossoms, and curious, two-lobed leaves. It helps to bind the sand together, as do also, the large, yellow-flowered *Hibbertia volubilis,* and several maritime grasses. Although *H. volubilis* is offensively fetid, in English green-houses, I could never perceive that it had any smell, either here, or at Sydney. Some of the smaller species of the genus, are offensive in Tasmania. Many interesting shells are found upon the shores of this bay; among them, the Crowned Melon Shell is much esteemed for its beauty. The Blacks watch for it, and take it as the tide ebbs, before it has time to bury itself in the sand, or they probe for it, with a bone skewer, in the places where its track is seen.

The Blacks on Stradbroke Island, like those resorting to Brisbane Town, are fine-personed, in comparison with those about Sydney. Some of them can speak a little English. Their intercourse with the white people, at this station, has not increased their virtue, but it has evidently advanced them a few steps towards civilization, beyond those of Brisbane Town. Pride produces its painful effects among these people, as well as among those who profess civilization and Christianity, among whom it is less tolerable. The males of this tribe of Aborigines, ornament themselves, by cutting their flesh, and keeping it from healing, till it forms elevated marks. They cut nineteen ridges, that look like ribs, right across their breasts, from the line of their armpits, downwards. One man, about six feet high, had them as wide as my thumb, and half as much elevated. Their

A A

backs and thighs are thickly marked, with lighter, zigzag
lines, of great regularity.   The right shoulder is marked
with lines, like epaulettes, and the left with irregular scars,
received in combat with stone-knives; with which, on such
occasions, they wound one another on the left shoulder,
left thigh, or left leg; considering it a point of honour not
to deface the ornamented portions of the frame!   Some
of them have curly hair, but others have it, lank, and wear
it tied up, often forming a knot at the top of the head,
and decorated with feathers.   In this knot they stick their
bone skewers, and other implements; for being without
clothing, this is the only place in which they can carry an
implement not in the hand, except under the strips of skin
that they occasionally wear round their arms and loins.

12th.   The wind not favouring our departure, we went
on shore, and had a religious interview with the White
people.   We met them in the boat shed, which afforded
good accommodation, and was pleasantly cool for this almost tropical climate, in which the heat is still great, notwithstanding the summer is past.   A considerable number of
Blacks came also into the boat-shed, and as we could not
convey to them our sentiments of Christian good-will, in
words, we presented them with a few handkerchiefs.   Some
of these useful articles were also given to the boat's crew,
as an acknowledgment of their attentive services.   Though
prisoners, they may be allowed to wipe the perspiration
from their faces with them; but so strict is the discipline,
that they would not be allowed to tie them round their
necks!   They are not allowed to wear any thing but the
slop clothing, provided by the Government.   Perhaps this
may be a good regulation, tending both to keep up the
feeling that they are prisoners, in consequence of their
crimes, and to prevent their stealing.   Some of the soldiers
and prisoners, applied for tracts, which they received gratefully, along with a few books, including a testament.
They are very destitute of books, the only Bible I heard of,
at the station, belonged to the pilot.

The wind continuing adverse, I accompanied a party
from the Isabella, to Moreton Island, with a view of

examining its vegetable productions. Bordering the sands, there were a *Scævola*, with brilliant, blue flowers, and black berries, *Ipomæa maritima*, some of the shoots of which, were fifty yards long, *Canvallia Baueriana*, a kidney-bean-like plant, with rose coloured flowers, and another leguminous plant, with yellow blossoms, both of which, grow also on Norfolk Island, and several other plants, with trailing stems. The part of the Island, that I crossed, was sandy, with swamps and lagoons. Most of it was covered with trees, such as *Callitris arenosus*, a large *Tristania*, *Banksia æmula*, and *integrifolia*, and *Melaleuca viridiflora*, which attains a large size. Here, in sandy places, *Pandanus pedunculatus*, a species of Screw Pine, forms a singular tree, fifteen feet high. Its leaves, resemble those of the Pine-apple; its fruit, is as large as a child's head, yellow, and composed of clustered, oblong nuts, fleshy at the base, which separate in attached groups, when ripe. The fleshy part, is eaten by the Blacks; but it has an unpleasant smell, and though sweetish, is rather acrid. The trunk, is supported securely, by roots, that descend from various parts of it, into the sand, and are as thick and straight, as broom-sticks; they look rather like the stays of a ship. In returning from the west side of the Island, my attention was diverted, by a multitude of butterflies, and by a large lizard; and after walking for some time, I again, and again, found myself on the west coast. Taking therefore my compass, I determined, to make my way direct to my companions, whom I succeeded in reaching, after some fatigue, by wading through a lagoon, and crossing some steep sand-hills. The latter, were overgrown by *Myrtus tenuifolia*, a Myrtle, of low stature, with narrow leaves, and sweet, aromatic, white berries, spotted with purple. These are the most agreeable, native fruit, I have tasted in Australia; they are produced so abundantly, as to afford an important article of food, to the Aborigines. Near the east coast, there were a yellow *Crotolaria*, and *Lygodium microphyllum*, a beautiful, climbing fern, also *Pteris esculenta*, and *Blechnum cartilagineum*, ferns, the roots of which, are eaten by the Blacks.

On the shore, there were herds of crabs, covering many
acres of sand: they were globular, and about an inch in
diameter; their bodies roundish, and of a bluish colour,
and their legs long; they made a noise, like the pattering
of rain, while filing off, in all directions, to allow us to pass;
in doing this, they scraped the sand into masses, like peas.
A few of them buried themselves, by a rotatory movement,
like their smaller allies seen at Circular Head, in V. D.
Land. The Moreton Island species is also found on the
shores of Port Jackson, but in much smaller numbers.

13th. We again went on shore at Amity Point, where
some of the Blacks were amusing themselves, during a rainy
portion of the day, with dancing. One of them beat two
of their Boomerings together, for music, and produced a
deafening clack. The men danced, or rather, stamped, to
the tune, often changing the position of their hands, and
using great exertion, till every part of their bodies and limbs
quivered: they chanted at the same time, with a loud voice,
and in this the women assisted, adding also to the noise by
means of their hands. Once they sent the women out, that
they might not witness a dance, which had nothing about
it particularly striking; they also collected bushes, and
danced with them in their hands, and under their arms,
concealing themselves partly by them. They seemed to
enjoy this boisterous child's-play, for such it greatly resembled. If custom did not render people in some measure
blind to folly, many of the amusements practiced in circles
of society, considered highly civilized, might perhaps, seem
as absurd, and almost as barbarous. I consider the Society
of Friends to have made great advances in true civilization,
beyond the rest of the world, in having abandoned such
amusements, as well as in some other particulars. By this
abandonment, they also avoid much that is inimical to
Christian sobriety, and turn their relaxation into channels
more rational, and conducive to domestic happiness. I
believe no people in the world realize so much temporal
comfort as they. When the rain ceased, we walked to a
native village, on the coast. It consisted of a number of
huts, formed of arched sticks, and covered with tea-tree

bark, so as to form weather-tight shelters, just high enough to allow the inmates to sit upright in them, and equal in comfort to the tilts, inhabited by the Gipsies, in England. One of these is represented in the accompanying wood-cut.

Openings were left at their larger ends, opposite to which at the outside, there were little fires, at which many of the women were roasting fern-root. This, after it was roasted, was held by one hand on a log of wood, while its whole length was beaten, by a stone, held in the other hand, so as to break the woody fibre. In this state it is eaten, without removing the charred surface; its taste is something like that of a waxy potato, but more gelatinous. In most instances, there were a man and a woman in each hut, and in some of them there were also a few children; but the number of the children is small, in comparison with what it is in the families of Europeans. Many of the huts had shelters of leafy boughs placed so as to keep off the wind. We were informed that these people had several such villages on the Island; and that they resorted to one, or to another, according to the weather, the season of the year, and the contiguity of food. At present they are near the opening between Moreton and Stradbroke Islands, depending chiefly on the shoals of Mullet for food. A few weeks ago, they went further into the interior, collecting honey. At some seasons they resort to places producing wild fruits; and in wet weather, to elevated situations, contiguous to those parts of the coast, abounding with oysters. In these last situations, their huts are said to be large enough for a man to stand up in.

Some of the native dogs appeared to be in a half-domesticated state, among the Aborigines. One was shot to-day, by a sergeant, in the act of stealing his fowls: he said the women would make great lamentation over it. It was about the size of a cur, but slenderer, and of a reddish colour.

14th. Our company again went to Moreton Island, to fish, with a view to economizing the stock of provisions. The kinds they caught are known here, by the names of Mullet, Pimbore, and Guard-fish. Pimbore is the native name of a superior fish, larger than the Mullet of these seas. We also picked up a few shells, and saw some Gigantic Cranes and Fishing-eagles, a considerable number of Pelicans, and large flocks of Curlews, Terns, and Redbills. In the evening, we again visited the village of the Natives, on Stradbroke Island. One of them was busy, twisting rushes, to make a dilly or bag. The base of the rushes is of a pale colour, the portion included in the sheaths, at the base, or just emerging from them, is of a pinky hue, and the top green. By arranging the knots, so as to form diagonal lines across the bag, the colours are brought into a tasteful order, by these poor creatures, who have been erroneously represented as below all other human beings in capacity. In forming huts, and making nets and bags, and various implements, those here excel their more southern neighbours.

15th. We took a walk, along the inner shore of Stradbroke Island. Here we observed *Hibiscus tiliaceus*, with its fine, yellow flowers, like those of Hollyhock, but with crimson eyes, growing to the size of a pear-tree; and near it, *Edwardsia nuda?* a pretty bush, with yellow flowers, but inferior in beauty to the Edwardsias of New Zealand. On the muddy land, within the reach of high tide, there was a small species of *Rhizophora*, or true Mangrove, and a *Bruguiera*, another shrub of a nearly allied genus. The Mangrove resembles a thick-

leaved Laurel, and has roots from its stem above ground,
like the stays of the mast of a ship: its fruit is about
an inch in diameter, and it vegetates, as it hangs on the
bush, and sends out a green radicle, about a foot long,
and swollen toward the pointed base ; this, bearing the
germ on its top, drops from the fruit, and either sticks in
the mud, and vegetates, or floats in the sea, till landed on
some congenial spot, or till it perishes. The *Bruguiera*
forms a fine bush, eight or ten feet high, and has the bell-
shaped cup to its evanescent petals, in substance, resembling
red-morocco leather, and cut into ten narrow segments.
Its mode of propagation is similar to the former, but its
radicle is shorter, and not swollen toward the base. These
gay, red-leather-like flowers, and long, green, spindle-like
radicles, were washed up abundantly on the shore, ·and till
I saw them growing, they puzzled me not a little.

16th. We took a walk upon a part of the beach, where
the variety of shell-fish was great. The Rock Oysters were
attached to the portions of the various Mangroves, within
the influx of the sea. Drift Oysters were in large masses,
below the high-water mark ; among them were various species of *Cyprœa*, Cowrie, *Conus*, &c. Common and Pearl
Oysters were thinly scattered, lower down on the shore.
While walking on the beach, a native Black, who, in
answer to a question respecting his name, said " Tommy
Green," came dancing toward us, the picture of good nature ; he made signals to us to put on our shoes. This we
found, was to save our feet from being cut by fragments
of shells, in a mud-flat, which we were about to cross, and
in which there were a large *Pinna*, a sort of wedge-shaped
Muscle, and a strange thing, without a head, somewhat
like a lady's riding whip, as well as many other creatures,
of unusual form, that might reward the investigation of a
diligent naturalist. By the instruction of our black friend,
we obtained specimens of a large *Cardium*, or Cockle ;
the impressions of the margin of the shells of which, were
visible on the sand under which it was buried.

On our return, two Natives were fighting, at the village.
One of them, according to their custom, had seized a

woman from another tribe, for a wife, and had been chal-
lenged by one of her connexions. The combatants, wore
white fillets round their heads, and had boomerings in their
belts, and wooden shields, and waddies, in their hands;
with the latter, after some fencing, they gave each other
heavy blows, upon the head. They then retreated a few
paces, but maintained a vociferous contest, in which, the
women of the village joined. It was painful, to witness
this affray, which we could not interfere, to put an end to,
on account of not knowing their language. At length,
to our great relief, a shoal of mullet was announced. The
people took their nets, and hastened to the beach; and
when there were no abettors, the contest ceased, and the
company, belonging our boat, who had been standing in
the rain; to witness this painful spectacle, no longer delayed
returning on board the Isabella. It is said, the battles
sometimes become very general, on occasions of this sort,
but that they are seldom attended by loss of life. Several of
the men, at this time, were armed with spears, and boomerings; and seemed only to wait, for a little more excitement,
to join in the combat; others, paid little attention to the
fight, and one continued, quietly building a hut, notwithstanding, the combatants were often close by him.

On the borders of Moreton Bay, into which, several small
rivers discharge themselves, there are said to be four tribes
of Natives, of about one hundred each. Those, about Point
Skirmish, to the northward, are reported, to be remarkably
pugnacious, and cruel. Possibly, they may have been
influenced by runaway prisoners. The ornaments, of those
we met with, were necklaces, of short pieces of reed, pieces
of nautilus, or other pearly shell, feathers, and bands of
kangaroo sinews, or of opposum-fur: of the latter material, some of the female children wore short, fringe aprons.
They smear their bodies, with charcoal, pipe-clay, or
ruddle, and grease. Some of them, are affected with
disease, said to have been communicated, from an American
Whaler; but most of them seem, healthy, and robust.

While in Moreton Bay, we were surprised, by hearing
the Blacks call biscuits, Five Islands. This we learned,

arose from some men, who, several years ago, were driven
from the part of the Illawarra coast, called the Five Islands,
having held up biscuits, to the Blacks, and said, Five
Islands, in the hope, of learning from them, the direction
of their lost home.   The Blacks, however, mistook this,
for the name of the biscuits, and hence have continued
to call them by this name.   The lost men remained among
the Natives, for several years, and were kindly treated.
At length, they were brought away, by a vessel that put
in here, and subsequently, one of them was returned hither,
as a prisoner.

17th.   The weather having become more favourable, the
anchor was up, at an early hour; we parted from Lieut.
Otter, the officer, whose duty it was, to see the vessel
off, and who had shewn us much kind attention, and
soon crossed the bar, by a shallow passage.   At sea, the
wind was adverse, and the rolling of the vessel, was such,
as to produce much sickness.   This continued to be the
case, till the 20th, when we had a fine breeze, and were
off Port Macquarie; but the sea was too high, to admit of
our being put on shore there, without risk to the vessel.
In the night of the 22nd, there were violent squalls, and
in the morning, a gale commenced.   We were then to the
south of Port Jackson, having been unable to make the
land.   In standing off, during the night, we were driven
by a current, to the north, so that in the morning, we were
off the mouth of the Hunter River.

The gale continuing, and our provisions being reduced to
four days consumption, we concluded to run for Newcastle,
in Port Hunter.   On coming opposite the port, a gun was
fired, and a signal made, which was answered by one that
perplexed us, signifying that the tide had begun to ebb.
We therefore again beat off the land; but on referring to
the tables, it was found that the ebb could not have commenced, and that the tide would yet flow for several hours;
we therefore again approached the shore, fired another gun,
and made another signal, shewing that the vessel belonged
the Government.   This was answered by one such as we
desired, and quickly by a second, indicating that the pilot

had left the shore to board us; he soon reached the vessel, and made an excuse for the wrong signal, that was not very satisfactory; but under his prompt directions, we beat into Port Hunter, tacking first to one side, and then to the other, close to the breakers, until we reached a place of safety, under a natural, though imperfect breakwater, terminated by an islet, called The Knobby. The Tidewaiter, and another officer, soon boarded us to know our business; and after they, with our captain, and our fellow passenger, had gone on shore, we mustered such of the people as inclined to meet with us, to whom we read a chapter, and addressed some counsel. It was far from a bright time, and there is reason to fear, that more of a disposition to murmur, at the privations that had been endured, existed among them, than of one to give God thanks for the unmerited mercies, continued to us, and by which we had now been delivered from being driven to sea, in a famishing state. Last night the topping-lift of our mizen sail broke, when two men were on the boom, which swung over the side, but they kept their hold, and escaped injury. Another man received a severe bruise by it, and would have gone overboard, had not his leg got jammed between a water-cask and the bulwark. This poor fellow, though now unable to turn in bed from the injury, seemed thankful for his escape from a watery grave; from which, in a dark night, with a high sea, he could not have been rescued, had he been precipitated into the ocean.

25th. The gale continuing we went on shore, and were kindly welcomed by George Brooks, the Colonial Surgeon. Newcastle in New South Wales, like the town in England from which it is named, is famous for the production of coal; but Newcastle in N. S. Wales, is only a village of about forty houses, inclusive of a jail, a hospital and military barracks. It stands at the mouth of the Hunter River, on a sand-stone promontory, on the point of which, there is a lighthouse. The harbour is not of easy access; the river, which is shallow in this part, widens beyond it, and forms several channels, separated by low, Mangrove islands. There being no prospect of the Isabella getting to sea again for a few days, we embarked in the Ceres steamer in the evening, but the sea proved too high for her to proceed, and she put back to Newcastle about midnight.

26th. Most of the day was spent with our kind friend the Surgeon, in company with a gentleman in the Survey department and a settler, who were, like ourselves, delayed here by the storm. In a walk, we passed the burial ground, in which a detachment of an ironed-gang was at work, under an overseer, and three sentries. These men had been occupied here about a month, in making improvements, that a quarter of their number of industrious men, would have effected in the same time. Work without wages proceeds slowly, by a natural consequence that is not at all reversed, by the work being imposed as the punishment of crime. The state of the weather rendering it unlikely we should be able to proceed to Sydney for some days, we concluded to visit Ebenezer, on Lake Macquarie, where Lancelot Edward Threlkeld is employed by the Government, as a Missionary to the Aborigines, With this view we engaged as our guide Beerabahn, or M'Gill, a tall, intelligent man, the chief of the tribe of Blacks resorting thither.

27th. We set out with our black conductor, who could speak a little English, and one of his countrymen named Boatman or Boardman. These people had contracted a debasing appetite for strong drink, which was often given them by the military and other persons, perhaps from mistaken notions of kindness. Boatman some years afterwards, lost his life in a drunken fray.

M'Gill was dressed in a red-striped shirt, not very clean, a pair of ragged trowsers, and an old hat. Suspended from his neck, by a brass chain, he had a half-moon-shaped, brass breastplate, with his native and English name, and a declaration of his kingly dignity, engraven upon it: his nose and part of his cheeks were besmeared with ruddle, but he had few cuttings upon his flesh: he carried one of our bundles, and took a young dog upon his shoulder, on this journey, of twenty-six miles through the bush. In passing his hut, he stripped off his shirt, which he left behind to avoid encumbrance. Boatman, who is represented in the accompanying wood-cut, in the act of throwing a spear, by

means of a womera, an implement used to increase the
impetus, wore a ragged, blue jacket, and trowsers.—On the
way through the bush, our guides stopped to seek wild

honey, but without success.   Sometimes the Blacks capture
bees, and stick small pieces of feather to them, with gum; this
makes them fly heavily, and enables their pursuers to watch
them in their flight, until they reach their nests. Many of the
open places in the forest, abounded with Gigantic-lily; the
flower stems of which rise from 10 to 20 feet high.   These
stems are roasted, and eaten by the Aborigines, who cut them
for this purpose, when they are about a foot and a half
high, and thicker than a man's arm.   The Blacks also roast
the roots, and make them into a sort of cake, which they
eat cold: they likewise roast and pound the seeds of *Zamia
spiralis*, and then place the mass for two or three weeks,

in water, to take out the bitter principle, after which it
is eaten. M'Gill thought potatoes were better than most
vegetables they used: he said, the Blacks, in this neighbourhood, had "thrown away" the use of fern-root. These
people find maize, potatoes, bread, and other articles produced by the industry of white people, so much better than
their own native articles of diet, that they stay much about
the habitations of the European population, and do little
jobs, for which they get these articles in return : they also
find this kind of provision more certainly to be relied upon,
which induces them to keep near to the usurpers of their
country, notwithstanding the abuse and indignity they sometimes meet with, and their liability to be fired upon, if
seen helping themselves among the growing Indian corn.

The sun had just set, when we reached the residence of
L. E. Threlkeld and his numerous family, from whom
we received a kind welcome.

28th. L. E. Threlkeld has applied himself diligently to
attaining the language of the Aborigines, and reducing it
to writing, compiling a grammar, preparing a translation of
the Gospel according to Luke, and some smaller selections
from Scripture, also a vocabulary. He has been employed
several years in the mission, in which he has been unassisted by any other Missionary. He has had, at the same
time, to provide for his own family, which now consists of
nine children, and is living on his own land, a portion of
which he has cleared, with much labour. In the afternoon,
we walked to a woody point, extending into the lake, which
is twenty-five miles long, and seven broad, and has a narrow opening into the sea. Some Blacks were fishing, to
whom L. E. Threlkeld spoke a few words, in reference to
the Deity, to which they attended with gravity.

29th. We accompanied L. E. Threlkeld, in a boat, rowed
by three Blacks, to the site of the old missionary station,
at the head of the Lake, where we landed on a fine seam
of coal. This station was abandoned some years ago, by
the London Missionary Society, on account of its expense,
and the misrepresentations of persons who had never been
upon the spot ; and thus an opportunity was lost for

benefiting the Blacks, such as will never occur again in this part of N. S. Wales. Those who were collected here, have become dispersed among the settlers, toward Newcastle; and through the acquired love of strong drink, and other causes, such as occasion Black men "to fade away," have become greatly diminished in number. The Natives obtain fish and oysters in the lake; which they exchange for flour, tobacco, &c. In the forest, at the north end of the lake, the variety of trees is considerable; among them is *Achras australis*, which bears a fruit like an inferior plum: its seeds are something, in form, like the handle of a gimlet, but are pointed and polished. The Blacks scratch various figures upon them, and amuse themselves by guessing what the figure is, on the one held in the hand of another person.

30th. Was very rainy: it was spent in examining into the labours of L. E. Threlkeld, which have been very persevering and disinterested. He has succeeded in imparting to the Blacks, some general ideas respecting the Deity and the responsibility of man; but so far as yet appears, without that effect by which, under the influence of the divine Spirit, such knowledge becomes practical, in leading to repentance and faith in Christ. We have come to the conclusion, that no impediment exists, to the Aborigines of New South Wales becoming civilized, or receiving the Gospel, beyond what applies to other tribes of human beings, destitute of civilization. In these, the wandering habits, induced by living on the wild produce of the earth, are uncongenial to the settlement requisite for instruction; but this might be overcome, especially in the rising generation. But there have been impediments of another class, in New South Wales, such as the demoralizing influence of the white population, and the prejudices of benevolent persons, who had given way to discouragement, in consequence of individual Blacks, who had been brought up among the Whites, returning to their own tribes. This circumstance has arisen from the feeling that such had, that they were looked down upon as black men among Whites; while they were looked up to, because of their enlarged knowledge, among their own people. The amount of the Black population of Australia has been a subject of much variety of opinion; but it has probably been greatly over-rated.   On comparing the number of Aborigines, known to exist between Batmans Bay and Port Macquarie, with the whole extent of N. S. Wales, and this with the whole of Australia, making large allowance for the reduction of the tribes, by European influence, and doubling the amount for contingences, we came to the conclusion, that the whole Black population of Australia, probably did not exceed fifty thousand; and nothing that we subsequently saw in Southern or Western Australia altered our impression on this subject.

5th mo. 1st.   We were present during the season devoted to public worship, in the mission family, in which opportunity was afforded us, for the expression of what was upon our minds.   It is seldom that any of the Blacks are present on these occasions.   Among the marks of improvement, in regard to civilization, exhibited by the Natives of this neighbourhood, none of whom can be said to remain permanently here, may be noticed, their wearing clothes, and their consequent abandonment of the practice of ornamenting themselves by cutting their flesh; their ceasing to knock out a tooth, on their youths attaining to manhood; their intelligence and friendly feeling toward the white population, and their willingness to do little turns of work, for rewards in flour, tobacco, clothing, &c.

2nd.   Taking leave of Ebenezer, L. E. Threlkeld, conveyed us in a boat, to the head of the lake; from whence we proceeded by a road, originally cut from the old missionary station to Newcastle, through forest of Red Gum, *Angophora lanceolata*, Apple-tree, *A. augustifolia*, Iron Bark, Stringy Bark, Blood-tree, Bastard Box, Spotted Gum, and other species of the genus *Eucalyptus*.   About two miles from Newcastle, there is a singular spring of water, that rises a few inches above the surface of the ground, inside of the trunk of a Spotted Gum-tree, a root of which has probably tapped the spring: the water is accessible by an inversely heart-shaped hole in the tree, and occasionally flows out in wet weather.   The beautiful *Blandfordia grandiflora*, with yellow, bell-shaped, lily-like flowers, was growing in the forest, along with many other pretty plants. In the course of our walk, we fell in with some regiments of hairy caterpillars, following one another in long lines, the head of each, except the first, touching the tail of the one before it. A friend of mine told me, that once, on meeting some of these caterpillars, traversing a rock, he directed the head of the first, with a stick, to the tail of the last, and they continued following one another in a circle, for several hours, without seeming to discover the trick that had been played upon them! Our sable guides were joined on the way through the forest, by another of their tribe, whose name was Macquarie, and we saw several other parties, passing backward and forward. They sometimes amused themselves and us, by throwing their boomerings, which made circuits, almost like the flight of birds. On reaching Newcastle, they received their wages in bread, tea, sugar, and tobacco. This kind of payment, they seemed to understand better than one in money; of which it has not been the policy of the settlers to teach them the value; perhaps more from seeing that they appreciated more readily the worth of useable commodities, than from an intention to keep them in ignorance of a point, that would have been desirable for them to understand, in order to save them from imposition, in regard to the value of their own labour.—In the afternoon, we embarked on board the Ceres, a fine vessel, built on the Williams River, carrying two engines, each of forty horse power, and once more put to sea, with a contrary wind.

3rd. We landed at Sydney, after a rough passage of sixteen hours, and were kindly welcomed by our friends. The Isabella, on board of which was our luggage, arrived before us, having beaten up, against the wind, in three days.

CHAPTER XXXIV.

5th mo. 7th. WE had the satisfaction of hearing of our dear friends, D. and C. Wheeler, through the medium of a letter from Charles Barff, to William P. Crook, of this place, dated "Huaine, Jan. 19th, 1836;" he says, "I mentioned in my last, that I accompanied Mr. Daniel Wheeler and Son, to Pora Pora, as interpreter. The Natives listened with profound attention, to their pious, pointed, and Scriptural addresses."

8th. Very wet. Only seven persons were at our meeting in the morning, and eight in the afternoon. Both were silent seasons, except that I gave expression to a few sentences in prayer, in the morning.—Our black guides, M'Gill and Boatman, called to see us. They are in town, in consequence of the trial of some Aborigines, to whom, on behalf of the Government, in conjunction with L. E. Threlkeld, M'Gill acts as interpreter. We gave them some articles of clothing, with which they were much pleased.—These poor creatures called upon us several times afterwards, during their stay in Sydney. They were mostly in a state of excitement, from strong drink; which they are easily persuaded to take. The Blacks are not like the same people,

B B

when in towns, as they are, when remote from places where they are incited to vice, into which many of the white population take a pleasure in leading them.

12th. The week-day meeting was very small. To me it was a season of comfort, notwithstanding a prevailing sense of my own weakness and poverty. The clear perception of these, is the direct work of the Holy Spirit. If we have any just sense of the state of man before his Maker, it must be of his helplessness, and that, without Christ, the best of men can do nothing for the glory of God, the edification of one another, or the salvation of their own souls. It is by waiting upon God, in the depth of humiliation, that we have the evidence confirmed to us, from season to season, of being reconciled to him, through the death of his Son, and know a union, one with another, and with Christ, and through him, with the Father. It is thus that we experience, the fulfilment of that, for which our holy Redeemer prayed, not for his immediate disciples alone, but for all who should believe on him, through their word: "That they all may be one, as thou Father," said he, " art in me, and I in thee; that they also may be one in us;" "that they may be one, even as we are one; I in them, and thou in me, that they may be made perfect in one."—John xvii., 21, 22, 23.

13th. In consequence of the decease of a child belonging to parents, one of whom was brought up among Friends, and has a religious objection to the modes of burial, in common use, and who could not, on that account, attend the interment of her own babe, we made an application to the Governor, for a burial place for Friends, in the land reserved for Burial Grounds, adjacent to Sydney. This request was afterwards granted.

14th. On behalf of a reformed prisoner, who has for some time been associated with us, in religious fellowship, we remitted to the persons who prosecuted him, the sum of £20, toward the expense they incurred in the prosecution.

19th. At the suggestion of my Brother, who has kindly taken care of my temporal concerns during my absence, I made some needful provisions, by a codicil, in my will.

I have often regretted not having brought a copy of this document with me, as I cannot recollect with certainty its contents. When in England, it was my practice to read it once a year, to see that it was according to my mind and conscience; and more than once, I have seen occasion to alter it. Before I had a proper will made, I was a few times unwell, when from home; and though favoured with peace in looking toward eternity, I was nevertheless uncomfortable at not having a satisfactory will. It is well to attend to such subjects in proper season, and to remember, that in the Day of Judgment, account will as surely have to be rendered, for the right use, and the disposal, that has been made of the talent of property, as for that of any other talent.

24th. We received a call from L. E. Threlkeld, who is about to return to Lake Macquarie. The Black who was tried lately, was acquitted, and some others have been discharged. In the course of this trial, one of the barbarous, white evidences, stated in open court, that he considered the Blacks as no more than the beasts of the field. This is a sentiment too prevalent among many of the Whites of the Colony. The presiding Judge expressed his abhorrence of such a sentiment, and his conviction, that they were human beings, responsible before God, in whose sight, killing them was as truly murder as killing human beings of any other description : he stated also, that they were responsible to the laws of the Colony, and must be protected by them ; and said he was glad, that through the medium of a respectable Missionary, their causes were capable of being pleaded in that Court.

27th. On visiting the Bible Society's Depot, to obtain an Irish Bible, for an old Hibernian, in the interior, both the Depository and myself were at a loss, among the variety of languages, in strange character, to distinguish the Irish. This difficulty was at length overcome, by reference to the word, New Testament, in forty-eight languages, forming the frontispiece to Bagster's Polymicron New Testament. This circumstance suggested, that the name of the language in which each Bible was printed, might be advantageously introduced, in English, in the titlepages of foreign Bibles.

6th mo. 12th. Since returning to Sydney, we have been much occupied in sending books, and tracts to persons whom we visited in our late journey. In the prospect of again leaving this place, for a season, we felt a debt of Christian love toward the inhabitants, which it seemed time to endeavour to discharge, by inviting them to a meeting for public worship, which was held this morning. I was much oppressed in it, by a sense of a lamentable want of a true hungering and thirsting after righteousness, in the congregation, among whom there were nevertheless some pious persons. I had to address them on the passage, " It is a fearful thing to fall into the hands of the living God." At the conclusion, notice was given of the hours of meeting, on First and Fifth-days. At three o'clock about thirty persons assembled, with whom we sat an hour and a half in silence. My own state was one of great emptiness, and under such circumstances, I dared not to attempt expression, much as the people seemed to need religious instruction. Tracts were distributed at the close of the meetings.

14th. Being furnished with letters of introduction, from our kind friend, the Colonial Secretary, to several settlers on the Hunter River, we sailed by the Ceres steamer, for Maitland, and had a fine passage, the sea being so smooth as scarcely to give motion to the vessel.

15th. About five o'clock in the morning, the steamer anchored at Newcastle. After waiting an hour for daylight, it proceeded up the Hunter, to the Green Hills or Morpeth, the port of the embryo town of Maitland, which is about twenty miles from Newcastle, by land, and forty by water. The Hunter is here of considerable width; its banks are low, alluvial land, but little of which is cleared. A thick scrub, containing a variety of trees and shrubs, extends to the water's edge. Some of the trees are clad with shaggy Lichens, and many of them support the Golden Mistletoe, and a species of Loranthus. The Elkshorn Fern, *Acrosticum alcicorne*, which in Port Jackson, generally grows on decomposing, sandstone rocks, forms here protuberant girdles, round the trunks of trees, among the branches of which *Ipomœa pendula*, and *Marsdenia fragrans*, are striking climbers. Water-fowl are numerous, near the bushy islands, at the mouth of the river, especially Pelicans. The Williams River and the Paterson, both of which are navigable, join the Hunter from the north. In proceeding up the river, the depression of the waters, before the packet, occasioned by the elevation produced behind, by the action of the paddles, made the reeds of the margin, bow to our approach, with an amusing regularity.—Maitland is about three miles from Green Hills: it consists of a considerable number of houses, scattered by the sides of a soft road, for upwards of two miles, some of which are substantially built of brick. We found good accommodation at an hotel, between Green Hills and Maitland. There are also several decent inns in the town. We had been told, that we should find a large proportion of the inhabitants of this place, drunken with rum and prosperity; and this description was not without ground, in regard to many; for the place has of late, become one of importance, in traffic between the coast and the interior, and at the time of our visit, devotedness to the world, and drunkenness, were awfully prevalent.

16th. We made several calls in the town; in which a considerable number of the native Blacks, were working for the inhabitants, as hewers of wood and drawers of water. We also visited the Jail, a place of temporary confinement, till the prisoners are examined and transferred to Newcastle: it consists of a few cells, enclosed within a high, wooden fence, and is said to be sometimes so crowded, that prisoners have to be brought into the yard to avoid suffocation.

17th. At sunset, several Night Hawks, in flight resembling owls, were soaring in various directions. Plovers were crying, and frogs croaking in the marshes. Large Bats, called Flying Foxes, are common in this neighbourhood. It is now nearly mid-winter, but the frost has scarcely touched the leaves of the Pumpkins and Potatoes, and the second crop of Maize is not yet fully harvested. The springing wheat is beautifully green, and the "brushes," on the sides of the river, scarcely vary from the verdure of summer, except in the yellowness of the foliage of *Melia Azedarach.* The evenings and mornings are chilly, but the middle of the day is as warm as that of an English summer, and Swallows are numerous.

19th. We had a meeting in the Court House, and notwithstanding the roads are very soft, from late rains, about 150 persons assembled; to whom, after a considerable period of silent waiting upon God, we were enabled to bear a clear testimony to the truth, with expressions of earnest desire, that our auditors might become individually acquainted with the blessings, proposed to mankind in the Gospel. In the afternoon, we visited an ironed-gang, employed on the roads, under a military guard; we found them locked up in their caravans, out of which only one-third were allowed to come at a time, for exercise. When locked in, only half of them can sit up, on the ends of the platforms, on which half of them sleep; the rest must sit back, with their legs at a right-angle with their bodies. On our arrival, they were all turned out, counted, and then marched to a place, at a short distance, where they stood, with the guard of soldiers, under arms, behind them. After a pause, we addressed them, inviting their attention to the convictions of the Holy Spirit, as the witness in their own minds, against sin; by neglecting which, they had fallen into transgression before God and man, until they had been permitted to commit the sins which had brought them into grievous bondage, among their fellow-men; when, if they had attended to this warning voice of the Most High, they would, on the other hand, have been led to repentance, and faith in Christ, and through him, would have become of the number of his reconciled and obedient children, free from the bondage of Satan. They were invited to turn at the reproofs of instruction, as at the voice of Him who desires not that any should perish. In commenting on the passage, "Eye hath not seen, nor ear heard, neither have entered into the heart of man, the things which God hath prepared for them that love him; but God hath revealed them unto us by his Spirit; for the Spirit searcheth all things, yea, the deep things of God;" it was mentioned, by way of illustration, that our ideas of all things, are liable to be very defective, till we see or feel them; that thus, though themselves might have heard of the sufferings of prisoners, they had had a very defective idea of them, till they felt them; and though they might have seen men in chains, they had had a very imperfect notion of the suffering of this punishment, till they felt it; and that so, likewise, though of an opposite nature, the blessings of the Gospel required to be felt, to be understood. These comments excited a significant assent, in the countenances, and movements of the heads of the prisoners, expressive of their sense of the suffering under which they have brought themselves, by having multiplied their offences, so as to incur the extra-coercive discipline, of this part of our penal laws.

20th. Was occupied in connexion with a lecture, on temperance, held in the Court House, in the evening. The evils of strong-drink seem scarcely to have claimed the notice of the people here, notwithstanding they suffer grievously under them.

21st. We travelled westward through open, grassy forest, toward Harpers Hills, where another ironed-gang is stationed. In the evening, we were overtaken by a settler, professing with the Church of Rome, who kindly invited us to his house, and readily assembled his family and servants, in order that we might express to them our Christian desire for their present and eternal welfare.

22nd. In the morning, we had an interview with the Ironed-gang, at Harpers Hills, who were working on the road, at a place where, I think, there were marine fossils, sparingly imbedded in basalt. The officer in charge, promised to send me some, to Sydney; but those received from him, had evidently come out of an argillaceous rock, and seemed to have been selected on account of their beauty.

We pursued our route for a few miles further, along the course of the Hunter River, which here flows through a rich, alluvial vale, in some places spreading into extensive flats, and in others narrowed by ranges of hills, which, in the distance, rise to mountains of three or four thousand feet high. The whole country is still one vast wood, except here and there, a patch of a few hundreds of acres, where the forest has yielded to the axe. In the evening, we reached Dalwood, the dwelling of a pious and hospitable settler, by whom we were kindly welcomed.

23rd. We proceeded to Kirkton, the residence of a settler, who has a considerable vineyard. In the course of the day, we saw a Kangaroo, an animal that has become scarce in the settled parts of N. S. Wales; where flocks of sheep, and herds of cattle, now consume the thin grass of the continuous forests. *Kennedia ovata,* a blue, pea-flowered climber; a species of *Tecoma,* or Trumpet-flower, with small, pale blossoms and bright leaves; *Sicyos australis,* a little plant of the Cucumber tribe; *Nicotiana undulata,* a species of Tobacco, with flowers, that are fragrant in an evening; a species of Hemp, possibly *Cannabis indica,* and several other striking plants, were growing on the banks of the Hunter.

24th. Continuing our walk, we passed the dwellings of several considerable settlers, and crossed Patricks Plains, an extensive flat, partially cleared, with some small scattered houses upon it. At the further end of the plain, the Hunter is fordable, close to a little rising town, called Darlington, where we were kindly received by a family of the name of Glennie. From Darlington, we proceeded over low, gravelly hills, thinly covered with grass, to Dulwich, where, as well as on other parts of our journey, we were received with hospitality.

25th. We passed through a beautiful, park-like property, called Ravensworth, belonging to a gentleman in Sydney. Oranges were ripe in the garden, but the crop was thin, from continued drought. The rains nearer the coast, have scarcely reached this part of the country. Between this place and Muscle Brook, our route lay over sandy, gravelly, poor, clay hills, thinly clothed with grass and Iron-bark trees, and with some other species of *Eucalyptus,* and the Forest-oak. The town reserve, of Muscle Brook, is marked by a small, weatherboard inn. Near this place, we came again upon the rich, alluvial soil of the Hunter, and a few miles further, reached Arthurs Vale, a large farming establishment, belonging to Henry Dumaresq, by whom we had been recommended to the kind notice of his agent. This morning, the country was white with hoar frost, but a swallow flew into the house at Dulwich, and took a fly off the ceiling.

25th. We had some religious service with the family of the agent, and the prisoner-servants of the establishment, in which their attention was directed to the teaching of the Holy Spirit, by which alone, the truth of the Gospel can be practically understood. The prisoner-servants were numerous, and under excellent management. The greater proportion of them are lodged in ten, neat cottages, with gardens attached. The wives of several of those, of good conduct, have been permitted to join their husbands. The cottages of the married people, present a neater appearance, than those in which the different classes of single men reside. Classifying the single men, and placing the married men with their wives and families, and at the same time, maintaining a good superintendence over the whole, has a decidedly beneficial effect upon them ; and were they brought to entire abstinence from intoxicating drinks, much might reasonably be expected in regard to moral reformation.

27th. We proceeded to St. Aubins, the residence of William Dumaresq, from whom we received a most kind welcome. This establishment is conducted on a similar plan to that at Arthurs Vale, and with similarly beneficial results. In this family we met a pious person, much interested in the state of the female Convicts, and who, since her return to England, has published an intelligent, little volume respecting them, entitled "The Prisoners of Australia." In the course of our journey, we crossed the Hunter, at a shallow ford, and passed over a series of low hills, covered with thin, grassy herbage, and open forest, of small trees. Among the trees were species of *Eucalyptus,* known in the Colony as Box, and Bastard Box. *Lotus australis,* with pink or white, vetch-like blossoms, was scattered, in pretty tufts, among the thin herbage. The quantity of rain that falls in this part of the country, is often very small, in proportion to the evaporation. The grain crops are consequently, too uncertain to be calculated upon. Few settlers aim at growing more wheat than may support their own establishments. Sheep form the great object of the attention of the settler of the Upper Hunter; and far beyond this district, they are extensively fed, on the open tract, called Liverpool Plains. The flocks consist of about 400 each: several of these flocks are often folded at one place, the folds being slightly separated by a few rails. The sheep are counted into the folds, and committed to the charge of a night-watchman, to be protected from thieves and wild dogs: in the morning, they are re-counted to the respective shepherds, who travel with them, several miles, in the course of the day over the thin pasturage.

28th. The night was very cold. In the morning, the adjacent mountains were covered with snow, a phenomenon that had not occurred in this part of the country, for a long period. Snow also fell in Sydney at this time, which it is said not to have done previously, for more than thirty years. After having a religious interview with the family and establishment, at this place, we walked in the direction of Mount Wingen, or the Burning Hill, a pseudo-volcano, distant about fourteen miles, It would have been interesting to have visited this and some other objects of curiosity, had our time admitted, but as our object was to visit the people, we were not disposed to go out of our way, even to see the wonders of creation, unless when delayed at a place longer than was necessary for the primary object. But when the wonders and beauties of creation, fell in our way, we counted it a privilege, to be able to admire them, and to remember that " our Father made them all."

29th. Not apprehending it to be our duty to proceed further in this direction, we returned by way of Henry Dumaresq's house, at St. Helliers, to Arthurs Vale, and from thence, on the 30th, we crossed through the forest, to Ravensworth, using the compass and a map to direct our course. When the weather was clear, we more frequently resorted to the sun and a watch, than to the compass for this purpose. The country about St. Aubins, is on porphyritic rock; about Arthurs Vale it is on Sandstone.

7th mo. 1st. On leaving Ravensworth, we were assisted with horses, in fording the Hunter. We continued our journey on foot, passing the habitations of some settlers, to Cock-fighters-bridge, on the Wollombi Rivulet; where we were hospitably entertained, at the house of a person belonging the Survey Department, under whose charge, a party of prisoners were employed in the erection of a bridge.

2nd. The Bridge-party here, were lodged in huts of split timber. The numerous fissures in the walls of which, admitted much air; but fires were allowed, to keep out the frost. The men had only one blanket each, in which they slept, on large sheets of bark, put up like berths in a ship. No religious instruction was provided for these men, nor any suitable occupation, for the first day of the week. Bibles were distributed among them about three years ago, but none are now to be found. Men in such situations often take to card-playing, or other demoralizing occupation, to fill up vacant time. In some places in these Colonies, they have been known to convert the leaves of their Bibles into cards, and to mark the figures upon them with blood and soot! After a religious interview with these people, we returned to Darlington, and again met a kind reception from the Glennies.

3rd. At eleven o'clock, we walked about two miles, to the school-house, which we found a miserable slab-building, in a ruinous condition, with seats fixed into the ground, much exposed to the weather, and without doors or windows. By half-past twelve, about twenty-five persons had assembled, among whom were some of the more respectable settlers of the neighbourhood; to whom we were strengthened to point out the "way of life." We learned that the Presbyterian Minister, from Maitland, was in this neighbourhood to-day, and that he had only the family in whose house he preached, as a congregation. The indisposition of people to think of eternal things, which is increased by the approximation of the races, at Maitland, and the want of a convenient place to assemble in, were probably the chief causes of the smallness of our congregations.

We arrived at Maitland, on the 5th. On re-visiting a settler on the road, he told us, that he had long leaned a little toward the Society of Friends, although his acquaintance with them had been small, but that he had not supposed their principles to be so decidedly scriptural, as he now had found they were, on reading some of the tracts that we had given him.

6th. Maitland was in a state of great excitement yesterday, from the races, and to-day, from a large sale of live stock, belonging to the Australian Agricultural Company. From rain, and the treading of the cattle on the rich soil of the road, through the eastern part of the town, it had become so cut up, as to make a journey to the post-office, distant from our inn, one mile and a half, a difficult task. I succeeded in effecting it, and returning, in two hours.

8th. On expostulating with a store-keeper, against his practice of selling spirits, the evil of which he acknowledged, as well as, that temporal and eternal injury might accrue to his family, through this means; he pleaded the necessity of doing it for their maintenance. Thus, people too often delude themselves, and as it were, sell themselves to the devil, and those with whom God has intrusted them, under the pretext of obtaining a supply for their temporal necessities, even in the midst of other means. Such practically deny their professed belief in the promise of Christ, that the things needful for the body, shall be added to those who seek first the kingdom of heaven and its righteousness. They shrink from following his example, in denying themselves of the glories of this world, when offered on condition of falling down to Satan, and worshipping him.

CHAPTER XXXV.

7th mo. 9th. AFTER attending to some subjects of importance, we took a walk into one of the luxuriant woods,
on the side of the Hunter, such as are termed Cedar
Brushes, on account of the colonial White Cedar, *Melia
Azedarach*, being one of the trees that compose them.
Eugenia myrtifolia and *Ficus Muntia*, are among the variety
of trees in these brushes. The former resembles a large,
broad-leaved Myrtle, and attains to twenty feet in height; its
fruit, which is now ripe, is about the size of a cherry, but
oblong and purple, with a mixture of sweet and acid. *Ficus
Muntia* is a spreading Fig, growing as large as an Apple-
tree. Where its branches touch the ground, they root, and
send up erect shoots, forming a succession of trees. The
insipid fruit, which is about the size of a Gooseberry,
is sometimes produced from the bare trunk and boughs,
as well as from the leafy branches, giving the tree a very
unusual appearance. These Cedar Brushes are also thick
with climbers, such as *Cissus antarctica*, the Kangaroo Vine,
Eupomatia laurinæ, a briary bush, allied to the Custard-
apple, but with an inferior fruit, and several *Apocineæ*.

10th. We held a meeting with about fifty persons, in

a school-house, at Green Hills, or Morpeth, in which the Gospel was preached, with much warning. We afterwards dined with the benevolent individual, who let us have the use of the school-house, which he built for the benefit of the neighbourhood. He belongs to a class that is pretty numerous in these Colonies, who, having been brought up to a military life, have beaten their swords into plough-shares, and have proved, that the pecuniary profits of the arts of peace, as well as their comforts, are much greater than those of war. The eldest son of this person, when between two and three years old, wandered into the bush, and was lost; he would probably have perished, but for a faithful spaniel, that followed him, and at midnight, came and scratched at the door of one of the servants' huts, and when it was opened, ran toward the place where the child was. A man followed the dog, which led him to a considerable distance, through a thick brush, by the side of the river, where he found the little boy, seated on the ground, almost stiff from cold, but amused with watching the sport-ing of some porpoises and sharks. The dog afterwards lost its life, from the bite of a snake, which proved fatal in fifteen minutes, much to the sorrow of its little master, who pointed out the corner of the room where it died, with evident emotion, though several years had now elapsed since the event.

11th. We proceeded by the steamer Ceres, to the mouth of the Williams River, and walked from thence to Ray-monds Terrace. Here we had a meeting, in the evening, with the assigned-servants of a considerable establishment, in an overseer's cottage, situated among some trees, in con-tact with the forest. The large Bats, called Flying Foxes, and the black, Flying Opossums, made considerable noise among the over-hanging trees, but this did not seem to divert the attention of our congregation.

12th. There is a manufactory of superior, brown earthen-ware, at Raymonds Terrace; it is one of the most successful, of the few attempts that have been made to manufacture pots, in the Australian Colonies.—From a hill in this neigh-bourhood, there is a fine view of the surrounding country, which, like most other parts of N. S. Wales, is one vast wood, interrupted by a few open swamps. Near this place, *Sarcostemma australe*, a remarkable, leafless shrub, with green, succulent, climbing stems, as thick as a quill, and bearing clusters of white flowers, resembling those of a *Hoya*, was growing on some rough, conglomerate rocks. In the more fertile spots, by the sides of brooks, there was a species of Yam, the root of which is eaten by the Aborigines, as well as *Eugenia trinervis*, and another shrub of the Myrtle tribe, and *Logania floribunda*, a Privet-like bush, with small, white, fragrant blossoms. The country toward Port Stephens, whither we next proceeded, was decorated with *Acacia longifolia*, and some others of that genus, with lively, yellow flowers, and with *Bursaria spinosa*, which is fragrant and white, *Lambertia formosa*, a stiff bush, with beautiful, deep crimson flowers, and *Dillwynia parvifolia* with pretty, orange blossoms.

We were accompanied a few miles on our way, in this direction, by a prisoner, who had been the subject of religious impressions in early life, but had yielded to temptations, which led to the forfeiture of his liberty. The trials to which he had been subjected, by association with wicked men, had become, under the divine blessing, the means of stirring him up to watchfulness and prayer; and here, he met with kindness, from those under whom he was placed, whose hearts became opened toward him, as his own became again turned to the Lord. A boat, belonging to the Australian Agricultural Company, conveyed us from Sawyers Point, on the south-west of the estuary of Port Stephens, to Tarlee House, the residence of Henry Dumaresq, the Company's First Commissioner, by whose family we were received with much Christian kindness.

13th. Much rain has fallen lately. Our journey through the forest, yesterday, was a very wet one, and to-day we were almost confined to the house by rain.

14th. We visited the little village of Carrington, which is situated on the north shore of Port Stephens, and is composed of a few weather-board cottages, occupied by officers and servants of the Agricultural Company, with whom we had a meeting, in the evening, in a carpenter's shop, which was used also as a place of worship, by the Episcopal Minister. There were a few Aborigines in the village, where they are kindly treated. Their number is very small in this neighbourhood. Port Stephens is studded with a few, little islands, which, with the contiguous Porphyritic hills, give it a pretty appearance; but the country is not of the most fertile description. The territory of the Australian Agricultural Company consists of detached tracts, amounting together to 1,000,000 acres. The parts where their sheep and cattle are chiefly kept, are on Liverpool Plains and the Peel River, distant 150 miles from Port Stephens.

15th. We proceeded to Booral, up the Karua River, which is wide and navigable to within a short distance of this place, and flows through a sandstone country. Where the water is salt, it is margined with Mangroves, which give place, where it is fresh, to various species of *Eucalyptus*, *Ficus*, *Casuarina*, and a number of climbers. We were kindly received at Booral, by the Second Commissioner and his brother, and had a religious interview with the people of the settlement, in a neat little chapel.

16th. Passing a small settlement, called Alderley, we continued our journey to Stroud, where we were hospitably entertained by an intelligent, medical man, having the superintendence of the stock of the Company, which consists of about 60,000 sheep, 3,000 horned cattle, and 500 horses. At the sale of some of their stock, last week, sheep averaged 28s. each, cows with calves £8, and horses £20; which are high prices for this Colony. Their last year's dividend was three and a half per cent. and they have now a prospect of a progressive increase. The Speculations of Companies, in land, in the Australian Colonies, have not answered the expectations of the parties who have embarked in them; nor is it very likely that they should, as the salaries of officers alone, amount to more than the profits of most private settlers. The Company have about 300 acres in cultivation here, and 200 at Booral. The population of Stroud is considerably greater than that of the other stations.—This evening, a large party of Blacks were singing and dancing around some fires, near the village. Their number is considerable on the territory of the Company; and if its object had been as much to do justice to the people, whose lands they have occupied, as it has been to enrich themselves, they would, doubtless, have made more effort than they have done for their civilization.

17th. We had a meeting in the evening, with the people of the settlement, in a chapel built by Sir Edward Parry, the former First Commissioner of the Company. The service of the Episcopal Church is read by a pious overseer, except once a month, when the clergyman from Carrington visits the place.

18th. A young German, in the employment of the Company, and a Native, accompanied us part of the way to Dingadee, at the confluence of the Carowery Creek and the Wilson River, to help us over some swollen rivulets, by means of horses. These being cleared, we passed over some high land, on a narrow ridge, and over several lower hills. The forest was open, but in places, rather thick. In the gullies, there were large Myrtle-like Eugenias, of handsome form, with Cedars, and other trees, not occurring on the face of the open, forest hills, which were of poorish soil, and thinly covered with Kangaroo-grass, besprinkled with various plants, among which *Swainsonia galegifolia*, forming a low, suffruticose bush, with white or pink pea-flowers, was strikingly pretty. At Dingadee, which forms a peninsula of rich, alluvial soil, nearly surrounded by the Williams River, and which has been partially cleared of thick brush, we met a kind reception from a settler, with whose establishment we had an interesting religious interview, and who, in his solitude, seemed glad to converse on subjects of eternal importance. The distance between Stroud and Dingadee is about seventeen miles. When these places were first occupied, the parties went to them from different points, and our friend at Dingadee said, that when he first saw a white man come from the hills behind him, his surprise was excessive, as he had no idea that his countrymen had penetrated the woods, in that direction.

c c

19th. We proceeded down the Wilson River, to Dungog, where the site of a town is marked by a small, weatherboard Court-house. The brush by the side of the river is very rich, and ornamented by numerous, fan-leaved palms, *Corypha australis*, some of which are about sixty feet high. On leaving the river, we passed over a hilly country, of poorish soil, clothed with open forest and thin grass, to Wallaroba, where we were very cordially received, by a settler and his wife, whose connexions, we were well acquainted with in England, and who emigrated to this country in a time of great depression in agriculture. In this land, they have exerted themselves, with a spirit of independence, that led them to decline the help of money on loan, and by persevering industry, they are now possessed of a comfortable home, and a location of land, on which they have a fair stock of cattle. They have also maintained a kindly feeling toward the Aborigines, who live about them in quietness and confidence, but who have been reduced, in this neighbourhood, by various causes, among which has been the Small Pox, from about 200, to 60. These kind-hearted settlers say, they are convinced, that the misunderstandings between the Blacks and Whites, always originate with the latter; many of whom would destroy the Blacks if they happened to take a few cobs of Indian-corn, from the fields, enclosed from their own country; they also strongly deprecate the indiscriminate vengeance, often returned upon this hapless people, when any of their number have committed outrages, by the Government sending armed police, or soldiers upon them, often before the merits of the case can be properly ascertained. One of the Blacks brought our host a present, of a small species of kangaroo, called in this part of the Colony, a Paddy-melon: it is about the size of a hare, which it is said to resemble in flavour, when roasted.

20th. After a wet walk of ten miles, over hills and flats, of open grassy forest, we reached a little settlement, called Paterson, consisting of a few houses, on a river of the same name, and were kindly entertained by a settler whom I had met in London, and at whose house, we had a meeting with such persons as could be assembled to receive our gospel message. Our friend here had brought with him a good library. This is a point which a few other settlers have also attended to ; but emigrants are not generally a reading people, their rural pursuits occupying most of their time and energy.

21st. Much rain having fallen, many parts of the road to Maitland were inundated, and strong currents were flowing through the hollows. Some of these, we crossed, upon logs, such as, from the woody nature of the country, frequently happen to have fallen across the brooks and rivers. In other places, the post and rail fences, which commonly divide the located portions of the land, enabled us to cross the water ; and in others, we had to wade, after going a little out of the way, in search of fordable places. Some parts of the country bordering on the Paterson, were fine, and interspersed with houses and cultivated lands ; but we found the children of the lower classes here, as we have also found them in some other parts of this Colony, growing up in much ignorance. There was no school among them, and the only apology for public, religious instruction, was a sermon from the Episcopal Clergyman of Maitland, once a month, in a lock-up-house, on the site of the intended town of Paterson. Some of the settlers however, collect their servants on First-days, for devotional reading, but this is far from being a general practice.

On the 22nd, we were detained at Maitland, by rain ; on the 23rd, we proceeded by the Sophia Jane steamer, to Newcastle, where the Police Magistrate, who is a military officer, granted us permission to hold a meeting for public worship in the Police Office, and the Episcopal Chaplain kindly lent us some seats for the place.

24th. In the forenoon, we had a religious interview with about 120 prisoners, in the jail ; in the evening we had a crowded meeting with the inhabitants of Newcastle, in the Police Office. On this occasion, great freedom was felt, in preaching the Gospel, and in drawing a clear line, between the service of God, and the service of the devil, and in testifying to the grace of God that brings salvation, and to the manifestation of the Holy Spirit, sent into the world, of the Father, in the name of his beloved Son, to convince the world of sin, bring them to repentance, and lead them through faith in Christ, to reconciliation with God. There was a comforting sense of the divine presence with us, enabling us to bear witness to that justification by faith, through which we have peace with God, through our Lord Jesus Christ, and receive the spirit of adoption, whereby we cry, Abba, Father, knowing the divine Spirit to bear witness with our spirits, that we are the children of God.

25th. We breakfasted with a pious couple of Anglo-Australians, and inspected the Jail, which is a considerable building, but very badly arranged, for the complete separation of the male and female prisoners.—Between the Jail and the town, there is a sandy hill, that was once covered with brushwood. This was cut down, when Newcastle was a penal settlement, to prevent the concealment of prisoners; and ever since, the drifting sand has bid defiance to all opposition, burying walls, and all other impediments, raised to obstruct its course. In the afternoon, we had an interview with an ironed-gang, stationed here, who are chiefly employed in the formation of a break-water, at the mouth of this harbour; several soldiers were also present; the whole of the company were very attentive, while we discharged our debt of Christian love toward them.

26th. We visited a detachment of fourteen men, belonging to a bridge and road-party, at the Iron-bark Creek, about eight miles from Newcastle, toward Maitland, a part of whom we gathered up, by walking two miles back into the bush. They were at length collected in an overseer's hut; and we were strengthened to extend to them, an invitation, to turn to the Lord and live, calling their attention to the proofs of his unwillingness that they should perish in their sins, exhibited in his having freely delivered up his beloved Son for us all, and in the pleadings of his Spirit, by which he still convinces the rebellious of their transgressions, and warns them to repent and turn, that they may be saved.

The road to this place was sandy and heavy, but the fineness of the day made the walk pleasant. The bush, through which it lay, was gay with *Kennedia monophylla* and *rubicunda, Acacia longifolia* and *suaveolens,* and other shrubs, and the air was perfumed with their fragrance.

27th and 28th. We had religious interviews with the patients in the Upper and Lower Hospitals, and with the pitmen, of the Coal-works, of the Australian Agricultural Company, the last of whom are about ninety in number. We also took part in the organization of a Temperance Society, and a Branch Bible Auxiliary. Among the pitmen, there seemed an ear open to religious counsel. Several of them were formerly in connexion with a religious society, but were transported for offences, connected with "striking for wages."—A considerable quantity of good coal is raised here, and shipped to Sydney, Hobart Town, the Cape of Good Hope, &c.

29th. At the request of the Military Officer, in charge, we had an interview with the soldiers stationed here, for the purpose of giving them some hints on the importance of temperance.—I received a letter from India, from the young man to whose care we committed some of the writings of Friends; and respecting which he says: "The books which you entrusted to me, afforded me much pleasant, and I hope also profitable reading, during the voyage to Madras; and I will tell you frankly, that in many, perhaps in most things, I find myself satisfied that the truth is with you. I refer, in thus saying, chiefly to your application of the precepts of the Gospel to the every-day practice of life; in which, I have long felt, that Christians fail, and are content to fall very far short of what they ought to attain to."

30th. We embarked on board the William the Fourth steamer, which put in at Newcastle this morning, on the way to Port Macquarie, and early in the forenoon, we were in Nelsons Bay, Port Stephens, where the steamer had cargo to deliver to a whaling brig. Keeping close in with the land, the view of the coast was fine. The islets and headlands, about Port Stephens, present a remarkable, and ruggedly furrowed appearance, and have numerous vertical fissures. They are also much varied in colour, with red, yellow, and dirty white. The tide was running with great force, round some of the points within the port.

31st. We anchored under a head-land, on the south side of Port Macquarie, until the tide allowed the steamer to cross the bar; when we proceeded to the jetty, which is an overhanging, conglomerate rock, where we landed. After depositing our luggage at a small inn, we proceeded to Lake Cottage, seven miles distant, where we received a hearty welcome from Archibald Clunis Innis, and his wife, son-in-law and daughter of our kind friends, Alexander and Elizabeth M'Leay, of Sydney. On the way, we had a religious interview with a small road-party, in which there is a person, who was brought up a clergyman of the Episcopal Church. They were without a Bible, or any religious instruction.

8th mo. 1st. A. C. Innis drove us to Port Macquarie, and introduced us to the Episcopal Clergyman, and the Police-magistrate, both of whom received us kindly, and signified their willingness to assist us, in obtaining religious interviews with the prisoners and free population. Port Macquarie was a penal settlement, up to a late period, but is now thrown open to free settlers: it still is a depot for that description of educated prisoners, denominated "Specials," and for invalids, decrepit, and insane persons, and idiots, who are lodged in miserable, wooden barracks, about to be superseded by new ones of brick.

The town is prettily situated, on the side of a bay, with a sandy beach; upon which, the rocks are of Quartz, and mottled, green Serpentine. The soil is rich, and of a remarkably red colour. On the south of the town, the forest is very thick. The buildings are few, and chiefly of weather-board. The principal ones are, the Commandant's Quarters, Military and Prisoners Barracks, Hospital, a few stores and a windmill.

2nd. We visited the female prisoners, the ironed-gang, and the invalids. The Ironed-gang assembled in "the Punishment-yard;" in which, three men were shortly after, to be flogged. They were all very quiet, while we set forth to them, the way of salvation, and pleaded with them on the folly of sin.

3rd. We visited the specials, operative prisoners, patients in the Hospital, a free overseer who had brought on dropsy by drinking strong liquors, a prisoner who had attempted to commit suicide, under the mortification produced by the restraints imposed upon him, and some of the specials, individually. Neither their association here, nor that of the other prisoners, seems likely to produce reformation.

5th. We had a meeting with the free inhabitants, in a room in the Colonial Hospital. It was not numerously attended, neither was it a season of much brightness. There is reason to fear, that in this place, as well as in many others, the people are much more concerned about their temporal things, than about those that are eternal; forgetting that temporal things will soon pass away, and that then, those who are not rich toward God, will be poor indeed.

6th. We rode to the Plains, on the Wilson River, and on the way visited a road-party, at Blackmans Point, where there is a ferry across the Hastings River, at its confluence with the Wilson. By an order from the Commandant, the road-party met us at the ferry-house, where a few other persons also assembled with them, and we had a satisfactory season of gospel labour. These people have no appointed religious instruction, but had borrowed a Bible, from which, on First-days, one of their number, who had been a clergyman of the Episcopal Church, read to them. At Balingara, where there is a ferry across the Wilson, we met another road-party, in a large barn, used as a barrack for them. The quietude of our meeting was much interrupted, by the passing of a herd of cattle, and by the swearing of their drivers, but we were favoured with a sense of the divine presence, both while silent, and in preaching the Gospel. This company, consisted of from twenty to thirty men, some of them persons of education; they had not a Bible, nor were they assembled, even on First-days, for religious instruction.

The brushes on the border of the Wilson, are very

magnificent. The trees, some of which are of gigantic size,
are overrun with climbing, evergreen shrubs, twisted about
them in fanciful coils, or wreathed around them, like huge
serpents, or hanging from them like ropes; their leafy tops
being enlivened by gay and fragrant blossoms, and often
hanging pendent to the ground, which is covered thickly
with beautiful shrubs, ferns, and flowering plants, nourished by the moisture of the rich alluvial soil, and kept
from the parching influence of the sun, by the exuberant
foliage. Mosses, epiphytes of the Orchis tribe, and splendid
Ferns, as well as various species of Fig-tree, support themselves on the trunks and branches of the larger timber, and
add greatly to the richness of this kind of forest scenery;
among which, gay Parrots, Cockatoos, and other birds,
unlike those of our native land, sport and chatter in harmony with the rest of the surrounding objects, which are
strongly calculated to remind an Englishman, that he is far
from home, even though he may have made this, his adopted
country. But to one who, feeling reconciled to God through
the death of his Son, can, with a sense of the divine presence
in his mind, look upon these objects, and with filial love to
his and their Creator, say, "My Father made them all;"
even though such a one may be reminded by them, that he
is far from his nearest connexions in life, they have an
interest which cannot be understood by those who are living
at enmity with God. In some sense of this interest, we are
often favoured to feel the length of our journeys beguiled,
and our minds cheered. And with thankfulness, I would
add, that often, when withdrawn from these enlivening
scenes, and amidst various conflicts and exercises, both on
account of ourselves and others, we are favoured with such
a measure of peace, and such a· sense of the love of God
extended to us, poor, unworthy, and of ourselves, helpless
creatures as we are, as reconciles us to our allotment, and
restrains us from wishing to be anywhere but where we are,
at the time, willing to leave the morrow to the morrow,
knowing that sufficient for the day is the evil thereof, without adding to it, by useless anticipation.

7th. We proceeded along a line of little alluvial plains,

intersected by the windings of the Wilson River, still margined by rich brushes, among which numerous Cockatoos
were screaming, Parrots chattering, and the singular and
loud-voiced, snake-killing bird, called the Laughing-jackass,
was at intervals, setting up its rolling note, until we reached
the house of a settler, at which we had a meeting appointed,
that was attended by several young persons of the neighbourhood, and a considerable number of assigned prisoners. It
was held in the verandah, and was satisfactory, notwithstanding the wind was strong and cool. The auditory
listened attentively to the doctrines of truth, which commend themselves to the conscience, according to the measure
of light, and the experience of those that hear; who, at
least, can trace in themselves, the work of the Spirit of God,
as a witness against sin.

In returning, we called on a settler of our acquaintance,
on Rollins Plains, which is one of a series of rich alluvial
flats, adjoining the river, and backed by wooded, grassy hills.
Considerable alarm was existing at this time, in consequence
of some of the native Blacks having speared some cattle,
and committed other outrages. Two little boys, who were
staying at the house of our acquaintance, durst not venture
off the road, into the adjacent brush, lest they should be
killed by their countrymen, who, on account of some pique,
had destroyed all the rest of their tribe. The impression
among the settlers is, that the Blacks spear the cattle to
eat; and as the locating of the land by Europeans, has
greatly diminished the Kangaroo, and other food of the
Natives, this seems highly probable. Maize is the principal
crop now grown on these plains, which are liable to be
flooded, and were naturally clear of timber or scrub. A
few years since, the Government tried the growth of sugar
upon them. The canes came to good perfection, but before
arrangements were made for harvesting them, they were
injured by frost, and the growth of sugar was abandoned.
The land here has been sold by the Government, to the
persons who have located it, at from 7s. to 67s. per acre.

8th. Hoar frost was strong in the night, and the open
grounds were very white in the morning. While the

house of the settler with whom we lodged, was got ready, the room used as a dormitory at night being the sitting-room during the day, as is often the case in a newly-settled country, I walked into a copse, for shelter from the cold, and met with a beautiful little palm, resembling a South American *Geonoma*, in form. It was from six to ten feet high, and had pinnate leaves, three feet long, and bore its minute flowers, in long, simple spikes.

The vegetation here is very striking. On our return to Port Macquarie, we noticed a shrubby, white-flowered *Helichrysum*, two species of *Cassia, Tasmania insipida, Ficus macrophylla, ferruginea,* and another species, *Hibiscus splendens,* with blossoms six to nine inches across, *Hibiscus heterophyllus,* and a shrub, with white flowers, allied to *Sida,* but of a distinct genus, having five red glands at the base of the common filament, also a singular, climbing plant, belonging the *Aroideæ,* adhering to the trees along with *Dischidia numularia, Polypodium quercifolium* and *attenuatum, Dendrobium tetragonum, linguiforme, æmulum* and *calamifolium.* In some places the country is undulating and grassy. It is adapted for horned cattle, and suffers less from drought, than many other parts of N. S. Wales.

9th. I took a walk into the wood, on Tacking Point, on the coast, south of Port Macquarie. The road from Lake Cottage lay through the Cathi Marsh, part of which was crossed by a long and imperfect bridge of logs. *Blandfordia grandiflora* decorated some of the open forest, in which several of the Gum-trees were supporting a variety of parasitical Figs. A grass-tree swamp, intervened between the bridge and the shore. On the borders of the swamp, where the ground was sandy, with a small mixture of vegetable matter, several species of *Boronia, Epacris,* and *Euphrasia,* were in flower, along with *Sowerbea juncea,* a handsome *Comesperma,* a species of *Sprengellia,* &c. On the drier sand-hills, there were *Banksia serrata* and *spinulosa, Platylobium formosum, Ræperia pinifolia,* a species of *Pultenæa,* which formed dense patches, and *Kennedia ovata* and *rubicunda,* &c. Close upon the coast, *Pandanus pedunculatus,* was of inferior growth to that at Moreton Bay.

In a marsh, at Tacking Point, chiefly occupied by *Melaleuca paludosa*, and bordered by a large, silver-flowered, willow-leaved *Helichrysum*, *Todæa africana?* had become arborescent, and formed a beautiful tree-fern, with fronds six feet long, on a trunk three feet high. It was growing with an *Alsophila*, the trunk of which was much slenderer than that of the *A. australis* of V. D. Land, and with a large *Crinum* and *Calladium glycyrrhizon*. In the forest, there were many noble trees, similar to those in the neighbouring woods, but here, they were intermingled with abundance of *Seaforthia elegans*, a noble, feather-leaved Palm, forty feet in height. The small Palm already noticed, was also here, and a tall, cyperaceous? plant, growing into the trees, and again bending toward the ground, with a stem as thick as a Ratan. One of the parasitical Figs had sent a root down from a lofty bough, remote from the trunk, and the root, which must have swung like a rope, had a diagonal direction, and was adhering at its lower extremity to the foster tree! Some *Casuarinæ* were encircled by masses of *Acrosticum alcicorne*. This fern retains much moisture in its dead, sterile fronds, which form large scales, rising one over another, it generally grows on the upper portion of the trunks of the *Casuarinæ*, and in stormy weather, they are sometimes thrown down by the weight of water and vegetable matter, thus accumulated about them. Many thus circumstanced, were lying in the forest, having a profusion also of *Davallia pyxidata*, growing out of the masses of *Acrosticum alcicorne*. Other trees, ferns, and flowering plants, were here in great variety.

Whilst admiring the rich profusion of the vegetable productions, and conversing with some wood-cutters, I insensibly got turned round, and toward evening, on referring to my compass, found myself making rapid progress, in a direction opposite to the one I ought to have pursued. What gave to this place the name of Tacking Point, I know not, but its name harmonized with my present circumstances; and to use a sea phrase, I "tacked," without delay, being desirous to escape from the dense forest, before sunset.

I had become hungry, and looked longingly to the tops

of the majestic palms, without the hope of reaching one of them; but at length, I came at one, which, from some accident, had turned its head downward, so that it seemed to be put exactly into my path. I cut it off, stripped away the base of the leaves, to the tender heart, and went along, enjoying my grateful meal, thankful to Him who had brought me and the crooked palm, as by accident, into contact. The supply was so ample, that when I reached my friends, at the Lake Cottage, after a toilsome journey through the marsh, in the dark, I had a piece, as thick as my wrist, and a foot and a half long, under my arm, reserved for supper, in case I should have found it impracticable to reach my quarters, and have been under the necessity of remaining among the bushes of the sand hills, on the coast, during the night.

Among the sedgy plants, in the margin of Lake Innis, there is a large species of *Eriocaulon*. Several other species of this genus, occur in N. S. Wales, and one in the west of Scotland, but its maximum is in America. Plants are subject to a remarkable, geographical distribution, which it is very interesting to trace out. The remarkable section of the genus *Acrosticum*, which includes *A. grande* and *A. alcicorne*, has at least one species in India, and another in Western Africa. *A. grande*, which is represented in the accompanying cut, grows to a large size, on trees bordering on Lake Innis. One measured, had the upper, or barren fronds, three feet across, and as much in height. There were two mature, barren fronds, that had strong, black nerves, and the same number of fertile ones. From the opposite extremities of the appendages of the latter, the measurement was seven feet. Some of these appendages were of ten, ribbon-like divisions, many of which were bifid. The central portion might be compared to a jockey's saddle, attached by the pummel. From this point, to the extreme margin, was a foot and a half, and this portion was two feet across. The fructification formed a half-moon shaped patch, under the exterior portion, that extended one foot from the margin, toward the point of the attachment, and was a foot and a half across. A young, white, barren frond, almost circular, was placed in front of the two older ones, to which it was closely pressed. Behind these, there were several dead, spongy, old fronds, that retained much moisture, and were penetrated by numerous, spongy roots, such as were also spread behind them, on the bark of the tree that supported this remarkable fern, the colour of which was bluish green, covered with a whitish powder.

10th. We again visited Port Macquarie, where we were glad to find that an individual, in an influential station, had resolved to adopt temperance principles. The use of intoxicating drinks is a sore evil here, as well as in other parts of N. S. Wales. It is the bane of all classes of society. The number of educated prisoners, called Specials, at this depôt, is about 160. Of these, only 25 can be considered as orderly or thoughtful men. About as many more are of equivocal character. The residue are dissolute and drunken. The prisoners who are operative mechanics, are allowed to earn money, at least by connivance; but they have no private places, in which to keep anything, and if they even purchase clothes, to give themselves a more respectable appearance than that of prisoners generally, they are sure to have them stolen, by those with whom they are associated. To avoid this risk they therefore, almost universally, spend their earnings in rum and tobacco.

14th. After a solemn parting from our friends at Lake Cottage, with whom we have sympathized in their affliction, by the loss of a beloved sister, who devoted herself much to the good of others, we proceeded to Port Macquarie, and embarked, on board the William the Fourth, which left the wharf about noon, the day being beautifully fine. Shoals of fish in some places darkened the water, out of which many of them were continually springing. They were followed by numerous Gulls and Terns, notwithstanding the fish themselves, seemed quite too large for these birds to prey upon.

15th. We were off Newcastle early, but unable to enter the Hunter for some time, in consequence of a dense fog. At noon, we again put to sea, and entered Port Jackson late in the evening. Passing the new floating-light, on the shoal, called The Sow and Pigs, we came to anchor in Darling Harbour, after ten o'clock, and quietly retired to our berths for the night.

CHAPTER XXXVI.

WE remained in Sydney a month, during which, we were chiefly occupied, in caring for the few persons professing with us, circulating books and tracts, and preparing for a journey southward. The spring was now considerably advanced, and in our walks, in the country, intervening between Port Jackson and Botany Bay, many beautiful shrubs and plants were in flower, some of which were also remarkable for their fragrance. Many of these plants, which are amongst the most lively decorations of our English green-houses, present a strikingly gay appearance in their native locality, where they grow on a poor, sandy soil, thinly intermixed with vegetable matter, and very uncongenial to horticulture or agriculture.

9th mo. 13th. We went to Liverpool, in a four-wheeled car, on springs, drawn by three horses. The journey of nineteen miles, was accomplished in three hours. Having taken up our quarters at the Ship, a comfortable inn, we called upon several of the inhabitants, and made arrangements for a meeting with them, which was held in the Court House, in the evening; it was but thinly attended in consequence of the wetness of the weather. In the course of the day, we visited a patient in the Colonial Hospital, who had been confined to bed nearly three months. During the first seven weeks he was here, no one called upon him, and as he was very ill, one of the attendants inquired, if he would not wish to see some pious man, to which he replied in the affirmative. He was then asked, whom he would wish to see. He answered, he knew no one, but would be glad to see any good man. The attendant then mentioned a person, who he said was a good man, and very kind in visiting some of the patients in the wards. He was introduced accordingly, and proved to be a Roman Catholic priest. On his first visit, he expressed sympathy with the sick man, and advised him to exercise himself in prayer, as a means of obtaining spiritual comfort. On being told, that the young man had been educated among Friends, and entertained the views of that people, he inquired what their views were ; on being informed upon some leading points, he said, they appeared to differ little from Roman Catholics, except in regard to transubstantiation. On this subject, he brought a book, which he requested the young man to read. Subsequently the priest debated with him on water-baptism, and urged his reading a book on that subject. After a few days, he proposed his submitting to that rite, and intimated that it might be administered by the hands of their bishop, who was expected in Liverpool, from Sydney. He also assured his hoped-for proselyte, that if he received baptism from this prelate, however great a sinner he might have been, he would become as spotless as a new-born babe, and would go direct to heaven, without passing through purgatory, if he died the next moment. As an additional inducement, he proposed also, that the bishop should bring with him a relic of a saint, which he said, had been of service, in the restoration of some other person, from grievous sores, such as the patient was suffering from. The young man found these importunities very unpleasant, in his weak state, and became rather alarmed, at the idea of a visit from the bishop, with his " old bones ;" but was relieved by receiving a call from a pious Protestant, to whom he communicated these circumstances, as he did subsequently, to George W. Walker and myself. His Protestant friend proposed, that a letter should be written to the priest, acknowledging his kindness in calling, and stating, that as a Protestant acquaintance, living in the neighbourhood, would now visit the young man, he had no further occasion for the visits of the priest. This step was taken, and the books were returned, accompanied by the letter, which had the desired effect. This may be regarded as a specimen of some of the attempts, used in this land, to gain proselytes to the church of Rome; and by which, many are lulled into false rest. Superstition is propagated and nursed, with a degree of persevering industry, that would ornament a better cause; and many of its dupes appear to go on carelessly in sin, regardless of its consequences, or presuming on receiving absolution before they die. Carelessness prevails to a lamentable extent, both among professed Protestants and Roman Catholics, to a large majority of whom it might be said, "Ye are of your father, the devil, and the lusts of your father ye will do." Cursing, swearing, drunkenness, and other open profligacy, proclaim, that Satan, and not Jesus, is their Lord.

14th. After breakfasting with the Surgeon of the Colonial Hospital, and having a religious meeting with the patients, we walked to the Quarries, where the military officer in charge, met us, and we had a religious interview with an Ironed-gang, consisting of sixty men, employed in raising stone, which is conveyed up the Georges River, to Lansdowne Bridge. We next proceeded to the bridge, where there is another Ironed-gang, of fifty men, and had a religious opportunity with them, and a few prisoners, out of irons. A few of the military and their wives, were also present, on both occasions. Some of these recognized us, having been stationed on Norfolk Island, when we were there. It was pleasant to find that some of them had adopted the principles of the Temperance Society, and that both these gangs were visited weekly, by the Episcopal Chaplain of Liverpool, and by a Wesleyan local preacher. At both places, the men are lodged in caravans. The

D D

married soldiers have built themselves very small, slab-huts, covered with sheets of bark, and white-washed. Some of the ground we passed over to-day was sandy, and produced many of the beautiful shrubs, common to similar situations in this country. The Lansdowne Bridge, which is on the road from Liverpool to Sydney, is a handsome structure, of sandstone, with one elliptical arch; it is the first of the kind, that has been erected in this country. The road over it, is metalled with a bluish, argillaceous stone, having vegetable impressions.

15th. We visited a few prisoners in the Jail, a brick-building, containing two large rooms for prisoners of common order, one for debtors, a small one for females, and three good cells, all opening into one common yard, along with the dwellings of the turnkey and overseer, and the cooking-place, and other offices! The number of prisoners varies, from a very few to about fifty. We next went to the Male Orphan School, about three miles distant, which is under the charge of a pious, retired lieutenant, of the navy. This establishment contains about 160 boys, of from twenty months, to fourteen years of age. They are chiefly the children of prisoners; many of them illegitimate. They exhibit, in numerous instances, the effects of the drunkenness and profligacy of their parents; many of them are unhealthy for two or three years after coming to the institution. They receive a plain, English education, and are taught the rudiments of tailoring, shoe-making, gardening, and husbandry. The premises are on a reserve, of 10,000 acres, in a district that is badly supplied with water, the springs being salt. This circumstance, with the distance from the town, and other inconveniences, renders the removal of the institution to another site, desirable. The buildings are of a very temporary structure. It is inconvenient to have the children from the Factory brought hither so very young; but when they remain longer at that nursery of vice, they learn so much iniquity, that their early removal proves the less evil. In the evening, a few persons met us, at the Court House, at Liverpool, to whom we addressed some remarks on temperance. Most of them had previously signed the declaration.

16th. We took places in an open coach, for Campbell Town, distant thirteen miles. On the way, there is a considerable extent of cleared land: the country is undulating, but the soil does not appear rich, though in some places, it seems to overlay basalt. Campbell Town consists of an Episcopal worship-house, of brick, with a steeple, and a Papal one, of stone, without a tower, and scattered houses, on both sides of the road: some of them are of brick, but most of them of wood; a large proportion are public-houses. We called on a young man, from England, who was just recovering from an attack of pleurisy, and was laid on a mattress, covered with blankets, on the floor of a little room, behind his shop, where he had been for a fortnight. He made some feeling remarks on the privations to which persons so situated are subjected, and on the pain felt when, on reflection, they are sensible of having deprived themselves of the comforts of a home among their relations, and he expressed regret at having left his connexions in England. Almost all persons in this land, call Great Britain *Home*, and speak with desire respecting returning thither, casting "a longing, lingering look, behind," on that which they have left. While in Campbell Town, we took our meals with the family of the Police-magistrate, who was the first Commandant of Port Macquarie, when it was a Penal Settlement. He remained in office three years, during which, he prevailed on the military to commute their rations of spirits, by having it sold for them in Sydney, being aware of the difficulty of managing them, if they had access to strong liquors. The soldiers found no want of them, though living, much of the time, in bark huts, and at close service. This was before the existence of Temperance Societies. At that period, the Commandant of a Penal Settlement was not required to keep a record of punishments, but could flog any man at his own discretion. Happily such a toleration of tyranny no longer exists, but every man must be tried before he is punished, and his sentence must be recorded.

17th. We visited the Jail, which is under the Court House, and below the level of the ground, in front. It

has five, badly ventilated cells, and a room for the general
prisoners, 20½ feet long, by 12½ feet wide, and 8 feet high,
with two insufficient, ventilating tubes, and two grated windows, opening into a low, covered place, that thoroughly
obstructs the fresh air.   There is no airing-court.   The
place is damp, and its atmosphere excessively oppressive
and offensive, even now that there are only two prisoners
here.   Sixty persons are sometimes confined, and ninety
have been shut up in it!   The stench arising through the
floor of the Court House, is so bad, that the windows have
to be kept open, during the time of business, and sometimes, the court is obliged to adjourn to another place.
This is the worst prison we have seen in the Colony, notwithstanding many others are very bad, in proportion to
the number of prisoners occasionally confined in them.   As
the weather, in this country, is very warm in summer, the
thermometer occasionally rising to upwards of 100° in the
shade, the prisoners, not unfrequently, strip off all their
clothes, for relief from the oppressive heat, when crowded
in such places.

18th.   While conversing with a man, whom we casually
met, when walking through the bush, to give notice of a
meeting, a large limb dropped from a tree, apparently from
the increasing weight of the foliage, for there was no wind
at the time, and the limb appeared sound.   It fell so close
to us, as to impress us deeply, with a sense of the uncertainty of life, which might quickly be taken, even by such
an accident as this, in the interminable forests of Australia,
in which, many times, and occasionally in calm weather,
we have heard the thunder of timber falling from natural
causes.

We had a meeting, in the Court House, but it was thinly
attended, notwithstanding the notice was extensively given.
The windows could not be closed, on account of the noi-
some effluvium from the Jail beneath, though the wind
was boisterous at the time.   Drunkenness, profligacy, and
dishonesty, are notoriously prevalent in this district, in
which a large proportion of the lower class profess with
the Church of Rome; but they too generally, like many

others, make a profession of religion, to quiet their consciences, while living in open sin.

19th. We proceeded on foot to Appin, near which, we
became the guests of a respectable widow, with a large
family. The village of Appin, consists of two public-
houses, a few slab huts, and a wooden lock-up house.
The country between this place and Campbell Town, is
undulating, and the soil strong. It is more extensively
fenced, cleared, cultivated and settled, than any other part
of the Colony, we have visited. There are, however, few
respectable settlers: most of them are low Irish. We
felt but little liberty in distributing tracts among the be-
nighted population; and in a few cases in which we
offered them, they were received with a sort of fear,
the evident result of Popish restrictions. The people are
afraid to receive religious instruction, lest their priests
should find fault; and though the priests visit them, with
an attention that binds the people to them, many of them
seem to exercise much more care, to prevent their leaving
the Church of Rome, than to turn them from the service of
Satan.

20th. A son of our kind hostess, conducted us through
an intricate part of our route, to Illawarra. The road for
several miles lies over an elevated, sandstone country, covered with low forest, intermingled with a great variety of
beautiful shrubs, and interspersed with marshy flats. The
elevation above the level of the sea, is about 2,000 feet.
Among the shrubs of this district were four species of *Grevillea,* one of which had brilliant, scarlet blossoms, also a gay
Mirbellia, with bluish, purple flowers, and several species of
Dillwynia, Pultenæa and *Boronia.* On some of the rocky
ground, there was a profusion of the Gigantic Lily, *Doryan-
thes excelsa,* which bears a compound head, of dull-crimson,
lily-like blossoms, among large floral-leaves of the same
colour, upon a lofty stem, furnished with numerous, dagger-
shaped leaves, diminishing in size toward the top. The stem
rises from the centre of a large crest, of upright, sedgy leaves,
about four inches wide, and as many feet long. It was not in
blossom here. The vegetation is much more luxuriant on

the top of the coast-range of mountains, the precipitous fronts of which, and the low ground, between their base and the sea, are covered with forests of the greatest luxuriance, and richest variety. Cedar, Sassafras, Swamp-mahogany, Cabbage-palm, large Fig trees, and numerous climbing-shrubs, with Tree-ferns, form a striking contrast to the low forest, of the sandy tract just left behind. The rich prospect, bounded by the ocean beneath, and exhibiting some bold, mountain projections, and a spot of cultivated land on the coast, affords a treat to the eye, such as is seldom enjoyed among the vast forests of Australia. We descended by a rough track, called the Bulli Road, the sides of which were ornamented by a gay *Prostanthera, Pimelia hypericifolia, Pittosporum undulatum*, and another fragrant species of this genus, and a handsome, white *Clematis*. This road is difficult for horses, and impracticable for carts, except by the assistance of ropes, passed round conveniently situated trees, by means of which, in a few instances, they have been got down. After reaching the beach, our way, for eight miles, was along loose sand, to Wollongong, near which, our toils for the day, found an end, in the hospitable dwelling of Charles Throsby Smith, the chief proprietor of the place, which we reached when it was nearly dark, after a walk of twenty-seven miles.

21st. We went to Wollongong, which is situated on a small boat-harbour. The buildings, at present erected, are, a police-office, two stores, two public-houses, a Roman Catholic chapel, and a few dwelling-houses; a barn is also fitted up for an Episcopal place of worship. In the afternoon, we met a large road-party, under the charge of a military officer, at a place, a mile and a half from the town. They were assembled in a large, open shed, where they take their meals: the officer and his wife, with a number of military, who were under arms, and their wives were also present; the whole company was quiet and attentive, both while we addressed them, and while we remained with them in silence. The prisoners here, are those sentenced from Great Britain, to work on the roads, for certain periods, before being assigned. They were, at one time, ordered to work in chains, and for periods as long as seven years, but this excessive, and injurious severity, has been relaxed, and they are now exempted from chains, unless as a punishment for improper conduct; and if they behave well, they are assigned, at the expiration of two years. Hope being thus kept alive, while strict discipline is likewise maintained, their conduct is generally good; only three cases have occurred to be subjected to flagellation, within the last month. They are lodged and guarded, in the same manner as the ironed-gangs. Though this station is called a stockade, there is no defence around it; but no prisoner can wander off the premises, on account of the military guard. The whole place is remarkable for its cleanliness and order. The prisoners are employed in the formation of roads and bridges: they have already formed a road, from the top of the mountains, wide enough for one carriage; but it is yet only available for horses, as a creek on the way to Appin, remains impassable for carriages, without a bridge. This part of the Colony has much of the features of Cleveland, in Yorkshire. The mountains, however, are more precipitous, and as well as the low land between them and the sea, are covered with lofty, dense forest, except in a few places, in which, in most instances, human industry has cleared the fertile soil. This seems to consist of decomposed basalt, and dark, argillaceous rock, from the base of the mountains, mixed with washings from their sandstone tops, and much vegetable matter. The Blacks in this district are not numerous; a group, many of whom were afflicted with sores, were seated on the ground, when we returned into the town.

22nd. Being furnished with horses, by some of our friends, we accompanied a young physician, a few miles from the coast, off which there are five small islands, that give this district the name of The Five Islands, by which it is familiarly known among the lower class, in the Colony. Along the shore, there are several lagoons, some of which are fresh, being separated from the sea by narrow portions of land. The two largest, the Illawarra Lake, and Tom Thumbs Lagoon, are salt, the sea breaking into

them, in high tides. The former of these, is of considerable extent, and ornamented by a few little islands. The
surrounding scenery is very fine ; the contiguous land being
undulating, and clothed with grassy forest, and rich brushes,
in which many Cabbage Palms are interspersed, and the
lofty trees are overhung with climbers. The back ground
is formed by the woody steep, of the low mountain range,
which extends for many miles along the coast, at from five
to ten miles from the sea.

On a little spot of cleared land, near the margin of a
lake, is the habitation of a settler, in humble life : it is a
very rustic hut, covered with bark, and internally having
much of the sombre hue, common to the dwellings of the
lower classes of the Scotch and Irish, and which too often
prevails also, in those of the English, in this Colony. But
the mother of this family is of a character, rarely met
with in these wilds ; she is pious, and abounding in Christian goodwill to all around her. It was a treat to visit
her, and to receive her hearty blessing. She is an honour
to her country, Scotland, and an ornament to the community to which she belongs. Our medical friend had been
called in professionally, when she was ill, but he found that
he had come, rather to receive than to give advice. From
this place, we went to the hut of our friend, to dine. It was
of rough slabs, covered with bark, rustic, in the full sense of
the word, and scarcely protecting his valuable library from
the weather. Here he is superintending a flock of sheep,
the joint property of himself and one of his friends, who
is also temporarily dwelling in the same habitation. But
Illawarra not being a favourable country for sheep, though
a delightful climate, and fine soil, well adapted for agriculture, and which will, no doubt, become the Egypt of
Australia, our friend is about to remove with his flock, to
one of the more elevated southern districts.

23rd. We accompanied some of our friends in a ride,
along the newly-formed road, up the mountain, which is
a few miles south of the one by which we descended into
the district. The whole ascent is about five miles, through
rich forests, abounding with Cabbage Palm, and other

striking trees. The vegetation of the country, is of similar appearance to that within the tropics. This arises from the nature of the climate, which is mild, from the contiguity of the sea, and from the protection afforded by the precipitous mountains, from the frosts and hot winds of the interior ; these mountains also cause rain to fall much more abundantly here, than is common in other parts of N. S. Wales. Dripping sandstone-rocks project, at the top of the mountain, and are decorated with ferns, and *Dracophyllum secundum*, a remarkable plant of the Epacris tribe, with white flowers. One of our party killed a large Diamond Snake, which is considered venomous, but its bite is said to be rarely fatal. It is a beautiful species, and very different from the small one, known by the same name in Tasmania. The Bush Turkey, *Alectura Lathami*, inhabits these forests: it is somewhat less than the female of the Common Turkey ; its general colour is dark brown, but the head and neck, which are almost bare of feathers, are red, and it has a large, orange-red wattle, attached to the lower part of the neck. This bird is remarkable for using a hot-bed for hatching its eggs. It scratches together a conical heap of sticks and leaves, in which it deposits its eggs, distantly one from another, with the small end downward. From the quantity of eggs found in these heaps, several females are supposed to lay in the same place. The birds, both male and female, are said by the Natives, to watch the heaps during the period of incubation, and the latter diminishes or adds to the heated, vegetable matter, according to the instinct given her by her Creator.

In the evening, a meeting for the promotion of temperance, was held in the Police-office. Several persons addressed the audience, and a settler made some sensible remarks, on the desirableness of establishing a Savings' Bank, as an additional mode of promoting temperance. A man lately perished from spontaneous combustion, in this neighbourhood, and a woman was smothered in a hay-loft, under most abhorrent circumstances, consequent on intoxication.

24th. We took a walk into the forest, and examined some of its beauties, more particularly. Some large species of Fig are met with, as well as large Gum-trees, and species of *Tristania;* also *Metrosideros capitata,* called here Turpentine-tree, which attains a large stature, and *Sterculia acerifolia,* which has large clusters, of small, flame-coloured flowers, that produce a striking appearance in spring. The Cabbage Palm, *Corypha australis,* represented in the margin, abounds by the sides of water courses. Great numbers of this Palm, which has elegant, fan-like foliage, and hard, purple seeds, the size of a marble, are destroyed for the sake of their trunks and leaves. The trunks, which are sometimes 80 feet high, and are rough with scars, where the leaves have fallen of, are occasionally split, and converted into posts for fencing; they are also used for slabs in temporary buildings. The inside being rather sweet, and not hard, though fibrous, is eaten by pigs. The mature leaves are used for thatching, those just beginning to expand, for making hats, and the heart, or cabbage, of the young, unexpanded leaves, is eaten either raw or cooked. A heart-leaved species of Pepper, climbs like Ivy, among the lofty trees, and hangs in festoons from their branches, almost to the ground. Ferns and orchidaceous plants, abound on the trunks and limbs of many of the trees. One of the latter, *Sarco-chilus falcatus,* with blossoms nearly as white as Snowdrops, is now in flower.

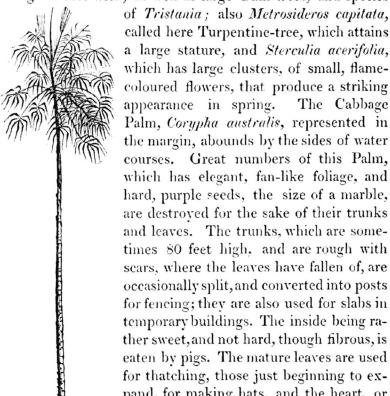

In these forests, there are many epiphytes of the orchis tribe, the habits of which are worthy of notice, both as exhibited here, and in other parts of the Colony. *Dendrobium speciosum* generally grows in fissures of the sandstone rocks, among the loose fragments, mixed with vegetable matter, but I once met with it, of extraordinary size, in the cleft of an old fig-tree, among vegetable remains. *D. linguiforme*, generally creeps on grit rocks, rarely on the living bark of figs and *Casuarinæ*. The other species of *Dendrobium*, with the genera *Sarcochilus* and *Gunnia*, grow on the bark of living trees. Once I saw *Dendrobium cala-mifolium* on a rock; but both this and the other species growing on living trees, begin to languish when the trees to which they are attached, die, probably from the portion of their roots adhering to the bark, becoming dried; a circumstance that is prevented, when they are cultivated in England, by the moist atmosphere of an orchideous-house. The Australian species of *Cymbidium*, universally strike their roots into the decaying portions of trees, in which they may sometimes be traced many feet. Once only, I met with one growing from among the paper-like laminæ of the bark of *Melaleuca viridiflora*, and it looked sickly.

25th. Accompanied by two of our acquaintance, we proceeded to the little settlement of Dapto, where a meeting was held, in the house of a widow, at which, a few people, from scattered houses in the vicinity, were present, to whom we were enabled to extend the gospel message, inviting them to seek the knowledge of the Lord, through submission to the teaching of the divine Spirit, and the diligent reading of the Holy Scriptures. In the afternoon, we reached Marshall Mount, where we were kindly entertained by a respectable settler, with whose family and servants, we had an open opportunity for religious communication.

26th. Rain, in the early part of the day, detained us at Marshall Mount. In the evening we walked to the top of a conical, basaltic hill, and had a view of Illawarra Lake, the sea, the mountains in the western back-ground, topped by sandstone crags, emerging from the boundless forest, and of the intervening plain; some parts of which are naturally clear. It is beautifully varied by forest, of trees, of different hue, and groves of Cabbage Palms, along the margins of the streamlets, and by Peach-trees, now in full blossom, in the gardens of the settlers.

27th. When at Dapto, we engaged a native Black, named Tommy, of the Kangaroo Ground, to be our guide to Bong Bong. He was of middle stature, rather broad-shouldered, and had a depressed nose, through the cartilage of which, he wore a bone. His eyes were drawn obliquely toward their inner angle, probably from the same cause which occasioned an elevated ridge downward, from one of them. When he came to us, he was dressed in a suit of ragged, European clothing; but as a part of his wages, he was fitted out with a striped shirt, a pair of canvass trowsers, and a grey, woollen jacket.—On the way to Kiama, we called on several small settlers, and left them tracts. We also fell in with some of the Aborigines. The females had their hair ornamented with kangaroos' teeth. They inquired of our guide, who we were, and where we were going, and appeared well satisfied with his explanations. All the men had the cartilage of the nose perforated: and through the perforation, they will sometimes stick the stem of a tobacco-pipe, when they have no other convenient place for carrying it! The Cabbage Palms are very numerous in this part of Illawarra; forming groves by the sides of the ground which has been cleared. *Seaforthia elegans*, known here by the native name of Bangalee, is also plentiful, but it grows in shady places. Many parts of the forest are gay with a species of *Goodia*, which forms a large shrub, and is covered with racemes of yellow, pea-like blossoms, tinged with orange. Some of the open, grassy forest is covered with a species of Indigo, *Indigofera australis*, three feet high, which is now clothed with rosy-pink flowers. Some of the species of fig, have established themselves on other large trees, and shut them in, and like those described at Moreton Bay, have become enormous, forest trees. Tree-nettles are numerous, and require care in passing; we measured the trunk of one, sixteen feet in circumference. The Australian Pheasant, celebrated for its splendid tail, on account of which, it is sometimes called, the New Holland Bird of Paradise, and various species of Pigeon and Parrot, as well as the White Cockatoo, abound here. We only saw one small species of Kangaroo. The Lory Parrot, of crimson and blue, mixed with dark colours, and the King Parrot, of crimson and green, were sitting in flocks, on the post-and-rail fences; they are very mischievous in the gardens.

Kiama is situated on the coast, at a little boat-harbour: it consists of about a dozen cottages, built of wood, occupied by a blacksmith, a carpenter, a shoemaker, &c. and a constable's house, where the police-magistrate holds his court. We passed a mile beyond it, to the house of a settler, where we were hospitably entertained, and had a religious interview with his establishment. The roads were too miry, to allow other persons to meet with us after sunset. Our black guide, who speaks English intelligibly, and is of an industrious disposition, joined some of his country-people in the bush, notwithstanding the inclemency of the night, preferring their company, and the shelter of a few sheets of bark, to the company of white people, in a house.

28th. The day was showery, but we prosecuted our journey, in the course of which we passed several Blacks, with whom our guide was acquainted, and called on a few settlers. One of the latter spoke very respectfully of the Society of Friends, in Ireland, but said she knew little of their principles, as they did not admit persons of other persuasions into their places of worship. We endeavoured to correct this mistaken idea, which there is reason to believe, prevails in some quarters, assuring the party, that our meetings for worship were always open to the public, notwithstanding we sometimes invited a special attendance, at the request of a minister, feeling specially the constraining influence of the love of Christ, toward persons not connected with the Society.

In the course of our walk we noticed large masses of *Acrosticum alcicorne* and *Asplenium Nidus*, growing upon the limbs of enormous Fig-trees; the latter is a large fern, with a circle of long, entire leaves. Even some of the lofty Cabbage Palms were encircled by the *Acrosticum*. *Polypodium tenellum* and *quercifolium*, and *Niphobolus rupestris* were climbing the trunks of trees, adhering to them like Ivy, and on the ground, there were *Adiantum formosum* and *assimile*, *Doodia aspera*, *Lomaria Patersonii*, and a tree-fern, of the genus *Alsophila*. *Calanthe veratrifolia*, and several other terrestrial, orchidaceous plants, also attracted our attention, in the rich district of Illawarra, from which we emerged on the coast, about seven miles north of Shoal Haven. The beach was sandy and firm, and separated from a grassy swamp, by sand hills, covered with Honeysuckle, *Banksia integrifolia*. At Colomgatta, in Shoal Haven, we were received with great hospitality by Alexander Berry, the proprietor of an extensive territory in this district, which, like that of Illawarra, is much more favourable for the grazing of horned cattle than for sheep. Among the enemies of the latter in these rich, coast lands, is the Wattle Tick, a hard, flat insect, of a dark colour, about the tenth of an inch in diameter, and nearly circular, in the body; it insinuates itself beneath the skin, and destroys, not only sheep, but sometimes foals and calves. Paralysis of the hinder quarters often precedes death in these cases. Sometimes it occasions painful swellings, when forcibly removed from the human body, after having fixed its anchorlike head and appendages in the skin. To prevent this inconvenience, we several times, made them let go their hold, by smearing them over with oil, or with wet tobacco-ashes.

29th. I did not feel comfortable in having proceeded to Shoal Haven, without having made an attempt to assemble the few persons, settled about the boat-harbour at Kiama. An undue fear of prolonging our visit beyond its proper bounds, and discouragement at the state of the roads, induced me to put by, a little exercise on their account, which I afterwards felt a painful burden, though I did not apprehend it required of me to return to the place; I felt it the more, when I found we could not assemble the people at Shoal Haven before the 2nd of 11th month.

We walked with our intelligent host, to the top of Colomgatta hill, from which his house takes its name. From this elevation, which is basaltic, there is a fine view, embracing the inlets of Shoal Haven and Crook Haven, and the Pigeon House Peak, to the south. In the distance, in this direction the country changes from flat, into low ridges, and becomes less fertile. About the Pigeon House Peak, is probably, the limit of the Australian Palms. The Cabbage Tree of Tasmania is a *Richea*, and only allied to palms, in bearing a single head, on a tall stem. On Colomgatta, a *Zamia* supposed to be *Z. spiralis*, forms a trunk, or root-stock, three to four feet high, and as much round. Its crests of palm-like, pinnate leaves, are very beautiful. The Rock Lily, *Dendrobium speciosum*, was in blossom on a rock, on the side of the hill; the spike of white flowers fading into pale yellow, was as thick as my arm, and a foot long. In returning from gathering it, I encountered a N. S. Wales Black Snake, *Coluber porphyryaceus;* and destroyed it by throwing large stones at it. It is accounted a very venomous species.

From the first settlement of this place, Alexander Berry has succeeded in maintaining a good understanding with the natives, who, he says, believe in a transmutation, after death. This first claimed his notice, when he had wounded a Porpoise, which some Blacks, who were with him in the boat, tried to dissuade him from firing at. On landing, the men told the women what had been done, at which they made great lamentation; and he learned from them, that they regarded the Porpoises, as having been the ancient chiefs of the neighbourhood, who, when they had died, had changed into these animals; and who, they said, drove fish on shore for them, sometimes whales, when the people were very hungry!

10th mo. 1st. Yesterday, we took some steps to invite the persons on the opposite side of the Shoal Haven River, to a meeting for public worship, to be held at Colomgatta, on First-day. In walking in the brush, we measured three Stinging-trees, *Urtica gigas*, eighteen, twenty, and twenty-one feet in circumference. Probably these are the largest nettles in the world, and possibly the most severe. Happening to come in contact with the leaf of one, with my hand, it occasioned about as much pain as the sting of a wasp. The leaves are large, some of them six inches across, and heart-shaped. The stinging hairs are not the most numerous; they are readily distinguished from the others, by the poison vesicles, at the base, on holding them between the eye and the light. We killed several Black Snakes, that were basking on a sunny bank. When disturbed, they

raise their heads, and distend their necks, presenting a terrific aspect; but a smart blow across the back, with a
stout switch, soon despatches them.   One of the Aborigines,
who has learned to saw, at A. Berry's sawing establishment, came to Colomgatta to-day, and asked for some seed
potatoes.   He said, he had cleared a piece of land, and
sowed some pumpkins, and he wanted to grow some potatoes,
and " sit down," for it was " no good " to wander about,
as his countrymen did.   A. Berry was much pleased with
this spontaneous offer to settle, he having often tried in vain,
to persuade some of these people to adopt such a course.

2nd.   About ninety persons assembled under the verandah, at Colomgatta, with whom we had a satisfactory meeting.   The only native Black who was present, was Lewis,
a man we became acquainted with in V. D. Land, who was
employed in assisting to collect the Natives.   No families
in N. S. Wales, who assemble for public worship, appear
to take any pains to collect the Blacks along with them.
The idea that the Blacks cannot understand a dissertation
in English, is one obstacle, and their want of personal
cleanliness is another; but neither of these are insurmountable difficulties.   I feel persuaded, that if worldly emolu-
ment was to be had by civilizing and instructing the
Aborigines, they would soon be civilized and instructed;
but generally, there is a great neglect, on the part of the
white population, with regard to their own spiritual state,
and consequently with respect to those around them, especially the Blacks.

3rd.   We again proceeded on our journey, having two
Blacks, Lewis and Sam, as guides, Tommy having left
Shoal Haven, without notice.   We were so amply provided with food for two days, by our kind host, that the
services of one of these men was required, to carry it on
his head, in a sack.   A circuit of about six miles, over
grassy, forest hills, between two marshes, brought us to
A. Berry's sawing establishment, on Broughtons Creek,
which is under the superintendence of a respectable, Scotch
family, who do not think they have improved their situation in life, by emigrating.

At the foot of the Cambewarra mountains, we met half-
a-dozen Blacks, dressed in blankets, and in the old clothes
of Europeans.   One of these sons of the forest had an
expressive countenance, and
remarkably fine features: he
spoke English tolerably, and
said that he went occasionally, as a seaman, on board a
vessel belonging to A. Berry.
These people were accoutred
with hunting and fishing
spears, and weapons of war,
some of which are here represented.   Figure 1, is a
heavy, wooden, offensive
weapon: Fig. 2, a throwing
stick, or womera, used for
projecting spears; the after
extremities of which, are
placed against the hook, behind the combatant, as represented at page 380: Fig.
3, a single-barbed spear, used
in war: Fig. 4, a death-spear,
barbed with a row of pieces
of glass.   Fig. 5, a shield, of
wood, having a handle in the
centre, under which is a piece
of soft, tea-tree bark, to defend the knuckles. This shield
was whitened, and marked
with red lines: sometimes
they are blackened with
blood and soot, under the
idea of rendering them proof
against injury: and on this
black surface, the figure of a

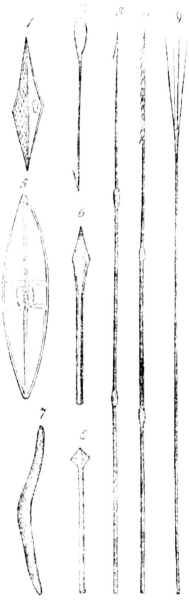

hand is occasionally depicted, by means of a white powder,
thrown on before the black is dry, or the whole is dotted

with white. At Moreton Bay, the shields were oblong, and made of the light wood, of the Gigantic Nettle: Figs. 6 and 8, are clubs of heavy wood: Fig. 7, a Boomring, Boomering, Barragan, or Kyler, described at page 319: Fig. 9, a four-pronged fishing-spear, described at page 288.

Upon trees on the ascent of the Cambewarra mountain, *Dendrobium ruscifolium* was in flower. Two other orchideous epiphytes, but of minute size, grew on mossy logs, near the top of the mountain, where there were several other remarkable plants. The Cabbage Palm grew to the top of the mountain, and on the descent toward the Kangaroo River, the Zamias were fine.

After ascending about 2,000 feet, we descended nearly half as much, and pursuing our route, through almost trackless forests, reached a stock-station on the Kangaroo Ground before sunset. This place is an open, grassy plain, inaccessible to carriages, and surrounded by mountains. In this sequestered spot, we were recognized and welcomed, by a man in charge of a hut, who was a prisoner, in a bridge-party, at Windsor, when we visited that place, a year ago; in the mean time he had become free. We were also recognized by an Anglo-australian youth, who had been at one of our meetings in Illawarra. In this land of strangers, a very slight knowledge of a person is sufficient for claiming acquaintance. In passing through some of the more open forest, on the Kangaroo River, and contiguous plain, Buttercups, Violets, and Geraniums, resembling those of English fields, but not identical with them, reminded us pleasantly of our native land, while Red-tailed Black Cockatoos, numerous Aborigines, and many plants of truly Australian features, proved that we were still at the antipodes of the land of our birth. The men residing on the Kangaroo Ground, had no Bible. The only religious treatise in their possession, was a Prayer Book; but they were not destitute of compassion for the afflicted. A poor, aged, black woman, who had lost the use of her legs, and was living near their hut, under a slight shelter, formed of a few sheets of bark, was chiefly supported by milk and scraps of food, which they gave her.

4th. We found our old guide on the Kangaroo Ground, where he had been engaged in a fight, had got his head severely broken, and had then made peace with his antagonist. Three tribes of Blacks were assembled here last night; one belonging to the neighbourhood, and the others to Shoal Haven and Bong Bong. There were forty men in one of these tribes : they were going to the Cow-pastures, to learn a new song, that had been invented by some of their country people there! For an object of this kind they often travel great distances. Several of them speak tolerable English. They were attired either in skin garments, fastened over one shoulder and under the other, or in blankets, or articles of European clothing; one having on a pair of trousers, another a shirt, a third a jacket, and so on. Few of them had any covering for their heads, and none had shoes. All the men had undergone the ceremony of having one front-tooth knocked out, on being admitted to the privileges of manhood; and they had the cartilages of their noses perforated, and bones, the thickness of a quill, and about four inches long, through them. They wore fillets of net-work around their heads, and beads, formed of short pieces of reed, around their necks. They prop up large sheets of bark with sticks, for shelters to sleep under, having fires in front. They are very peaceable, when kindly treated : we felt no fear in sleeping in a rude hut, without a fastening to the door, which blew open several times in the night, though about 200 of them were only a few hundred yards distant. In the morning eight of them, in addition to the three we had engaged, chose to accompany us on our journey. Our party did not commence their march till after a considerable time had been spent in conversation between our sable companions, and their countrymen : to this delay we were obliged to submit patiently. They carried with them, their arms, and a musket, which one of them had received as a present from a settler, for whom he had done some service. The ascent of the mountain, toward Bong Bong, was steep, and covered with Cedar, Swamp Mahogany, Sasafras, Cabbage Palm, and large climbers. The stem of a *Tecoma*, that we met with, having blossoms like *T. australis,* but differing considerably from that species in foliage, was two feet in circumference, and reached the head of the tree that supported it, at about seventy feet from the ground, a species of *Cissus;* and some other climbers, were also very large. One of the Natives ascended a Cabbage Palm, and with a hatchet, cut off its head, which he soon stripped of leaves, to afford us the opportunity of tasting the heart. Not having that of the *Seaforthia* to compare it with, at the time, I could not decide that it was superior, though it is generally reputed to be so. The Natives informed us that they were not aware that the hearts of these Palms were wholesome, till White people came among them; they now form a considerable item of their food, in this part of the country. The Blacks are greatly afraid of being poisoned, by eating articles to which they have not been accustomed. Though sometimes pressed with hunger, they seem not to have tried several vegetable productions, likely to afford sustenance; and those of V. D. Land will not eat any kind of fish, but shell-fish, probably from fear of being poisoned by them. We halted at the Waterfall Brook, after descending a little from the summit of the mountain, and divided the residue of our provision, which, though ample for the number that we amounted to when we left Shoal Haven, was somewhat small for thirteen, but all appeared content, being made equal partakers. We passed a waterfall, reported to be 500 feet, from the top to the bottom, without being aware that we were near it. On descending, the country became sandy; Stringy Bark, and other upland species of *Eucalyptus,* as well as of *Banksia, Hakea, Grevillea,* and some of the *Legumenosæ,* of the sandstone districts, succeeded to the richer forest, and toward the conclusion of our journey, the country became more grassy. Some Pheasants and a Kangaroo were espied in the bush by the Natives, who were very cheerful companions. They were amply supplied with food, on arriving at the noble mansion of Charles Throsby, at Throsby Park, near Bong Bong, where we also were received with great hospitality.

CHAPTER XXXVII.

10th mo. 5th. BEING kindly supplied with horses, by
Charles Throsby, we visited the Ironed-gang at Berrima,
and a neighbouring Road-party. The prisoners forming the
Ironed-gang are employed in erecting a jail and court-
house. They have Bibles and Prayer Books lent to them, on
First-days, by the military officer, who takes some pains in
regard to their religious instruction. Berrima is upon a
new line of road, to the southern parts of the Colony.
It is on a poor, sandy soil, but is better supplied with
water than Bong Bong, which is now abandoned, as the
site of a town, though in a richer country, and on basalt.
We spent the evening pleasantly with the large family of
Charles Throsby, whose wife was rescued from the New
Zealanders, when a child, by Alexander Berry. They had
destroyed and eaten the company of the ship, with the
exception of the cabin-boy and herself; in consequence of
the captain having beaten the son of one of their chiefs,
when on the voyage, because he suspected him of stealing a
silver spoon, that was probably thrown overboard, by accident.

6th. An aged man, named Wyld, who accompanied

E E 3

Robert Brown, in his botanical researches in N. S. Wales
and V. D. Land, and who discovered the district of Illawarra, was sent with us as guide, to Black Bobs Creek,
and to bring back the horses on which we rode, as we
wished to pursue our journey southward, on foot, after
visiting a Bridge and Road-party. This part of the Colony
is about 2,000 feet above the level of the sea. The forest
is open and grassy. Apples, Cherries and Gooseberries,
thrive here, but it is too cold for Oranges and Lemons.
From Black Bobs Creek to Paddys River, the soil is poor
and sandy, and grass is scanty in the open forest, which
is chiefly of Stringy Bark, White Gum, and *Eucalyptus
pulverulenta*, the Peppermint-tree of this part of the country. The last seldom reaches fifty feet in height; it has a
remarkably crabbed appearance, white, perfoliate leaves,
and soft bark, very obnoxious to the effects of fire, so that
most of the trunks are partially charred. *Acacia homomalla,
tenuissima*, and another species, occur in this country, in
which some of the birds of V. D. Land abound; such as
the Piping Crow, *Cracticus hypoleucus*, the Jay or Black
Magpie, *Coronica fuliyinosa*, the Butcher Bird or Miner,
Myzantha garrula, and the Rosella, Rosehill, or Nonpareil
Parrot, *Platycercus eximius*. There are several sandstone
rocks, and pools of water, near the road. From behind
one of the former, persons have sometimes been shot
by bushrangers; but their depredations have been greatly
checked of late, by a more efficient police, and the stricter
discipline of the Ironed-gangs, from which it is now difficult to escape. The short herbage, which characterizes the
sheep lands of this Colony, became more abundant near
Wingelow, where we were kindly received by a settler, to
whom we had a letter of introduction.

7th. We visited an Ironed-gang at Marulan. The prisoners had lately been supplied with Bibles and tracts, by
order of the Bishop of Australia. The Episcopal service
is read to them on First-days, by the officer in charge.
Prisoners who are not of good character, are assigned into
service, in places remote from Sydney, in order that they may
be separated more completely from their old associates. The

Marulan gang consists of such as have committed offences
after such assignment. They present strong marks of depravity in their countenances, and not a few have defectively formed heads. This circumstance, which is not uncommon among convicts, and is probably among the causes
of their turpitude, ought, in some points, at least, to be
taken into account; some of them appear to be in a state
bordering on insanity or idiotism. Had they yielded to a
good influence, their untowardness would probably have been
softened or diminished; beyond a doubt, it has been aggravated by yielding to evil. Their case is a very affecting one,
and their moral responsibility must be left to the Judge of
all the earth. Here the punishment to which they are subjected, for misconduct in the gang, is flagellation; and
in some instances they have received, from 600 to 800
lashes, within the space of eighteen months, at the rate
of not more than fifty lashes for one offence! The Ironed-
gangs in this Colony may now be said to be placed under
a rigid, military discipline, and kept closely guarded, day
and night, by soldiers. No smoking is allowed among
them: they are kept closely to work, at least, that is the
case with such as are stationed on the roads, in the interior, and are locked up in caravans, from sunset to sun-
rise.

After leaving Marulan, the country for about ten miles,
was very poor, and covered with low Gum-trees, and very
thin grass. It then improved; and on emerging from the
forest, at the location of a settler, on a branch of the Wollondilly River, the corn fields looked beautifully green.
Our track now led, for about three miles, through a narrow
hollow, of good soil, in which there was a chain of pools;
it then continued eight miles further, most of the way,
through deep hollows, and over low hills, of conglomerate
sandstone, basalt, or dirty white quartz, mixed with red
or brown, breaking into cubic gravel. We passed a few
small huts, forming the village of Towrang, before reaching Goulburn or Strahallen, at the junction of the Mul-
warie Ponds, and Wollondilly Rivers. The old town of
Goulburn consisted of a court-house, of slabs, covered

with bark, a lock-up house, a few huts, occupied by the mounted police and constables, a cottage of roughly cut timber, and a small inn, affording tolerable accommodation for such a place, as well as a better house or two, at a short distance.

8th. A neighbouring settler, and the Police-magistrate, called upon us. From the latter, we obtained leave to hold a meeting in the court-house: he also accompanied us to the new township, about a mile distant, where a few scattered buildings of brick, and others of wood, had been erected. One of the latter is an hospital, affording accommodation for about thirty patients. Like other places of this kind, in remote situations, it was pretty fully occupied, by stock-men, and others of the lower order; victims of immorality, the scourge of this class, in sequestered parts of the Colony, frequented by the Aborigines. Goulburn Plain is an extensive down, besprinkled with small herbs, and thin grass, and clear of trees, for several miles. In some places, it runs into gentle undulations, with thinly scattered trees, such as Weeping Gum, White Gum, Box, and Bastard Box. On the margin of the plain, there are woody hills of white, quartzose rock. The plain, and low hills, afford excellent pasturage for sheep, but as each sheep requires from two to three acres, or more, for its support, a large extent of land is required for a considerable flock.

9th. The meeting in the Court House was attended by only seventeen persons. The population of the neighbourhood is much scattered; and many shew a much stronger inclination to resort to a public-house than to a place of worship. In the afternoon, we had a religious interview with the establishment of a young settler, who emigrated a few years since, and has a fine property, and a good flock of sheep; and who has read and thought more than many, both on natural and religious subjects.

10th. Near a place, where Mountain Limestone crops out, by the side of a chain of ponds, we fell in with a tribe of Blacks, resting by a fire, under the shelter of some bushes; two of whom frequently do turns of work, in hewing wood, drawing water, &c. for the settler at whose house we lodged.   One of the women was eating raw sow-thistles, as salad, with avidity.

In the course of the day, we walked over a continuance of the plain country, more thickly covered with herbage, near the course of the Sully Ponds, to Rossiville; where we met a courteous reception, and joined a company of opulent settlers. The proprietor of this comfortable mansion, like most other extensive wool-growers, in this part of the colony, occupies a portion of the unlocated territory, called Menaro Plains, to the south west. The plains of this district, succeed each other, for upwards of 200 miles. They are upon Granite, Mica Slate and Quartz, with here and there, Limestone and Basalt. The parts overlaying the granite are generally free from trees, and from extensive downs.   The intervening hills are more or less covered with wood. Snow falls frequently in winter, but it seldom lies many hours; hoar frosts are also prevalent, and they sometimes occur in summer. The country is watered by rivers, generally forming chains of ponds, except in rainy weather. These are of great importance to the Australian shepherd, whose flocks must drink twice a day, in the warm weather. In some seasons, a disease called Influenza, makes great havoc among the sheep. Our worthy host, lately lost about two thousand; but not being aware that this mortality could have been prevented by any care on the part of himself or his shepherd, he bore it with becoming patience, as a dispensation of Him, who is Sovereign Lord of all, and who has a right at his pleasure, to give proof that temporal possessions are held subserviently to his will.

11th. We did not think it our duty to proceed further among the scattered inhabitants of this sheep country; who are spreading into the interior, like a mighty flood; fixing themselves in temporary huts, until the Government shall survey and sell the land they occupy; when many of them will move still further onward; we therefore returned to Goulburn, after having a meeting with about forty persons, in the wool-room, at Rossiville. We next proceeded to Lumley, taking advantage of the guidance of a soldier, who was going that way, and who led us by a route of sixteen miles, instead of twenty three, by the road. We crossed a portion of the plain, upon which a shepherd was feeding his flock, and at the same time driving them gently along, as they consumed the thin herbage. In this manner, a flock has to travel a considerable distance, daily, to obtain food and water. Leaving the plain, our route lay through some barren, quartzose forest, and along a narrow valley, with a chain of large ponds, which wound among the hills, for many miles. The water was very grateful to us; for being a little fatigued with the walk from Rossiville, and with the heat, we took some bread and cheese and porter, at Goulburn, which on again walking in the sun, created intolerable thirst. This circumstance brought us to the conclusion, that though porter might seem to revive at the time it was taken, its effects upon the system were most uncongenial to continued exercise, and in no way really beneficial; and in our long and laborious travels, subsequently, we were abundantly confirmed in the great advantage of abstaining from all intoxicating liquors, which, however, we did not entirely abandon the use of, till nearly two years after this period.

In the pools, in the neighbourhood of Goulburn, there are some plants, nearly allied to those found in the waters of England, such as a few species of *Potamogeton* and *Villarsia*; others such as *Typha latifolia* and *Myriophyllum verticillatum* are supposed to be identical with the English species. Here there is also, a species of *Marsilea*, the foliage of which sometimes floats upon the water, and resembles that of a four-leaved clover. *Acacia graveolens* and a holly-leaved *Grevillea*, with greenish flowers were growing on the quartz hills, and a rosemary-leaved *Grevillea* with crimson flowers, near Rossiville. A few Ducks, Parrots and Cockatoos were the principal birds that attracted our attention.

Lumley, is the residence of an opulent settler. The surrounding country is open forest, affording good sheep-pasture, and interspersed with small plains, clear of trees. The Shoal Haven Gullies, which are ravines in a limestone formation, and said to be 1,600 feet deep, are a few miles to the east.

12th. After a meeting, at an early hour, in one of the rooms of the commodious house, at Lumley, our kind host set out for his sheep station, on the Menaro Plains, in a four-wheeled carriage, on springs, attended by a servant on horseback. With a little care, in choosing the road, and places for crossing rivers, a carriage may be driven for a few hundreds of miles, in the untracked country. In the Colony generally, most of the acknowledged roads, are merely cart tracks, with the bad places cut through, or filled up. They are bad to travel upon in wet weather; but the weather is so generally dry, and free from strong frost, that these tracks are much less cut up, than they would be in a climate like that of England.—In the forenoon we visited Bungonia, a rudimentary town, and had a religious interview with a road-party, seated on some logs, by the way-side. Here, a gentleman, visiting this country from India, on account of his health, whom we met at Lumley, took us up in his carriage, with the view of expediting our journey; but the pole breaking, in crossing a rut, occasioned some delay. While this was repairing at the station of the Marulan Ironed-gang, two men were brought up by the guard, charged with throwing pieces of tobacco to the prisoners, at work on the road. Being strangers, they were reprimanded, and allowed to proceed. For this offence, free persons are often fined, and prisoners in assigned service are flogged, to the amount of fifty lashes. The carriage being repaired, we proceeded, but sometimes had to hold it back, in descending the hills, on an almost trackless road, until at a later hour than if the journey had been performed on foot, we reached Arthurslee, a fine station for agriculture and sheep feeding, belonging to an opulent gentleman, whom we had met near Goulburn, and who now welcomed us as his guests. The country, though more clothed with wood, and more hilly than that near Goulburn, was still on a basis of granite, which projected in some places, above the surface. Two acres were on an average required for a sheep, on the better pastures. Near the house, White Clover, Trefoil, a spinous-seeded Medic, Rib-grass, Rye-grass, Shepherds Purse, *Erodium cicutarium* and *moschatum*, and some other English plants, had established themselves, as they have in many other parts of the Colony, where they spread and thrive, often more vigorously than in their native country.

13th.   After a meeting with the numerous people of this establishment, we again set forward, and proceeding over some open-forest hills, and across the Wollondilly and Paddys Rivers, entered the Wombat Brush, a forest of Stringy-bark, Peppermint-tree, and low scrub, upon barren, quartzose hills, in which a species of White Ant was numerous.   The conical habitations of this insect, were from four to six feet high, and very solid : sometimes four of these were in sight, at a time.   A more ferti¹ tract, on Whinstone or Basalt, succeeded, upon which a few settlers were located, whose little fields and orchards, with Apple and Plum-trees in blossom, presented a cheerful aspect.   We next came again upon the sandstone of Black Bobs Creek, on the rocky borders of which, *Epacris cerinthoides* was clothed with a profusion of white flowers.   Here we got a drink of water, the only refreshment we had, in a walk of twenty-two miles, to Oldbury, where another religious opportunity concluded the labours of the day.

14th.   We again reached Throsby Park.   On calling at a cottage, where some shoemakers were at work, to inquire the road, I was recognised by a man from York, who said he enlisted for a soldier, about ten years since, and went to India ; where he was " unfortunate," that is committed a crime for which he was transported, and was sent to this Colony ; here, after seven years' bondage, he had become free, and was working at his trade.

16th.   In the forenoon, we had a meeting at Bong Bong, which consists of a few scattered houses, on the Wingee-carabee River, and in the afternoon, at a small settlement, called Sutton Forest, where there is a weather-board, Episcopal chapel.

17th.   Many persons are now on their way southward, to their sheep shearings, and the number of drays, conveying their provisions is considerable.   On the way to Mittagong, we fell in with two young men, with whom we had become acquainted, who were on a twelve days'

journey, toward their sheep stations, on the Doomut River,
far southward, beyond the located part of the Colony.
They were resting by the side of the road, having two
saddle horses, and a tilted cart, in which they slept and carried their provisions, drawn by other two horses, their two
attendants sleeping under the cart. After taking coffee
with them, in gipsy style, we pursued our route over the
Mittagong Range, which, like much of the adjacent country, is basaltic. The Gum-trees upon it are of several
species. One called here, the Woolly-butted Gum, seems
identical with the Black-butted Gum of Tasmania. The
White Gum was beginning to drop its manna, in small
pieces, of pure white, from the increased warmth of the
weather, which also occasioned the merry Tettagonias, here
called Locusts, to keep up a continual rattle, in which, in
the species inhabiting these forests, there is a remarkable,
undulating harmony.

Between Bong Bong and Mittagong, we passed the huts
of several veterans, who had grants of 100 acres each, in
this fine neighbourhood, where the soil is rich, in many
places, overlaying basalt; but drunkenness and profligacy
have kept these wretched people in poverty, where industry
and sobriety would have been rewarded with plenty. At
Mittagong, we became the guests of Charles Sturt, a benevolent and enterprising man, well known on account of
his long, exploratory journies, to the southward, in company with George M‘Leay, of which an account is published. Their courage among the native Blacks, by which
they were preserved from hostility, is an interesting feature
in their narrative.

18th. After a religious interview with the family and
establishment, we again set forward on our journey: the
track lay through an inhospitable territory, called Bargo
Brush, which is a thick forest, on a sandstone formation.
The timber is chiefly Stringy-bark, of tall and slender
growth. A fire had blackened the trunks of the trees, and
consumed the scrub; but many of the gay shrubs that ornament these desolate forests, were again springing, and
putting forth their lively blossoms. We met several

companies of Blacks.   Some of the women had considerable quantities of Native Currants, the fruit of *Leptomeria acida*, that they were carrying in vessels scooped out of the knots of the gum-tree, some of which will hold several quarts. We dined at an inn, the landlord of which was killed, a few days before, by a fall from his horse, when intoxicated; the following night, the wife of an innkeeper, nearer to Goulburn, died from excessive drinking, which is the bane of these Colonies.   After sunset, we passed through a small settlement, called the Stone-quarries, and at length, reached Jarvis Field, the residence of a pious Police-magistrate, from whom we received a a cordial welcome, after a tedious walk of twenty-five miles.

19th.   We had a religious interview with the family and servants of the Magistrate, in a room upon his premises, erected for a court-house, in which this worthy man, not only assembles his family and establishment, for public worship, but also a neighbouring road-party, with the ticket-of-leave men, and others who reside near; on First-days, he reads the service of the Episcopal Church to them, with a sermon; he also assembles his own household twice a day, for the reading of the Scriptures and prayer.   We were present this morning on one of these occasions, to our comfort.—Departing from Jarvis Field, we had a religious opportunity with a neighbouring road-party, and then crossed the range of hills, called Razor-back, and proceeded through open, grassy-forest, to the Cow-pastures, where, at Brownlowe Hill, we were welcomed by George and James M'Leay, sons of our kind friend the Colonial Secretary.

20th.   In clearing the land about the tasteful, genteel, cottage, and garden, at Brownlowe Hill, more care has been taken not to destroy its beauty, by cutting down the trees indiscriminately, than is usual in these Colonies; where trees, being the encumbrance of the land, are generally cut away unsparingly.   Much of the land in this part of N. S. Wales, has been cleared by human industry; it is now covered with luxuriant crops of wheat and barley, in ear, but not sufficiently advanced to be out of danger, from a single day's hot wind, such as not unfrequently blights

the hopes of the husbandman, in this sunny climate.—
We visited the agricultural establishment of the M'Leays,
on the Mount Hunter Creek, where they have a garden,
producing Oranges, Apples, Loquats, Pears, Plums, Cherries, Figs, Mulberries, Medlars, Raspberries, Strawberries,
and Gooseberries, and where Roses are in great profusion.
We then proceeded to Cawdor, where, at the Court House,
the magistrates sentenced a young prisoner-shepherd, to
receive fifty lashes, for carelessly suffering his flock to get
mixed with another.

From hence, we accompanied William Macarthur, to
his noble mansion, at Camden, which is of two stories,
built of beautiful sandstone, and finished in style equal
to that of the dwellings of the upper class, in England.
The gardens are extensive, and well laid out. Many of
the beautiful, native plants, are here cultivated successfully,
for ornament; and a grassy lawn looks very English, but
to preserve it, much watering is required in summer. The
seasons have latterly, been so dry, that not more than
10,000 sheep can now be kept here, where formerly 30,000
were maintained; the flocks have consequently, to be driven
to the higher lands, to the south, for pasturage. Some
families of Blacks are regularly rationed at Camden, on
the score of justice; the present proprietors, and their father,
to whom they succeeded, rightly considering, that this was
due to the people, whose lands themselves had occupied.

21st. We visited the Camden farm-establishment, a mile
distant from the house, and had a meeting with about 100
of the men, who are now busy with the sheep shearing.
Both here and at Brownlowe Hill, the Episcopal prayers
are read to the men by their masters. These establishments are also occasionally visited by the exemplary and
diligent, Colonial Chaplain, from Cobbity, on whom we
made a call, and then returned to Brownlowe Hill. In
some fields, on the road, the people were making hay, from
oats and barley, cut green. Grass rarely becomes fit for
the scythe, in this country. The thermometer to-day was
at 90°, in the shade. I walked into the forest by moonlight, along with George M'Leay, to see the Opossums.

The Vulpine, *Phalangista vulpina*, and some other species are common here, including flying ones. There is also in various parts of this Colony, an animal, called the Koala, *Phasclaretos fuscus*, which like the Opossums, feeds at night, in the Gum-trees; but it is without a tail, and somewhat resembles a small bear: the pupils of its eyes are vertical, and its ears are large.—Several of the intelligent settlers, in this part of the country, have paid some attention to Natural History. Studies of this kind do not generally gain much attention in new countries, where the mind becomes much engrossed by clearing, building, and obtaining the necessaries of life; but some of the settlers in N. S. Wales, have risen above this point, and occupy a position analogous to that of English gentlemen. The growth of wool is however, the prevailing object of attention.

22nd. The thermometer rose to 100°, in the shade, which rendered travelling, even for a short distance, very oppressive; but we proceeded to Cobbity, where we became the guests of Thomas Hassal, the Episcopal Chaplain. Many people in the neighbourhood were affected with fever, which was so prevalent that it had obtained the name of Influenza, and this good man was diligently ministering to their temporal relief, and spiritual instruction. In one family, to which I accompanied him, the father, in a state of high fever, was in the same bed with two of his own children. The crowded state of some of the huts of the poorer settlers, renders them extremely uncomfortable in times of sickness. In the evening, we had a meeting in a school-room, near the chapel; it was a satisfactory opportunity, notwithstanding the heat continued to be great.

23rd. Being mounted on ponies, by our kind friend T. Hassal, we proceeded through the beautiful vale of the Nepean River, assembling the establishments of some considerable Colonists, on the way to Winbourn, the residence of George Cox, by whom we were received in a very friendly manner, and who conveyed us in his carriage, to a place used for public worship, on the premises of one of his brothers, at Mulgoa, where he had appointed a meeting for us, at which about forty persons were present. After a solemn silence, of considerable duration, in which the divine presence was comfortingly with us, strength was afforded to proclaim the gospel message, with much warning and encouragement.   After the meeting, we returned to Winbourn, which is a substantial mansion, having the features of an English gentleman's seat; it is situated in a country resembling an English park; such indeed, is much of the district, which includes Camden, the Cowpastures, and Mulgoa.

24th.   Passing several fine estates, which are as verdant this year, as they were parched a year ago, we came to Penrith, and went forward to Duneved, the residence of Captain Philip King.   Here we received a kind and Christian welcome, and had a meeting with his large and interesting family, in which the benign influence of maternal piety was clearly to be traced.

25th.   This morning, I witnessed the operation of milking some cows, that had been brought up wild in the bush. They were driven into a fold; where, with some difficulty, their calves were separated from them.   A noose, at the end of a rope, was then thrown over their horns, by means of a long pole, and the rope was drawn through a ringbolt, in a wall, so as to bring the cow tightly up.   In this position she was milked; but from the time occupied, the risk of injury from the untractable beasts, and the small quantity of milk obtained, I thought it a very dearly bought article.— We proceeded down the western road, to Parramatta, and after calling on some persons there, went to the Vineyard, where we became the guests of Hannibal H. Macarthur, from whom we received an invitation, when at his house, in the district of Argyle.   The mansion at the Vineyard is an excellent one, of two stories, with a capital garden, pleasantly situated upon the navigable part of the Parramatta River, or to speak more correctly, near the extremity of the estuary of Port Jackson, to which the Parramatta River is but a small, tributary brook.

26th.   We returned to Parramatta, and paid our respects to the Governor, and to his son, John Bourke, who made

many inquiries relative to our visit to the southern part of
the Colony. We called also at the Factory, where the
female prisoners are now under improving discipline. Many
improvements are visible in Parramatta, since we visited
it, a little more than a year ago. The demand for lime, has
raised that article to 1s. 6d. per bushel. In the evening,
we returned to the Vineyard, and had a religious opportunity with the family and servants.

Hannibal H. Macarthur is one of the members of the
Legislative Council of the Colony, for which office he is
well qualified; being an intelligent, upright man, who has a
large interest in the country.

27th. We returned to Sydney, calling on the way at
Pennant Hills, where we had a religious interview with
an Ironed-gang, and Invalid Road-party, and at Kissing
Point, where we dined with Isaac Shepherd, a good, old
man, who has a son, a missionary in New Zealand, and a
daughter, the wife of a missionary in Tahiti. I. Shepherd
has resided forty-two years in this Colony, and has prospered temporally, as he has grown in grace, in which he
has exceeded most of his cotemporaries. He is the proprietor of an Orange-grove, the trees in which, exceed in
size, any other Orange-trees, that we have seen in N. S.
Wales. We called also at Tarban Creek, to see the new
Lunatic Asylum, which is in progress, and taking the steam-
packet, at the adjacent ferry, arrived in Sydney, in good
time in the evening; we took up our quarters for the night
at a comfortable hotel.

CHAPTER XXXVIII.

On returning to Sydney, at this time, we engaged apartments in the upper part of Pitt-street; for which, with
board in the family, we paid £2 a week, each. Here we
remained till we finally left the Colony, in the 3rd month,
1837.

10th mo. 29th. I had some conversation with an Independent Minister, appointed to Norfolk Island, who left
England single, by the advice of his friends. In the majority of cases, great advantages arises to persons emigrating, from taking suitable wives before leaving their own
country. Many have discovered their mistake, in coming
out single, after arriving in these Colonies. Even if a
man go into the interior, he is much more likely to succeed,
if he have a wife to take care of what he may leave in his
dwelling, be that ever so humble a one, while he is out
attending to his flocks; if his residence be in a town, such
a care taker is still necessary, for respectable house-keepers
are not easy to be obtained, because persons of this class
are generally soon sought out, by those wanting wives.

29th. A high wind raised such clouds of dust, as rendered it nearly impracticable to pass along the streets. The
frequency of this annoyance in summer, is a great objection
to a residence in the town, at this season.

30th. About twenty persons were present at our meeting. A large proportion of them, were of one family, lately arrived in the Colony, from amongst whom, a promising daughter died on the passage. In a little vocal service, I had to point out the imperative claims of religion, and the necessity of attending to the convictions of the Holy Spirit, if we would be led to Christ, and know him to abide with us.

11th mo. 1st. This morning, an assigned servant, who had resided some time in the family, and was remarkably sober, honest, and industrious, and possessed an unusual share of muscular strength, was suddenly taken ill, and died in about an hour and a half, in consequence of an affection of the heart. He had three attacks of spasm, and in the last exclaimed, "If I was only prepared to die!" he then cried for mercy, and almost instantly expired.—I was absent when the awful event took place, having a short time before taken a seat on the Liverpool coach, in order to visit the young man noticed on the 13th of 9th mo. On the coach, I met with a man, who was going to catch a horse, that had killed its rider, by dashing his head against a tree. After some very profligate persons, who, from their appearance and bad language, might be prisoners, had left the coach, I found an openness to speak with this individual, on the necessity and advantage of living in a state of preparation for death, and to explain to him the way of salvation. This man also left the coach before we reached Liverpool, and a woman got up, so drunk that I could not sit by her, either with propriety, or any degree of satisfaction; I therefore stepped over the roof, and found a place among some more sober people. The coach was not very strong, and the roads were rough, so that to some of the other passengers, as well as to myself, it was a great satisfaction to arrive safely at the end of our journey: this was perhaps, not an unfair specimen of Australian coach-travelling. Many of the roads are still mere tracks, and the practice of taking large quantities of strong drink, is very prevalent, and the proportion of persons of low morals, is great.

4th. I had some conversation with an intelligent settler,

who was awakened by shipwreck, to a consideration of the importance of eternal things; but like many others, he shrinks from taking up the cross, and practicing self-denial, and would rather trust solely to the death of Christ, for salvation, than esteem his propitiatory offering, as the means of redemption from sins that are past, and of perfecting for ever, those who submit to the sanctification of the Spirit unto obedience, and who consequently, seek divine help continually, to keep the precepts of Christ. Such persons would be saved by what Christ has done for them, without troubling themselves much about the practice of what he has enjoined; they seem to settle themselves down under a kind of systematic delusion, forgetting the declaration of the Redeemer, " Not every one that saith unto me Lord, Lord, shall enter the kingdom of heaven, but he that doeth the will of my Father which is in heaven."

12th. The day was very warm, with a strong wind from the north, of the character called in the Colony, a Hot Wind. These Hot Winds often injure the crops greatly, especially those of wheat, which they have already blighted, in the Hunter and Bathurst districts. In the latter, the wheat crops are so completely destroyed, that the inhabitants will be dependent upon Sydney for supplies. The abundance of grass will, however, render this less inconvenient, than it would have been last year. A frost cut off the chief part of their crop, in the tenth month, and the remainder, in the lower grounds, was destroyed by a hot-wind in the eleventh month. Much of that which escaped, in the higher grounds, was destroyed by hail; and that which escaped the hail, was soon after, devoured by caterpillars! In the evening, the wind changed suddenly to the southward, blowing with violence, as is usual in such cases, as noticed at p. 236.

In the course of the 11th and 12th months, we held meetings of a religious character, with the inhabitants of Sydney, who were invited to our meeting-house, in Macquarie Street, by notice from house to house, the town being divided into districts. The young man who gave the notice, distributed tracts at the same time, and frequently entered into conversation on religious subjects. He found several persons in Sydney, who had escaped from their creditors in the adjacent Colony, and many, in an exceedingly degraded, ignorant, and demoralized state. One man, who professed to be a Roman Catholic, told him, that he liked his own religion best, because he could get drunk two or three times a week, and then confess to one of their priests, and obtain absolution, which set all to right again! Another, calling himself a Protestant, said, he supposed no one would engage in such labour without being pretty well paid for it; but he thought the diligence of the young man, in going from house to house, was more than most would exercise for their money, and that he therefore deserved attention. In one of the districts of the town, two New Zealanders were found lying, without shelter, in a yard, exposed to the rain, and very ill: medical assistance was obtained for them; but one of them died before morning, as another had done a short time before. On the case being made known, an order was immediately given, to admit the survivor into the Benevolent Asylum, to which, however, he declined going.

We also visited the prisoners retained in the employment of the Government, in the Hyde Park Barracks, the Carters' Barracks, the Tread Mill, the New Jail, and the Hulks, as well as those on Goat Island, and in the Old Jail, and the patients in the Colonial Hospital, having the sanction of the Governor, in this service. In these visits, we were accompanied, to our comfort, by John C. S. Handt, who was at Wellington Valley, when we visited that Missionary station, and who was now, remaining with his family, in Sydney, for an opportunity to proceed to Moreton Bay, on a mission to the Aborigines there. The Hyde Park Barrack is the principal depôt of prisoners, in the Colony. It is a substantial, brick building, rather handsome, and of three stories, enclosed in an open area, formed by buildings of one story, with sloping roofs resting against the outside walls, at the angles of which there are circular, domed, small buildings. Some taste is also displayed in the gateway and other parts. The lower story of the central building,

is chiefly devoted to the offices of the Assignment-board,
&c. The second and third stories are divided into large
wards, in which the prisoners sleep in hammocks, in single
tiers. Those who arrive by one ship, occupy one ward, till
taken away by the masters to whom they are assigned.
This is a good regulation ; it keeps them in some measure,
from the contamination of the "old hands." The mechanics,
retained in the employment of the government, and some
others, are also lodged in separate wards. One ward, in a
side-building, has a barrack-bedstead, or platform, on which
the prisoners sleep side by side, without any separation.
There are only ten solitary cells in this prison, in which,
flagellation is the usual punishment. One of the officers,
who had been there only about fifteen months, said, that
upwards of one thousand men had been flogged in the course
of that period !   He stated his opinion to be, that how much
soever men may dread flagellation, when they have not been
subjected to it, they are generally degraded in their own esteem, and become reckless, after its infliction. This, we have
found to be a very prevailing opinion, in the Colony.

The Carters' Barracks are at the south end of Sydney,
and are now used as a debtors' jail, and as a barrack for an
ironed-gang, of about one hundred men, who, like the other
ironed-gangs in the district of Sydney, are under the superintendence of a military officer. The prisoners sleep on
platforms, that allow only one foot and a half to each man ;
they are under a close, military guard, in brick buildings,
opening into a separate yard, and the place is very clean.
The treadmill is contiguous, but is under distinct superintendence. It has one wheel, for eighteen men, and another,
for ten ; and when the mill is not at work, the men are kept
running round a circle, in the yard. There are now about
eighty men, under sentence to this punishment.

The new Jail is an unfinished building, upon a good
plan. It is at present occupied by an Ironed-gang, and
about 130 prisoners, employed in the Mineral Surveyor's
Department. The Ironed-gang is employed in quarrying
stone, &c. They are lodged in "boxes," in the Jail-yard,
accommodating twenty-five men in each, and are under

the same kind of guard and discipline, as the Ironed-gangs in the interior. On our visit, they assembled in the mess-shed; at first, the Roman Catholics separated them-selves, to be locked up, while we addressed the others; but on being informed, that we belonged to no class of ordained clergymen, and received no pecuniary remunera-tion for our labours, and that persons of their persuasion had often assembled with us, in other places, they joined the rest, and the whole were very attentive and orderly.

After visiting the men, in the department of the Mineral Surveyor, we accompanied the person filling that office, to a tunnel, which he is forming, from the Botany Bay Swamps, which is nearly completed, and brings the water to Sydney. This tunnel is arched with hewn stone; it is two feet wide, four feet high, and about two miles long. The water from it is laid in iron pipes into various parts of Sydney, but it is not yet distributed to private houses. The Botany Bay Swamps are natural reservoirs, being ex-tensive basons, in sandstone rock. One of them occupies about 1,000 acres, and is filled with sand, which keeps the water pure; it is overgrown with shrubs, but is of great depth, and contains a vast body of water. Few of these reservoirs exhibit water on the surface, beyond what renders the soil a little boggy; but some small streams ooze from them, and in two or three cases, their surface is pure white sand. Most of them are ornamented with gay shrubs and plants, which also abound on the adjacent sandy hills, in many places on the sides of which, the sandstone rocks are bare. The marshes are now gay with *Callistemon lan-ceolatus,* a low, rigid, willow-like shrub, with clusters of crimson flowers, like bottle brushes, surrounding the stem, and with *Blandfordia nobilis,* a plant with an erect stem, about a foot and a half high, crowned by about a dozen pendent flowers, an inch long, tubular, and as thick as a swan's quill, sealing-wax red, tipped with orange at the six-cleft mouth. There are also upon these swamps, several other striking shrubs and plants, among which may be enu-merated *Melaleuca thymifolia,* and *armillaris, Epacris obtusi-folia, Drosera pedata, Villarsia elata,* and *Utricularia speciosa,*

and *violacea*. On the low hills there are *Correa speciosa,
Stenanthera pinifolia, Roeperia pinifolia*, and several species
of *Banksia, Leptospermum, Leucopogon*, &c. The shrubs
on these low hills and swamps, gave the name of Botany
Bay, to the bay by which access was first gained to
them. Some of the swamps are formed into gardens,
which, retaining their moisture, supply the Sydney market
in summer.

The Phœnix Hulk is moored off a small island, in Port
Jackson, and is occupied by men, sentenced to Penal Settlements, who work on shore, in chains, under a military
guard. At the time of our visit, it contained about 200
men.—The prisoners on Goat Island also amount to about
200, most of them are in irons; they are employed in
erecting a powder-magazine, which is nearly completed,
and is of sandstone. Internally, it is an arch, of 25
feet wide, and 100 feet long. The prisoners are lodged
in twelve wooden "boxes," which are whitewashed inside
and out, and are very clean. Each of these boxes is furnished with a few Bibles, Testaments, and Prayer Books.
When addressing the people, in the mess-shed, in which
one of the Colonial Chaplains preaches to them every other
Seventh-day, and J. C. S. Handt occasionally, they were
very attentive, and there was more comfort, in preaching
to them the glad tidings of the Gospel, with warning and
exhortation, than is sometimes the case. Among prisoners,
under such discipline as keeps them entirely from strong
drink, we are generally sensible of more openness for receiving religious instruction, and of a more comforting
sense of the divine presence, while communicating it, than
among the generality of the free people of the Colony.

After this visit, and the publication of an Address to the
Prisoner Population of New South Wales and Van Diemens
Land, which was read to the people on Goat Island, by a
pious young man, who frequently visited them, a remarkable
letter was addressed to us, anonymously, by one of the prisoners, and placed in the Bible of the Catechist, who communicated it to us, and promised to endeavour to make out
the writer, with a view of attending to his case.—For the

Address to the Prisoner Population, and the letter here referred to, see APPENDIX. L. and M.

The Old Jail was an inconvenient building, in George Street, the principal street in Sydney, and was soon to be superseded by the new one, which was a little out of the town. At the time of our visit, it contained about 180 prisoners, male and female : the number had often been nearly 300. They were visited by a Colonial Chaplain, at least once a week, and occasionally by J. C. S. Handt, or some other pious person. Five men were under sentence of death, two of whom expected to be executed the following week. The number of executions in N. S. Wales was, at this period, very great, in proportion to its population, compared with the number in Great Britain.

The Colonial Hospital is a commodious building, in Macquarie Street, forming a portion of the same range with the Council Rooms, &c. It has seven wards, and at the time of our visit, contained 130 patients, most of whom were, or had been, prisoners.

The Benevolent Asylum is an institution for the support of the indigent; it is under the care of a committee, chosen at an annual, public meeting, of the subscribers toward its maintenance. Any deficiency in its funds, is made up by the Government, in consideration of most of the inmates having been brought out as prisoners. On our visit, the Roman Catholics were invited, but they declined coming, saying they could not without leave from their priests. There were at this time, upwards of 200 inmates in this institution, about one-third of whom were females   Several of them were very aged, and lamentably depraved. Strong drink has brought many of them, both young and old, to the state of destitution they are in ; and some of them have so strong a desire for liquor, that they abscond from this comfortable refuge, climbing over the fence to obtain it.

Early in the 12th mo. we received a quantity of books and tracts, unapplied for, from our friends in Yorkshire. We could not but regard this free-will offering, on their part, as a special favour from the Lord, who, we doubt not, stirred them up to make it. Without such a supply, we should have been without the means of continuing to disperse religious information, as we have hitherto done, during our visit to these Colonies, which would have been painful to us, at this juncture, when we have a better opportunity for this description of service, than we have before had.

12th mo. 19th. We received a pleasant letter from a person at Maitland, whose faith had been put to the test, with regard to taking an oath: he had previously become willing, if called to do so, to suffer for bearing a testimony against the practice of swearing. He was summoned as a juryman, at the Quarter Sessions. When his name was called, he stood up, and said he could not take an oath. Why? asked the chairman. Because the book, on which you swear me, tells me not to swear at all, was the reply. The chairman looked angry, and said he could not take such an excuse; but an attorney, who sat by, said, an affirmation could be taken, if the party were a Quaker. Are you a Quaker? asked the chairman. I cannot say I am, was the answer, but if there was a Quakers' meeting here, I would certainly attend it. It was then decided that the affirmation of the party should be taken, and he affirmed accordingly, and served as a juryman, upon two trials.

About this time, a young man, who had filled the office of clerk to one of the Colonial Chaplains, in the interior, but had resigned this office, on conscientious grounds, was subpœned to Sydney, as a witness on a trial, and declined taking an oath. When called upon to state his grounds of objection, he referred to the command of Christ, " Swear not at all;" and when it was urged, that an oath was only a solemn declaration, calling upon God to witness, (a mistaken view which was entertained by the pious Judge on the bench) the young man replied, that if it could be made to appear, that to take an oath, was not to swear at all, he would willingly take the oath; but that till that was done, he could not take it conscientiously. On inquiry being made, if he were a Quaker, a Moravian, or a Separatist, he signified that he was brought up in the Episcopal Church, and remained in its communion, though he did not believe in all the thirty-nine articles, and that he was ignorant of the sentiments of the Moravians

and Separatists.   One of the absurdities of the English
law, which still exists, construes such a refusal into contempt of court! and the Judge was consequently under
the necessity of committing him to the charge of the Sheriff's Officer; but the young man was not removed out of
court.   He had, however, made up his mind to suffer imprisonment, rather than violate his conscience; but when
the court broke up, the Judge discharged him, saying, he
had no doubt respecting the young man's objection being a
conscientious one.   A Magistrate, in another court, in this
Colony, of a different spirit to the Judge who was on the
bench on this occasion, threatened a young man, with imprisonment, who objected to swear, in obedience to the commands of his Lord and Saviour, and succeeded, in connexion with the expostulations of deluded friends, in turning
the young man from his steadfastness.

Among the tracts which we circulated extensively, at this
time, was " A Christian Address to the Free Inhabitants
of New South Wales and Van Diemens Land," written in
the prospect of an early departure from these Colonies, and
which is introduced in APPENDIX. N.   Large editions of
this Address, as well as of that, to the Prisoner Population,
were printed in Sydney, in very respectable style, and at
a moderate charge.

CHAPTER XXXIX.

North Harbour.—Pumice-stone.—Animals, &c.—School and Temperance Societies.—Tidings of D. and C. Wheeler.—Report to the Governor.—Sense
of Unprofitableness.—Botany Bay.—La Perouse.—Circumnavigation.—Butterflies.—Fishermen.—Silent Meetings.—Drunkenness.—Convict Servants.—
Arrival of D. and C. Wheeler.—Visit to the Governor.—Refraction.—Factory.
—Aborigines.—Elizabeth Macquarie.—Departure from N. S. Wales.—Voyage
to V. D. Land.—Jervis Bay.—Sheds, &c. of Aborigines.—Jelly-fish.—Storm.
—Lying to.—Albatross.—Arrival at Hobart Town.

1st mo. 5th, 1837. WE walked to the North Harbour of
Port Jackson, to visit a family who frequently attended our
meetings. On the way, we met with many beautiful insects,
upon the flowers of *Anyophora cordifolia,* such as *Buprestis
grandis, variabilis* and *macularia,* and *Cetonia frontinalis.*
Many of the insects of New South Wales are of splendid
appearance. We also saw several interesting plants, among
which was *Dendrobium ruscifolium,* a large tuft of which
was growing on the sandstone rock.

6th. We visited one of the bays, north of Port Jackson,
on the north shore of which, there were banks of Pumice-
stone. This volcanic production has, at some period,
drifted with a south-east wind and a high sea, into many
similar places on this coast. A lizard, three feet long, was
running among the rocks. On G. W. Walker's attempting
to catch it, he received a blow from its rough tail, that
brought the skin off his hand. Within the influence of the
salt water, the beautiful *Crinum pedunculatum* was producing heads of fragrant, white, tubular, lily-like blossoms.—
In a morning walk, I set up a Wild Dog, which made off
with speed. These animals, though of wolfish appearance,
are very shy. We returned to Sydney in the evening.

A few mornings ago, in a walk before breakfast, I fell in with a large Emu, at a short distance from Sydney, which probably had been domesticated, as it exhibited no signs of fear on my approach. The Emu retreats from the haunts of man, and is now rarely seen, except in remote places in the interior.

9th. We attended the meeting of the Committee of the Australian School Society, at which, information was received, that Government had granted a piece of land, for the site of a school-house. The Girls' School is in a prosperous state, the prospect of that for boys is improving.

10th. We were present at a Committee of the Temperance Society, which is about to issue a twopenny, monthly publication, on the plan of the Temperance Penny Magazine. While the Committee was sitting, there were repeated cries of "Murder," to which no one gave any attention, for some time. At length, one of the persons present remarked, with a sigh, that he saw that the rest of the company had, like himself, become callous to such cries, from their frequency, in consequence of the prevailing intemperance.—Subsequently to this period, the question of Total Abstinence from all intoxicating liquors, was successfully taken up in Sydney; and in 1841, the members of the Total Abstinence Society, amounted to 1,842.

17th. We received from Henry Bobart, a Missionary, just returned from New Zealand, the pleasing intelligence that our dear friends Daniel and Charles Wheeler, had arrived in safety at the Bay of Islands, and were likely soon to return to this Colony. Their visit had been very reviving to the New Zealand Missionaries, who, on both sides of the island, had been greatly cast down by the misconduct of some of their own body, and by contentions among the native tribes.

21st. Through the medium of the Colonial Secretary, we forwarded to the Governor, "A Report, on various subjects connected with the state of the Colony of New South Wales," which we thought it our duty to submit to his notice before our departure, and which is inserted in APPENDIX. O.

22nd. The weather lately, has been very wet. To-day it rained nearly without intermission; generally, there are fair intervals in the course of the day. Our meetings were small, and held in silence. Now that our labours in New South Wales are nearly concluded, it is my lot to dwell much under the feeling of emptiness and unprofitableness. For this I desire to be thankful, for were it otherwise, I might be in danger of taking to myself, the glory of any little services that I have been enabled to perform, instead of giving it to the Lord, who gave the qualification, and in whose sight no flesh may glory, without condemnation.

27th. We went to Botany Bay, to pay a farewell visit to a family of our acquaintance. On the way, we got upon a newly-drained marsh, the surface of which was dry, and so light, that we often broke through, to the water which remained underneath.

28th. We walked to the north head of Botany Bay, to visit the Custom-house officer, stationed there; who, we were glad to find, had strictly adhered to temperance principles, for the last thirteen months. The officer at the Light-house, at the heads of Port Jackson, and one of the pilots, have also adopted temperance principles, greatly to their advantage. At the north head of Botany Bay, stands the monument, erected by the French Government, on the spot from which La Perouse embarked, when he last sailed from this land, in 1788. No tidings respecting him were obtained from that period, till within a few years, when Chevalier Dillon ascertained, that he was wrecked on a small Island, near the Fegee group. Contiguous to the monument, is a rude tomb, containing the remains of a French priest and physician, who was attached to the party of La Perouse, in their expedition to circumnavigate the globe. This exploit, so much thought of at that period, is now performed by almost every vessel from England, to N. S. Wales or V. D. Land; as these come out by way of the Cape of Good Hope, and return by Cape Horn, in consequence of the wind, in the latitudes of the Southern Hemisphere, in which they have to sail, blowing almost constantly from the west. Near the Heads of Botany Bay,

gay butterflies were numerous. Some of those in this part of
the Colony, are remarkable for having the upper sides simply white, or mottled, while the under sides are exceedingly
gay with various colours. Two noble, dark coloured,
species are frequent about Sydney; where they, with many
others, are occasionally to be seen in the streets. In returning, we passed a row of fishermen's huts, near to which two
men were mending their nets. We had some conversation
with them, reminding them of the fishermen of Galilee, and
of that Gospel which they were chosen to proclaim. Not
being unmindful of their temporal interests, we instructed
them in the art of making shrimp-nets, and taking shrimps;
of which there are plenty on the neighbouring shoals, but
they are rarely brought to the Sydney market.

29th. Twenty persons were present at meeting, in the
forenoon, and eighteen, in the evening. Both meetings
were held in silence. This seemed hard for some of the
company to bear: three of them left in the evening, before
the meeting concluded: such an occurrence is by no means
unfrequent. It is lamentable to see how little idea, even
the professors of Christianity generally, have of communing
with their own hearts, in silence before the Lord, or of
quietly waiting upon him, in stillness. Their religion is
too much a temporary excitement, produced by external
influence; and their waiting in public worship, it is to be
feared, is rather upon man, that he may produce this excitement, than directly upon God.

30th. On returning to our lodgings, last evening, we
found the family in a state of alarm. While some of them
were at a place of worship, two of the servants had gone out,
and got drunk, and on their return, had cruelly beaten a poor,
Mauritian Black, who was also a prisoner-servant, in the
house: his cries brought in a neighbour, who by the free
use of a horse-whip, made the drunkards desist; but they
had severely bruised the object of their spleen. Subsequently, the black man preferred a charge against the others,
before the Magistrates, and they were sent to prison.
Servants of the convict class, are amongst the greatest
drawbacks upon domestic comfort, in these Colonies; and

by their drunkenness, they clearly shew, that the use of intoxicating liquors has been a principal cause of their becoming convicts.

31st. We were greatly comforted, by the return of our dear friends, Daniel and Charles Wheeler, who, in the course of the forenoon, arrived in Sydney Cove, on board the Henry Freeling. They seemed in more vigorous health than when they left, and their crew had behaved remarkably well, during their voyage among the islands of the Pacific; where the religious labours of our friends appear to have been well received.

2nd mo. 15th. Having received a note from the Private Secretary, informing us that the Governor was shortly to leave this part of the Colony, on a visit to Port Phillip, from which he would not be likely to return before the departure of G. W. Walker and myself, and inviting us to visit him again at Parramatta, we took the steamer, in the evening, and joined him and a few of his friends, at tea, at the Government House. The Governor courteously acknowledged our Report, made many inquiries respecting the subjects of our observations, conversed freely respecting the state of the Aborigines, and inquired, as he had also done on former occasions, if we remembered anything in which he could forward our views, or be helpful to us. This visit made way for our addressing to the Governor subsequently, the letters respecting the Aborigines, introduced at APPENDIX. P. We were politely invited to lodge at the Government House; but having previously engaged to accept the hospitality of P. L. and B. Campbell, whose relatives we expected to meet in Africa, we returned to their dwelling. On the way, we were amused with the refraction of the moon's rays, on the dewy grass, presenting a luminous radiation, around the shadows of our heads. This appearance is sometimes also produced by the rays of the sun, when a person is in a position to see his own shadow in the sea, over the side of a ship; in both cases, he sees little, if anything of it, on the shadow of any one except himself.

16th. We called at the Factory, the superintendent of

G G

which has been changed, and many alterations for the better have been introduced, but the difficulties are considerable, in managing so many women, of this class, in a building, badly arranged, especially with slender help, from persons imbued with a feeling of Christian benevolence toward its unhappy inmates.—In the evening, we returned to Sydney, and on the passage had the company of the Episcopal Bishop of Australia, who also was on board yesterday: he is an agreeable man, and seems desirous of promoting the religious welfare of the Colony.

19th. Twenty-five persons were present at the forenoon meeting, and twenty-three at that in the evening. In the former, D. Wheeler bore a short testimony, to the necessity of knowing Christ, by the revelation of his Spirit, as a light within, reproving for sin, and making known the way of holiness, as well as giving ability to walk therein. I also added a few sentences, confirming the same, from my own experience, under a fresh sense of that divine mercy, which not only grants us access to the Father, through his beloved Son, but also heals our backslidings, forgives our iniquities, restores our souls, and leads us in paths of righteousness for his name's sake. The Epistle from the Yearly Meeting, held in London, in 1836, was read by G. W. Walker, at the conclusion of the meeting.

20th. We received a letter from Lancelot E. Threlkeld, with copies of his Report on the Mission to the Aborigines at Lake Macquarie, for 1836. By this document, it appears, that little success, of an obvious kind, has attended the labour bestowed, and much has occurred to discourage. In the remote parts of the Colony, a spirit of discord between the black and the white population, seems to be increasing, in consequence of the Blacks spearing the cattle of the Whites, the flesh of which they smoke-dry, and thus preserve for food. This is said to have been taught them by a run-away prisoner, and in consequence, several lives have been lost. Some of the Blacks have been destroyed, both by the police, and by stock-keepers, and a few of the latter have fallen by the Blacks.

28th. We visited the School of Industry, in which

twenty-five poor girls are boarded, clothed, and educated. It was established by Elizabeth Macquarie, the wife of Governor Macquarie, and is one of the many good works of this excellent woman, that remain a testimony to her benevolent zeal. She also established a school for the Aborigines, at Parramatta, which was afterwards abandoned; and laid out some extensive public walks, leading round a picturesque, wooded point, adjacent to Sydney, and projecting into Port Jackson; and she laboured diligently to promote good morals, in regard to marriage, at a period when they were lamentably low in the Colony.

Several groups of Blacks are now in town, from districts of the coast, to the southward. As is too commonly the case, they are much intoxicated. When walking this morning, I saw several parties of them by little fires, around which they had been sleeping. One of them, who had his hand in a sling, said he cut it, when drunk, yesterday. I asked another, whose shirt was besmeared with blood, what made him in that condition. He replied " Drink, sir." Thus, these poor creatures are injured by the profligacy of the white population, who give them drink, till their tribes are fast perishing from the face of the earth.

3rd mo. 5th. Twenty-five persons were present at meeting in the forenoon, and about twenty in the evening. D. Wheeler bore short and lively testimonies in both. In the morning I also expressed a few sentences, both in testimony and supplication, under a continued exercise for the welfare of those assembled, and an impression, that we might meet many of them, no more again, in this world.

12th. We went on board the Francis Freeling, a barque, of 190 tons burthen, lying in Darling Harbour. The wind, though light, being favourable, we sailed, and glided gently along the smooth waters of Port Jackson, the Heads of which, we cleared about three o'clock. The only devotional exercise of a public kind that we were equal to, was that of reading a chapter in the New Testament.—In leaving New South Wales, I was favoured with a peaceful mind, under the feeling of having discharged the religious duty required of me, toward its inhabitants, and with the hope that the labour bestowed, had not been altogether in vain in the Lord.

Voyages from N. S. Wales to V. D. Land, at this season of the year, are often tedious and stormy. Ours proved of this character. On the 13th, we were off Jervis Bay, but were driven back to Shoal Haven. During the following two days, we made little progress. On the 17th, we passed Montague Island. The wind being adverse on the 18th, and a heavy sea getting up, we beat off the land. The 19th was very stormy and wet. We ran back before a high sea, and at noon, descried land, and the Pigeon-house Hill; we then stood for Jervis Bay, within the friendly shelter of which, we came safely to anchor, just as the day closed. We read a chapter in the New Testament, in the morning, with a few of our cabin passengers, all of whom were sober, orderly persons, and some of them decidedly pious. A larger number assembled in the evening, when, after another chapter had been read, most of the company retired to rest, being fatigued and exhausted, in body and mind, by the continued rolling of the vessel, and the excitement of looking out for the land. It was a great comfort to be among those who bore these things patiently, and a greater, to remember that we were under the notice of Him who, when his disciples were afraid, because of the agitation of the billows, said, "Peace, be still, and there was a great calm," and without whose knowledge not a sparrow falls.

20th. Being nearly out of water, a few of us went on shore, with the boat that went for a supply. We landed near a rude building, used at the proper season for the salting of beef. Large herds of horned cattle are fed in the wilds of this part of N. S. Wales, from which beef is extensively exported, especially from Twofold Bay, to Hobart Town. The forest on the sides of Jervis Bay was much like that of other sandy soils in the Colony, and abounded with Parrots and Bell-birds. The tinkling note of the last, is only heard in low grounds, and near water. We saw some Blacks fishing: some of their hooks were formed of pieces of shell, but they preferred English ones, of steel.—In the evening, one of them commenced making a shelter for the night, of slabs of bark set up against sticks in the form of a pyramid, such as is represented in the accompanying cut. Shelters of this kind, or of bark,

raised in the form of a roof, are amongst the best habitations of these people, in this part of Australia; most commonly, they only prop up a large sheet or two of bark, with sticks, and thus make a shelter to windward, with a fire in front.

21st. We renewed our stock of beef from the shore, and again put to sea, the wind having become favourable.—In coming out of the Bay, we passed some Jelly-fish, of a hemispherical form, with fringed margins and long tentaculæ, of a remarkably deep purple: they appeared to be of the form represented in the margin, but I had not the opportunity of examining them closely.

On the 23rd, the wind again became adverse, and on the 25th the vessel became unmanageable, from the violence of the storm; the helm was therefore lashed, and we lay-to, under a close-reefed topsail, and a portion of a trisail. The latter soon became so torn as to require to be taken in. The wind now roared awfully in the rigging, but as the vessel yielded a little to it, and presented no resistance to the raging sea, she rode lightly, like an Albatross, over the tops of the foaming billows, and rarely caught, even the spray; notwithstanding the force of the wind, carried it, like a sheet of rain, near the surface of the broken water, which formed streaks of white, on the deep-blue ocean. A large shark kept near us, for the sake of the shelter of our lea, as did also many Stormy Petrels. The scene was magnificently grand, and the state of the Francis Freeling, afforded a lively emblem of the efficacy of pacific principles. Under the divine blessing on her non-resistance, she rode safely through the gale, notwithstanding the probability seemed to be, that the sea would have swallowed her up, had she continued to contend against the rage of its billows. The gale moderated on the 26th. During its continuance, as well as for some time after, large numbers of a species of Albatross, about the size of a large Gull, and which is common in these seas, accompanied the vessel; often soaring around it, or resting under its lea.

On the 31st, we sighted the land, off which we had been driven, without nautical instruments to detect our position, and on the 1st of 4th month, we came safely to anchor in Sulivans Cove. Thus terminated this memorable voyage, in which, though our patience was exercised by its length, the ground of our eternal hopes proved, by its storms, and many kinds of provision had become low, by its protracted duration, we had great cause to commemorate the goodness of our Heavenly Father, who sustained our minds by a sense of his mercy in Christ Jesus, when from the oppression of the animal spirits, occasioned by continued nausea, in consequence of the rolling of the vessel, there was a physical tendency to depression.

CHAPTER XL.

On landing in Hobart Town, we found that our old friends,
T. J. and S. Crouch, had removed from their former residence, into Harrington Street, and their family had increased,
so as to render them unable again to receive us as their
lodgers; we therefore took apartments at the Freemasons
Hotel, a quiet, clean house, next door to them.

The day after landing, we had again the privilege of
meeting for worship, with the persons professing the same
religious principles as ourselves. Their number was still
but small, but some of them had evidently grown in grace,
and a few more of them occasionally spoke in the line of
Gospel ministry. The family of Mathers had removed into
the town, greatly to their own comfort, and the satisfaction
of their friends. Some of them were very helpful in our
little church; the members of which, by seeking to the
Lord for help, had been enabled to maintain the ground of
true gospel-fellowship, and to deal with a few of their number, who had turned out of the right way. Some of this
class had been convinced of their error, and restored to
unity, and others, on whom labour proved unavailing, were
testified against and disowned.

We took an early opportunity of paying our respects to
Sir John Franklin, the new Lieutenant Governor, who

received us kindly, and offered to forward, what he was
pleased to call, our objects of " benevolence and philanthro-
phy," in any way in his power. We were glad to see a
man, whose intention appeared to be to do good, succeed to
Colonel Arthur ; but we felt no sympathy with a great part
of the Colonists, with whom the latter had become un-
popular, through the influence of dissatisfied men, of party
spirit, who being in a wrong mind themselves, took great
pains to prejudice others against this worthy man.

The cause of Temperance had made some progress during our absence. The town had been divided into districts,
in which meetings for the promotion of this object were
held periodically, in rotation.—Since this time, a further
step has been taken with a view to stem the torrent
of iniquity, connected with the use of intoxicating drinks,
and a society has been formed to promote total abstinence
from them; which it is devoutly to be hoped, may be
blessed, to the removal of the example of respectable persons using that, which often proves a deadly snare to their
own souls, and which presents one of the greatest impediments to the moral and religious improvement of mankind.

A few of the pensioners who came to the Colony with
us, in the Science, were still in this neighbourhood, but
several had been removed by death, chiefly from drinking
intoxicating liquors. A very small number of the remnant,
maintained themselves above poverty.

4th mo. 14th. One of the pensioners called upon us,
presenting a forlorn specimen of the effects of instability
and inebriety. According to his own statement, he gave
up a little farm in England, on which he was doing well,
to follow a vicious woman, who forsook him upon the
voyage, after having wasted all that he had. Since he
came to this Land, his propensity for strong drink had
been a constant hinderance to his prosperity. About two
years ago, a tree fell upon him, on Bruny Island, from the
effects of which he still suffers. Thus, "a stranger in a
strange land," and half a cripple, he is a burden to the
public and to himself.—Bitter indeed is the fruit of sin!
But when sin is forsaken, great is the mercy extended, and

sweet is the fruit of righteousness! Of this we had an interesting illustration, in a visit we paid to-day, to John Johnson, of Glenorchy, who is now in his seventy-seventh year. He is an affecting picture of human infirmity, so tottering as scarcely to be able to walk, and when he falls, he is unable to rise again without help; his speech is so nearly gone, as scarcely to be intelligible; and he has a bleeding-cancer on his breast, that often pours out blood till it runs into his shoes; but he has many who care for him, out of Christian love, and on whose beneficence he is entirely dependent. The state of his mind, though not exempt from occasional conflict, is generally peaceful. Often he is favoured with the aboundings of the consolations which are in Christ Jesus, which, in his simple language, he describes, as being as if heaven broke over his head; such an overflowing as he cannot convey an idea of. He says he is quite willing to go, whenever his Master shall be pleased to call him, but is endeavouring to wait patiently, knowing that he shall be called, when the Lord sees him to be fully prepared.

While we were with this good old man, some of his pious neighbours came in, who occasionally hold a meeting at his house, as he is unable to go out. He says he has now many comfortable " blanket prayers," not being able to get out of bed to kneel down, as was formerly his practice. The necessity of this, he was led to question, by his inability, and his views have become much more simple and scriptural, both upon the nature of prayer, and of worship generally.

18th. While in Sydney, I was reduced in weight, by the heat of the climate, to 111 lbs. nevertheless my health was good. At the time of our last arrival in V. D. Land, I weighed 112 lbs. and to-day I weigh 119 lbs. having gained 7 lbs. in two weeks, in this cooler climate. I continued to gain flesh rapidly, till reaching my usual weight of about 124 lbs. which I never much exceeded.

22nd. The Aurora australis was very brilliant, notwithstanding the moon was shining brightly. This beautiful, electric phenomenon presented vivid shades of crimson, yellow and white; the last was in columnar streaks. It was also striking, in the same colours, on the 1st instant, when we landed from the Francis Freeling. The common appearance of the Aurora australis, in this latitude, is a diffuse, yellowish light, on the horizon. It rarely presents bright corruscations, or a columnar figure, like the Aurora borealis, as seen in England.

25th. We joined Philip Palmer, one of the Colonial Chaplains, in a visit to the schools for boys and girls, that are under his superintendence, and are conducted on the plan of the British and Foreign School System. They are supported by the Government, and by the payments of the children, who are admitted at from 6d. to 9d. a week. In the boys' school, the average attendance, is seventy-three, out of one hundred and five, on the list. The school for girls has a daily average of forty-six out of fifty-six. The premises, which are not well adapted, were not erected for the purpose; but the experiment of the application of the system, has proved satisfactory, notwithstanding a little opposition from the prejudice of some persons, that it has to contend with. In the institution of these schools, we furnished a stock of lessons, &c. from those committed to our care, by the committee of the British and Foreign School Society.

30th. Our meetings were held at half-past ten and three o'clock, these hours being convenient to many of those who attend. In the forenoon twenty-two adults were present, with nine children; and in the afternoon about the same number of adults. Many of the children who are brought to meeting here, are infants, the mothers of which have no suitable persons with whom to leave them. They occasion, surprisingly little disturbance, and the children derive a great advantage from being thus habituated from infancy, to quietness, and consequently to self-denial.

On the 1st of 5th month, we set out on horseback, to visit some other parts of the Island, and were absent from Hobart Town till the end of the month. We made interesting calls on several of the settlers. Their circumstances had generally become greatly improved, since our former visits. This improvement was not generally attributable to any thing resulting from their own industry, or good management, but from the increased value of Australian wool in the English market, from the demand for sheep to export to the new settlement of Port Philip, from the increase of Emigrants, bringing capital into the Colony, and from the extension of Banks, supplying more copiously a circulating medium. These changes had occasioned such an advance in the value of property, as placed many persons in comparative affluence, who were before, in embarrassed circumstances. Many of these, however, increased their expenditure proportionately to their improved income, and subsequently felt severely, the pressure of a falling market.

We travelled to Kelvedon, by way of Richmond and the Eastern Marshes. A small road-party was employed in improving the rugged path, across the Rocky Hills, in Great Swanport, which was yet impassable for carriages.

On reaching the peaceful habitation of our dear friends, Francis and Anna Maria Cotton, and their large family, we found them in good health, and in sitting in silence with them, before and after their frugal meals, as well as at their family readings of the Holy Scriptures, and in their meetings for worship, we were permitted to partake with them, of a sweet sense of our Heavenly Father's love.

We held a few meetings in this neighbourhood, to which the inhabitants were invited, and in which Francis and Anna Maria Cotton, Dr. Story, and a young man, formerly a prisoner, sometimes joined us in Gospel labour. In some of these meetings, the exercise of our minds was much of the character of being baptized for the spiritually dead. But this ought to be borne with patience, and even with thankfulness, " if so be that the dead be raised" through this means; and as " the servant is not greater than his Lord," it is to be expected, that where the government of Christ is rejected, his servants will feel painfully oppressed in spirit; for to them it is given, even in this sense, not only to believe in Christ, but also to suffer for his sake.

On the 16th, we set forward toward Launceston, by way of Waterloo Point, St. Pauls Plains, and Perth. So little rain had fallen for several months, in this part of the country, that the water-mills were almost useless, and the cattle were distressed for want of grass: that which remained of the abundant growth of last spring, was dry upon the ground, and the ploughing and sowing of the land were much retarded. Since the Aborigines were removed from V. D. Land, the Opossums and Brush Kangaroos have increased in many districts, and are very troublesome to the agriculturist, making incursions on his grain and turnip-crops.

Among the settlers whom we visited in this part of our journey, some had evidently grown in grace. An affecting accident had occurred in one of their families, calculated to excite solemn reflection. A gay young man had been expostulated with, by an affectionate relative, on his thoughtlessness respecting the state of his soul. He had replied, that he was yet young, and it was time enough for him to think of such things. A few days after this, his horse ran off with him, from the door of this relative, and dashing his head against a tree, killed him on the spot!

Near Perth, we passed a gibbet, lately erected; on which the body of a prisoner who committed a murder near the spot, was suspended, with a view of deterring from crime. But so unsuccessful was this first experiment of the kind in Tasmania, that pocket-picking and drunkenness occurred among the crowd, who resorted thither to view the hideous spectacle. Popular feeling was so strong, against the transfer of this political barbarism to the Australian regions, that it was officially resolved, that this first experiment should be the last.

We arrived at Launceston on the 19th. I again became the guest of my friends Isaac and Katharine Sherwin; while G. W. Walker availed himself of the opportunity of visiting some of his relatives, who were now residing a few miles from this town.—The Factory, lately erected here, for female prisoners, is very superior for the purpose, to the one it superseded, at George Town; but it is already found to be too small. There are now one hundred prisoners within its walls. —The town of Launceston is greatly improved since our first visit. Its population, which included the district, and amounted in 1831, to 2,500, is now 7,185. Many good, brick houses have been erected, and several public buildings, as well as large meeting-houses, belonging the Wesleyans, Independents, and Presbyterians; and the place seems as much improved in morals as in other respects.

We left Launceston on the 24th, and, visiting some pious persons on Norfolk Plains, on the way, reached Barton, on the Isis, the residence of Andrew Gatenby, an old Yorkshire acquaintance, on the 25th; intending to proceed on our journey the following day; but feeling the constraining influence of the love of Christ, toward the settlers in this neighbourhood, we obtained leave to invite them to meet us at Barton, on the 28th. A member of our own Society, from Yorkshire, was now living with a relative, at a house near to Barton, named Skelton Castle. With this individual, as well as with several persons of our former acquaintance, not making the same religious profession, we had much interesting converse on the things belonging eternal life.

Andrew Gatenby left Yorkshire, at a period of difficulty among farmers, in that county, and settled for a time in Wales. Here he found his rent too high, to admit of his making a livelihood for his family, even with his industrious habits; he therefore determined to emigrate to V. D. Land. When his landlord found that he was really intending to leave his farm in Wales, he offered to lower the rent; but A. Gatenby had already made arrangements for his projected voyage; and he now says, that it has been better for his circumstances, that he has emigrated, than it would have been, to have accepted the farm in Wales, as a gift. On arriving in Tasmania, he obtained a good grant of land, under the regulations then existing; upon which, himself and family, several of whom were sons, worked diligently with their own hands. Perhaps in no country, is the adage more true than in this, " He that by the plough would thrive, himself must either hold or drive." They tilled their own land, made their own bricks, and built their own house, with the help of a few prisoner-servants; and they have now one of the most complete farming

establishments in the Island.   In the early part of their residence here, their house was attacked by Bushrangers, one
of whom was shot by one of A. Gatenby's sons; and one
of his sons lost his life, by some hostile Aborigines.   These
causes of alarm and distress are now removed from the
country, in which life is nevertheless much more frequently
terminated by accidents, than in England.   In speaking
respecting a neighbour that A. Gatenby had in Yorkshire,
and whom he esteemed very highly, and would gladly have
had for a neighbour, in Tasmania, he said—"You may
tell him how I have done, but do not say I advise him to
come.   You know all have not done so well as I have, and
I do not know how he might succeed."

On the 28th.   A considerable number of persons attended
the meeting at Barton.   A comforting sense of the divine
presence was with us, and we felt much freedom, in directing
the company to the revelation of the Spirit in the secret of
their own hearts, leading those who yield to its guidance, out
of darkness into light, and bringing them from under the
power of Satan, to God.   The spirit of infidelity which has
deluded some in this neighbourhood, was shown to be of
Satan, and its destructive tendency was variously illustrated.
Eighteen of the company afterwards partook of the hospitality of A. Gatenby, in his large and well-furnished dining-
room.   The arrangements, dinner, and Yorkshire dialect
of many of the party, forcibly reminded us of our dear
Native Land, and of some of its scenes and inhabitants.

29th.   Pursuing our journey, we passed through Campbell Town and Ross; both of which are considerably increased in size, and have had Episcopal places of worship
erected in them, since our last visit to this part of the
Island.   In the evening we reached Mona Vale, calling on
the way upon our patriarchal friend, George Parramore, and
upon a few other settlers.

30th.   The morning, was very cold.   There was thin
ice on the pools, and the vegetation was beautifully whitened,
with hoar-frost, especially the leaves of the Acacias.   The
fog scarcely admitted the houses at Green Ponds to be
distinguished, in riding through the village.   When the sun

broke through, it was pleasant, though the wind was still sharp. Observations on the temperature of Tasmania, taken from eight o'clock in the morning, to six in the evening, give no idea of the frosty nights, which are almost constant in winter, and sometimes occur so as to injure wheat, potatoes, &c. in summer, especially in the interior of the Island. We breakfasted at the Saracen's Head, a good inn, in the Vale of Bagdad. This extensive valley, presented a pretty appearance for winter. The cultivated grounds were generally covered with stubble. Gay Parrots were perched in great numbers on the post-and-rail fences, by the sides of the road, upon which many poor prisoners, in their party-coloured garments, of grey and canary-yellow, were labouring with an assumed air of cheerfulness, such as sometimes makes superficial observers imagine, that their sufferings are light. Many of them were in irons, and were " whistling to keep their spirits up." We crossed the Derwent, at Bridgewater, by a large punt, or flying-bridge; on board which, there were two carts, with their teams of bullocks yoked, a gig with the horse yoked, several riding horses, and a considerable number of passengers. The wind blowing from the Dromedary Mountain, was so piercingly cold, on the Green Point side of the estuary, that I was glad to keep my hands around my horse's neck, for the sake of warmth, and to avail myself, at the same time, of the lea of one of the carts, for shelter. We landed on the causeway, raised by the Chain-gang, on the Bridgewater side, on which, being sheltered from the wind, by the adjacent mountains, it was like a warm, English, spring day. On arriving at Hobart Town, we again took up our quarters at the Freemasons Hotel, under feelings of reverent gratitude to the Author of all our mercies, who condescended still to bless and to preserve us.

CHAPTER XLI.

WE remained in Hobart Town more than three weeks,
and made many unsuccessful inquiries, respecting vessels
proceeding to the Mauritius, and touching at the Settlements on the south coast of Australia, and at the Swan
River; believing it would be right for us to proceed in
that direction, for the Cape of Good Hope, as soon as way
should open. In the mean time, we continued our labours,
for the edification of those, united with us in religious profession, and for the welfare of the Inhabitants of the Colony
generally.

6th mo. 1st. Our monthly meeting was a season, to be
remembered with thankfulness to the Shepherd of Israel,
who was pleased to grant a sense of his presence, and in a
remarkable degree to unite our spirits, especially in delib-
erating upon the important subject of recording two individuals as approved ministers. Great unity of sentiment prevailed in taking this step, and under a sense of the importance
of the office, much weighty counsel was conveyed by various
persons.

13th. We had a pleasant visit from James Allen, the
surgeon of the Establishment for the Aborigines, on Flinders Island. He gave an interesting account of the progress of civilization among the Blacks. They have left off

their dancing and hunting, and are acquiring the English language, and useful arts, as well as an historical knowledge, at least, of Christianity. They still, however, diminish in number, the mortality being considerable; and in one case of a birth, among them, a strong disposition was shown by the parents, to destroy the child.

18th. The meeting this morning, was a very remarkable one. The early part of it was attended by a deep feeling of poverty. The weather being wet, and the roads miry, it was long before the congregation was fully assembled. Soon after the meeting became settled, the sense of the divine presence gradually overshadowed us, gathering our minds into reverent, silent adoration, and preparing many to magnify God with their voices. Silence was first broken by one of our women friends, of whom we have some that, like Tryphena and Tryphosa, labour in the Lord: she expressed a few sentences, on the marvellous condescension of our Holy Redeemer, in taking upon him the nature of man, and submitting to be tempted as we are, that we might know, that in him, we have a High Priest, touched with a feeling of our infirmities. This testimony was followed by others, from seven different persons, in which the way of life, through Jesus Christ, was clearly set forth, with various exhortations, admonitions, and praises, and with allusions to the importance of being instant in prayer, and steadfast in faith, not only in the propitiatory sacrifice of Christ, but in all that he said and did, and in that light which comes by him, and by, and in which, he leads his disciples into all truth, and now " speaketh" to them " from heaven."—A person who held Unitarian principles, came casually into this meeting, and became convinced of the unsoundness of his principles: he said, that the feeling of divine influence was so powerfully felt by him, as soon as he entered the door, and before a word was spoken, that it would have been in vain, from that time, for any one to have tried to persuade him, that there was no such thing to be felt, as the perceptible influence of the Holy Spirit. This influence opened his understanding to receive also, the doctrine of Christ crucified, to the unspeakable comfort of his own soul.—The afternoon meeting was small and silent; a season to prove to us, that mercies, such as we were favoured with this morning, are not at our command.

23rd. We set out, on horseback, on another journey into the interior.—At New Norfolk, we met an elderly woman of our acquaintance, who, after a residence of many years in Tasmania, made a voyage to Europe, and visited her native country, Scotland. She found the more humid and cloudy climate of Great Britain, uncongenial to her feelings, and was glad to get back to this, her adopted country. It is however, the clouds and rain of Great Britain, that render it so much more fertile than these sunny, southern climes. Though the clouds, and rain, and cold, of Britain, give rise to diseases, that often put a period to life, I much question, whether the average longevity is greater here, than in Great Britain. Consumption is less frequent in the Australian regions, but acute diseases and sudden death, are more frequent. Perhaps this may result from the more free use of intoxicating liquors, and the much more abundant consumption of animal food, in Australia and Tasmania. Nervous diseases are also very common in these Colonies; possibly they may arise from drinking such large quantities of green tea, as are generally taken by persons of all ranks.

24th. We visited a couple, who are strongly attached to the principles of the Society of Friends, and had a religious interview with the patients in the hospital. Of latter time, the Wesleyans have paid attention to the religious state of New Norfolk, which is now much more of a town than when we first visited it; they have erected a chapel, and are building one at the Back River.

25th. We held meetings with the inhabitants of the Back River, and of New Norfolk. In the former, one of the persons noticed yesterday, expressed a few words in prayer, and afterwards, informed the congregation, that he had at his house, a collection of books for gratuitous loan, illustrative of the principles of the Society of Friends. A comforting sense of the divine influence prevailed in this meeting; and after it, a man, who had formerly been very

unsteady, but had become reformed, expressed the comfort
he had derived from the manner in which the doctrine of
Christian self-denial had been urged.

26th. We proceeded by way of Hamilton, to Green
Valley. Hamilton is considerably improved since we were
last there. In addition to several other buildings, a neat,
brick, Episcopal place of worship, has been erected. The
day was cold; the hoar frost did not melt in the shade, and
the roads were frozen in places.

We parted from our friends at Green Valley, and went
to Bothwell, on the 28th, and from thence to Ansty Barton,
on the 29th. The cold still continued severe. The Clyde
and the Jordan were frozen over, but not sufficiently to
bear a person to walk upon them. On the 30th, as we
travelled across the Eastern Marshes: the horses tried to
drink at some ice-covered pools, and did not seem at all
to understand why they could not get their noses into the
water. Soon after sunset, a brilliant meteor appeared in
the east, like a large star, with a coloured train, descending
in an oblique direction. Falling stars are of frequent occurrence, in these southern latitudes.

We reached Kelvedon on the 1st of 7th month. The
weather was much milder on the coast, but stormy. On the
4th, we went a few miles along the beach, to see a Whale,
that was killed on the 1st instant, by a whaling party,
who have a station on Schouten Island, that is attended by
a schooner, which rode out the gale of yesterday, with
difficulty, and was obliged to let go the Whale, which was
about forty feet long. It drifted on shore, and they were
now endeavouring to tow it off, for the purpose of " cutting
it in." It was a Right Whale, the species affording whalebone and oil. As is generally the case, it had a great many
flattened Barnacles, adhering to its smooth skin, on which
there were also a number of small animals, holding on by
hooked claws; these were about half an inch long, and
might be regarded as the lice of the Whale. The Right
Whale is wonderfully constructed for taking large quantities
of fish into its capacious mouth, and retaining them there,
while it ejects the water taken in along with them, by sending

it out between the numerous plates of whalebone: these
are articulated to the upper jaw, like the laths of a venetian blind, but fixed only at the upper extremity; the lower,
when the mouth is partially, or completely closed, being
included within its enormous lips. The whaling season is
a time of excitement among young men on these coasts;
they sometimes join the whalers, who are generally reckless,
dissipated men.

6th. The Monthly Meeting was one, in which the sense
of the presence of Him, who condescended to promise
to be with the two or three, met together in his name,
was sensibly felt, both in the time occupied in worship,
and in that employed in conducting the discipline of our
little church. Two young men, who had for some time
past occasionally laboured in the Gospel, to the edification
of their brethren, were recorded as approved ministers, and
a person who had been separated from the church, was
restored to membership.—These decisions were subject to
the approval of the Monthly Meeting, to be held next
month, in course, in Hobart Town, and by which they were
confirmed.

8th. I am this day forty-three years old; an age to
which, at one time, I little expected to attain, nor when I left
England, to reach in this part of the world. It is of little
consequence where we are, if only in our right places; and
I am not aware that we could rightly have been, at this
time, in any other, than the one in which we are. Though
we have long been separated from our dear friends, in Europe, we have much to be grateful for, and nothing to
murmur at. May our dedication to the service of the best
of Masters, increase with the claims upon our gratitude.

After again visiting the settlers in Great Swan Port, we
took a solemn leave of our friends at Kelvedon, and on the
17th, set out for Hobart Town, where we were favoured to
arrive in safety, on the 19th, having made the journey by
way of Spring Bay and Richmond; we crossed the Derwent,
at some risk, in a sailing boat, that was scarcely large
enough to hold ourselves and horses. The steamer now
used in this passage, was laid off for repair.

In the family of a settler, at whose house we lodged upon the way, we had much interesting conversation, on the importance of minding eternal things, and on the manner in which the kingdom of heaven is brought near to us, by the in-shining of the light of Christ, the witness of the Holy Spirit against sin, which, being attended to, enables mankind truly to receive Christ, and gives them power to become the sons of God by adoption; so that they "are no longer strangers and foreigners," in regard to the kingdom of heaven, but "fellow-citizens with the saints, and of the household of God," to whom they "have access by one Spirit, and are built upon the foundation of the apostles and prophets, Jesus Christ himself being the chief corner-stone." This experience would doubtless be more known, if those who profess to believe in Christ, were more generally to receive the truth as it is in him, in simplicity, and to seek help through him, to obey it, in sincerity.

We now remained in Hobart Town nearly four months, before the way opened clearly, for our departure from the Colony. In the mean time several subjects of importance claimed our attention.

We had some correspondence with Captain Maconochie, on the state of the Penal Discipline of these Colonies, and on his views of a better system of managing Convicts. The best plan that had been pursued, was one of restraint, accompanied by religious instruction, so far as the means were found, for carrying out the latter object. But whether in prisons, or in assigned service, the prisoners exercised an influence over each other, that was generally far from reformatory, and often very deteriorating. Nevertheless, the greater separation and occupation of the prisoners, and the hope of the indulgence of a Ticket-of-leave, had a salutary effect upon them, compared with that produced by shutting them up in jails, in England. But there was still another evil in the Assignment System. It engendered feelings, both in the minds of servants and of masters, nearly allied to those produced by slavery. Notwithstanding the prisoner had forfeited his liberty by his crimes, he did not easily reconcile being sent to work for a settler, without wages;

he therefore generally tried to get off with doing as little work as he could; while the master, having to support and clothe him, was consequently irritated, by finding his work neglected, unless he were himself constantly present.

The system proposed by Captain Maconochie, provided a remedy for these evils, by removing unpaid labour, and making the prisoners answerable for the conduct of their associates, in such a way, as to make it their individual interest to discourage what was evil, and to encourage what was good, in each other.

Captain Maconochie's system of penal discipline proposed: That transportation should not be for specified periods, lest the offender should be returned upon the public unreformed, but that the recovery of freedom should depend entirely upon the conduct of the prisoner: That all prisoners should be first sent to Penal Settlements, to work in Government employment, as a punishment for their offences: That their original sentence should, generally determine the least period of such punishment, and should amount to one or two years: That removal from Penal Settlements should, in all cases, depend on good conduct: That on leaving these Settlements, the prisoners should enter Probational Road-gangs, in groups of about six persons, who should select one another as companions, and be answerable for the conduct one of another: That these gangs should ascend a progressive scale, toward freedom, at a rate, to be determined by the acquirement of certain numbers of tickets for good conduct, which tickets should be daily awarded, and should be the common property of the gang, who should thus, unitedly, and daily, feel the effect of any neglect of any one of their number, or of any forfeiture of tickets for the misconduct of such a one: That, in case of any one of the gang, proving so refractory as to render it necessary for his companions to complain of him, he should, on conviction, be returned to the Penal Settlement, there to remain till the period for which he should be returned, should expire, and further, until he could gain the confidence of five others, in his future good conduct, so as to induce them to try him as a companion, in attempting to ascend the scale of reformation : That the five parting with such a refractory companion, should descend on the scale, to meet the one who should be taken from the Penal Settlement, to supply the place of their former companion : That having passed this probational scale, which should be so modified as to require, with the original sentence, about seven years, the prisoners should become so far free, as to be allowed to hire themselves to masters of their own choosing, and to reap the reward of their own labour, out of which they should provide their own food, clothing, and lodging : And that, having proved their reformation by good conduct, for a sufficient period, under these circumstances, they should become free.

The principles of this system, appearing to us to be sound, we entertained a hope of benefit arising from their adoption, notwithstanding many difficulties might occur, in carrying them out, especially, in finding persons for this purpose, imbued with the moral principle, to which it was the design of Captain Maconochie to lead the prisoner. The best projects for the reformation of human beings, must fail in accomplishing their object, if the persons on whom the carrying of them out, depends, be taking a lower moral standard than that proposed for the parties to be reformed. And this is likely to be the case, where persons engage as the agents of such reformation, merely from secular motives. But taking all the anticipated difficulties into account, we still thought this System worthy of attention, because it is not only based upon sound moral principles, but arranged so as to call the common feelings of human nature into useful operation, by making it the interest of one man, to try to reform another, instead of leaving him in such a position, as to facilitate his corrupting his fellow for his own gratification.

On the 11th of 8th month, we were comforted by the arrival of our dear friends, Daniel and Charles Wheeler, from Sydney, by the " Mary Ann Watson." They took a private lodging in Liverpool Street; and soon after their arrival, we removed to a lodging near to them.

The accompanying view of the entrance of the Derwent,

a few miles below Hobart Town, with the Lighthouse, on Iron-pot Island, is from the pencil of Charles Wheeler.

The room occupied for a meeting place, by Friends, in Hobart Town, proving too small for their accommodation, and being the sixth into which they had moved, within four years, I determined, on my own responsibility, to purchase some convenient premises that were offered for this purpose, in Murray Street; my English friends now here, concurring in the opinion, that such a purchase was desirable.—The sum which was required for this object, was kindly raised by some of our Society in England, soon after they were informed that the premises had been bought; those in Van Diemens Land not being, at that time, in circumstances to warrant their paying for the property, notwithstanding they were disposed to be liberal in proportion to their means.— A person who attended our meetings had previously presented us with a piece of ground for a burial place, and had himself been interred in it.

Our meeting had received an accession of a few members, who had adopted the principles of the Society of Friends, on conscientious grounds; and when assembled for public worship, we were often favoured with a comforting sense of the influence of the Holy Spirit, contriting our hearts before the Lord, and exciting among us a concern for the growth of each other in grace.

On the 28th of 9th month, old John Johnson, of Glenorchy, peacefully breathed his last, whilst one of his neighbours was reading to him, the thirty-first Psalm, to which he had frequently recurred with much comfort. I saw him on the 2nd instant, when he was very weak, and his articulation very feeble. He made many pertinent remarks, both on his own state, and on the state of many others, and inquired, if I thought it could be right for bad men to use the Lord's Prayer, as he thought they could not properly say, "Our Father, which art in Heaven," when the devil was their father. George W. Walker and Joseph B. Mather visited him the evening before he died, and found him in a very comfortable state of mind, hoping in the Lord, and anticipating everlasting happiness. His

disease-worn remains, wore striking traces of that calmness
and serenity, with which he had long waited for his change,
which he had often said, he felt would be a happy one.
This feeling, arose out of a sensible communion with his
Maker, the result of unfeigned penitence, combined with
Faith in Christ, and patient endurance of the sanctifying
operation of the Holy Spirit. In answer to a question, as
to whether he felt comfortable, that was put to him, only
a few minutes before he died; he replied, " Yes, I shall
soon be happy in Heaven." He added something respecting his friend John Leach, with whom he had often praised
his Saviour on earth, and whom he hoped to join in prais-
ing him everlastingly; seeing, as he often said, how wonderful it was, that the Lord should have looked down with
compassion, upon one who had been so long living in sin,
and have drawn him to himself, and given him a place
among his servants. Precious indeed, is the memory of this
poor, but righteous man, notwithstanding he entered the
Lord's Vineyard, only at the eleventh hour!

On the 28th of the 9th month, G. W. Walker and
myself went again to New Norfolk, and paid a farewell visit
to our friends, at that place. We had a meeting with them
in the Court House, on the 1st of 10th month, in which
the uncertainty of human life was illustrated, by a reference
to the case of the Police Magistrate, who had, on the
previous day, granted us the use of the house. At that
time he was on the bench, and occupied the chair, in which
I was seated at the meeting. Subsequently, he attended a
sale, and purchased a house and some land. Now he lay at
the point of death, having been seized with illness, that left
no hope of recovery. He survived the seizure only twenty-
three hours. We likewise held a meeting with the patients,
and aged and infirm paupers, in the hospital, to whom also,
I had much to communicate; illustrating to the poor invalids, the power and the blessings of the Gospel, as exhibited in the declining years, and last hours of the late
J. Johnson; and pointing out to them the importance of
cherishing a hunger and thirst after righteousness, as he did,
even in the days of his outgoings, and to which the Lord

had respect, who ultimately filled him with the joys of his salvation.

We returned to Hobart Town on the 2nd of 10th mo. and were brought under some concern, by the Pusine Judge refusing to accept the affirmation of a person professing with our Society, because the person was not a member. I pointed out to the Judge, that the Act of William the Fourth, chapter 49, intituled "An Act to allow Quakers and Moravians to make Affirmation, in all cases where an oath is or shall be required, dated 28th August, 1833," was passed, for the relief of the consciences of persons of those persuasions, without regard to membership, and that, in order to this being made clear, the words, "Or of the persuasion of the people called Quakers," were introduced. To this he objected, that these words could only mean, *bona fide* Quakers, members of the Society, because persons of the persuasion of the people called Quakers, were not distinguished from Quakers, in the absolute sense, in the title of the Act! Thus, the plain, common-sense object, and meaning of the Act, were made to give way to an imaginary, or capricious, difficulty. Other law officers, however, accepted the obvious intent of the Act, and admitted the affirmations, both of members of the Society, and of persons "of the persuasion of the people called Quakers."

Our Yearly Meeting commenced, on the 6th, and held by adjournments, till the 10th. It was a comforting season, to such as have learned to take comfort under a sense of the helplessness of man, unassisted by the Spirit of his Maker; and especially, when this sense of helplessness is attended by an evidence to the mind, of the fulfilment of the gracious promise of the Lord Jesus, "Where two or three are gathered together, in my name, there am I, in the midst of them."—At the conclusion of the meeting, the following minute was made:—"We believe it right to place upon record, before we separate, that through the gracious extension of divine regard toward us, we have been made sensible of feelings of quietness and peace, resting upon us during the several sittings of

this meeting; under which we have been enabled to conduct the business which has come before us, in brotherly
love, to our edification and comfort, and under a renewed
feeling thereof, we now conclude."

Our dear friends, Francis and Anna Maria Cotton, were
in Hobart Town, on this occasion, and lodged at the same
house with G. W. Walker and myself. A few days after
the meeting, they took a solemn leave of us, and returned
to Swan Port.   They, with Esther Dixon, from Skelton
Castle, near Campbell Town, were all the strangers professing with the Society of Friends, who were present at
the Yearly Meeting, which is a very small one.   The number of persons generally present at its sittings, was fifteen.
Our usual congregations for worship, were of about forty
persons, many of whom were not members of the Society,
but were attached to its principles.

12th.   We attended an interesting, and satisfactory
meeting of the Temperance Society.   Major Ryan, the
Commandant of Launceston, took the chair.   While we
were at this meeting, the cook of a vessel, in Sulivans
Cove, fell into the water, in a state of intoxication, and was
drowned.

18th.   James Allen, lately the Surgeon of the Establishment for the Blacks, on Flinders Island, took tea
with us.   He gave an interesting account of the progress
of civilization among the Natives; but said, that the mortality continued to be great among them.   Four have died
since he was here three months ago.   He thinks the change
in their habits, has something to do with this circumstance,
and that a residence in an open and somewhat exposed
situation, after having grown up in the recesses of the forest,
is uncongenial to them ; and that their remaining very constantly on the Settlement, (which they are encouraged to
do, in order to promote more rapidly, their civilization,)
instead of making frequent excursions, for a few days together, into the bush, also tends to deteriorate their health.

In the course of our present visit to Hobart Town, we
received much kindness from Sir John and Lady Franklin,
and from other members of their family.   On the 28th of

10th month, we took our last dinner with them, at the Government House.   Our friends, Daniel and Charles Wheeler, were also of the company, as was likewise Dr. Foreman, who had lately arrived in Hobart Town, in charge of a cargo of female prisoners.   The Doctor is an intelligent man, and a strict disciplinarian.   In three instances, during the voyage, he was obliged to gag some of the women, for persisting in violent and abusive language.   One of them, had previously shown a disposition to be very unruly, but after suffering this punishment, for a short time, and subsequently, a few hours' solitary confinement, she became so orderly as to give no further trouble during the remainder of the voyage.   The Doctor spoke with warm approbation, of the "Ladies' Committee," and of the beneficial effect of the supply of work, given to the female prisoners, at the commencement of the voyage.

29th. We received a visit from a man, formerly a prisoner, who gave us some striking particulars of his life. He said, the first occasion on which he took spirits, was, when going a short voyage ; a little was then given him, in a small vial, which he was charged to drink, lest he should take cold !   His father was a man who endeavoured carefully, to inculcate honest principles into his children, both by example and precept, and who used to ejaculate, in a low tone, on leaving his house, " The Lord preserve my going out and my coming in, from henceforth, and for evermore ;" but he was a drunkard ! and his son was sometimes sent to the public-house, to bring him home.   On such occasions his father often gave him "a little sup," in the bottom of the glass, and was amused at the wry-faces that his son made on drinking it.   When the boy was able to drink a whole glass full, his father expressed great pleasure ! little anticipating that he was training his son, not only to drunkenness, but through drunkenness, to dishonesty.   At length, his son became both a drunkard and a thief, and was transported for a robbery.   He was now a prisoner, in bondage, in a foreign land ; but years rolled on, and the term of his transportation expired ; he regained his freedom, but not from the bondage of habitual drunkenness ; this, to him, was more powerful than the bondage, under the laws of his country. Many times he sold his shirt for drink, and, to use his own expression, parted with the flesh off his back for it also; for while a prisoner, he was several times flogged for being drunk. As soon as he was loosed from the triangles, he hurried on his clothes, and with his back bleeding, went to the first place where drink was sold, and drunk again! Often the declaration, "Drunkards shall not inherit eternal life," came awfully before his mind: he was alarmed, miserable, and ashamed of himself, and he cried to God for deliverance. He joined the temperance society, resolved he would leave off the use of spirits, and drink only a little wine or beer, but these kept alive his depraved appetite. He bagan to attend the Methodist meeting, hoping thereby to gain strength; but in a few weeks, he was again overcome by his old enemy, and being ashamed to be met in that condition, he left the road, and lost himself in the bush, where he remained all night, in confusion. Still, in the anguish of his soul, he cried unto the Lord for deliverance, and in this state, he attended a meeting that we held, at the Back River, New Norfolk, where his attention was directed to the Holy Spirit, as a witness against sin, revealed in the secret of the heart, and as a guide, leading those who attend to its convictions, to repentance, and to the bearing of the cross, in the practice of self-denial, and giving them a sense of their weakness, in order that they may place their trust in the Lord alone, obtain strength from him to perform his will, and receive remission of sins through Jesus Christ. These doctrines made a deep impression upon this individual, and under the conviction, wrought upon his mind, he sought divine help to leave off the use of all stimulating liquors. He not only forsook the use of spirits, but of wine and beer; he also left off smoking, and chewing tobacco; and to enable him the sooner to pay his debts, he likewise left off the use of tea and sugar. These privations were trying to him for a few weeks, after which, the desire for such indulgence left him; and he is now in better health and spirits than before. Several persons have brought liquor to him, and tried to persuade him to drink, saying that as he had drunk, chewed, and smoked so long, he would certainly die from leaving off these practices! The poor man is now working for 10s. per week, as a builder, and is in a very humble, thankful state of mind: he walks eight miles into town, to attend our meetings, and is likely to stand his ground, so long as he continues in humility and watchfulness.

Having engaged a passage to King Georges Sound, by way of Port Phillip and South Australia, on board the barque Eudora, of 208 tons, Stephen Addison, of Hobart Town, master, we embarked, on the 3rd of 11th month, taking rather a hasty leave of many of our friends. A few of them accompanied us on board, among whom were Daniel and Charles Wheeler, to whom we had been much united in the fellowship of the Gospel, and who sailed for England a few days afterwards.* The vessel was quickly got under weigh, our friends bid us farewell, and before we had well arranged our luggage, we were at the mouth of the Derwent. After watching the places, in which we continued to feel a deep interest, recede from our view, till they disappeared, we retired to rest, overpowered by nausea and fatigue.

* See Memoirs of the Life and Gospel Labours of the late Daniel Wheeler, published by Harvey and Darton, London, 1842.

CHAPTER XLII.

11th mo. 6th. THERE were ten cabin passengers on board the Eudora, eight of whom were persons in the prime of life, going to Port Phillip, with a view to improving their circumstances; either by obtaining a more extended range for their flocks, than they had commanded in Tasmania, or in the expectation of obtaining more lucrative situations in this new settlement, on the south coast of the Australian Continent. In the steerage, there were several mechanics and their families, who were hoping to obtain better wages at Port Phillip, than they could get in Van Diemens Land.

At the entrance to Bass's Straits, we passed large flocks of Mutton-birds, some of which were on the wing, and others, resting on the water. The latter could not rise without difficulty, on account of the smoothness of the sea. On the Eudora coming among them, they afforded an amusing spectacle, diving in all directions, around and under the vessel, and using their long wings under the water, as if flying in that element. When the ship had passed them, they fluttered along the surface, for a considerable distance, and at length rose into the air. When once upon the wing, they can continue their flight for a great length of time, being more at home in the air, than either upon the water or the land.

7th. The weather was beautifully fine. We passed within a short distance of the Fourneaux Islands, which looked interesting. The desolate mountains of Cape Barren, the rugged peaks of Flinders, the smooth pyramid of Chapel Island, and the low, flat surfaces of Preservation, and Green Islands, and others of similar character, revived pleasant recollections, unaccompanied by the fatigues, and other drawbacks upon enjoyment, that attended our former voyages in these Straits. The Blossom and the John Pierie, which sailed from Hobart Town a few days before us, were just leaving the anchorage under Preservation Island, with a press of canvas, that rendered them beautiful objects. They had taken refuge under this island, from a gale that we escaped. We passed to the southward of a high rock, called The Pyramid. The evening was very fine and moonlight, with a freshening favourable breeze.

A visiter who came on board the Eudora, from one of the other vessels, was much habituated to the use of profane language, a practice, lamentably common among seafaring men. I was greatly pained with his conversation, on this account, and not seeing any opportunity for speaking to him privately, I enclosed two tracts, entitled A Christian Memento, and Thoughts on the Importance of Religion, in the following note, which was slipped into his hand, and which he afterwards acknowledged gratefully, on shore.

"Permit a stranger to commend to thy notice, the enclosed tracts, under the feeling that thy soul is precious in the sight of God, and that it ought to be precious in thy own sight, and that the days for securing its salvation are fast hastening away."

8th. The early part of the day was very foggy. We passed a little to the southward of Curtis's Islands, which are three, huge masses of rock, standing high out of the water, and having upon them no appearance of vegetation. In the same direction, we sighted the Rodonda Rock. The evening became clear, and the breeze freshened, so as to carry us along, at the rate of eight knots an hour.

9th. We passed in sight of Cape Schauck. While going at about four knots an hour, many Barracootas were taken from the stern, by means of large hooks, baited with pieces of red rag, or of their own gills: they are fine, large fish, in form, resembling Pike, but of a bluish, silver colour, and having long, slender bones; the texture of their flesh is like that of mackerel, but tougher. Toward noon we entered Port Phillip, having just sufficient breeze to carry us in, against the nearly spent ebb-tide, and we dropped anchor under Point Nepean, where some of the passengers immediately went on shore. The rock here is soft, and Calcareous, and rises into low hills. These are covered with Kangaroo-grass, trees, and shrubs; the beach is sandy, with shells, among which were the Zigzag Volute, and Paper Nautilus. *Casuarina quadrivalvis, Banksia australis,* and other Tasmanian trees grow here, also a N. S. Wales *Eucalyptus,* and several shrubs and plants that are found on Flinders Island. I likewise met with a shrub, belonging to the genus *Croton,* and two Goodenias, that I had not noticed before. We bathed in shallow water, to avoid sharks, and got on board again, after being wet by a heavy thunder-storm.

10th. We made a good passage, to the anchorage at Gellibrands Point, at the north-east angle of Port Phillip, passing up the eastern channel. Though it is not yet marked by buoys, we only once touched, on the end of a sand-bank, when the vessel was in stays, and she immediately worked off again. An officer, connected with the customs, who boarded us, and took our mail on shore, gratefully accepted a few tracts, intimating, that there was much need for the attention of the people here, to be stirred up to the importance of temperance and religion; both being greatly neglected. Our captain went up to Melbourne with this individual, but the hour being late, we remained on board. The day was very warm, the thermometer on ship-board 80°. We afterwards learned, that it had stood at 107°, on shore, during this and the three previous days, but several of those following were very cool. Port Phillip may be called a small, inland sea; the land is not visible across it, except where elevated. In the course of our day's sail, we were close in with the shore, below Arthurs Seat, a considerable range of hills, on the east side of Port Phillip, which are grassy, with trees thinly scattered upon them. These are chiefly the spherical-headed *Casuarina quadrival-vis,* of Tasmania, which I have only seen in one other place in N. S. Wales, viz. on Mount Arthur, Wellington Valley, where it grew sparingly, and was very small; here it is vigorous and abundant.

11th. Some horses and a bullock, belonging to our fellow-passengers, were landed on the beach, by means of boats. We left the Eudora, and entered the bush, at a place, marked by a red flag. A track toward Melbourne, led us through a wood, but upon reaching a salt marsh, we were guided by a way-mark, which had been previously described to us. Much of the land between the beach and the town, is sandy, and covered with grassy, open forest. The trees are chiefly like those of V. D. Land, as are also the plants, but the former are marked by several species of *Loranthus* growing upon them, none of which, I believe, exist in Tasmania.

We were conveyed across the Yarra-yarra, by a voluntary ferryman, whose practice was to make no charge, but to accept what his passengers pleased, finding, that in this way he got the best paid. On landing from the ferry boat, we were recognized by George Langhorne, whom we had known in Sydney: he was at one time employed as a Cate-chist, upon Goat Island, where a few Natives, who had become prisoners, were under his care. These made con-siderable progress in knowledge, but they were ultimately, either discharged or sent to the Missionary Stations, at Lake Macquarie and Wellington Valley; and George Lang-horne was appointed, by the Government of N. S. Wales, to form a Missionary Station, at Port Phillip, placed under the care of a committee of the Episcopal Church Missionary Society, in Sydney. When we met with him here, he was setting out for this Missionary Station, two miles up the Yarra-yarra River, in a boat, managed by four native boys, and a young man who became a proselyte to temperance views, on our first visit to Launceston. We accepted a pressing invitation to accompany this party, and took a hasty leave of our fellow-passengers from Hobart Town. After dining with George and Mary Langhorne, who are labouring diligently to civilize the Blacks, and to introduce Christianity among them, we were conveyed four miles further up the river, to the dwelling of John and Mary Gardiner, with whom we were acquainted in V. D. Land, and who have erected for themselves a comfortable house in this newly-occupied country. Here we consented to remain all night, in order to have the opportunity of conveying religious instruction to the establishment.

John Gardiner was one of the first persons who made an overland journey, from Sydney to Port Phillip, a distance of about 700 miles. Among other provisions, to facilitate his progress, he had a cart, so constructed, that the body could be taken off the wheels, separated from the shafts, and placed in a tarpawling, so as to serve as a ferry-boat. A native Black, from the Merumbidgee River, has become an efficient servant in his family, and shows more reflection than some of the white people who have been brought up, nominally, Christians.

In one of J. Gardiner's journeys from Sydney, one of his men was bitten by a venomous serpent. The wound was sucked, but the man showed symptoms of faintness, of alarming character. The party had received intimation, from a native woman, that some of her countrymen intended to attack them in the night; and at the juncture, when the poison seemed to be taking effect, the lights of the Natives, were seen approaching. The party were thrown into a state of alarm: they watched a favourable opportunity, seized the Blacks at unawares, and expostulated with them, against making such an attack, upon persons in no way disposed to injure them. The chief was detained as a hostage, and placed under the charge of one of the party, who, being overcome by fatigue, fell asleep, and his captive escaped, but returned no more to annoy them. These circumstances diverted the attention of the company from the envenomed man, and his case was forgotten till the next morning, when he was inquired of respecting his welfare. He also had forgotten his malady; fear seemed to have superseded the effect of the poison, and he said, he had felt nothing more of it, from the time that the lights of the Blacks appeared!

12th. We had a religious interview with J. Gardiner's household, last evening. This morning, the servants of his establishment were invited to meet with us, but except one man and his wife, they were too little interested in such matters, to get themselves dressed by eleven o'clock, so as to be ready for the occasion. This sort of negligence is said to be very prevalent among free-servants here.—In the afternoon, we returned to the Missionary Station, where we had a meeting with the family, some native boys, and a few individuals from Melbourne. A person from Melbourne, who reads the service of the Episcopal Church, in the School-house, on First-days, kindly offered us the use of this place, on any other day of the week. We returned home with J. Gardiner, and were present at the family reading of the Scriptures, when the servants also assembled, and we laboured to turn their attention to things of eternal importance. Great is the reluctance of man to live in the service of his Maker. To think of the multitudes who live without hope, and without God in the world, who, nevertheless, are within reach of the knowledge of the Gospel, and who are willingly, if not wilfully, ignorant, is truly awful!

13th. A boat conveyed us again to Melbourne. The Yarra-yarra River is deep; but it is difficult to navigate, for boats, on account of the quantity of sunken timber. It is about sixty feet wide, and margined with trees and shrubs. Among these are heard, the tinkling note of the Bell-bird, and the shrill whistle of the Coachman, which is ter-minated by a jerking sound, something like the crack of a whip. We also noticed the Nankin-bird, a species of Heron, which is cinnamon-coloured on the back, sulphur-coloured on the breast, and has a long, white feather, pendant from the back of the head. The river is fresh to Melbourne, where there is a rapid. The country on its banks is open, grassy forest, rising into low hills. The town of Melbourne, though scarcely more than fifteen months old, consists of about a hundred houses, among which are stores, inns, a jail, a

barrack, and a school-house. Some of the dwelling-houses
are tolerable structures of brick. A few of the inhabitants
are living in tents, or in hovels resembling thatched roofs,
till they can provide themselves with better accommodation.
There is much bustle and traffic in the place, and a gang of
prisoners are employed in levelling the streets. The town
allotments, of half an acre, were put up for sale, a short
time since, at £5 each, the Surveyor thinking £7 too much
to ask for them. But the fineness of the country has excited
such a mania for settling here, that they sold for, from £25
to £100 each!

Eighty thousand acres of land, suitable for cultivation,
and for the sites of dwellings for opulent settlers, have
already been surveyed, and are expected soon to be put up
for sale, by the Government, in sections of from fifty to one
hundred acres each. Larger tracts will also be sold, as soon
as the survey is sufficiently forward.

At this place we met several of our acquaintance, from
other parts of New South Wales, and from Van Diemens
Land, who had removed hither from various motives. Some
from an unsettled disposition, others from dissipated habits,
others with the hope of improving their circumstances, and
others from greediness of gain. Some of the great holders
of sheep and stock say, that they do not think their removal
hither has been, in the aggregate, advantageous. Though
they have increased their property, it has been at a great
risk, from the greater untowardness of their servants, and
from the enmity of some of the Blacks. A few have lost
their lives by the latter, and one had eight of his servants
murdered, either by them or by their fellow-servants.

Business was at this time, conducted on a very disagreeable and unsound plan, at Port Phillip. Almost every thing,
including labour, was paid for by orders on Sydney, or Van
Diemens Land; the discount required by the few persons
who had cash, was from £20 to £40 per cent! A mechanic
received half his wages in goods, charged at about 30 per
cent. profit, and the rest in an order, on which he paid his
employer 10 per cent. discount for cash!

After taking tea with a family of Wesleyans, with whom

we were acquainted in Sydney, we proceeded to a meeting in the School-house, to which the inhabitants of the place generally, were invited. About forty persons were present on this occasion, with whom we were enabled to labour faithfully, though under a deep sense of our own weakness; and our gracious Master was pleased to grant a more powerful sense of his presence, than we had ventured to hope for.

14th. Last night, we returned with our friends to the Missionary Station, to lodge. The reserve for the Missionary Institution is of 800 acres. This, though but a small extent of land for a pastoral country, was considered sufficient to devote to the object, at so short a distance from the town. The buildings are temporary ones, of mud and plaster, with thatched roofs; they are not yet sufficiently extensive to accommodate the mission family, and twelve native boys, who are already under tuition. The design is, to educate them in English, and to teach them useful occupations, and then to let them mix themselves with the European population; with whom it is hoped, by these means, to put them upon a level. The parents of the children come to see them at pleasure, and when they wish it, take them out to hunt; but for this, the children do not seem much inclined, preferring to be fed on easier terms, at the institution. The parents are not encouraged to make long visits; they are furnished with but a few meals gratuitously, and if they choose to make longer stops, they have to earn their victuals, at the rate of two hours' work, for eight ounces of meat and twelve ounces of flour. They are chiefly employed in cutting wood and drawing water. Clothing, chiefly consisting of canvass frocks, is furnished to them gratuitously. At another station, nearly twenty miles distant, about sixteen native families are marshalled as an armed police, and are clothed suitably for their occupation.

It is gratifying to see the Government disposed to make efforts, to benefit the people whose country they have usurped; but their effort in this case does not appear to us, to be of a character such as Christians ought to make, being contrary to "peace on earth and good will toward men."

At the first settlement of Port Phillip, a party of benevolent people attempted making a treaty with some of the
chiefs, and purchasing land from them; but this, the British
Government did not sanction, and the whole scheme fell
through, when the country was taken possession of, as a
part of N. S. Wales. There is reason to think, that the
state of society among the Aborigines, gave no power to
the chiefs to sell, on behalf of their respective tribes, and
they certainly had none, on behalf of other tribes. If Europeans occupy the country of savages, the former must
act justly, from principle, if they would act as becomes
Christians. The untutored natives, forming a thinly scattered and unorganized population, can neither assert nor
defend their own rights. It is in cases like this, that principle is put to the test; and it is lamentable to see, how
little principle, in this respect, has been exhibited, in these
cases, either by the British Government, or by its European
subjects.—People in England, maintaining a good character,
are little aware, how much of what gains them this character,
they owe to the oversight of those, by whom they are continually surrounded, and how little to principle. When they
emigrate to a country, where this oversight is withdrawn,
too generally, but little that has the appearance of principle
remains, especially in their conduct toward the defenceless
Aborigines.

In the afternoon, we went down the Yarra-yarra, in a
boat, to obtain some tracts from on board the Eudora.
The water continues fresh for a considerable distance below
the town. Its banks are low, and fringed with bushes.
Toward the mouth of the river, there are swamps, covered
with a narrow-leaved, white-flowered *Melaleuca*, drawn up
like hop-poles, to thirty feet in height. The river is navigable for small vessels, up to the town. We met several
boats, and the Rebecca, from Launceston, on board of
which was a person, with whom we made our first voyage
to Flinders Island. Though here, in a strange land, we
are not among strangers; we have some acquaintance
with most of the white inhabitants. Contiguous to the
river, there are some beautiful pieces of land, clear of trees,

and covered with green grass. On Gellibrands Point, there are a few houses, where Williams Town is laid out; but the place is badly supplied with water.

On returning to Melbourne, we attended a meeting for the organization of a temperance society, auxiliary to the one in Sydney.

15th. We called on John Batman, formerly of Buffalo Plains, in Van Diemens Land, who has been much of an invalid since his removal to Port Phillip. He continues to feel a deep interest respecting the Aborigines of these Colonies, and has now, in his employment, several Blacks from the vicinity of Sydney, and a woman and two boys from Tasmania, whom he finds useful servants. They are not disposed to indulge in wandering habits, now that they are removed from their native haunts. This may probably arise, from the fear they entertain of the tribes by which they are here surrounded. J. Batman showed us the skull of a Native, found near Gellibrands Point, which was perforated with slugs, and had some of the lead lodged in the bone, evidently proving, that the individual to whom it had belonged, had been shot. Though from its appearance, when picked up, the murderous deed did not seem to have been perpetrated above six months, yet, he said, no inquiry had been instituted, as to how the party had come by his death.

The number of Blacks in the vicinity of Port Phillip, including its whole circuit, with Western Port, is estimated at from three to five hundred. They are said to be more healthy than those of many other parts of New South Wales, and most of the women have children, though their families are far from large. These circumstances are attributed to the consumption of a much larger proportion of roots, than is eaten by their country people in many other parts, and to their having had less intercourse with Europeans.

One of the plants which yields them sustenance is *Podolepis acuminata,* which is about a foot high, and has flowers, in some degree, resembling Sweet Sultan, but of a deeper yellow: it abounds in rich soils, especially about the margins of salt marshes, and has a thickened root, compared by some to a potato. Another resembles a Dandelion, but has very

narrow leaves, and a nodding bud; its roots resemble Scorzo-
nera, to which it is allied; it is generally diffused in grassy
lands. These roots are cooked, by heating stones in the fire,
and covering them with grass, laying the roots upon the
grass, and a covering of grass upon them, and lastly, one of
earth over the whole. When roasted, the last especially, are
said to be sweet, and are very delicious. Kangaroos and
Opossums, Emus, and other birds, are also generally eaten
by the Blacks, and are abundant. The Emus are fast retir-
ing before the white population, and their flocks and herds.
The large bird of the crane kind, called here, the Native
Companion, and a Bustard, denominated the Wild Turkey,
are plentiful; there are also Yellow-tailed and Red-tailed
Black Cockatoos, Round-headed White Cockatoos, Parrots
of various kinds, Pelicans, Black Swans, Ducks, White
Hawks, Laughing Jackasses, Kingfishers, Quails, and various other birds, not to omit the Piping Crow, with its
cheerful note, and the Black Magpie.

In the course of the day, we walked about three miles,
on the way toward Geelong, a district where there are
several settlers, among whom is our friend David Stead;
but which we had not opportunity to visit. The country,
as far as the eye can reach, has the appearance of a continued series of parks, even to the ascent of the distant hills.
In many places, it is clear of trees; the grass is verdant,
and pretty thick for a country which has not been subjected
to the fostering hand of man. The flocks and herds seem
in the full enjoyment of life, and are very fat. The only
formidable enemies they have to contend with, are wild dogs,
which are numerous, and are destructive among the sheep
and calves.

We dined with Captain Lonsdale, the Police Magistrate,
and commanding officer of the troops, with whom we had
some conversation, on the importance of inquests being
held on the bodies of Blacks, who may come by violent
or doubtful deaths, and of inquiry being made into cases of
reported injury. This, he assured us, had in some measure,
been attended to, particularly in one case, where several
persons had been said to have been killed, but which proved

a false report. On returning to the Missionary Station, we observed the Aurora australis, very brilliant, in columns of yellow, on a diffuse, pale, crimson ground.

16th. After taking leave of the Mission family, I walked through the bush to the beach, and spent much of the day in fruitless efforts to obtain attention from the Eudora, which was at anchor about two miles from the shore. The signal agreed upon was two fires, that were to be lighted on the sand; but the strong wind carried the smoke so close to the ground, that I concluded they could not be seen. I therefore joined G. W. Walker at Melbourne, where we put a few books and tracts into circulation, and after some time, returned to the beach, but with no better success. We therefore abandoned our object at sunset, and went back, to spend the evening with J. Batman, who presented us with some oval baskets, of neat and strong construction, the manufacture of the Blacks of this district. These baskets differ, in some respects, from any we have seen of native manufacture, in other parts of the Colony, being stronger and better calculated for general use; some of them are like reticules, others like fishing-crails, and others of larger dimensions. Possibly the Blacks of this district, may excel their countrymen in the manufacture of baskets, from the instruction of William Buckley, a prisoner, who was left at Port Phillip by Colonel Collins, in 1802, and who remained among the Natives till the settlement of the country in 1835: he had forgotten his own language, which he soon recovered: he is a man of large stature, and now fills the office of constable at Melbourne.

The Blacks often bring in, the splendid tails of the Lyrebird, *Menura superba*, which is called in Australia, the Pheasant, or the Bird of Paradise: it is said to abound among the hills of this district. J. Batman has some fine Emus, captured here.

17th. We returned to the Eudora, but the sea breeze setting in before we were ready to sail, we remained at anchor during the rest of the day.

18th. We made sail early, and cleared Gellibrands

Point before the sea breeze set in. The anchor was dropped in the evening, in a bay a little to the northward of Arthurs Seat. We are now the only passengers in the cabin. There are still thirteen in the steerage, who, not liking the arrangements for wages, at Port Phillip, have determined on proceeding to South Australia. The captain has also thirty dogs on board, which he brought from Hobart Town, and which he hopes to sell to advantage, in India.

19th. We beat out of Port Phillip, having been favoured to avoid running aground on the shoals, which is an accident of very frequent occurrence. When opposite Point Nepean, we saw a Dingo, or Wild Dog, upon the beach; he was of large size, brownish colour, had a bushy tail, and was of very wolfish aspect. These animals are numerous in this district, and very destructive among the flocks; which are already computed to consist of considerably more than 200,000 sheep. The entrance of Port Phillip is only about three quarters of a mile wide, and the tide runs in it, at from five to six knots an hour. On our first attempt to pass out, the current was too strong. When at length, we succeeded, the wind outside was adverse, so that we had to beat off the land.

CHAPTER XLIII.

FROM the 20th, to the 23rd, of 11th mo. the wind was adverse, and we beat backward and forward, between Kings Island and Cape Otway. Kings Island is low. In some places, sand rises far up from the beach, but the land is generally covered with scrub, among which trees were visible. We tacked, when about fifteen miles from its north coast, to avoid a reef, on which the convict vessel " Minerva," was lost, about two years since. A large Whale and an Albatross passed us on the 23rd, when we spoke with the " Thistle," from Portland Bay, on her way to Launceston, with oil. The whaling season is now over on these coasts. The land about Cape Otway is high and woody, with deep ravines.

On the 24th, we saw the flat-topped, roundish hills, to the east of Portland Bay, the table land of Cape Bridgewater, the low, extended hills of Cape Northumberland, and several other points of the coast.

25th. We passed in sight of a long series of sand hills, and took a considerable number of Barracoota. These fish had a small kind of Shrimp in their stomachs. Birds were numerous, especially Mutton-birds and Terns.

26th, The wind was very changeable, and there was lightning toward evening. Vast numbers of sea fowl, and some Seals of a yellowish colour, with black muzzles, were upon one of the two little islands, called The Pages, which are at the opening into St. Vincents Gulf, by the Backstairs Passage, by which we entered.

27th. We came to anchor, at about five miles from the shore, in Holdfast Bay, South Australia, which has a sandy beach, exposed to the south. As the evening was wet, with heavy rain, and thunder, we remained on board, while our captain went to Adelaide.

28th. The night was very boisterous, and the vessel pitched violently. The captain returned on board, along with the Port Officer, and we went on shore in the boat that brought them off, paying one pound each to the boatmen. The sea was so rough as to render it difficult to get into the boat, and the wind so high as to carry us rapidly before the sea, with only the aid of a small sail. The men desired us not to be alarmed, and said the boat never shipped a sea, but soon one made its way upon us. They then told us not to be afraid, for if the boat upset in the surf, they would take care of us, but we expected to have to take care of ourselves, in case of such an accident ; they succeeded, however, in keeping the boat before the sea, so as to escape this danger. We landed in a small creek, at Glenelg, a place consisting of a few rude huts, one of which was used as a store. A light, chaise cart, that brought the captain from Adelaide, was waiting for us, and we were quickly conveyed over a flat country, covered with grass, and scattered trees of *Eucalyptus*, *Acacia* and *Banksia*, to the embryo capital of South Australia. Here we received a kind welcome from John Barton Hack and his wife. The former of whom I was acquainted with in England, and the family connexions of the latter, were among the kind friends of my early youth. They were at this time dwelling, with their large family, in a wooden house that they brought from England, in which they realized much more comfort than most of the other settlers did, in their rude huts, of rushes or of sods.

29th. We called on the Governor, Captain John Hindmarsh, and on James H. Fisher, the Commissioner for the Sale of Lands, to both of whom we had letters of introduction from Sir John Franklin, and by whom we were

courteously received. The former offered to endeavour to
obtain a place for us to hold a meeting in; and in the
evening we received a note from him, to say, that he had
conferred with the Episcopal Clergyman, Charles B. Howard,
who was quite willing that we should occupy the place in
which he preached. This was a temporary, square erection
of planks, with a flat roof, raised and seated chiefly by the
minister's own hands. We also called at the tent of T. Q.
Stow, the Independent minister, who happened to be out:
his wife received us kindly; she and her family were busily
occupied in their frail, temporary habitation, a long marquee,
which was greatly agitated by the strong gale of wind that
continued blowing with increased violence. We likewise
spoke to Robert Cock, a prudent Scotchman, who was
living with his wife and several children, under a sort of
thatched roof, till he earned something to build a house:
this indeed he had already effected, but it was occupied
as a store and sale-room. We spoke likewise to several
other settlers. They generally appeared well satisfied in
having emigrated, but were disappointed in not being able
more quickly to have their land apportioned to them. They
had already found, that discord was peculiarly liable to find
its way into small communities, consisting of persons newly
settled, with the view of each promoting his own interest.

30th. We walked about seven miles, to Port Adelaide.
The way was over two level plains, separated by a slight,
sandy rise, covered with wood. The soil of the plains was a
reddish loam, having a slight admixture of sand and calcareous matter. They were covered with tufted grass and
small herbs. Among the latter was a species of *Eryngium*,
a foot high, the leaves of which are eaten with avidity by
cattle, and some small, yellow-flowered Everlastings. Near
Port Adelaide, the land becomes saline, and produces crimson *Mesembryanthemums*, of three species, along with numerous maritime shrubs. On a sand-bank separating the plain
from the salt marsh, which borders the creek or inlet that
forms the harbour, there are trees of a species of *Callitris*,
resembling Cypress. These are here called Pines, and have
trunks about 40 feet high, which are used for piles. *Casuarina*

quadrivalvis, and *Banksia australis,* likewise grow here.   On this bank there was an *Orobanche,* very like *Orobanche minor* of England.   At Port Adelaide there are two large stores, of corrugated iron, in the form of the halves of horizontal cylinders, and several smaller ones, of rushes, &c. and some huts and tents.   Shipping can come up the creek to this place; and by means of a cut, of 180 yards, across a salt marsh, boats can discharge their cargoes close to the stores.   The Eudora had not been able to move hither, in consequence of the violence of the wind, nor had any person got on shore from her.   The salt marsh was covered with two species of *Salicornia,* one of which was shrubby; interspersed among these, were two species of *Frankenia,* one of which was bushy, about a foot high, and besprinkled with rosy, pink blossoms, the size of a silver penny.   The creek was margined with Mangrove, *Avicennia tomentosa.*

12th mo. 1st.   Before breakfast, I walked along the borders of the Torrens, the river which supplies Adelaide with water, which is fresh, and of excellent quality.   Good water is also obtained from wells of about forty feet deep, in the open, limestone formation, upon which Adelaide is situated.   The stream of the Torrens, at the present season, is about one foot in depth, and four feet in width; there are numerous pools, of several fathoms deep, in its course, which are not likely to lack water in the driest seasons.   In some places there are reedy flats below the banks of the river, which are of red loam, and are ornamented by a variety of shrubs and flowers; among which are *Lavatera plebia, Verbena officinalis,* and two species of *Goodenia.*

A few miles back from Adelaide, there is a range of woody hills, the most elevated point of which is called Mount Lofty.   We walked a few miles in this direction, on a plain which is several miles wide, and extends from Cape Jarvis to the Head of St. Vincents Gulf.   It is covered with grass, and intersected with belts of Gum-trees, and a sickle-leaved *Acacia.*   Some of the Kangaroo-grass was up to our elbows, and resembled two years' seed meadows, in England, in thickness; in many places, three tons of hay per acre, might be mown off it.   I had not seen anything to equal it, in this part of the world, except in some of the places that had not been browzed, about Wellington Valley. Several small groups of honest-looking, English labourers were mowing; but their work was only to be seen as little patches, on coming upon them. Adelaide is laid out on both sides of the Torrens; it has an open space of park-land, reserved in the midst, and is divided into 1,040 acres, exclusive of the streets, which cross at right-angles, so as to give to every acre, one side of street-frontage, and to about half of them, two sides. The acres sold originally, at from £3, to about £12 each, and they are now bringing from £40, to £65 each! The population already amounts to about 1,200, but being scattered over so large an area, they make little show. Some of the immigrants are erect-ing comfortable dwellings of wood, stone, or terra-pisa, but many are living in rush huts, which are exceedingly obnox-ious to fire. The day was excessively hot, and every thing was consequently very dry. One of the huts caught fire, and was destroyed in a few minutes. So many persons settling together in an open, fertile country, and having generally brought good supplies with them, from England, and a few who had capital, having imported cattle from Tasmania, they have suffered but a small share of the privations to which the early emigrants to N. S. Wales and V. D. Land were subjected. Provisions are however high; fresh meat 1s. per pound, bread 20d. the four-pound loaf; but if made at home, it does not cost half that sum. Mechanics are obtaining 10s. a day, wages, in cash, or notes of the Bank of Australia, which issues 2s. 5s. and 10s. as well as larger notes, and receives small deposits at interest.

The Blacks about Adelaide are not numerous: they are much like those of other parts of Australia, and most per-sons admit, that the pictures which they have seen of them in England, are caricature likenesses, of much more for-bidding aspect than the originals. I think those here, have mouths, not quite so large as some in other parts. Only one European has lost his life from them, and this was the result of his own profligacy. Since we arrived here, some days have been so cold, that we have been glad of a fire.

2nd. We had conversations with the Governor, and other persons of influence, respecting the Blacks, whose rights there is a disposition to consider. It is greatly to be regretted, that these rights were not secured by the Act of the British Legislature, for the settlement of this Province; but instead of this being done, the country is described in the Act, "as certain waste and unoccupied lands;" and it has been disputed by men of the law, whether, from the tenor of the words used, these Aboriginal Inhabitants, could legally possess land in this country, which was their own by birthright, and which they have done nothing to forfeit.—Another fire destroyed much of the property of one of the immigrants.

3rd. In conversation with a pious settler, he acknowledged, that since coming to this country, he had not kept up the practice of reading the Holy Scriptures, daily, with his family. He said also, that he had observed many instances, in which persons, who bore a religious character in their native land, had sustained great loss in being broken off from their old connexions. Having to stand more alone in this country, they either departed from that to which they had attained, or having in time past, merely kept up the form of religion, from the influence of the society with which they were surrounded, their religious profession faded away, when this influence was removed.—In the forenoon, a meeting for worship was held, consisting of persons professing with the Society of Friends: these were few in number, amounting, with George W. Walker and myself, to only nine persons. I encouraged them to seek strength from the Lord, in order that they might be enabled to walk in the light, and enjoy true Christian fellowship, and know the blood of Jesus Christ to cleanse them from all sin.

4th. We spent some time in conversation with the Commissioner for Lands, respecting the Natives, and the importance of promoting temperance among the settlers. Some of these have got an idea, that, because the climate is hotter than that of England, they must use more stimulating diet and drink, and this notion has been promoted by an injudicious, medical man. The evil of this error is

K K

already becoming obvious.   Many people become drunkards
at sea, where they smoke and drink for want of proper
occupation.   In one vessel, in which the emigrants were
not to be allowed spirits, the captain sold them to them for
biscuit, which they saved from their rations.   The forenoon
was extremely hot, but a breeze from the south-east set in,
and cooled the atmosphere.   We walked to Port Adelaide,
where we became mediators in the settlement of a dispute,
in which some seafaring men were parties, and were more
difficult to reconcile, from being excited by strong drink.
The Eudora has now got into the creek; she was in a
trying situation in Holdfast Bay, during the gale.   The
violent pitching broke her windlass in two, and placed her
in danger of going on shore.

5th.   On going again to Port Adelaide, to obtain a supply of books and tracts from on board the Eudora, we
found one of the seamen in irons, on the bilboe-bolt, he
had refused to work, and had used threatening language
to the captain.   Expostulation with this man was useless:
he was obstinately sullen; and as there seemed no prospect
of peace with him on board, he was at length dismissed.
The thermometer rose to above 100°, and G. W. Walker
became so unwell, from heat and fatigue, that he was unable to attend the meeting in the evening, at which about
200 persons were present.   I was strengthened to labour
with them, and to point out the importance of yielding to
the convictions of the Holy Spirit, and of cherishing the love
and fear of God, as well as to show to them the connexion
of these with true repentance, and faith in Christ.   I also
pressed upon them, the consideration of their duty toward
the Black Population, and the danger of bringing a curse
upon themselves, if they neglected these things.   After being
engaged in vocal prayer, I made a few comments on the
favour granted to us, in the feeling of a precious solemnity,
produced, no doubt, by the immediate influence of the Holy
Spirit.   This continued over the assembly, not only during
the time appropriated to worship, but also while the company were invited to meet again, on the subject of temperance.   After the meeting, a number of copies of our

"Christian Address to the Free Inhabitants of New South
Wales and Van Diemens Land," and of a tract entitled the
"Sentiments of the Society of Friends on Divine Worship
and Gospel Ministry," were distributed.

6th. I walked with two of J. B. Hack's sons, to a place
called The Pines, about five miles from Adelaide. This is
a sandy tract, of limited extent and slight elevation, differing
considerably in its vegetation from the general features of
this district. Among the trees, is the species of *Callitris*,
here called Pine : the timber it affords is said soon to decay :
the tree is of pyramidal figure, and seems distinct from
any we have before seen. We also met with a Gum-tree
of low growth, with yellowish-white blossoms, an *Exocarpos*,
a *Myoporum*, a *Cassia*, and several other trees and shrubs
that were new to us.—In the evening, there was some
excitement among the Blacks, consequent upon two of them
having accidentally, received some injury from the gun of
a man, shooting a quail, who being intent upon his bird,
did not see them among the grass.

7th. A threat was made by the Blacks, that if either of
those shot yesterday, died, the others would burn the hut
of the man that shot them ; and he, in his fear, magnified
this, into an assertion, that they were coming to burn the
huts of the neighbourhood, and persuaded some of his
neighbours to watch with him. In the night, one of the
Blacks, accidentally going to the river to drink, took with
him a fire-stick, according to their usual custom, for they
do not move in the night without a light. This was mistaken for a design to set fire to the huts that lay in the
direction of the river, and a hue and cry was raised after
these people, who also were fired after, but it was alleged,
not with intent to hurt them ; they were, however, left in
a state of considerable excitement. Happily, this was ultimately allayed, and the matter explained to them by the
Protector, who bestirred himself, to see that the white
people were not taking the matter into their own hands.
—Robert Cock, who is much interested for their welfare,
also took some pains with them, and they were persuaded to
come to the Commissioner's store, where they received

some potatoes and other food. The Governor likewise took advantage of this occasion, to assure them of his protection, and to invite them, in all cases of uneasiness, to seek redress from himself and the Protector. He also informed the European population, that if they took the law into their own hands, in any cases of imagined intention of offence, or of actual injury, from the Blacks, they should be dealt with according to law. It is evident, that it is of the utmost importance, to impress upon both communities, that they will not be allowed to avenge themselves, but that the law is open for the redress of both. Something, however, requires to be done, to render the evidence of the Blacks available, or they will not stand on even ground, with the Whites.

The day was extremely wet, and very cool. About a score of the Aborigines took shelter under J. B. Hack's verandah. They were chiefly clad in rugs of skin, which they wear fastened over the shoulders, extending to the knees, or in fragments of European clothing. Their bodies are not so much cut as those of some other tribes of Australia, that wear no clothing. Some of the men wear red ochre and grease in their hair. They appear rarely to wash themselves, and consequently they have an unpleasant smell, much like what we have noticed among prisoners of filthy habits in N. S. Wales, and from this similarity I am disposed to attribute the unpleasant smell of Blacks, not to their colour, but to their want of personal cleanliness. The hair of these Aborigines is not woolly, but generally black, and it has a tendency to curl. Some of the men have more than one wife, and most of the women have children, of which they seem very fond, often embracing and kissing them very affectionately. One of them noticed Bridget Hack kissing her little son, and exclaimed, " Very good," with evident satisfaction. When their families become inconveniently large, they nevertheless sometimes destroy the infants : this seems a matter of regret with them, but is looked upon as one of necessary consequence. We heard of two female children being rescued, or rather of their destruction being abandoned, by the intervention of Europeans. The women do not appear to live in any dread of their husbands. Kangaroos' teeth are fastened to the locks of the children's hair, before and at the sides, as ornaments, and often tufts of feathers are appended behind. I do not think the Natives here, have jaws quite so prominent as some we have seen, but their noses are broad and rather depressed, and the men wear their beards short. Their spears are generally simple rods, but to some, they attach on one side, a sort of barbed ridge, of pieces of glass, by means of Grass-tree gum. We did not observe the boomring among them. In conversation with R. Cock, he suggested that advantage might arise, from the appointment of a committee to co-operate with the Protector, and I recommended him to confer with this individual on the subject.—At dinner, we partook of the flesh of an Emu, killed yesterday between this place and Port Adelaide; it bears some resemblance to tender stewed beef. These birds are yet pretty common here.

8th. Last night was extremely wet. The Blacks remained under J. B. Hack's verandah, where they slept much of yesterday, seeming to think it desirable to be as nearly torpid as possible, in such weather.

9th. Very stormy. Several of the Blacks still remain very quietly under the verandah; some of their children coughed much during the night. We accompanied Robert Cock, in making a call upon the Governor, to converse with him on the propriety of the appointment of a committee to assist the Protector of Aborigines, if such a measure should be acceptable to that officer. The Governor concurred in the opinion that such a committee might be useful, and the Protector expressed more than a willingness to receive the help of such a committee.

10th. Meetings for worship were held at J. B. Hack's, at eleven and six o'clock. They were attended by his family, and a few other persons. On these occasions, I was sensible of the influence of the love of God, extended to his poor, weak creatures. In the morning, I had a few sentences to express, relative to the importance of having the mind subjected to the government of the Holy Spirit, in order that we might not be condemned by our own hearts, but have confidence toward God, under the indispensable terms of discipleship with Christ, the practice of self-denial, and the daily bearing of the cross, and in the progress of this work, know Christ as the propitiation for our sins. The meeting in the evening was held in silence. The day was beautifully fine. The river is much swollen by the late rain. While watching some Blacks rolling up a cask of water, by means of a rope, attached to a pinion, at each end of the cask, so as to enable them to draw it after them like a garden-roller, I noticed some small Crayfish, in the river, of a dark colour, and about the size of those found in some parts of England. One of the Blacks caught some of these, and pulled off their legs, to keep them from running away. While here I saw another break the wings of some young Parrots, to keep them from flying; and when at Port Phillip, I saw two Native boys, holding two Ring-tailed Opossums together, by their tails, to make them fight. Thus, in acts of thoughtless cruelty, as well as in many other points, these people show, that they inherit the fallen propensities of man. This need not excite wonder when seen in savages, as it is so often exhibited in civilized society, and among persons professing to be Christians, who sometimes show as great cruelty, and thoughtlessness, in their sports. The Aborigines do little turns of work for the Settlers, from whom they obtain payment in bread, or some other food. Some attention has been paid to clothing them, and they have already learned, that they are expected to have on blankets, or some other covering, when they come near the houses of the Settlers.

11th. A meeting was held for the promotion of Temperance; and at its conclusion, one to consider of the propriety of appointing a committee, to assist the Protector of the Aborigines. The Governor was in the chair at the former of these meetings, and the Protector at the latter; at which a large committee was appointed.

But notwithstanding this was done, with much appearance of cordiality, I could not dismiss from my mind, an apprehension, that the poor Natives would yet feel themselves

reconciliation

rights 'talk' indeed!

placed in such a position toward the Settlers, as would excite feelings, inimical to the maintenance of a good understanding between them; and that the consideration of the rights of the original Inhabitants of the country, would ultimately be merged in the supposed interests of the Settlers. This arose from some sense of the general prevalence of self-interest among mankind at large, and especially among the emigrants to newly-settled countries, and of the annoyance that uncivilized human beings are apt to prove, to those from civilized countries.

12th. We visited a sawyers' station, among the hills, in the direction of Mount Lofty. After crossing the grassy plains of Adelaide, the first hills, which are nearly at a right-angle with the Mount Lofty range, are of limestone, with here and there, argillaceous rocks. These hills are grassy, with a few trees, and a variety of plants. The next hills are more purely argillaceous, and have trees scattered upon them, like the last, they run rather steeply, into valleys, which are well sheltered, and some of them have small streams at the bottom. Adjoining, there are slate hills, which have less abundant vegetation, and more scrub. The next hills are of old red-sandstone, with poor, sandy soil, but abounding in gay, vegetable productions, in forest, of various species of *Eucalyptus;* among these is the useful Stringy-bark, which some parties are sawing for boards, and splitting for fencing. The carriage from this place to Adelaide is easy, being all the way, down-hill. Beyond this point, the mountain range exhibits white quartz; and persons who have passed Mount Lofty, which may be 1,500 to 2,000 feet above the level of the sea, say, that between it and Mount Barker, the country is fine and woody, and that it also looks well toward Lake Alexandrina. On returning, we descended into a deep valley, at the junction of one of the slate hills, with one of the argillaceous ones, of less slaty character, and found a waterfall of about 160 feet, on a stream, called the White Hill Creek. Some of the hills, like the plains below, are covered with red loam, on which there is fine Kangaroo-grass, that is green, notwithstanding the thermometer has, several times lately, risen to 107° in the shade.

A white-flowered *Morna,* a downy, drooping-flowered *Pimelea,* a broad and a narrow-leaved *Xanthorrhœa,* and several other striking plants, were growing in the forest on the red sandstone. On the argillaceous hills, there was a shrub belonging the *Gentianæ,* with leaves resembling those of the Greater Periwinkle, and a *Pomaderris,* with pale leaves next to the heads of flowers. *Todea africana, Grammitis rutæfolius,* and some other ferns were also here. Upon the limestone hills, were a broad-leaved *Goodenia,* an *Orobanche,* and *Lobelia gibbosa,* this last is a singular annual, flowering after its leaves have faded.—A considerable number of curious insects were feeding in a thicket, on the blossoms of a *Leptospermum.* On the low land, there is a flat beetle, allied to *Silpha,* that is surrounded by a broad, projecting, horny margin, in which there is a hole, that the insect can raise its head through, at pleasure.

13th. We took leave of our friends at Adelaide, walked to the Port, and again went on board the Eudora. The heat was so great, that the thermometer stood at 102°, in one of the stern cabins, with the window and door open, and the deck above, wet. The heat at Adelaide often produces ophthalmia; but this disease generally gives way to the use of a greatly diluted solution of nitrate of silver, which is a remedy, only safe in the hands of a skilful person. The creek at Adelaide will scarcely allow of more than a single line of vessels, for most of its length. They make fast to the Mangroves, one of which was pulled up by the Eudora, in a gale of wind. The vessel went against the opposite bank, but was easily warped off again. There is some trouble in loosing the moorings, to allow other vessels to pass.

14th. The moschettos were very troublesome last evening, and during the night. The position of the Eudora is between two bushy, salt marshes, in which they abound. To-day I crossed one of these, partly covered by the tide, to the sandy beach of Holdfast Bay, where I amused myself by picking up some small and curious shells. I found a drier path to return by: there were, however, some places to cross, where the tide was running off the marsh; but

the heat being very great, it was pleasanter in the water
than out of it.   In my walk, I kept my eye on the base of
the trunks of the Mangroves, *Avicennia tomentosa,* in the
hope of finding some rock-oysters attached to them, but was
disappointed.   I conclude that this species of shell-fish does
not inhabit the south coast of Australia, as it is not met
with here, nor yet at Port Phillip: probably Jervis Bay,
on the east coast, may be about its southern limit, as it is
there very small.   On ship-board, a cotton shirt and a pair
of trousers, of thin drill, with slippers, constitute my clothing.   The heat is very oppressive, notwithstanding the decks
are often wetted.   The thirst of the persons on board was
such that I made them a bucket full of Cream-of-tartar
drink, which being sweetened, and having a flavour imparted
by a few drops of essence of lemon, is a good substitute
for lemonade; or, with the addition of a little carbonate of
soda, it affords a pleasant effervescent draught.   In the evening, with the high tide, and a light and pleasant breeze,
the Eudora proceeded about fifteen miles, to the mouth of
the creek.

CHAPTER XLIV.

12th mo. 15th. At day-break, we got fairly under weigh. The port-officer left us as soon as we entered St. Vincents Gulf. A fair breeze brought us, at eight knots an hour, to the entrance of Investigators Strait, where it failed, and was succeeded by variable puffs of wind, and calms.

16th. The wind being against us, we stood backward and forward, between Kangaroo Island and the small islands, off York Peninsula. The surface of Kangaroo Island is woody, with grass, in some places; its gullies appear to be deep. Its cliffs are lofty, dark, and horizontally stratified. A few months since, some persons landed from a vessel, at the western end of the island, being tired with a long voyage, and thinking to make their way easily to Kings Cote, a settlement of the South Australian Company, on the eastern extremity. Some of the party reached this point, in a very exhausted state; but the surgeon, and another person perished in the intricate bush. Much danger attends strangers in any country, attempting to make their way from the coast, to distant places; many have narrowly escaped death, in such attempts, in other parts of Australia.

17th. This morning we left the Gambier and Thistle Islands, in Spencers Gulf, to the northward, and one of the Neptune Islands, to the southward. Mutton-birds and Terns were numerous about this island, on which there were also some

Seals. We spent much of the day in private, religious retirement, and placed books of a religious tendency, in the way of the officers of the vessel, who now and then looked into them. The position of the Eudora, in regard to the land, was unfavourable to collecting the ship's company, for religious purposes.

18th. We made 224 miles, between the noon of yesterday and to-day, and were out of sight of land.

20th. The wind was unfavourable yesterday, but favourable to-day; though fresh, it was not so strong as to prevent the rigging of the vessel being tightened. Birds were numerous: among them were the Wandering, the Black, and the Small Brown-winged Albatross, the Mutton-bird and another species of Petrel. A shoal of Porpoises passed westward, in the morning.

22nd. A heavy squall, attended by loud thunder and vivid lightning overtook us. The evening was fine.—A gale which reached us last night, was heavy in the early part of the day, in Encounter Bay, to the east of St. Vincents Gulf, where it occasioned some injury to shipping, and was attended by loss of life.

25th. Yesterday we again came in sight of land, sail was shortened last night, and this morning, we were a few miles south of Bald Island. We soon got sight of Mount Gardener and Bald Head, and passed between them, into King Georges Sound, which is a fine bay, surrounded by hills, with an opening into an inner harbour, called Princess Royal Harbour, near the entrance into which, we anchored. The little town of Albany, the only one on the south coast of Western Australia, is situated within the inner harbour, at the foot of Mount Melville and Mount Clarence, two small, rock-capped, granite hills. Here we became the guests of George Cheyne, who, with his open-hearted wife, gave us a kind welcome. Though Albany, is laid out as a town upon some maps, it is a poor place, consisting of a few, scattered cottages: there is no baker's shop in it, but there are four public-houses. The population is very small.

After taking some refreshment, we walked about a mile and a half, to call on the Government Resident, Sir Richard

Spencer, who received us kindly, and made many inquiries for intelligence, which every body, in this sequestered spot, seemed desirous of receiving. In the course of our walk, we were struck with the variety, and gaiety of the shrubs and plants of this poor country, which seems to be chiefly peat and sand. *Banksia coccinea,* and several other species of this genus were in blossom; also several species of *Pimelea, Sphenotoma, Callistachys, Anigozanthos,* &c. The most striking object was *Nuytsia floribunda,* a low tree, belonging to the same natural order as the Mistletoe and Loranthus, but growing out of the ground. Its thick, narrow, green leaves formed a fine contrast with the deep, golden blossoms that covered the whole upper half of its head. We dined with George and Grace Cheyne, at whose table there was a plentiful supply of Green-peas, and of Potatoes, of excellent quality. In the afternoon, we met a small congregation, in the house of a person from India, sojourning here, and who kindly afforded us this accommodation. I found it my place to proclaim briefly, the gospel message, with solemn warning, beginning with reference to the passages of Scripture, "It is appointed to all men once to die, but after this the judgment." And "some men's sins are open before hand, going before unto judgment, and some they follow after." There was a sense of the divine presence, perceptible to my mind throughout the meeting, but it was not a bright time. A few remarks were made at the conclusion, on the importance of temperance, but we did not see our way open to appoint a meeting for this specific object, which, nevertheless, greatly wants attention here. It is said, that every sixpence, not wanted for absolute necessaries, by the labouring class, who get great wages, goes in strong drink, and by this means the settlement is impoverished, while in a peculiar degree, it needs capital. There seems to be a great lack of industry also among the people; and poor as the land is, it yields good supplies of vegetables, with a little attention. Few of the cottages have their gardens fenced in, so as to protect them; and ships putting in, for wood, water, &c. can rarely get supplied with vegetables, notwithstanding that traffic by sea is what the inhabitants chiefly depend upon.

In the evening, I had some interesting conversation with a magistrate from Oyster Harbour, respecting the Blacks of this immediate district, commonly known here by the designation of the King George tribe. They are about fifty in number, are very docile, live on good terms with the European inhabitants, and exhibit few of the vices that prevail among their countrymen, in the older settlements, on the eastern side of Australia. From what we have seen and heard of those of the south coast, I incline to the opinion, that many of the most atrocious vices of those in the older settlements, are the result of a contact with a depraved, white population. Infanticide is said to be unknown among the King George Blacks. No case is known of a white man having been speared by them, nor by any other tribe within about seventy miles. Their dwellings are rude shelters of leafy boughs, about four feet high; they wear a garment of Kangaroo-skin, or a blanket, fastened over the shoulders, and reaching about to the knees, and smear their heads, faces, and necks, with grease and red ochre, and dust a little of this article, or of a yellow earth, upon the cheek-bones. Their countenances, generally, are not unpleasant, but some of them have very prominent mouths; they use their teeth in straightening their spears, which are simple rods.

A few of these people have been employed by the settlers, in carrying wood and water, and in some other domestic occupations; but taking into account, the length of time that the British Settlement of King Georges Sound has existed, and the docility of these people, it is remarkable that no systematic attempt at their civilization, has been made. There is one solitary instance, of a childless couple of white people, adopting a little, black, orphan girl, to which they seem much attached, and she is forward for her years, with her book and her needle. One reason that the Blacks of King Georges Sound have not come into hostile collision with the Whites, is probably, that, from the nature of the country, few of the latter live off the Settlement, and consequently, they are seldom from under notice of the other settlers; and another, that as the land is so unfavourable for agriculture or depasture, the country of the Blacks has suffered but little, actual invasion.

There is no religious teacher of any denomination, at King Georges Sound, unless a person can be called one, who "reads prayers," to all who will go to hear him, in a little chapel, that he has erected at his own expense, and who retails spirituous liquors, but does not allow persons to sit down in his house to drink! There is but one family professing with the Wesleyans, and they say, that seldom more than two or three persons meet with them for devotional purposes.

Many inquiries were made, if our Captain had clothing, shoes, flour, or live-stock to dispose of, all of which are scarce here; even some of the children of the Government Resident have been obliged to go barefoot. This however, is not a serious evil here, as the roads, or rather tracks, are generally soft. The climate is so fine as to admit of three crops of potatoes being obtained in the year; the heat is seldom oppressive. It is said, that there is little good land, within seventy miles of this place; but there are patches of strong, red loam, in the neighbourhood, probably where the granite is interrupted by basalt. In some places there is lime-stone, but upon this, the land is said to be poor. Near the coast, pure white sand prevails to the tops of the hills, which may be from three to five hundred feet high.

26th. We breakfasted with Sir Richard and Lady Spencer, and walked with them, over their fine garden, and little farm, which are on one of the little patches of good land. In the garden, Grapes, Figs, Almonds, Peas, Potatoes, &c. are very thriving. On the farm, there is a good crop of Wheat, where the land has been manured; that, on fresh broken-up land, is very thin and poor: Maize will also grow here. A decent cottage, with a little garden, was pointed out to us near Albany, as the possession of a man, who was upon the parish when in England; but I believe, a much greater number have become poorer than richer at this place.

A poor, heathy country, which does not produce grain enough for its inhabitants, and in which, except in a few spots, neither bullocks, sheep, nor even goats thrive, and where, when fresh meat is to be had, it costs 1s. 6d. per lb. and bread, is proportionately dear, is not the place in which persons without capital are likely to improve their circumstances. The climate, however, is salubrious, and adapted for persons who have lost their health in India; but to make this their retreat, they ought to have a tolerable income, and to be fond of solitude. We were informed that no European had died a natural death here, since the formation of the settlement. Rum has slain some of its votaries, three persons have been speared by the Blacks, far into the interior, and a few have been drowned. Small as is the community of this place, it is said to be much disturbed by discord. A little business is done here in whaling and sealing. Plenty of good fish is to be had, in the harbours and the sound: the Blacks catch a singular, bearded species, about one foot and a half long, among the sea-weed, with their spears. Among their articles of food, is the long bulb, of *Hemodorum teretifolium,* which they call Mean; and poor fare, it truly is, occasioning their tongues to crack grievously: it is prepared for eating by being roasted, and beaten up with the earth, from the inside of the nest of the White Ant, or with a red substance, found on burnt ground. We held ourselves in readiness to return on board this evening, but were prevented by a strong wind, which upset one of the boats in coming on shore; the men narrowly escaped drowning, but were rescued by another boat from the ship, from which providentially they were seen.

In the course of a walk, we examined some of the remarkable plants of this district. Among these may be enumerated *Kingia australis,* which resembles a Grass-tree, of about eight feet high, but differs in its flower-stems and blossoms; *Solya heterophylla,* which produces elegant, blue flowers, on a privet-like, half-climbing bush; *Anthocercis viscida,* which forms a large, bushy plant, with striking, white flowers, and grows close upon the beach; and *Cephalodea folicularis,* which has small, whitish flowers, on a stalk a foot and a half high, and which produces pitcher-like vessels among its leaves, at the base of the flower-stem: the pitchers have lids, are an inch deep, contain water, and often, drowned insects, and are of very singular structure.

27th. Our kind friend, George Cheyne, offered to convey us to the Eudora, in his whale-boat, at an early hour, but some of the men who were to have rowed us, were too early intoxicated. When we got off with others, some of them were incapable of managing the boat, from the same cause, and G. W. Walker and G. Cheyne were under the necessity of taking to the oars. We had agreed with Stephen Addison, to touch with us at the Swan River, on his way to India, for fifty pounds, provided he could effect this without a delay of more than a fortnight, and that, in case the wind should be so against him as to prevent him touching, we should go with him to India, for the same sum. When we reached the vessel, all was bustle on board, to get her under weigh, her position being near the lee shore. Prompt exertion soon effected this important object, and we beat out of the Sound, shortening sail when near the Seal Rock, to allow G. Cheyne to board the Alice, which had been lying here for a few days, and was going to Swan River, but by which we had not felt comfortable to proceed. We were favoured to get nicely to sea again, and in the afternoon, passed inside Vancouvers Reef and the Eclipse Island; by night we were also past the White-topped Rock, with a fair breeze.

28th. We made good progress, the wind following us round Cape Leeuwin, near to which, a remarkable patch of sand, of considerable width, runs from the coast, up the adjacent hills.

29th. Some flying-fish were seen this morning. The day was fine, the wind brisk and fair. We passed to the west of Rottenest Island, and came to anchor in Gages Roads, at the Swan River, about half-past seven o'clock in the evening, having been favoured to make this voyage, in little more than two days, from King Georges Sound!

CHAPTER XLV.

12th mo. 30th. OUR luggage was sent on shore, by a large
boat, at the charge of £3! We obtained lodgings at a
tolerable inn, at Freemantle, to which we were recommended
by Thomas Bannister, with whom we became acquainted,
when he was Sheriff of V. D. Land, and from whom we
received much kind attention, both at that period, and during our sojourn at the Swan River, Western Australia.

The town of Freemantle is situated behind a little promontory of limestone, at the mouth of an estuary, called
Melville Water, into the head of which, near Perth, the
Swan and Canning Rivers flow. These rivers form an inland navigation, to a considerable distance, but the opening
of Melville Water into the sea, is so choked with rocks,
that it is only passable for boats, in fine weather. Vessels
discharge their cargoes at a jetty, in a small bay on the
south of the town. A tunnel is formed through the
promontory, to a place where boats can land with more
security, in stormy weather. The houses of Freemantle
are of limestone. Many of them have been left unfinished,
in consequence of the seat of Government having been removed to Perth; these, as well as others that are occupied,
are going to decay. Freemantle resembles some of the

little coast-villages, on the limestone of the county of Durham, but it is even whiter than they, and it is greatly inconvenienced by the drifting of sand. Fresh water is obtained in shallow wells, in the limestone. The population is about 200.

Having learned that the Governor, Sir James Stirling, was likely to make an exploratory voyage, to Port Leschenault, we concluded to pay him a visit before he set out, and for that purpose, proceeded to Perth, in a passage-boat, which reached that place in about two hours. A fine sea-breeze made the sail up Melville Water very pleasant, the weather being hot. This estuary widens, in many places, into large bays. The limestone hills on its margin are covered with trees and scrub, and are broken here and there, into picturesque cliffs. On landing, we were welcomed to the Colony, by Major Irwin, a pious, military officer, who invited us to his house. After tea, we called upon the Governor, who, with Lady Stirling, received us kindly. We were also introduced to the Colonial Chaplain, and to several other persons; and the Governor gave us leave to hold a meeting for public worship, in the Court House, which is a neat building, conveniently fitted up, and used as a place of worship, by the Episcopalian congregation. The windows have white calico, in place of glass, and are fitted with Venetian shutters, outside.

At Perth, we became lodgers, in the homely dwelling of the widow of a Colonial Surgeon; in whose house, several other persons were also inmates. The bed-rooms were without plaster on the walls, or glass in the windows, and fleas were very numerous. Circumstances like these are not uncommon in newly-settled countries, in warm climates. But we had learned to put up with inconveniences of this kind, and gratefully acknowledged the endeavours of our landlady, to do her best to accommodate her guests.

The town of Perth consists of several streets, in most of which there are but few houses. Some of these, as well as the fences about the gardens, appear to be going to decay. The streets are of sand, mixed with charcoal, from the repeated burning of the scrub, which formerly covered the ground, on which the town stands. The principal street has a raised causeway, slightly paved, by which the toil of wading through the grimy sand may be avoided. Many beautiful, native shrubs grow in the borders of the gardens, most of which are in a neglected state. A few, on the slope to the head of Melville Water, have the advantage of being moistened, by filtration, from some lagoons, at the back of the town; these are well cultivated, and produce fine crops of Grapes and Melons. The lagoons are much filled with the Cats-tail Reed, *Typha latifolia*, the root of which is eaten by the Natives. They are margined with blue Lobelias, and various species of *Drosera* and *Villarsia;* and other pretty plants. Moschettos are numerous, and very troublesome in the evening.

31st. We met a congregation of upwards of two hundred persons, a large number for the place, the population being only about six hundred. Several of the influential inhabitants were present. I had an open season of religious labour, and endeavoured to turn the attention of the audience to "the gift of God," and to Him who is able to give the "living water," "which they who drink of, shall never thirst."

In conversation respecting the Aborigines, with a medical man, from the country, he stated his opinion to be, that they were a people who deserved no consideration, but whom it would be best to destroy whenever they were troublesome! To this sentiment, we replied, that neither Christianity, justice, nor even common sense admitted such an idea; and that though, according to the notions of these people, blood was required for blood, yet that persons who voluntarily settled in a country, which the British Government had usurped, ought, with that Government, to labour for the civilization of the Native Inhabitants, and to bear patiently the inconveniences resulting from their customs, until these could be changed. There is reason to fear, that many other persons entertain similar sentiments, but the Colonial Chaplain, with whom we dined, at the table of the Governor, said, he believed that in almost every case, where any of the white people had been destroyed by the Blacks, the Whites were the faulty party.

The native Blacks, who are numerous about Perth, are a
fine race, and far from defective in intelligence : they have a
few, irregular, elevated scars upon their bodies, generally
about their shoulders ; their teeth are not injured, as a token
of manhood, as in N. S. Wales; they usually wear a small rug,
of Kangaroo-skin, about their shoulders, but not unfrequently,
the men walk about Perth and Freemantle in a state of nudity, and custom appears so to reconcile this practice, that little
pains is taken to discourage it. They cut wood, draw water,
and perform many other little offices, for the European Population; for which they obtain bread, or money, which they
lay out in bread, the two-pound loaf now costing 1s. They
have not acquired a taste for tobacco, or spirits, nor do they
show a disposition to wear English clothing. They are remarkably docile, but scarcely any attempts have been made
to civilize them. We are informed that the people here have
been discouraged from attempting any thing in this way, by
the ill success which they understand has attended such efforts in N. S. Wales. There seems a great willingness to
suffer the Aborigines to dwindle away, under the easy conclusion, that thus the Indians of North America, and the
Natives of Van Diemens Land, passed away, and that as
nothing could be done for those of New South Wales, any
attempt at so hopeless a task, as their civilization here, is not
of much consequence.

1st mo. 1st. 1838.   We returned to Freemantle, by land,
and found the journey very tedious. Though the road lies
over one of those portions of the Great Plain of Quartania,
marked on maps " gently undulating grassy country, thinly
timbered," it is difficult to find grass upon many parts
of it, but there is abundance of rigid herbage, chiefly of a
stemless *Xanthorrhœa,* called here the Ground Blackboy,
and a profusion of rigid shrubs, unfit for pasturage, except,
perhaps, for goats, camels, or asses. The distance, said
to be eleven miles, is over a loose sand, adorned with
curious trees, and gay shrubs and flowers. Thus, as in other
instances, the soil with the gayest productions, is the worst
in quality. The gay *Nuytsia floribunda,* attains to forty
feet in height, and six feet in circumference; it is called

in the Colony, Cabbage-tree, because of a faint resemblance, in the texture of its branches, to cabbage-stalks: its top, at this season, is one mass of golden, orange, or yellow flowers, while the lower portion is of a pleasant green. *Banksia grandis* attains to twenty feet, and some other species of this genus, to a greater elevation. A fine, yellow *Calythrix;* a yellow and red, and a sky-blue *Leschenaultia;* a crimson, linear-leaved *Callistemon;* a scarlet *Melaleuca;* a crimson *Calothamnus*, with several species of *Jacksonia*, &c. are now in blossom.

A Black was tried yesterday, and sentenced to death, for beating two boys, leaving them for dead, and driving off the sheep that were under their care. Dr. Guistiniani, a missionary, about to leave the Colony, pleaded for the Black, and compared the taking away of the sheep, by the Natives, with the destruction of the Kangaroos, by the Whites: he urged, that undue temptation was put into the way of the Blacks, by placing the sheep in the charge of such very young boys.

3rd. Much of the country near Freemantle, is of limestone, covered with sand; it is unproductive of herbage, adapted for flocks, and unlikely, in a state of nature, to yield any thing for the support of a new colony. With a little culture, it is said, however, to yield good vegetables. Potatoes are excellent, and in some situations, produce three crops in a year. Vines and figs thrive, even in the town, where the limestone rock, is covered with little but fragments and sand. Industry is not great in the Colony, and much of the land will yield nothing without it.

4th. In the evening, we took a walk, on Arthurs Head, the promontory, at the mouth of Melville Water, the top of which is rough, stony, and covered with scrub. From this point, we saw the effect of oil, in stilling the sea; some had been pumped out of a ship, with leaky casks on board, and it rendered the surface of the ocean strikingly smooth, for a great distance.—We had some conversation with two persons, who have known much of the Colony, from its settlement, and who consider that it has struggled through its first difficulties. One of them afterwards acknowledged, that he believed the whole population would have left it, had they been able; but that they were prevented, by having invested their whole capital in it.

5th. I walked to Woodmans Point, seven miles from Freemantle, where there is a sand-spit or projecting shoal, on which some interesting shells are found. A Crowned Conch was in the act of burying itself in the sand, in the shallow water, at sunrise. There were vast numbers of sea-fowl at this point, at day-break. The variety of shells found here is considerable, and a slug, more than a foot long, is also cast up on the beach, having a large, cartila-ginous, internal shell.

6th. A Shark with a round nose was harpooned to-day, from the Abercromby, a vessel by which we purpose to leave this Colony. It measured nearly ten feet in length. The head and shoulders of a sharp-nosed species, of not greatly inferior dimensions, that was killed on the previous day, were found in its stomach. Though these frightful animals are so numerous here, that in bathing, it is need-ful to keep a good look-out, and not to venture beyond the sandy-flats, where they can easily be seen, no accidents have yet happened by them.—The thermometer is often 103° in the shade, and where the water of the sea is not more than a foot and a half deep, the sand upon which the sun is shining through it, is perceptibly warmer than the water.

7th. We had a large meeting in the Court-house. On going thither, I felt very empty, and much discouraged, but in a short time, had to speak of the fear of the Lord, and to declare its fruits to be, watchfulness over our own hearts, and attention to the convictions of the Holy Spirit, by which alone, mankind come savingly to Christ, as the propitiation for their sins, and as the Shepherd and Bishop of their souls. Toward the conclusion, a comforting sense of the divine pre-sence overshadowed the meeting, claiming the tribute of thanksgiving and praise.

On the 8th and 9th. We circulated a considerable num-ber of tracts, and a few books, many persons calling for them at our lodgings. The little books, printed at Birming-ham, are very acceptable to the children here: we have had some applications for Bibles and Testaments. There is no bookseller in Western Australia, nor any Bible Society Auxiliary, nor even agent, at the Swan River.

12th. We returned to Perth on the 10th, and to-day, walked to the Peninsula, distant about four miles, along a road, so sandy as to require two hours to traverse it. Here we called upon Michael and Elizabeth Clarkson, the former of whom emigrated from Yorkshire; they have commendably, accommodated themselves to the circumstances of the Colony, and are industriously endeavouring to support themselves, by cultivating the land. The Peninsula is formed by a bend of the Swan River, and is a flat, of strong, but not rich soil. The river here is broad, and salt, and has samphire marshes on its margin. We crossed it, in a boat, on the way toward Guildford, where we became the guests of Alfred and Elizabeth Waylen, from whom we had received a kind invitation.

13th. Francis Whitfield, the Government Resident, or paid magistrate of the district, assisted us in giving notice of a meeting, to be held in the Episcopal chapel. We were joined by an Irish settler, from the York district, a grassy country, adapted for sheep, beyond the Darling Range, and upon the Avon River, which is identical with the Swan, and where many of the settlers have flocks of small size. In driving sheep and cattle, from the Perth side of the Darling Range, across that mountain territory, numbers of them have been taken ill suddenly, and have died almost immediately, it is supposed, from eating a species of *Lobelia*. No accident of this kind is said to have occurred, in driving fat stock, from the better lands of the York district, to the inferior, coast country. The largest flock of sheep in the Colony, is said to be of about 800, and the whole stock not more than 12,000. The whole of the sheep-country, discovered, is computed to be able to support about 200,000. In this, is included, the Toogee country, to which several settlers are now removing. East of the York district, there is a great range of extremely sterile country, almost destitute of water; but upon which the Bush Turkey, hatches its eggs, in hillocks of sand! We called on a pious Welshman, whose parents occupy a house licensed for the sale of spirits, and kept open for travellers. There are two other houses licensed for the sale of spirits, in Guildford, seven in Perth, and four in Freemantle, besides some others, in more remote situations!

It is difficult to estimate the ruin that has been brought upon this Colony, by the consumption of spirits. The whole revenue of the Government, amounting to about £7,000 a-year, is derived from spirits, in the form of duty on the imports; so that the amount of capital, annually paid for them, must be much more considerable. The Colony is so poor, as to be unable to import sheep in sufficient quantity, to stock its lands, so that the holders of grants of from 5,000 to 100,000 acres, have little stock of any kind upon them. Such grants are consequently, of so little value, as to occasion land to be sold, as low as from 1s. 6d. to 2s. 6d. per acre! Had the money expended in spirits, since the foundation of the Colony, been occupied in the importation of sheep, it is not improbable that land might now have been ten times its present value; and had no grants originally exceeded 5,000 acres, many more persons would have had the means of maintaining flocks, of about 1,000 sheep each. The wealth of the Colony would probably have been thus increased, so as to have rendered grants of this size, by this time, as valuable as those of 50,000 acres each, now are. Spirit drinking, and avarice in obtaining grants of large extent, have paralyzed the country, which, beyond a doubt, is naturally very inferior to what was originally represented. The exports of oil and wool, are yet very inconsiderable, perhaps, not amounting to £4,000 in any one year, and almost the only other sources of income to the Colony, are, the payments of Government salaries, the supply of provision to the few ships that put in here, and a little arising from private property. The persons, who have improved their circumtances by emigration to this country, are labourers, store-keepers, and a few others, into whose hands much of the capital that was originally in the possession of other Colonists, has passed; but by this transition, the capital of the Colony is not increased. Its population is said to be now, only about 2,000, or one third of what it was, three years after the Colony was first settled. Death, frequently the result of drinking, and emigration to Australia and Tasmania, have been the chief causes of this reduction.

14th. About sixty persons assembled in the chapel, which is a commodious room, of large dimensions, built of terre-pesée. We had an open opportunity of religious labour. There were some inquiring minds among the congregation, but I fear, little disposition to "seek first the kingdom of God, and his righteousness."

15th. In company with a respectable settler, we ferried ourselves across the Swan River, the ferrymen being so drunk that we could get no help from them, and returned through a sandy forest, to the Peninsula. By the way, we were constrained to turn into the house of a settler, to partake of such refreshment as she was able to set before us, which consisted of salt-beef, Cucumbers, Water-melons, and Cape-gooseberries, which last, were placed before us in a bushel-measure. Many interesting shrubs were in blossom, on moist places, in the forest, and beautiful insects were feeding on the honey of their flowers.

16th. We returned to Perth, and in the evening addressed the inhabitants in the Court House, on the subject of temperance. At the close of the meeting, a Western Australian Temperance Society was organized. In the course of the proceedings, a labouring man came forward, and inquired, how persons like himself, should become members of Temperance Societies, when their masters often paid them, to the amount of one-third of their wages, in spirits, and the remainder, in an order on some store, where little else was to be had. This led to some comments on the injurious practice, which appears to have arisen out of a kind of Government-order, before the formation of any Colonial law, that each servant should be allowed two glasses of rum daily! Servants, having acquired a strong appetite for stimulating liquors, frequently left their work and went to public-houses; masters, therefore, to obviate this inconvenience, and perhaps, it is not too severe to say, to avail themselves of a part of the profit of retailing spirits, obtained an Act of Council, to render it lawful for them, to pay their servants in spirits, to the amount of one-third of their wages; and this pernicious law is still in force.

17th. We had another interview with the Governor, who seemed much pleased with Port Leschenault; the country about which is represented as well adapted for the pasturage of horned cattle. We walked with him over his garden, in which the Olive, Vine, Fig, and Peach thrive luxuriantly. Bananas ripen tardily at Perth; Oranges and Lemons do not thrive, perhaps for want of a stronger soil and more shelter.

19th. Yesterday we returned to Guildford. Being again accompanied by the Government Resident, we went this morning to the upper part of the Swan River. Much of the country that we passed through, was poor, and covered with open forest of several species of *Eucalyptus*, called here Red-gum, Mahogany, White-gum, Flooded-gum, &c. The Red-gum has capsules as large as crab-apples, and is useful timber for fencing, &c. The Mahogany resembles, in some degree, the true Mahogany, but is rather darker and heavier. The ground of these forests is covered with low scrub of Acacia, Grass-trees, &c. Several species of Banksia and Acacia also form low trees. Along the borders of the Swan, there are narrow alluvial, flats, of good land, that are chiefly cultivated with grain. Adjoining these, there is a very limited extent of soil, of inferior quality, but capable of yielding good crops, by the aid of manure. In the range of this kind of country, there are several small farming establishments, and a few large ones, within sight one of another. Some portions of arable land, have lately been sold at £1. per acre.

We visited George Fletcher Moore, the Advocate-general, at his farming establishment, and went with him to see a little of the country, some of which, in this neighbourhood, is accounted the best in quality, in the Colony. Some of the estates are doubtless fine ones, or at least, have fine portions upon the river. A considerable number of the Blacks were assembled on one farm: we had met with several of them before, about Perth and the Peninsula;

they quickly recognized us again, and began to beg for "tickpens," as they call sixpences, to buy bread with. One woman showed me her eye, which she made me understand, that one of the men had injured. They frequently treat one another with great cruelty; and if one of them die, naturally or violently, one of the same tribe makes a point of killing some one of another tribe. Thus one death among them, leads to a series ; one, according to their notions, to avenge another, and to keep up a balance of power ! If a man quarrel with another, or be angry with one of his own wives, he will spear the wife of his enemy, or his own wife, through the leg or thigh.

20th. We took a walk to that part of the Swan, where its bed becomes dry in the summer, except in large pools, and is covered with scrub, among which is the handsome, shrubby *Hibiscus lilacinus.* The harvest is now over, and it is expected that there will again, be wheat enough to supply this little Colony. This was the case last year, but many of the agriculturists being needy, were obliged to sell their corn to the merchants, who appear to be a class of men, ready to take every advantage, to enrich themselves, and they contrived to raise the price from 5s. to 30s. a bushel, before the late harvest. This Colony, suffers from selfishness and discord, as well as the others, in this part of the world, and even in a pre-eminent degree.

In our walk, several places were pointed out, as sites of the destruction of Blacks, either by their own tribes, according to their barbarous customs, or by the White Inhabitants; and others, where white men had been destroyed by the Blacks. There is now a pretty good understanding between the Aborigines and the Europeans, on the Swan ; but across the Darling Range, persons do not feel themselves secure, and several Blacks have been shot, on the alleged ground of self-defence. Neither the Colonial Government, nor the Settlers generally, seem to understand, the advantage, that it would be to themselves, to bring the Aborigines into the state of an industrious peasantry, by instructing them in the relative value of money and labour, and by rewarding them proportionately to the White Labourers, for the work they

palm-like leaves, four feet long or more. They generally grow in considerable numbers, within a few feet of each other, either among the Gum-trees, or in pieces of richer and more humid soil, on flats, along with large Grass-trees, and large shrubs. In this part of Australia, the Natives bury, or macerate, the nuts, till the rinds become half decomposed, in which state they eat the rind, rejecting the kernel; but in N. S. Wales, they pound and macerate· the kernels, and then roast and eat, the rough paste.

I have heard, from persons of respectable authority, that in the Swan River Country, as well as at King Georges Sound, the Natives have their private property, clearly distinguished into hunting-grounds, the boundaries of which are definite, trees being often recognized by them as landmarks, and that the possession rests in the head of a family. Several of these families residing in a district, form what the white people call a Tribe; but these tribes are not subject to any recognized chief, though a man of prowess will often gain great ascendancy among them. A young man, who resided some years at King Georges Sound, told me, that several tribes of Blacks assembled there, once a year, and held a sort of fair; and that as different tribes excelled each other in the manufacture of weapons, such as spears, throwing sticks or woomeras, kylers or boom-rings, shields, and waddies, these formed the articles of exchange, as well as the red-ochre, with which, combined with grease, they besmear themselves, and which is only found in certain localities. In Western Australia, the Blacks perforate the cartilage of the noses of the boys, when about twelve, or fourteen years of age; a kangaroo-bone, of the thickness of a goose-quill, is occasionally worn through the hole; they also mark their bodies by cutting them; but those of the Swan River are not so tasteful in this respect, as those of some other parts of Australia.

CHAPTER XLVI.

Swan River.—Drunkenness.—Fights of the Aborigines.—Temperance Meeting.
—Evils connected with the use of Spirits.—Explorators.—Weapons of the
Blacks.—Retribution.—Amount of Black Population, &c.—Jelly-fish.—Edu-
cation.—Visit of the Blacks.—Birds, &c.—Aurora australis.—Intemperance of
Seamen.—Revenge and Expiation of Injuries among the Aborigines.—Em-
barkation.—Peaceful Retrospect.

1st mo. 23rd. WE returned by a boat, to the Old Ferry,
three miles from Freemantle, and walked the remainder of
the way, which is over rough limestone and sand, and were
glad to reach our former quarters again, notwithstanding, in
some respects, they are far from what we could desire;
especially in being at this time, the resort of a number of
noisy, drunken sailors, belonging to a whaler, and some
other vessels in the roads.

26th. Having received an invitation to attend another
temperance meeting, at Perth, we returned thither. A large
party of the Murray River Natives were crossing the Melville Water, at the Ferry, above Freemantle, as we passed.
They were returning from Perth, were they had been to
fight with the Natives of that neighbourhood, respecting a
woman who had been carried off by the latter, and who was
dreadfully speared by one of the party. While under excitement, they also killed a man, known by the name of Dobbin,
who had rendered himself an object of dislike, by committing
a robbery, some months ago, on a white man's premises.
The white man went out on the spur of the moment, fired
at the first Blacks he came at, and shot an unoffending
young man. For this offence he was tried, and though not
found guilty of murder, he was removed to King Georges

Sound, for his own safety. Many of the Blacks that we passed, were lame from spear-wounds in their legs or thighs, that they had received during their late conflict; this we also found to be the case with the Perth Natives, few of whom had escaped without injury. Before, and also some time after these battles, which appear to be affairs of honour with these untutored people, they have grand corroberries, or dances together! It is matter of surprise, that little care is taken by the civil authorities, to prevent these murderous combats, which sometimes take place in the towns, in the presence of white people, who remain passive spectators. In this instance, however, the chief constable drove them out of the town, got possession of some of their spears, broke them, and threatened to fire amongst them. I am aware that much difficulty attends interference with the customs of the Natives, but I am also satisfied, that if putting an end to these barbarous practices were an object of solicitude, on the part of the civil authorities, it would be effected.

At the Temperance Meeting, the provisions of the Act of Council, rendering it lawful for masters to pay one-third of the wages of their servants in spirits, were brought forward, by a person, who argued, that thus it was made compulsory on the servant, to accept one-third of the amount of his wages, in spirits. This sentiment was controverted by the Advocate General, who showed, that the Act only protected the master from penalty, in case the servant, at his own desire was paid in spirits, to this amount. There is reason, however, to believe, that the construction put upon it by the other party, is one, by which servants, in some instances, have been imposed upon. But too generally, the great avidity of servants to obtain spirits, has rendered it unnecessary, on the part of such masters, as wished them to take out a portion of their wages in this pernicious article, to force it upon them. The inducement of masters to sell spirits to their servants has been strong, from the large profit laid upon them. A settler on the Swan, who contracted to have a barn built for £80, acknowledged to a person of his acquaintance, that, in reality, the building only cost him £45, deducting the profit he derived from spirits and other articles, taken by the contractors in lieu of wages! Thus have the hirelings been oppressed. This class of persons complained further, that when they had received one-third of their wages in spirits, the residue was often paid to them, in orders upon store-keepers, from whom there was, not unfrequently, little but spirits to be had, so that, at times, it was difficult for them to obtain a loaf of bread for their families. The capital of this Colony appears to have been drained out in spirits. Under these circumstances, and other difficulties, with disappointments of no ordinary character, which the settlers of Western Australia have had to contend with, it is no matter of surprise that numbers of the labouring class, as well as of persons of other descriptions, should have left its shores, and sought to better their condition in New South Wales and Van Diemens Land. Many young men, who left their Native Country, with good characters for sobriety, have become drunkards, through the customs of the society to which they have been exposed, on ship-board, and after their arrival in the Colony. Numbers of these have filled the drunkard's grave, and others appear to be hastening thither, appalling examples of the debasing and enslaving influence of strong drink. It is generally admitted, that spirit-drinking is on the decline in the Colony, but a distillery has lately been established by a settler on the Swan River.

27th. We took tea with the Governor, in company with Captain Hardinge, of the Pelorus, and two young officers; also a young man named Smith, who came out by the Eleanor, intending to join an exploratory expedition to the northward. This young man ultimately lost his life, through hunger and fatigue, when returning to Perth, from a subsequent exploratory expedition, with Captain Gray.

28th. We had a meeting in the evening with the inhabitants of Perth, in which ability was graciously afforded, to point out "which are the first principles of religion," and to illustrate the objects and spirit of the Lord's Prayer, and the necessity of guarding against drawing nigh unto God with the lip only, in the use of it.

29th. We called upon a Wesleyan local preacher, who
is an interesting instance of reformation, from the drinking
habits that prevailed in the early stages of this Colony;
when it is said, that few persons went to bed sober. As
a specimen of some of their ideas of moderation, this person
related, that, having made some comment to three of his
men, respecting having taken more liquor than was good for
them, they replied, that they had only had two bottles of
rum among three of them, and they did not think that could
be called excess! The Wesleyans have a neat little chapel
in Perth.—In a walk, I passed a large tribe of Natives, who
were in a very agitated state, threatening, vociferating, and
occasionally raising their spears: they appeared to be verging toward a combat, but I could not learn the occasion;
groups of Blacks, and some white people were looking on,
at a short distance. I also met with a few, little, naked,
black boys, tending sheep. In this hot weather, the Blacks
sleep in large groups, on the loose sand of the streets,
drawing their cloaks over them. The men often wear bands
about their loins, into which they stick their hammers,
with the handle downwards, behind, which gives them the
appearance of having a short tail. These hammers, which
serve also, in some respects, as hatchets, are made of pebbles,
fastened together, and to the handles, with the gum of the
Grass-tree, mixed with ashes. The weapons of these Natives are of a more warlike character, than those of the
Blacks of many other parts of Australia. Most of their
spears are barbed with wood, and some have a ridge of
sharp splinters of quartz-crystal, or of glass; these they
call death-spears. The women dig up roots with a stick,
about the thickness of a broom-stick, but longer, and sharpened at one end; they carry their provisions, and also
their infants, for which they generally show great affection,
in square, skin-bags, at their backs.

Francis Armstrong, the Government Interpreter to the
Blacks, informed us, that when the young man, noticed on
the 26th, as having been shot, was on the point of death, knowing that the theft of Dobbin, had occasioned to himself the
fatal injury, that was fast hastening his dissolution, he was

overheard, requesting another of his countrymen to avenge his death; and though this was many months ago, yet when Dobbin was killed, the party who had been so charged, was overheard to address the departed youth, to this effect: —"There, my brother, his flesh is meat for thee." Some cases of cannibalism are said also to have been traced among these Natives.

It seems probable that the Aborigines, residing in different localities, within about 70 miles of Perth, and occasionally resorting thither, may amount to 1,000. The hunting grounds of these people, are the lands, of which the British Government has taken possession, without regard to the original proprietorship, yet professing to recognise the Blacks as British subjects. It is true, they are an uncivilized people, living on the wild produce of the earth, but they are, nevertheless, intelligent beings, and ought not to be treated with injustice. They have a strong claim upon the sympathies of the British public, and measures ought to be adopted for their instruction, and for preventing the effusion of blood, which sometimes takes place through mutual retaliation between them and the Whites, and at other times, through their own barbarous customs and superstitions. There are persons in Western Australia who would gladly co-operate in the work, but the Colony is too poor to do much, unless the principal supplies were furnished from Great Britain.

At one time, it was intimated, in a Swan River paper, that the language of the Aborigines was a mere jargon! but an intelligent individual acquired so much knowledge of it, as to prove its power of communicating ideas. Hostile views against these people, at one period proceeded so far, as to meditate a war of extermination against them, but the same individual made so powerful an appeal against the injustice and iniquity of such a measure, that the settlers, convened at Guildford, on the occasion, inquired what they should do in the case. To this, the friend of the Aborigines replied, "Do, my dear Sirs, what our Lord and Saviour Jesus Christ has commanded." And to the further question, "What is that?" he answered, "Whatsoever ye would that men should do to you, do ye even so to them." The

conviction produced, was so strong, that the war of extermination was abandoned.

30th. We returned to Freemantle, in a boat.
Previous to a breeze springing up, the heat was
very great. Numerous shoals of fish were sport-
ing in the sunshine, and multitudes of Jelly-fish
of great beauty, were floating just beneath the
surface of the water. One of these, Fig. 1, had a
pellucid cap, marked by a cross; with about ten,
brown, spongy masses, covered with shining globules, attached to it by four pellucid muscles: it had also about ten
whitish, obtusely-terminated tentaculæ, and numerous smaller
ones. Another, Fig 2, was like a glass
saucer, with a fine, fibrous margin. It
continually expanded and contracted, and
had a quadrifoliate mark in the centre,
above, and a number of short tentaculæ
beneath. Although this tribe of animals may be looked upon,
as among the first degrees of animal organization, they are
nevertheless, among the wonders of the Lord, to be seen in
the deep; and their remarkable forms and habits are worthy
of investigation. On arriving at Freemantle, we put up the
only set of lessons that we had left, and the remainder of
the school-furniture, with which we were intrusted, by the
British and Foreign School Society, and sent them to the
charge of Major Irwin; for a school at Perth, for which the
Government allows a salary. Exclusive of this school, the
Episcopalians and the Wesleyans, each have a sabbath school
at Perth. The Government School at Freemantle is at
present vacant, and that formerly existing at Guildford, has
been discontinued, so that education is at a low ebb in the
Colony.

In the course of the day, on going into a store, to get a
few biscuits out of one of our packages, I gave one to a
Native, who came in at the time. In a few minutes, I was
surrounded by such a number of his country people, applying for biscuits, as was quite surprising, considering how few
of them had been to be seen before. No doubt but they
had been lying among the adjacent bushes, to shelter

themselves from the powerful sun. They have no idea of the
resources of white people being liable to fail, but are disposed to draw upon their flour, bread, and sixpences, as long
as they can ; and bread being dear, they often beg for a
"tilling," as they call a shilling.　One of them kept very
close to me all the day, and as he had washed off his red-
ochre and grease, I allowed him to sit some time, on a box
in my room ; he was of the Murray River tribe, and had
received a wound in the late affray at Perth.　Sometimes I
have so many visitors of this description, that I have to
make an excuse to go out, and lock the door, to get rid of
them ; and they often come, and look in at the windows
when we are at meals.　Their preference for European food,
and indisposition to exert themselves, when they can obtain
a supply by begging, often keeps them about the town,
especially when what they call " Kibra men," that is
persons coming and going in ships, are numerous.　Some
of them express a wish to go with us, when the " Kibra
walk," as in their attempt to speak English, they describe
the sailing of a ship.　One of these men, who is very
intelligent and efficient, and is a good hand in delineat-
ing country upon paper, was engaged as a servant, by one of
our acquaintance, but so large a number of his countrymen
constantly resorted to the house, that he was obliged to
discharge him.

31st.　At an early hour, my young, black friend presented
himself at my door ; I invited him to take a walk with me,
which pleased him much, especially as on his return, he was
furnished with some biscuit.　The mornings are delightful for
taking exercise, but the middle of the day is generally too
hot ; yet the heat, in proportion to the elevation of the thermometer, which often rises to 103° in the shade, is said to
be much less oppressive than that of India.　We walked
about four miles on the road toward the Canning River ;
at first, it lies over sand and limestone, but further on,
through sandy forest, covered with Grass-trees or Black
Boys.　Large grubs are found in the trunks or rootstocks of
the Black Boys, which are esteemed a delicacy, both by the
Natives, and by such of the white people, as have learned to

eat them. The bases of the centre-leaves are also eaten in Western Australia. Zamias likewise abound here, and the scrub is overtopped by *Banksia grandis* and several *Eucalypti*. Parrots, Piping Crows, and Australian Magpies were the principal birds we saw. Emus are sometimes met with, in this district: one was chased a few days ago by the river-side. In the course of our walk we passed an old native man, and two women; the latter were digging up roots, and with their usual curiosity, they inquired whither we were going.

2nd mo. 4th. I had some conversation with a person who received his education at Ackworth, about the end of last century, but married from amongst Friends; he is a carpenter, and might improve his circumstances, were he to act upon the principles in which he was educated; but from these he has greatly departed. There is, however, some recollection of better days, which I endeavoured to encourage. We had a meeting in the evening, which was well attended, and we were again favoured with some sense of the divine presence. I was enabled to preach repentance, and faith in Christ, as the fruit of attention to the inshining of the light of his Spirit, and to press upon the congregation, the importance of laying up treasure in heaven.

5th. I again walked to Woodmans Point, at an early hour. Aurora australis was beautifully marked in broad streaks of yellow light, at three o'clock in the morning. On the sand-hills of the coast, there is a bushy *Callitris*, with warted fruit, very distinct from the other Australian species of this genus, of the Pine tribe.—The door of my room opening into a yard, which is also the way to the tap-room, I have had much opportunity of witnessing the baneful effects of spirituous liquors upon the seamen frequenting the port, who are often drunk by seven o'clock in the morning. I am abundantly confirmed in the conviction, that the sale of strong drink to this useful class of men, injures, degrades, and destroys them, more than any other thing. Their appetite for stimulants is kept alive by their allowance of grog at sea, and they are encouraged to drink them, by dealers on shore. The commanders of two American, Temperance Whalers, lately here, kept their

crews much on board, and they were generally sober. The
police at Freemantle is very inefficient in this point; there
are some good laws to prevent drinking, but they are left as
a dead letter.

7th.   Several of the natives came to us, to sell us some of
their implements; in addition to their red-ochre and grease,
some of them had their thighs dappled with large spots of
red or yellow; others had a broad ring of black, displayed
upon a red ground, crossing the forehead and nose, and enclosing the eyes.

8th.   Most of the day was occupied in getting our luggage
on board the Abercromby, in which we have engaged berths,
for the Mauritius.   Several of the Natives assisted in removing it to the beach, and were much pleased at receiving sixpence each for their labour, which some of the bystanders
seemed to grudge them.

9th.   Several of the natives were lying about the town, one
of them, a female, was groaning grievously, from pain, occasioned by a spear-wound in her thigh.   At some period, one
of her ears had been cut off, but I did not learn, whether by
one of her own countrymen, or by a European.   If one of the
Blacks be angry with his wife, he will, for the most trifling
provocation, thrust a spear through her leg or thigh, or if two
of the men quarrel, they will revenge themselves by spearing,
in this manner, the wives one of another.   A person of our
acquaintance, told us, that he saw a Black, named Monday,
and his two wives, crossing the river in a boat, that was badly
trimmed, and which, by a lurch, spilt a little wheat into the
water, out of a bag, that was entrusted to one of the women.
Upon this, Monday exhibited violent anger, knocked the
woman down with his hammer, and ran a spear through
her thigh.   Though they thus punish others, they often
exhibit a stoical firmness, in receiving punishment themselves.   Thus, if by accident, they injure another person,
whether of their own nation or a European, they will immediately stand forward, and put out one leg, to have a
spear thrust through it, as a return for the injury; and if, as
is generally the case among themselves, the challenge, thus
to suffer in expiation, be accepted, the parties immediately

after the infliction of the retaliative wound, recognise each other as friends! Were proper means taken, much might, no doubt, be done toward leading the Aborigines to abandon these, and other cruel practices; but the notion exists among the Whites, that the Blacks must be made to fear you, before they will love you. This sentiment has even been promulgated by high authority, in the Supreme Court, notwithstanding it is an ancient barbarism, exploded in civilized society. Many a poor Black has been shot under this idea, in Western Australia, and Monday was at one time proscribed, and a reward was offered for his head by the Government.

10th. We took leave of our acquaintance at Freemantle, and went on board the Abercromby, which was lying in the roads, in company with some other passengers. The sea was rough and we got thoroughly wet, but as we had taken advantage of a fine day to ship our luggage, this was of small moment.

11th. On shipboard, with the expectation of sailing hourly. Much unsettlement prevailed, from persons passing backward and forward between the vessel and the shore. The captain and harbour-master did not come off till evening, when several other persons came with them, who had claims upon the seamen, for "grog," drank at public-houses in the town, where they had been freely plied with spirits, contrary to law, and often, when in a state of intoxication. The men, however, acknowledged the debts as just, and they were therefore paid into the hands of the harbour-master, by the captain, on their behalf. Some altercation took place between two of the passengers and the harbour-master, in consequence of the latter claiming the certificates of leave to depart from the Colony, that had been granted them by the Colonial Secretary; this was at length settled, by the harbour-master giving them attested copies of these documents. This is the only Australian Colony that requires such certificates to be produced, for the clearance of a vessel; and as the Colonial Secretary cannot know much of the affairs of private individuals, they are regarded by some, as mere pretexts for obtaining fees. The guarantee of a local magistrate is, however, of the same force; and as my companion and myself, had not provided ourselves with such documents, not having regarded ourselves as more than casual visiters in Western Australia, we understood that the Government Resident, at Freemantle, had voluntarily performed the friendly office, of becoming guarantee for us, as he had also for another passenger. We had some satisfactory Scripture reading, in the cabin, after breakfast, and furnished a coloured American sailor, who was casually on board, with some tracts, for which he had before made application. In the midst of the prevalent unsettlement, I felt it to be indeed, a privilege, to be able to retire in heart, to the gift of God, and to Him who giveth to drink of the "living water, which springeth up unto everlasting life."

12th. Toward noon we got under sail.

As the shores of Australia receded from my view, I was favoured to feel clear of them, and thankful, that I had been enabled, while possessing a fair share of health and vigour, to discharge a debt of Christian love, toward the inhabitants of these regions, for whom, both Aboriginal and European, I have felt much solicitude.

After leaving the Australian Colonies, we continued to feel a lively, Christian interest, in the welfare of their Inhabitants, and especially, in regard to those with whom we had been united in religious fellowship. When at Philippolis, in Southern Africa, in 1839, we addressed an epistle to those in Sydney, which is given at APPENDIX. Q. At the conclusion of our labours in Africa, which terminated in 1840, G. W. Walker returned to Hobart Town, where he believed it to be in the divine ordering, that he should settle. By his hand, I sent a letter to our little church in V. D. Land, which is introduced at APPENDIX. R. I also left Cape Town, in 1840, and was favoured to land in England, in safety, on the 15th of 2nd month, 1341, after an absence of nearly nine years and a half.

CHAPTER XLVII.

In concluding this volume, it seems proper to introduce some further notice respecting the Aborigines of Australia, as well as a few general observations on Emigration.

In some quarters, in Great Britain, an idea prevails, that as the land toward the coast of Australia becomes occupied by Europeans, the Blacks retire into the interior. This, however, is a mistake. These people have their hunting grounds, which are more or less defined, in the various parts of the country, and though their tribes can scarcely be said to be organized, or to be more than family compacts, led by some man of prowess among them, these tribes fear each other, and cannot fall back one upon another, without being in danger of destruction. Instead of the tribes who once inhabited the part of New South Wales, which has been longest occupied by the British, having fallen back, they have, to use the expressive language of the Episcopal Bishop of Australia, "faded away." They have become diminished, or have ceased to exist; from the combined influence of the habits of Europeans, which are uncongenial to them, the vices that have been introduced among them, the positive destruction to which they have often been subjected, and the reduction of their means of subsistence.

The Aborigines of the Australian Continent, differ from those of Van Diemens Land, in many of them having lank hair. This prevails most to the north and west, but occurs in some measure, in almost every direction; it may probably be occasioned by a mixture of Malay blood, derived from the contact of the Inhabitants of the north, with the Malays, who, from time immemorial, have annually resorted to the tropical shores of Australia, to collect Betle-nut.

All the races of Australia, confirm the remark of a pious and diligent observer of the state of the human family: That a belief in spiritual influence, is instinctive in the mind of man; and that where this is not directed to its right object, it is always found in the form of superstition. The Aborigines of Australia, in common with the rest of mankind, seem to have some consciousness of right and wrong; hence they will hide themselves, or leave a neighbourhood, after having committed mischief; but they have no distinct ideas of a Supreme Being. They are very superstitious, and are afraid, of evil spirits, on account of which they will not move at night, without a lighted stick: they believe in the efficacy of charms, and have a great aversion to speak of death. The following particulars, for some of which, I am indebted to my friend L. E. Threlkeld, will illustrate some of these points :—Koin, Tippakal, or Porrang, are their names of an imaginary being, who, they say, always was as he now is, in figure like a Black; and who, they believe, resides in brushes and thick jungles, and appears occasionally by day, but mostly by night, and generally before the coming of the Natives from distant parts, when they assemble to celebrate certain mystic rites, such as some dances, or the knocking out of a tooth, which is performed in a mystic ring. They describe him, as being painted with pipe-clay, and carrying a fire-stick, but generally, as being perceived only by the doctors, who are a kind of magicians, to whom he says, " Fear not, come and talk." At other times, they say, he comes when the Blacks are asleep, takes them up, as an eagle its prey, and carries them off: that the shout of the surrounding party occasions him to drop his burden, or he conveys it to his fire in the bush, by which he deposits it: that the person carried off, tries to cry out, but cannot, feeling almost choked; but that, at day-light, Koin disappears, and the Black finds himself safely conveyed to his own fireside!—In the latter part of this description, the nightmare is too aptly personified, to leave a doubt, who this person of savage terror is.

Tippakalleun, Mailkun, and Bimpoin, are names of the wife of Koin, whom they dread much more than her husband. They have also several other names of imaginary beings, who are objects of terror.

Kurrur-kurran, is a place at the north-west extremity of Lake Macquarie, where there is almost a forest of petrified wood. The tradition of the Aborigines is, that this was formerly one large rock, which fell from heaven, and killed a number of Blacks, who were assembled where it descended, by the command of an immense Guana, or Lizard, that came down from heaven for that purpose, in consequence of his anger, at their having killed lice, by roasting them in the fire! Those who had only cracked them, are said to have been previously speared to death, by a long reed, from heaven! At that remote period, they say the Moon was a man, named Pontobung; and they consider the Sun to have been a woman. When the great Guana saw that all the men were killed by the fall of the stone, they say, that he ascended again into heaven, where he now remains!

Nungngun, is their word for a song, such as is composed by their poets. These songs are first sung and danced to, by the tribe of the poet who composes them. They are then acquired by more distant tribes, throughout the country, as noticed at page 435, until by change of dialect, the very words are scarcely understood, by those who originally composed them.

Murramai, is their name for a ball, which the Aborigines carry in a small net, suspended from their girdles of opossum yarn. These balls contain pieces of quartz, agate, or carnelian, wrapped in cord, made of opossum-fur. They are used as charms against sickness, and are sent hundreds of miles for this purpose. The women are not allowed to see the contents of these balls.—While we were in N. S. Wales, a Black was hanged, at Dungog, for killing an Englishman, for showing a black woman the contents of one of these balls.

Respecting death, their ideas seem vague. The Natives of Tasmania, considered it contrary to good manners, to mention the name of a deceased person, and one of those of Australia, asked a friend of mine, who spoke to him of death, why he spoke to him of "tumbling down." One of the Tasmanian women, on Flinders Island, on being asked what she thought became of people when they died, replied, she supposed they went to some of the islands in Bass's Straits, and "jumped up white men!" Their ideas of a future state are dark and vague; but that they have ideas on this subject, is clear, from the circumstances noticed at page 105, 431, and 547.

The Aborigines of Van Diemens Land, had a tradition, that man was created by a benevolent being, or spirit, who came down from heaven; but that, originally, he was made with a tail, and had no knee joints. That in this state, he was very miserable; but another being who had compassion upon him, and also came down from heaven, cut off his tail, and softened his knees by rubbing grease into them, until the joints were formed. Those of the Swan River are thought to have traces of a tradition respecting the Flood, in connexion with the possession of a Yam, having an esculent root, as noticed at page 540.

The language of the Aborigines of Australia has various dialects, and is of remarkable construction. A friend of mine in Africa, well acquainted with the Caffer, said, after examining Threlkeld's Australian Grammar, that he thought a similarity was traceable in these Languages. Should this prove to be the case, persons studying the Australian, may derive advantage from the grammars of the Caffer or Sichuana, both of which are from one root. These grammars have been printed under the auspices of the Wesleyan Missionary Society.

The good intention of the British Government, is not to be doubted, in declaring that the Native Inhabitants of the

British Colonies should be regarded as British Subjects: but this professed recognition, served rather to blind the people of England, than to benefit the Natives of Australia, so long as their evidence could not be taken without an oath. Even now, that the authority of the British Government has been given, to take their evidence in such manner as they are capable of giving it, for whatever it is worth, they must often stand on an unequal footing, with the British occupants of their country, in consequence of their ignorance of our language, and want of opportunity to prosecute their causes in the Colonial Courts, notwithstanding help is afforded them in the provision of Protectors.

The want of investigation into cases of death, suspected to have proceeded from violence, left them much more open to outrage than they would have been, had it been made a part of the duty of coroners and magistrates, to investigate into these cases, in the manner in which they were bound to investigate into those relating to white men. Such a procedure might have deterred many a settler from imbruing his hands in blood.

Persons who, before they emigrated would have shuddered at the idea of murdering their fellow-creatures, have, in many instances, wantonly taken the lives of the Aborigines. And many of those who have desired to cultivate a good feeling toward them, have found them such an annoyance, as to have their benevolent intentions superseded by a desire to have these hapless people removed out of the way.

Strong Christian principle is required to keep down the bias of self-interest, both in regard to the Aborigines, and in regard to every circumstance, in which duty and interest are opposed to each other. And this strong Christian principle, it must be admitted, is too rarely to be met with, among the emigrants to new Colonies. On this account, associations, such as the Aborigines Protection Society, which help weak principle, by exposing delinquency, are highly to be valued. The very knowledge of the existence of such a Society, is, in itself, a protection to the Aborigines. And it is to be hoped, that the cultivation of a better feeling toward the uncivilized tribes of the human family, by this Society and many kindred ones, which marks the present day, will still extend itself, and be blessed of the Most High, to the effectual arresting of those deeds of atrocity toward them, which disgraced former times; and will be made subservient to bringing a remnant of the Natives of Australia, to the saving knowledge of Him who laid down his life for them, and before whom, their oppressors must finally render an account.

Emigrants from Great Britain are generally disappointed on arriving in the Australian Colonies, in consequence of the extravagant expectations they have formed. These are often such as no country on earth could possibly realize, and they are often injudiciously fostered by merchants, interested in the conveyance of emigrants from England, and by land speculators. Perhaps few persons thinking of emigrating, take into account the privations to be endured in settling in a new country, from want of the society to which they have been accustomed, from remoteness from the means of instruction, &c. as well as from having to provide themselves with dwellings in an uncultivated wilderness, to attend to their cattle, and to do many other things for themselves, which would have been done for them in their native land, and from their residence in contact with an uncivilized population, unaccustomed to distinctions of right of property, in consequence of living entirely on the wild produce of the earth, and accustomed to avenge themselves, if provoked.

People often emigrate from a restless spirit, arising out of their not submitting themselves to the government of the Prince of Peace While such are actively engaged in establishing themselves in the wilderness, their attention is much occupied, and diverted from themselves. On this excitement ceasing, even if it be from having obtained a competency, they again begin to feel the plague of their own hearts; but being unwilling to believe that the fault is in themselves, they give way to a disgust with the land of their adoption; its inconveniences, through which they had struggled, become magnified in their view; they remember, the land they left behind, the occupations and amusements of their youth, and in this recollection, they even fancy they were then happy, and they resolve again to encounter the perils of a voyage half round the globe, to seek a renewal of their imagined comfort. Many persons, under these circumstances, leave the Australian Colonies, but disappointment follows them to their Native Land. England is not to them what it once was. The friends of their youth are gone. They had gained a place among the people with whom they had spent the prime of their days, but they have become strangers in England, and cannot soon fill a similar place there; and in disgust, they return again to the Colonies, still bearing with them the curse of unrenewed hearts.

Persons thinking of emigrating should be well satisfied, that they have sufficient reasons for taking so important a step, as that of leaving their native land. Those who can obtain "food and raiment," in addition to peace of mind, in their own country, would do well to endeavour to be content therewith, rather than to incur the risks attendant on emigration, unless health, or some other sufficient motive, render a change desirable. While sober, industrious, and prudent persons have, in many instances, found it easier to obtain a livelihood in the Australian Colonies, than in England, many, from speculations of various kinds, have been ruined, and others from inefficiency or instability, have sunk into hopeless degradation.

Under all circumstances, it ought to be remembered, that man has no right to expect the divine blessing in any country, unless he be living in the fear of God; and that he can have no enduring peace of mind, unless through repentance and faith in Christ, he be reconciled to his Maker. That without this, the plague of his own heart will accompany him through all the regions of the earth, and at the end of time, will follow him into eternity. But in every land, the declaration will be found to be true, "Godliness is profitable unto all things, having promise of the life that now is, and of that which is to come."

APPENDIX.

A.

CERTIFICATES of JAMES BACKHOUSE and GEORGE WASHINGTON WALKER.

To the Inhabitants of the British Colonies and Settlements, in New Holland, Van Diemens Land, South Africa, and elsewhere.

At a Monthly Meeting of the Religious Society of Friends, commonly called Quakers, held in York, in Great Britain, on the Fifteenth day of the Twelfth Month, One thousand, eight hundred and thirty. Our friend James Backhouse, of this City, having, at a former meeting, communicated unto us a belief which has long deeply impressed his mind, that he was called to visit, in the love of the Gospel of our Lord Jesus Christ, the Inhabitants of the British Colonies and Settlements, in New Holland, Van Diemens Land, and South Africa, and to attend to such other religious duties as, in the course of his journeying, he may be required to perform; the subject has, at this time, as well as when first submitted to us, obtained our serious deliberation; and much sympathy having been felt with our beloved friend, in the prospect of this arduous undertaking, and he being of circumspect life and conversation, and a minister in good esteem among us, and this meeting feeling unity with him in the proposed engagement, liberates him for the work unto which he is called.

Commending him to the care of the Great Head of the Church, to the guidance of the Holy Spirit, and to the kind notice of those amongst whom his lot may be cast; and earnestly desiring that his labours may be blessed to their spiritual benefit, and to the extension of the Kingdom of our Holy Redeemer, and that he may

a

be favoured to return in peace to his native land, we remain, in the love of the Gospel, your Friends.

Mary Backhouse	John Tuke
Elizabeth Backhouse	Thomas Backhouse
Sarah Backhouse	Robert Waller
Elizabeth Janson	David Priestman
Alice Hornor	George Baker
Sarah Baker	John Bleckly
Sarah King	William Richardson
Sarah Allis	William Procter
Martha Richardson	Simeon Webster
Hannah Brady	Caleb Williams
Mary Allis	Thomas Smith
Ann Priestman	John Ford
Mary Hollingworth	Henry Ransome
Hannah Scarr	Robert Tuke
Hannah Wilson	Thomas Marshall
Elizabeth Tuke	Samuel Lay
Elizabeth Rowntree, jun.	Caleb Fletcher
Mary Knowles	William Webster
Martha Fletcher	Robert Jackson
Catherine Mason	John Parkinson
Jane Simpson	Joseph King
Mary Coates, jun.	Thomas R. Hills
Alice Webster	George Cartwright
Hannah Webster	John Thompson
Sarah Gummersall	Henry Richardson
Ann Davis	John Kitching
Hannah Wilkinson	George Baker, jun.
Hannah Richardson	Godfrey Waud
Maria Tuke	Nathanael Pasco
Ann Weatherald	Joseph Rowntree
Elizabeth Brown	William Simpson
Jane Cloak	Lovel Squire, jun.
	Henry Hipsley

To the Inhabitants of the British Colonies and Settlements, in New Holland, Van Diemens Land, South Africa, and elsewhere.

At a Quarterly Meeting of the Religious Society of Friends, commonly called Quakers, for the County of York, held at York, in Great Britain, the Twenty-ninth and Thirtieth days of Twelfth Month, One thousand, eight hundred and thirty. Our dear friend James Backhouse has, at this time, stated an apprehension, which has long attended his mind, that it is required of him in the discharge of his duty, as a minister of the Gospel, to pay a religious visit to the Inhabitants of your parts, as described in the within Certificate, from the members of our Society, constituting the Monthly Meeting of York, expressive of their unity and concurrence with him in the same prospect. This meeting has had the proposal under its serious and deliberate consideration, and fully participating in the feeling of near unity and sympathy with our dear friend therein, hereby liberates him to pursue the service to which he believes himself called.

Earnestly desiring that he may be preserved under the safe guidance, and protecting care of his Divine Lord and Master, and strengthened to be faithful to all his holy requirings, we humbly trust that his labours amongst you may be attended with the blessing of our Heavenly Father, and that, after having accomplished the work assigned, he may be restored to his family and friends in safety and peace.

Signed in and on behalf of the aforesaid Meeting,

LEONARD WEST, Clerk.

———

At a Yearly Meeting of the Ministers and Elders, of the Society of Friends, commonly called Quakers, held in London, the 16th, 17th, and 28th of the 5th Month, 1831.

Our dear friend James Backhouse, of the City of York, a minister of our religious Society, has stated to this meeting, that, for some years, an apprehension of religious duty has rested on his mind, to visit in the love of the Gospel, some of the Inhabitants of the British Colonies, of New Holland, Van Diemens Land, and South Africa.

He produced a Certificate of York Monthly Meeting, also one from the Quarterly Meeting for that County, expressing the sympathy and unity of those meetings with him in his concern.

The magnitude and importance of the engagement have claimed the solid consideration of this meeting; much Christian sympathy being felt and expressed with this our dear friend in the prospect before him, and this meeting feeling unity therewith, thinks it right to liberate him for the service.

Under a sense of the awful responsibility of the engagement, we reverently commend him to the protecting care of Almighty God,— earnestly desiring that he may, from day to day, abide in deep humility, watchfulness, and prayer, and be preserved in single dependence upon the leadings of the Holy Spirit; and may his Gospel labours be blessed to the spreading and exaltation of the kingdom of our Lord and Saviour Jesus Christ.

Signed in and on behalf of the Yearly Meeting of Ministers and Elders, held in London, the 16th, 17th, and 28th of the 5th Month, 1831.

WILLIAM ALLEN, Clerk.

To the Inhabitants of the British Colonies in New Holland, Van Diemens Land, South Africa, and elsewhere, where these may come.

The Religious Society of Friends, constituting the Monthly Meeting of Newcastle-upon-Tyne, in Great Britain, send greeting:

Our dear friend George Washington Walker having, in a solid manner, spread before this assembly, a religious concern which rests with weight upon his mind, to offer himself to go out as a companion to our dear friend James Backhouse, of the City of York, who is about to pay you a visit in Gospel love.

These are to certify, that he, the said George Washington Walker, is a member in good esteem with us, the Society aforesaid; and that, in this, his arduous engagement, he has the near sympathy and cordial concurrence of this meeting; trusting that in surrendering himself to this service, he is moving under the direction of Him who is Lord of Heaven and Earth.

We desire that these, our beloved Friends, may be preserved in the fear of God, daily walking in his counsel; that so their circumspect conduct, and their religious labours, may tend to the instruction and edification of those among whom their lot may be cast; that many may be brought to the knowledge of the Truth,—may be turned from darkness unto light,—from the power of Satan unto God; that receiving the remission of sins through the blood of

Christ Jesus our Lord, and by the sanctifying influence of the Holy Spirit, they may become meet to be partakers of that eternal inheritance, which he hath prepared for them who truly love and fear Him.

We commend these our beloved friends to the protection of the Lord God Omnipotent, through all the outward dangers, and the inward conflicts of spirit, which may be permitted to attend them; desiring that He may keep them in the way in which they should go, bless their labours for the honour of his name; and when their service is performed, be graciously pleased to permit them to return in peace.

Under the feeling of a measure of that Love which desires that all men may be brought to the knowledge of the Truth as it is in Jesus, and be saved, we are your friends.

Signed in and on behalf of our Monthly Meeting aforesaid, this 13th day of the 7th Month, 1831.

Michael Watson
George Unthank
John Burt
Joshua Ianson
William Grimshaw
Thomas Richardson, jun.
Edward Backhouse, jun.
Edward Richardson
John Hills
John Brown
George Baynes
Edward Ford
Henry Wilson
Joshua Wilson
James Gilpin
Abel Chapman
Henry Fearon
Edward Backhouse
Joshua Watson, Jun.
Joseph Watson
Thomas Robson
James Hills
William Noble

Solomon Chapman
George Richardson
Daniel Oliver
Thomas Richardson
Jonathan Priestman
William Richardson
Caleb Wilson
Anthony Clapham
George Brumell
Joshua Watson
William Brown
William Hotham
William Beaumont
John Richardson
John Hewitson
Joseph Procter
George Atley Brumell
John Allison
Caleb Richardson
William Richardson
John Mounsey, jun.
John Read Seekings

APPENDIX.

B.

A CONCISE APOLOGY for the peculiarities of the SOCIETY OF FRIENDS, commonly called QUAKERS, in their language, costume, and manners. By JAMES BACKHOUSE.

When any People adopt a style of Language, Costume, and Manners, differing from that of the community at large, it is reasonable to expect that they will appear singular, if not foolish, in the eyes of the uninformed. It is therefore incumbent on those who act in a manner at variance with common custom, to explain their reasons for so acting, in order that they may not be misunderstood.

It is well known that the Society of Friends, commonly called Quakers, has adopted, in many points, practices very different from those of the Christian community in general; but their motives for doing so, it is apprehended, are little understood by many of their fellow Christians: and as the Quakers believe that they have scriptural grounds for these variations from common usage, it is a matter of some moment, that their views should be explained, in order that they may not be regarded as visionary, and that Christians of other denominations may consider how far they are called upon to act according to the same principles. Explanations of this kind have been copiously given in several treatises on the principles of Friends, already published; but as these treatises, from their size, are necessarily limited as to their circulation, the following reasons, in a more compendious form, are submitted to notice.*

* For further information on the principles of Friends, see Barclay's Apology;—Tuke's Principles;—Gurney on the Distinguishing views of Friends.

One of the first peculiarities in the manners of a Quaker likely to arrest attention, is his disuse of Complimentary Modes of Address. These, it is presumed, originate in a disposition to gratify that principle in the human mind, which loves to be thought something of: and this principle, if examined into, will be found to have its root in pride, either of circumstances, character, or station in life. But as "the Lord knoweth the proud afar off;"* and "hateth a proud look;"† and "will destroy the house of the proud;"‡ and "every one proud in heart is an abomination to the Lord;"§ and a proud heart is sin;"‖ and "God resisteth the proud;"¶ it is inconsistent with that love which "worketh no ill to his neighbour;"** and which it is the duty of Christians constantly to exercise, to cherish this pride. For this reason, the Quakers do not use those complimentary titles, and addresses, which, by exciting and fostering the pride of those to whom they are addressed, are calculated to produce feelings the very opposite to christian humility.

The Society of Friends conceives the use of Complimentary titles to be clearly forbidden to Christians, by the exhortations of their great Lord and Master; "Be ye not called Rabbi; for one is your master, even Christ; and all ye are brethren. And call no man your Father upon earth; for one is your Father which is in heaven." And, in the following verse, the disciples are forbidden to desire such compliments; "Neither be ye called Masters: for one is your Master, even Christ."†† The pride of the Scribes and Pharisees, in loving such compliments, and in seeking gratification in other ways, is further denounced by the Saviour; "But all their works, they do, to be seen of men: they make broad their phylacteries, and enlarge the borders of their garments, and love the uppermost rooms at feasts, and the chief seats in the synagogues, and greetings in the markets, and to be called of men Rabbi, Rabbi."‡‡ The injurious effect of a desire for worldly honour, is also pointed out by our Lord, in the following expressions: "How can ye believe, which receive honour one of another, and seek not the honour that cometh from God only?"§§

It must be obvious to every considerate person, that in making a stand against any wrong practices, even where these merge by slight gradations into right ones, a line must be drawn somewhere, to commence from; and unless this line be drawn from the commencement of the evil, it is very difficult, if not impossible, to find another place

* Psalm cxxxviii. 6. † Proverbs vi. 17. ‡ Ibid. xv. 25. § Ibid. xvi. 5. ‖ Ibid. xxi. 4.
¶ James iv. 6. 1 Peter v. 5. ** Romans xiii. 10. †† Matthew xxiii. 8, 9, 10.
‡‡ Matthew xxiii. 5, 6, 7. §§ John v. 44.

where such a line can be drawn. The depravity of the human mind continually inclines it to risk cherishing evil in others, rather than to hazard giving offence, by adopting a course of conduct calculated in any degree, to correct the evil. Hence, a testimony against an evil practice is almost sure to be evaded, unless it have a clearly defined line to commence from. The Society of Friends has therefore drawn this line of commencement, from the complimentary style now prevalent, of addressing single persons in the plural number, which is supposed to have originated in the practice of addressing emperors and princes, in the plural term, You, by way of adulation,—a form of address, which, in this day, has become extended to the lowest classes of society, spoiling also the beauty, and the distinctive operation of our language.

The appellatives Mr. Mrs. and Miss, have likewise been avoided by the Quakers, for the same reasons. At the period of the origin of this People, these appellatives were considered complimentary; but, like the address of the plural pronoun, You, to an individual, they have at this day, pervaded all ranks, This circumstance may be traced to the operation of a principle in the human mind, prompting persons in the lower walks of life, to desire the same gratifications that are indulged in by those in the higher circles;—a principle which is constantly striking death-blows at distinctions not existing in rank or merit, by inducing the lower classes to imitate those things, invented to gratify the pride of the higher classes. The effect of this principle is so unvarying, that it may be regarded as one of the laws of God, to prevent man retaining distinction from his fellow man, by such unworthy means.

Complimentary modes of address are often a mere cloak for insincerity, they do not constitute an integral part of true politeness, or of genuine courtesy of manners. These have their origin in love towards our fellow creatures, and in proper consideration for the feelings of those around us;—in doing, in short, as we would be done by. Where such dispositions are cherished, they will be continually prompting their possessor to the spontaneous exercise of the minor offices of disinterestedness and benevolence, and they will cause " the law of kindness" ever to dwell on his lips. These are the characteristics of the true gentleman; and it must be admitted, that they greatly enhance the sweets of social intercourse, and the comforts of human life.

It may perhaps be thought too much, by some persons in the present day, to style the forms of address that have been adverted to, complimentary, unless in a negative sense, since they have been adopted in all ranks of society; for we now have Mrs. the Milk-Woman, and Miss, her daughter; as well as Mr. the Shoe-Black, or the Chimney Sweep; who are also addressed by the plural pronoun, You: but these circumstances do not alter the fact, that the terms in question, generally express a relation of superiority and servitude not existing between the persons using them, and those to whom they are addressed, and consequently, they are not strictly consistent with Christian sincerity. Instances, also, are not wanting of persons considering themselves insulted on being addressed by their first names, or even by the singular pronoun, Thou.

It is sometimes asked, what benefit the Quakers derive from keeping up their style of address, in the disuse of what has so nearly ceased to be complimentary? It may be replied, that, in addition to the motives before mentioned, in the present state of the world, retaining this style of language, which at once marks them wherever they go, has considerable effect in preserving those amongst them, of little religious strength, from mixing in the dissipations of that part of mankind which professes christianity, but does not practice it; and, that to protect its youth, and the weak among its members from the influence of injurious company, is no unimportant part of the duty of a Christian community. The inconvenience which they avoid by the practice they have adopted, is also a recommendation to it.

Our remote ancestors used only single names; but as civilization increased, it was found expedient to add a surname, in order that families and individuals might be more easily identified: but a disposition to flatter soon invented an appellation, to take the place of the first-name; and this has prevailed, until people of the present day, are put to as much inconvenience as our single named forefathers, and, in some instances to more. The names of the whole series of males in a family, are often confused by the indiscriminate use of the common term Mr., and those of the females by that of Mrs. or Miss: and though the younger branches have frequently their first names added, by their near connexions and domestics, who, being in constant association with them, must have some mode of distinguishing one from another; yet the knowledge of their first-names seldom extends far beyond these. And so easy a substitute being found in the terms alluded to few persons take the trouble to enquire what are the first names of those they meet with: or, if they disregard the trouble, they are afraid to ask, lest they should be thought rude. Hence, in a large family mistakes are frequently occurring, especially if that family be separated into several branches

residing in the same neighbourhood ; and bills, messages, &c. are
continually reaching individuals to whom they do not belong ; and
if some time have elapsed since the former were contracted, it often
proves difficult to make out to whom the debt is chargeable. Added
to this, it is presumed, that no honest person should be ashamed of
his own name ; nor is it any proof of a good understanding to be
offended on being addressed by it.

The appellations of Your Majesty, Your Grace, Your Excel-
lency, My Lord, and numerous others of a similar class, clearly
rank under the head of complimentary titles ; and are to be distinguished from those of station or office, such as, the King, the
Governor, the Duke of, the Earl of, the Lord Chancellor, Doctor,
&c. which the Quakers, as a body, have never considered it their
duty to abstain from.

Complimentary ecclesiastical titles are considered by the Society
of Friends, as calculated to produce pride in those who ought to be
examples of humility ; they therefore do not style, a Bishop, The
Right Reverend, &c. a Dean, The Very Reverend, or a Priest or
Minister of Religion, The Reverend.

The Quakers do not use the ordinary names of days and months,
on account of their being relics of idolatry. They consider the
naming of days and months after heathen deities, as inconsistent
with " the form of sound words" recommended by Paul to Timothy:*
and contrary to the spirit of the injunction given to the Israelites,
as a preservative from idolatry : " In all things that I have said
unto you, be circumspect : and make no mention of the name of
other Gods; neither let it be heard out of thy mouth:"† It may also
be remembered, that when the reformation of the Jews was foretold
by the prophets, these among other things were stated as a part:
" I will take the names of Baalim‡ out of her mouth, and they
shall no more be remembered by their name ;§ " I will turn the
people to a pure language ;"|| and "I will cut off the names of the
idols out of the land, and they shall no more be remembered :"¶
These prophecies are to be regarded as applicable to those becoming Jews spiritually ; and the Society of Friends has therefore
substituted numerical, instead of idolatrous names, which are at
once simple, definite and scriptural. Nor does the Society stand
alone in this view of the subject : Thomas Wemys, formerly of
York, a man of great piety and learning, in a tract published some

---

* 2 Timothy 1—13   † Exodus xxiii. 13.
‡ This word is used here in a general sense, to denote the Gods of the Heathen.
§ Hosea ii. 17. || Zephaniah iii. 19.   ¶ Zechariah xiii. 2.

years ago, entitled " A Catechetical Treatise on the Jewish and Christian Sabbath," has enlarged upon the evident impropriety of calling the day set apart for the worship of the true and living God, Sunday; a name it received in honour of the Sun, one of the idols of our Saxon ancestors. When we call to mind that all the other days of the week are the Lord's, though given us to provide for our temporal necessities, as well as for religious purposes,—no day being exempt from its religious duties; and that it is required of a Christian to keep a conscience void of offence toward God and man upon all days, this writer's arguments against the appellation of Sunday being given to the first day of the week, bear with equal force against

Monday, the day on which the Saxons worshipped the Moon.
Tuesday, ... their idol Tuisco.
Wednesday, ... Woden.
Thursday, ... Thor.
Friday, ... Friga.
Saturday, ... Seater or Saturn.

Bourne Hall Draper, of Southampton, the author of several valuable publications for young people; in the preface to one named " The Youth's Almanack," says, that when Christians shall become divested of prejudice, we may reasonably expect to see them abandon the use of the heathen names of days, &c.

The convenience of correct numerical names for months has been admitted in various quarters; and they are now used in many of the Government and other offices, on account of the brevity and precision with which they can be written in a contracted form.

January derives its name from Janus, a deified king of Italy.

February, from Februa, an imaginary goddess of purification.

March, from Mars, the heathen god of war.

April, supposed to be from a Greek name of Venus, an imaginary goddess of the Romans.

May, from Maia, the pretended mother of Mercury, worshipped this month.

June, from Juno, another heathen goddess.

July, from Julius Cæsar, who gave his own name to this month in honour of himself!

August, from Augustus Cæsar, deified by the Romans.

September, October, November, and December, retain their Latin numerical names for the seventh, eighth, ninth and tenth months; but in consequence of the change in the calendar in 1752, they now occupy the places of the ninth, tenth, eleventh and twelfth months ; so that if misnomer be any ground for correction, there is also sufficient cause for changing their names.

The Society of Friends objects to the use of the terms Michaelmas, Martinmas, Christmas, &c., considering them the offspring of popish superstition, and connected with the recognition of the anti-christian sacrifice of mass.

The practice of drinking healths, having originated in offering libations to the gods of the heathens, and tending to lead persons to intemperance, has likewise been discountenanced by the Society, from its origin.

The dress of the Quakers is also likely to attract attention, as peculiar ; they have, however, no rule as to the manner in which they shall dress. They are expected to attend to the apostolic commands ; " that women adorn themselves in modest apparel, with shamefacedness [modesty] and sobriety ; not with broidered hair, or gold, or pearls, or costly array ; but (which becometh women professing godliness) with good works."*   " Whose adorning let it not be that outward adorning of plaiting the hair, and of wearing of gold, or of putting on of apparel ; but let it be the hidden man of the heart," " even the ornament of a meek and quiet spirit, which is in the sight of God, of great price."†

Had the men professing Christianity, in the nations to which these injunctions were addressed, sought the gratification of the carnal mind in continually changing their mode of dress, according to the fashions of the world, such as now so rapidly succeed each other, no doubt, the apostles would have extended specific counsel to them also ; and the spirit of such counsel is contained in the injunction, " Be not conformed to this world, but be ye transformed by the renewing of your mind, that ye may prove what is that good, and acceptable, and perfect will of God."‡   Acting conformably to the spirit of these exhortations, the early members of the Society dressed according to the style of plain, sober people of that day ; but people of this description being in some degree influenced by the prevailing customs of the age, changed their costume, and soon left the Quakers singular in their appearance ; they themselves, have also changed, in some measure, by adopting such alterations in their dress as they have considered improvements, in point of comfort or convenience ; for improvements they by no means object to : but it is easy to see, that if changes proceed as rapidly as they have done, and they were, this year, to adopt the same habit as that

---

* 1 Timothy ii. 9, 10.   † 1 Peter iii. 3, 4.   ‡ Romans xii. 2.

of the plain, sober people of the present day, and to retain it, they would, in a few years, be left as singular as they now are. Friends have also this additional reason for retaining their style of dress. Experience has proved, that like their language, it has a preserving effect upon their young and weak members, and so powerful has the conviction of its usefulness been with persons who have joined the Society, that there are very few who have not thought it best for them to conform to the mode of dress commonly adopted in it.

Connected with the subject of dress, the complimentary practices of uncovering the head, and of bowing, come properly under review.

It will require no argument to prove that these practices are liable to the same objections as complimentary language. With regard to the custom of taking off the hat, the Society of Friends retain it, as a token of homage to the Most High, only in the most solemn acts of public worship. The congregations of this people stand with their heads uncovered in time of vocal prayer; the person thus praying being the only one who kneels; and they consider it would be an impropriety to use a sign of reverence to their fellow mortals, which they make to their Creator, only on the most solemn occasions. Their ministers take off their hats when they preach, as standing before God, and proclaiming the Gospel of His Son, and as publicly making mention of His Holy Name; but the congregations do not adopt the practice in assembling for worship; they believe it right for them, by sitting in their places of worship with their hats on, to bear a testimony against that superstition which represents buildings set apart for the worship of God, as intrinsically holy, and therefore to be reverenced by taking off the hat upon entering;—a view diametrically opposed to that maintained by the martyr Stephen; "Howbeit the Most High dwelleth not in temples made with hands."* †

This superstition appears to have arisen from the mistaken notion, that other places of worship partake of the same character of holiness, that, under the first Covenant, existed in the Temple of Jerusalem, in which the Lord specially placed his presence, and commanded it to be reverenced; a notion that seems to have been kept up, along with many others, through the influence of persons who have been taught to think that this was the case, but who have not submitted their views to a strict comparison with the New Testament.

---

* Acts viii. 48.

† Friends do not think themselves bound to keep their hats on in their places of worship when personal convenience dictates otherwise.

The Society of Friends are convinced, that by giving this kind of reverence to the externals with which, since the days of the apostles, the religion of the New Covenant has been invested, and which belongs only to God, a superstitious, and in many instances, an idolatrous feeling is excited in the mind; and the attention of the people is proportionably diverted from that worship of the Father, which is in spirit and in truth; and which is performed under the influence of the Holy Spirit, bestowed on us freely of the Father, through the mediation of Jesus Christ, his Son.

This Holy Spirit convinces mankind of sin; leads to genuine repentance, and to faith in Christ as the propitiation for sin, and as our Advocate and High Priest at the right hand of the Father as well as in all his other offices; and constitutes those who yield implicit obedience to the will of God, thus revealed in the secret of the heart, spiritual worshippers—"lively stones," that "are built up, a spiritual house, a holy priesthood, to offer up spiritual sacrifices, acceptable to God by Jesus Christ."*

The following testimonies of the apostle Paul afford a further elucidation of this important doctrine:

"Know ye not that ye are the temple of God, and that the Spirit of God dwelleth in you? If any man defile the temple of God, him shall God destroy; for the temple of God is holy, which temple ye are."† "Ye are the temple of the living God; as God hath said, I will dwell in them, and walk in them; and I will be their God, and they shall be my people. Wherefore, come out from among them, and be ye separate, saith the Lord, and touch not the unclean thing; and I will receive you, and will be a Father unto you, and ye shall be my sons and daughters saith the Lord Almighty."‡

Agreeably to the foregoing exhortation, the Society of Friends esteem it to be the privilege, as well as the duty of Christians, not only to renounce every thing obviously wrong; but every thing even of an ambiguous character,—to "abstain from all appearance of evil;" § they nevertheless, are far from judging censoriously of those who do not see eye to eye with them, in these and other things, in which they believe it their duty to persevere in a line of conduct different from that, pursued by other bodies of Christians. On the contrary, they desire to regard with Christian love, all who fear the Lord, and work righteousness; and constantly to bear in remembrance the saying of the apostle : " Who art thou that judgest another man's servant? to his own master he standeth or falleth." ‖

---

* 1 Peter ii. 5.   † 1 Corinthians iii. 16, 17.   ‡ 2 Corinthians vi. 16, 17, 18.
§ 1 Thessalonians iv. 3.   ‖ Romans xiv. 4.

APPENDIX.

C.

The Question, "ARE JUDICIAL OATHS LAWFUL?" Answered; with some Observations on the Moral Influence of Judicial Oaths. By JAMES BACKHOUSE.

IN a country professing the Christian Religion, but having laws that require evidence in courts of justice to be given upon Oath, the question, Are Judicial Oaths Lawful? is necessarily to be understood as the enquiry ;—Is it in accordance with the laws of God, as revealed in the New Testament, for men to swear in confirmation of evidence, before magistrates? and this enquiry is necessarily involved in the more general one—Are Oaths of any description lawful under the Gospel?

In order to determine this question, it is necessary, in the first place, to define what an oath is ; much confusion having arisen, in connexion with this subject, from not distinguishing between Oaths and Solemn Affirmations.

An Oath may be defined to be, a declaration combined with an imprecation—a conditional calling down upon one's self some dreaded penalty. A man either swears by something which is dear to him, or by some object of his reverence or dread. In the former case, the penalty he means to attach to himself, on the supposition that he swears falsely, is the loss of that which is dear to him ; and in the latter case, it is the wrath of him whom he reverences or fears. When the ancient Grecian, for instance, swore by his head, he professed to subject himself to the loss of his head ; and when the Jew swore by the Lord God of Israel, he cursed himself by the wrath of the Lord, provided his oath should be false or broken. This feature in the constitution of an oath is observable in all the cases in which the Saviour of men has commented on swearing.

The British law also makes this distinction betwixt oaths and affirmations; refusing to accept evidence upon the latter, even when most solemnly made, except in a few cases, in which, in deference to the conscientious scruples of certain religious communities, by special laws, their evidence is received on simple affirmation.

Solemn appeals to the Deity, unaccompanied by imprecations, do not constitute oaths, from their very nature; they do not invoke the special wrath of God should they be broken; but only call to mind, whether formally or by inference, the great truth, that God is ever the witness of our motives and actions; and that for all these we must give account to Him in the Day of Judgment.

The Jews under the First Covenant were limited in the use of oaths, to swearing by the name of the Lord: "Thou shalt fear the Lord thy God, and serve him, and thou shalt swear by his name."* —"Be ye therefore very courageous, to keep and to do all that is written in the book of the law of Moses, that ye turn not aside therefrom to the right hand or to the left; that ye come not among these nations, these that remain among you: neither make mention of the name of their gods, nor cause to swear by them.†

When Jesus Christ, in his Sermon on the Mount, promulgated the perfect standard of morality belonging to the New Covenant, he said, "Ye have heard that it hath been said by them of old time, Thou shalt not forswear thyself, but shalt perform unto the Lord thine oaths: but I say unto you, swear not at all; neither by heaven, for it is God's throne: nor by the earth, for it is his footstool: neither by Jerusalem, for it is the city of the great King: neither shalt thou swear by thy head, because thou canst not make one hair white or black: but let your communication be, Yea, yea, Nay, nay: for whatsoever is more than these cometh of evil."‡

The words of Jesus, on this occasion, appear to contain a plain and unqualified interdiction of all swearing. In the first place, the command to the Jews not to forswear or perjure themselves is mentioned: "Ye have heard that it has been said by them of old time, Thou shalt not forswear thyself." In the next place, the only form of oath allowed under the law of Moses is alluded to: "But shalt perform unto the Lord thine oaths." Then comes the emphatic distinction between the Law and the Gospel, in the words, "But I

---

* Deut. vi. 13.   † Joshua xxiii. 6, 7.   ‡ Matthew v. 33, 37.

say unto you." Immediately following this and the preceding allusion, is the command of Jesus—"Swear not at all;" which, from the construction of the whole paragraph, prohibits, primarily, the oaths which of old time, were to be performed unto the Lord; and secondarily, those which had been introduced among the Jews by the traditions of the Pharisees; these being connected with the former by the conjunctions "neither" and "nor." Jesus then adds, in conclusion, "But let your communication be, Yea, yea; Nay, nay: for whatsoever is more than these, cometh of evil:" thus, after having forbidden all swearing as tolerated under the Mosaic Law, he established, by a positive, clear, and definite precept, the use of simple affirmation, as that form of communication which alone belongs to the dispensation of the Gospel.

The Apostle James appears to have understood the above command of our Lord, to be absolute; and in accordance with this view, he uses the exhortation, not less clear and emphatic than that of his Divine Master: "But above all things, my brethren, swear not, neither by heaven, neither by the earth, NEITHER BY ANY OTHER OATH: but let your yea be yea, and your nay, nay, lest ye fall into condemnation."*

The primitive Christians, for some ages, refused to take oaths: being called upon to swear, they constantly answered, "I am a Christian, I do not swear." Some of the advocates of judicial oaths have urged, that this refusal was on account of the nature of the oaths tendered them; but there is no proof that this was their sole ground of objection; on the contrary, their answer favours the conclusion, that they considered all oaths as unlawful for Christians. They appear to have objected, not to the species of oath only, but to swearing; in obedience to HIM who said, "Swear not at all."

That the judgment of the early fathers, both Greek and Latin, was, that the words of our Lord and his Apostle James, forbid all oaths, without any exception, is abundantly evident from their writings. "I say nothing of perjury," says Tertullian, "since swearing is unlawful to Christians;" "The old law," says Basil, "is satisfied with the honest keeping of an oath: but Christ cuts off the opportunity of perjury;" "He who has precluded murder by taking away anger," observes Gregory of Nysse, "and who has driven away the pollution of adultery by subduing desire, has expelled from our life the curse of perjury, by forbidding us to

* James v. 12.

b

swear; for where there is no oath there can be no infringement of it." " Let the Christian entirely avoid oaths, in obedience to our Lord's prohibition;" says Chrysostom, " do not, therefore, say to me, I swear for a just purpose : it is no longer lawful for thee to swear, either justly or unjustly. Let us preserve our mouths free from an oath." " It is our absolute duty," says Gregory Naziansen, " strictly to attend to the commands of our King, and by all means to avoid an oath, especially such an one as is taken in the name of God." See also Justin, Clement Alex., Origen, Cyprian, Hilary, Theophylact, Ambrose, Jerom, and Isidorus Pelus. Barclay's Apology, Prop. xv. sec. 12. Gurney's Peculiarities of Friends, &c.

Notwithstanding the plain interdiction of all swearing by our Saviour and his Apostle James, many attempts have been made to prove that some exception is implied in these interdictions; and that swearing before a magistrate is compatible with the Gospel; it becomes necessary, therefore, to consider, separately, the arguments used in support of Judicial Oaths.

In order to support the assumption, that Christ intended to except swearing by the name of the Lord from his interdiction, " Swear not at all;" it is urged, that when he used these words, he was merely combating the perversions of the Pharisees, in which they taught, that to swear by heaven, or by the earth, or by any of God's creatures, was no breach of the command, " And ye shall not swear by my name falsely, neither shalt thou prophane the name of thy God: I am the LORD,"* nor an infraction of the Third Commandment: " Thou shalt not take the name of the Lord thy God in vain."† But though Jesus had previously told those around him that, " except their righteousness should exceed the righteousness of the Scribes and Pharisees, they should in no case enter the kingdom of heaven ;"‡ and, though he noticed, also, the oaths introduced by the Pharisees, and forbade them, after having first forbidden swearing by the oath that, under the Law of Moses, was to be performed unto the Lord, it by no means appears that the general tenour of this part of his Sermon on the Mount was exclusively, or even principally, directed against those traditions of the Pharisees, by which they made the commandments of God of none effect. The general scope of his discourse, on this occasion, was obviously, to call the attention of his audience to the imperfect morality of various precepts in the Mosaic Law, that related to

---

* Leviticus xix. 12.   † Exodus xx. 7.   ‡ Matthew v. 20.

conduct, and to inculcate a perfect standard of morality, affecting motives, as well as actions; the allusion to Pharisaical perversions being merely incidental.

"Ye have heard," said He, "that it was said by them of old time, Thou shalt not kill; and whosoever shall kill, shall be in danger of the judgment: but I say unto you, that whosoever is angry with his brother without a cause, shall be in danger of the judgment: and whosoever shall say to his brother, Raca, shall be in danger of the council; but whosoever shall say, Thou fool, shall be in danger of hell fire."* The Saviour proceeds to speak, in like manner, of the motives to adultery, swearing, and revenge, commenting upon the requisitions of the Levitical Law: hence, the fair conclusion is, that he was not combating merely the views of the Pharisees, but chiefly, pointing out what were to be the motives and actions of men, under the Gospel, in contradistinction to those allowed under the dispensation of the Law.

Had the Lord intended that a special exception should be made to his command, "Swear not at all," it is reasonable to presume he would have expressed it, as he has done in the case of a man putting away his wife:"† but no exception being expressed, and the command being absolute, it is not to be assumed that any such exception is implied.

It has been urged in favour of Judicial Swearing among Christians, that the Almighty is sometimes said, in the Holy Scriptures, to have made use of an oath. To this it may be answered, that the Almighty could not swear as man swears, there being none greater than Himself, to whom he could appeal; and that what he might do as Sovereign Lord, may not be proper for us to do as dependent creatures, whose highest perfection is obedience to his will. When the Almighty confirmed his own assertions or promises by an oath, he spoke to the Jews, or to others of old time, who regarded an oath as increasing the solemnity and verity of a promise, in accordance with their imperfect views, and the inferior dispensations under which they lived. In various parts of the Scriptures, the Almighty is thus represented as condescending to the weakness of his creatures, using language adapted to their imperfect ideas, and even, in some instances, to their prejudices and misconceptions. When he says, "Unto whom I sware in my wrath, that they should not enter into my rest;"‡ the passion and chagrin of a man chafed by the obstinacy and perverseness of those with

---

* Matthew v. 21, 22.   † Matthew v. 22.   ‡ Psalms xcv. 11.

whom he has to deal, and prompting him to declare with an oath that he will withhold the good he had designed to confer on them, are assumed by Him, " with whom is no variableness neither shadow of turning ;"* in order to render his decrees more clearly intelligible to the human race, whose ways are not as his ways, nor their thoughts as his thoughts.† No case, however, occurs, in which the Almighty is represented as swearing, after the introduction of the perfect standard of morals enjoined by his beloved Son, whom He hath commanded mankind to hear,‡ and who has exhorted his disciples "not to swear at all :" an exhortation, which no instances of adaptation to a less perfect order of things, in days of old, can in the least invalidate.

It has been advanced, as a ground for supposing that an exception in favour of Judicial Swearing was intended by the Lord Jesus ; that if no such exception were meant, the words, "For whatsoever is more than these cometh of evil," or " of the evil one," as some ancient copies of the Scriptures have it, would cast upon the Most High, the imputation of having instituted of old time that which was of the evil one. This objection, however, is grounded on the supposition that God was the original institutor of oaths ; which no where appears. The case of God swearing to Abraham is not the first instance of an oath recorded in the Scriptures ;§ and it is evident from the expressions of the Apostle Paul, that on this occasion, as well as on many others, some of which have been already alluded to, God condescended to express himself in a manner according with the imperfect views of those to whom his promise appertained : " For," says the Apostle, " when God made promise to Abraham, because he could swear by no greater, he swore by himself, saying, surely, blessing I will bless thee, and multiplying I will multiply thee. For men verily swear by the greater, and an oath for confirmation is to them an end of all strife. Wherein God, willing more abundantly to show unto the heirs of salvation the immutability of his counsel, confirmed it by an oath,"‖ &c. It is clearly to be inferred from these expressions that "an oath for confirmation " was customary among men at the period when God confirmed his promise, in this manner, to Abraham.

It is to be observed, that the standard of morality held up to the Israelites under the Law of Moses, though far superior to that of the heathen nations which surrounded them, was still inferior to

---

* James i. 17.   † Isaiah lv. 8, 9.   ‡ John v. 22—Matthew xvii. 5.

§ See Genesis xiv. 24—xxi. 23, 24.   ‖ Hebrews vi. 13, 17.

that of the Gospel, to which it served, nevertheless, as a sort of stepping-stone, or as the Apostle terms it, "A schoolmaster to bring us unto Christ"* and yet all its inferiority was of evil, or of the evil one, and was tolerated in condescension to human weakness, and not instituted, by the Most High. Of this, we have specific information from the lips of Christ himself, in a case strictly parallel with that under consideration, in his comment on the practice of divorcement, as allowed under the law: "For the hardness of your heart," says He, "Moses wrote you this precept; but from the beginning of the creation, God made them male and female. For this cause, a man shall leave his father and his mother, and cleave to his wife; and they twain shall be one flesh: so then they are no more twain, but one flesh. What therefore God hath joined together, let not man put asunder."†

If He then, whose name is Holy, tolerated, consistently with his attributes, the custom of the Jews with regard to divorcement, because of the hardness of their hearts, and in adaptation to an inferior standard of morality; his righteousness cannot be impugned, in supposing that the custom of swearing was tolerated on the same grounds. Both practices may be traced to the hardness of men's hearts; both imply a defective standard of morality to render them necessary; and both, therefore, come of the "evil one."

Until Christ had promulgated his Gospel, which included a pure standard of morality, and was about to offer himself a propitiatory sacrifice for the sins of mankind, and to send the Holy Spirit to convince the world of sin, and to lead those who should receive him, and believe in Jesus into all truth; Satan appears to have retained a power, of which, at that remarkable crisis, he was deprived: it was then that Jesus exclaimed, "I beheld Satan as lightning fall from heaven."‡

This accords with the declaration of the Almighty, referred to by the Apostle, "Yet once more I shake not the earth only but also heaven; and this word, Yet once more, signifieth the removing of those things that are shaken, as of things that are made, that those things which cannot be shaken may remain."§ The "things that are shaken," here, obviously refer to the things belonging to the inferior dispensation of the Law of Moses; and "the things that cannot be shaken" to the perfect dispensation of the Gospel, the morality of which, being pure, rests on an immoveable foundation.

---

* Galatians iii. 24.   † Mark x. 5, 9.   ‡ Luke x. 18.   § Heb. xii. 26, 27.

The passage in the Epistle to the Hebrews, already adverted to,
—" For men verily swear by the greater, and an oath for confirmation is to them an end of all strife,"* has also been urged as an
apostolic countenance to judicial swearing, under the Gospel: but
surely, the incidental mention of a general practice among men,
having reference also to what occurred in the days of Abraham, is
not a sufficient argument for the rectitude of that practice, under
the dispensation of the Gospel: nor a proof that it was allowed
by Christians, who, in comparison with the rest of " men," at the
period when the Apostle wrote, were few in number.

The circumstance of our Lord being silent before the High
Priest, until he adjured him by the Living God, has been advanced
in defence of swearing before a magistrate.   It does not, however,
appear in this instance, that Jesus either swore himself, or was
sworn by his judges.   He was not attending the court as a witness,
neither was there any fact, to which he was called to depose.   He
was accused of having assumed the divine character: the evidence
brought in proof of the point was of a suspicious and unsatisfactory
description; and it was evidently for the purpose of entrapping
him into the repetition of the supposed crime, that the High Priest
solemnly enjoined him to declare to the Sanhedrim, whether he
was, or was not, the SON OF GOD.   With this solemn injunction
Jesus complied: and no sooner had he uttered his answer, than
the " High Priest rent his clothes, saying, he hath spoken blasphemy; what further need have we of witnesses? behold now ye
have heard his blasphemy."†   The verb rendered in this passage
" I adjure," is admitted by some of the ablest Greek scholars not
to mean, I make to swear, or put upon oath, but only, I solemnly,
and in the name of God, enjoin.

It is sometimes argued, that the Apostle Paul has made use of
oaths in some parts of his epistles.   By a reference to the definition
of an oath, in the commencement of this essay, it will be seen
that his expressions want the essential features of an oath.   " God
is my witness," says he to the Romans, " that without ceasing I
make mention of you always in my prayers."‡   And to the Thessalonians, " Neither at any time used we flattering words—God is
witness."§   To the Galatians, he says, " Now the things that I
write unto you, behold before God, I lie not."|| And to the Co-
rinthians, " Moreover, I call God for a record upon my soul,"¶ &c.

---

* Hebrews vi. 16.   † Matthew xxvi. 65.   ‡ Romans i. 9.   § 1 Thes. ii. 5.

|| Galatians i. 20.   ¶ 2 Corinthians i. 23.

These solemn affirmations appeal to the Omnipresent Deity, as privy to the secrets of men's hearts; but they include nothing of that which being of old time, added to yea and nay, came of evil. The most scrupulous Christians who would object to all oaths, would hardly assert that there are no occasions in which appeals of this kind may be made with propriety. Great care should however be used that the sacred name of the Most High, or of his holy attributes, be not lightly uttered by mortals, lest his great name should be taken in vain : the danger of this sin is a sufficient objection to such an appeal being used to supersede an oath in judicial cases.

The example of the Angel who "lifted up his hand to heaven, and sware by him who liveth for ever and ever, that there should be time no longer,"* has been adduced in support of the opinion, that swearing is lawful under the Gospel. Upon this it may be remarked, that what John here records, was only what he saw in a vision. Had he seen a reality, instead of the representation of the things which should come to pass, exhibited in a manner adapted to the views and capacities of those, for whose warning and instruction, he was commissioned to write them, what was done by an angel in heaven, beyond the reach of error and sin, would be no authority for a man upon earth, who is liable to both, to do the same; especially when, in taking the angel for an example, he would be transgressing the commands of his Lord and Master.

In aiming to discuss the leading arguments brought forward in support of the practice of judicial swearing, it would be improper to omit noticing the sentiment, promulgated in the thirty-ninth Article of the Episcopal Church of England. The writer is not aware of the existence of any other authorized document of that community of Christians, explanatory of the view there taken on the subject in question; he can, therefore, only advert to it as it stands in the Article itself. The words are these :—"As we confess that vain and rash swearing is forbidden Christian men by our Lord Jesus Christ, and James his apostle, so we judge, that the Christian Religion doth not prohibit but that a man may swear when the magistrate requireth, in a case of faith and charity, so it be done according to the Prophet's teaching, in justice, judgment, and truth." It may be observed, no sufficient reason is here given, why such a judgment is come to : for with respect to the circumstances and manner in which, it is here assumed, oaths may

* Revelations x. 6.

be taken, reference is made, not to any precept under the Gospel, but to one by a prophet, addressed to a people living under the Mosaic dispensation, which certainly admitted of swearing, though only in truth, and by the name of the Lord.

Attempts are also made to defend judicial oaths, by the assumption that they are indispensable in obtaining true evidence, in courts of justice. Few persons are, however, to be found in the present day, so unenlightened as not to perceive, that it is rather the fear of the penalty, than the solemnity of the oath, that influences people of bad principles, on these occasions, to speak the truth. Were swearing in courts of justice to be superseded by the use of simple affirmation, and the same penalties attached to false affirmations that are now attached to perjury, there is no reason to fear that the difficulty of obtaining true evidence would be increased: but for causes which will shortly be explained, there is ground to expect this difficulty would be greatly diminished.

It is a sound maxim, that nothing which is morally wrong, can be politically advantageous. Mistaken views of expediency may induce legislative bodies to adopt measures that are unsound in moral principle, with a design to promote the interests of a state; but such measures will ever be found to demoralize the people, and to weaken the influence of the Government. That such is the effect produced by the practice of legalized swearing, may be made to appear; but it will be of advantage before illustrating this part of the subject, to take a view of the evidence which further tends to confirm the conviction that the command of Christ; " Swear not at all," is absolute, and admits of no exception.

It is an acknowledged principle in morals, that it is an immorality for a man to engage himself to the performance of an obligation in any bond that exceeds his actual possessions, or beyond what is properly under his control. This principle is recognized by our Saviour in his command not to swear by the oath which was of old time to be performed unto the Lord; neither by heaven, because it is God's throne; nor by the earth, because it is his footstool; neither by Jerusalem, because it was the city of the great King; neither by thy head, because thou canst not make one hair white or black. The conclusion is obvious: all these oaths involved more than any man had control over, and consequently more than he could stake without guilt. But a simple affirmation involves no such consequence, and is therefore perfectly consistent with the pure morality enjoined in the Gospel of Christ.

The sentiment that the commands of Christ and his Apostle

James were intended to forbid all oaths, receives strong confirmation from the moral influence of swearing, even when limited to judicial oaths.

It must be admitted, that in proportion as an allegation is supposed to be increased in solemnity and weight, by the addition of an oath, in such proportion the solemnity and weight of simple affirmation is diminished; and the idea encouraged, that declaration without an oath, is not to be regarded as so binding as declaration with an oath.

That the use of oaths produces such a sentiment is often proved by the assertion of persons charged with lying: "I did not swear to it." Expressions of this sort are apt to be looked upon as proving, than an oath gives a higher tone to moral feeling than simple affirmation can do. But on investigation, it will be found, rather, that the standard of simple truth has been lowered in the estimation of the people; and that a serious inroad has been made for wanton, or careless prevarication and lying, by ecclesiastical and legal institutions having fostered the idea that truth was confirmed by an oath.

Who, it may be asked of the advocates for swearing, are the persons most ready to confirm their assertions by an oath? Is it not uniformly those whose veracity is least to be depended upon, and who also have the least respect for the solemnity and responsibility of an oath? A readiness to swear in confirmation of an assertion, is proverbially considered an indication of laxity with regard to truth in the individual; for he who fears not to lie, fears not to swear.

Many heathens have been so far enlightened as to be deeply sensible of the demoralizing influence of oaths, and to discourage the use of them on that account. Epictetus says, " Avoid swearing altogether;"—Plato, " Let an oath be avoided on every occasion;"—Chœrilus, " No oath, whether a just or an unjust one, ought to be allowed;"—Menander, " Abstain from swearing; even though it be justly;"—Solon, " A good man ought to be in that estimation, that he need not an oath; because it is to be reputed a lessening of his honour, if he be forced to swear;"—Pythagoras, " Let no man call God to witness by an oath; no not in judgment; but let every man accustom himself so to speak, that he may become worthy to be trusted, even without an oath." Similar sentiments were also expressed by other heathens.* If, therefore,

* See Grotius on Matthew v. 34; Barclay's Apology, prop. xv. sec. 12.

the commands of Christ be construed to admit of swearing under the Gospel, it must also be admitted that the standard of morality, proposed to mankind in the Gospel, in regard to speaking the truth, is inferior to that upheld by many heathens; and will not the advocates of Judicial Swearing revolt from an admission so derogatory to Christianity?

Lowering the standard of moral truth is not the only demoralizing effect of Judicial Swearing: it opens the way to profane and colloquial swearing. A careful investigation into the subject may convince any unprejudiced person, that there is no line of demarcation betwixt the most solemn and the most frivolous oaths; and that there is every conceivable gradation between the two extremes. Who then shall undertake to say, where profane swearing begins? If it be answered, It is only before a magistrate that swearing is allowed to Christians: it may be replied, Jesus Christ makes no mention of a magistrate, in any supposed exception in favour of oaths; and there are certainly many other occasions, equally solemn and important with the greater part of those on which an oath is required before a magistrate.

So decidedly subversive of the morality enjoined by our holy Redeemer is the influence of Judicial Swearing, that this circumstance alone might have been sufficient to have proved all oaths inconsistent with the Gospel, if neither our Lord, nor his Apostle James, had said a word upon the subject. And there is reason to apprehend, that neither the lax regard to truth, nor the practice of " vain and rash swearing," so lamentably prevalent, will ever be successfully opposed, so long as judicial, or any other oaths, are enjoined by the Government, and receive the sanction of ministers of the Gospel, and the support of ecclesiastical establishments. Till it be admitted, on all hands, that " Swear not at all," means " Swear not at all;" and, that in swearing by heaven, or by the earth, OR BY ANY OTHER OATH, men fall into condemnation; and that Yea is to be yea, and Nay, nay, on all occasions :—because of swearing the land will mourn, and because of lying, the heart of the righteous will be made sad.*

It is a remarkable fact, that the advocates for Judicial Swearing all endeavour to prove, that swearing by the name of the Lord alone, as allowed to the Jews, is to be tolerated under the Gospel; while they overlook the circumstance, that the oath prescribed by the English Law, is of a widely different character; and that

* Jeremiah xxiii. 10; Ezekiel xiii. 22.

in taking this oath, they break the command they propose to establish.

The penalty which the swearer calls down upon himself in taking the common judicial oath, in an English court of justice, on the supposition of his swearing falsely, is one of infinite weight and severity; it is nothing less than the eternal punishment of his immortal soul. He swears that " he will tell the truth, the whole truth, and nothing but the truth ;" and adds, " So help me God." This imprecation was, in former days, more intelligibly expressed by the additional words "at his holy dome," which are now omitted in the form, though the spirit of them of them is fully implied. These expressions he accompanies by the significant act of kissing the Bible or New Testament. Thus, in effect, he says : Let the condition on which God shall help me in the day of judgment, or grant me an interest in the salvation proposed in the Gospel, be, that I now speak the truth, the whole truth, and nothing but the truth. When we consider the circumstances of mental excitement and perturbation, so frequently experienced by the person taking the oath, and which are peculiarly fitted to deprive him of his self-possession, and of the calm exercise of his judgment, and when we reflect upon the very comprehensive nature of the promise, that he will speak the truth, the whole truth, and nothing but the truth, and upon the tremendous import of the pledge that is at stake, the practice of Judicial Swearing assumes a truly awful character.

In this respect the English Judicial Oath far outweighs that used among the Jews. If an Israelite inadvertently swore falsely, when the circumstance came to his knowledge, he was to look upon himself as guilty, and was to confess his sin : and he was commanded to bring a trespass offering unto the Lord, for the sin which he had sinned; a female from the flock, a lamb or a kid of the goats, for a sin-offering; and the priest was to make an atonement for him, the man laying his hand upon the head of his sacrifice, when it was killed.* By this act the sinner was regarded as confessing that his sin deserved death, and as identifying himself with his sacrifice, the life of which he offered as a substitute for his own life; for " without shedding of blood is no remission."† But in the English Oath, the swearer proposes, in case he swear falsely, to forfeit his interest in that sacrifice which Christ offered of himself once for all, and by which alone there is remission of sin under the Gospel !

---

* Leviticus iv. 32, 35; v. 13.   † Hebrews ix. 22.

No doubt can exist as to the right of legislative bodies to secure true evidence in Courts of Law, so far as it can be secured, by the infliction of civil penalties upon false affirmations; but surely, nothing can justify them in requiring persons to transgress the commands of Christ, or to stake that salvation which he died to purchase, for the convenience of those on whose account evidence is required. If the persons giving evidence be Christians, they have no right, on any considerations, to transgress the commands of their Lord and Master, or to stake their salvation: for " they are not their own: they are bought with a price."*

It is the duty of the Christian who entertains a doubt respecting the propriety of swearing under the Gospel dispensation, to avoid the practice; for as "whatsoever is not of faith is sin:"† he is bound to avoid all active compliance with measures that are of doubtful propriety, and thus to "abstain from all appearance of evil:"‡ and " to have always a conscience void of offence toward God and toward men."§ At the same time he must bear in mind the injunction; " Let every soul be subject unto the higher powers."‖ And, where he cannot conscientiously comply with the laws, he ought patiently to submit to the penalties consequent upon his non-compliance, according to the example of the Apostles.¶

That the injunction, " Let every soul be subject to the higher powers," is not intended to enjoin active obedience, where a good conscience would be violated, is plain from the example of Peter and John, who, when ordered to act in a manner contrary to the Divine commands, replied, " Whether it be right in the sight of God, to hearken unto you more than unto God, judge ye."**

As the British Law regards a refusal to swear, as contempt of Court, without taking into account the motives of the persons refusing, a judge may be placed under the painful necessity of committing to prison a person refusing to take an oath from conscientious motives. It may reasonably be expected, however, in the present enlightened age, that such an imprisonment would not be of long duration; but should it prove otherwise, a good conscience is worth suffering for, even in a prison.

It is a solemn truth, and worthy of the serious consideration of Christians, that every individual who conforms to the practice of swearing, voluntarily renders himself responsible for the continuance of the custom with all its attendant evils.

---

* Corinthians v. 20. † Romans xiv. 23. ‡ 1 Thes. v. 22. § Acts xxiv. 16.
‖ Romans xiii. 1. ¶ Acts iv. ** Acts iv. 19.

Were those who see the inconsistency of Judicial Oaths with the commands of Christ, to act conformably with their convictions, we might confidently hope, that the Legislature itself would recognize the absolute nature of the command of Christ, " Swear not at all ;" and in accordance with his exhortation, " Let your Yea be yea, and your Nay, nay ;" adopt a form of simple affirmation, in the place of that system of swearing which has so long dishonoured God, and demoralized the people.

Such a measure would powerfully contribute to raise the standard of truth in public estimation, and thus to reduce the amount of national sin ; and while it would diminish the difficulty attendant on the administration of the laws, by rendering evidence less uncertain, it would add to the stability of the Government, which stability must ever be proportioned to the soundness of the moral tone of its people.

A conviction of the importance of being faithful to the command of Christ, " Swear not at all," has induced many Christians, at various periods, to refuse compliance with laws requiring oaths : and to submit to tedious imprisonments, and grievous sufferings, rather than violate a good conscience. The Society of Friends, called Quakers, especially, endured much persecution on this account during the Commonwealth, and in the reign of Charles the Second, &c. At length their affirmations were tolerated in civil cases by the Legislature ; and the penalties consequent on their refusal to swear were removed. By the 3rd and 4th of William the Fourth, cap. 49, intituled "An Act to allow Quakers and Moravians to make Affirmation in all cases where an Oath is or shall be required, their affirmations have been admitted in criminal cases, and for all other legal purposes, and the same penalties have been attached to them, in case of falsehood being proved, as to perjury." This exemption from swearing has also been extended, by a recent Act of the British Parliament, to the Separatists, a body of Dissenters from the Episcopal Church, of modern date. And it becomes all professing the name of Christ, and who are therefore bound to depart from iniquity, to weigh this subject seriously, endeavouring to divest their minds of all bias and prejudice : and should their deliberations result in the conviction of the unlawfulness of swearing, ought they not to urge, when pressed to take an oath, as was practically urged by the conscientious individual who recently refused to take an oath, in the Supreme Court of Van Diemens Land ; Christ has said, " Swear not at all," and God hath commanded me to " hear him :" "Whether," therefore, "it be right in the sight of God to hearken unto you more than unto God, judge ye?"

Though much more might be advanced in support of the sentiments of the writer, enough, he apprehends, has been said in the preceding pages, to prove—than an Oath differs essentially from a Solemn Affirmation,—that the British Law recognizes this distinction,—that the Jews, under the First Covenant were limited to swearing by the name of the Lord,—that Jesus Christ has forbidden the use of this and of every other oath,—that the Apostle James enjoined men above all things not to swear,—that the early Christians acted in obedience to these commands, and refused to swear,—that ancient Christian authors of great eminence denounce all swearing,—that the various arguments used in favour of Christians swearing before a magistrate are futile,—that the Episcopal Church of England, in its 39th Article, adduces no sufficient warrant for Judicial Swearing, though professing to consider it not prohibited by the Christian Religion,—that oaths are not necessary for the accomplishments of the ends of justice,—that they belonged to an inferior and defective system of morality, and are so obviously demoralizing in their effects, that even heathens were sensible of their demoralizing influence,—that there is no line of demarcation between the most solemn and the most frivolous oaths, —that their demoralizing effects alone are sufficient to prove them inconsistent with the Gospel,—that the oath prescribed by the British Law is widely different from, and much more awful in its character than that allowed to the Jews, and is highly objectionable, even according to the views of the advocates for Judicial Swearing, —that legislative bodies have no proper right to enjoin Christians to swear,—that by abolishing the use of Judicial Oaths, the administration of the laws would be facilitated,—that Christians are not required by the Gospel actively to obey, in violation of a good conscience,—and finally, that they ought to be willing to suffer rather than to take an oath, when convinced of its unlawfulness under the Gospel.

In endeavouring to establish these positions, it is presumed, that the Question, "Are Judicial Oaths Lawful?" has been satisfactorily answered; and sufficient evidence adduced to prove, that they are not lawful; and that every other kind of oath is likewise forbidden under the Gospel.

Note.—In the foregoing essay extracts have been freely introduced from Tuke's Principles of Friends, and Gurney on the Distinguishing views and practices of Friends.

APPENDIX.

D.

Remarks on the Indigenous Vegetable Productions of Tasmania, available as Food for Man. By James Backhouse, amended, by Ronald C. Gunn.

In the Van Diemens Land Annual, for 1834, edited by Dr. Ross, a paper appeared, " On the Roots and other indigenous Esculents of the Colony." That account met with attention in Europe, from the remarkable circumstance that so few of the indigenous plants of these Colonies yield any fruit suitable for human subsistence. In this respect, the Australian regions stand singularly apart, from every other portion of the known world.

The present article is chiefly a republication of the paper alluded to, but with such additions as a longer residence in the Colony enabled, the last editor to make.

Originally the plants were classified into those yielding Roots, Fruits, and Leaves, available for the sustenance of man, but here they are noticed according to their Natural Orders.

DICOTYLEDONES.

Natural Order Cruciferæ. Cress family.
Genus, *Cardamine.*

C. heterophylla is a small cress, common in good, light soil, in most parts of the Colony. *C. nivea* is a larger species, found growing on the South Esk, near Launceston, and at the base of Mount Wellington. *C. tenuifolia* is an aquatic species, common about Norfolk Plains and the western parts of the Colony.

These, as also a few other plants of this well-known family, might be eaten like the Common Cress; although generally, when in a wild state, or not growing luxuriantly, they are slightly acrid.

Nat. Ord. PITTOSPOREÆ. Pittosporum family.
Billardiera. Apple Berry.

B. mutabilis has a green cylindrical fruit, becoming of a lighter green, or amber colour, when ripe, possessing a pleasant, sub-acid taste; but the seeds are numerous and hard. This species is common about Launceston, growing among stones, in dry places; and is very abundant on Flinders Island. The fruit drops off immediately, on becoming ripe, and must usually be picked off the ground, but is not produced in sufficient quantity to be useful.

Nat. Ord. GERANIACEÆ. Geranium family.
Geranium parviflorum. Small-flowered Geranium.

The Aborigines were in the habit of digging up the roots of this plant, which are large and fleshy, and roasting them for food. It was called about Launceston, Native Carrot. This species is very widely distributed over the Colony, and is usually found in light, loamy soil.

Nat. Ord. OXALIDEÆ. Wood-sorrel family.
Oxalis microphylla. Small-leaved Wood-sorrel.

This little plant, which displays its lively, yellow blossoms on almost every grassy spot in the Colony, and has acid leaves, in form resembling the leaves of clover, is very pleasant eaten raw, to allay thirst; and made into tarts, it is almost equal to the barberry. *O. lactea*, a white flowering species, is found about the Hampshire and Surrey Hills, and western parts of the Colony; but is too sparingly distributed to be generally serviceable, like the preceding species.

Nat. Ord. RUTACEÆ. Rue family.
Corræa alba. Cape Barren Tea.

The leaves of this species, which is common all along the sea-coast, forming a shrub from two to four feet high, have been used by the sealers on the islands in Bass's Straits, as a substitute for tea.

Nat. Ord. LEGUMINOSÆ. Pea family.

Although we possess about 60 species of this family, exclusive of the *Acaciæ*, none of them yield good edible seeds. The Aborigines were in the habit of collecting the ripening pods of *Acacia*, *Sophora* or the Boobialla, and, after roasting them in the ashes, they picked out the seeds and eat them. This is a common shrub, growing from 6 to 15 feet high, on the sand-hills of the coast. The seeds of *A. verticillata*, Prickly Acacia, and some other common species, might doubtless be eaten in the same way. A gum, resembling in character and properties the Gum-arabic of commerce, which is produced by a species of this genus, exudes abundantly, at certain seasons, from the bark of several species of *Acacia*, particularly from those known as Silver and Black Wattles, *A. mollissima* and *affinis*, and might be collected in considerable quantities.

Nat. Ord. ROSACEÆ. Rose family.
Rubus macropodus. Tasmanian Bramble.

The common Bramble of the Colony, has a sweetish, red fruit, but the seeds are large and hard: it bears abundantly in many situations in the 1st and 2nd months. The finest fruit in the Colony, however, is produced by *Rubus Gunnianus*, a small species of this genus, bearing yellow flowers, and found commonly on the summits of all the mountains, and also in the level country of the Hampshire and Surrey Hills. It is a small creeping plant, seldom exceeding an inch or two in height, but covering patches of ground, of several feet in extent. The soil in which it bears most fruit, is composed principally of decayed wood. The fruit, which is large, of a fine red colour, and formed like that of the *Rubus arcticus*, is hidden from sight under the leaves, which densely cover the ground, and is also often partially buried under the light soil. The flavour resembles that of the English Cranberry.

Acæna Sanguisorba. The Burr of the Colonists.

The leaves of this plant are said to be an excellent substitute for tea. It is common every where, and well known from the annoyance caused by its seeds hooking to the stockings, and other parts of the dress of pedestrians.

Nat. Ord. MYRTACEÆ. Myrtle family.

The genera *Leptospermum* and *Melaleuca* are, in the Island, indiscriminately called "Tea-tree," without reference to species. The leaves of some of them have been used as a substitute for tea; but the flavour is too highly aromatic to please the European taste.

c

Nat. Ord. FICOIDEÆ.   Fig-marigold family.

Genus, *Mesembryanthemum.*

M. æquilaterale, Pig-faces, the Canagong of the Aborigines.   The seed-vessel of this plant is about an inch and a half long, of a yellowish, reddish, or green colour, and somewhat ob-conical. The pulp is sweetish and saline.   Robert Brown a celebrated botanist observes, that this is the most widely diffused plant in Australia, being found on all the coasts.   It seldom extends many hundred yards inland, except along the margins of rivers, like the Derwent and Tamar, which may indeed be called estuaries.   The fruit is ripe in the 1st, 2nd, and 3rd months.

Nat. Ord. CAPRIFOLIACEÆ.   Honeysuckle family.

Sambucus Gaudichaudiana.   Tasmanian Elder.

The Elder of this Colony has an annual stem, seldom exceeding three feet in height, and it is only found in the richest soil, in shady, humid situations.   It bears very large cymes of a white fruit, of sweetish taste.   In some places they may be collected in large quantities.

Nat. Ord. CINCHONACEÆ.   Peruvian Bark family.

Genus, *Coprosma.*

Of this genus, which belongs to the Coffee section of *Cinchon-aceæ,* there are three species in the Colony, all bearing esculent berries.   *C. hirtella* or *cuspidifolia* (both being the same species), called Native Holly, is a shrub growing from four to eight feet high, in rocky places; it bears a large, dark-red or purple drupe, almost the size of a small cherry, containing two seeds resembling in form, flat grains of coffee.   The pulp, or succulent coating of the seeds, is of a sweetish flavour, but not very agreeable.   This species seldom bears much fruit, nor is it sufficiently plentiful in one spot, to be so useful as either of the two following species. *C. microphylla,* one of the many plants called in the Colony by the name of Native Currant.   This grows from six to twelve feet high, in almost every umbrageous ravine, and in many places, forms the principal underwood in dense forests.   The fruit is a red, round drupe, about the size of a small pea; and these it bears abundantly.   Some years ago, when our British fruits were scarce, it was made into puddings by some of the settlers; but the size and number of the seeds were objectionable. *C. nitida.*   This species is smaller than the last, growing more erect and dense, and seldom exceeding from four to six feet in height. It exists on the sides and near the summits of all the mountains; but also abounds in the open country about the Hampshire and Surrey Hills. The fruit, which it bears in profusion, is elliptical, of a coral-red colour, sometimes approaching to amber. Persons suffering from excessive thirst, have been relieved by eating the berries of this species.

Nat. Ord. ERICEÆ. Heath family.
Genus, *Gaultheria.*

G. hispida, or Wax-cluster, is abundant in the middle region of Mount Wellington, and in other elevated and moist situations in the Colony. The fruit is formed by the thickened divisions of the calyx, inclosing the small seed-vessel: when ripe, it is of a snowy white. The flavour is difficult to describe, but it is not unpleasant. In tarts, the taste is something like that of young gooseberries, with a slight degree of bitterness. It usually grows from three to six feet high.

In 1834, R. C. Gunn found on Ben Lomond *G. antipoda,* a small shrub, bearing white fruit of a superior flavour, and as large as a small Gooseberry.

Nat. Ord. EPACRIDEÆ. Epacris family.

All the fruits of the berry-bearing section of this extensive natural order, are esculent; but the seeds are too large, and the pulpy covering too thin, to render them very available for food; the following, therefore, only are noticed:—*Astroloma humifusa,* the Tasmanian Cranberry, is found all over the Colony. It has a fruit of a green or whitish colour, sometimes slightly red, about the size of a Black Currant, consisting of a viscid, apple-flavoured pulp enclosing a large seed. This fruit grows singly on the trailing stems of the plant, which resembles Juniper, bearing beautiful, scarlet blossoms, in winter. The fruit of *Styphelia adscendens,* a small prostrate shrub, found near Hobart Town, resembles in appearance and character that of *Astroloma humifusa.* *Leucopogon Richei,* called Native Currant, is a large, dense shrub, growing only on the sea coast, and attaining to a height of from four to seven feet. The berries are small, white, and of a herby flavour. In D'Entrecasteaux's voyage, in search of La Perouse, a French Naturalist named Riche, was lost for three days on the south coast of New Holland, and supported himself principally upon the berries of this plant; in commemoration of which circumstance, it has received its specific name.

c 2

Nat. Ord. Solaneæ,   Potato family.
Solanum laciniatum.   Kangaroo Apple.

This is a shrub growing from four to six feet high, with large, deeply-cut leaves; it bears blue flowers, succeeded by a large fruit, resembling that of the potato. This fruit when perfectly ripe, which is indicated by the outer skin bursting, may be eaten in its natural state, or boiled or baked. It has a mealy, subacid taste, and may be eaten in any quantity with impunity; but until the skin bursts, although the fruit may otherwise appear ripe, it has an acrid taste, and causes an unpleasant, burning sensation in the throat. The Kangaroo-apple flourishes best near the coast, but grows on the Derwent, ten miles above New Norfolk. It is a perennial of rapid growth, but is injured by slight frost.

Nat. Ord. Chenopodeæ.   Goosefoot family.

Many of the plants of this family may be used as pot-herbs; and some, such as *Atriplex Halimus,* are called " Botany Bay Greens;" from having been very generally so used, many years ago, during a season of scarcity in N. S. Wales, and V. D. Land. The genera existing in this Island, are *Chenopodium, Atriplex, Rhagodia, Threlkeldia,* and *Salicornia.*   The young shoots of *Salicornia indica* are sometimes pickled.

Nat. Ord. Polygoneæ.   Buckwheat family.
Polygonum adpressum of Hooker, in the Botanical Magazine.
   Macquarie Harbour Vine or Grape.

This large climber was introduced into Hobart Town from Macquarie Harbour about 1831 or 1832; but it also abounds in almost every other humid forest in the Colony. The fruit, which is formed of the thickened divisions of the calyx of the flower, enclosing a triangular seed, of unpleasant flavour, hangs in racemes, and is of a sweetish taste. At the penal settlement of Macquarie Harbour, it was made into pies, puddings, &c.

Nat. Ord. Calycantheæ.   Allspice family
Atherosperma moschata.   Tasmanian Sassafras.

This forms a beautiful tree in many parts of the Colony, attaining to a height of 150 feet, and is from 6 to 7 feet in circumference. Its mode of growth resembles many •*Coniferæ,* in being conical, and in having all its branches of the same year's growth, radiating from one point on the trunk. A decoction of the bark, either when in its green state, or after having been dried, is used in many remote parts of the Colony, as a substitute for tea, and, when taken with plenty of milk, has a pleasant taste. Its effects are, however, slightly aperient. This tree delights in humidity, and is therefore only found on the margins of streams, in deep valleys, or in the southern and western parts of the Colony, which possess a more humid climate than the centre and eastern side of the Island.

Nat. Ord. OSYRIDEÆ. Osyris family.
Exocarpus cupressiformis. Cypress Cherry Tree.

This very handsome cypress-looking tree, usually grows in the open forest, under the slight shade of the *Eucalypti;* but it is scarce in other districts. The fruit is red, of a sweet taste, oval, and not exceeding the size of a currant, it produces the seed outside. *Exocarpus strictus* is a smaller shrub, with white fruit, similar in other respects to *E. cupressiformis.*

Nat. Ord. SANTALACEÆ. Sandal Wood family.
Leptomeria Billardieri. Native Currant.

This shrub grows about six feet high, and resembles Broom: it is devoid of leaves, but the branches are roundish, slender, and delicate. It bears its numerous spikes of small white flowers, and subsequently its green fruit, at the extremity of the branches. The whole plant, as well as the fruit, is of an acid taste, with a certain degree of astringency, but well suited when chewed, to allay thirst. This plant is usually found in light, sandy soil, Although not abundant, it is widely distributed.

Nat. Ord. CASUARINEÆ. She-oak family.
Casuarina quadrivalvis. Common She-oak.

The leaves, or rather young branches, and the young cones of this tree, when chewed, yield a pleasant acid; extremely useful to persons in want of water. Cattle are also exceedingly fond of them. This tree does not exist in the north-western parts of the Colony.

MONOCOTYLEDONES.

Nat. Ord. ORCHIDACEÆ. Orchis family.

A number of plants of this family have small bulbous roots, which were formerly eaten by the Aborigines, as they still are by Cockatoos, Bandicoots, Kangaroo-rats, &c. Little holes are often seen where the latter animals have been scratching for them.

Gastrodia sesamoides, or the Native Potato—see page 119. The genera *Pterostylis, Caladenia, Microtis, Prasophyllum, Diuris, Thelymitra,* &c. bear small bulbs; they are generally diffused over the open and thinly-wooded parts of the Colony.

Nat. Ord. ASPHODELEÆ.   Asphodel family.
Xanthorrhœa australis?   Grass Tree.

The base of the inner leaves of the Grass-tree is not to be despised by the hungry. The Aborigines beat off the heads of these singular plants by striking them about the top of the trunk with a large stick; they then strip off the outer leaves and cut away the inner ones, leaving about an inch and a half of the white tender portion, joining the trunk : this portion they eat raw or roasted ; and it is far from disagreeable in flavour, having a nutty taste, slightly balsamic. There are some other species of grass-tree in the Colony, the base of the leaves of which may also be used as food: those of the Dwarf Grass-tree, *Xanthorrhœa humilis,* which is abundant about York Town, may be obtained by twisting the inner leaves firmly together, and pulling them forcibly upwards ; but care is required not to cut the fingers, by slipping the hand. The different species of *Xanthorrhœa* are only found on the poorest soil, and usually in quartzose sand, in very open situations.

Astelia Alpina.   Mountain Astelia.

This plant forms large patches on the summits of mountains, and has light-green, silky leaves springing from the root, and covered underneath with a white down. The fruit is red, of a sweet taste, growing in the centre of each plant, and about the size of a large pea.

Nat. Ord. CYPERACEÆ.   Cyperus family.
Lepidosperma gladiata.   Broad-leaved Lepidosperma.

The blanched portion of the base of the inner leaves of some rushes, and of this sedgy plant, which grows on the sand-hills of the coast, and has the mature leaves an inch wide, and of a deep green, are eatable, and of a nutty flavour. The flowers of this plant, to the eye of a common observer, resemble those of rushes. They grow in clusters, on a stem as flat and broad as the leaves.

ACOTYLEDONES.

Nat. Ord. FILICES.   Fern family.
Pteris esculenta.   Tara or Eatable Fern.

The most extensively diffused, edible root of V. D. Land, is that of the Tara-fern. This plant greatly resembles *Pteris aquilina*, the Common Fern, or Brake, of England; and, like it, throws up its single stems at short distances, covering great extents of light or rich land. The Tasmanian plant is *Pteris esculenta*, and is known among the Aborigines by the name of Tara. The inhabitants of the South Sea Islands call a variety of esculent seeds and roots by this name. *Pteris esculenta* is known among the European inhabitants of the Colony, by the name of Fern, in common with many other plants of the same tribe; none of which, however, spread over extensive portions of open land in the same manner. It varies in height from a few inches to several feet, according to the richness of the soil in which it grows; and in some parts of the Colony, especially on Table Cape, it is so tall as to conceal a man on horseback. The root is not bulbous, but creeps horizontally, at a few inches below the surface of the earth, and where it is luxuriant, attains to the thickness of a man's thumb. Pigs feed upon this root where it has been turned up by the plough; and in sandy soils, they will themselves turn up the earth in search of it. The Aborigines roast this root in the ashes, peel off its black skin with their teeth, and eat it with their roasted kangaroo, &c. in the same manner as Europeans eat bread. The root of the Tara-fern possesses much nutritive matter; yet it is to be observed, that persons who have been reduced to the use of it, in long excursions through the bush, have become very weak, though it has prolonged life. Whether this arose from an insufficient supply, from eating it raw, or from some other cause, is doubtful. It is quite certain, that when this root is grated, or reduced to a pulp by beating, and mixed with cold water, a large quantity of fecula, resembling arrow-root, is precipitated. This adheres to the bottom of the vessel, and may easily be prepared for use by pouring off the water and floating matter, adding fresh water, stirring up the white powder, and again allowing it to settle. It may then be cooked by boiling, or the powder may be spread on cloths and dried in the sun, or hung up in linen bags where there is a free circulation of air.

Cybotium Billardieri. Tree Fern.

The native Blacks of the Colony used to split open about a foot and a half of the top of the trunk of the Common Tree-fern, and take out the heart, a substance resembling a Swedish turnip, and of the thickness of a man's arm. This they also roasted in the ashes, and eat as bread; but it is too bitter and astringent to suit an English palate. It is said that the Aborigines preferred the heart of another species of tree-fern, *Alsophila australis*, found at Macquarie Harbour, and in other places on the northern side of V. D. Land. The tree-fern is very generally diffused over the Colony, in humid, umbrageous ravines, and also to the southward and westward, growing more extensively in the dense forests, where the climate is moist, as at the Huon River, on the sides of mountains, and towards Emu Bay and the Hampshire Hills.

Nat. Ord. Fungi. Fungus family.
Agaricus campestris? Common Mushroom.

This, which seems to be precisely similar to the Common Esculent Mushroom of England, needs no description. It is very plentiful in many parts of the Colony, and has a fine flavour.

Mylitta Australis. Native Bread.

This species of tuber is often found in the Colony, attaining to the size of a child's head: its taste somewhat resembles boiled rice. Like the heart of the Tree-fern, and the root of the Native Potato, cookery produces little change in its character. On asking the Aborigines how they found the Native-bread, they universally replied, "A Rotten Tree." On the dry, open hills about Bothwell, it is to be detected in the early part of summer, by the ground bursting upwards as if with something swelling under it, which is this fungus.

For another esculent fungus, see page 119.

In closing this list of those vegetable productions of Tasmania, which can in any way be rendered available for the sustenance of man, it may be remarked, that not one of them is of sufficient value to be worthy of the attention of the agriculturist or the horticulturist.

APPENDIX.

E.

Extract from a REPORT, on the STATE of the CHAIN-GANGS, and ROAD-PARTIES in VAN DIEMENS LAND. By JAMES BACKHOUSE and GEORGE W. WALKER.

To the Lieutenant Governor, GEORGE ARTHUR.

Having visited all the Chain-gangs and Road-parties in V. D. Land, we proceed to make a report upon their State, Discipline, &c. according to the request of the Lieutenant Governor.

The State of the Chain-gangs and Road-parties is such as to render them effective as means of punishment, but not equally so as regards reformation. The privations experienced in them are keenly felt by the Prisoners; yet, for want of discipline and instruction, these privations have a tendency to produce recklessness of character.

Attention to prevent persons in these gangs, and road-parties from earning money, by employing the time allowed them for washing their clothes, &c. in the service of Settlers, or other persons, has had a beneficial effect. Before this measure was carried into operation, the money which some of the prisoners earned, was a bonus to them, to bear the privations of their situation, and an inducement to some of the more vicious, to prefer a Road-party to private assigned-service.

In most of the Chain-gangs and Road-parties, there is a great want of classification. A large number of persons are usually crowded together in one hut, or room, and those who would willingly conduct themselves in an orderly manner, are kept in a state of excitement by those who are determined not to care for their situation; and who continually keep up noise and other disturbance, to prevent their own minds from dwelling on the circumstances in which they are placed.

There is, in most of the gangs, and parties, a want of attention to the state of their lodging. Whatever the previous character of the prisoners may have been, they are indiscriminately crowded together in their lodging places, in a way by no means calculated to preserve a sense of decency, where it has not been previously extinguished.

At present, the arrangements of the huts, in some of the parties, is such, that, notwithstanding the attention of the watchmen, if a man only be present at the muster, morning and evening, he would have no great difficulty in being absent during the night. The frequent, petty depredations, committed upon the neighbouring Settlers, but too plainly prove how often such absence occurs.

Absentees from the Road-parties, on predatory excursions, in the day time, are not easily detected, in consequence of these Road-parties being stationed in the Bush, and not having any boundary marked to their liberty, when not at work; and from the creeks at which they wash, &c. often being out of sight of the huts. Were the boundaries stockaded, or even marked by a post and rail fence, beyond which it should be considered an offence for any man to be found, out of work hours, without proper authority, it might be attended with advantage.

Great evil arises from a half-day being allowed in a week, for washing and repairing clothes. If the men be at all diligent, they have no occasion for this amount of time, for these purposes; and many of them, where they are located in the Bush, for want of having it properly occupied, waste it in other objects; strolling to a distance, often to the great annoyance of the neighbouring settlers; neglecting also, the objects for which it is allowed. Thus, in one party we observed many of the men on the Sabbath morning, washing their shirts, and attending to other secular concerns, which ought to have been done on the previous afternoon.

In the Launceston Penitentiary, experience proves how much time may be saved, by appointing a few men to wash for a party, during the week, and how much their proper comfort may be promoted by having a change of clothes, so as to admit of this arrangement.—In this case, two men employed in washing, during six days, save the labour of 200 men for a half-day. This arrangement also greatly promotes cleanliness, and prevents the men from getting into mischief.

The delivery of several days' rations at once, to the prisoners, individually, in the Road-parties, is very undesirable, especially where it is done only once a-week, as was the case till lately, in Notmans Road-party. In the other parties, it takes place, for the most part, twice a week, and though in all of them, one or more persons are appointed as cooks, yet, in most of them, the prisoners are allowed to cook for themselves, because, it is alleged, they prefer doing so; a preference which, we submit, ought by no means to be consulted. Having this liberty, their meat is usually cooked in a wasteful manner. It is on this account that the rations allowed, have often proved insufficient. The men in one party, were often without food for two or three days at the end of the week, notwithstanding the rations were half as much more as in the Launceston Penitentiary, where, being differently managed, they were found sufficient. Having a week's provisions beforehand, greatly facilitates absconding, and is also an evil in this respect.

The men having their meat delivered to their own individual charge, without having any place to keep it in, except the huts in which they cook, live, and sleep, alleged that the meat soon spoiled, and that they therefore cooked it in the early part of the week, and consumed it whilst it was good. This mismanagement, however, combined with the too rapid consumption of their flour, when made into damper, which is a temptation too strong for healthy men with keen appetites to resist, left them no alternative in the latter part of the week, but to starve, or to steal; and there is ground to believe, that this state of things has been the cause of many taking to the bush. We have reason to suppose that the men, who escaped from the Constitution Hill Road-party, a few months ago, and committed depredations at Waterloo Point, were driven to this extremity, by hunger succeeding the imprudent consumption of their rations, under circumstances in which it was not reasonable to expect that men of this class would do otherwise.—The practicability of a plan being adopted, by which the ration of meat should be daily delivered to the cook, and distributed to the prisoners, when boiled, having been fully proved at Launceston, we would recommend the same plan being carried into effect in the other parties; and also, that the chief part of the flour should be converted into bread, as at Launceston, before being delivered to the men.

A fruitful source of desperation of character, in one Road-party, has been, the tasking of the men to break a cubic yard of whinstone or ironstone, daily, for the roads. This quantity, if well broken, is a full day's work for a skilful hand, with a good tool; but in this party, many unskilful hands have been required to do it, with hammers much worn. As tasking the men is contrary to a Government order, they have not been charged with the specific fault of not breaking a yard of stone, but with neglect of duty, or with insolence; and multitudes of them have been flogged upon these charges, upon the evidence of overseers, who had urged the men, in many instances, to angry replies, by opprobrious and irritating language. It must be allowed, that where the men, at this kind of work, are not tasked, many of them are very idle. It is, therefore, our opinion, that at such employment, tasking them is a good plan, where it is done with judgment. But it must be obvious, that what a skilful hand, accustomed to hard labour, will easily effect, will be oppression to a man whose pursuits have been in a shop, or a counting-house.

Many prisoners are sent to the Chain-gangs, and Road-parties, almost destitute of clothing; and, arriving after the regular time of supply, they remain long, almost in a state of nudity. Many come also with very bad shoes, and suffer much in consequence, from the nature of the work they are engaged in. The shoes supplied by Government are frequently of too slight a kind for road making, and the men are often in a bad state for working, before the time arrives for the delivery of new shoes.

Retaining men in the Road-parties, or Chain-gangs, after the period of their sentence to confinement in them has expired, or subjecting them to an indefinite sentence, has, in our opinion, a decidedly prejudicial effect. To leave a man in a situation to which he has been sentenced as a punishment, after the period for which he was sentenced has elapsed, is in itself an act of injustice; and however patiently a man may bear a punishment that he feels he has brought upon himself, as the just reward of his crimes, the moment he feels himself unjustly dealt with, his evil passions become excited, and we may expect to find him becoming stubborn, and promoting insubordination.

Loss of hope of alleviation from punishment, has a strong tendency to produce recklessness of character; and if no fixed time can be looked to, when a specific punishment shall cease, this loss of hope will exist to a great degree, even where it is known that general good conduct may, at some indefinite time, produce remission of sentence. On this account, we would recommend that every man committed to a Chain-gang, or Road-party, should know exactly, what his sentence is; and that no man should be kept in any of these parties a day beyond the period of his sentence; but that every man should be returned to his former employer, or into the public-works, for re-assignment, &c. immediately that his sentence expires. This would not only prevent the impression of injustice, but would occasion the Road-parties to be looked upon as institutions for specific punishment. We would also suggest, that the men who commit offences in the Road-parties, be not remanded to them on indefinite sentences; but that, in such cases, the sentence should be regularly lengthened for a specific period, or the party be sentenced for a fixed time, to a higher penal station. This we believe would be found to promote that resigned submission to the punishment, which is essential to reformation.

We are likewise of opinion, that certain acts of delinquency, such as disobedience of orders, and neglect of duty, should be punished by the specific addition of a month, or some other definite period, to the original sentence, in place of subjecting the individual to the degrading and demoralizing punishment of flagellation; and that a recommendation from the Superintendent to the Police Magistrate of the District, for extraordinarily good conduct, should reduce the original sentence according to a regular scale, say one month in six.

Some of the Road-parties are destitute of those most important agents of reformation, Moral and Religious Instruction. Many of them have been so neglected as to be entirely without Bibles.

JAMES BACKHOUSE.
GEORGE WASHINGTON WALKER.

Hobart Town, 16th 10th mo., 1833.

APPENDIX.

F.

REPORT upon the STATE of the PRISONERS in VAN DIEMENS LAND, with Remarks upon the PENAL DISCIPLINE, and Observatians on the GENERAL STATE of the COLONY, in 1834.

☞ In presenting the subjoined Report, James Backhouse and George Washington Walker feel that some apology is due for having introduced many particulars, with which the Lieutenant-Governor must necessarily be already acquainted: this seemed almost unavoidable, not only to render the subject connected, and that the data on which conclusions and suggestions are founded, might be brought under review; but also, that the document might be made more generally intelligible, should it meet the eye of any less familiarly acquainted than the Lieutenant-Governor, with the subjects under discussion.

Hobart Town, 19th of 6th mo., 1834.

To Colonel George Arthur, Lieutenant-Governor of Van Diemens Land, and its Dependencies.

The Report of James Backhouse and George Washington Walker, upon the State of the Prisoners in Van Diemens Land; with remarks upon Penal Discipline, and observations upon the General State of the Colony.

The Lieut-Governor having repeatedly expressed a desire, that we would furnish him with a report on the state of the Prisoner Population of Van Diemens Land, with remarks on the Penal Discipline, and observations on the general state of the Colony, we now venture to attempt a compliance with his wishes, after a visit of upwards of two years in the Colony; undertaken with the single purpose of endeavouring, according to a sense of religious duty, to benefit our fellow men, in any way that might be opened before us, but especially, in regard to their eternal interests.

We arrived in Van Diemens Land with the prepossession so common in England, that transportation is little of a punishment, beyond the circumstance of exile. This impression, which has probably had its origin in the circumstances of the earlier times of the Australian Colonies, and in the wilful, and interested misrepresentations of prisoners, as well as in the superficial observations of travellers, and other persons who have had little intercourse with prisoners, was soon removed from our minds by observation, and frequent conversation with prisoners; and a further and more intimate acquaintance with the subject, has greatly increased our estimate of the severity of the punishment to which criminals are subjected by transportation; and, also, of the advantage of Colonial transportation, as exhibited in Van Diemens Land, contrasted with other systems of prison discipline practised in the British dominions.*

But before entering further upon the subject, it may not be improper to make a few observations, upon what we conceive to be the nature and design of penal discipline, and on the degree of influence which the fear of punishment might be expected to produce in the prevention of crime.

Penal discipline may be regarded as a medicine for the remedy and removal of moral evil; its paramount objects being the good of the community, and of the individuals subjected to its operations.

When a man has broken such of the laws of his country, as have been instituted in strict justice, for the protection of persons and

* In the early times of the Australian Colonies, prisoners were frequently allowed, from their first landing, to work for themselves during a great part of the day. At this period wages were high, and there was little restraint upon intemperance and licentiousness.

Prisoners frequently represent their situation to their friends to be much better than it really is, by letters which they contrive to get conveyed to them. This is often done to induce their friends to emigrate, in the hope that they may be a benefit to themselves.—A case of this kind is fresh in our recollection, in which a man wrote home to his wife, entreating her to come to him, and stating that he had an excellent situation, with good wages. The poor woman and her children, aided by the benefactions of the magistrate who had committed her husband, and by other benevolent individuals at Liverpool, accomplished the voyage; but found when she landed in Hobart Town, that her husband was two hundred and fifty miles distant, and was without wages; and having no means of reaching him, she took to immoral courses. Several other cases of a similar kind came to our knowledge.

Persons arriving in the Colony, and travelling hastily through it, are apt to form very erroneous conclusions respecting the state of prisoners. They too often forget, that many men are disposed to make the best of trying circumstances, particularly when they have become inured to them, and know that they cannot escape: and that they will even make admissions to strangers as if they were pretty well off, when their comforts are few indeed. Persons in public offices, and in business, are generally remarkably ignorant of the condition of the prisoner population; seldom speaking to prisoners except about matters of business, or when giving orders to such as are in their service. Magistrates are also liable to be unfavourably impressed with regard to the general characters of prisoners; their duties rarely bringing them into contact with any but the most vicious and depraved.

property, and for the preservation of the good order of society, three things appear requisite.   1st. That he be rendered incapable of doing further mischief, by being placed under restraint.   2nd. That he be compelled to make restitution; to the parties aggrieved, if practicable, if not to the community.   3rd. That endeavours be used for his reformation.

The use of means adapted to promote these ends, though the means may involve a large portion of suffering, are yet strictly in accordance with the divine precepts, "Be not overcome of evil, but overcome evil with good;" (Rom. xii. 21.) and, "All things whatsoever ye would that men should do unto you, do ye even so to them;" (Matt. vii. 12.) for every man of sound mind must, on reflection, approve of measures by which he, or his neighbour, becoming injurious to the public weal, shall be restrained from further evil, shall be compelled to make just restitution, and shall have his own reformation promoted.

But an idea is extensively entertained, especially by some members of the British Legislature, as may be inferred from their frequent observations on prison discipline, that severity towards convicted offenders has a reformatory tendency, and particularly, that it has a powerful influence in deterring from crime, through the excitement of fear.   This, we conceive to be a sentiment radically erroneous, and one that if practically adopted, would lead to acts of vengeance toward criminals, opposed to sound reason, and to the Christian religion.   The comparative effects of the prison discipline respectively adopted in England, and the United States of America, shew that the increase of crime in those countries has uniformly kept pace with the severity of the Penal Code.   This affords strong presumption, that mere severity is ineffectual to restrain from the commission of crime.

It is sufficiently obvious that a system of coercion, calculated to promote the legitimate objects that have been adverted to, viz.: restraint, restitution, and reformation, will necessarily include much suffering.   But this suffering not being inflicted for its own sake, or on the principles of retaliation, but being a necessary consequence of measures founded on the immutable principles of justice and mercy, and therefore, essentially adapted to recommend themselves to the conscience, the minds of most men will secretly acquiesce in the propriety and justice of the punishment, or to speak more properly, of the discipline of which suffering is an unavoidable concomitant; and by the production of this subdued state of mind in the offender, a most important step is made toward reformation, and the other appropriate ends of Penal Discipline.

On the contrary, every species of suffering that is inflicted merely as a punishment, on the principle of retaliation, and with a view to strike terror into the culprit, or into the minds of others, tends only to excite feelings of resistance, if not of revenge, in the individual subjected to it; and will certainly promote obduracy of heart, rather than amendment, both in the culprit, and in the evil-disposed part of the community.—The propensity to commit evil originates in a vitiated state of mind; and, when men are morally diseased, they need a moral remedy.—Besides, the administration of abstract punishment is a usurpation of the divine prerogative: "Vengeance is mine, I will repay saith the Lord." (Rom. xii. 19.)*

If the mere dread of punishment had a powerful effect upon the human race, generally, surely the dread of eternal punishment

---

* It is worthy of observation, as a fact well known to those acquainted with School Discipline, that the receipt, or forfeiture of a Single Ticket, a certain number of which entitles the possessor to a Specific reward of insignificant value, has a far greater influence in exciting to good conduct than the old, and now nearly exploded system of corporal punishment. And prisoners, generally, are but children in point of moral attainment, or true understanding of their own interests. If a plan, therefore, on a somewhat similar principle to the foregoing, were to be adopted with reference to them, we are of the opinion, that it would be attended with happy effects. The Tickets might be dispensed at the monthly musters, every prisoner having no offence recorded against him for the past month, should be entitled to a Ticket; and on the other hand, he should be required to forfeit one, or more, for misconduct, according to the nature and number of the offences that might have been committed. If every prisoner were to be thus continually reminded, that three tickets would shorten his period of servitude for a Ticket-of-leave, say one month, while the forfeiture of the same number would lengthen it for a like period, and that so long as he possessed no tickets, he had no chance of obtaining a Ticket-of-leave, a certain number of the former being the price of that indulgence; we conceive, that it would operate as a powerful incentive to self-control, and would be more influential than the present mode of holding out inducements for good conduct. A modification of the same principle, might be adopted in dispensing Conditional, or Free pardons, or in removing from a Road-party, a Chain Gang, or a Penal Settlement; for it is equally applicable to the various conditions of the prisoner.

The following remarks extracted from the writings of a modern author, further elucidate our views on the nature of punishment, in connexion with Penal Discipline :—

"The law seems to go on the principle of ' Lex talionis :' Eye for eye ; tooth for tooth; &c. Life for life, seems to be only consistent with this. The Gospel, as said John the Baptist, lays the axe to the root of corruption. Its spirit leads not to injure, much less to kill the body, but to mend the mind ; therefore punishments on a Christian plan, must have the latter in view always, the former never, except in subserviency to the latter. This, I think, will utterly abolish all capital punishments, stripes and public stigmas. Restraint, labour, and solitude are chiefly admissible, because they tend to make the culprit better, and may therefore be proved not only consonant to the Gospel in their nature, but really so to the golden, Gospel rule, ' Do unto others, &c.' for every enlightened, upright man (and such only are fit to judge) must wish, that should he ever slip from the right way, and be obnoxious to his country's laws, those laws may rather operate to bring him back, than either to destroy him in a sinful state, or to stigmatize him to such a degree that honest men will shun him. As to the wish that some have had to suffer death, lest they should again be tempted, it seems to prove them in some degree penitent and humble, and such are fit to live."— J. G. Bevan, on the nature of punishment.

d

would deter from sin, more than it does. But attentive observation
may convince us, that this dread is chiefly operative upon persons
who have already some regard for the laws of God, by inducing
them to guard against temptation, and hence, it is to be expected
that the anticipation of temporal punishment will chiefly influence
those who have been trained to habits of reflection, and who
have been taught to respect institutions for the preservation of
good order. That these are the persons, on whom the dread of the
suffering consequent on transportation, usually operates, if it operate at all, may be inferred from the fact, that few of our criminals are of this class.

By far the larger proportion of those sentenced to transportation, consists of persons whose moral perceptions have become
blunted by spirit-drinking, In general they may be arranged
under the following sub-divisions :—

1st. The uneducated.

2nd. Persons who have been trained to thieving from their
youth.

3rd. Licentious persons, whose means would not enable them
to indulge their corrupt propensities, without resorting to fraud,
or theft.

4th. The idle, who by loitering in the streets, and about public-
houses, especially on the Sabbath, have formed vicious connexions.

5th. Gamblers.

6th. The indigent, who from the pressure of extreme poverty,
have committed theft; or, under the influence of designing men,
have been prompted to acts of outrage.

All these may be considered, either as persons of little, or no
reflection, or of such perverted minds as constantly to calculate
on the probabilities of evading the penalties, attached to infractions
of the law.

Taking this view of the subject, it would not appear that the
prevention of crime is to be expected, in any great degree, from
the dread of punishment; but rather, from counteracting the
causes that lead to the commission of crime. By extending the
means of education; by discouraging the sale and use of ardent
spirits; by removing juvenile thieves, as well as older adepts;
by stimulating magistrates to suppress houses of ill-fame, and to
remove profligate women from the streets; by promoting a due
observance of the Sabbath; by discountenancing every species of
gaming; and by remedying those evils by which the labouring
poor are oppressed in their wages; the principal avenues to vice

would be closed, and the benefit would be incalculable in the prevention of crime.

The legitimate objects of Penal Discipline appear to us to be, in considerable measure, accomplished by transportation to Van Diemens Land.

In the first place, the removal of the prisoner from Great Britain, and consequent restraint from further outrage there, is, in most instances, effectually secured.—It is computed that only one in fifty returns to his native land.

Secondly. As by the Government regulations, no wages are allowed to the prisoner, in the assigned service of the colonist; but he receives merely food and clothing, his labour is rendered subservient to the progress of a rising Colony, and some restitution is thus afforded to the injured public.

Thirdly. A door of hope is opened to the prisoner, which operates as a powerful stimulus to industry and good conduct. For, while conscious of some mitigation in the rigour of his bondage, when in assigned service, he is also aware, that by a certain continuance of good conduct, he will become eligible for a Ticket of Leave, which will enable him to appropriate his own earnings; and that by a continued perseverance in a course of amendment, he may obtain the further indulgence, of a Conditional or a Free Pardon.

Fourthly. The bulk of the prisoners are dispersed in small groups over the Colony, where they are generally under the immediate cognizance of their respective masters: and as it becomes the strong interest of the assigned-servant to please his master, in like manner, it is that of the master to watch over his assigned-servant, for his good, and to treat him with a certain degree of kindness; which, in general, has some ameliorating effect on his character.

Fifthly. Should these inducements fail to produce good conduct; should the prisoner in assigned-service become refractory and ill-conducted, more irksome restraint, and a much severer discipline await him, in a Road-party or a Chain-gang; and should he continue to sink in the scale of conduct, he ultimately finds his level in the lowest grade of Penal Discipline, in the Public Works, or at a Penal Settlement; where he is still more effectually restrained, and is doomed to toil out his days, in irons, at the lowest species of drudgery.

Sixthly. Even at a Penal Settlement, and in a Chain-gang, or a Road-party, an incitement to good conduct is still presented, in the hope of removal to assigned-service, after a certain period of amendment.*

As a medium of reformation, the assignment of prisoners as bond-servants, holds a pre-eminent place in Colonial Prison Discipline; and for the reasons previously advanced, it has great advantage over confinement in Jails and other Public Prisons, or in Road-parties and Chain-gangs. It would hardly be practicable by any other method, to bring them under the charge, and surveillance of so great a number of persons, many of whom are men of education and moral worth.

It must, however, be admitted, that the incitements to moral reformation are very unequally brought to bear upon prisoners in assigned service, from the varied character of their masters While some endeavour to improve their servants, by imparting moral and religious instruction, and by holding out hopes of recommendation for Tickets of Leave, or by rewarding the well-conducted with additional clothing, tea, tobacco, &c. others chiefly aim at keeping them in subjection by threats, and by bringing them under summary punishment, by complaints to the Magistrate.†

Some of the prisoners in assigned-service are very industrious, but a much larger proportion are of a very different character, and require constant attention to keep them at work.—On an average they do not effect nearly so much work as the labouring population of the northern parts of England. This may be accounted for on several grounds :

First. The greater number of persons transported, are of the idle, intemperate, and dissolute, to whom regular labour is peculiarly irksome.

Secondly. Many, who have grown up in idleness, or in town occupations, are here put to rural employments.

* In our remarks on prison discipline, we have not had reference to the Auburn system, having had no opportunity of witnessing its operations. We are far from asserting that it may not be superior, in some respects, even to transportation.

The right of man to separate married couples, by transporting one of the parties, and thus exposing both to temptation, appears to us extremely equivocal. The practice does not seem reconcileable, with the injunction, " What therefore God hath joined together let not man put asunder." (Matth. xix. 6.)

† There is necessarily a great variety of character among the settlers to whom prisoners are assigned, and consequently they are exposed to an equal variety of treatment. Few masters attend to their moral and religious instruction ; many treat them with some degree of kindness, combined with judicious firmness ; a larger proportion treat them with disdain and harshness ; and a few are still more unreasonable and severe.

The commendable vigilance of the Government, extending to the private admonition of the Master, and even to the removal of assigned servants from settlers who may have proved themselves unworthy of such indulgence ; and also to the careful weekly revision of all Magisterial Sentences, operates as a salutary check to tyranny and oppression.

Thirdly. The idea that prisoners are the aggrieved parties, which is industriously impressed upon new comers, when in the Penitentiary, also has its influence.

Yet, in spite of all these obstacles, it must be admitted that a great number of prisoners, who have been brought up in ignorance, idleness and profligacy, acquire improved habits, in assigned-service; and that cases of radical reformation occur, under the discipline to which they are subjected.

Nothing can afford more convincing proof of the estimate prisoners form of their punishment, whether in assigned service, or in the public works, than the universal anxiety they exhibit to obtain a ticket-of-leave; and when they have been enabled, by this indulgence, to avail themselves of their own earnings, their further solicitude, to obtain a conditional pardon, by which they may be at liberty to travel any where in the Colony without a pass, and be exempted from summary punishment, for being out before sunrise, or after eight o'clock in the evening, for being too far from their residence, absent from muster, or for other trivial matters, which are a constant restraint upon the liberty, even of a man possessing the indulgence of a ticket-of-leave.*

The punishments of transportation are many and considerable. Among the more grievous may be enumerated, the privations to which every prisoner is exposed, during a tedious voyage; the annoyances he has to experience after his arrival, during his sojourn in the Penitentiary.† If assigned as a bond-servant,

* As the influence of the hope of indulgence, is of powerful agency in promoting reformation; so a want of promptitude, such as, in some instances, occurs, on the part of the Government, in fulfilling its promises of indulgence for particular services, disheartens the prisoners in striving to merit Tickets-of-leave or Emancipation.

The discouraging effects of allowing prisoners to remain in Penal Road-parties, after the expiration of their sentence, we have commented upon in a former report; we would suggest the immediate removal of those whose sentences are expired, into the newly established Road-parties of Assignable Prisoners; and that the assignable parties should have rations different from the others. A trifling allowance of tea and sugar, or of vegetables, would make a great difference in the estimation of a prisoner.

† The prisoners, in the Penitentiary for males, in Hobart Town, are about 750 in number. They occasionally exceed that amount by several hundreds. A proportion of these, usually from about 120 to 140, compose the Chain-gang. Another Chain-gang comprising upwards of 200 men, not included in the 750, but rationed from the Penitentiary, are lodged in the Hulks.

The ration of victuals, per diem, is as follows; 1¼ lbs. flour, from which 12 per cent of bran has been subtracted, 1¼ lbs. Fresh meat; ½ oz. salt; and ⅓ oz. soap. No tea nor vegetables are allowed. When divided into three meals this proves barely sufficient to satisfy the cravings of a working man, in Van Diemens Land: and the prisoner who does not keep a close watch upon his provisions, is almost sure to be robbed by his comrades. Some have been deprived of their rations to such an extent, through this means, as to have been on the verge of starvation. In road-parties and chain-gangs, others have even absconded from this cause.

the prisoner has no choice in the selection of his master; yet to all lawful commands, he must yield him implicit obedience; he has not even the choice of an occupation; he receives no wages for his daily labour; his comforts are very few, and for these he is entirely dependent upon his employer, who is not bound to allow him any thing beyond the bare rations of food, clothing, and bedding, prescribed by the Government.* The prisoner is constantly liable to suffer summary punishment, on conviction before a magistrate, whether for intemperance, absence without leave, insolence, or any other species of insubordination; as well as for more flagrant breaches of the law. For misconduct, he may be sent to a Road-party or Chain-gang, and if repeated, to a Penal Settlement, where his privations will be greatly increased.† He must have for his companions such other prisoners as happen to be associated with him in servitude, however degraded and disagreeable their company and character may be; and in the midst of all these trials, he is continually reminded of the sweets of liberty, by numbers around, who are free, and by

---

* The accommodations of assigned servants are usually far removed from comfort. They generally live in huts constructed of logs, apart from the dwellings of their masters, having wooden shutters instead of windows, and inferior to the commonest stables in England; they are frequently so open to the weather, as only to be rendered habitable for human beings, even in the mild climate of V. D. Land, by means of large fires of the wood, with which the Island so universally abounds; they are generally untidy and dirty, and the sleeping accommodations are of the meanest kind. Few settlers limit their assigned servants to the ration of provisions prescribed by the Government, viz: 10½ lbs. meat, 10½ lbs. flour, 7 oz. sugar, 3½ oz. soap, and 2 oz. salt, per week, for males; and 5½ lbs. meat, 8½ lbs. flour, 2 oz. tea, ¼ lb. sugar, and 2 oz. salt per week, for females; but many allow vegetables, tea, sugar, and tobacco. Though the Government ration is more in quantity than many mechanics in England consume, of the same articles, yet, when without vegetables, and cooked in a frying-pan or made into "damper," which are wasteful modes of preparing food, it is not sufficient to satisfy the appetite of many prisoners. The opportunities that agricultural and other servants have of pilfering from their masters, render it in general, a matter of policy not to limit them in the necessaries of life: but it is a great advantage to the settler, to be able to revert to Government rations, in cases of discontent or misconduct.

In many instances in which settlers, have tried to increase the comfort of their assigned servants by cooking for them, they have been very ungrateful for the attention, and have appeared to regard it as an attempt to save something from their rations. Prisoners generally, refuse to eat Kangaroo, or other provision which they think costs their employers nothing; and though they often take Kangaroos themselves, for the sake of the skins, which they sell, or exchange for tobacco, and too often secretly for spirits, &c. they rarely cook the flesh when in assigned service; but when they have obtained tickets-of-leave, and in consequence of receiving wages for their labour, have to maintain themselves, they frequently live almost entirely on Kangaroo flesh.

---

† A prisoner may be convicted of insubordination, or insolence, and receive punishment when some angry speech of his master or mistress, may have temporarily excited his passion. And this punishment may be flagellation, solitary confinement, or even sentence to a Road-party; in the latter case, if provoked by an unreasonable Overseer, such as prisoner Overseers often prove, so as to be induced to abscond, it may bring him to a Chain-gang, or a Penal Settlement, absconding from the latter of which, brings him under the sentence of death!

contrast, of the irksomeness of his miserable bondage, with their freedom. With reference to prisoners sentenced to seven, or fourteen years transportation, the fact should also be mentioned, that few ever attain the means of returning to their native land, so that, to them, transportation for a limited period, generally proves banishment for life.

The reformatory effect of the Penal Discipline, enforced in Van Diemens Land, may be estimated by the good order, and general security of persons and property that prevail throughout the Colony. The number of persons that have been brought up in idleness and vice, who have acquired habits of industry, by which they maintain themselves decently in the Colony, is considerable; a few have become prosperous, even to affluence; and others having become reformed upon sound Christian principles, have realized more " durable riches," and are ornaments to both civil and religious society. It is deserving of remark, that a considerable proportion of the latter class have been at Penal Settlements, during a period in which they have had the benefit of moral and religious instruction, through the medium of sincere and devoted men, placed there for the purpose, by the Government.*

The idea, that persons transported are so depraved that they cannot be at large without danger to the public, must be received with much limitation. The safety of persons and property in Van Diemens Land, affords collateral proof of this position, and of the justness of the sentiment, that many of them are criminals rather from the peculiar circumstances under which they have been placed, than from their own confirmed depravity. The attentive inquirer will be led to take this view, by an acquaintance with their history. It must, however, be admitted, that the Penal Discipline adopted, contributes much to this state of security. Though the settlers are surrounded by persons, in the stations of domestic, agricultural, and other descriptions of servants, who have been convicted of nearly every species of violation of the laws, they live among them in comparative safety; generally in greater safety than when in

* Whilst we would acknowledge with gratitude, the ready access that has at all times, been granted to ourselves, in visiting the prisoners under the immediate charge of the Government; we consider it a duty to state our conviction, that the objections which have been made by some of the Colonial Chaplains to the voluntary labours of others, have been unreasonable, and have tended to hinder a good work. This remark chiefly refers to objections made to the labours of the Wesleyan Minister, in Hobart Town, and to those of a respectable Independent Minister, residing some time ago in Launceston. Both these individuals offered gratuitously to visit some of the prisons, weekly, without interfering with the duties of the Chaplains, by whom they were refused; and there are other sincere and suitable persons in the Colony, who would engage in the same work of Christian philanthropy, if way were made for them.

England. There are exceptions, particularly, as regards sheep stealing, and, in some cases, purloining, to exchange the stolen goods for
strong drink : yet, taking all these exceptions into account, it must
still be acknowledged, that many of the prisoner class, do not exhibit
greater depravity than the " unconvicted public " of Great Britain.
Attention to the moral and religious instruction of prisoners is of
vital importance in promoting reformation.   It has afforded us much
satisfaction, to observe the increasing attention of the Government
to this point ; and we have no doubt that it is a measure of
sound wisdom, to appoint persons of piety, who are sincerely
interested in the work, as instructors to the Road-parties, and
other prisoners under the immediate charge of the Government,
without restriction to any peculiar denomination of Christians,
provided the fundamental doctrines of the Gospel are but zea-
lously inculcated.

Having expressed our opinions on the influence of the Penal Discipline of Van Diemens Land, generally, we venture to offer some
remarks upon what appear, in our view, to be its imperfections; and
to suggest a few improvements, not, however, designing to supersede those proposed in our former report, on the state of the Road-
parties, Chain-gangs, &c. some of which, we observe, have been
already acted upon by the Colonial Government.

From what we can learn, the discipline of prison ships, on the
passage out, is calculated to promote the good of the prisoners.
Most of the Surgeon Superintendents are reputed to be attentive
in teaching the prisoners to read ; and some of them endeavour to
impart moral and religious instruction ; but these important parts
of their duty appear to be neglected by others.

The allowance of so large a quantity of wine to prisoners on the
passage, is productive of great evil, and we would submit that it
ought only to be administered as medicine.   On the present plan,
a regular allowance is provided for each person, and it is commonly
distributed daily, from the time of approaching the tropical regions,
to the termination of the voyage.   If, at a certain daily rate, the
stock laid in, promises to last beyond that period, the quantity
distributed daily is increased.   Thus an appetite for stimulating liquors is nourished, to the end of the voyage, and this
frequently proves an insurmountable obstacle to future reformation.

Prisoners are furnished with Bibles on their passage out, which
are taken from them on their arrival in Van Diemens Land, and
lodged in the ordnance store ; from whence they may be obtained

again by application through the medium of a Colonial Chaplain. But a large proportion of the prisoners are assigned into parts of the Colony, where they seldom come into contact with the Chaplains; and few of the latter make it their business to see that the prisoners in their respective districts, are supplied with Bibles; few also of the settlers attend to this subject: the consequence is, that for want of Bibles, the inclination and the power to read them, that had been acquired on the passage, are often lost. We would suggest that the Bibles should have the names of the prisoners marked upon them; and that they should be no longer consigned to the ordnance store, but that the prisoners should be required to produce them at their monthly muster.

When prisoners arrive in the Colony, and are transferred from the prison-ships to the Penitentiary at Hobart Town, though the time they remain there, previously to entering upon assigned service, is usually short, we have reason to believe, that they almost universally sustain great injury in the course of it, by mixing with a large number of prisoners who have been long in the Colony, and who are also the inmates of the Penitentiary, having, for misconduct, and other causes, been returned upon the hands of the Government. The male prisoners of mechanical callings, who are retained in the public service, and continue to lodge in the Penitentiary, are still more exposed to this contaminating influence. In this place prisoners on their first arrival are diligently instructed by the " old hands," in all the tricks prevalent among them.* They are taught to look upon themselves as the aggrieved parties, and are encouraged to think that they will, in some manner, revenge themselves by wasting the provisions of their employers, and doing as little work as they can. These instructions, though disregarded by the more considerate among the prisoners, produce an effect upon the thoughtless and idle, that is felt in almost every establishment in Van Diemens Land, and is highly inimical to reformation. Female prisoners, on their arrival, are subjected to the same kind of contamination, from collision with the " old hands" in the Penitentiary for females, as in the case with the other sex.

When women are assigned into the service of families, the habits of smoking and drinking, which they have acquired, are very frequently indulged in, to the great annoyance of their employers, and the hinderance of their own reformation: and in order to gratify their propensity to smoking and drinking, they not unfrequently ,

---

* "Old hands," is a term in frequent use, to designate prisoners who have been long in the Colony; and especially those of notoriously bad character.

give way to pilfering, and other immoralities.   Many of them contract the habit of smoking in English prisons, where, as well as on the passage out, it ought to be carefully guarded against.   The greater number have acquired the habit of drinking at home, which has led to the crimes for which they have been transported; and this unhappy propensity has been fostered during the latter part of the voyage, by the daily allowance of wine.

The practice of paying a sum of money to female prisoners, as a compensation for clothing, which generally prevails, is a great evil: they often conduct themselves well till the first payment, which they spend improperly, and thenceforward are unmanageable; and the style of dress they adopt is frequently unbecoming their station.

In the transfer of female prisoners from place to place, throughout Van Diemens Land, under charge of constables, &c. an exposure exists, demanding the most serious attention of the Government.   The difficulty of applying an efficient remedy, will be admitted by every one acquainted with the circumstances of the Colony.   Improvement in the jails and lock-up-houses, would in some measure, counteract the evil; and the erection of a good central prison at Oatlands, by which a great deal of travelling might be avoided, would also conduce to that effect.   Such a prison is greatly wanted, both as a jail and a penitentiary for males and females.

The insecurity of the jails of the Colony, universally, is an evil needing correction.   Owing to this circumstance, it is common to put free persons into irons as soon as committed; and if confined in the jail at Launceston, they are often kept in irons, among convicted felons, for several months before trial, on account of the long intervals that occur between the times of holding the sessions at that place.   This injustice to untried prisoners, we submit, ought to be speedily remedied.*

---

* The jails in V. D. Land are, all of them, ill adapted for the purposes designed.   Those at New Norfolk, Hamilton, Bothwell, Campbell Town, Oatlands, and Waterloo Point, are rude wooden buildings; the two last mentioned are without airing courts of any description; and most of them are without proper convenience for the separation of the sexes: this is also the case with the one on Norfolk Plains, which is built of brick, and has one day-room, with two cells on each side, in which all that is said in the day-room can be heard.   The jail at Richmond is of stone, and has a stockaded airing-court; those at Hobart Town and Launceston have more internal accommodation, but, like that at Richmond, they have not sufficient to admit of the untried prisoners being kept apart from the convicted; both are crowded together in the same rooms, in which they also sleep, spreading their beds on the floor: and as there are no inner court-yards, neither the convicted nor unconvicted, have the benefit of fresh air, except for about two hours in the day, when they are allowed to exercise themselves in the common yard, under the eye of a guard.   The prisoners in the Penitentiary at Hobart Town, vary in number from 700 to 1,000, all of whom have to associate in one common airing yard.

The very general disposition, on the part of persons transported, to regard themselves as aggrieved, is greatly to be regretted, because such a feeling is hostile to reformation. But when the severity of the punishment is contrasted with many of the comparatively trivial offences to which it is attached, it cannot be denied, that there are cases in which some ground for such a feeling exists. These cases afford convincing proof, that a punishment disproportionate to the offence, and which is consequently a violation of justice, tends to frustrate its own object. This remark also applies to many of the Colonial punishments.

Most prisoners have a dread of flagellation, and of road-parties, and chain-gangs, till they have once suffered such punishments: after this, the generality of them exhibit a decided deterioration of character. Flagellation especially, is degrading, and excites revengeful feelings. Solitary confinement has a much better influence, when properly carried into effect. Settlers, however, generally prefer flagellation, because it occasions less interruption to the work of their servants. We have often observed that the most strenuous advocates of flagellation, are given to the practice of swearing. It is worthy of notice that this punishment, under the law of Moses, was limited to "forty stripes save one;" because of its degrading nature; (See Deuteronomy xxv. 3.) and yet, that dispensation was one of a less merciful character than the Gospel; and no precept of the latter, in any way, justifies the infliction of flagellation at all, much less allows of its extended administration.* This was the corrective administered from the cradle to the grave, in the semi-barbarous ages, but the progress of civilization and Christianity has corrected the error in many quarters, and we doubt not, will, ere long, universally stamp it as barbarous and unchristian, as well as inefficient.

Solitary confinement is calculated to awaken reflection. Reformed prisoners, who have been subjected to this punishment, and have remarked its effects on others, say, that, how much soever a man may be disposed to set at nought the power of those appointed to punish evil-doers, he is almost sure, when he comes to be for a few days on low diet, without exercise to dispose him for sleep, and to be left to his own cogitations, to feel self-condemnation, and to bow under his punishment. It is, however, to be

* In some parts of the Colony, when a prisoner is sentenced to flagellation, the strokes are inflicted after the lapse of half a minute, by which means, inflamation takes place, to a considerable degree, before the execution of the sentence is completed, and the torture is thus greatly augmented; while in others, including the Penitentiaries in Hobart Town, and at Port Arthur, the less barbarous plan, of administering the lashes in quick succession, is adopted.

expected, that the good resolutions of those long habituated to evil, will be more frequently broken than kept, under the renewed influence of strong temptation.

The effect of solitary confinement cannot be considered to have been fairly tried, in Van Diemens Land. Few of the Colonial prisons at present admit of it, either in its most rigorous form, or as it may be administered for longer periods, combined with silent labour. In most of them, the cells are within hearing of the other prisoners, or of persons outside; and in many, the cells are so few in number, that four, or more persons, sentenced to solitary confinement, have been placed in the same cell at one time.

The practice of sentencing men to work in chains, as a punishment, apart from the mere purposes of restraint, appears to be contrary to the sound principles of penal discipline. It is a practice, beyond doubt, borrowed from a barbarous age, when those principles were little understood. It has no direct tendency to promote reformation; but on the contrary, is calculated to increase desperation of character; it is a part of that system of abstract vengeance, which man is not authorized to inflict upon his fellow man. While such punishments fail to deter from crime, in the Mother Country, their tendency is decidedly to increase it in the Colony. We cannot, therefore, but lament the promulgation of the late regulations, by which numbers of men have been sentenced to work, for long periods, in chains, from their first arrival in Van Diemens Land, without having committed any offence, subsequently to conviction in England. We cherish the hope, that no Chain-gang will long exist, except such as shall be composed of men who have absconded from other service, who may be worked in chains, not to make their labour more galling, but to prevent them from running away; unless some better mode of restraining them can be applied.

Extension of sentence, on the plan at present adopted, is not a very influential punishment. This may arise from the infliction of the penalty being remote from the commission of the crime to which it is attached, and the hope of remission, for good conduct intervening. We would propose for consideration, immediate removal to a Chain-gang, as the punishment for absconding from a Road-party, and removal to the Chain-gang at Port Arthur, for the punishment for absconding from other Chain-gangs.

Capital punishments appear also to be far from effectual, in deterring from crime; and without reference to their conformity to

the principles of the Gospel, or otherwise, they are certainly inde-
fensible, on the grounds of sound justice and humanity, in many
of the cases in which they are awarded. The proximate cause of
their want of influence may be, that, in the majority of instances,
the men who commit crimes to which capital punishment is attached, have persuaded themselves into unbelief respecting a future
state, and consequently the anticipation of death is to them, only
that of extinction of life, without further consequences, unless coming
under its sentence should awaken them to a sense of their delusion. It
is the eternal consequences that render death a greater punishment
than transportation. Separate from these, transportation, even to
Van Diemens Land, under its present system of penal discipline,
is, in our opinion, more to be dreaded than death itself.

Many of the objections which exist with regard to the association
of large numbers of prisoners in jails and houses of correction, in
England, apply with equal, and in some respects, with greater force,
to the Penitentiaries, Road-parties, and Chain-gangs, in Van Diemens Land.* The chief superiority of the latter, consists in the
daily employment of the prisoners out of doors, and in the encouragement to good conduct, held out by the hope of assignment
to settlers ; or, to mechanics, retained in the public works, the
hope of a ticket-of-leave.

The employment of prisoner overseers in the Chain-gangs and
Road-parties, is liable to many objections. It has been ascertained,
that in many instances, their conduct toward the men placed under
them, is very oppressive, especially, where they think they can
extort money by oppressing some and favouring others ; and that,
in some cases, they act in collusion with prisoners who abscond ;
agreeing with them, that they shall give themselves up to certain
constables, with whom, and the absconding parties, they divide the
reward for their apprehension.

In spite of the Government regulations, many of the prisoners,
both in Chain-gangs and Road-parties, and in other situations,
contrive to obtain money : this, in a Penal system like that of Van
Diemens Land, in which the prisoners often come necessarily into
contact with the free population, it appears to be next to impossible
entirely to prevent.

Some of the provisions of II and III William IV. Chap. 62,

---

* The arrangements for sleeping, and the association in the prisons, are universally admitted to have a depraving effect. It is worthy of notice, in connexion with this fact, that
in the provisions of the Mosaic Law, bond service, which was consequently not in prisons,
was the only kind of restraint provided in penal cases.

intituled " An act for abolishing the punishment of death, in certain cases, and substituting a lesser punishment in lieu thereof," if carried into operation, would have a very detrimental influence upon the reformation of prisoners. To prohibit those from holding property, who by good conduct, had obtained tickets-of-leave, would have a great tendency to drive them to spend their earnings in profligacy and drunkenness. To extend this prohibition to those whose sentence had expired, would be to make transportation for seven or fourteen years, confer a disability for life, which would be opposed to every principle of justice.

To preclude prisoners holding tickets-of-leave from suing or being sued, is on the one hand, to expose them to be robbed of their wages, and otherwise imposed upon, in a way that might render a ticket-of-leave more of an evil than a benefit ; and on the other hand, to enable them to commit fraud with impunity. And to deprive the Governor of a Penal Colony of the power of conferring indulgence on a prisoner, for special service, or peculiarly meritorious conduct, until after the expiration of a prescribed and lengthened period, is to render nugatory one of the most powerful means of preserving order in the Colony.

Licensing so many Public Houses, notwithstanding the plea, that this measure prevents the illicit sale of spirits, is a great evil in Van Diemens Land, both as regards the prisoners, and the free population ; many of whom will make any efforts, and run any risks to obtain strong drinks. Wherever a fresh Public House is opened, there the settler finds his servants more difficult to keep in order than before, whether they be bond or free. According to the common admission of prisoners, the larger proportion of them have given way to the temptations to commit the crimes that have resulted in their transportation, under the influence of ardent spirits ; and it is evident, that the majority of the offences committed in the Colony, occur under the same kind of excitement. It ought ever to be remembered, that in licensing houses for the sale of spirits, the Government countenances, if it does not patronize, the chief incitement to crime.

There is ground to believe, that in the earlier times of the Colony the vicious example of some of the Officers of Government, from those in the highest stations downward, and of most of the settlers, when open profligacy and intemperance pervaded all ranks, tended greatly to increase the demoralization of the prisoners ; but through the divine blessing upon the exertions of the present Lieutenant Governor, to promote reformation by his own example and influence, and by his endeavours to remove immoral persons from office, and to prevent profligate settlers having assigned servants, very extensive improvement has taken place, both in the character of the settlers and in that of the prisoner population. The religious labours of Christians of various denominations, and the emigration of persons of respectable character, to this Colony, have also materially contributed to promote reformation. An encouraging advancement is now observable, both in the improved standard of morals, and in the increasing spirit of religious enquiry.*

The early settlers of Van Diemens Land, availed themselves of the plains and valleys, that were naturally unencumbered with timber, and most readily brought into cultivation: these form a very small portion of the Island, and are, with little exception, located. It is chiefly locations of this character that have been sold for considerable sums from one settler to another; in a few instances, nearly without any expense having been bestowed upon them, but frequently, when nearly as much had been incurred in fencing and other improvements, as the price obtained for the land, with the improvements.

The territory yet unlocated is so thickly timbered, that the clearing would, in most instances, cost more than the land when cleared, would be worth: but where the capital of settlers consists chiefly in their physical power, they do not begrudge its expenditure, if by this means, they can obtain a subsistence. The major part of the unlocated land is not nearly worth five shillings an acre, even to men of capital, being mountainous, stony, and covered with trees, and probably not capable, on an average, of maintaining, in a state of nature, one sheep to four acres, nor one bullock to ten acres. Yet, in our opinion, a much larger proportion of the Island will ultimately be found available for the purposes of agriculture, than is generally calculated upon; but it will only be as Population becomes more dense, and by the expenditure of immense exertion in clearing.

There is much appearance of prosperity among the settlers of Van Diemens Land, where, without doubt, the sober, prudent, and

* The assignment of female prisoners to public-houses, is obviously injurious to the morals of the Colony: We are decidedly of opinion, that no exceptions whatever should be made to the prohibition of such assignments.

Among the prominent impediments to good morals now existing, are Races and Theatrical exhibitions; the latter of which are of modern introduction. The associations connected with these and some other kinds of public amusements, are always detrimental to good morals; and races are peculiarly adapted to interfere with the moral order of the prisoner, as well as that of the free population of a Penal Colony like V. D. Land.

industrious, find it easier to obtain the necessaries, and a moderate share of the comforts of life, than in England. Yet the fact, that upwards of two thousand three hundred writs were issued from the Sheriff's Office, in 1833, proves, that the semblance of prosperity exists to a greater degree than the reality; this is also confirmed by some acquaintance with the circumstances of the settlers. The chief causes of want of success, appear to be intemperance, and a disposition to embark in larger concerns than the capital of the parties renders warrantable. Many, who, in the earlier days of the Colony, practised fraud on the Government, and by fictitious representations of capital, obtained large grants of land, had to borrow money to stock their land, at a higher rate of interest than its produce was equal to: these have, consequently, failed of success, and are struggling with adversity, or their locations have passed into other hands.

A want of the means of education has been greatly felt, in many of the thinly-settled districts, but this is generally obviated by the institution of Schools, as the population increases. Those established by the Government are calculated to be useful, where the number of children is insufficient to induce private individuals to open Schools; but we think, most of the Government Schools might be rendered much more extensively useful, if they were organized on a better plan.

The Orphan School, at Newtown, is an admirable establishment; but we think, it also might be improved by introducing a more systematic plan of education; and by placing a Superintendent over the whole of its operations, in no way engaged in teaching. Such an arrangement has been adopted in many Public Schools, with advantage.

It is also very desirable, that the children, from the Female Factory, should be removed to the Orphan School, or to some other suitable place, as soon as they are weaned, and be put as early as possible, under Infant School discipline.

We apprehend, that advantage would arise to this class of children, if the persons who nurse them in the Factory, were assigned to the Nursery, and encouraged to the right performance of their office, by the hope of a Ticket-of-leave, for faithful servitude; instead of being frequently removed. And more justice might be done to the infants, if the mothers were sentenced to a year's imprisonment, from the time of their arrival in the factory, rather than to six months, in the crime class, from the period of the children being weaned; and if such only as misconduct themselves in the Factory, were to be removed into the crime class. On the present plan, there is a strong temptation to the mothers, to keep their infants in a weakly state, that the time, apparently necessary to nurse them at the breast, may be lengthened, and that the time of entering upon their own punishment, may be delayed; as well as to instigate the nurses to neglect the children, in order that it may be needful to bring their mothers back to them. The punishment now falls much more severely upon the woman who is sent into the Factory three months before her confinement, than upon one who gives birth to her infant immediately after her arrival.

The Colonial Hospitals, at Hobart Town and New Norfolk, are very useful establishments, and appear to be under good management. That at Launceston is very inadequate to the purpose designed, and when we visited it a year ago, most of the beds were on the floor, and every thing about the place bespoke neglect.

The little Hospital, at George Town, is much dilapidated, but it appears to be as comfortable as the state of the building admits. It is very useful for the reception of patients afflicted with chronic diseases, who often recover in it speedily, after having been long at Launceston, without amendment. This circumstance probably arises from the difference in the air and climate, of the two places.

If the hope of early indulgence by a ticket-of-leave, were held out to the wardsmen, and attendants of the Hospitals, as a reward for the faithful discharge of their respective duties, it would contribute greatly to the comfort of the patients.

The situation of the Colonists in Van Diemens Land, has been rendered abundantly more comfortable, by the transfer of the Aboriginal Population, from the main land to Flinders Island, while the circumstances of the poor Blacks also, have been materially improved. The exertions of George Augustus Robinson, in this arduous work, which he appears to have effected without any mixture of violence, have been characterized by a degree of perseverance and success, that demands the gratitude of the public.

We would express our decided conviction as to the expediency of all the Aboriginal children, whose parents can be brought to acquiesce in the measure, being placed in the Orphan School, at New Town, that in future, they may be trained up in the habits of the Europeans, and in knowledge that may qualify them for usefulness in the community. By this early separation from their countrymen, all fear of their returning to their former savage state would be precluded, and they would be prepared to maintain themselves by their own industry.*

While we cordially approve of the benevolent intentions of the Government, in the removal of the Native Blacks to Flinders Island, a measure, we believe, the most judicious that under existing circumstances, could have been adopted; we cannot but deprecate the short sighted policy, by which, in the Colonization of New Countries, the lands of the Aboriginal Inhabitants have been wrested from them, with little, or no regard to their natural and indefeasible rights. Had these been duly considered, by establishing an amicable intercourse with the rightful owners, and rendering them an equivalent for their lands, they would have been retained as friends of the Colonists, instead of being transformed, by provocation, into implacable enemies. Such a proceeding, which, in the history of America, has been proved to be practicable, and attended with the happiest results, would not only have been accordant with justice, which knows not the distinction of clime, or of colour, but with a sound and enlightened policy.

The misery, and waste of human life, that have ensued in this Colony, from the adoption of a different course, convey an instructive warning to present, and future generations, which, it is to be hoped, will never be forgotten.

JAMES BACKHOUSE.
GEORGE WASHINGTON WALKER.

Hobart Town, 19th of 6th mo., 1834.

---

* We have noticed, with much satisfaction, the progress made by the few Aboriginal youths, who have already been placed in the Orphan School. Among these, Arthur and Friday, the two lads who were at Flinders Island, during our first visit there, and who were then sunk in the barbarous habits of their race, have made considerable improvement since their removal. The former writes a hand, that would not disgrace a European youth of the same age.

APPENDIX.

G.

TESTIMONIALS of HOBART TOWN MONTHLY MEETING of FRIENDS, respecting the RELIGIOUS LABOURS of GEORGE WASHINGTON WALKER.

HOBART TOWN MONTHLY MEETING of FRIENDS, held on the 7th of 8th Month, 1834.

Third Minute.—This meeting having had under its serious consideration, the religious labours of our dear friend George Washington Walker, and feeling unity with them, hereby records him as an approved Minister of the Society of Friends; and expresses its satisfaction with his proceeding, in this capacity, as the companion of our dear friend James Backhouse, in his religious visit to this Colony, and other parts of the world, as noticed in his Certificate, from Friends in England.

HOBART TOWN MONTHLY MEETING, held at KELVEDON, GREAT SWAN PORT, on the 4th of 9th Month, 1834.

Third Minute.—The subject of the Third Minute, of the 7th of 8th Month, having been read, this Meeting, after having solemnly considered the same, is of the judgment, that the minute be confirmed. The Clerk is desired to hand a copy of the said minute, to George Washington Walker.

FRANCIS COTTON,

(Copy.)   Clerk.

e 2

To the Inhabitants of the British Colonies in New Holland, Van Diemens Land, South Africa, and elsewhere.

At a Yearly Meeting, of the Religious Society of Friends, commonly called Quakers, in Van Diemens Land, held at Hobart Town, on the 3rd, and by adjournments, on the 6th and 9th days of the 10th Month, 1834. Our dear friend George Washington Walker, who came amongst us as the companion of our dear friend James Backhouse, in a religious visit to these parts; in the course of which, the said George Washington Walker has been constrained from time to time, under a sense of religious duty, to labour in the work of the ministry; and has been recorded as an approved Minister of the Society, by Hobart Town Monthly Meeting of Friends, has informed us, that he now believes it his duty, in the capacity of a Minister of the Gospel, to continue to accompany James Backhouse in his travels amongst you. He has also produced copies of two minutes of Hobart Town Monthly Meeting, signifying its unity with his proceeding under these circumstances; and this meeting feeling unity with him in this prospect of continued religious labour, liberates him for the work, and desires his encouragement therein.

Recommending him, with our dear friend James Backhouse, with whose Gospel labours we have had much unity, to the kind regard of those amongst whom they may come; and desiring that their labours may be blessed of the Most High, to the honour of his great Name; and to the turning of many to the inward teaching of the Holy Spirit, in order that they may come savingly to believe in Christ, and to know their sins to be blotted out for his sake, and receive help through him to do the will of God, we remain in the love of the Gospel, your friends.

Henry Cotton	Abraham Charles Flower
William Rayner	William Holdship
Anna Maria Cotton	Thomas Squire
Robert Andrew Mather	Theophilus Pollard
Sarah Benson Mather	Daniel Wheeler
Isabella Rayner	Charles Wheeler

Francis Cotton, Clerk.

APPENDIX.

H.

A LETTER to COLONEL ARTHUR, respecting SPIRITUOUS
LIQUORS.

To Colonel George Arthur, Lieutenant-Governor of Van Diemens
Land, and its Dependencies.

Observations of James Backhouse and George Washington
Walker, on the Distillation, Importation, and Sale of Ardent
Spirits, as sanctioned by the Government.

Our attention having been frequently called to the habit of spirit
drinking, so destructively prevalent in the Colony, we venture to
submit to the notice of the Lieutenant Governor, the following
observations :—

That the practice of spirit-drinking is a sinful practice, is a
position so clearly proved by the evidence brought before the
public, through the medium of Temperance Societies, and other
channels, as to require no arguments here.

That this practice often entails upon its votaries, curses, such
as injury of health, of mental powers, and of morals, in this life,
with perdition in the world to come ; and by its prevalence, burdens the community with pauperism, insubordination and crime, is
clear to every person of reflection.

And that those who make use of Spirits, in small quantities, as
beverage, are but the voluntary tamperers with this sin, and are,
generally, themselves verging towards an awful vortex, that involves inevitable ruin, the experience of ages has unequivocally
decided.

With these views and convictions, we cannot but look upon the countenance, by the Government, of the produce, importation, and sale of Spirits, as sinful; nor regard, but with dread, the accumulating evils entailed upon society by this countenance; being assured, that, in proportion as any Government renders itself a party to national sin, however popular that sin may be, such a Government must also render itself, and the people under it, obnoxious to the Divine displeasure, and to consequent instability and embarrassment.

The principles of Justice and Righteousness, according to the Gospel of Christ, are the only principles of sound Government; and every act of legislation, whether upon a small, or a large scale, will be found, in the end, to work well, in proportion as it approximates to these principles. On the other hand, every act will be found to work badly, in proportion as it departs from these principles, how greatly soever such a departure may, to the short-sighted views of mere human policy, at first, appear to be expedient. The history of mankind, from the earliest ages of the world, clearly proves this position.

We are, nevertheless, aware, that it requires much faith in the wisdom of God, practically to admit, that his laws are, in the end, invariably the most congenial to our welfare, when the end may be removed far beyond our perception. But this circumstance does not alter the fact: and the laws of God admit of no participation in sin.

We conceive, that to license Distilleries, and Houses for the sale of Spirits, and to admit the importation of Spirits, on the payment of a duty, is, on the part of the Government, an obvious participation in the sin, connected with Spirit-drinking; for to allow of sale by license, and on the payment of duty, implies voluntary sanction by the Government.

We therefore venture to suggest, that it is the duty of the Government, to interdict the Distillation, Importation, and Sale of Spirits; and thus, to withdraw its countenance from the sin of Spirit-drinking; and to impose penalties upon these acts, in order to stamp them with its disapprobation.

Believing that decided measures, to prevent the Distillation, Importation, and Sale of Spirits, would be in strict accordance with sound and enlightened policy, (even though compensations to individuals, might, in a few cases, in equity, be required,) we cannot but strongly recommend their adoption; and we have no doubt, that in the course of a single year, the improved comfort and prosperity of the community, which the banishment of this noxious fluid would produce, would silence the clamours that, at first, might be raised by the inconsiderate, against such measures.

But, if the Government be not prepared to act with this decision, we would respectfully suggest, the propriety of imposing a fine upon ships bringing Spirits into the Colony, and upon distilleries; also a penalty, per gallon, upon Spirits imported or purchased, whether by wholesale or retail, and upon all houses, per month, convicted of the Sale of Spirits; also rendering them liable to search by the Police, by day or by night, for twelve months from the time of conviction. Thus the Government would punish, instead of encourage, this sin, even though the penalties, at first, might amount to little more than the present duties and licenses. These penalties might from time to time be increased, until they amounted to a total prohibition. Nevertheless, we beg leave to state our decided conviction, that to pass an Act, to take effect from a period not very distant, totally prohibitory in its first operation, would be the wiser, safer, and more righteous measure.

JAMES BACKHOUSE.
GEORGE WASHINGTON WALKER.

Hobart Town, 15th of 11th mo. 1834.

APPENDIX.

I.

A LETTER to the CATECHIST, at PORT ARTHUR.

Hobart Town, 27th of 11th Mo. 1834.

To   *   *

Though much of a stranger to thee, I am disposed, in Christian freedom, to address thee, on the subject of thy mission to Port Arthur; where, the fervent desire of my heart is, that fruit from thy Gospel labours and exercises, may be produced abundantly, to the glory of the Most High.

In our late visit to the Settlement, I was disappointed, in not finding more cases of decided reformation among the prisoners, on the ground of sound, religious principle, than the very few, if they amount to above a solitary one, that have occurred at Port Arthur. Such cases amounted to about 5 per cent. upon the whole number of prisoners at Macquarie Harbour, for some time previous to the abandonment of that Settlement.

Many of the prisoners, so reformed, are still pursuing a humble, religious life, in the Colony, with a great measure of consistency. They form a class, perfectly distinct from those who have improved in conduct, on the ground of mere worldly policy; and who exercise restraint over themselves, in those points which rendered them obnoxious to human laws, because they have found the operation of these laws, painful to themselves.

I am far from attributing the lack of cases of religious reformation, to neglect of duty on the part of the late Missionary: I am prepared to believe that his labours were beneficial, though not marked by such heart-cheering cases of reformation. I am also aware, that many of the individuals, who became reformed, at Macquarie Harbour, were first awakened to a sense of their lost state, and of their need of a Saviour, and of the constant help of the Holy Spirit, to enable them to resist temptation, and to work righteousness, by remarkable circumstances, permitted, or ordained, in the overrulings of a merciful Providence. Yet those who were thus awakened, were, in many instances, encouraged and confirmed by the Christian care of the first Missionary.

The services of this individual, in the latter part of the time of his residence at Macquarie Harbour, were nevertheless, rendered much less influential, by his giving way to complain to the Commandant, of the omission of some one, to pay him the customary, and empty token of respect, of taking off the hat to him as he passed.—In so doing, those around him, perceived the operation of a spark of the pride of unregenerated man, such as ought not to be seen in a Christian minister; and I am persuaded, that however consistent it may be thought, with the military, or the civil discipline, to require such tokens of respect from prisoners, whether the respect exists or not, it will not do for religious men to require them, if they regard their own usefulness in the Divine hand, for the reformation of the unrighteous. If religious persons conduct themselves with humility and sincerity, manifesting a christian interest in those around them, in the fear of the Lord, they will be respected by those who are in any degree capable of appreciating that which deserves respect; and they will generally receive the tokens of it in the usual forms, except in cases where persons cannot use the common forms conscientiously, on account of many of them being tokens of homage to God, and of their general insincerity, as applied to men; and in these cases, the respect will be shown in more marked attentions, even from prisoners.

What I want chiefly to impress upon thy attention, is the absolute necessity of a minister, keeping his mind under the power of the Holy Spirit, in order that his ministry may baptize others "into the name of the Father, and of the Son, and of the Holy Ghost:" for unless the Lord's power accompany our ministry, however sound our doctrine may be, it will not awaken the spiritually dead. If the dead be raised by the Lord, through our instrumentality, we must first be baptized of the Holy Spirit, for the dead; and if the sick in spirit be healed, we must sympathize with them, under the operation of the Holy Spirit. We must be willing, in our measure, to follow the Captain of our Salvation, who took our sicknesses, and bare our diseases, and who, having been tempted in all points like as we are, though without sin, is able to succour them that are tempted. Many of the baptisms of Christ belonged to his office of a minister, in which he was an example for all ministers. These baptisms are to be distinguished from the offering of his life upon the cross, for the sins of mankind. In patiently bearing our measure of such sufferings, on behalf of others, we fill up our portion of " that which is behind, of the afflictions of Christ in our flesh, for his body's sake, which is the church." See Col. i. 24.

I want also to impress upon thee, the importance of being "instant in season; out of season;" for I am persuaded, that where religious labours are only used in set seasons for public worship, they will be of comparatively little effect. The mind of the labourer will, in the intervals, get from under the power of the Holy Spirit, and his ministrations will lose the savour of life. On the other hand, if the mind be kept in a close walk with God, attentive to the pointings of his Spirit, he will frequently open to the view, out of set seasons, opportunities for speaking a word to restrain evil, or to direct in the way of holiness, by turning people's attention to the inward manifestation of the Holy Spirit, as a witness in the conscience, against sin; and as a Comforter to those who work righteousness, and seek daily for the renewed, or continued evidence that their sins are blotted out in the blood of the Lamb. In these opportunities, " out of season," much is to be done, under the putting forth of the True Shepherd, in the way of remark, conversation and example.

It is well to be cautious of impeding such services, by too readily clothing these simple exercises in the formal garb of preaching or prayer; nevertheless, we must preach, and pray too, when these services are opened before us, of the Lord. Where the mind is kept under the power and guidance of the Spirit of Truth, there is often, in fields of labour like Port Arthur, a right opening for reading small portions of Scripture, and for making comments, in simplicity, on such passages as may impress the mind for instruction, or on other passages or subjects, that may not at the time have been read. At other times, there may be no such openings for expression; and then, it is safest to let the simple reading, with a pause, for inward exercise of soul, suffice.

I wish particularly to commend to thy Christian sympathy and notice, the poor creatures, sick in the hospital, or in the exempted building, and those in solitary confinement. Often, " man's extremity is God's opportunity;" and I believe, if thou give thy mind to exercise before the Lord, for these, he will reward thee with fruit from among them. I would also recommend thy visiting, as frequently as can be done, the out-stations, including the constables' huts, &c. The men on Woody Island, told G. W. Walker and myself, that they had no Bible, nor any books : we gave them a few tracts, and promised to mention their situation to thee. On lending books, or receiving them again, it would be well to take the opportunity to converse a little on their contents : this would tend to increase the attention and interest of the men, in reading them.

I would also recommend thy taking a lively interest, in unison with the Commandant, in classifying the prisoners. Much evil may be prevented, by putting men who shew signs of religious reformation, by themselves, as, I think, is done in your school-room. Those whose conduct is improved, or improving, from inferior motives, ought to be separated from the more vicious; and so on, in different grades, till the worst, not sleeping in cells, are left by themselves; and those sleeping in cells should be apart from the others, in a day-room, unless their cells be used also as day-rooms.

When we put a good, or a well-conducted man, among those who are worse, we ought always to calculate upon his becoming as bad as his companions; for such is the evil tendency of human nature, that nothing but a miracle of grace can preserve such a man from contamination; and we cannot insure such a miracle. No doubt, but God would afford the needful grace, if the man were to seek it; but who among the sons of men, can assure themselves that such a man will never get off his watch, and fall into the snare of the devil.

I think the Catechist ought to consider it as one of his official duties to superintend the School, every time it is conducted. If he neglect it, the interest of the teachers and pupils will be sure to flag.

George W. Walker joins me, in the salutation of Christian regard; and in desires, that thou mayst so walk with God, and labour in his fear, and in the ability that he giveth, as to receive his blessing abundantly thyself, and as to be made of the Lord, abundantly, a blessing to others.

Thy sincere friend,

JAMES BACKHOUSE.

APPENDIX.

J.

PRISONERS LETTERS.

No. 1.

"Norfolk Island, 25th April, 1835.

" Affectionate Parents,

"An unfortunate Son, now embraces the afforded opportunity, of imparting to you, in the strongest terms, his fervent desires for your welfare, &c. Since the receipt of your last letter, I have, through the want of a friend, and which I shall long feel the need of, become convicted to Norfolk Island. * * * My present situation here however, unfortunately, for me, dear Parents, [is such] that nothing but pure conduct, and the help of God alone, can afford me again the opportunity of meeting with you in this world. * * Dear Father and Mother, mine is a bitter lot in life; but I, myself, am alone to blame. Bid my brothers and sisters ever to bear my situation in mind, ever to refrain from drinking and loose company; and bid my sister M. to be careful over her son, lest he meet with my present unfortunate situation. * * * And may every blessing that God can impart, attend you all through life, is the prayer of your unfortunate, though affectionate Son,"

* *

No. 2.

"Norfolk Island, 26th April, 1835.

" My dear Father,

"It is the heart-felt duty of me, to write to you at all opportunities. * * * What will be your surprise, when I inform you, that upon my arrival in the Colony of New South Wales, I was immediately forwarded to this Penal Settlement, an Island in the South Seas, about 1,000 miles distant from Sydney. * * * I cannot for a moment, imagine, that it was the intention of the British Government, for me to be forwarded here; and this most particular and important point, I have most earnestly to beg of you, to find out. I am quite aware, that certain Prisoners are so sentenced, to be forwarded to this penal place of punishment; but such persons are generally old offenders, and individuals who have been more than once convicted. * * * If such is the law of my Country, that I, for the first offence, be transported to a Penal Settlement, (and that, the most severe in their dominions,) I must humbly submit to the same, and endeavour to obtain by my good conduct, a removal; but I cannot become reconciled to so strange a proceeding as yet; however, I shall most patiently wait for your reply, which I hope will be favourable."

"I am much concerned respecting the welfare of you, my dear father and mother, and my dear brothers and sisters. Tell them, I most earnestly hope, that my misfortune will be an everlasting warning to them; and whatever they do, strictly to obey your commands, and live an honest, upright, and religious life; for ill-gotten booty, only tends to make people miserably unhappy, instead of comfortable. Had I my time again, I would lead a very different life indeed, to what I have hitherto accustomed myself to. * * * Accept yourself, my dear father, the kind love of your ungrateful Son,

* * *

No. 3.

"Norfolk Island, 11th April, 1835.

"My dear Wife and beloved Children,

"Through all the chances, changes, and vicissitudes of my chequered life, I never had a task so painful to my mangled feelings, as the present one, of addressing you from this doleful spot,— my sea-girt prison, on the beach of which I stand, a monument of destruction; driven by adverse winds of fate, to the confines of black despair, and into the vortex of galling misery. I am just like a gigantic tree of the forest, which has stood many a wintry blast and stormy tempest; but now, alas! I am become a withered trunk, with all my tenderest and greenest branches lop'd off.

My head begins to assume an honourable colour, and will ere long be silvered o'er; but I am not now wearing my country's uniform, as a veteran soldier, after having carried arms through an eventful war, and having braved the field, under victorious Wellington, in battle's doubtful day.† Nor am I filling an enviable and honourable, civil post, with credit and respect. All which I have done. No, L——, I am wearing the garb of degradation, and the badge or brand of infamy, N. I. which being interpreted, is Norfolk Island, the "Villain's Home." I am with heart rending sorrow, and anguish of soul, which no language can convey, now ranged and mingled with the veriest outcasts of Society. My present circumstances and picture, you will find truly drawn, in the 88th Psalm, and the 102nd commencing with the 3rd verse to the 11th inclusive; which you and my dear children, I request will read attentively, before you proceed any further. * * * * I shall take leave of this subject, by requesting you and my sons, to pay particular attention to the several passages I have selected from Scripture, all of which are applicable, either to my own or your situation, past or present. Now L——, as you value the good things of this world, and the salvation of your own and our dear children's souls, you will forthwith, study and reflect upon these awful and solemn truths. You and I have lived a long time without God in our hearts: and injured as I am, I entertain but one opinion on the subject of my conviction; viz. That it was permitted, to bring me to a sense of my depravity and wickedness. * * * * * *

"You will make our children read, and get off, the above Scripture passages. [A number having been marked down.] Never let them read any political works. Keep their minds from being entangled with political men, and their productions. This, you need not be told, has been the prelude to all my present misery. * * * Party spirit runs very high in Van Diemens Land. A licentious press evinces, invariably, a great degree of contumely towards all authority, endeavouring to bring it into the hatred and contempt of the people. Yet they must acknowledge such authority was wisely instituted, for the furtherance of even-handed justice, between the several members of a community. No just citizen, no honest man, or well-wisher of his country, will lend his hand to such an engine, that wields such weapons; for it always injures, if not destroys, the cause and party, it pretends

---

† The writer was once a non-commissioned officer in the army, and was first transported for insurrection in Yorkshire, and subsequently, for forging a name to a deed in Van Diemens Land.

to advocate; and it, ultimately, works its own cure, by destroying its own existence; and brings its supporters into that contempt, it so industriously endeavours to hurl upon that authority, to which, finally, its supporters so meanly cringe. Never permit our children to read any leading articles in any Colonial Newspapers. There is so much scurrility, vituperation, and perfidy amongst their productions. * * * I am exceedingly anxious that my dear children should have the cause of my present privations, and humiliating and degrading situation, constantly pressed upon their attention, that they never may be exposed to the same fate as that which has overtaken me, but be preserved from it. * * * * I am aware that you will expect to hear an account of the cruelty and tyranny, which is supposed to be inflicted, and in existence here; but, to be candid, this is not that 'earthly hell,' which it has been represented, by vindictive writers. If credit is to be given to the stories of men here, there has been a very great degree of severity exercised by the authorities, and if I may judge, or venture an opinion, on the measures which put such severity in execution, I have no hesitation in saying, that the insubordinate state of the prisoners fully warranted the exercise of such rigorous discipline. But our present Commandant, (who was not here when the mutiny took place,) has given humanity a fair trial; and it has had a very good effect. There was an attempt made to abuse his goodness, by a few misguided individuals, and such are never wanting in any community. They took to the bush, for a few days; but he proved himself no waverer, but a very determined and prompt officer. And although his public duty was painful, and trying to his feelings, yet as a Public Functionary, he could not, and did not, let his private feelings step between himself and his duty; but by a partial and momentary severity, to two or three individuals, he shewed an infinite degree of humanity to every prisoner on the Island; for he put a full and effectual stop to that crime. * * * * * * *

" I remain,
" Your ill-fated Husband,"

* *

APPENDIX.

K.

An Epistle to Friends in Hobart Town, &c.

To Friends of Hobart Town, and such other persons as habitually
attend their Meetings.

Dear Friends,

      Our hearts have been made sad, by the information we
have received, respecting the departure of one, who was of your
little company, from the paths of rectitude; and by the offence
which his misconduct has occasioned. While we mourn over
him, as over one that has fallen into the snare of the devil, to
his eternal perdition, unless he repent, and turn from his iniquity, and obtain pardon of the Lord, we cannot but feel an
anxious solicitude, for the rest of the little flock in Van Diemens
Land, who, being turned to the teaching of the Holy Spirit,
as manifested in man, have been brought to sit down together
in silence, to wait upon the Lord, in their public worship.

May all these watch and pray, that they enter not into temptation. If we neglect to keep our minds open to the convictions
of the Holy Spirit, we shall not perceive our spiritual wants, and
how then can we ask to have them supplied? The imitation of
prayer may indeed be uttered in words, or presented in the language of thought, but it will not ascend with acceptance before
the throne of God; it will form no part of that worship which
is in spirit and in truth, and which alone is acceptable to God.

Be careful, then, dear Friends, that you do indeed watch over
your own hearts before the Lord, and as you feel your own
souls' necessities, pray unto the Father, in the name of his beloved

Son, for the supply of your need,—for pardon, or help, or strength, or preservation, as you feel you require these blessings.

How great is the privilege, of being permitted to ask of God, in the name of Christ, when, because of past transgression, we are universally unworthy, to receive anything that we may ask in our own names, or for our own sakes! And seeing that the Lord Jesus so loved us, that he gave himself for us, how ought we to cherish love to God, and one to another!

Christ himself hath declared, that it is impossible but that offences will come; therefore, let us not be discouraged by them, nor act as the world, who refuse to come unto him, or to walk with him, because of these offences. For "Woe," is still "unto the world because of offences," and "woe," is also "unto him by whom the offence cometh."

Be not shaken from steadfastly following the Lord, by what has happened, we entreat you; but rather, be stirred up to diligence thereby, that so you may be enabled by a holy, chaste, conversation and conduct, to exhibit proof to those around you, that the fall of such as go astray, is not the fault of the Foundation, on which you have builded, but their own fault, in departing from this Foundation. Remember, for your encouragement, that "truth is truth, though all men should forsake it," and that "the foundation of God standeth sure, having this seal, The Lord knoweth them that are his."

And dear Friends, have compassion on those, who through unwatchfulness, and human infirmity, are overtaken with a fault; and seek to "restore such in the spirit of meekness, considering yourselves, lest ye also be tempted:" yet deal faithfully and impartially, with those, who persist in a course contrary, to sound doctrine or practice.

Much as we value gospel ministry, when it is exercised under the divine anointing and putting forth, both in testimony and in prayer, we are solicitous, that none among you may be trying to live upon vocal labour, in meetings, or thinking that meetings cannot be profitably held without vocal expression. Such temptations are very dangerous, both to those who speak, and to those who hear; and if given way to, they weaken the establishment of those who give way to them, till their ministrations destroy the life of religion, instead of strengthening it, and the hearing becomes the object waited upon, instead of the Lord. Be not therefore, ashamed of silent meetings, neither be discouraged at their occurrence; but let your hearts be to the Lord, both in them and out of them, and be diligent in attending them; then you will profit under the Lord's own teaching, and if, at seasons, he put forth any to speak in his name, there will also be a preparation of heart to hear with profit; and those who speak under such impressions, keeping within the measure of their exercise, will edify the Church, and be strengthened themselves.

We remain, with much love,

Your friends,

JAMES BACKHOUSE.
GEORGE WASHINGTON WALKER.

Sydney, New South Wales,
   23rd of 5th mo., 1835.

APPENDIX.

L.

An Address to the Prisoner Population of New South Wales and Van Diemens Land.

The Address of James Backhouse and George Washington Walker, to the numerous Persons who compose the Prisoner Population, of New South Wales and Van Diemens Land.

Suffer, we entreat you, two individuals, who have spent nearly five years, in New South Wales and Van Diemens Land, in labouring to promote the temporal and eternal welfare of their fellow-creatures, without any other motive than that of endeavouring to discharge a Christian duty, to call your attention to the present Address. Seriously peruse it, and reflect upon it; and accept it as their parting expression of sincere concern for your well-being, now that they are about to leave these shores, for other fields of religious labour, into which they believe themselves called of the Most High.

During our sojourn in these Colonies, we have felt much for you, who are in bondage; and have often, when opportunity presented, expressed our fervent desire, that you might act as rational men, and as Christians; and we continue to feel for you, under the humiliating circumstances in which you have been placed, through sin. We would therefore entreat you to keep in remembrance, that it was sin which brought you under the punishment you suffer; and that, as sin brings a measure of its own punishment in this world, sometimes in the form of bondage, and always in one

f 2

form or other, so, if it be not forsaken, it will certainly bring ever-lasting punishment, in the next. " For the Son of Man shall come in the glory of his Father, with his angels, and then he shall reward every man according to his works."* " The Lord is known by the judgment which he executeth. The wicked is snared in the work of his own hands. The wicked shall be turned into hell, and all the nations that forget God."†

We are far, however, from looking upon you, as being necessa-rily sinners above all others, because you have so suffered; but we know, that, all men shall perish, who do not repent.‡ Do not by any means deceive yourselves, by imagining, that, because you receive a portion of the punishment of sin, in this world, you will escape the wrath of God in the next. For when the prophet Isaiah pronounced grievous judgments from God, upon the Israel-ites, because of their sins; he said, " For all this, his anger is not turned away, but his hand is stretched out still."§ This was because the people turned not to him that smote them, neither sought the Lord of Hosts.‖ None can escape the just judgments of God, without repentance; and none who truly repent can will-ingly continue in the practice of sin. Sin becomes a grievous burden to the penitent; and if, through unwatchfulness, they at any time fall into it, they are deeply humbled before God, under the sense of their transgression, and they cannot rest, till through renewed repentance and faith in Christ, they know the Lord, again, to lift them up,¶ and give them the evidence, within themselves, of the forgiveness of their sin.

John the Baptist said to the multitude that came forth to be baptized of him, and thus made public profession of their belief in the doctrine of repentance :—" O generation of vipers! Who hath warned you to flee from the wrath to come? Bring forth, therefore, fruits worthy of repentance ; and begin not to say within yourselves, We have Abraham to our Father: for I say unto you, that God is able of these stones to raise up children unto Abraham. And now also, the axe is laid unto the root of the trees: every tree, therefore, which bringeth not forth good fruit, is hewn down, and cast into the fire."** As none, therefore, in that day, might hope to be saved, because they were the children of Abraham, unless they brought forth fruits meet for repentance, and thus did the works of Abraham; so, in this day, none may hope to be saved,

---

* Matthew xvi. 27.   † Psalm ix. 16. 17.   ‡ Luke xiii. 1, 3.
§ Isaiah v. 25—ix. 12, 17, 21—x. 4.   ‖ Isaiah ix. 13.   ¶ James iv. 10.   ** Luke iii. 7—9.

because they call themselves Christians, unless they bring forth fruits worthy of repentance, and follow Christ.* " He that covereth his sins shall not prosper: but whoso confesseth and forsaketh them shall have mercy."†

Let not any, therefore, who do not forsake their sins, deceive themselves, by supposing that their sins are forgiven, even though they may have confessed them, and had absolution pronounced upon them: for God never gave to any man, authority to pronounce absolution upon unrepented-of sin, but he complained of such as assumed it, saying, "From the least of them, even unto the greatest of them, every one is given to covetousness; and from the prophet, even unto the priest, every one dealeth falsely: they have healed also the hurt of the daughter of my people slightly, saying, Peace, peace, when there is no peace." " Therefore they shall fall among them that fall: at the time that I visit them, they shall be cast down, saith the Lord:"‡ such are but " blind leaders of the blind," who, Christ has said, " shall both fall into the ditch."§

We are aware, that some among you, profess to deny the being of a God, but the unbelief of such, does not make void the faith of those who do believe, or alter the fact of the existence of God: any more than the sun would be blotted from the heavens, by a man shuting his eyes, and saying there was no sun. This would indeed prove the man to be a fool: and it is " the fool who has said in his heart, there is no God."‖

Others there are, who assume that they are lost by an eternal decree, being predestinated to destruction, and that it is in vain for them to strive against sin. Thus, in their folly, these charge their destruction upon God, and madly persevere in the service of the devil. But the language of the Most High, to a people who turned to iniquity, in former ages, was, "O Israel, thou hast destroyed thyself, but in Me is thy help."¶ " Have I any pleasure at all, that the wicked should die? saith the Lord; and not that he should return from his ways and live?"** " The Lord is long-suffering to us-ward, not willing that any should perish, but that all should come to repentance."†† Others, again, remain in a sinful course, who yet acknowledge that sin makes them unhappy, and that it is their duty to forsake it; but they say, it is useless

* Mark viii. 31.   † Prov. xxviii. 13.   ‡ Jer vi. 13—15—viii. 10—12.

§ Matthew xv. 11.   ‖ Psalms xiv. 1—liii. 1.

¶ Hosea xiii. 9.   ** Ezek. xviii. 23.   †† 2 Peter iii. 9.

for them to try to do better, while they are surrounded by evil example, and by persons who scoff at every thing good.

We entreat you to reflect upon these excuses for not turning to God, and for remaining the servants of Satan: they are merely the temptations of Satan, by which he strives to keep you in his service, in order that your portion may be with him, in that awful state of suffering, which shall be the reward of the wicked, in the world to come; and which is compared to a lake, burning with fire and brimstone, where the worm dieth not, and the fire is not quenched.* These excuses will not avail in the day of judgment; for God is willing to give grace to all who seek to him for it, sufficient to enable them to resist temptation. He "resisteth the proud, and giveth grace to the humble;"† and his "grace is sufficient" for those who trust in him; for his "strength is made perfect" in delivering those who are sensible of their own weakness, and confide in him as their helper.‡ The language of Christ is: "I am Alpha and Omega, the beginning and the end. I will give to him that is athirst, of the fountain of the water of life, freely. He that overcometh shall inherit all things, and I will be his God, and he shall be my son." "God himself shall be with them, and be their God: and God shall wipe away all tears from their eyes; and there shall be no more death, neither sorrow nor crying, neither shall there be any more pain;" for the former things shall have passed away, and God himself shall have made all things new. "But the fearful, and unbelieving, and the abominable, and murderers, and whore-mongers, and all liars, shall have their part in the lake which burneth with fire and brimstone, which is the second death."§

We have no doubt, that on serious reflection, all of you desire peace to your immortal souls, both in this world and in the next. Be wise then, and seek it, where it is to be found. It is not to be found in sin; for "the wicked are like the troubled sea, when it cannot rest, whose waters cast up mire and dirt; there is no peace, saith my God, to the wicked."|| It is the same Almighty Being, who ordained, that the sun should rise in the east, and set in the west, who has ordained, that there shall be no peace to the wicked; and it would be just as rational, to expect the course of nature to be changed, in accommodation to our wishes, as to expect that peace can be attained, while living in sin. Sin ever will bring trouble, and only trouble; for "there is no peace, saith the Lord,

---

* Rev. xxi. 8.—Mark ix. 48.   † 1 Peter v. 5.   ‡ 2 Cor. xii. 9.
‖ Rev. xxi. 3—8. || Isaiah lvii. 20, 21,

to the wicked !"* May you constantly bear this in remembrance, and that "all unrighteousness is sin."†

"The fear of the Lord is the beginning of wisdom: a good understanding have all they that do his commandments."‡ "By mercy and truth iniquity is purged: and by the fear of the Lord, men depart from evil." "The fear of the Lord tendeth to life; and he that hath it shall abide satisfied; he shall not be visited with evil."§ Those who fear the Lord, regard his law, both as it is recorded in Holy Scripture, and as it is revealed in their hearts; and they obtain an inheritance in the new covenant of God; the covenant of life and peace, in Jesus Christ: for, "Behold, the days come, saith the Lord, that I will make a new covenant with the house of Israel, and with the house of Judah, [with all who turn unto the Lord.] I will put my law in their inward parts, and write it in their hearts, and will be their God, and they shall be my people; and they shall teach no more, every man his neighbour, and every man his brother, saying, Know the Lord; for they shall all know me, from the least of them unto the greatest of them, saith the Lord, for I will forgive their iniquity, and I will remember their sin no more."‖

This "Law of the Lord," is written in the hearts of mankind by the Holy Spirit, or "Holy Ghost, whom," said Christ, "the Father will send in my name; he shall teach you all things, and bring all things to your remembrance, whatsoever I have said unto you."¶ "When he, the Spirit of truth, is come, he will guide you into all truth." "And when he is come, he will reprove [or convince] the world, of sin, and of righteousness, and of judgment."** The operation of this Spirit on the mind of man, is continually referred to in the Scriptures, as essential to religion; and it is described under a great variety of similitudes and terms, according to its diversified effects. The work of the Holy Spirit is ever, to enlighten the mind, and to lead man in the paths of righteousness and peace. It is therefore called "Light." "All things that are reproved," says the Apostle Paul, "are made manifest by the Light: for whatsoever doth make manifest is Light. Wherefore, he saith, Awake thou that sleepest, and arise from the dead, and Christ shall give thee Light."††

Now, have you not all, at times, known sin to be made manifest

---

* Isaiah xlviii. 22.   † 1 John v. 17   ‡ Psalm cxi. 10.
§ Prov. xvi. 6—xix. 23.   ‖ Jer. xxxi. 31—34.   Heb. viii. 8—12.   ¶ John xiv. 26.
** John xvi. 8, 13.   †† Ephes. v. 13, 14.

to you, so that you have been convinced in your own minds, that some things you were tempted to commit, were offensive in the sight of God? And when you have neglected this warning, and have committed the sin, have you not felt an inward consciousness, though no man might know of its commission but yourselves, that it was known unto God? and a secret dread, has attended you, that "your sin would find you out,"* if not in this world, at any rate in the next; and thus you have felt uneasy in your minds. We boldly appeal unto every one of you, as having felt thus, at one season or other, though you may not hitherto have known what it was, that thus secretly convinced you of sin: it may·have been as a light shining in darkness, and not comprehended: for, said the Evangelist John, "The Light shineth in darkness, and the darkness comprehended it not." Know, however, that that which convinced you, was the light of the Holy Spirit, the Light which cometh by Jesus Christ. "In him was life, and the life was the Light of men." He is the "true Light, which lighteth every man that cometh into the world."†

The object for which He who is the true Light, enlightens mankind by this Light, is clearly set forth by the apostle Paul, in the passage already referred to‡ and again in these striking expressions: "God who commanded the light to shine out of darkness, hath shined in our hearts, to give the light of the knowledge of the glory of God, in the face [or appearance] of Jesus Christ." And, "If our Gospel be hid," he adds, "it is hid to them that are lost: in whom the god of this world hath blinded the minds of them which believe not, lest the light of the glorious Gospel of Christ, who is the image of God, should shine unto them."§ Precisely parallel to this testimony, is the spirit of the following declaration of Christ himself: "This is the condemnation, that Light is come into the world, and men loved darkness rather than Light, because their deeds were evil; for every one that doeth evil, hateth the Light, neither cometh to the Light, lest his deeds should be reproved: but he that doeth truth, cometh to the Light, that his deeds may be made manifest, that they are wrought in God."‖

The term Grace is variously used in the Holy Scriptures, in which the plan of salvation is called the "Grace of God." It is so called, because this salvation is received through the mercy of God, in Christ Jesus; and for his sake, not for our own, "lest any

---

* Numb. xxxii. 23.   † John i. 5, 4, 9.   ‡ Ephes. v. 13, 14.
‡ 2 Cor. iv. 3, 6.   ‖ John iii. 19, 21.

man should boast." It is likewise declared, that it was by grace, through faith, that the saints of old were saved, and that this grace came by Jesus Christ, "By grace are ye saved, through faith, and that not of yourselves; it is the gift of God: not of works, lest any man should boast: for we are his workmanship, created in Christ Jesus unto good works, which God hath before ordained, that we should walk in them."* "The law was given by Moses, but grace and truth came by Jesus Christ."† The Psalmist addresses Christ in this prophetic language: "Thou hast ascended on high, thou hast led captivity captive; thou hast received gifts for men; yea, for the rebellious also, that the Lord God might dwell among them."‡

The Holy Spirit is also alluded to under the appellation of Grace, and its teaching, as the teaching of the Grace of God, and it is declared that this "Grace of God, that bringeth salvation, hath appeared to all men" (for all are thereby convinced of sin), "teaching us, that, denying ungodliness and worldly lusts, we should live soberly, righteously, and godly, in this present world; looking for that blessed hope, and the glorious appearing of the great God, and our Saviour Jesus Christ; who gave himself for us, that he might redeem us from all iniquity, and purify unto himself a peculiar people, zealous of good works."§ This grace is sufficient to enable a man to overcome all evil, "My grace is sufficient for thee," were the words of the Lord Jesus, to Paul; and without this grace, none can know Christ to be their Saviour; who came to "save his people from their sins,"‖ or can know him to destroy in them the works of the devil.¶

Let none therefore remain in blindness, hating the Light; and disregarding the Grace of God, or continue at enmity with God by wicked works; but may all believe in Christ, who is the "Light of the world," "the way, the truth, and the life,"** and come unto the revelation of his Grace, or good Spirit, manifested in the heart, as unto that, without which, they cannot be saved. The words of our gracious Redeemer himself are: "I am come a Light into the world, that *whosoever* believeth on me, *should not abide in darkness.*" "I am the Light of the world, *he that followeth me shall not walk in darkness,* but shall have the *Light of life.*" "I am come *that they might have life,* and that they might have it more abundantly."††

He directed the attention of mankind to the "Light," or

* Ephes. ii. 8—10.   † John i. 17.   ‡ Psalm lxviii. 18.   § Titus ii. 11—14.
‖ Matth. i. 21.   ¶ 1 John iii. 8.   ** John xiv. 6.   †† John xii. 46—viii. 12—x. 10.

" Grace," or " manifestation of the Spirit,"* by many similitudes, in order that this important doctrine might be rendered plain to all sincere inquirers after the truth. He compared the Kingdom of Heaven to " a grain of mustard seed, which indeed is the least of all seeds, but when it is grown, it is the greatest among herbs, and becometh a tree, so that the birds of the air come and lodge in the branches thereof."† The seed of Divine Grace, though easily overlooked in its first appearances, when not resisted, but suffered to prevail in man's heart, not only regulates the affections and unruly passions of men, but brings " into captivity, every thought, to the obedience of Christ."‡

The Kingdom of Heaven is also declared by the Saviour, to be " like unto leaven, which a woman took and hid in three measures of meal till the whole was leavened;"§ because, when suffered to work, it gradually leavens the heart of man into its own pure and heavenly nature, until the whole becomes leavened, or changed. This change is alluded to in Christ's conversation with Nicodemus, as being " born again," and being " born from above," without which, it is declared, " a man cannot see the kingdom of God."‖ It is that " treasure hid in a field, which when a man hath found," when he has once become convinced of its divine nature and origin, and the glorious end for which it appears in his heart, viz.: that through this medium, God may " work in him both to will and to do of his good pleasure,"¶— " he hideth, and for joy thereof, goeth and selleth all that he hath, and buyeth that field ;"** he prizes it as something exceedingly precious, as " a pearl of great value ;" and willingly parts with every thing that may hinder his access to this inestimable treasure, or that may endanger its continuance in his heart; in other words, he renounces all his beloved lusts, and denies himself of every sinful gratification, that he " may win Christ."††

Where Christ's dominion is thus established in the heart, that sublime prophecy of Isaiah is fulfilled, in the experience of the Christian : " Unto us a child is born, unto us a son is given; and the government shall be upon his shoulder, and his name shall be called Wonderful, Counsellor, the Mighty God, the Everlasting Father, the Prince of Peace : of the increase of his government and peace, there shall be no end."‡‡ This is that

---

* 1 Cor. xii. 7.   † Matth. xiii. 31, 32.   ‡ 2 Cor. x. 5
§ Matth. xiii. 33.   ‖ John iii. 3.   ¶ Phil. ii. 13.   ** Matth. xiii. 44, 46.
†† Phil. iii. 8.   ‡‡ Isaiah ix. 6. 7.

spiritual kingdom or government, for the coming of which, Christ taught his disciples to pray: "Thy kingdom come, thy will be done, in earth as it is in heaven;"* and which he declared, "cometh not with observation." "The kingdom of God cometh not with observation, neither shall men say, lo here! or lo there! for behold, the kingdom of God is within you."† "The kingdom of God is not in word, but in power."‡ It "is not meat and drink, but righteousness and peace and joy in the Holy Ghost."§

Salvation by Jesus Christ, is, indeed, "the mystery which has been hid from ages and from generations, but now is made manifest to his saints [and all are called to be saints], to whom God would make known what is the riches of the glory of this mystery, which [says the Apostle Paul] is Christ in you, the hope of glory,"‖ Those who rightly estimate this "unspeakable gift,"¶ will be solicitous to have their hearts made clean; for the heart in which Christ takes up his abode, must be holy. "If a man love me," is the language of our blessed Redeemer, "he will keep my words, and my Father will love him, and we will come unto him, and make our abode with him."** It is thus that the Christian becomes "the temple of the living God." "Know ye not that ye are the temple of God, and that the Spirit of God dwelleth in you: if any man defile the temple of God, him shall God destroy; for the temple of God is holy, which temple ye are."†† "For ye are the temple of the living God; as God hath said, I will dwell in them, and walk in them; and I will be their God, and they shall be my people. Wherefore come out from among them, and be ye separate, saith the Lord, and touch not the unclean thing, and I will receive you, and will be a father unto you, and ye shall be my sons and daughters, saith the Lord Almighty."‡‡

Thus, ever since the Gospel began to be preached, those who have believed in the Light, who have had faith in the Grace of God, who have been led by the Spirit; have uniformly been enlightened thereby, to perceive their fallen and sinful state, have attained unto true repentance, and been enabled to look upon Jesus, "the Lamb of God which taketh away the sin of the world," so as to have peace with God through him; being strengthened, to walk in the Spirit, not fulfilling the lust of

---

* Matth. vi. 10. † Luke xvii. 20, 21. ‡ 1 Cor. iv. 20.
§ Rom. xiv. 17. ‖ Col. i. 26, 27. ¶ 2 Cor. ix. 15. ** John xiv. 23.
†† 1 Cor. iii. 16, 17. ‡‡ 2 Cor. vi. 16—18.

the flesh ; but glorifying God in their body and in their spirit, which are God's.*

Greatly do we desire that you may become of this happy number, who constitute " so great a cloud of witnesses " to the efficacy of faith in the power of Divine Grace ; that thus, " laying aside every weight, and the sin which doth so easily beset you, you may run with patience the race that is set before you, looking unto Jesus, the Author and Finisher of [all true] faith ; who, for the joy that was set before him, endured the cross, despising the shame, and is set down at the right hand of the throne of God."†

" God so loved the world, that he gave his only begotten Son, that whosoever believeth in him, should not perish, but have everlasting life : for God sent not his Son into the world, to condemn the world, but that the world through him might be saved "‡ Believe, therefore, in the mercy of God which is freely offered you in the Lord Jesus Christ : for, as " God spared not his own Son, but delivered him up for us all, how shall he not with him, also, freely give us all things ?"§ " He was wounded for our transgressions, he was bruised for our iniquities, the chastisement of our peace was upon him ; and with his stripes we are healed. All we like sheep have gone astray ; we have turned every one to his own way ; and the Lord hath laid on him, the iniquity of us all."‖

If you repent, God is willing to forgive you your sins, for Christ's sake, who died for you, " the just for the unjust, that he might bring us to God."¶ " Him hath God exalted with his right hand, to be a Prince and a Saviour, for to give repentance and forgiveness of sins."** Christ said, " No man can come to me, except the Father which hath sent me, draw him ; and I will raise him up at the last day."†† Have you not been thus drawn? Have you not often felt convinced of sin, so as on many occasions, clearly to distinguish the difference between right and wrong ? These convictions, then, were the drawings of the Father, by his eternal Spirit seeking to lead you unto his Son, that you might obtain eternal life through him.

We read in the Scriptures, that under the law of Moses, when a man had sinned, he was commanded to take his sin-offering

---

* John xii. 36.   Ephes. ii. 8—10.   Rom. viii. 14.   John i. 29.   Rom. v. 1.   Gal. v. 16.
1 Cor. vi. 20.   † Heb. xii. 1, 2.   ‡ John iii. 16, 17.   § Rom. viii. 32.
‖ Isaiah liii. 5, 6.   ¶ 1 Peter iii. 18.   ** Acts v. 31.   †† John vi. 44.

to the priest, to lay his hand upon its head, and to slay it; and the priest was to take of its blood, and to put in on the horns of the altar, and to pour out the rest at the bottom of the altar, and to burn its body upon the altar, to make an atonement for him, that his sin might be forgiven.* In taking his sin-offering to the priest, the sinner thus confessed that he had sinned: by laying his hand upon its head, he made himself, as it were, one with his sacrifice: in slaying it, pouring out its blood, and offering its body on the altar, he acknowledged the justice of God, in passing sentence of death on sin. "In the day thou eatest thereof, thou shalt surely die."† "The soul that sinneth, it shall die."‡ "The wages of sin is death."§ Hereby the sinner offered the life of his sacrifice, in the stead of his own life, its blood in the place of his own blood; for "without shedding of blood, there is no remission."‖

This is a lively type or representation, of the way of salvation, under the Gospel. The sinner is to confess his sins unto God; to remember, that the awful death which Christ, "who did no sin"¶ suffered on the cross, was due to sin;** and that it is for his sake, that forgiveness of sin is offered to those who repent:†† for He is "the Lamb of God that taketh away the sin of the world;"‡‡ and, "there is none other name under heaven, given among men, whereby we must be saved," but the name of Jesus Christ.§§ The conditions of our acceptance are, "repentance toward God, and faith toward our Lord Jesus Christ."‖‖

But he who truly repents and believes, or has faith in Christ, believes in the truth of all his sayings, and feels the necessity of obeying his precepts: he is baptized with the baptism of Christ, even with the Holy Ghost and with fire. "I indeed baptize you with water," said John the Baptist, "but one mightier than I cometh, the latchet of whose shoes I am not worthy to unloose; he shall baptize you with the Holy Ghost and with fire; whose fan is in his hand, and he will thoroughly purge his floor, and will gather the wheat into his garner, but the chaff he will burn with fire unquenchable."¶¶ Christ, who is the "Power of God,"*** like a "consuming fire,"††† is revealed in the hearts of true believers, cleansing them from every corruption, even as gold is

---

* Lev. iv.   † Gen. ii. 17.   ‡ Ezek. xviii. 4.   § Rom. vi. 23.   ‖ Heb. ix. 22.
¶ 1 Peter ii. 22.   ** 2 Cor. v. 21.   †† Luke xxiv. 47.
Ephes. iv. 32.   ‡‡ John i. 29.   §§ Acts iv. 12.   ‖‖ Acts xx. 21.   ¶¶ Luke iii. 16, 17.
*** 1 Cor. i. 24.   ††† Deut. iv. 24.   Heb. xii. 29.

purified by fire, "for the trial of their faith is much more pre‑cious than of gold that perisheth."* Such know from heartfelt experience that, the baptism which now saveth, is not the putting away of the filth of the flesh [not any outward washing], but the answer of a good conscience toward God, by the resurrection of Jesus Christ ;† who cleanses them from every defilement "by the spirit of judgment, and by the spirit of burning."‡

Those who thus believe and are baptized, whatever name they may bear, as to religion, among men, constitute that "one body," "the Church," of which Christ is "the Head ;"§ "all such are the children of God, by faith in Christ Jesus."‖ "For by one Spirit, are we all baptized into one body, whether we be Jews or Gentiles, whether we be bond or free, and have all been made to drink into one Spirit."¶ "Through him," said the Apostle, "ye have access, by one Spirit, unto the Father; and are no more strangers and foreigners, but fellow-citizens with the saints, and of the houschold of God; and are built upon the foundation of the apostles and prophets, Jesus Christ himself, being the chief corner-stone; in whom all the building, fitly framed toge‑ther, groweth unto an holy temple in the Lord: in whom ye also are builded together, for an habitation of God, through the Spirit."**

Our Heavenly Father is willing to give the Holy Spirit, to those who sincerely ask it of him. "Ask," says Christ, "and it shall be given you; seek, and ye shall find; knock, and it shall be opened unto you: for every one that asketh, receiveth; and he that seeketh, findeth; and to him that knocketh, it shall be opened. If a son shall ask bread, of any of you that is a father, will he give him a stone? or, if he ask a fish, will he for a fish, give him a serpent? or, if he shall ask an egg, will he offer him a scorpion? If ye then, being evil, know how to give good gifts unto your children, how much more shall your Heavenly Father give the Holy Spirit to them that ask him?"†† O, believe, that God is willing to hear, and to answer the prayers of them that desire to be made what he would have them to be, how weak and unworthy soever they may feel themselves! "Like as a father pitieth his children, so the Lord pitieth them that fear him; for he knoweth our frame, he remembereth that we are

* 1 Peter i. 7.   † 1 Peter iii. 21.   ‡ Isaiah iv. 4.
§ Ephes. i. 22, 23. Colos. i. 18.   ‖ Gal. iii. 26.   ¶ 1 Cor. xii. 13.
** Ephes. ii. 18—22.   †† Luke xi. 9—13.

dust."* And he will regard the prayer of the heart, for, "He knoweth the secrets of the heart."†

Many of you, we know, have no private place, or closet, to retire into, to "pray to your Father who is in secret;" but all may pray in the closet of their own hearts, and the Lord will hearken to the sincere breathings that arise from thence, and will regard them as acceptable incense, whether they be expressed with the tongue, or not. Lift up your hearts, therefore, unto him, whenever, and wherever you may feel your necessities, whether it be by night or by day, in the house or in the field; "pray unto your Father which is in secret, and your Father which seeth in secret, will reward you openly."‡ Be not discouraged from staying your souls upon God, by any sense of your past delinquencies; for you are not invited to pray in your own names, but in the worthy name of Jesus,§ who "is able to save them to the uttermost, that come unto God by him, seeing he ever liveth to make intercession for them."‖ Wherefore, all are invited to "come boldly to the Throne of Grace, that they may obtain mercy, and find grace to help in time of need."¶

Be cheered by the remembrance, that Christ became a prisoner for the sake of prisoners; that he was, "in all points, tempted like as we are, yet without sin;"** that therefore, he "can have compassion on the ignorant, and on them that are out of the way;"†† and, "in that he himself hath suffered, being tempted, he is able to succour them that are tempted."‡‡ May you, therefore, be willing to seek reconciliation with God, through him.§§

Some of you have but few of the outward means of religious instruction; but if you desire to learn righteousness, God is willing to teach you himself, by the Holy Spirit, the Spirit of Truth, who will guide you into all truth.

It is a profitable exercise, to wait upon the Lord in stillness, to feel after his presence, with the attention turned to the state of the heart before him, remembering that he is ever with us: for, "God that made the world, and all things therein, seeing that he is Lord of Heaven and Earth, dwelleth not in temples made with hands; neither is worshipped with men's hands, as though he needed anything; seeing he giveth to all life, and breath, and all things; and hath made of one blood all nations

---

* Psalm clii. 13, 14.　　† Psalm xliv. 21.　1 Sam. i. 13.　　‡ Matth. vi. 6.
† John xiv. 13, 14—xv. 16.　　‖ Heb. vii. 25.　　¶ Heb. iv. 16.　　** Heb. iv. 15.
†† Heb. v. 2.　　‡‡ Heb. ii. 18.　　§§ 2 Cor. v. 18—21.

of men, for to dwell on all the face of the earth; and hath determined the times before appointed, and the bounds of their habitation: that they should seek the Lord, if haply they might *feel after him, and find him,* though he be not far from every one of us; for in him we live, and move, and have our being."* And he has commanded us, saying: " Be still, and know that I am God."† " Keep silence before me, O islands, and let the people renew their strength; let them come near, then let them speak; let us come near together to judgment."‡ " It is good for a man that he bear the yoke in his youth; he sitteth alone and keepeth silence, because he hath borne it upon him; he putteth his mouth in the dust, if so be there may be hope."§ If we thus wait upon him, he will make himself known unto us, as our God and our deliverer: for it was declared by the prophet Isaiah, in referring to the dispensation of the Gospel, that " it shall be said in that day, Lo, this is our God, we have waited for him, and he will save us; this is the Lord, we have waited for him, we will be glad, and rejoice in his salvation."||

Many of you, have also the Holy Scriptures, and can read them. Let this be your frequent employment: for " all Scripture is given by inspiration of God, and is profitable for doctrine, for reproof, for correction, for instruction in righteousness: that the man of God may be perfect, thoroughly furnished unto all good works."¶ " They are they which testify of me," said Christ. As you give attention to his Light and Grace in your hearts, thus coming unto Christ, that you may have life,** he will open your understandings, and enable you to understand these precious records aright; and you will know, from happy experience, that they are able to make " wise unto salvation, through faith which is in Christ Jesus.††

If you were diligently to read the sacred writings, and to attend to the Light of Christ, to which they direct you, you could not continue in bondage to Satan. That many of you are under this grievous yoke, is too clearly proved by your sinful practices; " for of whom a man is overcome, of the same is he brought in bondage;"‡‡ and by cursing, swearing, and other profane language, by fornication, uncleanness, and theft, and by numerous other sins, it is but too plain, that many of you are " taken

---

* Acts xvii. 24—28. † Psalm xlvi. 10. ‡ Isaiah xli. 1. § Lamen. iii. 27—29.
|| Isaiah xxv. 9. ¶ 2 Tim. iii. 16, 17. ** John v. 39, 40.
†† 2 Tim. iii. 15. ‡‡ 2 Peter ii. 19.

captive by the devil at his will."* But we entreat you to remember, that thereby you dishonour God; and that, before him, you must shortly give account: for it is he who "shall judge the secrets of men by Jesus Christ."† "We must all appear before the judgment-seat of Christ; that every one may receive the things done in his body, according to that he hath done, whether it be good or bad."‡

"Behold the judge standeth before the door."§ "The Son of Man cometh at an hour when ye think not."‖ Defer not, therefore, the work of repentance, under the delusive notion that you will repent when drawing near unto death. "Boast not thyself of to-morrow, for thou knowest not what a day may bring forth."¶ "This night," it may be said unto any of you, "thy soul shall be required of thee."** Many have gone on in sin, thinking they would repent before they died, who have either been cut off suddenly, or prior to death, have been given up to hardness of heart, so as to be wholly indifferent about the state of their souls. These have indeed died "as the fool dieth;"†† the end of the beasts that perish, would have been infinitely preferable to theirs.‡‡ "For what shall it profit a man, if he shall gain the whole world, and lose his own soul? Or what shall a man give in exchange for his soul?"§§ Though a few have appeared to become penitent, when in anticipation of death; yet, when unexpectedly to themselves, the life of some of these has been prolonged, how large a majority of them have failed to bring forth fruits meet for repentance, and instead thereof, have relapsed into habitual sin. The inference is plain, that though some of these might possibly be cases of sincere repentance, yet that the greater number of those, who, in the prospect of death, seemed penitent, deceived themselves, and others also, who had hoped better things of them.

To trust to the approach of death, for opportunity to repent and seek reconciliation with God, what is it, but to make a league with the devil, to serve him as long as a man can, and thus to wrong his own soul? Remember with awe, the declaration of the Most High: "My Spirit shall not always strive with man, for that he also is flesh."‖‖ "Despisest thou the riches of his goodness, and forbearance, and long-suffering, not knowing that the

---

* 2 Tim. ii 26. † Rom. ii. 16. ‡ 2 Cor. v. 10.
‖ James v. 9. ‖ Luke xii. 40. ¶ Prov. xxvii. 1. ** Luke xii. 20. †† 2 Sam. iii. 33.
‡‡ Psalm xlix. 11—20. ‖‖ Mark viii. 36—37. ¶ Gen. vi. 3.

goodness of God leadeth thee to repentance; but after thy
hardness and impenitent heart, treasurest up unto thyself wrath,
against the day of wrath, and revelation of the righteous judgment of God?"* As none of you know how short may be the
day of the Lord's merciful visitation to your souls, beware that
you "do not frustrate the Grace of God;"† for if his Grace be
withdrawn, you may seek "a place of repentance," when too
late.‡ To-day, therefore, "to-day, if ye will hear his voice, har-
den not your hearts."§

Before we conclude this Address, we would offer a few more
observations for your consideration, on some subjects which we
deem also essentially connnected with your welfare.

From what we know of your feelings, with regard to bondage,
we do not doubt, that most, if not all of you, regard it as a
grievous punishment. Now, as nothing happens but under the
providence of God, without whose notice, not a sparrow falls to
the ground, we would entreat you to consider the cause, and the
end, for which he has suffered you to be afflicted. The cause, you
must be convinced, has, in general, been, that you cast the fear
of the Lord behind you, and therefore, were at length, so given
up to your own hearts' lusts, as to disregard also the restraints
of human laws. Was it not either neglect of the Sabbath, intemperance, lewdness, gaming, pride, or disregard of the Divine Law
in some other respect, that paved the way for those offences, which
have resulted in the loss of your liberty? If conscience constrain
you to admit this, let the consideration humble you before God.
For, "Hast thou not procured this unto thyself, in that thou hast
forsaken the Lord thy God?" "Know, therefore, and see, that
it is an evil thing and bitter, that thou hast forsaken the Lord
thy God, and that my fear is not in thee, saith the Lord God of
Hosts."‖ And let this conviction make you watchful against the
sins that have "so easily beset you," and have already brought
so much suffering upon you; lest, should you still cleave to
them in heart, they should become the means of plunging you
further into the depths of degradation and misery.

Consider also, that the end for which affliction is dispensed to
man, while in a state of probation, is, that he may turn to the
Lord; who, though a God of judgment, in the midst of judgment
remembereth mercy. Hence, to the very people, to whom the

* Rom. ii. 4—5.   † Gal. ii. 21.   ‡ Heb. xii. 17.   ‖ Heb. iii. 7—15.
‖ Jer. ii. 17, 19.

language, quoted above, was addressed, the following gracious invitation was at the same time extended: " Return, thou backsliding Israel, saith the Lord, and I will not cause mine anger to fall upon you; for I am merciful, saith the Lord, and I will not keep anger for ever. Only acknowledge thine iniquity, that thou hast transgressed against the Lord thy God." " Return, ye backsliding children, and I will heal your backslidings."* We have no doubt, that the design of the Lord respecting you, is likewise one of mercy. Is it not proved to be such, by your having been arrested, in a course that must have ended in your destruction, if you had been permitted to have gone on in it?

Convinced then, that your bondage is a dispensation of mercy, designed to restrain you from following that which is evil, you ought not to regard it, as some do, unhappily for themselves, as a state of oppression, but rather as one of salutary discipline, in which you have a duty to discharge, before God, in faithfully serving those persons to whom you are assigned; according to the apostolic exhortation: "Servants, obey in all things, your masters according to the flesh: not with eye service, as men pleasers, but in singleness of heart, fearing God: and whatsoever ye do, do it heartily, as to the Lord, and not unto men: knowing that of the Lord, ye shall receive the reward."† Moreover, whatever station a man may fill in the world, if he take an interest in the service allotted him, and perform it cheerfully, he will have a measure of enjoyment in it: but if he give way to a dissatisfied disposition, and consider his employment as a task, he will be uncomfortable in himself, and will continually provoke the displeasure of others.

When persons, circumstanced as you are, take no interest in their employments, but perform them merely from compulsion, what is the general consequence? Do they not embitter their state of bondage, and often prolong it; or by adding to their transgressions, bring themselves to an untimely end? herein fulfilling the declaration of an inspired writer:—"He that being often reproved, hardeneth his neck, shall suddenly be destroyed, and that without remedy."‡

It is not one of the least of the Lord's mercies, that banishment from our native country, is now the penalty of many offences, that a few years since were visited with death, which left little time for repentance. This alteration of the laws, has been attended in its effects, with great expense to the Nation, but the

---

* Jer iii. 12, 13. 22.   † Colos. iii. 22. 24.   ‡ Prov. xxix. 1.

Lord has made your countrymen willing to bear it, rather than
to run the risk of plunging their transgressing fellow-creatures,
into perdition.

Your comfort, we conceive, would be greatly promoted, by
considerations of this kind; and by looking upon your labour,
whilst serving out your sentence, as a reasonable return to the
public, for the injury they have sustained, by your crimes, and
for the expense incurred in consequence, not only in your prosecution, but also in your present maintenance. We are persuaded,
that many of you have sufficient candour and good sense, to admit
the justness of this mode of reasoning. For your own sakes, may
you be concerned to act upon it.

Let none among you be discouraged from striving to serve the
Lord, by the scoffs, or solicitations to evil, of others: for "though
hand join in hand, the wicked shall not be unpunished."* And
though "fools make a mock at sin:"† if their scoffs turn us aside
from righteousness, it is ourselves who will have to bear the
consequence of our own folly. It will be no excuse for us, in
the day of judgment, that we feared to serve the Lord, because
of the sneers, or solicitations to evil, of our associates. The
exhortation of Christ, who "endured the contradiction of sinners
against himself,"‡ and who set us a righteous example, is, "Fear
not them which kill the body, but are not able to kill the soul:
but rather fear Him, which is able to destroy both soul and body
in hell:" and he likewise added, "Whosoever, therefore, shall
confess me before men, him will I confess also, before my Father
which is in Heaven: but whosoever shall deny me before men, him
will I also deny, before my Father which is in Heaven."§

It has been a satisfaction to us, to find a few among you, walking in the fear of the Lord: these we have been glad to recognise
as brethren in Christ; and we heartily desire their encouragement,
in every good word and work; and that, by the continued exercise
of faith and patience, they may inherit the promises; having,
according to their own testimony, already found the consolations
of the Gospel to lighten their bondage among men, and to comfort
them in all their tribulation.‖ If others were to seek comfort, in
this way, they also would find it. But none can understand the
joys of God's salvation, until they taste of them, in their own
experience. "Eye hath not seen, nor ear heard, neither have

* Prov. xi. 21.   † Prov xiv. 9.   ‡ Heb. xii. 3.   ‡ Matt. x. 28, 32, 34.
‖ 2 Cor. i. 4.

entered into the heart of man [in an unregenerate state], the things which God hath prepared for them that love him: but," added the Apostle Paul, speaking of those who were turned unto the Lord, " God hath revealed them unto us by his Spirit: for the Spirit searcheth all things, yea, the deep things of God."* There are no joys worthy to be compared to these ; and all others must soon come to an end. Come, therefore, " taste and see " for yourselves, " that the Lord is good. Blessed is the man that trusteth in him."†

In conclusion, to such of you as are not yet turned to the Lord, we would address the emphatic exhortation : " Seek ye the Lord, while he may be found, call ye upon him, while he is near. Let the wicked forsake his way, and the unrighteous man his thoughts; and let him return unto the Lord, and he will have mercy upon him, and to our God, for he will abundantly pardon."‡

JAMES BACKHOUSE.
GEORGE WASHINGTON WALKER.

Sydney, 12th of 12th mo., 1836.

* 1 Cor. ii. 9—10.   † Psalm xxxiv. 8.   ‡ Isaiah lv. 6—7.

APPENDIX.

M.

A LETTER addressed to JAMES BACKHOUSE and GEORGE WASHINGTON WALKER, by a CONVICT, confined on GOAT ISLAND, PORT JACKSON, NEW SOUTH WALES.

"Goat Island, Feb. 4th, 1837.

"Gentlemen,—Your humane Address to the Prisoner Population of New South Wales and Van Diemens Land, has just been read to this portion of the objects of your kind solicitude, by the officiating minister; from which I gather, that you are about to leave these shores, for other fields of religious labour.

"Had you remained in this country, I should not have ventured to address you, lest I should have been suspected of having other motives than the one I have in view; which is, to convey to you the sincere thanks of a grateful heart, for the interest you take (and in your prayers, I have no doubt, will continue to take) in our eternal welfare and happiness; an interest which I feel persuaded, is shared in common, by members of your benevolent Society. And I feel confident, it will not be among the least consolations on your dying bed, that the Almighty graciously vouchsafed to incline your hearts to sacrifice your home, your social comforts, and in some degree, your happiness, to mix in scenes of misery and distress, in a distant land; to bring home the glad tidings of peace and deliverance, to the unhappy exile; to sympathize with the wretched and unfortunate; and point us to a gracious Saviour, and assure us, that God is a very present refuge in time of trouble; to proclaim liberty to the captive; to open the prison-doors of our minds, and point us to the redeeming blood

of the Lord Jesus Christ, to wash us from all our sins and wickedness, and make us meet for the inheritance of the kingdom of
heaven. I feel confident your pious efforts have not been altogether in vain, but that many a heart has been melted and moved,
under your discourses, that had neither the power nor opportunity
to express their feelings. Continue then, gentlemen, to go forward
in your work of mercy; and though you may not see the fruits
of your labour in this world, trust the event to the Almighty, who
can, and I have no doubt, will, in his own good time, bring forth
an hundred fold.

"It may probably occur to your minds, to ask, how the writer
came to take the liberty to address you. I will tell you, gentlemen, I am aware the very best of people are sometimes apt to
become discouraged, at the seeming hopelessness of the cause in
which they have embarked their most anxious hopes. It is this
consideration, coupled with a sincere desire that my fellow-pri-
soners should not lose the benefit of any future exertions you may
employ in your work of mercy, in their behalf, (either in your
prayers, or in books of instruction,) that has induced me to do so.
And I feel confident, you will excuse the liberty, and pardon the
manner, for the sake of the matter.

"It may not, perhaps, be altogether uninteresting to you, to hear
a few words that more immediately concern the unhappy person
who addresses you, as we shall most probably never see each other
again in this world.

"I had the very great privilege to be born of pious parents,
whose anxious endeavour it was to train me up in the paths of
piety and virtue. But, notwithstanding all their prayers, and all
their cares, I have lived, the greatest part of my life, in open rebellion against my Maker; and though scarcely a day has passed,
without my receiving some special mercy at the hand of my in-
dulgent Maker, I have still added ingratitude to ingratitude, and
sinned with a high hand; all which time he was graciously trying
every means to reclaim me, and even heaped his blessings on my
ungrateful head; which, (next to his boundless mercy,) I think I
am justified in attributing to the constant and earnest prayers in
my behalf, of a pious, afflicted, and most affectionate mother.
But still, all this was without effect; and I was at length given
up to the deceivings of my own wicked heart, and suffered to be
led captive at the will of the devil, and finally to the commission
of a crime, which has brought punishment and infamy on myself,
and misery and disgrace on all my friends.

" Yet even in this dire place, at the thought of which, in happier days, my heart would have recoiled with horror, even here, (strange to say) I think I have spent the most peaceful, and certainly the most innocent moments of my life. Here, removed from temptation, I have been enabled to review, with bitter anguish, the folly of my mis-spent life; and here, I trust, the Almighty has been graciously pleased to pardon and forgive, even the vilest of his creatures. I am aware it may be said, with much truth, There is always reason to distrust that repentance which is forced from us by punishment; and I confess, I am sometimes tempted to think that I have been flattering myself, and that the great enemy of mankind is only instilling this opinion into my mind, to lull me into the greater security. But still I must, I will have hopes: they are founded on this—the boundless mercies of my God and Saviour, who has watched over me from earliest childhood, and encompassed me with his goodness and protecting care. Yes, his mercy has followed me, even to this place; where, on my landing, my heart sunk within me, and I was ready to give up all for lost, in hopelessness and despair, at the seeming severity, and the nature of the employ, for I had always been brought up within doors. Even here, useless as I was, compared with other men, with my spirits broken, in poor health, and without a friend, the Almighty, in whose hands are the hearts of all the children of men, graciously inclined the heart of my overseer towards me, who placed me in a situation (turning a wheel) where attention rather than extreme labour, was required.

" This, to me, appeared one of the most extraordinary interpositions of Providence, in my favour, I almost ever knew; as I was taken from two hundred men, when I had been but a short time on the island, and nothing to recommend me, and never having spoken to that officer; and it was the only place of the kind on the island. May God return his kindness to me, in blessings on his own head! Thus you see, gentlemen, at a time when I least expected it, and least deserved it, the Almighty, in tender compassion, kept a watchful eye over me; proving to my ungrateful heart, that—

> When lowest sunk in grief and shame,
>   Fill'd with afflictions bitter cup;
> Lost to relations, friends and fame,
>   His powerful hand can bear me up.

Verifying in me, the truth of his word: " I will have mercy on whom I will have mercy." Surely, if my heart is not of stone, I have cause of thankfulness and gratitude. Oh! for the sanctifying influences of his Holy Spirit, to enable me to walk before him in spirit and in truth. What numbers of men, who never enjoyed the means of grace I have, nor have been the subject of the prayers of pious ministers as I have, have I seen, since I have been here, severely punished for crimes, the magnitude of which I have exceeded a thousand fold. With what truth can I exclaim—

> Whilst justice, armed with power Divine,
> Pours on his head what's due to mine!

"I must not omit to mention, that while a child, my father, who took a lively interest in establishing a Sunday School, in his neighbourhood, and devoted much of his time in instructing the children, while his health permitted, took me occasionally with him; and I can truly say, the virtuous instruction I then received, and the hymns I then learned, though I was under six years of age, have never, during all the vicissitudes to which I have been exposed, been eradicated from my mind, and have been of much use to me, in this hour of distress and misery. I mention this circumstance, because I think, Sunday School teachers, particularly the younger part of them, are sometimes discouraged, by the thoughtlessness of the children under their charge, which I think should not be the case; as, I doubt not, thousands of happy spirits now in heaven, will have cause to bless the day, to all eternity, that Sunday Schools were ever established.

In conclusion, allow me, gentlemen, to express a hope, that the Almighty may be graciously pleased to prolong your lives, and bless you with health, and increased success, in the cause of humanity and love; and late, very late, may he receive you to himself, finally to mix with that happy, thrice happy number, unto whom it shall be said, at the last great day of account, "Come, ye blessed children of my Father, receive the kingdom prepared for you from the foundation of the world."

"WM. * * * *."

APPENDIX.

N.

A CHRISTIAN ADDRESS to the FREE INHABITANTS of NEW SOUTH WALES and VAN DIEMENS LAND.

The Christian Address of James Backhouse and George Washington Walker, to the Free Inhabitants of New South Wales and Van Diemens Land.

The time has nearly arrived, when we believe it will be right, to leave these Colonies, for other fields of religious labour; after having spent five years among you, in the discharge of what we have apprehended to be our religious duty. The Lord has opened many of your hearts toward us, and has favoured us, everywhere, with a hospitable reception; for which, we have great cause to be thankful to him, and to you. And now, under the continued feeling of that love which desires the salvation of all men, we are disposed, before we depart, to visit you with this, our Christian Address; in order to bring before you some subjects which deeply concern you, and to keep you in remembrance of others, to which your attention may have been directed, while we were personally with you.

Though, in the course of our sojourn, in these lands, we have visited a large proportion of the inhabitants, in their own dwellings; or have had communication with them, in public assemblies, for moral and religious purposes; yet this Address will probably fall into the hands of some with whom we have not met: we wish such, and indeed all whom it may reach, to accept it as a token of Christian good-will, from two individuals, who have no other motive for being in this part of the world, than a desire to discharge their duty toward God and man; their Gospel labours being entirely gratuitous, in accordance with the precept of Christ: "Freely ye have received, freely give."*

We think it proper, here to remark, that the greatest proportion of the large quantity of Books and Tracts, which we have circulated in these Colonies, was placed at our disposal by the Society of Friends, in Great Britain; with whom we are in religious fellowship: who have not only thus proved, that they participate in the deep interest we feel for your welfare, in time and in eternity; but who, uniting with us in the belief, that we were called of the Lord, to discharge this duty towards you, have cheerfully defrayed the expenses attendant on its accomplishment; with the desire, that our Gospel labours among you, might be blessed, to the spreading and exaltation of the kingdom of our Lord and Saviour Jesus Christ.

We cannot but consider you, collectively, as Communities, already occupying very important stations in the world; and we fervently desire that you may be blessed of the Most High. He has permitted many of you to become prosperous in temporal things; and if you seek wisdom from him, he will enable you to act the part of good stewards over that which he has committed to your trust; and for the right use of which, you must give account unto him.

The blessing of the Lord will be with you, in proportion as you walk in his fear; but if you refuse to serve him, he will even "curse your blessings:"† for though he may give you that which you desire, he can send with it, "leanness into your souls."‡ Has not this already been the experience of many of you? so that, though you have been outwardly prosperous, you have continued in bondage to sin, have been strangers to peace of mind, and have remained without hope in the prospect of death.

We would remind you, that in the history of the world, no nation has ever maintained a state of prosperity, or of true freedom, whilst the people who have composed it, have rejected the government of God. In proportion as they have refused to serve him, they have been permitted, either to oppress one another, or to be oppressed, by their rulers, or by other nations; or he has suffered them to fall under the influence of ecclesiastical tyranny,—the oppression of men, or of bodies of men, who, contrary to the

‡ Matt. x. 8.   † Mal. ii. 2.   ‡ Psalm cvi. 15.

precepts of the Lord Jesus and his Apostles, have assumed to themselves the lordship over God's heritage.*

The injustice of one nation toward another, has often been signally punished, under the providence of God. This is strongly exhibited in the historical portion of the Holy Scriptures, as well as in more modern histories; and it was strikingly exemplified, a few years ago, in the case of Van Diemens Land; when a mere handful of the Aborigines, whose territory had been usurped, and who had been, in many instances, cruelly and brutally treated by the White Population, were permitted to spread terror over the Island, and to introduce mourning into the families of a large portion of the Settlers, through the destruction of the lives of one or more of their household. This awful judgment is now withdrawn; the residue of these oppressed people having been taken under the protection of the British Government: but the example remains, a warning to the Inhabitants of Australia, who are not clear in the sight of God or man, with regard to the charge of injustice and cruelty, toward the Native Black population; whose territory has been wrested from them, and toward whom, little of that feeling has been shown, which ought to actuate Christian men. Upon you, the Native Blacks have indeed, a strong claim: they have been dispossessed of their soil, and you have occupied it; it is, therefore, your duty, to provide for their support and instruction, as well as for their protection; that they may neither perish through want, nor in ignorance, with the added vices which have been introduced among them; nor remain liable to be shot, while helping themselves to the produce of the land that has been taken from them; nor to be destroyed promiscuously, because acts of retaliation or aggression may, occasionally, be committed by individuals among them.

We regret that some benevolent persons, for want, we apprehend, of taking a sufficiently comprehensive view of human nature, should have become discouraged, with regard to the use of means for promoting civilization, and the knowledge of Christianity, among this degraded portion of our race: principally, because several of the Aborigines, who had been introduced to civilized customs, again returned to the barbarous habits of their countrymen. We think this was no just cause of discouragement; for these carried back into their tribes, many ideas which they would not, probably, so soon have received, had the individuals in question remained among the White Population. We have observed a marked difference, between the tribes that have been thus benefited, and others that have not had a similar advantage, And where religion has been introduced to their notice, there is reason to fear, that it has been too often, as a form, rather than as an operative principle: need we wonder, then, that it has failed to produce practical effects? The history of man, however, proves, that there is no means so effectual, for attaching human beings to civilized habits, as the introduction of vital Christianity among them. And those nations that have received the Gospel, and have become civilized, even in a small degree, have, in most instances, been the subjects of patient labour, for several generations; and have furnished many grounds of discouragement, during this season of probation; at the same time, that the imputations, of defect of capacity, treachery, and incorrigible barbarism, have been heaped upon them by their oppressors, seconded by the misinformed and the ignorant, as reasons why further attempts for their amelioration should be abandoned.

You hold a no less responsible position, in regard to the Prisoner Population. These unhappy persons having become obnoxious to the laws of their country, through giving way to peculiar temptations; as a part of the punishment of their crimes, are assigned to you, as servants; and you are not only required to exact from them, a due portion of labour, but it is expected by the British Nation, that you should strive to promote their reformation. This is likewise your duty before God, who will be your judge, as well as theirs, and who " is no respecter of persons."*

Many of you, also, have families, and free servants, dependent upon you, for moral and religious instruction; who may become righteous or wicked, according to the principles you may inculcate, and the good, or evil example you may set them.

May you consider, seriously, what your duty, in these several respects, is; and may you be enabled faithfully to discharge it: remembering, that, as it is the Almighty who has given you an influence over others, which may be turned to a good or an evil account, so you are answerable to him, for the use you make of it; for he will " reward every man according to his works."†

It must be evident to any who reflect, that none can effectually teach others, that which they themselves have not learned: and if a man have not learned his duty toward God, so as to practice it,

---

* Acts x. 34.   † Matt. xvi. 27.

surely, he is in an awful situation. How prosperous soever he may be, in temporal things, how much soever esteemed by the world, hell yawns beneath his feet! he has no certainty of life; and should death overtake him, in this state, it brings him before the bar of an insulted God;—insulted by the neglect of his laws, of his offered mercies, and of his threatened judgments.

And if a man perform not his duty toward God, he will inevitably fail in his duty toward man; for the right discharge of the one, is inseparably connected with the due fulfilment of the other. There is no excuse for ignorance of our duty to God, and to one another; nor for want of capacity to perform it; for we are promised wisdom and strength, if we apply unto God for them: "If any of you lack wisdom," says the apostle James, "let him ask of God, that giveth to all men liberally, and upbraideth not; and it shall be given him;"* and the Lord Jesus Christ has said: "If ye, then, being evil, know how to give good gifts unto your children, how much more shall your Heavenly Father give the Holy Spirit to them that ask him?"†

In the patriarchal ages, heads of families, many of whom were persons following pastoral and agricultural occupations, like those in which some of you are engaged, were the teachers of their own families, as is strikingly exemplified in the cases of Abraham and Job; of the former of whom, the Almighty said: "I know him, that he will command his children and his household after him; and they shall keep the way of the Lord, to do justice and judgment; that the Lord may bring upon Abraham, that which he hath spoken of him."‡

Under the Law of Moses, also, the observance of this duty was strongly inculcated: "Hear, O Israel! the Lord our God is one Lord: and thou shalt love the Lord thy God with all thine heart, and with all thy soul, and with all thy might. And these words, which I command thee this day, shall be in thine heart; and thou shalt teach them diligently unto thy children, and shalt talk of them, when thou sittest in thine house, and when thou walkest by the way, and when thou liest down, and when thou risest up."§

And under the Gospel, men are no less strictly enjoined, "to rule well their own houses, having their children in subjection, with all gravity;" and "to bring up their children in the nurture and admonition of the Lord."‖ Nor is there the shadow of a reason,

* James i. 5. † Luke xi. 13. ‡ Gen. xviii. 19. § Deut. vi. 4—7.
‖ 1 Tim. iii. 4. Ephes. vi. 4.

for supposing, that, under this last dispensation, God has taken the responsibility off the heads of families, and transferred it to any other description of persons, such as the public ministers of the Gospel, or teachers of schools. The labours of these are to be valued in their places, but are by no means, to supersede those of parents and others, who may have charge of domestic establishments.

We feel for such of you, as may be sensible of the responsibility involved in these important duties, and who, discouraged under the sense of their inability, of themselves, rightly to discharge them, may be ready to exclaim: " Who is sufficient for these things?" Let such perseveringly wait upon God, under the feeling of their own weakness, for strength to perform their respective duties; and he will assuredly impart the needful qualifications.

We would earnestly recommend the practice of assembling your families and servants, daily, as well as on the first day of the week; and of reading the Holy Scriptures to them (which is generally found to be practicable, where there is a proper sense of the importance of the duty): for, " they are able to make wise unto salvation, through faith which is in Christ Jesus;" and " all Scripture is given by inspiration of God, and is profitable for doctrine, for reproof, for correction, for instruction in righteousness; that the man of God may be perfect, thoroughly furnished unto all good works."*

Spend also a portion of time, on these occasions, in seeking communion with God in silence, that you may worship Him, who " is a Spirit, in spirit and in truth."† And at these seasons, should any pertinent counsel be presented to your minds, whether it be little or much, be willing to express it, on behalf of those assembled with you, in simplicity, and in the fear of the Lord; who will be as " a mouth and wisdom" to such as put their trust in him.‡ But be careful that nothing be expressed, either in exhortation or in prayer, but what weightily impresses you at the time; and that it be, with the single aim of discharging your religious duty to God, and to your families. And be not discouraged from reading to them, though you may not often have anything to say in addition.

Were you thus to cherish a concern for the spiritual welfare of those entrusted to your care; being solicitous, also, in your

---

* 2 Tim. iii 15—17.   † John iv. 24.   ‡ Luke xxi. 21—15.

own conduct, to walk as becometh the Gospel, the divine bless-ing would attend you: and it would be found, that to this day, the declaration of the Apostle Paul is verified: "Now, there are diversities of gifts, but the same Spirit: and there are differences of administrations, but the same Lord: aud there are diversities of operations, but it is the same God which worketh all in all. But the manifestation of the Spirit is given to every man to profit withal: for to one is given by the Spirit, the word of wisdom; to another the word of knowledge, by the same Spirit; to another faith by the same Spirit:"—"But all these worketh that one, and the self-same Spirit, dividing to every man severally as he will."*

It has been a cause of sincere regret to us, to find so little practical Christianity among the inhabitants of these Colonies; and we wish strongly to urge upon you, individually, the important inquiry: Whether you really are Christians, or are only pro-fessing to be such, whilst living out of the fear of God, and not subject to the government of Christ; and are thus deceiving your own souls: for this, we cannot but fear, is the state of many amongst you. The inquiry is an infinitely important one: not only your present, but your everlasting happiness, is involved in the subject. For, "Know ye not, that to whom ye yield your-selves servants to obey, his servants ye are to whom ye obey; whether of sin unto death, or of obedience unto righteousness?"†

The Apostle John has declared, that "all unrighteousness is sin." "Let no man deceive you," says he, "he that doeth righteousness is righteous, even as he is righteous; he that committeth sin is of the devil; for the devil sinneth from the be-ginning. For this purpose the Son of God was manifested, that he might destroy the works of the devil."‡ Sin, then, is the service of the devil, who is the enemy of God; and "No man," said Christ, "can serve two masters; for either he will hate the one, and love the other; or else he will hold to the one, and despise the other."§ Those who live in sin, reject Christ; they "will not that he should rule over them;" and they are in the "way that leadeth to destruction."‖ But those who are Christians in deed and in truth, take up the cross to their sinful inclinations, and follow Christ, in the practice of self-denial: for, said he, "If any man will come after me, let him deny himself,

---

* 1 Cor. xii. 4—11.   † Romans vi. 16.   ‡ 1 John v. 17.—iii 7, 8.
§ Matt. vi. 24.   ‖ Luke xix. 27.   Matt. vii. 13.

and take up his cross, and follow me."* He that taketh not his cross, and followeth after me, is not worthy of me."† " Whosoever doth not bear his cross, and come after me, cannot be my disciple."‡

Are not many of you conscious, that you are living in habitual sin? some in drunkenness, adultery, fornication, or other unhallowed indulgencies; some in the practice of cursing and swearing, and taking the divine name in vain; and some in dishonesty; if not in actual theft, yet in over-reaching and defrauding one another? And are not others, who are more upright among men, living, notwithstanding, out of the divine fear, and in forgetfulness of God; placing their affections on temporal things, and thus making them their idols; so that their hearts go more after their families, their lands, their flocks, and their merchandise, than after the Lord?

Let none who live in these practices, deceive themselves, by supposing that they are true Christians. " He that loveth father or mother more than me," said Christ, "is not worthy of me: and he that loveth son or daughter more than me, is not worthy of me."§ " Know ye not," says the Apostle Paul, " that the unrighteous shall not inherit the kingdom of God? Be not deceived: neither fornicators, nor idolaters, nor adulterers, nor effeminate, nor abusers of themselves with mankind, nor thieves, nor covetous, nor drunkards, nor revilers, nor extortioners, shall inherit the kingdom of God." There is hope, however, for those who repent, and turn from these things: for the Apostle adds, in addressing the Christian converts, at Corinth; " And such were some of you: but ye are washed, but ye are sanctified, but ye are justified, in the name of the Lord Jesus, and by the Spirit of our God."‖

We believe that many of you are visited, from season to season, with serious impressions, of the origin of which you may not be fully aware. Have you not felt, that something more than you have yet attained to, is wanting, to render you peaceful and happy? Have you not had some painful convictions of the vanity of human pursuits, and of their insufficiency to satisfy the desires of an immortal being? We beseech you, stifle not these impressions. They are the work of the divine Spirit upon your minds, rendering you uneasy in yourselves, that you may know, that this is not

---

* Mark viii. 34. † Matth. x. 38. ‡ Luke xiv. 27. § Matth. x. 37.
‖ 1 Cor. vi. 9—11. See also Gal vi. 7, 8. 1 John ii. 15—17.

h

the place of your rest; and that you may "acquaint yourselves with God, and be at peace."* Seek not, as too many unhappily do, under the idea of driving away melancholy, to dissipate these impressions, by resorting to company and music, to smoking and drinking, or to other transient enjoyments, even should any of them be such, as under other circumstances, might be regarded as inno-cent; for if by so doing, you "quench the Spirit"—that Spirit which would draw you nearer unto God; what might otherwise seem for a moment, to be gain unto you, would be indeed to your eternal loss. These things cannot afford you peace. The world and its pleasures, as regards your participation in them, will speedily pass away. And "what shall it profit a man, if he shall gain the whole world, and lose his own soul? Or what shall a man give in exchange for his soul?"† Be wise then, and lay up for yourselves treasure in heaven, by making the Redeemer of men your friend; that, when called before the Judge of quick and dead, he may admit you into one of the "many mansions" that are prepared for the righteous.‡ It is through the goodness and mercy of God, who seeks to lead you to repentance, and to the knowledge of himself, and of his Son Jesus Christ, that you are thus disquieted in yourselves. Turn, then, unto him, who has smitten the root of your enjoyments. Those who give their hearts unto the Lord, have the foundation of true happiness laid in themselves. " Using this world without abusing it,"§ they realize the full measure of happiness that it can afford; and a much larger measure than they ever realize, who make the world their only enjoyment: for, "Godliness is profitable unto all things, having promise of the life that now is, and of that which is to come."‖

We lament, that amongst those, who, in these Colonies, profess to be vital Christians, so little of the fruits of righteousness should be found; that a large proportion of such, should be living, in a great degree, conformed to the world, and in accordance with its maxims, having something of the "form of godliness," but prac-tically, to a great extent, "denying the power thereof;" and re-luctantly, if at all, denying themselves, taking up their cross, and following Christ. The words of the Lord Jesus convey a solemn warning to such as these: "Not every one that saith unto me, Lord, Lord, shall enter into the kingdom of heaven; but he that doeth the will of my Father, which is in heaven."¶

---

* Job xxii. 21.   † Mark viii. 36, 37.   ‡ John xiv. 2.   ⸗ 1 Cor. vii. 31.
‖ 1 Tim iv. 8.   ¶ Matth. vii. 21.

We have often felt for a class of persons amongst you, who admit that they are out of the right way; and who attribute their want of religion, to the absence of what they call "a Church, and a regularly ordained ministry;" not considering, that their defect originates in their own want of diligence, in seeking the Lord for themselves. In several instances, where such a ministry has been established, and such places of public worship have been erected, we have observed, that many of the persons who formerly lamented the want of them, were still dissatisfied, not having come unto Jesus for themselves; who said, "I am the Way, and the Truth, and the Life: no man cometh unto the Father, but by me." "I am the Bread of Life: he that cometh to me shall never hunger; and he that believeth on me shall never thirst."*

We would remind persons of this description, that the Gospel of Christ is of universal application; and is, therefore, not dependent upon any system of religious instruction, of human institution; neither is the propagation of it limited to places set apart for public worship: nevertheless the Lord is pleased to bless such ministry as is of his own appointment, as an important means of conversion and edification. An essential characteristic of this ministry is, that it is "neither received of man, nor taught, but by the revelation of Jesus Christ,"† whatever may be the religious denomination of the persons who exercise it: nor can it be restricted to one person in a congregation, without infringement upon the privileges of the rest; "for," says the Apostle Paul, "Ye may all prophesy one by one, that all may learn, and all may be comforted:" and, "He that prophesieth speaketh unto men, to edification, and exhortation, and comfort."‡ The apostle, however, shows, that all are not called to speak in this manner, when he describes the gifts of the Spirit (to some of which we have already alluded), and declares, that "God hath set some in the Church; first apostles, secondarily prophets, thirdly teachers, after that miracles, then gifts of healings, helps, governments, diversities of tongues.§

We are also instructed, that, "the Most High dwelleth not in temples made with hands,"‖ and, that, where neither ministry, nor a place specially set apart for worship, exists, the blessings of the Gospel are, through the great mercy of God, provided for all; whether they be solitary individuals, solitary believers, in

---

* John xiv. 6—vi. 35.   + Gal. i. 12.   ‡ 1 Cor. xiv. 31—3.   ‡ 1 Cor. xii. 28.
‖ Acts vii. 48—xvii 24.

h 2

families, or those associated in numbers. "Thus saith the Lord; The heaven is my throne; and the earth is my footstool: where is the house that ye build unto me? and where is the place of my rest? For all those things hath mine hand made, and all those things have been, saith the Lord: but to this man will I look, even to him that is poor and of a contrite spirit, and trembleth at my word."* This was the encouraging language, to the humble and sincere-hearted, though solitary, worshipper, under the Law; and the gracious words of Christ, are no less full and consolatory, under the Gospel: "Behold, I stand at the door, and knock: if any man hear my voice, and open the door, I will come in to him, and will sup with him, and he with me."† Again, "Where two or three are gathered together in my name, there am I in the midst of them."‡

It is, however, the indispensable duty, of Christians, to assemble for the public worship of God, wherever they are so situated as to be able to meet with others, whose views accord with their own, on this important point: "not forsaking the assembling of ourselves together, as the manner of some is," says an apostle; "but exhorting one another; and so much the more, as ye see the day approaching."§

———

We would now invite your attention to a few Scriptural positions, that involve very important practical consequences, in connexion with the "faith which is in Christ Jesus."‖

1. When the Gospel was ushered into the world, it was with the message; "Repent ye: for the kingdom of heaven is at hand."¶

2. John the Baptist, who was as "the voice of one crying in the wilderness, Prepare ye the way of the Lord, make his paths straight," and who, as well as the Lord Jesus himself, preached repentance; "came for a witness, to bear witness of the Light, that all men through him might believe."**

3. So essential was it that men should believe in Christ, the Light of the World, that though "John was not that Light, he

---

* Isaiah lxvi. 1, 2.   † Rev. iii. 20.   ‡ Matth. xviii. 20.   § Heb. x 25.
‖ 2 Tim. iii. 15.   ¶ Matth. iii. 2—iv. 17.
** Matth. iii. 3—11. Mark i. 4. Luke iii. 3. Acts xiii. 24—xix. 4. John i. 7.

was sent to bear witness of that Light: that was the true Light, which lighteth every man that cometh into the world."*

4. It is also testified of Jesus Christ, "The Word," who "was in the beginning with God, and was God;" by whom all things were made, and without whom was not any thing made that was made: that "in him was life; and the life was the Light of men."†

5. It is this Light which cometh by Jesus Christ, the true Light, that makes sin manifest unto man; and the object of God, in causing it to shine into the heart of man, is, that he may awake out of sleep, with regard to the concerns of his soul, and arise from a state of death "in trespasses and sins," that Christ may give him Light, that he may obtain the forgiveness of his sins, through Jesus Christ; and that this Light of Christ may abide with him for ever. The testimony of the Apostle Paul is, "All things that are reproved are made manifest by the Light; for whatsoever doth make manifest is Light:" wherefore he saith, "Awake thou that sleepest, and arise from the dead, and Christ shall give thee Light."‡

6. Though Christ, the true "Light, lighteth every man that cometh into the world;" there is a state of darkness in which the Light that cometh by him is not comprehended: "The Light shineth in darkness; and the darkness comprehended it not."§

7. Christ himself bore witness to the Light received through him; exhorting people to believe in it, and walk in it, and promising it to those who should follow him, saying; "I am the Light of the world: he that followeth me, shall not walk in darkness, but shall have the Light of life." He also shewed, that they who reject it, are in danger of being given up to total darkness, as regards the way of salvation: "Yet a little while is the Light with you: walk while ye have the Light, lest darkness come upon you: for he that walketh in darkness knoweth not whither he goeth. While ye have Light, believe in the Light, that ye may be the children of Light."‖

8. Christ pointed out the inseparable connexion between practically believing in the Light, which cometh by him, (and consequently examining our deeds by it,) and savingly believing in his name; saying: "God so loved the world, that he gave his only

---

* John i. 8.   † John i. 1—4.   ‡ Ephes. ii. 1—5.—v. 8, 13, 14.   § John i 5—9.
‖ John viii. 12.—xii. 35—36.

begotten Son, that whosoever believeth in him, should not perish, but have everlasting life; for God sent not his Son into the world to condemn the world; but that the world through him might be saved. He that believeth on him is not condemned: but he that believeth not is condemned already, because he hath not believed in the name of the only begotten Son of God. And *this is the condemnation,* that *Light is come into the world, and men loved darkness rather than Light, because their deeds were evil;* for every one that doeth evil hateth the Light, neither cometh to the Light, lest his deeds should be reproved; but *he that doeth truth cometh to the Light,* that his deeds may be made manifest, that they are wrought in God."*

9.   The Apostle John, likewise, exhibits, in the following expressions, a close connexion between walking in the Light, and being cleansed from sin by the blood of Christ: "This, then, is the message which we have heard of him," that is, of Christ, "and declare unto you, that God is light, and in him is no darkness at all. If we say that we have fellowship with him, and walk in darkness, we lie, and do not the truth; but if we walk in the Light, as he is in the Light, we have fellowship one with another, and the blood of Jesus Christ his Son cleanseth us from all sin."†

10.   From the foregoing, it is plain, that the Light, to which the attention of mankind is so emphatically directed by Christ and his Apostles, is the " manifestation of the Spirit," "the Spirit of Truth, which proceedeth from the Father," cometh in the name of Christ, testifies of him, "convinces the world of sin," teaches his followers all things, and brings his sayings to their remembrance, guides them into all truth, and, as the Comforter, abides with them for ever: he dwelt with the disciples of Christ, while Christ himself was with them, who also promised, that he should be in them: he is not, however, received of "the world, because it seeth him not, neither knoweth him;" nevertheless, it was declared, that he should "reprove the world of sin, of righteousness, and of judgment."‡

11.   This Light, or manifestation of the Spirit, as " the Grace of God that bringeth salvation," "hath appeared to all men, teaching us that, denying ungodliness and worldly lusts, we should live soberly, righteously, and godly, in this present world."§

---

* John iii. 16—21.   † 1 John i. 5—7.   ‡ John xv. 26.   xiv. 26, 16, 17.   xvi. 8—13.
§ Titus ii. 11, 12.

12. It was by Grace, through faith, that the early believers in Christ were saved: "by Grace are ye saved, through faith; and that not of yourselves; it is the gift of God: not of works, lest any man should boast; for we are his workmanship, created in Christ Jesus unto good works, which God hath before ordained, that we should walk in them."*

The doctrine that salvation is obtained through Jesus Christ, by believing in the Light, being guided by the Spirit of Truth, and having faith in the Grace of God; is strictly in accordance with the declaration of the apostle Paul: "Believe on the Lord Jesus Christ, and thou shalt be saved."†

For when mankind believe in the Light, so as to bring their deeds unto it, and walk in the way of holiness, according to its manifestations; they attain unto "fellowship with the Father and with the Son," and being reconciled unto God through him, and walking in the Light, as he is in the Light, they have fellowship one with another, and the blood of Jesus Christ his Son cleanseth them from all sin."‡ By submitting to the guidance of the Spirit of Truth, which convinces mankind of sin, and excites them to repentance, they are drawn unto him who is their "Advocate with the Father, Jesus Christ the righteous, who is also the propitiation for their sins." These obtain the remission of sins through him, and walk in the spirit, not fulfilling the lust of the flesh :§ and "there is no condemnation to them which are in Christ Jesus, who walk not after the flesh, but after the Spirit; for the law of the Spirit of life in Christ Jesus hath made them free from the law of sin and death."‖

Thus through faith in the Grace of God, mankind are taught, "that denying ungodliness and worldly lusts, they should live soberly, righteously, and godly, in this present world; looking for that blessed hope, and the glorious appearing of the great God and our Saviour Jesus Christ; who gave himself for us, that he might redeem us from all iniquity, and purify unto himself a peculiar people, zealous of good works :"¶ and those who are thus taught, ascribe all "to the praise of the glory of his Grace, wherein he hath made them accepted in the Beloved: in whom they have redemption through his blood, the forgiveness of sins, according to the riches of his Grace."**

It is for want of attention to the teaching of divine Grace, that

* Ephes. ii. 8—10.   † Acts xvi. 31.   ‡ 1 John i. 3—7.   § Gal. v. 16.
‖ Rom. viii. 1, 2.   ¶ Titus ii. 12—11   ** Ephes. i. 6, 7.

so large a portion of mankind remain "dead in trespasses and sins," "having no hope and without God in the world."* Indeed, it is evident, from the whole tenor of the New Testament, that without attention to the Light, Spirit, or Grace, of our Lord Jesus Christ, we cannot believe in him, so as to be saved.

When the apostle Paul declared to the Athenians, " the Unknown God, whom they ignorantly worshipped," he said: " God that made the world and all things therein, seeing that he is Lord of heaven and earth, dwelleth not in temples made with hands; neither is worshipped with men's hands, as though he needed any thing, seeing he giveth to all life, and breath, and all things; and hath made of one blood, all nations of men, for to dwell on all the face of the earth; and hath determined the times before appointed, and the bounds of their habitation; that they should seek the Lord, if haply they might *feel after him, and find him*, though he be not far from every one of us: for in him we live, and move, and have our being."†

This holy exercise of " feeling after God," in order to " find him," we know by experience, that he blesses, both in seasons of private devotion, and in those of public worship; for when, in stillness, the attention is reverently turned to the Light, or manifestation of the Spirit, the mind being kept quiet before the Lord, or if it wander, being re-called to watchfulness, and calm dependence upon him; a sense of the Divine Presence is often granted, under which, a lively perception of the sinfulness of sin, as being rebellion against the Most High, and of the goodness, forbearance, and mercy of a long-suffering God, is imparted to the soul; so that, in brokenness and contrition of heart, confession is made unto him, and the healing virtue of·the blood of Jesus is experienced. For if thus " we confess our sins, God is faithful and just to forgive us our sins, and to cleanse us from all unrighteousness."‡ The soul, at such seasons, being humbled under the feeling of its necessities, is also quickened, in the true spirit of prayer, to ask in the name of Jesus, for the supply of its wants; or in the silence of all flesh, is bowed in reverent adoration, before the Divine Majesty, even the language of thought being suspended. In this state, pre-eminently, pure, spiritual worship is rendered to the Most High; the lowly worshipper resting in quietness and confidence, in the Lord, as a child on the bosom of its father.

Among the numerous exhortations and encouragements, recorded

---

* Ephes. ii. 1, 12.   † Acts xvii. 23—28.   ‡ 1 John i. 9.

in the Holy Scriptures, inciting to diligence in thus waiting upon the Lord, are the following: " Stand in awe, and sin not; commune with your own heart upon your bed, and be still."* " Be still, and know that I am God."† " Wait on the Lord: be of good courage, and he shall strengthen thine heart; wait, I say, on the Lord."‡ " Rest in the Lord [or as in the Hebrew, be silent to the Lord] and wait patiently for him."§ " My soul, wait thou only upon God; for my expectation is from him."‖ " They that wait upon the Lord shall renew their strength; they shall mount up with wings as eagles; they shall run and not be weary; and they shall walk, and not faint. Keep silence before me, O islands! and let the people renew their strength: let them come near; then let them speak: let us come near together to judgment."¶ " Thus saith the Lord God, the Holy One of Israel: In returning and rest, shall ye be saved; in quietness and in confidence, shall be your strength."** " Who is among you that feareth the Lord, that obeyeth the voice of his servant, that walketh in darkness, and hath no light? Let him trust in the name of the Lord, and stay upon his God."†† " The Lord is good unto them that wait for him, to the soul that seeketh him. It is good that a man should both hope, and quietly wait for the salvation of the Lord. It is good for a man that he bear the yoke in his youth. He sitteth alone, and keepeth silence, because he hath borne it upon him. He putteth his mouth in the dust; if so be, there may be hope."‡‡ " I will stand upon my watch, and set me upon the tower, and will watch to see what he will say unto me, [or *in me*, according to the marginal reading] and what I shall answer when I am reproved." " The Lord is in his holy temple: let all the earth keep silence before him."§§ " Be silent, O all flesh, before the Lord! for he is raised up out of his holy habitation."‖‖ " What, could ye not watch with me one hour? Watch and pray, that ye enter not into temptation."¶¶ " What I say unto you, I say unto all: Watch."*** " Continue in prayer, and watch in the same with thanksgiving."††† " Praying always with all prayer and supplication, in the Spirit, and watching thereunto with all perseverance."‡‡‡

Through not attending sufficiently to these scriptural injunctions, and thus seeking communion with the Father of spirits, who

---

* Psalm iv. 4.   † Psalm xlvi. 10.   ‡ Psalm xxvii. 14.   § Psalm xxxvii. 7.
‖ Psalm lxii. 5.   ¶ Isaiah xl. 31.—xli. 1.   ** Isaiah xxx. 15.
†† Isaiah l. 10.   ‡‡ Lam. iii. 25—29.   §§ Hab. ii. 1, 20.   ‖‖ Zech. ii. 13.
¶¶ Matth. xxvi. 40, 41.   *** Mark xiii. 37.   ††† Col. iv. 2.   ‡‡‡ Ephes. vi. 18.

must be worshipped in spirit and in truth; the religious exercises of many professing Christians are lamentably superficial: and their attention being continually diverted from the state of their own hearts, to something outward, they seldom "come to the Light, that their deeds may be made manifest that they are wrought in God;" but they rather content themselves with ceremonial observances, which are not in accordance with the spirituality of the Gospel; so that the language of the Most High is often too applicable: "This people draweth nigh unto me with their mouth, and honoureth me with their lips; but their heart is far from me."* And again: " Behold, all ye that kindle a fire, that compass yourselves about with sparks: walk in the light of your fire, and in the sparks that ye have kindled, This shall ye have of mine hand; ye shall lie down in sorrow."†

But, on the contrary, where the Lord is waited on daily, for the knowledge of his will, and for strength to perform it, watchfulness unto prayer being perseveringly maintained; Divine teaching is known; strength is received of God to do his will; and the voice of Christ, "the Shepherd and Bishop of souls," is distinguished from the "voice of the stranger:" for " Christ's sheep hear his voice;" and "he goeth before them, and the sheep follow him; for they know his voice." " The Lord being their shepherd, they do not want; he maketh them to lie down in green pastures; he leadeth them beside the still waters; he restoreth their souls; he leadeth them in the paths of righteousness, for his name's sake. Yea, though they walk through the valley of the shadow of death, they fear no evil: for he is with them; his rod and his staff, they comfort them:" " he giveth unto them eternal life, and they shall never perish; neither shall any man pluck them out of his hand."‡ These have " received the Spirit of adoption, whereby we cry, Abba, Father: the Spirit itself bearing witness with our spirit, that we are the children of God."§ These have the Holy Spirit as " an Unction from the Holy One;" and to them it may be said, " the Anointing, which ye have received of him, abideth in you; and ye need not that any man teach you; but as the same Anointing teacheth you of all things, and is truth, and is no lie."‖ And thus, the promise to the Church of Christ is fulfilled in their experience : " All thy children shall be taught of the Lord; and great shall be the peace of thy children."¶

---

* Matth. xv. 8.   † Isaiah l. 11.   ‡ John x. 3, 4, 28—1 Pet. ii. 25—Psalm xxiii. 1, 4.
§ Rom. viii. 14—16.   ‖ 1 John ii. 20—27.   ¶ Isaiah liv. 13.

Fervent is our desire, that you, the Inhabitants of these Colonies, may attain to this practical Christianity; that the fruits of righteousness may appear among you, and that you may reap the rich blessings thereof, in time and in eternity. "The fruit of the Spirit is love, joy, peace, long-suffering, gentleness, goodness, faith, meekness, temperance: against which there is no law."* "If these things be in you and abound, they make you that ye shall neither be barren nor unfruitful" in that knowledge in which is life eternal: "for so an entrance shall be ministered unto you abundantly into the everlasting kingdom of our Lord and Saviour Jesus Christ."†

We would now bid you Farewell, in the Lord! regarding as our Christian brethren, "all them that love our Lord Jesus Christ in sincerity,"‡ notwithstanding their religious views may differ from our own; not doubting that, though it is our duty to "prove all things, and to hold fast [only] that which is good;"§ yet they who fear God, and work righteousness," what name soever they may bear among men, "are accepted with him."||

May "the Lord direct your hearts [universally] into the love of God, and into the patient waiting for Christ:"¶ so as that you may be enabled from heartfelt experience of the Divine Presence being with you, to adopt the language of the inspired penman: "Lo, this is our God, we have waited for him, and he will save us! this is the Lord; we have waited for him, we will be glad and rejoice in his salvation!"**

JAMES BACKHOUSE.
GEORGE WASHINGTON WALKER.

Sydney, 4th of 1st month, 1837.

* Gal. v. 22, 23.   † 2 Peter i. 8. 11.   ‡ Ephes. vi. 24.   § 1 Thes. v. 21.
|| Acts x. 35.   ¶ 2 Thes. iii 5.   ** Isaiah xxv. 9.

APPENDIX.

O.

A REPORT ON NEW SOUTH WALES.

To Major General Richard Bourke, K. C. B. Governor in Chief of the Colony of New South Wales, &c. &c.

The Report of James Backhouse and George Washington Walker, on various subjects, connected with the state of the Colony, of New South Wales.

Having devoted nearly two years, to visiting the Colony of New South Wales, with a view to promote the moral and religious welfare of its inhabitants, and being now on the eve of departing from its shores, we think it incumbent upon us, to express the gratitude we feel to the Governor, for the facilities he has been pleased to afford us, in the prosecution of our object, and to present him with a few remarks, on some subjects that have attracted our attention, in the course of our sojourn in this land.

Being convinced, that, how prosperous soever, in general, the population of a Colony, such as New South Wales, may be, in the acquisition of property, nothing can secure the stability of the Government, or the true well-being of the community, short of the divine blessing; and being satisfied that there is no ground to expect this blessing, where the morals of the people are generally bad, we cannot but regard, with mournful interest, the low state of morality, and necessarily consequent defect of religious principle, in the generality of the Inhabitants of this Colony, and look upon them as demanding the serious attention of an enlightened Government.

The prevailing immorality of the population of New South Wales is, no doubt, to be attributed, primarily, to their neglect of the fear of God. Many secondary causes, however, contribute to foster, if not to induce a state of reckless impiety, in the community.

Foremost in the rank of these, we apprehend, is the encouragement given by the Government, to the consumption of spirituous liquors, by the sanction of their distillation and importation, and by the licensing of houses for their sale.

We would respectfully state our conviction, that the prohibition of the sale of all spirituous liquors, as beverage, would promote the reformation and prosperity of the population, in a greater degree than any other measure, in the power of the Government to adopt.

In an object of such vital importance to the true interests of the community, the influence of such a measure upon the revenue, scarcely deserves consideration; yet, as this may have weight in the estimation of some, it is to be observed, that a reduction of the revenue, from the prohibition of spirits, would be attended by a corresponding reduction in the expenses of police; and that whatever might be the ultimate deficiency in the revenue, it would be much better made up in some other way, than by continuing to sanction the use of spirits, and by this means, to promote the demoralization of the people.

The pernicious influence of evil example, in regard to the use of profane language, may, perhaps, rank next to that of drunkenness, in the promotion of bad morals, in this Colony. It is a subject that calls loudly for magisterial interference, both as respects the free, and the convict population; for whilst the former are allowed to indulge in unrestrained profanity, the latter cannot reasonably be expected to refrain from it; and while open violations of the divine law, in this respect, prevail, no rational hope of reformation of character in other respects, can be entertained; for no man can be expected to regard with increasing attention, the laws of God in other things, who daily breaks them wantonly, in this particular.

Other evils also exist, to a great extent in New South Wales, to which it is desirable the attention of the Government should be directed, that it may adopt such measures as may tend to suppress them. Among these evils may be enumerated, a want of regard

to the sanctity of the marriage bond, and other allied immoralities, as well as an avaricious disposition, which would compass
its own ends, at the expense of what is strictly honest; especially
if the dishonesty be of a character, not easily cognizable by law.
To the latter may be referred, a disposition to introduce lotteries,
and to countenance other species of gaming.

It would be superfluous, to make much comment upon the pecuniary circumstances of the free Colonists, as these must be better
known to the Governor, than to ourselves. It may not be im-
pertinent, however, to remark, that so far as our own observations
have extended, sober, honest, and industrious persons, of ordinary
abilities, and moderate expectations, readily obtain a livelihood in
New South Wales, and many of this class, become prosperous.
But among those who emigrate to these Colonies, is a large proportion of persons, who, for want of some of the requisites
mentioned, were unsuccessful in their native land; and these remain inefficient and unprosperous here, and from them, is often to
be heard, an assertion, by no means true, that a free emigrant has
no chance of making a livelihood in New South Wales, because of
the competition of prisoners.

The education of the rising generation, in the Colony, is a
deeply interesting subject. We regret that it has so frequently
been discussed, on various occasions of late, in the spirit of party
politics. As regards our own view, of the merits of the respective
systems of education, we give a decided preference, for general
purposes, to that of the British and Foreign School Society; but
we would respectfully suggest, that the greatest amount of benefit
to education, from the assistance of the Government, might be
expected to accrue, if none but such institutions as orphan-schools,
or such others, as might be established, in districts where the population was very limited, were to be supported exclusively, from the
funds of the Government; and the latter, without reference, either
to the peculiar religious views of the persons establishing them, or
to the system of instruction pursued; and that, where the population becomes sufficiently numerous, only a certain quota, up to a
specific amount, should be contributed by the Government; the
amount to be proportioned to that contributed by the settlers, or
raised by the payments of the children. Teachers of schools are apt
to become negligent, when rendered independent of the payments
of their pupils; and parents, among the lower orders, who do not
pay any thing toward the education of their offspring, are very
generally careless, in enforcing their regular attendance at school.

We have rejoiced to observe a disposition, on the part of the Government, to attend to the state of the Black Population, and by establishing missions, in different parts of the Colony, to promote their civilization, and the introduction of Christianity amongst them. We have no doubt, that these objects are to be accomplished, if suitable means be employed; and we believe, that much would have been already effected, had equal zeal been exercised with respect to the amelioration of the condition of the Blacks, with what has been displayed, in driving them from their lands, and in protecting the White People, who occupied them, from the petty depredations of the original possessors of the soil.

Indeed it is probable, that not more expense would have been incurred by the Government, if it had, from the first, properly considered the rights of this oppressed people, and obtained territory from them by treaty, and at the same time, had provided sufficient means for their civilization, than has been incurred, by the measures that have been adopted, many of which have been derogatory to the character of the British Nation, both as regards Christianity and common justice. We would respectfully submit, that the means yet employed in this Colony, for the civilization of the Aborigines, are extremely small, in proportion to the end proposed, even taking into account, the stations about to be occupied, at Moreton Bay, by John and Mary Handt, and at Port Philip, by George Langhorne, in addition to that already filled, at Wellington Valley, by William and Ann Watson, and the partial assistance, afforded to Lancelot Edward Threlkeld, at Lake Macquarie. If these be compared with the number of labourers, employed by the Church Missionary Society alone, in the part of New Zealand, contiguous to the Bay of Islands, it will be seen, that notwithstanding the more settled habits of the New Zealanders present greater facility for their civilization, the effect produced has been, in great degree, commensurate with the means made use of, for the promotion of the object.

We venture to point out the neighbourhoods of Port Macquarie, or of the M'Leay River, of Shoal Haven, and of Two-fold Bay, as desirable stations, at which, to place other instructors of the Aborigines, who, in general, resort much more to the coast, than to the interior. And we would suggest, for their better protection by British law, that provision should be made, for their evidence being received on affirmation, in courts of justice; for it is obvious, that while their evidence can only be taken on oath, and their oath cannot be received, on account of their ignorance of the Gospel, they are, to a great extent, virtually, placed out of the protection of British law.

The more we have seen of the state of the prisoners, in these Colonies, the more fully we are satisfied, that transportation is a severe punishment. The state of the prisoner is, in most instances, one of privation, and to him, of painful restraint, as well as of separation from his connexions and country. And if he be a disorderly man, and in consequence, be sentenced to an ironed-gang, we can scarcely conceive a situation more miserable. To be locked up, from sun-set to sun-rise, in the caravans or boxes, used for this description of prisoners, which hold from twenty to twenty-eight men; but in which, the whole number can neither stand upright, nor sit down at the same time, (except with their legs at a right angle with their bodies,) and which, in some instances, do not afford more than eighteen inches in width, for each individual to lie down in, on the bare boards, and to be marched out, and kept to a monotonous employment, under a strict, military guard, during the day, and to be liable to suffer flagellation, for even a trifling offence, such as an exhibition of obstinacy, that may be excited by the capricious conduct of an overseer, is truly a miserable state, and one, to which death itself, would be greatly preferable, were it not for the eternal consequences that await the unprepared.

Although the convict population, of New South Wales, are kept under a considerable degree of subjection and discipline, yet the measure of reformation among them, evinced by the adoption of better principles, is exceedingly small. This need not excite surprise, when the paucity of the means employed for their reformation is considered, in connexion with the facilities for obtaining strong drink, that are placed in their way, notwithstanding the regulations prohibiting the sale of spirituous liquors to prisoners. The opportunities open to them, from the vast number of licensed public-houses, and of places where spirits are sold covertly, are available to a large proportion of the prisonors, who are constantly committing petty thefts, to enable them to gratify their propensity for strong drink.

In visiting the various Penal Establishments of the Colony, and observing the limited means made use of for moral and religious instruction, we must conclude, that restraint, rather than reformation, has been the object of the British Government, in the institution of the penal discipline of New South Wales. There is no religious instructor, at the Penal Settlement, at Moreton Bay, and it is but very lately, that one has been provided for

Norfolk Island. Few of the Ironed-gangs have any other semblance of religious instruction, than the reading of "the prayers" of the Episcopal Church, by the military officers in charge. Though this means is deplorably inefficient, yet, being, in the estimation of the officers, the best at their command, it is persevered in, in a manner that is creditable to them. Except in a few instances, in which are included the prison establishments, in the vicinity of Sydney, little attention appears to be given by the paid clergy, of any denomination, to the state of the convict population, who remain under the charge of the Government ; and at the periods in which we visited them, several of the stations, especially of the Road-parties, were destitute of the Scriptures, as well as of other books, calculated to promote religion and morality. Of latter time, we have observed with satisfaction, that some of the Ironed-gangs have been supplied with Bibles, and some other religious books, through the means of the Episcopal Bishop of Australia.

We think advantage would result, from a report being regularly made, in the periodical returns from the penal stations, of all the visits made to the prisoners, for moral and religious purposes, whether by paid ministers, or by volunteers ; and also of the number of Bibles and Testaments, and of other books and tracts, belonging to the several stations, at the end of each quarter : and it occurred to us, that the books and tracts, might not only be distributed on the first day of the week, but that a few might, with advantage, be placed on a shelf, in each caravan, for daily use, according to the plan that has been adopted on Goat Island.

We conceive, that the inefficiency of the reading of the prayers of the Episcopal Church, as a medium of religious instruction, arises from the mere formality, which must necessarily attend the continual repetition of the same words, how excellent soever they may have been, in the mouths of those who originally used them, or may still be, when adopted by persons in the state of mind, which they represent. And we have no doubt, that if, instead of attempting to put into the mouths of prisoners, devotional expressions, which their state rarely allows them to adopt in sincerity, a few chapters from the Holy Scriptures were to be read to them, to which a simple address, or the reading of some plain narrative, or exhortatory treatise might be added, and if a little time were also to be spent in silence, to allow of serious reflection, more real and permanent benefit would be the result.

The frequency of flagellation in some of the Ironed-gangs, as well as in other stations of prisoners, including the Hyde Park

i

Barracks, Sydney, is a subject deserving notice; for, as a punishment, flagellation is generally admitted to have a degrading effect. In some of the Ironed-gangs, this punishment has, on an average, been administered four times round, to each man, many of the cases being of fifty lashes each, in a period of less than eighteen months. And we have been informed, that upwards of one thousand men have been flogged, in the Hyde Park Barracks, within the same period.

In the large Road-gang, in Illawarra, the punishment of flagellation is comparatively rare, and the conduct of the men is generally good. In this instance, two cells for solitary confinement have been erected, in the rear of the boxes, in which the prisoners sleep, and within the range of the sentries, and this is the punishment usually resorted to. We are of opinion, that it might, with great advantage, be generally substituted for flagellation, at the stations of the Ironed-gangs, and that much benefit would result, from the universal adoption of solitary confinement, in the place of flagellation.

The practice of mustering prisoners, holding tickets-of-leave, once a quarter, is attended with some disadvantages, on which we venture to offer a comment. Many of these persons have so strong a propensity to indulge in drinking spirituous liquors, that they fall into temptation, almost as certainly as it comes in their way. Some of them, conscious of their own weakness, engage in situations, remote from public-houses, and in the intervals between musters, conduct themselves in an orderly manner. But being from ten to twenty miles, or more, from the place of muster, they have to leave their homes once a quarter, for one, two, or more days, to present themselves at the place appointed, which is generally contiguous to a public-house, and few of them return to their work, without having been intoxicated; and instances are not unfrequent, in which, under the influence of inebriation, brought on from these circumstances, they commit some misdemeanour, which results in their privation of the hard-earned indulgence, of a ticket-of-leave.

We have visited most of the prisons in the Colony, and would respectfully state our conviction, that not one of them is on a plan calculated to promote reformation. In the whole of them, prisoners are congregated in considerable numbers, in day-rooms, in most of which they also sleep; in many instances, side by side, on the floor, or on platforms, and in but few, in hammocks. None of the prisons have any adequate provision for solitary confinement, and in some of them, the cells are so few, that prisoners sentenced to solitary confinement, have to wait a considerable time, in the common rooms, for their turns, otherwise, more than one person would have to be in a cell, at the same time.

Some of the prisons do not effectually exclude communication, between the male and female prisoners, as for instance, those at Port Macquarie, Newcastle, and Liverpool. That at Maitland is sometimes so crowded, as to render it necessary for some of the prisoners, occasionally, to spend the night in the yard, to avoid suffocation. That at Campbell Town, under the Court House, is unfit to place human beings in, of any description, even for an hour, however small their numbers may be; the effluvium from it renders the Court House above, untenable, if the windows be closed; and with the number occasionally placed in this prison, their health must be seriously endangered. Many of the prisons in the interior, have no airing courts, and it would be difficult to describe, in a few words, the contamination, which must be the inevitable result, of placing a number of persons without employment, in association, often for several months at a time, in such places.

We have been gratified, in observing the adoption of better plans, in the jails, now erecting, at Sydney and Berrima, having no doubt, that separation and seclusion, are most important auxiliaries in prison-discipline. Solitude is much dreaded by persons of depraved character, while those in whom reformation is begun, feel it a privilege, to be secluded from evil company.

The addition of tread-mills to gaols, or of other means of furnishing employment to the prisoners, confined in them, is much to be desired. But we would remark, that when the sentence to a tread-mill, or to solitary cells, is lengthened out, to a great number of days, it materially diminishes the salutary effect. In the former, the stiffness, induced at first, begins to subside, after a week's exercise; and at the expiration of a fortnight, many persons of the labouring class, would leave the tread-mill, with less disgust, than at the expiration of a week. Persons often sleep a considerable portion of the first two or three days, in solitary confinement, but want of exercise soon renders them wakeful, and they then begin to feel their situation painfully; but the human mind, as well as the body, quickly accommodates itself to circumstances, and a large proportion of persons would be released from this punishment also, with less abhorrence of it, at the end of a month, than at the end of a week.

On the same principle, the female prisoners, in the factories, at Parramatta and Bathurst, and in the gaols, at Newcastle and Port Macquarie, being generally kept without employment, as was the case when we visited those establishments, become inured to idleness, often in such a degree, as not to be again recovered to industrious habits.

We cannot but regard the prison-discipline of the females, as even more defective than that of the males. We are aware, however, that more attention has of late been paid, to the state of the factory at Parramatta, and that some improvement has been the consequence; much, nevertheless, remains to be done. Great benefit might reasonably be expected, from the erection of a prison for the reception of female prisoners on their arrival, as well as for such as are returned from service, without any complaint against them, who ought not, however, to have any communication with the newly arrived. It is also desirable, that the separation of female prisoners, by means, such as are intended to be adopted in the new gaol at Sydney, should be carried into effect, in all other prisons, throughout the Colony.

At Port Macquarie, we saw a little of the situation of the class of prisoners, termed Specials. Many of these are very liable to be drawn into mischief, through their easy access to public-houses; and considering the state of the Penal Settlement at Moreton Bay, and its accommodation for prisoners, we think, many of the Specials might be more advantageously placed at that station, where they might be employed as gardeners to the settlement, or at such other work as they might be adapted for.

In visiting the Colonial Hospitals, we have been much gratified with the good order which prevails in them, and the proofs of attention, on the part of most of the medical officers. The lunatic establishment at Liverpool, though made the most of, is so defective in regard to accommodation for the patients, that their removal to Tarban Creek, as soon as the new asylum can be made ready for them, is much to be desired.

In concluding these observations, we take the liberty of stating our conviction, that the undue measure of punishment, that is yet attached to many offences, by the British Law, has a direct tendency to frustrate one of the chief ends designed to be answered by it, viz. the reduction of crime. This severity, in numerous instances, deters from prosecution, so that many offenders become hardened by repeated transgressions; and others, being associated with culprits more vicious than themselves, become confirmed in depravity, at the same time that they are rendered greater adepts in crime. And how much soever ideas of human expediency may have led to the adoption of a scale of punishment, more severe than is sanctioned by the Divine Law, experience has not only proved the hopes founded on such measures, to have been fallacious, but that in proportion as this sacred standard of human action, has been departed from, the consequences have uniformly been injurious.

In taking leave of these Colonies, we would express our fervent desire, that the Governor may be enabled to live and rule, in the fear of the Lord, maintaining a constant regard to his glory, and that he may be blessed with prosperity in his government, and peace in his own mind, in this world, and with everlasting happiness, in the world to come.

JAMES BACKHOUSE.
GEORGE WASHINGTON WALKER.

Sydney, 18th of 1st mo. 1837.

evangelical Spirit.

APPENDIX.

P.

LETTERS to the GOVERNOR of NEW SOUTH WALES, respecting the ABORIGINES.

To Major General Richard Bourke, K. C. B. Governor in Chief of New South Wales.

Frequently, since G. W. Walker and myself had last the privilege of being guests at the Government-house, at Parramatta, my attention has been recalled to a remark of the Governor, respecting the desireableness of doing something for the Aborigines of New South Wales, and the difficulty of knowing what to do, in order to promote their improvement; and some ideas have impressed my mind, on this subject, which I believe it my place to submit to the Governor's notice, in the hope that they may tend to the removal of the difficulty, and to the opening of the way, for the amelioration of the condition of this injured race of our fellow-men.

In order to make myself clearly understood, it seems necessary for me to advert to the original state of the Black Population of the Colony, and to several other subjects connected with their history, with which, I cannot doubt, that the Governor is already well acquainted. This may be necessary, for the illustration of the subject, to any person whose eye this letter may meet, who may not be so well acquainted with the state of the Aborigines of Australia, as the Governor of New South Wales.

The native Blacks, of New South Wales, are a people of very simple habits, and few wants: existing, in their original state, without clothing, and having, in the southern and middle parts of the Colony, no habitations, beyond rude shelters formed for the night, or against rain, and subsisting on such food as they can obtain with ease, in fine weather, in the wilds of the country, or along the coast; consisting of Kangaroos, Opossums, Emus, and other birds, with fish, grubs, roots, &c.

In those parts of the Colony, in which the White Population have taken possession of the lands, the Kangaroos and Emus, which were among the chief animals, on which the Blacks subsisted, have been generally destroyed, and the ground on which those animals fed, is now depastured by the flocks and herds of the usurpers of the country; who have also introduced profligate habits among the Blacks, that are rapidly wasting their race, some tribes of which have already become extinct, and others are on the verge of extermination.

It is scarcely to be supposed, that in the present day, any persons of reflection will be found, who will attempt to justify the measures adopted by the British, in taking possession of the territory of this people, who had committed no offence against our Nation; but who, being without strength to repel invaders, had their lands usurped, without an attempt at purchase by treaty, or any offer of reasonable compensation, and a class of people introduced into their country, amongst which were many, both free and bond, who, regardless of law, and in great measure exempt from its operation, by the remoteness of their situation, practised appalling cruelties upon this almost helpless race. And when any of the latter have retaliated, they have brought upon themselves the vengeance of British strength, by which, beyond a doubt, many of the unoffending have been destroyed, along with those who had ventured to return a small measure of these wrongs, upon their white oppressors.

Upon every hand, it is evident, that a heavy responsibility has thus been brought upon the British Nation; in which also, the Colonial Government is deeply involved; and that it is their bounden duty, to make all the restitution in their power, by adopting efficient measures for the benefit of the Aborigines of Australia, in affording them protection and support, and in endeavouring to civilize and settle them.

These desirable objects are, however, difficult to accomplish, in consequence of the wandering habits of the Aborigines, and the few motives they have for attaching themselves to places, where such means can be made to bear upon them; but it is to be observed, that Stockmen in all parts of the Colony, by availing themselves of these few motives, prevail upon as many of the

Blacks, as they wish for the assistance, or the company of, to spend a large portion of their time at their stations, and in some instances, permanently to remain with them.

The Blacks are universally fond of bread, potatoes, and beef, and of tea, highly sweetened; and they soon acquire a liking for tobacco and spirits; they are also glad of better shelter, in inclement weather, than that afforded by their own frail erections of bark; and they soon become sensible of the comfort of clothing, though on first being supplied with garments, they have no idea of taking care of them, and will often throw them off entirely, when too warm.

The Stockmen take advantage of these predilections, and thus gain their object; and there seems no ground to doubt, that if the same means were used, so far as they could be with Christian propriety, which would necessarily avoid the use of spirituous liquors, an influence might be produced upon the Aborigines, highly favourable to their civilization and settlement.

I would therefore suggest, that the Government should afford the means for supplying the Blacks with food, clothing, and shelter, at all the Mission Stations; where every Black who chose to be there, at the known meal-times, which should be, at least, three times a day, should be liberally supplied with wholesome and properly cooked victuals; and that such as chose to remain for longer, or shorter periods, should be accommodated and clothed, in such a way as to give them a taste for comfort. This is scarcely at all effected, by the mere supply of blankets, distributed annually to each of the Blacks, by the Government, as is the general practice in New South Wales, or by the donation of a little boiled wheat, by the Missionaries, as at Wellington Valley. In the first adoption of such a plan, a considerable loss, by want of care for articles of clothing, ought to be patiently borne. The clothing should be considered as the property of the Government, and it ought to be of such a character as to be easily identified, in order to prevent its being purchased from the Blacks; many of whom, it is also to be observed, have a great objection to wear such, as is the common garb of the prisoners in the Colony.

At each of these Stations, provision ought also to be made, for the board, clothing, and education of any children, that the Aborigines might be disposed to leave, for longer or shorter periods, for instruction; as it is chiefly, upon the children, that the most decided impression of civilization, may be expected to be made.

Encouragement should likewise be held out to other persons

than missionaries, to engage in this work of benevolence, who ought to be liberally provided for by the Government, until a sufficient number of Stations should be occupied, to afford the assistance and protection, needed by the whole Aboriginal Population ; who, by these means, would be drawn away from towns, and from the habitations of Settlers and Stockmen, where they are now debased and demoralized.

To prevent collision with Settlers, in the time of the maize-harvest, the Blacks ought to be liberally supplied, at that season, with maize, in the state in which they so much like it, as now to induce them to steal from the fields.

No work ought to be exacted from the Aborigines, for a considerable period ; nor at all, except in assisting on the Establishments, at such labour as might be made to appear to them to be reasonable ; but every encouragement of industry should be held out to them, by rewarding their labour, perhaps, chiefly by payments in money ; in order to teach them its use and value ; but only in cases where they might be willing to lay it out in suitable things, a store of which should be kept on each of the stations, for the purpose. As soon as any of the Blacks might be disposed to cultivate land for themselves, or in other ways, to adopt settled and civilized habits, they ought to receive encouragement to do so, by the allotment to them, of portions of land, or by other suitable means ; and no discouragement, in the pursuit of the desired object, ought to be given way to, either by the Government, or by the parties employed by it, in consequence of occasional, or frequent disappointments, even if, for some time, at the first, these should occasionally threaten, the forsaking of some of the Establishments by the Blacks.

Every person employed in this service, should be regarded as a servant of the Government, in this description of labour, and should be paid as such ; and where it might be combined with religious instruction, this should, on the part of the Government, be regarded as gratuitous : yet every individual, engaged in this service, should be expected, religiously to fulfil his various duties, before God and man, in this work of benevolence and humanity.

The expense of carrying into operation such a plan, as is thus briefly sketched, would obviously be considerable ; but seeing the state to which the Blacks are reduced, and the vast pecuniary advantage, derived by the Whites from the possession of their soil, the expense ought not to stand in the way of the amelioration of their condition, especially, when it may be amply provided for, out of the proceeds of the Government sales, of the very lands, which were the natural possession of the Blacks, and to which, their right has been only questioned by a foe, too powerful for them to contend or to argue with.

The priority of claim for the benefit of the Blacks, upon the funds arising from the sale of lands, by the Government of New South Wales, to whatever extent, it may be required for their benefit, must, I conceive, be admitted, by every person who regards equity, or common justice. I therefore trust, that I shall not be counted as improperly interfering in a political question, in thus plainly, yet respectfully, urging it; seeing my plea is in the cause of humanity, and on behalf of the oppressed,—of a people  who require to have justice done them speedily, or the opportunity will be gone for ever, and the unmitigated guilt before God, of their extermination, will be fixed, irremediably, upon the British Nation and its Australian descendants.

JAMES BACKHOUSE.

Hobart Town, Van Diemens Land,
    25th of 4th month, 1837.

To Major General Richard Bourke, K. C. B. Governor in Chief of
New South Wales.

On a subject so deeply important, as that which suggests means for rescuing from destruction, an entire race of human beings, such as the Aborigines of Australia, I trust the Governor will not deem me intrusive, in giving expression to my individual concurrence, in the views submitted by my friend James Backhouse, in the accompanying communication. Having shared with him, in the opportunities he has had, of ascertaining the real condition of these unhappy people, I have been forcibly struck with their deep moral and physical degradation.

The encroachments of Europeans have curtailed their means of subsistence, and consequently augmented the misery of the Blacks; and the vices that have been grafted on their native habits, through association with Europeans, have not only contributed to this end, but have also sunk them considerably below their former level, in the scale of morals. A fearful responsibility, therefore, lies at the door of the British occupiers of the soil, a responsibility which it must be their interest to discharge, in such a manner as to relieve them from the weight of Divine displeasure, which must inevitably rest on the head of injustice and oppression. The practical effects of this displeasure are already apparent, in the evils entailed on the White Population, from collision with the Blacks. One of the most appalling and extensive of these, is the number of victims to vice and disease, who constantly crowd the hospitals of the Interior, solely from this cause, sufficiently demonstrating, that the oppressors and the oppressed are liable to be involved in the same common ruin, though the preponderance of guilt is greatly on the side of the former.

Aware of the feelings of interest, entertained by the Governor, on behalf of the Aborigines of Australia, I am not without hope, that the measures now suggested, or others promising to be equally efficient, that may hereafter be devised, will, at no distant period, be carried into effect.

GEORGE WASHINGTON WALKER.

Hobart Town, Van Diemens Land,
    25th of 4th month, 1837.

APPENDIX.

Q.

An Epistle to Persons attending the Meetings of
Friends, in Sydney.

To the Persons in Sydney, New South Wales, assembling for
Public Worship, after the manner of the Society of Friends.

Dear Friends,

Your situation, as a little company, meeting for the
public worship of God, according to the practice of the Society of
Friends, continues deeply to interest us; and often draws forth
aspirations to our Heavenly Father, that you may not rest in a
form of godliness, without knowing the power thereof; that you
may not be contenting yourselves with coming together, and sitting
in silence before the Lord; but that your hearts may be stayed
upon God, truly waiting upon him, in humble dependence and
fervent prayer; and that this may likewise be the habit of your
minds out of meetings. For those who live in forgetfulness of
God, or not in subjection to his Spirit, in their daily walk, cannot
reasonably expect to be enabled to draw near unto him, in seasons
of public worship.

Blessed be the name of the Most High! we have in Jesus
Christ, a Mediator and Advocate with the Father, touched with a
feeling of our infirmities, who ever liveth to make intercession for
us; not that we should live unto ourselves, but unto him; that
we should become his humble, self-denying followers; and through
him, be delivered from the power of Satan. May each of you
reflect upon your state, and examine whether you know anything

of the work of the Lord upon your souls; and if you have known
it, whether it be making progress, or declining. Remember the
declaration of the Saviour, "Many are called, but few are chosen."
None become of the chosen, or elect of the Lord, who do not
yield to the convictions of the Holy Spirit, and witness unfeigned
repentance, and consequent departure from sin, through the help
of the Grace of God, which is freely offered to all, through the
Lord Jesus Christ; and which will be increasingly received by all
who wait upon, and pray to God perseveringly, for it; trusting in
his mercy, set forth, and offered to mankind, in his well-beloved
Son.

"Be not deceived, God is not mocked: such as every man
soweth, such shall he reap. If ye sow to the flesh, ye shall of
the flesh, reap corruption; but if ye sow to the Spirit, ye shall of
the Spirit reap life everlasting." Those who do sow to the Spirit,
will continually come to the Light, that their deeds may be made
manifest, that they are wrought in God: and if any hate the
Light, and come not to it, lest their deeds should be reproved, it
is because they are evil doers, and in a state of condemnation
before God.*

We often feel for your situation, in regard to the lack of spiritual fathers and teachers among you; but we desire that you
may seek diligently to God, that you may become truly his adopted
children, know him as your reconciled Father, through the redemption that is in Christ, and the Holy Spirit, given through
him, as your Teacher. Then shall you be complete in Christ;
God shall supply all your need; and you shall be faithful witnesses in life and conversation, of his goodness and power to save;
and being guided into all truth, you shall not fail to receive of
him gifts, for the edification one of another, whether vocal in the
congregation, or otherwise. For the measure or "manifestation
of the Spirit, given to every man to profit withal," is not designed
merely for our own deliverance from sin, but for the edification
of the body of Christ; being differently administered, and operat-
ing diversely, according to the self-same Spirit, which divideth
to every man severally as he will.† But if the grace received, be
not suffered to reign in the heart, it will be as a talent wrapped
in a napkin, and buried in the earth; and how then shall the
Lord be met at his coming, when he shall call to account before
his Judgment Seat?

* John iii. 19—21.   † 1 Cor. xii.

Let the spirit of love, and of a sound mind, prevail amongst you: for "love is of God;" and as we become renewed in the image of Him who created us, through "the washings of regeneration and renewings of the Holy Ghost," with which the disciples of Christ are baptized, we shall love God and our neighbour the more, and shall have the evidence that "we have passed from death unto life, because we love the brethren:" it will also be evident to all men, that we are "the disciples of Christ, because we have love one to another." This love will not make us blind to the faults one of another; but it will bring us, in a sound mind, to labour with those who halt, or are out of the way, in the spirit of love, and solicitude for their restoration.

Your example before the world is of unspeakable importance. The eyes of many are upon you, as persons professing to be led by the Spirit of God; and if, while you are thus professing, you should be found walking in the spirit of the world, you may become stumbling-blocks in the way of others, and cannot then escape the judgment of God. "Beware lest any of you be hardened through the deceitfulness of sin." Remember the uncertainty of life, and that it is only while the Lord calls, that we can answer; and that, if we turn a deaf ear to his reproofs, we know not how soon he may give us up to hardness of heart.

That you may "not forsake the assembling of yourselves together, as the manner of some is," whether vocal ministry be exercised or not; but that gathering in "the name of Christ," in his authority and power, you may know him to be in the midst of you, who is the great Minister of ministers, and may experience him to be the Shepherd and Bishop of your souls, is the prayer of your friends, in the love of the Gospel,

JAMES BACKHOUSE.
GEORGE WASHINGTON WALKER.

Philippolis, South Africa, 27th of 6th mo. 1839.

APPENDIX.

R.

A LETTER to VAN DIEMENS LAND YEARLY MEETING of FRIENDS.

To Friends of Van Diemens Land Yearly Meeting.

Dear Friends,

In the anticipation of my dear companion, George Washington Walker, being present at your next Yearly Meeting, and delivering up the Certificate you granted him, in the year 1834, to proceed with me, in the capacity of a Minister of the Gospel; in which you commended me also, to the kind regard of the Inhabitants of this land, and of other countries where we might come; I think it right to inform you, that we have, very generally, met a kind reception from the people among whom we have travelled, and among whom we have been favoured, unitedly, to labour, in much harmony, in the Gospel of our common Saviour; that we part from each other in love; and we believe, in the counsel of Him, who brought us together in his work, and to whom we look for guidance and blessing, in our separate allotments. To Him be the glory for ever. Amen.

In thus addressing you; and as it were, bidding you Farewell! an earnest desire attends my mind, that you may be careful to walk watchfully before the Lord; waiting upon him daily, yea continually, for the renewal of your strength; that you may not leave your first love to Christ, nor suffer it to wax cold, either because of offences, or because of the cares of the world : but that while "not slothful in business, you may be fervent in spirit, serving the Lord:" not neglecting your gifts, but keeping in that exercised state of mind, in which the weapons of your warfare may be kept bright; not only seeking your own daily growth in grace, and diligently stirring up the pure mind one in another, but also, waging a holy warfare against the kingdom of Satan, by testifying against sin; and holding high the standard of the love of Christ, both toward one another, and toward the world.

Carefully watch over your own hearts, and diligently direct your fellow-mortals to that heavenly treasure, the manifestation of the Spirit of Christ in the soul of man, which you have felt to be precious, and to lead you to repentance, and to reconciliation with God, through the death of his Son, and to guide your feet in the way of peace.

O, my friends! a great and responsible trust is committed unto you. Examine daily how your account stands with God, before whom it must be rendered in his own time, be that soon or late. His long-suffering and forbearance are great; and he is ever ready to forgive our haltings and backslidings, for Jesus' sake, if we truly repent. But if we live in the spirit of true repentance, we shall continually aim at the fulfilment of the divine will, both in regard to personal holiness, and to the promulgation of the Gospel; for which we shall be zealous, according to the diverse gifts bestowed upon us, whether for public or for private use; and we shall abide in love, and in compassion toward those that have erred, or that may be out of the way.

Be not content in a dry, barren state; for this is generally the result of spiritual sloth, or of disobedience, or of a defective trust in the Lord, who alone is the strength and confidence of his dedicated children. Dwell, therefore, in the Fountain of Life; that ye may continually draw water with joy, from the wells of salvation.

In the flowing of that love which would gather all to Christ, and which springs from him, I remain,

Your Friend and Brother,

JAMES BACKHOUSE.

Cape Town, South Africa,
  17th of 9th mo. 1840.

YORK: PRINTED BY JOHN L. LINNEY, 15, LOW OUSEGATE.

THE WORLD
ON MERCATOR'S PROJECTION

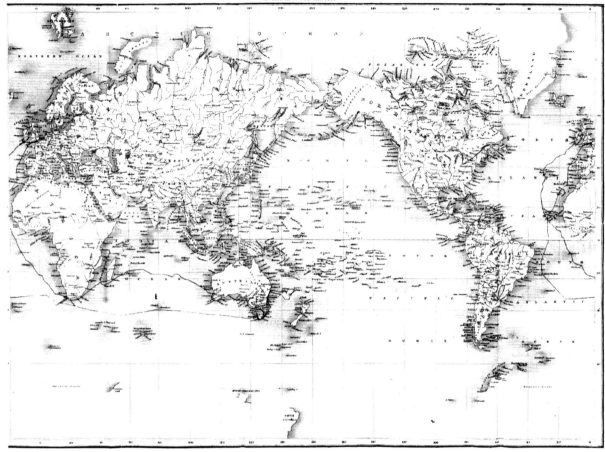

B L

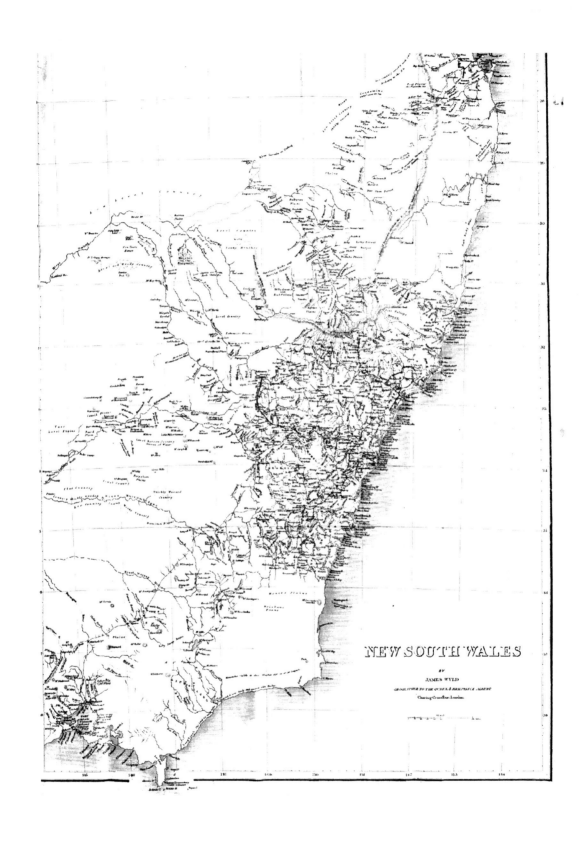

NEW SOUTH WALES

BY

JAMES WYLD

GEOGRAPHER TO THE QUEEN & H.R.H. PRINCE ALBERT

Charing Cross East, London.

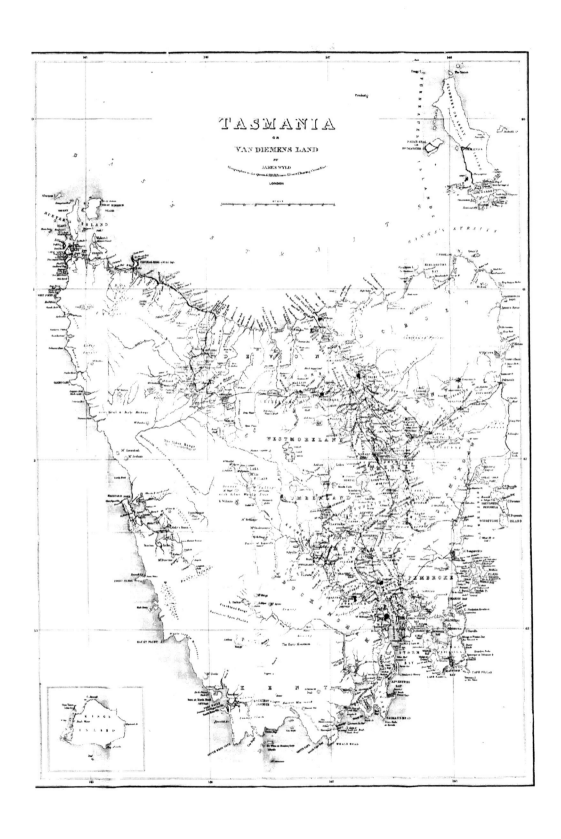

TASMANIA
OR
VAN DIEMENS LAND
BY
JAMES WYLD
Geographer to the Queen & H.R.H. Prince Albert Charing Cross East
LONDON

Lightning Source UK Ltd.
Milton Keynes UK
178572UK00005B/97/P